Happy Fifth
Birthday, Julian!
Your friend,
Lee

GREAT BOOK
OF THE
ANIMAL KINGDOM

GREAT BOOK
OF THE
ANIMAL KINGDOM

CRESCENT BOOKS
New York • Avenel • New Jersey

This single volume edition was compiled from the original
Italian series GRANDE ENCICLOPEDIA ILLUSTRATA DEGLI ANIMALI
edited by Maria Pia Mannucci and Alessandro Minelli

This 1993 edition published by Crescent Books, distributed by Outlet
Book Company, Inc., a Random House Company,
40 Engelhard Avenue, Avenel, New Jersey 07001

Random House
New York • Toronto • London • Sydney • Auckland

Printed and bound in Spain by Artes Gráficas,Toledo
D.L.TO:840-1993
ISBN 0-517-08801-0

h g f e d c b a

CONTENTS

The success of any book on natural history depends on the quality of the illustrations. In the United States a shining example of this sort of achievement is the work of John James Audubon, the great ornithologist and unrivaled watercolor painter whose representations of birds are universally regarded jointly as classics of science and art.

Even during the Renaissance, the botanists who compiled the first herbals illustrating plants possessing medicinal qualities, always sought the collaboration of competent painters who could give a true to life portrayal of individual species. And it is for these illustrations that the books concerned are chiefly prized today.

Illustrated volumes on natural history have benefited from advances in color printing and, more recently, in photography. Yet even today it is hard to surpass the high standards of certain classics of the eighteenth and nineteenth centuries, such as the South American butterflies painted by Sibylla Meriam or the animals of Indonesia as portrayed by Hermann Schlegel. And even now drawing and painting have the advantage over photography not only for the way in which they can depict rather dull anatomical detail but also because they are able to convey the living likeness of an animal in its typical natural environment.

It is for this reason, therefore, that we have chosen to employ that method in this *Great Book of the Animal Kingdom*. These color illustrations are remarkable for their realism and accuracy of detail, and the accompanying text, concise and clear, provides the most up-to-date information on the life and habits of hundreds of the most representative species of the entire animal world.

By reason of the way it has been structured, the *Great Book of the Animal Kingdom* will appeal to two types of reader. The numerous plates, with their short captions, are likely to be of immediate interest to everyone, whereas those who wish to delve more deeply into the subject will find more detailed information in the texts which closely complement the illustrations.

The identification and comparison of different animal species dates back to ancient times; but it is only comparatively recently that the observation and study of the animal world have begun to be organized along truly scientific lines.

Toward the middle of the eighteenth century, the great Swedish naturalist Carl von Linné or Carolus Linnaeus (1707-78) propounded a general classification of all living species thus far known; and this system formed the departure point for all subsequent developments in the science of zoology.

Linnaeus, admittedly, was only familiar with several thousand species, a small proportion of the catalog of countless organisms which still remain to be described.

Within little more than two centuries, our knowledge has been greatly broadened, so that today we possess descriptions of about 1,200,000 animal species.

Yet this immense task of cataloging is still far from being complete. Each year, in fact, 10,000 new species are added to the list of forms not so far included in zoological classifications, and it is estimated that more than 10 million, even as many as 30 million, different animal species may actually exist on Earth.

To get some idea of the diversity of animal species, however, it is not necessary, fortunately, to count them all. Many species, in fact, are very like one another, so much so that it takes the experienced eye of the specialist to tell them apart.

Likenesses and differences are indeed fundamental aspects of natural history. Why, for example, do some animals have six or eight legs, some only two or four, and others none at all? Why don't all animals have teeth? Why, among those that do, are some equipped with small, sharp teeth and others with powerful grinding teeth? And why do some birds possess a long, slender bill whereas others have a short, broad, strong beak?

To answer these and similar questions we need to know at least two "secrets" about each species concerned: firstly, its origin, its relationship and its racial history, often dating back thousands of years; and secondly, the characteristics of the environment in which it lives, its daily diet, the dangers to which it is regularly subjected, and the habits and cycles of its family life.

The bill of the flamingo, for example, is a sort of filter or sieve which enables this stately bird to collect large quantities of tiny organisms (algae and microscopic animals) from the lakes and swamps which it frequents. This is why its bill is quite different from that of an eagle, which is designed to tear the flesh of its prey, or that of a parrot, which is ideally formed to break open the tough husks that protect the big seeds of tropical forest trees.

There is a different type of beak for every species of bird according to the jobs they must perform and the lifestyles they need to adopt.

It is true, nevertheless, that along the banks of lakes patrolled by flamingos or in the dense tree canopy that conceals chattering crowds of parrots there are many other animals that have neither a beak nor a body protected by feathers. Snakes, for example, have a strong body, no legs and a mouth full of teeth; some of them can swim in shallow water among the swamp vegetation, while some have learned to climb trees, entwining themselves around the branches like a liana, ready to lash out at some passing bird or unsuspecting lizard.

The different types of beak, therefore, represent adaptations by birds to life in various environments where there are, in particular, different food opportunities. But other animals which live in the same surroundings have also developed a range of adaptations which enable them to feed, to defend themselves and to survive.

In the course of the last couple of centuries naturalists have come to adopt two different forms of investigation and comparison. Firstly, they have studied the question of adaptation to the environment, the significance of diverse structures and behavior patterns among animal species, and the reasons why these different modes of behavior and lifestyles enable animals in different surroundings to survive.

Secondly, naturalists have tried to recognize affinities and relationships between the various species; they have attempted to identify the "family likeness" that often exists among species which live in different environments and are therefore quite unlike one another in outward appearance.

As a result of all this research, scientists have built up a system of classification which places every animal species in a particular category, according to its relationships.

Individually related *species* are thus grouped into the same *genus* and the most closely related genera into the same *family*; the related families are then grouped in an *order*, the orders into a *class*, and the classes into a *phylum*. Species, genera, families, orders, classes, and phyla are then given an official Latin name; and the so-called *scientific name* is applied to each individual animal so that it can immediately be identified in conversation or in writing, no matter in what country or what language.

The coyote, for instance, is described by zoologists as *Canis latrans*, namely a species of the genus *Canis*, as are the wolf (*Canis lupus*) and the domestic dog (*Canis familiaris*). The genus *Canis* forms part of the canine family (known by the Latin name Canidae), together with several other genera including *Vulpes* (the common foxes) and *Lycaon*, which comprises the ferocious African hunting dog (*Lycaon pictus*).

The Canidae, in their turn, represent one of the families that belong to the order Carnivora, along with the Ursidae (bears), Felidae (cats, lions, tigers, lynxes, etc.), Mustelidae (badgers, otters, martens, etc.) and other families.

At a still higher level of zoological classification, the Carnivora are grouped in the class Mammalia, together with orders such as the Primates (comprising monkeys and humans), Rodentia (mice, hamsters, squirrels, beavers, etc.), Artiodactyla (deer, antelopes, cattle, giraffes, camels, pigs, etc.) and various other orders.

Mammals (Mammalia), birds (Aves), reptiles (Reptilia), amphibians (Amphibia), bony fishes (Osteichthyes), cartilaginous fishes (Chondrichthyes) and sharks, skates and rays (Selachii) make up the subphylum of vertebrates (Vertebrata); and this, together with two groups of marine animals (Tunicata and Cephalochorda) constitute the phylum Chordata, one of thirty or so phyla presently recognized by zoologists.

In the following pages, we shall illustrate a number of species that are representative of the most important phyla, classes and orders, beginning with the simplest and most primitive forms, the protozoans (Protozoa).

These are very tiny creatures whose body consists of a single cell. For this reason the Protozoa are often regarded, rather than true animals, as constituents of a group of living beings separate not only from animals and plants but also from two other groups of lower organisms, the bacteria, algae, etc. (Monera) and the funguses (Fungi).

Traditional classification groups animals above protozoans as metazoans (Metazoa), whose body is made up of many cells. The simplest of these multicellular animals are the sponges (Porifera) with a body which is merely a sac with a porous wall, generally supported by a frame of elastic fibers or by a network of tiny calcareous or siliceous needles.

The coelenterates (Coelenterata) are aquatic (mostly marine) organisms which have developed two basic forms: that of the polyp, sedentary and similar to a fleshy flower, and that of the jellyfish, mobile and transparent. The marine ctenophores (Ctenophora) somewhat resemble the jellyfishes and are equally delicate in structure.

Our survey continues with the flatworms (Platyhelminthes), numerous species of which live freely both in water and on land but which are better known for containing parasitic forms such as tapeworms and flukes.

All the animals that belong to the Mesozoa, Nematomorpha and Acanthocephalia are parasites, while those that make up the Nemertina, Rotifera, Gastrotricha and Kinorhyncha are free forms living in water, more or less wormlike in appearance.

The Entoprocta, the Bryozoa and the Phoronida all live freely in water, usually in the sea, and look like polyps.

The roundworms, (Nematoda), with a cylindrical, unsegmented body and no appendages, are extremely varied in habit, containing a large number of species that parasitize animals and plants in addition to others that lead a free life in water or in the earth.

Other wormlike marine forms, of uncertain relationship, constitute the Priapulida, the Sipunculida, the Echiurida and the Pogonophora, some of which may have affinities with the Annelida, i.e. the typical segmented worms that are found in many different surroundings (sea, fresh water, land) and which are subdivided into various classes, including the polychaetes, earthworms and leeches.

Then we have the mollusks (Mollusca), a very large phylum with about 100,000 species distributed in the oceans but also well represented in fresh waters and lands above sea level. The members of a small, exclusively marine phylum, the Brachiopoda, bear some resemblance to the bivalve mollusks.

The largest of all the phyla is that of the arthropods (Arthropoda), which alone comprises approximately one million known species, most of them insects, (Insecta), but also including the crustaceans, scorpions, spiders and millipedes. Related to the arthropods are the small phyla Tardigrada, Onycophora and Pentastomida.

The strange creatures that represent the phylum Echinodermata all live in the ocean: they include the sea lilies, sea stars, sea urchins and sea cucumbers. Despite their outward appearance, however, the echinoderms may be quite closely related (in addition to the small marine groups Chaetognatha and Hemichordata) to the chordates (Chordata), the important phylum which, as already mentioned, includes, among others, the Vertebrata.

According to the most modern systems of classification, the name "animal" belongs, in the strictest sense, only to the Metazoa. But we have followed tradition in commencing our journey through the animal kingdom with a quick look at the Protozoa.

Here we can already see how an organism deals with and solves all the main problems likely to arise in its daily struggle for survival.

Above all else there is the problem of food. Animals do not enjoy that special prerogative of plants, namely the capacity to manufacture their own food, building up the complex organic molecules that constitute their body from the simplest inorganic compounds such as water and carbon dioxide, and from that universally available source of energy, sunlight. They, quite differently, have to find their food in ready-made organic materials that are present in the tissues of plants or of other animals, or in the remains (more or less reconstituted) of other organisms.

In order to obtain its daily ration of food, an animal must, as a rule, move around; it cannot expect food to reach its mouth automatically. Movement, therefore, is a prime necessity for almost all animals, especially for satisfying hunger.

Even tiny protozoans consisting of a single cell make use of special organs for locomotion: these are slender appendages known as flagella or cilia. Some are equipped with one or perhaps two flagella, others have their cellular body entirely covered with hundreds of regularly arranged cilia. In every case the beating of these flagella and cilia permits the organism to move with ease through the water, to find a mouthful of food, to reach a better lit area or even to make contact with a partner at those rare times when a tiny protozoan is ready to go through the complex sexual maneuvers of its species.

Certain protozoans, however, can move without either cilia or flagella: they are the amoebas, which move very gradually simply by changing shape, slowly making themselves longer or shorter. The leucocytes (white blood cells), incidentally, are also capable of this kind of movement.

With the transition from single-celled to multicellular organisms, such simple methods of locomotion soon become insufficient. Only a few tiny worms and small aquatic larvae are still able to move around by beating the cilia of their epidermic cells.

More possibilities exist among multicellular organisms. The body of each individual is made up of many cells, whose tasks will then vary: some will make up protective body cover, some are concerned with locomotion, some are involved with the acquisition and processing of food, and others have the responsibility of reproductive functions and future of the species.

For locomotion, metazoans make use of muscle fibers which can be lengthened and shortened depending on need, almost always under the precise control of the nerve centers.

In order for these muscles to perform their functions efficiently, the single strands of tissue have to be firmly inserted at particular points and the body must therefore take on and retain a precise form. This is provided by the skeletal structures, external in the case of crabs or insects, internal in the case of humans and other vertebrates.

These skeletons are often mineralized, containing variable quantities of calcium carbonate (crabs) or calcium phosphate (vertebrates); but the typical insect skeleton is composed only of organic substances, without any mineral addition. Furthermore, certain animals have developed skeletons comprised merely of sacs filled with liquid, without any further support: this applies to earthworms and other wormlike invertebrates.

With the appearance of muscles and skeletons, the way was open to further specializations: for example, the development of legs for walking, fins for swimming or wings for flying.

Some animals, nonetheless, are sedentary and still find it possible to obtain food. They are exclusively aquatic, such as sponges or oysters. These animals procure food by continuously filtering large amounts of water and collecting (generally by means of a sort of sieve, which in the case of the oyster consists of the gills themselves) tiny organisms and scraps of detritus which are present in the water in sufficient quantities to satisfy nutritional needs.

This type of life would, of course, be inconceivable out of water: too much energy would be expended to filter large amounts of air, nor would it be possible to extract from it tiny traces of organic matter.

For the majority of animals, therefore, food does not consist of minute particles obtained by filtration. It may be represented by agile, swift-moving prey which can only be caught by developing tactics of ambush or pursuit; or it may comprise leaves, flowers, and seeds which have to be sought, selected and then chewed, gnawed or sipped, according to the mechanism of the mouthparts of the species concerned. There are also the parasites, which can enjoy abundant food when they have a suitable host but which usually have the problem of finding such a host either for themselves or their offspring.

The different animal species also have very different ways of coping with reproduction and growth.

Among protozoans, reproduction almost invariably entails the division into two parts of the cellular individual. Specific molecular mechanisms ensure that each of the daughter cells receives a complete copy of all the instructions which have formed the hereditary material of the parent cell. It may be that combinations of the hereditary makeup are gradually created, whereby a few characteristics of one cellular individual are linked with those of another individual of the same species. These are standard phenomena of sexuality which from time to time occur even among protozoans.

Progressing to multicellular organisms, there is, for each individual, a fundamental separation between two distinct cell types: those that will form the body with all its organs and systems (e.g. brain, intestine, muscles, etc.), and, those destined to form the gametes, namely the cells from which the new generation will originate.

In every species two different and complementary types of gamete are formed: the small male gametes, or spermatozoa, and the large female gametes, or egg cells, The union of a male gamete and female gamete produces a zygote (fertilized egg) which is usually the departure point for the creation of a new individual.

In many animal species (as, for instance, almost all vertebrates and insects) the two types of gamete are produced by distinct individuals. Zoologists describe such animals as *gonochoric*, i.e. of separate sexes, with males that produce spermatozoa and females that produce eggs. It is not rare, however, to come across the condition known as *hermaphroditic*, in which the same individual is capable of producing both types of gamete. Animal hermaphrodites include, for example, virtually all the land snails, the earthworms, the leeches, and even certain species of fish.

Among the wide variety of solutions adopted by the diverse animal species to ensure their future, there are cases in which the development of a new individual does not originate in a zygote.

In certain species, the egg produced by the female may develop even without having being fertilized by the spermatozoon. This kind of reproduction is known as *parthenogenesis*. The phenomenon is fairly common and may often alternate seasonally with normal bisexual reproduction. Among aphids and daphnia (water fleas), for instance, there may be a rapid succession of parthenogenetic generations, usually consisting only of females, throughout the summer, while with the approach of fall both males and the new generation will originate from fertilized eggs.

Cases of true vegetative reproduction, whereby an individual originates from cells that are not gametes, are rare among animals. This phenomenon occurs in sponges, in polyps (as in the common freshwater hydra) and in several other groups of lower animals.

However, in virtually all animals, new individuals develop from a fertilized egg. This is a rather special cell, sometimes of enormous size, as we can easily see if we look at a bird's egg (particularly that of an ostrich). These unusual dimensions, which differ considerably from one group to another, derive from the fact that the egg contains an abundant supply of nutritive materials, which are gradually used for making a new multicellular individual. Nor should it be forgotten that the fertilized egg is itself a cell which, like all cells, is capable of dividing, so forming two daughter cells.

This procedure of division is repeated again and again until the single huge, original cell is converted into a mass consisting of numerous smaller cells: these cells are known as *blastomeres* and collectively make up an *embryo*. The latter represents a rough version of the future animal and it rapidly changes and develops until the new individual is capable of leading its own active life.

Embryonic development, in the majority of instances, occurs outside the mother's body. Sometimes, as happens in birds and some animals, the mother (more rarely the father or both parents) takes care of the eggs, at least until the young hatch; but very frequently, especially among invertebrates, the eggs are simply left to their fate. All these animals, therefore, are described collectively as *oviparous*, or producers of eggs.

In some cases, however, the eggs are retained inside the mother's body, so that the embryos are protected, although when they hatch they have no particular links with the mother. This applies to many snakes, sharks, scorpions and other animals, all of which are considered as *ovoviviparous*, or producers of eggs that are hatched within the body.

The majority of mammals (and a few other animals) have evolved a more elaborate process which not only ensures protection of the embryo inside the mother's body but also provides it with nutritive substances so that the baby is born already well developed. These animals are *viviparous*, giving birth to live young.

At the moment of birth, many animals are already miniature versions of future adults: all they have to do is to grow in size and to develop characteristics appropriate to maturity, including the capacity to reproduce and the adoption of attributes which are often essential if individuals of either sex are to recognize each other or to engage in competition for winning a partner (bright colors, crests, horns, etc.).

Among certain animals the youngster which hatches from the egg is completely different from the future adult. Examples include moths and butterflies, bees, flies, beetles and many other insects, which are born in the form of *larvae*, without wings and generally wormlike, quite different from the winged insect that will subsequently develop. This also happens among frogs and toads, which begin their active life as tadpoles with no legs, but equipped with a long tail that is shed in the course of growth.

The process of major transformation from larva to adult is called *metamorphosis*. An animal which begins life as a larva and is then metamorphosed into an adult is described as undergoing *indirect development*, whereas an animal which is born as a miniature version of the adult is said to undergo *direct development*.

Animals live all over the world, wherever there is any chance of survival. Even among the icefields of the highest mountains and on the fringes of the desert wastes of Antarctica it is possible to find various forms of animal life.

Distribution of the diverse species, of course, has its own logic; and it is thus possible to describe both the fauna that occupies different types of surroundings and the fauna that inhabits different geographical regions.

From the latter viewpoint, the continents can all be broken down into a given number of zoogeographical regions.

The Holarctic region comprises much of the land surface of the northern hemisphere: North America to the northern provinces of Mexico (the Nearctic subregion) and then all of Europe, Africa north of the Sahara, and central-northern Asia, virtually to the boundary of the great mountain peaks of the Himalayas (the Palearctic subregion)

The Neotropical region comprises the remaining parts of the Americas, from around the isthmus of Tehauntepec to the most distant stretches of Tierra del Fuego.

The Paleotropical region takes in most of Africa and all southern and southeastern Asia.

Finally, the Oceanic region consists of Australia and most of the islands and archipelagos strewn about the Pacific Ocean.

PROTOZOA

By and large the Protozoa are unicellular animals consisting of a cytoplasm which is differentiated in various ways and possesses one or more nuclei. The phylum also contains forms which behave as a single organism but which consist of several cells that may even differ. This single cell divides, producing first two daughter cells, then four and so on, all remaining connected to a greater or lesser extent.

The shape and size of a protozoan's cell body varies greatly. Each species has its typical form which remains unchanged regardless of size but which, in some groups, may vary with environmental conditions. As a unicellular organism, the protozoan's body consists of a nucleus and cytoplasm and therefore, at the very least, also of a membrane which is similar in structure to the plasma membrane of any metazoan cell. Matters become more complicated with the presence of further membranes in addition to the plasma membrane. These form pellicles which, in many cases, can be fairly rigid.

In addition to the pellicle, many phytoflagellates secrete cellulose and deposit it as scales and plates. In other protozoans siliceous or calcareous scales are laid down in the pellicle and these give the body greater rigidity. Inorganic tests, which usually form external skeletons, are found in the Chrysomonadida and in the Sarcodina, excepting the amoebas. The structure of these shells varies and they may be either siliceous or calcareous in composition, although in the case of the Acantharia the shell is formed from strontium sulphate.

The contractile vacuole is a cytoplasmic structure present in many freshwater protozoans but which occurs less frequently in marine and parasitic species. Its principal function appears to be the removal of excess water from the organism.

The Protozoa possess one or more nuclei. Of the forms with more than one nucleus, it is only in the Ciliata and in some Foraminifera that there may be a clear morphological and functional division of the nuclei into two separate types.

Among the Protozoa there is also sexual reproduction, characterized by the fusion of nuclei (karyogamy) and

The Protozoa, which includes the most primitive and the smallest animal forms, has been the subject of careful study since the development of the techniques of microscopy. If one looks at a drop of water taken from a pond or a marsh under a microscope one can observe numerous protozoans. The largest measure $\frac{1}{32} - \frac{1}{16}$ in (1mm) while the smallest are only a few micromillimeters across. The drop pictured here contains some of the commonest freshwater Protozoa: *Paramecium, Vorticella, Stentor, Amoeba proteus, Trichodina pediculus* and *Volvox*.

this may or may not be associated with the fusion of the cytoplasm of differentiated cells known as gametes. Karyogamy is always accompanied by meiotic division of the nuclei, in much the same way as in the multicellular animals (Metazoa).

Protozoans live in a wide variety of habitats. The free-living forms are common in any sort of water, including temporary pools, soil water, and damp mosses. Some species are capable of encysting in response to adverse conditions.

Colorless protozoans, which may be regarded as primary consumers in the broad sense, feed off organic substances, whether they be dissolved in the medium which surrounds the protozoan or whether they be particles, as in the case of organic detritus (the minute remains of other organisms), bacteria, algae, protozoans or small metazoans.

In the Sarcodina, whose members appear to have fairly varied diets, the food particles are usually swallowed by means of the pseudopodia which are also used in locomotion. The way in which these particles are ingested may vary from one group of the Sarcodina to another. The Foraminifera, for example, tend to form a dense network of thin reticulopodia in which motile prey such as algae, ciliates, and bacteria are easily trapped. Digestion takes place in the network which enfolds the prey and the digested products are carried to the cytoplasm by the protoplasm which is continuously flowing both outward and inward along the reticulopodia. On reaching the cytoplasm, the food substances are assimilated.

The Protozoa are constantly active, either moving about generally or, in the case of forms fixed to the substrate, altering their position. They move by means of locomotory organelles which are differentiated to varying extents and, like metazoans, they use up energy as they move. In this respect, it is best to discuss each group separately. The amoeboid movement, typical of the Sarcodina, to which the amoebas belong, involves structures known as pseudopodia. The mechanism of contraction and relaxation also provides the basis for food capture in the amoebas, whether this be by pinocytosis or phagocytosis. The Ciliata move by means of cilia; and the Flagellata move by means of one or more flagella. Flagellar movement

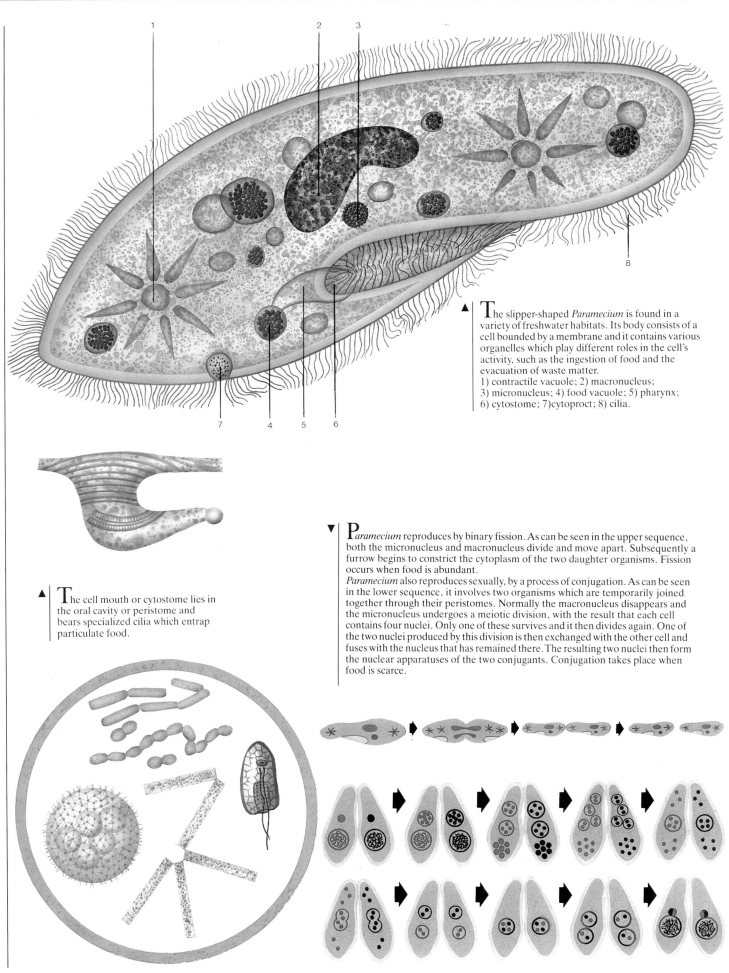

The slipper-shaped *Paramecium* is found in a variety of freshwater habitats. Its body consists of a cell bounded by a membrane and it contains various organelles which play different roles in the cell's activity, such as the ingestion of food and the evacuation of waste matter.
1) contractile vacuole; 2) macronucleus;
3) micronucleus; 4) food vacuole; 5) pharynx;
6) cytostome; 7) cytoproct; 8) cilia.

The cell mouth or cytostome lies in the oral cavity or peristome and bears specialized cilia which entrap particulate food.

Paramecium reproduces by binary fission. As can be seen in the upper sequence, both the micronucleus and macronucleus divide and move apart. Subsequently a furrow begins to constrict the cytoplasm of the two daughter organisms. Fission occurs when food is abundant.
Paramecium also reproduces sexually, by a process of conjugation. As can be seen in the lower sequence, it involves two organisms which are temporarily joined together through their peristomes. Normally the macronucleus disappears and the micronucleus undergoes a meiotic division, with the result that each cell contains four nuclei. Only one of these survives and it then divides again. One of the two nuclei produced by this division is then exchanged with the other cell and fuses with the nucleus that has remained there. The resulting two nuclei then form the nuclear apparatuses of the two conjugants. Conjugation takes place when food is scarce.

shows certain similarities with ciliary motion.

A first group of Protozoa are the Mastigophora flagellates. These organisms possess one or more flagella during the greater part of their life cycle. They may be grouped in colonies which have a fixed spatial arrangement of the component individuals. They reproduce asexually, typically by longitudinal binary fission. Sexual reproduction is rare but is well known in some groups. They are divided into two classes: Phytomastigophorea and Zoomastigophorea. Typically the members of the first group contain plastids which give the cell a yellow, green or brown coloration. They can synthesize sugars from carbon dioxide and water, like higher plants. They are all free-living. The class contains ten orders, the majority of which include freshwater and marine species. Well-known genera are Euglena, Chlamydomonas, and Volvox.

The Zoomastigophorea are colorless, do not contain plastids and possess from one to many flagella. The majority are symbionts and there are parasitic forms. The class contains nine orders, some of which are amoeboid forms, either with or without flagella. Sexual reproduction is known, particularly among the Hypermastigida.

The important order Kinetoplastida takes its name from the kinetoplast (or blepharoplast) which occurs in the cytoplasm closely associated with the basal body of the flagellum. It may be thought of as a large mitochondrion, being bounded by a double membrane, the inner one of which is invaginated to form ridges. The order contains many parasitic forms which cause diseases in humans; *Leishmania donovani* causes "kala azar" or visceral leishmaniosis, while *L. tropica* is responsible for oriental sore or skin leishmaniosis. *Trypanosoma gambiense* and *T. rhodesiense* cause sleeping sickness in humans, and they are transmitted by *Glossina palpalis* and *G. morsitans*. These dipterans also transmit *Trypanosoma brucei* which causes nagana among domestic animals in Africa. In Central and South America *T. cruzi* causes Chagas' disease and it is transmitted by hemipterans of the genus *Triatoma*.

A second major group of Protozoa, the Opalinata, are all parasites, living in the terminal portion of the alimentary canal of fishes and amphibians, and sometimes reptiles. The best known

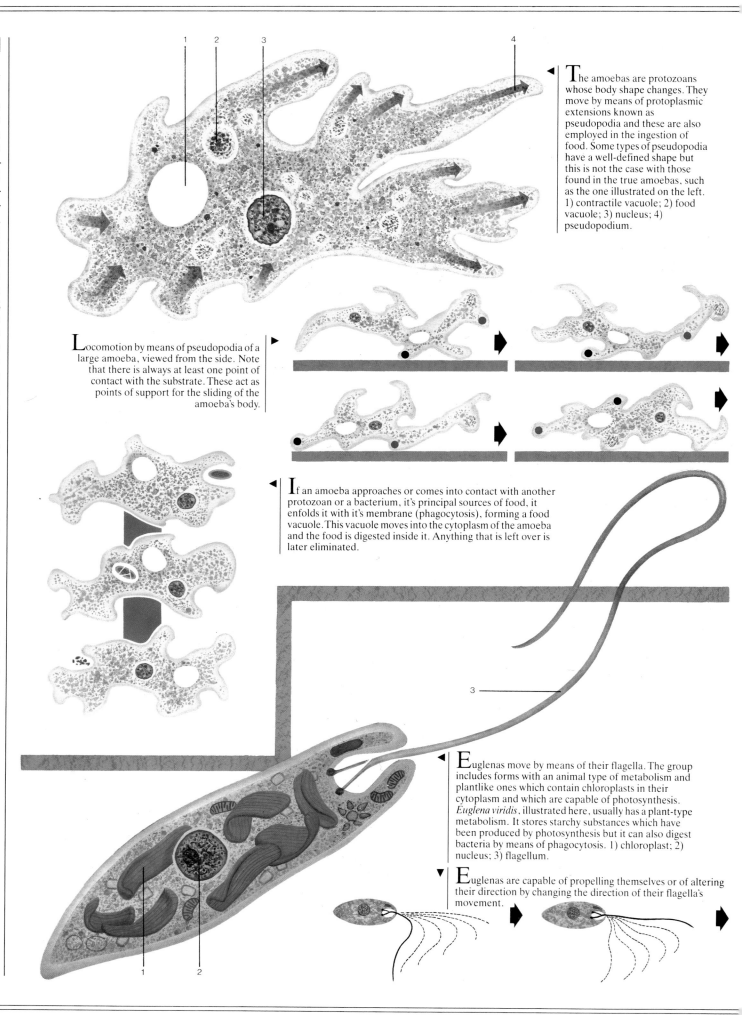

The amoebas are protozoans whose body shape changes. They move by means of protoplasmic extensions known as pseudopodia and these are also employed in the ingestion of food. Some types of pseudopodia have a well-defined shape but this is not the case with those found in the true amoebas, such as the one illustrated on the left. 1) contractile vacuole; 2) food vacuole; 3) nucleus; 4) pseudopodium.

Locomotion by means of pseudopodia of a large amoeba, viewed from the side. Note that there is always at least one point of contact with the substrate. These act as points of support for the sliding of the amoeba's body.

If an amoeba approaches or comes into contact with another protozoan or a bacterium, it's principal sources of food, it enfolds it with it's membrane (phagocytosis), forming a food vacuole. This vacuole moves into the cytoplasm of the amoeba and the food is digested inside it. Anything that is left over is later eliminated.

Euglenas move by means of their flagella. The group includes forms with an animal type of metabolism and plantlike ones which contain chloroplasts in their cytoplasm and which are capable of photosynthesis. *Euglena viridis*, illustrated here, usually has a plant-type metabolism. It stores starchy substances which have been produced by photosynthesis but it can also digest bacteria by means of phagocytosis. 1) chloroplast; 2) nucleus; 3) flagellum.

Euglenas are capable of propelling themselves or of altering their direction by changing the direction of their flagella's movement.

species is *Opalina ranarum*. It spends part of its life cycle in the adult frog and the other part in the tadpole. The third major group of protozoans, the Sarcodina, are capable of forming pseudopodia or a particular kind of pseudopodium, the axopodium. Flagella may be present to a limited extent at certain stages of the life cycle. Asexual reproduction is by binary or multiple fission. Sexual reproduction has only been observed among the Foraminifera and the Heliozoa. A first subgroup of Sarcodines consists of the amoebas, whose cell bodies are continuously changing shape as they move. Most amoebas are free-living and are common in the slime at the bottom of ponds, etc, but there are also many commensal and parasitic forms which are mainly found in the guts of animals. *Entamoeba hystolitica*, which causes amoebic dysentery, can be found in the human large intestine along with *E. coli*, which is non-pathogenic.

A second subgroup of sarcodines, the Foraminiferida, owe their name to the numerous openings (foramina) which connect the chambers of the "shell" where the cellular body is enclosed. The shell has an organic matrix, rich in mucoproteins. It is strengthened by the addition of calcium and magnesium carbonate as well as, to a lesser extent, grains of sand. The dimensions of these shells range from a few tens of microns to several centimeters.

Sarcodines also include the Radiolaria, planktonic marine organisms whose bright coloration is due to the presence of inclusions and phytosynthetic symbionts. They may live singly or more rarely they may be colonial, reaching sizes of up to 1.2 in (30 mm). They normally possess an extremely delicate siliceous skeleton.

A further major group of the Protozoa, the Sporozoa, are organisms that are exclusively parasitic, living both inside the cells and the body cavities of a wide array of animals, from other protozoans to mammals.

The Ciliophora (ciliates) form the last major group of Protozoa. This markedly homogeneous group of highly differentiated protozoans contains about 7,200 species and is found in all types of aquatic habitat as well as damp soil.

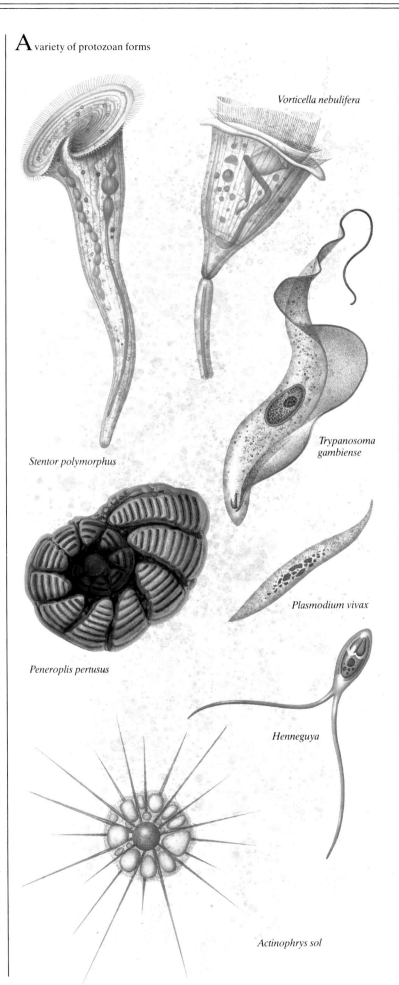

A variety of protozoan forms

Vorticella nebulifera

Stentor polymorphus

Trypanosoma gambiense

Peneroplis pertusus

Plasmodium vivax

Henneguya

Actinophrys sol

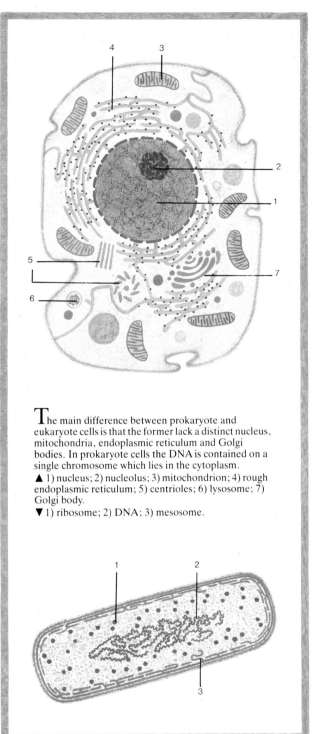

The main difference between prokaryote and eukaryote cells is that the former lack a distinct nucleus, mitochondria, endoplasmic reticulum and Golgi bodies. In prokaryote cells the DNA is contained on a single chromosome which lies in the cytoplasm.
▲ 1) nucleus; 2) nucleolus; 3) mitochondrion; 4) rough endoplasmic reticulum; 5) centrioles; 6) lysosome; 7) Golgi body.
▼ 1) ribosome; 2) DNA; 3) mesosome.

Protozoans have evolved along numerous lines, and as unicellular organisms this evolution has been achieved by the specialization of portions of the protoplasm or, in other words, by the evolution of organelles. Apart from its unicellular organization, there are no other characteristics which can be used to define the phylum since among its members there are examples of all types of symmetry as well as a variety of structures and adaptations to meet every kind of environmental condition. The members of this phylum are found wherever there is water, whether it be in the sea, in fresh water or in soil. There are commensal, symbiotic, and parasitic species. The majority of protozoans are solitary but there are also colonial forms.

PORIFERA

The Porifera, or sponges as they are commonly known, constitute a vast phylum of primitive animals whose organization sets them apart from the other multicellular animals. Because of this they are often placed separately in a group known as the Parazoa. The differences lie in the fact that their cells do not form well-defined tissues and organs but are instead relatively independent and retain a considerable amount of mobility. In addition, they lack a nervous system, muscle cells and sense organs. When adult, the Porifera are fixed to the substrate and they do not display any extensive body movements. As a result, they were regarded as zoophytes or plant animals until the eighteenth century.

The members of this phylum are all aquatic animals and the vast majority are marine. Most sponges have a body pierced by a network of canals in which the food-bearing water circulates. Bacteria make up a large part of their diet, but they also feed on other micro-organisms suspended in the water and on organic detritus. It also appears that sponges can absorb dissolved organic matter. The water flows in through the excurrent canals. These join to form larger and larger ducts and they finally open through exhalent apertures incorrectly known as oscula. Sponges are highly efficient filter feeders, filtering several hundred liters and square meters of substrate per day and extracting almost every particle of the size of a bacterium from it.

Although the choanocytes do not form a true tissue they do form a continuous layer, the choanoderm, which lines some of the cavities inside a sponge. Another type of cell; the pinacocyte, forms a continuous layer covering the entire surface of the sponge and the canal system. On the surface of the sponge, there are also specialized cells known as porocytes, which enclose the ostia and control their diameter. An intermediate layer, the mesohyl, lies between the pinacoderm and the choanoderm.

With a few exceptions, all sponges possess a skeleton. This is generally composed of mineral elements, the spicules, which vary in shape and which are divided into the megascleres and the microscleres. The former determine the overall structure of the

▲ Population of *Halichondria panicea* in a rocky, mid-littoral habitat.

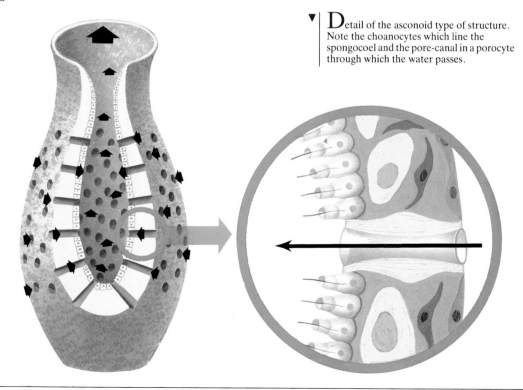

► Asconoid structure. The arrows indicate the direction of the water as it flows through the sponge, entering through the pores and leaving through the osculum.

▼ Detail of the asconoid type of structure. Note the choanocytes which line the spongocoel and the pore-canal in a porocyte through which the water passes.

skeleton while the latter are involved in secondary roles such as protecting the surface of the sponge or binding together the megascleres, etc. The mineral skeleton may be combined with a scleroprotein known as spongin and this may form sleeves around the spicules, binding them together and giving the skeleton strength and elasticity. Alternatively, the mineral skeleton is completely replaced by horny fibers of spongin, although in the majority of the members of this order the spongin fibers are strengthened by the inclusion of grains of sand. It is only in a few species, such as *Spongia officinalis*, *Spongia zimocca*, *Spongia agaricina*, and *Hippospongia equina*, that the fibers are completely free of foreign bodies and it is this which gives their skeletons the softness, making them commercially valuable as bath sponges.

Sponges that live in deep water, particularly those belonging to the class Hexactinellida (the glass sponges), have delicate lacelike skeletons of siliceous spicules. At the base of the sponge these spicules are clustered together to form a long peduncle anchoring the sponge to the muddy seabed. Close to the surface, on the other hand, it is the horny sponges which abound, and the elasticity of their spongin fibers protects them from the blows of the waves.

The sponges may reproduce sexually through eggs and spermatozoa, but also asexually; this latter form of reproduction is particularly well known in the freshwater Spongillidae. Several marine species, for example members of the genera *Tethya* and *Suberites*, form buds and these may be either inside or on the outside of the parent sponge.

The majority of marine sponges live on rocky bottoms in the littoral zone at depths of between 0 and 650 ft (200 m). There are, however, numerous forms occurring down to depths of 6,600 ft (2,000 m). On bathyal bottoms below this level the Porifera are represented by specialized forms that belong to the orders Tetractinellida and Monaxonida of the Demospongia and the class Hexactinellida. Some species penetrate into the abyssal and hadal zones below 20,000 ft (6,000 m) and even reach 26,000 ft. (8,000 m). There are over 5,000 living species of sponges.

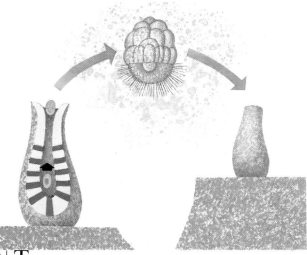

▲ The production of amphiblastula larvae by a member of the Calcarea. These larvae then attach themselves to the substrate and give rise to new sponges.

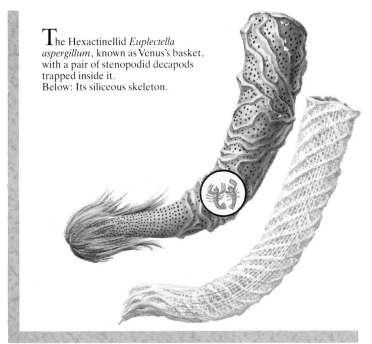

The Hexactinellid *Euplectella aspergillum*, known as Venus's basket, with a pair of stenopodid decapods trapped inside it.
Below: Its siliceous skeleton.

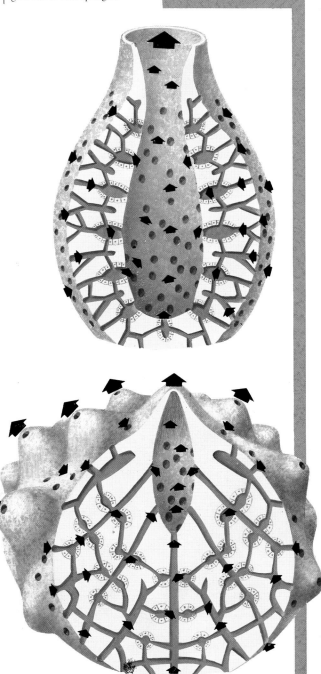

Examples of Demospongia

Halichondria panicea

Tethya aurantium

Spongia officinalis

Hymeniacidon sanguinea

Haliclona mediterranea

◄ Above: The syconoid structure. After having entered through pores, the water passes down the canals which open into the choanocyte chambers. These, in turn, open into the spongocoel and the water leaves through the osculum.
Below: The leuconoid structure. The choanocyte chambers lie inside the body and communicate with the spongocoel by means of a system of canals. There are numerous oscula, through which the water flows out of the sponge.

CNIDARIA

The organization of the Cnidaria is extremely simple. The body wall is composed of two layers of epithelial tissue in between which there lies a layer of gelatinous substance (a protein gel) impregnated with water. This layer is known as the mesogloea. It is both viscous and elastic, so it is able to provide support for the body and an anchorage for the muscle cells. Water is able to enter the coelenteron, (or gastro-vascular cavity as it is also known), through the mouth, and it is because this cavity is full of water that the turgor of the body is maintained. The outer cell layer is called the epidermis and the inner one is known as the gastro-dermis. The cells which make up these layers are only differentiated to a slight extent and the majority of them have many functions. There is only one class of highly specialized cells – the stinging cells or cnidoblasts, which are found only in the Cnidaria and which constitute both an effective means of food capture and of defense. About 10,000 species of Cnidaria are known at present.

Within the phylum two quite different body forms, the polyp and the medusa, occur. Each of these is adapted to a different way of life. The polyp is sessile or only slightly motile (benthic) and is basically cylindrical in shape, with the basal part, the pedal disk, being attached to the substrate while the mouth lies at the center of the upward pointing apical end and is surrounded by symmetrically arranged, hollow tentacles. The tentacles bear numerous stinging cells and they use these to ensnare prey which they then carry to the mouth.

The medusa swims or floats freely (planktonic) and is rather like an upside-down polyp which has been flattened and broadened out sideways. In shape it resembles a mushroom or an umbrella, and the body of a medusa is in fact known as the umbrella, with the convex upper surface being the exumbrella and the concave under surface being the subumbrella. Such a flattened and expanded form is well adapted to a floating way of life. Unlike the polyp, the medusa's mouth is pointed downward and it opens at the tip of a projection of varying length, the manubrium, which extends from the center of the subumbrella.

The Cnidaria are distinctive invertebrates which are found in all seas and which are adapted to different ways of life. The corals, sea anemones, and jellyfish are their principal representatives. Some members of the Cnidaria spend the whole of their life cycle as polyps, others spend the whole of it as medusae, and others still alternate polypoid and medusoid stages. The medusae are usually planktonic and solitary, while the polyps are benthic and may be either solitary or colonial. However, there are benthic medusae, planktonic polyps, and, finally, planktonic colonies which are composed of both polyps and medusae.

Jellyfish (*Aurelia aurita*)

Hydromedusa (*Obelia*)

Coral (*Corallium rubrum*)

Sea anemone (*Anemonia sulcata*)

Sea anemone (*Anthopleura xanthogrammica*)

The tentacles hang down from the margins of the umbrella. The cnidoblasts of these oral arms are used in the capture of prey.

The difference in the positions of the mouth and the tentacles in the polyp and the medusa is related to the different way in which they feed. The former lives on the bottom and catches prey which passes over it while the latter lives on the surface and preys on organisms which are found at lower levels. The medusa is well adapted to a planktonic life, possessing an extensive mesogloea (generally poorly developed in the polyp) as well as sense organs (absent in the polyp). The mesogloea gives the umbrella body and its low density helps the organism to float. As the medusa moves freely in all directions it must have a means of knowing its position in space, where the light is coming from and how strong that light is. To meet this need two types of very primitive sense organs are arranged around the margin of the umbrella. These are the statocysts, which indicate position, and the ocelli, which are photoreceptors.

Some members of the Cnidaria spend the whole of their life cycle as polyps, others spend the whole of it as medusae and there are also species which alternate a polyp stage with a medusa stage, the medusa being produced by the polyp asexually. The Cnidaria, therefore, display a great variety in their organization and in their way of life despite the simplicity of their structure. They may be benthic or planktonic, solitary or colonial. Generally speaking, the medusoid forms are planktonic and solitary whereas the polyps are benthic and may be solitary or colonial. There are, however, benthic medusae, planktonic polyps and planktonic colonies which are composed of both polyp and medusa-like individuals.

The phylum is divided into three classes: Hydrozoa including freshwater hydras and many marine forms; Scyphozoa including most well-known medusae; and Anthozoa including sea anemones and corals.

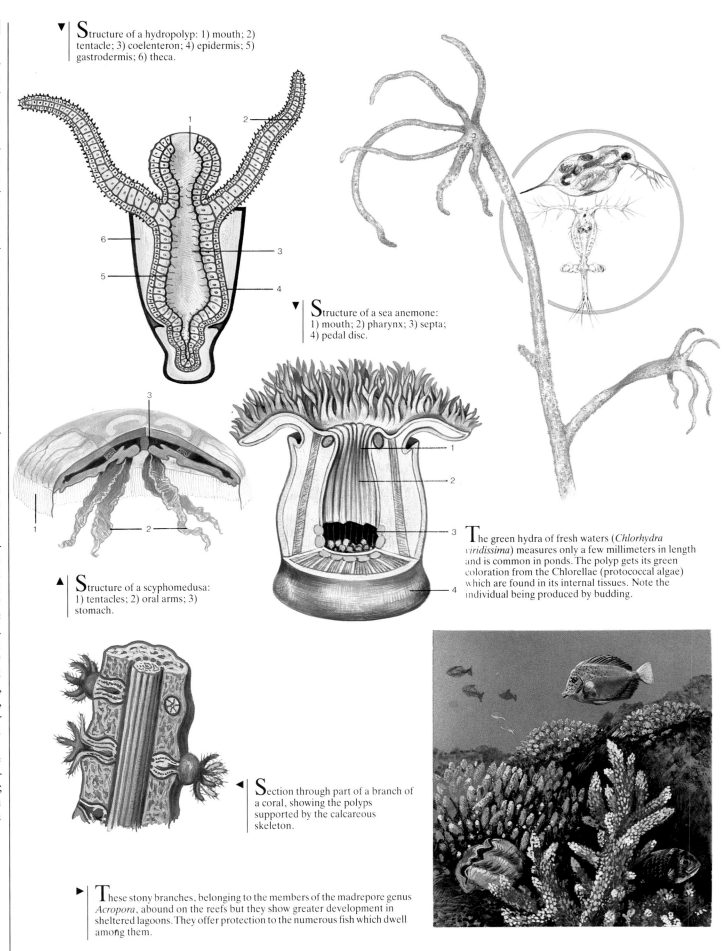

▼ Structure of a hydropolyp: 1) mouth; 2) tentacle; 3) coelenteron; 4) epidermis; 5) gastrodermis; 6) theca.

▼ Structure of a sea anemone: 1) mouth; 2) pharynx; 3) septa; 4) pedal disc.

▲ Structure of a scyphomedusa: 1) tentacles; 2) oral arms; 3) stomach.

The green hydra of fresh waters (*Chlorhydra viridissima*) measures only a few millimeters in length and is common in ponds. The polyp gets its green coloration from the Chlorellae (protococcal algae) which are found in its internal tissues. Note the individual being produced by budding.

◄ Section through part of a branch of a coral, showing the polyps supported by the calcareous skeleton.

► These stony branches, belonging to the members of the madrepore genus *Acropora*, abound on the reefs but they show greater development in sheltered lagoons. They offer protection to the numerous fish which dwell among them.

ANNELIDA

The Annelids are wormlike animals that possess a cavity between the alimentary canal and the body wall, and this is lined by a peritoneum. This cavity is known as a coelom and is divided into segments or meromes, within which lie the paired excretory organs and the blood vessels. The coelom contains a fluid which acts as a hydrostatic skeleton. The eggs of the primitive marine annelids give rise to a ciliated, pelagic larva known as the trochophore.

The common body plan of all annelids is of a vermiform animal divided into identical segments, whose body is supported by a hydrostatic skeleton. The pressure of the hydrostatic skeleton is balanced by an external cuticle. The nervous system consists of two ventral nerve cords linked by commissures to two cerebral ganglia.

The annelids possess chitinous bristles, the chaetae, and these play a role in locomotion when it involves lateral undulations or peristaltic waves of the body wall. The musculature of the body wall is typically arranged in two layers, a circular one and an inner, longitudinal one. The contraction of the longitudinal fibers causes the body to shorten and the contraction of the circular ones causes it to lengthen as the coelomic fluid is squeezed to the two ends. Annelids which dig (earthworms, lugworms) move along tubes or tunnels which are only slightly wider than themselves and their muscles contract in such a way as to produce waves of swelling which travel along the body from front to rear or vice versa.

The main classes of annelids are the Polychaeta (polychaetes) and the Clitellata (clitellates). The polychaetes are marine annelids that posses a pair of appendages known as parapodia on each segment with the exception of the first and the last. These parapodia are mostly supported by robust chaetae known as acicula. They also usually possess a variety of cephalic appendages. The sexes are separate and they have a pelagic, trochophore larva.

In most polychaetes the sexes are separate and fertilization is external. Most polychaete eggs produce a pelagic, trochophore larva. It is carried by currents in the water for quite a short time and then it settles on a

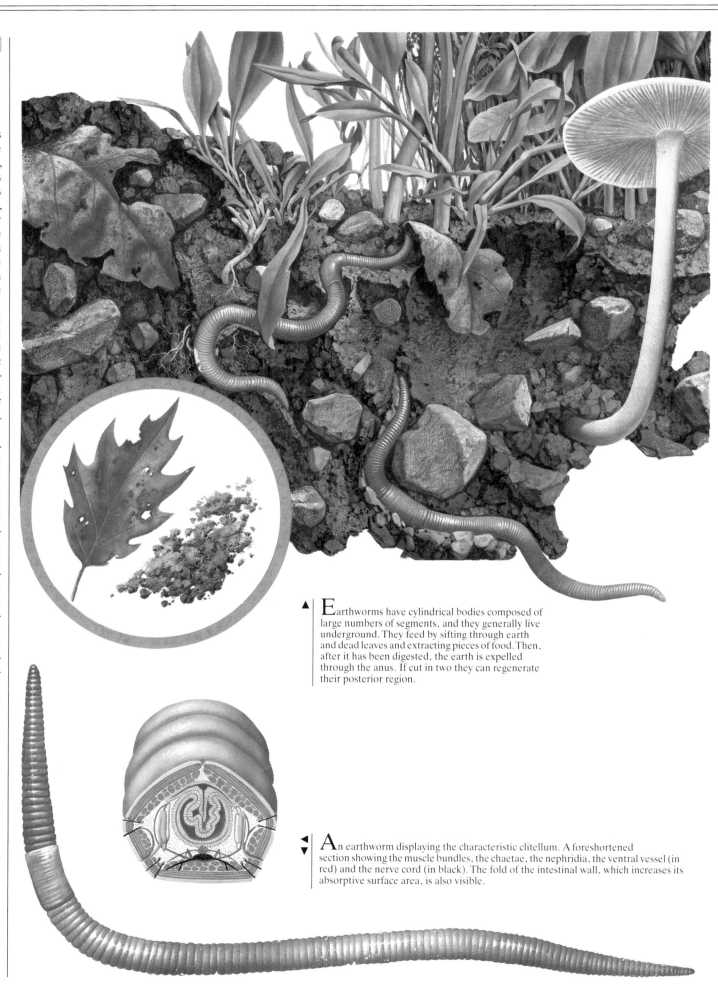

▲ Earthworms have cylindrical bodies composed of large numbers of segments, and they generally live underground. They feed by sifting through earth and dead leaves and extracting pieces of food. Then, after it has been digested, the earth is expelled through the anus. If cut in two they can regenerate their posterior region.

◄ An earthworm displaying the characteristic clitellum. A foreshortened section showing the muscle bundles, the chaetae, the nephridia, the ventral vessel (in red) and the nerve cord (in black). The fold of the intestinal wall, which increases its absorptive surface area, is also visible.

suitable substrate, where it metamorphoses into a young vermiform animal.

Errant polychaetes move by creeping over the sea bed and occasionally they burrow into the sand. Some have become pelagic and others live permanently buried in the mud in a tube. They are usually predators but some feed off marine plants and the smaller species devour micro-organisms which they find in the interstices between grains of sand. The sedentary polychaetes are characterized by fairly simple parapodia, which do not project far and usually lack acicula. Some of the members of this group are specialized for the gathering of detritus and small organisms which have accumulated on the sea bed. Others swallow mud or sand and digest the organic matter in it, just as earthworms do. Some pump water along the tube in which they live in order to filter out the micro-plankton. Finally, there are forms which are suspension feeders, capturing organisms by means of prominent crowns of thin tentacles which are borne on their heads.

The members of the Clitellata display a fair amount of diversity in their appearance and in their habits: in fact they include the Oligochaeta, the best known representatives of which are the earthworms, and the Hirudinea, better known as the leeches. They mostly live in freshwater habitats or in the soil. To survive in the former environment these animals had to permanently adopt internal fertilization and hermaphroditism, while at the same time losing their pelagic larval stage. Another clitellate adaptation to a hostile environment is that they lay their eggs in a cocoon and this then protects the eggs as they complete their embryonic development. The clitellates differ from the polychaetes in never having parapodia and in possessing, on average, fewer and smaller chaetae.

The subclass Oligochaeta (earthworms and allies) eat plant detritus and micro-organisms, usually swallowing these along with the mud or soil in which they live. A few freshwater species are carnivorous. The eggs of the aquatic oligochaetes are relatively large and a small number of them develop within each cocoon and then hatch out as small worms. The subclass Hirudinea contains clitellates which are specialized as predators and ectoparasites.

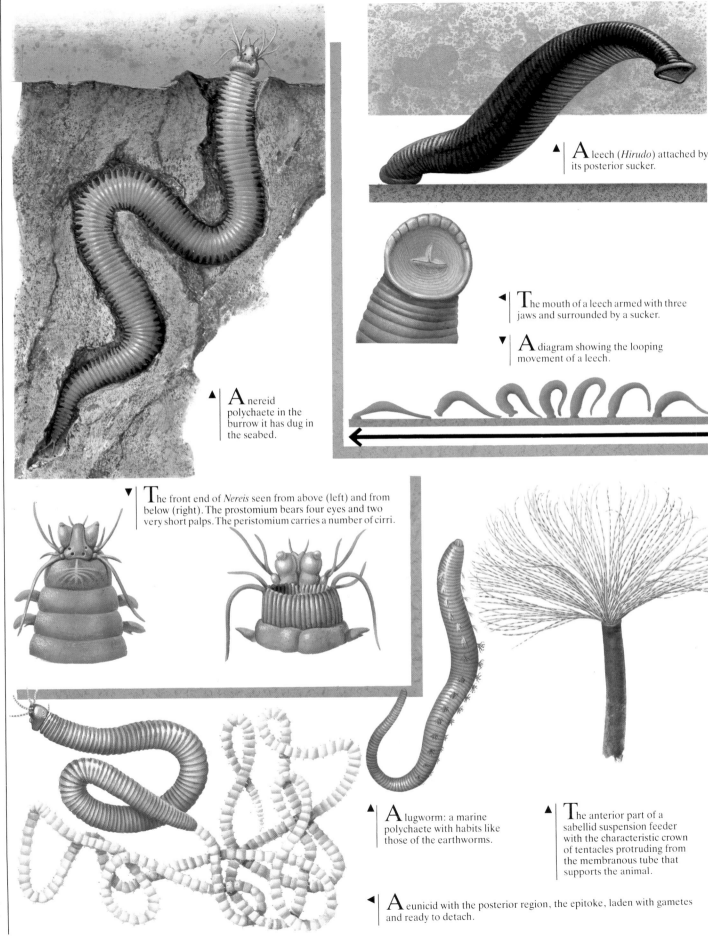

A nereid polychaete in the burrow it has dug in the seabed.

A leech (*Hirudo*) attached by its posterior sucker.

The mouth of a leech armed with three jaws and surrounded by a sucker.

A diagram showing the looping movement of a leech.

The front end of *Nereis* seen from above (left) and from below (right). The prostomium bears four eyes and two very short palps. The peristomium carries a number of cirri.

A lugworm: a marine polychaete with habits like those of the earthworms.

The anterior part of a sabellid suspension feeder with the characteristic crown of tentacles protruding from the membranous tube that supports the animal.

A eunicid with the posterior region, the epitoke, laden with gametes and ready to detach.

CRUSTACEA

The Crustacea is one of the richest animal classes in terms of numbers of species. A crustacean is an animal composed of a series of segments, each of which bears a pair of jointed appendages and is covered by a cuticle (the exoskeleton) heavily calcified. The appendages are forked, each one consisting of a protopodite from which branch an endopodite and an exopodite. The first and last segments do not bear appendages. The first six segments are fused into a head. The appendages of the second segment form the antennules and those of the third form the antennae, those of the fourth, the mandibles, the fifth, the first maxillae, and the sixth, the second maxillae.

In some cases the segments to the rear of the head may bear specialized appendages which assist the buccal ones by taking on the role of maxillae, and these are therefore known as maxillipeds. It is also quite common for a number of the segments which follow the head to be fused with it and for them to form a single region of the body known as the cephalothorax. Frequently, a fold of the exoskeleton known as the carapace covers a part or, exceptionally, the whole of a crustacean's body.

In all probability the Crustacea originated in the sea but they are now present in every aquatic environment. When they possess a respiratory system it is, with some exceptions, a branchial one. The first larval stage, the nauplius, is highly characteristic of crustaceans. It is a tiny larva which possesses three pairs of appendages and a simple, unpaired eye.

The Branchiopoda is a very ancient group of crustaceans. A characteristic of this group is the structure of the appendages, which are known as phyllopodia. They are flattened and held rigid by internal fluid pressure. Some branchiopods, the Notostraca, have a broad, flattened carapace which covers part of the body, leaving the posterior, appendage-less segments and the two long arms of the terminal furca uncovered. The segments which are protected by the carapace bear broad phyllopodia, which are continuously in movement. The members of this group can be relatively large in size and may exceed 4 in (10 cm) in length.

◄ **D**aphnia pulex belongs to the suborder Cladocera, a group of tiny crustaceans which, with some exceptions, form a part of the freshwater plankton. They are characterized by a carapace covering the whole of the body apart from the head, by long antennae and by leaflike appendages. Their reproductive cycles are also of interest. Known as water fleas, they are extremely common in any body of water. 1) antenna; 2) compound eye; 3) heart; 4) ovary; 5) thoracic legs; 6) brood chamber; 7) anus; 8); carapace.

▼ **A**n ostracod displaying the typical bivalved carapace.

► **T**riops cancriformis is a member of the Notostraca and it is found in temporary pools of fresh water.

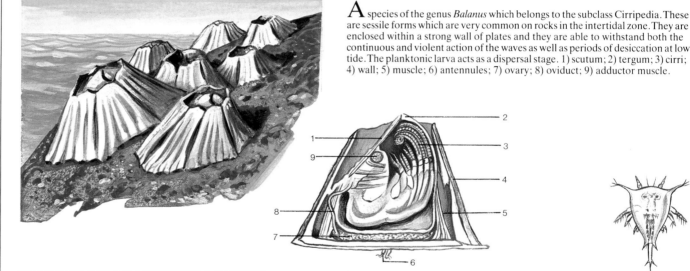

A species of the genus Balanus which belongs to the subclass Cirripedia. These are sessile forms which are very common on rocks in the intertidal zone. They are enclosed within a strong wall of plates and they are able to withstand both the continuous and violent action of the waves as well as periods of desiccation at low tide. The planktonic larva acts as a dispersal stage. 1) scutum; 2) tergum; 3) cirri; 4) wall; 5) muscle; 6) antennules; 7) ovary; 8) oviduct; 9) adductor muscle.

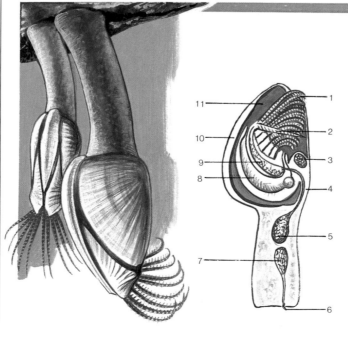

Another cirripede, belonging to the genus Lepas, with its distinctive fleshy peduncle. The goose barnacles are sessile hermaphrodites and, like the acorn barnacles, they pass through planktonic larval stages before attaching themselves to marine animals or floating objects. 1) cirri; 2) penis; 3) adductor muscle; 4) oviduct; 5) ovary; 6) antennule; 7) adhesive gland; 8) intestine; 9) seminal vesicle; 10) carina; 11) mantle cavity.

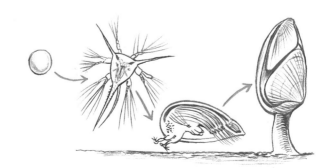

The members of this order form a prominent part of the faunas of short-lived pools. They are able to produce two types of egg. One kind, the thin-walled egg, is produced under favorable conditions, i.e. when the pool is full of water, and it develops rapidly. The second kind, known as the winter egg, does not develop and sinks to the bottom of the pool. There it waits while the pool dries out, until favorable conditions return.

The Cladocera is another interesting and important branchiopod group. Its members are the tiny and very common crustaceans known as water fleas, which are found in great numbers in any stretch of fresh water. In this group the carapace covers the whole body apart from the curiously shaped cephalic region, which resembles a bird's head. Inside the carapace the number of phyllopodia is greatly reduced and the segmentation of the body is no longer clearly distinguishable. The second pair of antennae is usually well developed and is used for swimming.

The members of another important group of crustaceans, the Ostracoda, have a bivalved carapace which encloses the whole body. The body itself is reduced to a small number of indistinguishable segments. The overall length of these organisms is generally a few millimeters. The majority of species are benthic and feed off detritus on the bottom. They live both in the sea and fresh water and some species populate temporary pools of water while others have been found at great depths in the Pacific.

Another major group, the Copepoda, are tiny crustaceans which, apart from a few exceptions, range from less than a millimeter to a few millimeters in size. They generally form the most important component of a community whether it be in the sea or fresh water, on the surface or the bottom, but they are particularly numerous in the plankton. Their populations can reach inconceivable levels and the entire food chain of the pelagic habitat is largely dependent upon them. The bodies of copepods are elongated and have a well-developed head which bears very long antennae. The final segment bears a furca. There is generally a single median eye situated dorsally at the anterior of the head and this is in fact the eye of the nauplius larva.

In a further group, the Cirripedia,

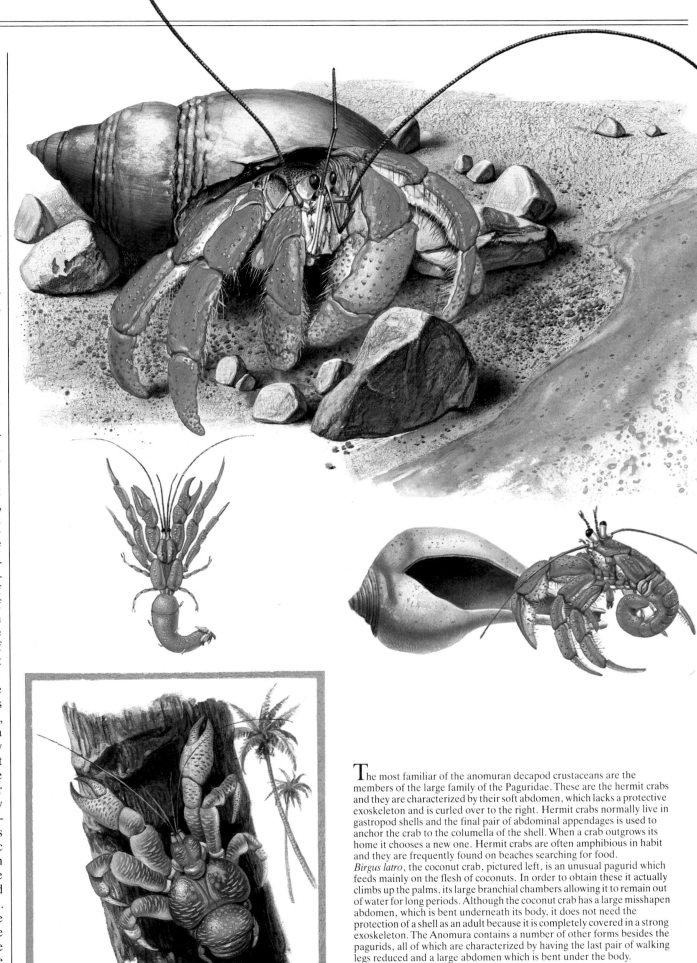

The most familiar of the anomuran decapod crustaceans are the members of the large family of the Paguridae. These are the hermit crabs and they are characterized by their soft abdomen, which lacks a protective exoskeleton and is curled over to the right. Hermit crabs normally live in gastropod shells and the final pair of abdominal appendages is used to anchor the crab to the columella of the shell. When a crab outgrows its home it chooses a new one. Hermit crabs are often amphibious in habit and they are frequently found on beaches searching for food.
Birgus latro, the coconut crab, pictured left, is an unusual pagurid which feeds mainly on the flesh of coconuts. In order to obtain these it actually climbs up the palms, its large branchial chambers allowing it to remain out of water for long periods. Although the coconut crab has a large misshapen abdomen, which is bent underneath its body, it does not need the protection of a shell as an adult because it is completely covered in a strong exoskeleton. The Anomura contains a number of other forms besides the pagurids, all of which are characterized by having the last pair of walking legs reduced and a large abdomen which is bent under the body.

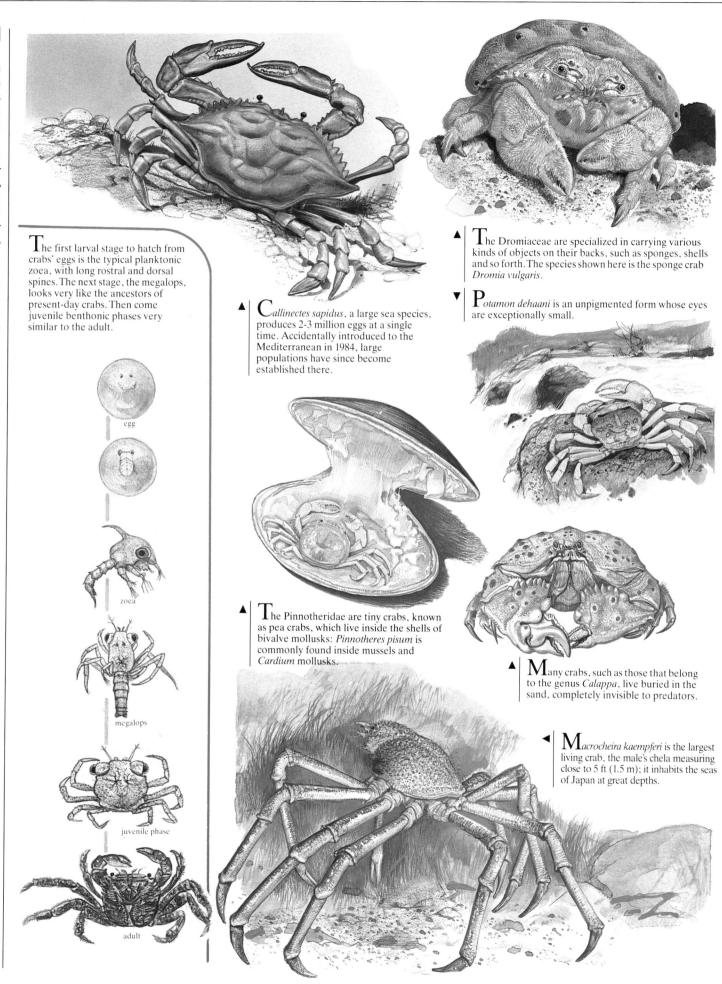

the adults are sessile, i.e. they live attached to the substrate, in the same way as sea anemones or sponges. This unusual mode of life for a crustacean has entailed considerable changes in their organization.

The goose barnacles are among the less extreme Cirripedes. A goose barnacle possesses a large, fleshy stalk, which attaches it to the substrate. At the top of this stalk there is what appears to be a sort of bivalved mollusk with a shiny, calcareous shell, formed from a series of five principal plates. These entirely enclose the body of the animal but there is an apical opening through which the cirri emerge when the animal is alive. The cirri are modified appendages which, when extended through the apical opening, set up water currents which trap the food particles on which the animal feeds. A goose barnacle hatches from its egg as a typical crustacean nauplius larva with three pairs of appendages. It is in fact the possession of this nauplius larva which reveals its crustacean nature. Goose barnacles attach themselves to floating objects and are carried about the oceans by currents

The acorn barnacles are a group of barnacles which occur along the low tidemark of rocky coasts, where they can form such thick encrustations as to make it difficult to walk in bare feet. They lack a peduncle and the capitulum is attached directly to the substrate.

The subclass of Malacostraca contains two-thirds of all crustaceans. The body of a malacostracan can be divided into three distinct regions: the head, the thorax or pereion, which is composed of eight separate segments, and the abdomen or pleon, which consists of seven segments. The final abdominal segment, the telson, lacks appendages.

The most important order of malacostracans is the Decapoda. The order derives its name from the presence of ten legs. These are arranged as five pairs of which the first pair is often transformed into a chela. The first three pairs of thoracic appendages are maxillipeds. The decapods are divided into two main groups, Natantia and Reptantia.

The first larval stage to hatch from crabs' eggs is the typical planktonic zoea, with long rostral and dorsal spines. The next stage, the megalops, looks very like the ancestors of present-day crabs. Then come juvenile benthonic phases very similar to the adult.

egg

zoea

megalops

juvenile phase

adult

Callinectes sapidus, a large sea species, produces 2-3 million eggs at a single time. Accidentally introduced to the Mediterranean in 1984, large populations have since become established there.

The Pinnotheridae are tiny crabs, known as pea crabs, which live inside the shells of bivalve mollusks: Pinnotheres pisum is commonly found inside mussels and Cardium mollusks.

The Dromiaceae are specialized in carrying various kinds of objects on their backs, such as sponges, shells and so forth. The species shown here is the sponge crab Dromia vulgaris.

Potamon dehaani is an unpigmented form whose eyes are exceptionally small.

Many crabs, such as those that belong to the genus Calappa, live buried in the sand, completely invisible to predators.

Macrocheira kaempferi is the largest living crab, the male's chela measuring close to 5 ft (1.5 m); it inhabits the seas of Japan at great depths.

SCORPIONS
Arachnida

The body of all scorpions appears to consist of a trunk and a tail. In reality the trunk comprises the prosoma, with the eyes situated dorsally, and the front part of the abdomen (the mesosoma), while the tail comprises the hind part of the abdomen (the metasoma). The circulatory system, the nervous system and the gut all continue into the tail and the latter ends in the anus beneath the sting or telson. The chelicerae are small and chelate while the pedipalps are very large and end in chelae. The genital aperture lies at the front of the abdomen and is followed by two curious structures, the pectines. These are undoubtedly sense organs but their exact function is still the subject of discussion. Four pairs of lung spiracles are visible on the abdomen behind the pectines.

All scorpions are solitary and show a tendency towards cannibalism. They usually spend the daylight hours in various kinds of burrows which they may sometimes dig for themselves, and at night they make short forays in search of prey. Catching their victims with the pedipalps, they hold the prey away from their bodies and sting it with their telson. As a result of possessing both pedipalps and poison they do not need to struggle much with their prey. The poison is produced by a gland in the telson. Contrary to what may be thought, scorpions are not generally aggressive and do not normally attack animals larger than themselves. The usual prey consists of other arthropods.

Scorpions only become more sociable during the breeding season, when there is a complex prenuptial ritual in which the two individuals grasp each other by the palps or the chelicerae and move backward and forward. The male deposits a spermatophore on the ground and then leads the female over it. Female gonads contain an unusual structure which functions somewhat like a feeding bottle. Very young scorpions attach themselves to it with their rudimentary chelicerae and suck up a nutritious glandular secretion produced by the mother. Scorpions are viviparous and the young are carried around on the mother's back until the first molt.

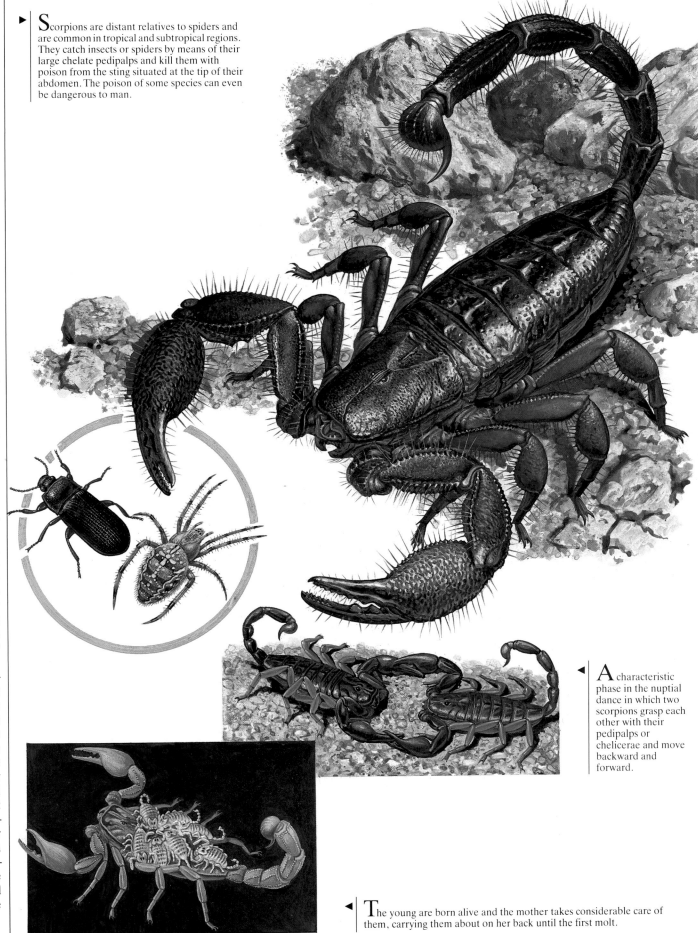

▶ Scorpions are distant relatives to spiders and are common in tropical and subtropical regions. They catch insects or spiders by means of their large chelate pedipalps and kill them with poison from the sting situated at the tip of their abdomen. The poison of some species can even be dangerous to man.

◀ A characteristic phase in the nuptial dance in which two scorpions grasp each other with their pedipalps or chelicerae and move backward and forward.

◀ The young are born alive and the mother takes considerable care of them, carrying them about on her back until the first molt.

SPIDERS

Arachnida

The body of a spider is clearly divided into a prosoma and an opisthosoma. These are linked by a pedicel which is often conspicuous. The prosoma is extremely variable in form. It is covered by a complete carapace and bears the eyes, which are usually 6 or 8 in number. There are, however, blind, soil or cave-dwelling forms. The abdomen is also highly variable in shape. It is only in the archaic Liphistiomorphae that it is still visibly segmented. The chelicerae are rather simple, consisting of a base and a fang which function rather like a hand with just a single finger. With the exception of some Uloboridae they contain poison glands. In the genus *Scytodes* the gland is modified to produce a sticky substance which the spider sprays over its prey to immobilize it. In females the pedipalps are like small legs, although in a few cases they are reduced or absent, whereas in males their tips have been transformed into a curious accessory copulatory organ known as the bulb.

Digestion is partly external, the digestive juices, which are of varying efficacy, being expelled and then taken back up. There are several types of silk glands and they produce various kinds of silk (non sticky, sticky, fluffy, etc.) which may sometimes differ in color. Silk is a protein which hardens on contact with air.

With the sole possible exception of some species which have adapted to living in ants' nests, all spiders are predators. They have three principal means of capturing their prey: by sight, by ambush or by using a web. Contrary to what might be thought, no more than half the existing spiders spin proper webs and only a minority construct the best-known geometrical form. This is virtually two-dimensional. The spider begins by building a four-sided or triangular frame which is stretched between branches or bushes. Diagonal threads are then run across the frame from one side to another in such a way that they all meet at one point, like the spokes of a wheel. These spokes are then connected together by a spiral of sticky thread. In many species the spider lives at the center of the web but in other forms it hides to one side and keeps in touch

Adult female of *Argiop bruennichi* (shown at natural size below), a common species which is found from Europe to Japan.

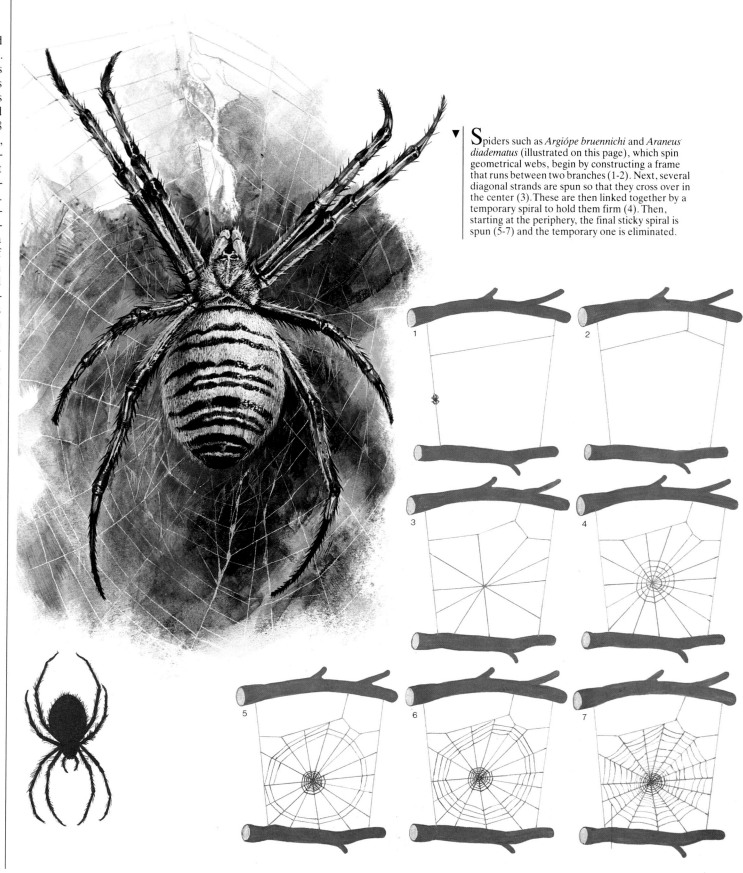

Spiders such as *Argiópe bruennichi* and *Araneus diadematus* (illustrated on this page), which spin geometrical webs, begin by constructing a frame that runs between two branches (1-2). Next, several diagonal strands are spun so that they cross over in the center (3). These are then linked together by a temporary spiral to hold them firm (4). Then, starting at the periphery, the final sticky spiral is spun (5-7) and the temporary one is eliminated.

with it by means of what Fabre called a "telegraph wire."

There are a number of other highly unusual ways of catching prey. Dinopids attach themselves to plants with their hindlegs and fish for small prey with a small web held between the tips of their forelegs and used like a trawl net. *Mastophora* sp. ensnare prey by using their forelegs to whirl a thread which ends in a ball of sticky silk, a habit which has earned them the name of bolas spiders. The great majority of spiders' victims are small and medium-sized flying insects such as dipterans, hymenopterans, lepidopterans, coleopterans, orthopterans and so on, together with other arthropods (arachnids, isopods and myriapods, etc.). Some large species living close to water catch tadpoles and small fish fairly regularly but the capture of other vertebrates is quite exceptional.

A large number of species are solitary throughout their lives; but there are, in addition to the numerous gregarious and social species, many species that display complex patterns of parental care or which tolerate young or males on their webs. The young often disperse by means of gossamer threads. The spider climbs up to a high point such as a branch or a blade of grass and, when the wind blows, emits a thread of silk to which, naturally, it remains attached. The thread is lifted by the wind and when it is fairly long the spider lets go of its support and is carried along like a kite.

Spiders generally like heat and humidity, and the majority of species live in tropical and temperate forests. In wooded areas a large number of species live among the detritus and run over the ground, while other species live on the vegetation and may be found at considerable heights. Some species live on mosses, under bark, in holes, in tree trunks, beneath stones or in burrows which they dig in the soil. All kinds of cavities, whether they be natural (caves, burrows, etc.) or artificial (mines, cellars, etc.), are inhabited by numerous species.

Argyroneta aquatica, has become virtually aquatic. It manages to live under the water by breathing air enclosed in a sort of silk bell, resurfacing every so often to replenish the air; however, it does not have to do so too often since it also has an underwater nest with a reserve of air.

▲◄ A*raneus diadematus*, the common garden or cross spider of the gardens of Europe, shown at natural size above.

▲ A male of *Philaeus chrysops* on the point of devouring a fly. It is one of the many salticid spiders capable of making small leaps. Note the pedipalps covered with white bristles. It has eight eyes and four of these are arranged in a row along the anterior margin of the prosoma.

◄ H*eteropoda venatoria* with a cockroach it has just captured. This is a large pantropical species which often reaches Europe in bunches of bananas (shown at natural size on the right).

▲ An *Atypus*, a distant relative of the tropical mygalids, lives in a tube of silk resting on the ground.

The spiders (Araneae) are the only chelicerate order so familiar that anyone will have seen at least one of its members. However, it is not the richest order in terms of species. They are familiar to everybody because of their webs which are common in even the cleanest houses. Very few species have a bite which is of danger to man.

▲ A large tarantula (*Lycosa*) with the egg bearing cocoon attached to its abdomen. It is a predatory spider with eight eyes arranged in three rows. The tarantula is virtually harmless to man but in Mediterranean regions its bite is connected with a collection of pre-Christian magico-religious practices. In these a central part of the ritual is a sort of frenetic dance which resembles the state of psychomotory agitation typical of people who have been bitten by *Latrodectus* (black widow) rather than the tarantula.

APTERYGOTA

The surface strata of the soil are inhabited by a teeming multitude of minute organisms, of which the most numerous are the apterygote insects. The common factors shared by all apterygotes are their originally wingless state, and their lack of metamorphosis. The creature which emerges from the egg differs from the adult only in size. This is known as ametaboly. The Apterygota comprise the Collembola, Diplura, Protura, and Thysanura. The Collembola or springtails are the most numerous and most widespread of the apterygotes. They are extremely small, some of them measuring only a few hundred microns in length, while others can be as long as a few millimeters. The head bears two antennae in which various sense organs are situated. The mouth parts are adapted for chewing.

Collembola differ from all other insects in having only six abdominal segments. On the ventral side of the first urite there is a prominent evagination known as the ventral tube. This allows the insect to stick to the smoothest surfaces even when it is vertical, since the end of the ventral tube from which two vesicles protrude is always covered with a sticky secretion. On the ventral surface of the third abdominal segment there is a two-pronged formation known as the tenaculum or clasp, designed to hold the saltatory organ. This organ is called the spring or furcula, and is an appendage of the ventral part of the fourth abdominal segment.

The Collembola are light-shunning creatures, and with only a few exceptions, such as *Seira domestica*, they inhabit damp and shady places where there is plenty of organic matter. Some, like *Anurida* and *Actaletes* live on the seashore. The majority of Collembola feed off the hyphae of fungi, spores, and bacteria.

The Protura are a strange group of small organisms discovered by the Italian entomologist Silvestri at the beginning of the present century. Protura are rarely as much as 2 mm long. Unlike all other insects, the head has no eyes and no antennae. The first pair of legs is not used in walking, but is raised above the head in an apparently threatening attitude. In fact, these legs are covered with a large number of

The Apterygota are small wingless insects which live under bark, beneath stones and among organic matter in the underbrush; some, like the thysanuran or bristletail pictured below (*Lepisma*, commonly called the silverfish), are often found in homes, living both on foodstuffs and old books, but more frequently feeding on bacteria and fungi. The abdomen of these insects terminates in a kind of three-pronged tail, made up of two long cerci and a median process.

sensillae and function as antennae. The abdomen in adults has twelve segments instead of the usual eleven. Unlike normal insects, Protura are born with only nine abdominal segments. The missing segments are acquired in the course of successive molts. This phenomenon is unique among insects, and is known as anamorphosis. Proturans, too, are light-shunning creatures, found in moist areas rich in organic matter.

Diplura have long, flattened bodies. They are small, and measure from 0.07 – 0.3 in (2 – 10 mm) in length. They are all blind, and except for a few rare species, unpigmented. The abdomen ends in two appendages called cerci, which are differently shaped in the Japygidae and Campodea. In the former the cerci form a pair of strong pincers, whereas in the campodeids the cerci are very long and delicate, are much segmented, and contain sensory organs. The mouthparts are contained within the buccal cavity, as in the Collembola and Protura. The first abdominal segments have vesicles on their ventral surface which can be evaginated. These are extremely important, and can absorb water, like the similar vesicles in the Thysanura. Diplura are found at every latitude, and in every biotope, so long as there is sufficient humidity for them to develop. Some of them are adapted to life in caves.

The Campodea are omnivorous and feed off mycelia, the leaves and bark of various trees, and small fragments of soil-dwelling Arthropods. The Japygidae are carnivorous and eat mites and the larvae of several beetles. The Thysanura constitutes probably the best-known order of Apterygota. Unlike the other apterygotes, the Thysanura are ectognathous, which means that the mandible and maxillae are externally visible. They are of medium size, and can reach 1 in (2 cm) in length. Some, such as *Zygentoma (Lepismatidae)* have a flattened body, while others such as *Microcoryphia (Machilida)* have more or less cylindrical bodies. The head has two very long antennae resembling those of the more evolved winged insects, which occupy most of the dorsal surface of the head, and the eyes. The thorax has three pairs of legs used for walking and jumping.

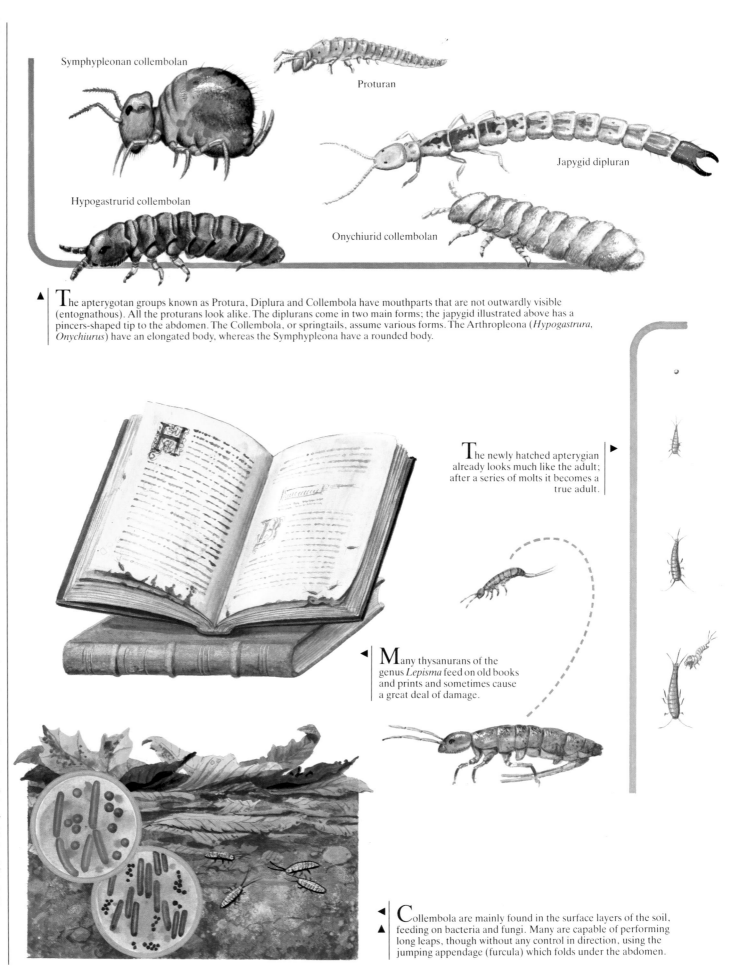

Symphypleonan collembolan

Proturan

Japygid dipluran

Hypogastrurid collembolan

Onychiurid collembolan

▲ The apterygotan groups known as Protura, Diplura and Collembola have mouthparts that are not outwardly visible (entognathous). All the proturans look alike. The diplurans come in two main forms; the japygid illustrated above has a pincers-shaped tip to the abdomen. The Collembola, or springtails, assume various forms. The Arthropleona (*Hypogastrura, Onychiurus*) have an elongated body, whereas the Symphypleona have a rounded body.

▶ The newly hatched apterygian already looks much like the adult; after a series of molts it becomes a true adult.

◀ Many thysanurans of the genus *Lepisma* feed on old books and prints and sometimes cause a great deal of damage.

◀ Collembola are mainly found in the surface layers of the soil,
▲ feeding on bacteria and fungi. Many are capable of performing long leaps, though without any control in direction, using the jumping appendage (furcula) which folds under the abdomen.

29

MAYFLIES

Ephemeroptera

The Ephemeroptera or mayflies are an ancient order of insects. They vary greatly in body size. Whereas the imagines of the smallest species are only about 0.07 – 0.12 in (2 – 3 mm) long, the body length of the biggest species may be as much as 2 in (5 cm). In many species the caudal filaments are as long as the body, or longer; the body of *Palingenia longicauda*, for instance, is 1¼ in (3.1 cm) long, and the cerci 2¾ in (6.9 cm).

The Ephemeroptera are distributed all over the world, except for some oceanic islands. Typically they are freshwater insects, almost entirely absent from marine biotopes and brackish inland waters. In the limnetic zone the nymphs are found in all biotopes from springs to stagnant water, but most species prefer fast-flowing, clear streams that offer coolness in summer. Most Ephemeroptera nymphs feed on vegetable material. The few predatory species eat small crustacea and gnat larvae.

The head of the adult has short, unsegmented antennae. The mouthparts are atrophied, so that they can no longer feed. The intestine is inflated with air and acts as an aerostatic organ. There are generally two pairs of wings. The nymphs have two long, segmented cerci and a single terminal filament. In many species the caudal filaments have bristles and are used in swimming. The abdomen has ten segments. In general, the first seven segments have gills at the sides. Most of the nymphs live in flowing water, in which they have to face a variety of conditions, the most important being the strength of the current. We can distinguish the different types of nymph by their living habit.

Burrowing nymphs, such as those of the Palingeniidae, Polymitaridae, and Ephemeridae, live in calm, slow-flowing water. They bore tunnels into the clay or muddy banks and live and find their food in them. The nymph's head has a pair of strong mandibles, specially adapted for digging, and the powerful legs are also well adapted for digging in sand and clay. The plumed gills close over the back.

Flat nymphs, such as *Ecdyonurus*, *Epeorus*, and *Rhithrogena*, are adapted to life in stronger currents. They mostly

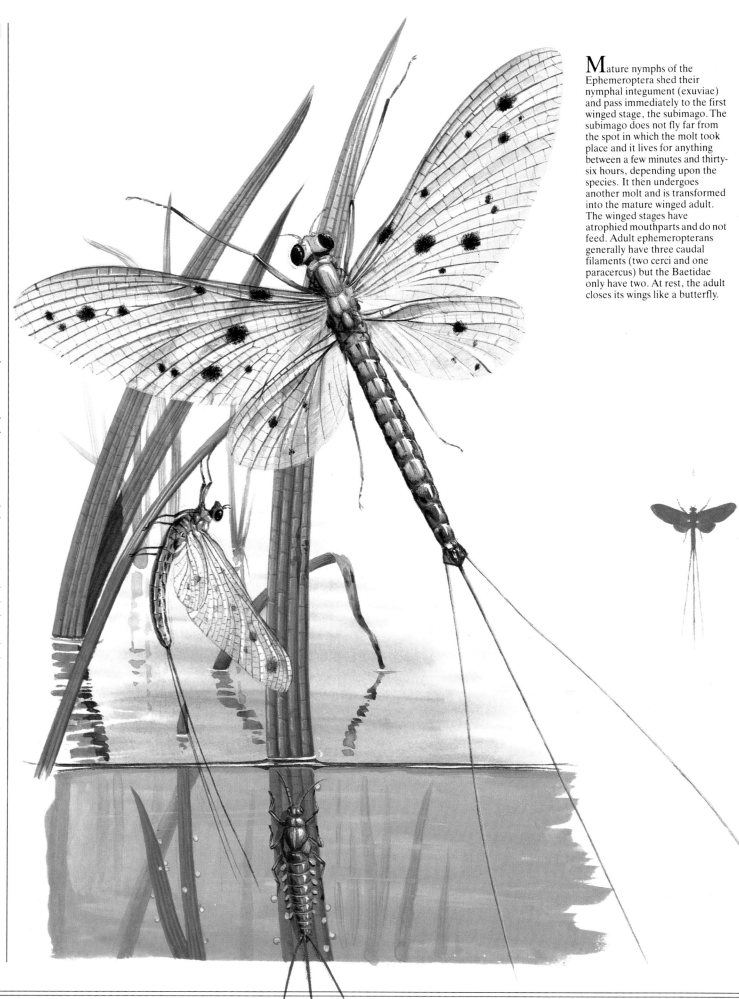

Mature nymphs of the Ephemeroptera shed their nymphal integument (exuviae) and pass immediately to the first winged stage, the subimago. The subimago does not fly far from the spot in which the molt took place and it lives for anything between a few minutes and thirty-six hours, depending upon the species. It then undergoes another molt and is transformed into the mature winged adult. The winged stages have atrophied mouthparts and do not feed. Adult ephemopterans generally have three caudal filaments (two cerci and one paracercus) but the Baetidae only have two. At rest, the adult closes its wings like a butterfly.

live in mountain or hill streams and on stony banks bordering big lakes. Their whole body is flattened dorso-ventrally. There are strong claws on the tarsi with which the animals can cling to the bed of the stream.

Swimming nymphs are slender, with streamlined bodies and soft legs. Examples are *Leptophlebiida*, *Siphlonurida*, and *Baëtida*. Some of these live in stagnant water, but they are also found in gently flowing water and in calm places in streams.

Crawling nymphs are found mainly in slow-flowing and stagnant water where the bottom is muddy and sandy, also among weeds and water plants. In flowing water they usually stay for the most part on the side of stones protected from the current. Examples are the Potamanthidae, Ephemerellidae, and Caenidae.

The duration of the nymphal stage varies from species to species. The tiny newly hatched nymphs still have no gills, but breathe through their skin. The nymphs molt 20 – 30 times in the course of their development before they are ready to emerge from the nymphal shuck.

These animals pass the majority of their lives under water; their life as flying insects lasts only a few days, in many species only a few hours. The first winged form emerges from the fully developed nymph. But this form, known as the subimago or "dun," is still not sexually mature. After emerging from the exuvia, the subimago flies up into nearby bushes on the bank, into the surrounding fields or into the foliage of trees in woods further from the stream. The lifetime of the subimago differs in different species; it may be only seconds, a few hours or even 2 or 3 days. The mouthparts are atrophied, and from then on the insects take no food. The same is true of the imago, which after a time emerges from the subimago. The sole task of the imago is the perpetuation of the species. The males gather in swarms, sometimes quite big, sometimes less so, and the females fly into them. Copulation takes place in flight and generally lasts only a few seconds.

Ephemeropteran nymphs always live in fresh water. Their mouthparts are well developed and they feed on plant tissues, algae and organic detritus. A few carnivorous species are known.

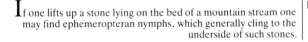

If one lifts up a stone lying on the bed of a mountain stream one may find ephemeropteran nymphs, which generally cling to the underside of such stones.

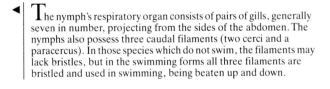

The nymph's respiratory organ consists of pairs of gills, generally seven in number, projecting from the sides of the abdomen. The nymphs also possess three caudal filaments (two cerci and a paracercus). In those species which do not swim, the filaments may lack bristles, but in the swimming forms all three filaments are bristled and used in swimming, being beaten up and down.

The nymphs are the favorite food of fish and the aquatic larvae of carnivorous insects. The adults are preyed on by birds, bats, dragonflies, and spiders.

ODONATA

The Odonata or dragonflies constitute an order of insects with incomplete metamorphosis. Some 5,000 species are known and – with the exception of the Poles – they are found in virtually every part of the world, although they are particularly common in temperate and warm regions. In the adult stage they are terrestrial, i.e. winged insects, but, their larvae (nymphs) are aquatic. All stages are predatory and when adult they are medium to large in size, ranging from ¾ – 5 in (18 – 130 mm) in length, with wingspans of between ¾ – 5½ in (19 and 140 mm). They are in general good flyers. Although the order Odonata is a homogeneous one it is divided into three well-defined suborders: the Zygoptera, the Anisozygoptera and the Anisoptera.

In the Zygoptera the head is extended transversely and the eyes lie at the two ends, whereas in the Anisoptera the head is spherical. This is due to the enormous development of the eyes, which are among the largest to be found in the insect world, with anything from 10,000 to more than 28,000 ommatidia each. Usually the membranous wings are transparent but in some species they are strikingly colored. A dense network of veins runs across them. The tip of the abdomen bears some appendages that play a vital role in mating.

In the Anisoptera the nymphs have elongated, roughly cylindrical, thick bodies or stouter, ovoidal bodies while in the Zygoptera they are more slender. A very distinctive feature is the enormous development of the labium, which is transformed into a prehensile organ known as the mask. This can be extended and retracted and is used for the capture of prey.

Dragonfly larvae may be found in various aquatic habitats, some preferring running water and others still water. Many tropical species lay their eggs in temporary pools of rain-water, while some use water-filled hollows in tree trunks or the cups formed by the overlapping leaf bases of certain Bromeliaceae. The development of certain species may take place in the brackish waters of coastal lagoons. Two exceptional cases are *Petalura gigantea* from Australia, which develops in very damp ground, and a Hawaiian member of the genus

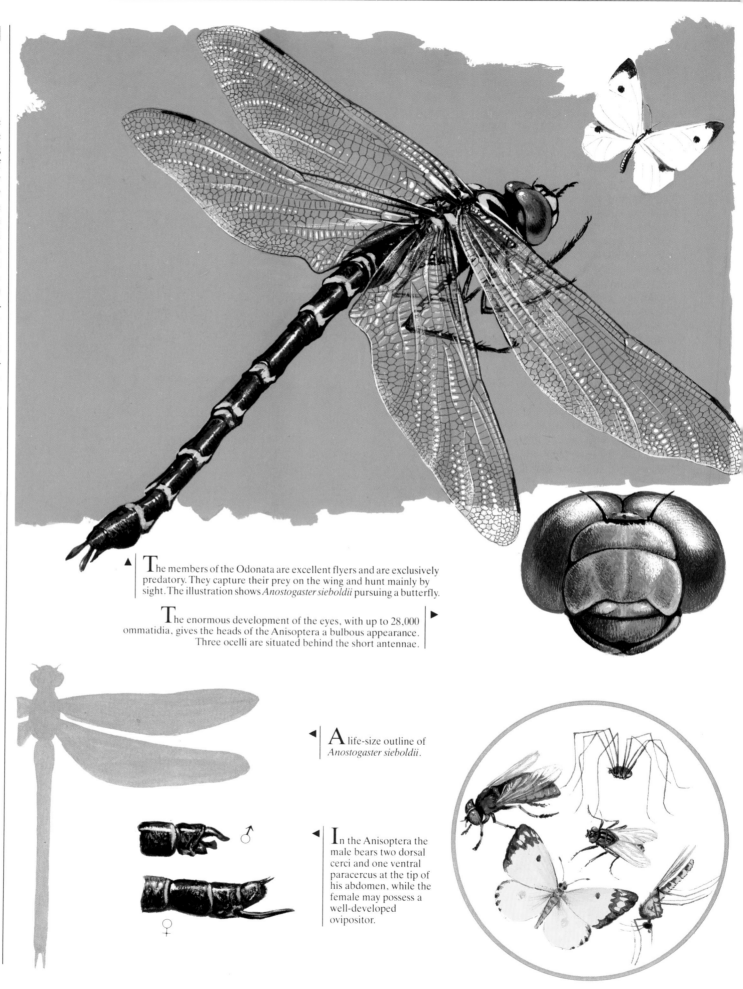

▲ The members of the Odonata are excellent flyers and are exclusively predatory. They capture their prey on the wing and hunt mainly by sight. The illustration shows *Anostogaster sieboldii* pursuing a butterfly.

The enormous development of the eyes, with up to 28,000 ▶ ommatidia, gives the heads of the Anisoptera a bulbous appearance. Three ocelli are situated behind the short antennae.

◀ A life-size outline of *Anostogaster sieboldii*.

♂

♀

◀ In the Anisoptera the male bears two dorsal cerci and one ventral paracercus at the tip of his abdomen, while the female may possess a well-developed ovipositor.

Megalagrion, which has become decidedly terrestrial in habit. The larvae are not normally very active, preferring to wait for some prey to pass within range of their mask as they rest on the bottom, hide in the mud or cling vertically to the stem of an aquatic plant. In the Zygoptera the lifespan of the larvae can vary from a few weeks to a year, and in the Anisoptera it lasts 2 – 3 or more years. During this period the insect molts 10 – 15 times and before each molt it becomes less active and stops feeding. When about to metamorphose, it slowly begins to emerge from the water.

Mating may be preceded by special courtship flights (parades). The male hooks the female's thorax with its cerci and they take a short flight in tandem, which ends with them clinging to the stem of a plant. If he has not already done so, the male bends his abdomen forward so as to bring his gonopore up to his copulatory organ and is then able to transfer the spermatophores containing the sperm. Once this operation has been completed the female curves her abdomen so that her gonopore is in contact with the male's copulatory organ. The linked abdomens of the two dragonflies form a characteristic heart-shaped figure. When mating is complete, oviposition begins. The eggs may be inserted into plant tissue or loosely abandoned in water. The egg hatches to produce a pronymph which after a short time becomes a nymph. This grows by a series of molts.

The early larval stages feed off infusorians and tiny crustaceans and then gradually move on to any other aquatic animal of a suitable size. The large larvae of Anisoptera can catch amphibian larvae, fish fry, and even small fish.

When the mature larva is close to the final molt, from which the adult will emerge, it abandons the water where it has lived until then. Various larvae climb up the stems of plants which emerge from the water or climb onto floating leaves or stones near the bank. Others move farther away from the water and undergo metamorphosis in nearby grasses.

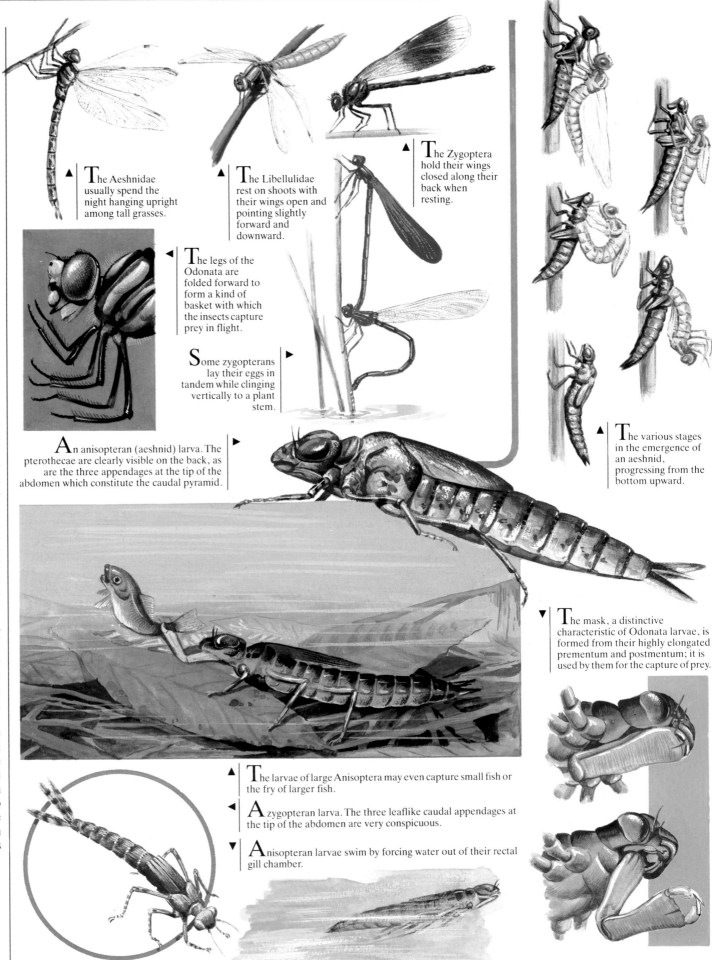

▲ The Aeshnidae usually spend the night hanging upright among tall grasses.

▲ The Libellulidae rest on shoots with their wings open and pointing slightly forward and downward.

The Zygoptera hold their wings closed along their back when resting.

◄ The legs of the Odonata are folded forward to form a kind of basket with which the insects capture prey in flight.

Some zygopterans lay their eggs in tandem while clinging vertically to a plant stem. ►

An anisopteran (aeshnid) larva. The pterothecae are clearly visible on the back, as are the three appendages at the tip of the abdomen which constitute the caudal pyramid. ►

▲ The various stages in the emergence of an aeshnid, progressing from the bottom upward.

▼ The mask, a distinctive characteristic of Odonata larvae, is formed from their highly elongated prementum and postmentum; it is used by them for the capture of prey.

▲ The larvae of large Anisoptera may even capture small fish or the fry of larger fish.

◄ A zygopteran larva. The three leaflike caudal appendages at the tip of the abdomen are very conspicuous.

▼ Anisopteran larvae swim by forcing water out of their rectal gill chamber.

MANTODEA

This order contains about 1,800 species of medium and large-size predatory insects; they are concentrated in tropical and subtropical regions. Extremely varied in form, they are striking in appearance and have attracted the attention of man since antiquity. It is the unusual structure of their forelimbs that is primarily responsible for this. These limbs are used for seizing prey and not for walking and this results in postures which are rather unusual for insects. Many people have seen the attack posture of a mantid as an attitude of prayer, and this has given rise to the common name of the praying mantis.

The body is usually farily elongated, green or brown, although there are often special features of morphology or color for the purposes of camouflaging the animal. Some tree-living mantids with flattened and highly variegated bodies (*Theopompa, liturgusa*) mimic bark and the lichens growing on it while other long, thin ones appear like small branches or twigs. Many species imitate leaves, even crumpled, dry ones (*Deroplatys, Acanthops, Toxodera*). Besides green, various shades of brown and ocher are common and indeed predominate among animals living on the ground or in dry grass. The result is a marked uniformity of color. Some species, however, do display chromatic polymorphism but this is due to environmental conditions rather than to any genetic mechanism.

Certain species are remarkable in that they exhibit the colors on the median surfaces of their expanded anterior coxae or have bodies which mimic the appearance of flowers in order to attract those insects feeding on them (*Gongylus gongylodes*). Numerous mantids possess processes and spines on various parts of their bodies, for example, on their eyes (*Oxyothespis, Toxodera*), on the vertex of their head (*Empusa, Phyllocrania, Sibylla*), and on the pronotum (*Junodia, Pseudocreobotra*). Others bear platelike expansions of the margins of their limbs, the pronotum and sometimes even the abdomen (*Deroplatys, Choeradodis, Idolomantis*).

Mantids have a relatively small, triangular head which is highly mobile. The antennae are normally filiform and the mouthparts are

The order of the Mantodea contains about 1,800 species of medium and large-sized predatory insects, concentrated in tropical and subtropical regions. Extremely varied in form, they are striking in appearance and have attracted the attention of man since antiquity. It is the unusual structure of their forelimbs that is primarily responsible for this. These limbs are used for seizing prey and not for walking, with the result that the posture of these animals are rather unusual for insects. The illustration is of a specimen of *Mantis religiosa* in a characteristic posture. It is well camouflaged among the grasses and its forelegs are ready to shoot out and seize prey, which are usually insects and may belong to any order.

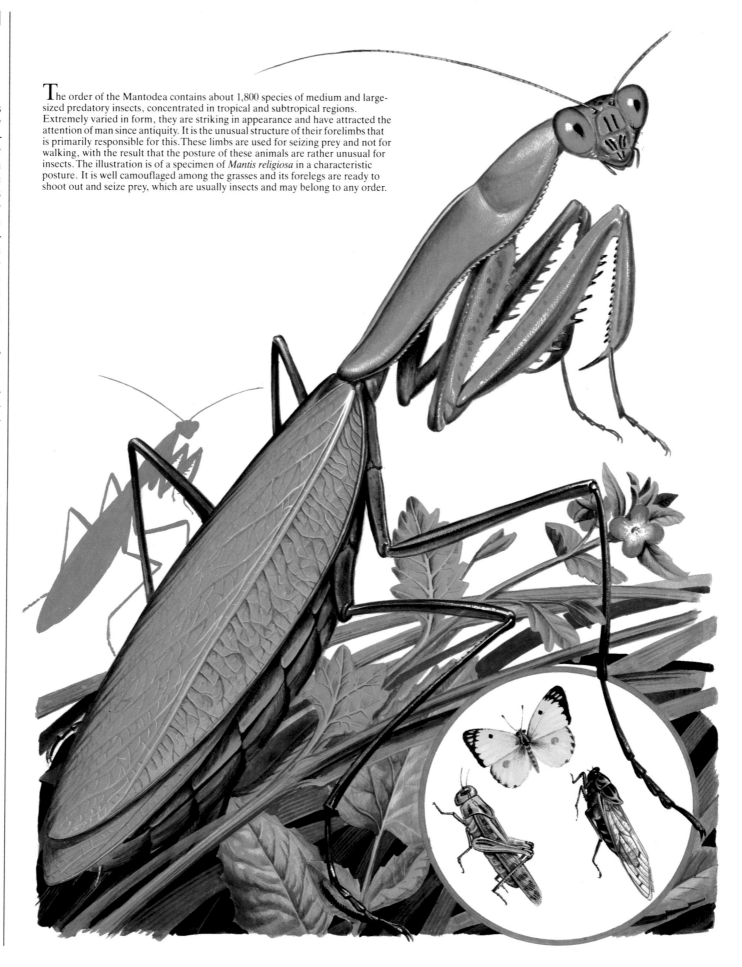

adapted for chewing. The mobility of the head is made possible by a highly extended neck region. However, the prothorax and its pair of legs is the most characteristic feature of the mantids. The forelegs are adapted for seizing prey and the manner in which they articulate with the prothorax allows them to make the most unexpected movements in all directions.

Another adaptation displayed by the raptorial legs is the marked elongation of their coxae, which may often be as long as the femora. The two ventral margins of the femora bear two rows of strong spines, some of which may be very long. The tibiae can be bent right back against the femora and they too bear two rows of spines along their ventral margins. These spines interlock with those on the femur and together they form a powerful vice in which prey is held and from which it cannot escape. The grip is further ensured by a strong, curved hook extending from the tip of the tibia and which, when the leg is closed, fits into a groove on the inner surface of the femur.

There are two pairs of wings, the anterior pair usually being leathery (tegmina) although they may be delicate and membranous like the hind pair. Reduction of the wings is common among the mantids and this may occur in the females only (*Ameles, Iris*) or in both sexes (*Eremiaphila*). The abdomen is extensively joined to the thorax and is somewhat flattened. Since a female will attack and kill a male as if it were prey, the overtures of a male intent on mating are extremely cautious.

The formation of the oöthecae, in which the eggs are deposited, is another highly complex operation. In dry environments the oöthecae generally have a delicate porous surface but in wetter climates their surfaces are hardened and smooth. The newborn larvae are very active and voracious and until they have dispersed they show a marked tendency toward cannibalism. Metamorphosis is gradual, being pseudoametabolous in apterous forms and paurometabolous in winged ones.

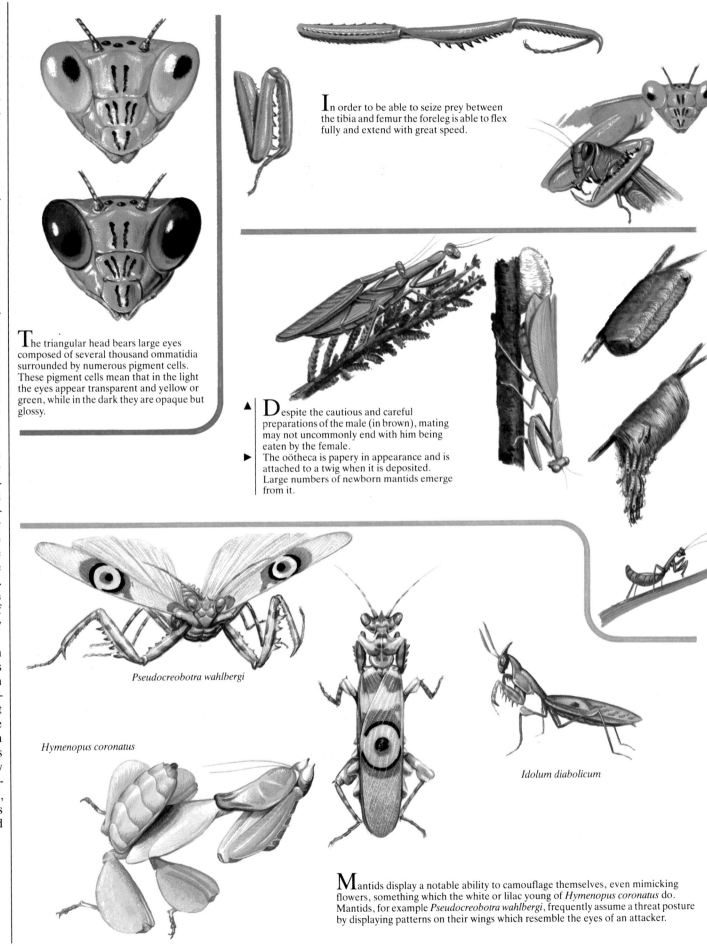

In order to be able to seize prey between the tibia and femur the foreleg is able to flex fully and extend with great speed.

The triangular head bears large eyes composed of several thousand ommatidia surrounded by numerous pigment cells. These pigment cells mean that in the light the eyes appear transparent and yellow or green, while in the dark they are opaque but glossy.

▲ Despite the cautious and careful preparations of the male (in brown), mating may not uncommonly end with him being eaten by the female.
► The oötheca is papery in appearance and is attached to a twig when it is deposited. Large numbers of newborn mantids emerge from it.

Pseudocreobotra wahlbergi

Hymenopus coronatus

Idolum diabolicum

Mantids display a notable ability to camouflage themselves, even mimicking flowers, something which the white or lilac young of *Hymenopus coronatus* do. Mantids, for example *Pseudocreobotra wahlbergi*, frequently assume a threat posture by displaying patterns on their wings which resemble the eyes of an attacker.

ISOPTERA

The Isoptera (termites) is an order of insects which live in societies characterized by caste polymorphism. The group is related to the Blattodea, with which it has common ancestors. The order contains more than 2,000 species, distributed mainly in the tropics and grouped into six families.

A prominent feature of the social organization of the termites is their caste polymorphism, which makes possible a marked specialization of function. Four basic castes are usually distinguished.

Winged individuals have the role of dispersing the species. They develop at certain times of the year, abandoning the nest in a dispersal flight, at the end of which they found a new colony, becoming the "founding royals" or "primary royals."

Replacement royals (supplementary, complementary, secondary or tertiary forms, etc.) are neotenous breeding individuals which develop from the juvenile stages and which retain a partly juvenile appearance. They develop within the colony and remain there as breeding individuals.

Soldiers are individuals with heads and mandibles radically modified to fit them for their task of defense. Soldiers are always sterile and their gonads are immature. They may sometimes be of both sexes (in a 1:1 ratio, *Kalotermes flavicollis*) or they may be just males (*Trinervitermes*) or just females (*Bellicositermes bellicosus*). They form a constant proportion of the population which is typical for each species.

The workers only constitute a well-defined caste in the Termitidae but there they often form two subcastes of large and small workers. Their presence in the other families is disputed. They are certainly absent from the Kalotermitidae, the Hodotermitidae and the Mastotermitidae, where their role is taken over by "pseudergates," juvenile forms which retain the ability to differentiate into any of the species' castes. Workers are sterile and their gonads are immature in structure. Workers carry out all the tasks needed by the society. They build the nest, look after and feed the royals and the soldiers, and care for the eggs, etc.

Winged adults develop within the nests at certain times of the year and their role is to disperse the species.

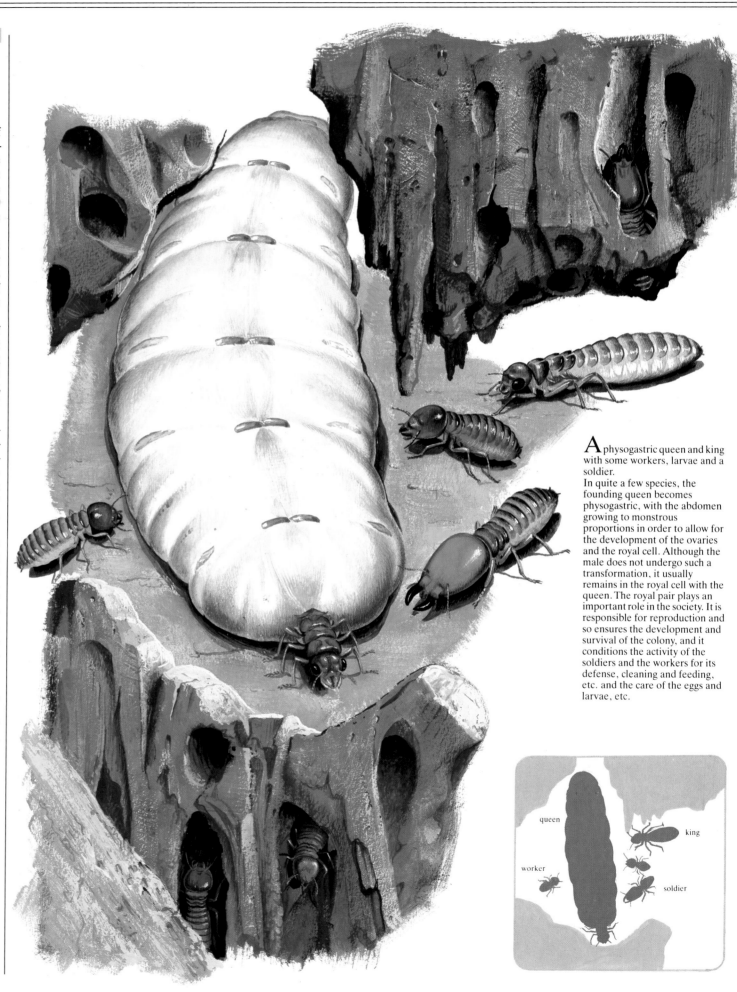

A physogastric queen and king with some workers, larvae and a soldier.
In quite a few species, the founding queen becomes physogastric, with the abdomen growing to monstrous proportions in order to allow for the development of the ovaries and the royal cell. Although the male does not undergo such a transformation, it usually remains in the royal cell with the queen. The royal pair plays an important role in the society. It is responsible for reproduction and so ensures the development and survival of the colony, and it conditions the activity of the soldiers and the workers for its defense, cleaning and feeding, etc. and the care of the eggs and larvae, etc.

queen

king

worker

soldier

After metamorphosing, the winged individuals remain in the nest for a while. Then they gradually gather in the chambers at the edge of the nest until the workers open passages in the walls of the nest and they are able to swarm.

At the end of their flight and usually before they meet, the male and female winged individuals break off their wing blades along the basal suture. When they do meet, the male and female form a pair and begin the nuptial dance. Once this is over they search for a suitable spot to found a new nest. In the majority of species both sexes cooperate in its building but in *Zootermopsis* the female alone digs and the male stands guard, perhaps to prevent the approach of other males. The founding pair must provide for the initial needs of the nascent colony, extending the nest, taking care of the eggs, feeding the larvae, etc. Gradually, as the colony expands, all tasks are taken over by the sterile castes.

Among the lower termites the founding pair feed actively, eating eggs and using the food reserves that derive from the fat body and from the lysis of the wing muscles. Subsequently, this feeding off stored reserves is gradually replaced by a diet based on the saliva of the larvae and the pseudergates. A diet of saliva, which is rich in protein, enables the queen's ovaries to develop and increases her fertility. This development may be so great as to swell the abdomen to 250 or 300 times its original volume. The number of eggs laid annually ranges form 220-300 in some kalotermitids to 30 million in *Odontotermes obesus*.

The nests of wood-eating Termites are generally very simple in structure, consisting of a seemingly disordered jumble of galleries dug into the wood, which affords the insects both food and shelter at the same time. Many species of termites, however, construct highly complex nests.

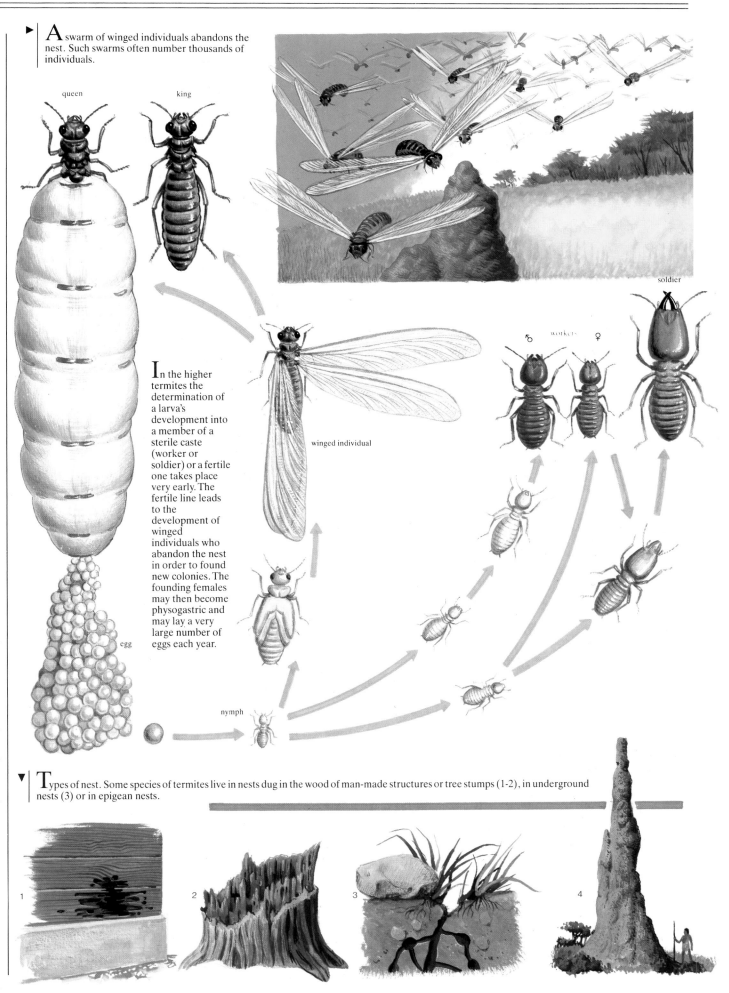

A swarm of winged individuals abandons the nest. Such swarms often number thousands of individuals.

queen

king

In the higher termites the determination of a larva's development into a member of a sterile caste (worker or soldier) or a fertile one takes place very early. The fertile line leads to the development of winged individuals who abandon the nest in order to found new colonies. The founding females may then become physogastric and may lay a very large number of eggs each year.

winged individual

egg

nymph

soldier

workers

♂   ♀

Types of nest. Some species of termites live in nests dug in the wood of man-made structures or tree stumps (1-2), in underground nests (3) or in epigean nests.

1   2   3   4

ORTHOPTERA

Commonly known as grasshoppers, crickets and locusts, the Orthoptera are characterized by their jumping ability and by the presence of stridulatory and acoustic organs. They are predominantly terrestrial and only occasionally semi-aquatic. Their bodies are elongated, subcylindrical, slightly compressed and less frequently depressed. Length varies from a few millimeters in the members of the genus *Myrmecophila* up to the 6 in (15 cm) of *Tropidacris* sp.

The head is normally large and rounded, although in the Conocephalidae, Pyrgomorphidae, etc. it may be conical. It has strong mouthparts. The antennae are inserted between the eyes and are normally filiform. They may consist of anything from a handful up to 500 joints and may be short (Caelifera), moderate in length or extremely long (Ensifera).

The first thoracic segment, the prothorax, is mobile and is always larger than the other segments. It bears a large pronotum which varies as to how far it reaches backward, although in some Tetrigidae it extends beyond the tip of the abdomen.

The forewings are normally elongated, narrow and similar in color to the rest of the body. They are tegmina, being poorly sclerotized and having prominent veins. In almost all ensifers they are modified in connection with the stridulatory organ. The hindwings are membranous, transparent or brightly colored, and broad, as a consequence of the marked development of the anal lobe. At rest they are folded like a fan beneath the tegmina, which normally cover them completely. The tegmina and the wings are often reduced, sometimes to differing extents in the two sexes, or absent altogether.

The legs are well developed, wih elongated tibidae and femora which often bear spines. The first and second pairs of legs are generally quite similar but in forms such as the Gryllotalpidae and the Cylindrachetidae the front legs are fossorial. In the majority of ensifers there is an auditory or tympanal organ at the base of each fore tibia. The hindlegs are typically saltatory and are always more highly developed than the other two pairs. In many species of acridoid caelifers the

The Orthoptera is an ancient group of insects and its members are normally characterized by the presence of stridulatory and auditory organs and by the considerable development of the third pair of legs.

In the suborder Ensifera the antennae are long or very long and consist of a large number of joints (sometimes more than 500). The stridulatory organ results from the specialization of the tegmina and the auditory organ lies at the bases of the fore tibiae. There are three or four tarsal joints. Apart from instances where it is secondarily reduced, all ensifers have a well-developed, ensiform, straight or curved (see inset below) ovipositor. They vary in coloration. The illustration is of *Metrioptera brachyptera* (Tettigoniidae).

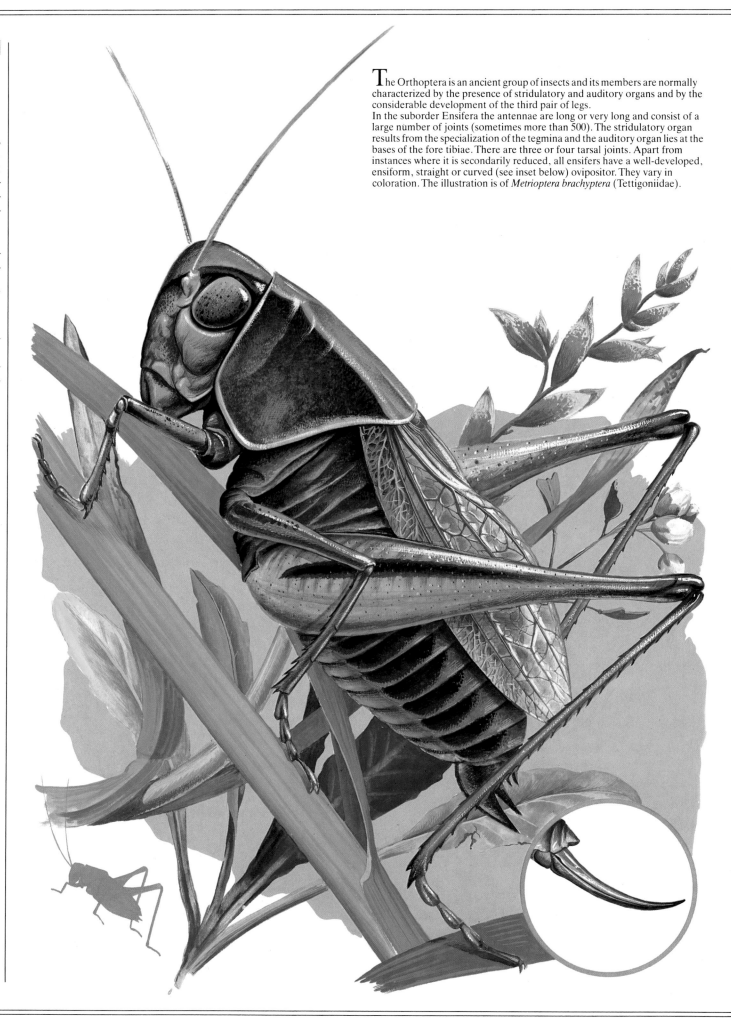

inner surface of the hind femur bears a longitudinal row of small tubercles which form part of the stridulatory organ.

In the females of the suborder Ensifera the ovipositor typically is well developed, compressed and ensiform – hence the name of the suborder – straight, curved upward or, less often, downward. It may sometimes reach a considerable size and in *Copiphora* and *Eurepa* it may be twice as long as the rest of the body. Caelifers generally have a short, stout cuneiform ovipositor. In most species eggs are only laid during a short period, normally at the end of the summer. Some species, however, do lay their eggs in the late spring and those forms living in houses will lay eggs at any time of year. The eggs are always hidden in sheltered spots, beneath bark, in plant tissues or in holes dug in the ground.

One of the best known and most typical characteristics of many orthopterans is their ability to emit sounds. In most members of this order it is only the males that do so. They use specialized structures known as stridulatory organs. In the ensifera parts of the tegmina are specialized to form the file, the scraper and the mirror of the stridulatory organ, and the insects stridulate by rubbing their tegmina together.

In the Caelifera the stridulatory organs are very different. There are also differences within this suborder and the sounds are not always produced by the vibration of the tegmina. In the majority of acridids, regarded as the true stridulatory Caelifera, the stridulatory organ consists of a row of quite pointed tubercles on the inner surface of the hind femora and the radial vein of both tegmina, the sound being produced by the passage of these tubercles over the vein.

Almost all the members of the order display a more or less marked tendency to congregate but it reaches its maximum development in only a few species, with the formation of immense swarms. The true migratory species belong to the acridid Caelifera. These include *Locustana migratoria* (Europe, tropical Africa, Asia), *Locustana pardalina* (southern Africa), *Schistocerca gregaria* (Africa, western Asia), *Schistocerca paranensis* (South America) and *Nomadacris septemfasciata* (central Africa).

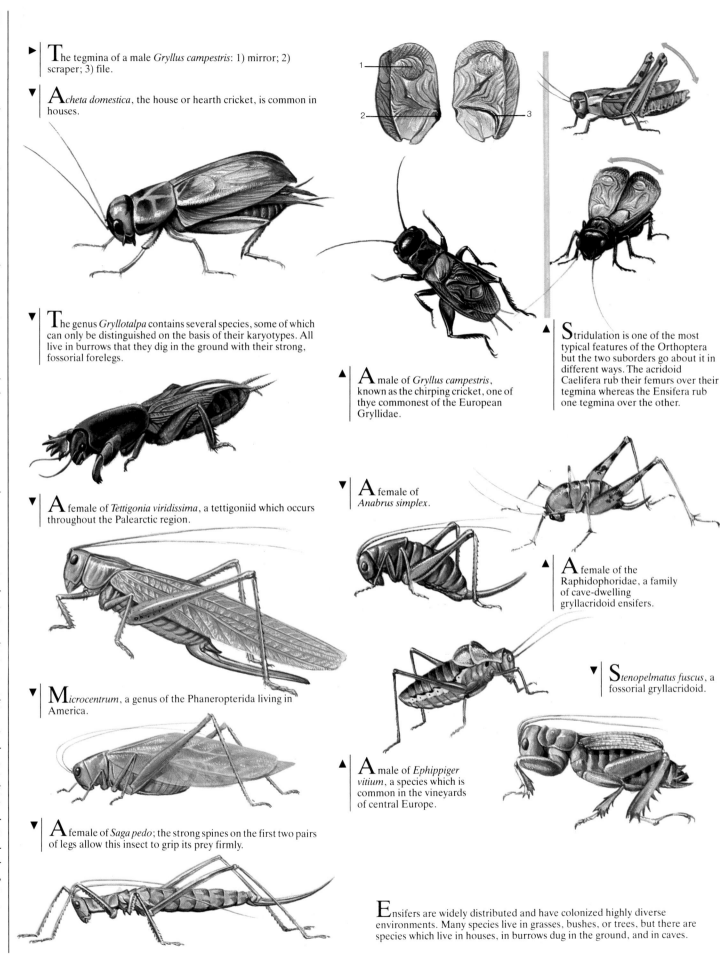

▶ The tegmina of a male *Gryllus campestris*: 1) mirror; 2) scraper; 3) file.

▼ *Acheta domestica*, the house or hearth cricket, is common in houses.

▼ The genus *Gryllotalpa* contains several species, some of which can only be distinguished on the basis of their karyotypes. All live in burrows that they dig in the ground with their strong, fossorial forelegs.

▼ A female of *Tettigonia viridissima*, a tettigoniid which occurs throughout the Palearctic region.

▼ *Microcentrum*, a genus of the Phaneropterida living in America.

▼ A female of *Saga pedo*; the strong spines on the first two pairs of legs allow this insect to grip its prey firmly.

▲ A male of *Gryllus campestris*, known as the chirping cricket, one of thye commonest of the European Gryllidae.

▲ Stridulation is one of the most typical features of the Orthoptera but the two suborders go about it in different ways. The acridoid Caelifera rub their femurs over their tegmina whereas the Ensifera rub one tegmina over the other.

▼ A female of *Anabrus simplex*.

▲ A female of the Raphidophoridae, a family of cave-dwelling gryllacridoid ensifers.

▼ *Stenopelmatus fuscus*, a fossorial gryllacridoid.

▲ A male of *Ephippiger vitium*, a species which is common in the vineyards of central Europe.

E nsifers are widely distributed and have colonized highly diverse environments. Many species live in grasses, bushes, or trees, but there are species which live in houses, in burrows dug in the ground, and in caves.

PHASMIDA

These medium to large-sized insects may sometimes be massive, as in the female of *Phoboeticus fruhstorferi* from Indochina, which is 12 in (30 cm) long and ranks as one of the largest living insects. Their bodies may be very thin and elongated, like a stick or a twig (*Bacillus*, *Carausius*, etc.), or broad and flattened, like a leaf (*Phyllium*) and as a result these animals are commonly known as stick or leaf insects. However, some species have stout and rather elongated bodies (*Prisopus*, *Haaniella*). The females are larger than the males.

Many Phasmids have well-developed wings but despite this they are poor flyers and numerous species are apterous or have rudimentary wings. The leathery forewings, tegmina, are prominently veined and markedly shorter than the hind pair. Indeed, they may sometimes be reduced to two small scales (*Orthomeria*) or they may be absent altogether (*Aschiphasma*, etc.) The hind wings are sometimes brightly colored and show varying degrees of development; they may even be missing. When present they comprise a narrow, well-sclerotized anterior region, the remige, and a more extensive, membranous hind region, which at rest, is longitudinally folded like a fan.

Phasmids normally reproduce sexually. Parthenogenesis, however, does occur in many species. It is usually occasional (*Carausius morosus*, etc.) but geographical parthengenesis is known in *Bacillus rossii*. In the latter species, the populations from the northern part of its range are parthenogenetic while from southern ones reproduce sexually. In the majority of cases parthenogenesis gives rise to females (thelytoky), rarely producing males (arrhenotoky). In some species males are particularly rare and in *Carausius morosus* it has been calculated that there is one male for every thousand females.

The eggs may be spherical, ovoidal or polyhedral and they have a thick coat, the chorion, which is variously decorated with ridges and prominences. Large in size, they have an operculum and with their unusual colors, they often closely resemble plant seeds. The females usually allow the eggs to fall one by one to the ground or

Many of the Phasmida are known as stick insects because of their sticklike bodies. The head is small, rounded, often depressed, is prognathous or hypognathous, and sometimes bears one or more large spines. The antennae may be short and moniliform or long and filiform, and they consist of between eight and one hundred joints. The wings are often absent, and the legs, which are used exclusively for walking, are slender and well developed, with two claws and a median adhesive pad (the arolium) at the tip of the tarsi. Many species, such as the *Carausius morosus* shown here, have the ability to alter their coloration under the influence of various environmental stimuli.

they may project them for some distance by means of movements of the abdomen. In some cases they place eggs in cracks in trees or stick them, singly or in small groups, to a substrate. Depending upon the species, each female may lay an average of between 100 and 400 eggs. The incubation period is long and may sometimes last more than a year. The juveniles are quite similar to the adults, especially in the wingless forms.

Phasmids are predominantly nocturnal and live almost exclusively in bushes, where their appearance allows them to be mistaken for twigs or leaves and to pass unobserved. They are scarcely mobile and when they are knocked they do not flee. Instead they assume a highly characteristic posture, with their forelegs stretched forward and pressed tightly together while the other two pairs are pointed back along the abdomen. They can remain in this position without the slightest movement for as long as four or five hours. Another defensive adaptation is the ability of certain species to alter their body coloration quickly and rhythmically, being pale during the day and becoming darker with the onset of evening.

Autotomy of the legs is another phenomenon which is very common among the members of this order. When they are subjected to a certain level of stimulation the leg is shed with a sharp muscular contraction and, except for a few species, this always occurs at a pre-existing breakage point between the trochanter and the femur. The diaphragm at this point allows only nerves and tracheae to pass through and minimizes the loss of haemolymph. The missing leg is subsequently regenerated unless the entire limb including the coxa is lost, in which case there is no regeneration. Broken antennae can also be regenerated, although if the base of the antennal nerve is damaged a leg will be regenerated in place of the antenna.

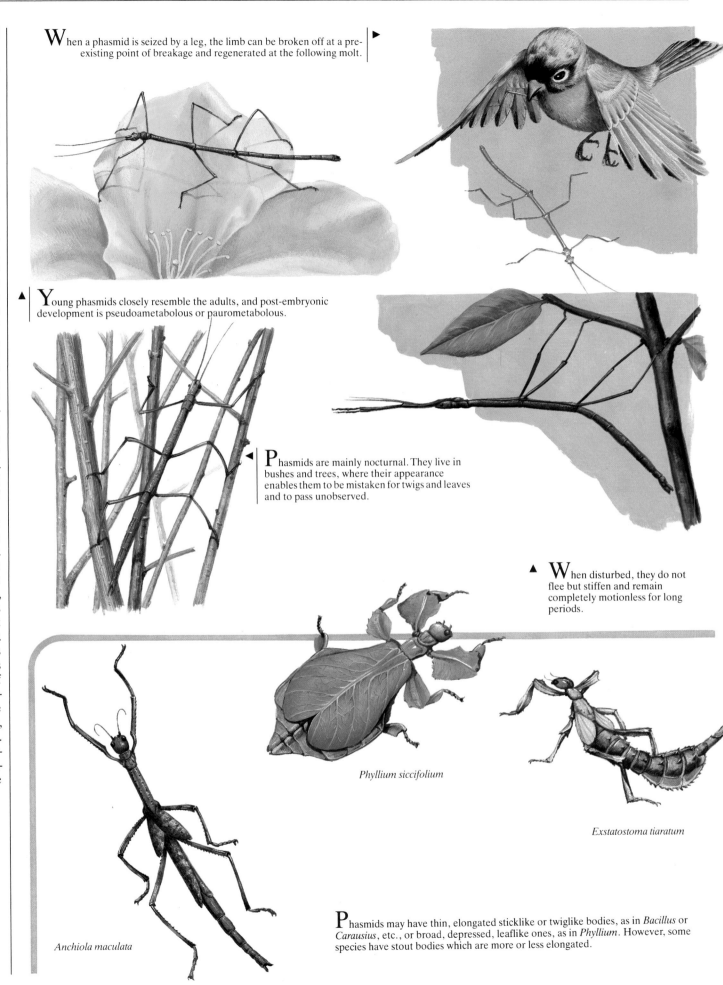

When a phasmid is seized by a leg, the limb can be broken off at a pre-existing point of breakage and regenerated at the following molt.

Young phasmids closely resemble the adults, and post-embryonic development is pseudoametabolous or paurometabolous.

Phasmids are mainly nocturnal. They live in bushes and trees, where their appearance enables them to be mistaken for twigs and leaves and to pass unobserved.

When disturbed, they do not flee but stiffen and remain completely motionless for long periods.

Phyllium siccifolium

Exstatostoma tiaratum

Anchiola maculata

Phasmids may have thin, elongated sticklike or twiglike bodies, as in *Bacillus* or *Carausius*, etc., or broad, depressed, leaflike ones, as in *Phyllium*. However, some species have stout bodies which are more or less elongated.

BUGS
Heteroptera

Bugs or Heteroptera are a large insect order characterized by the piercing-sucking mouthparts, enabling them to get every kind of fluid meal, and by the transformation of the forewing into the so-called hemielytra, with the basal half hardened like a beetle elytron. We shall deal here with a few families of bugs.

The Cimicidae is a well-known family of temporary parasites of warm-blooded vertebrates, characterized by an oval, elongated, flattened and slightly hairy body some 0.2 – 0.24 in (5 – 6 mm) in length, with a relatively short rostrum. The forewings are reduced to stumps and the hind ones are absent altogether. Both adults and young secrete a highly unpleasant repugnatorial fluid.

The females lay their eggs in a wide variety of locations, such as cracks in beds and other furniture or walls and in wall hangings, etc., but they carefully avoid cold or damp places. The nymphs, like the adults, are hematophagous and need at least one good meal of blood between each molt.

The Cimicidae contains a total of about 70 species worldwide. The majority are habitual parasites of birds. *Cimex lectularius*, which occurs everywhere up to 65 – 70°N., and *Cimex hemipterus*, from the tropics, are strictly tied to man. Besides humans, *Cimex lectularius* will greedily feed off any animals that it finds in the house, attacking dogs, cats, rabbits, mice, chickens, sparrows and swallows, etc. A horde of starving bedbugs may kill a small animal such as a mouse if it is unable to escape them, and if they have not fed for a long time they will even attack geckos and amphibians, etc., that have just died, provided the ambient temperature is high enough.

Cimex lectularius detests light, remaining hidden during the day and only moving in the dark if hunger forces it out into natural or artificial light to seek prey. It walks well, being able to cover more than 230 ft (70 m) in an hour and to climb large obstacles. Sometimes they will drop from the ceiling onto the sleeper's bed, aiming accurately for his face, thanks to the column of warm exhaled air which rises to the ceiling.

Many of the Heteroptera are phytophagous and live on cultivated plants, often causing damage. They have flat bodies, are brightly colored and many species emit unpleasant odors. Their mouthparts consist of long stylets which they use to suck up animal and plant fluids. Some species are hematophagous and feed on human blood. The figure on the right shows *Carpocoris mediterraneus* in the act of puncturing a leaf. This polyphagous species is widespread in southern Europe and may sometimes harm cultivated plants as does the related *Carpocoris pudicus*.

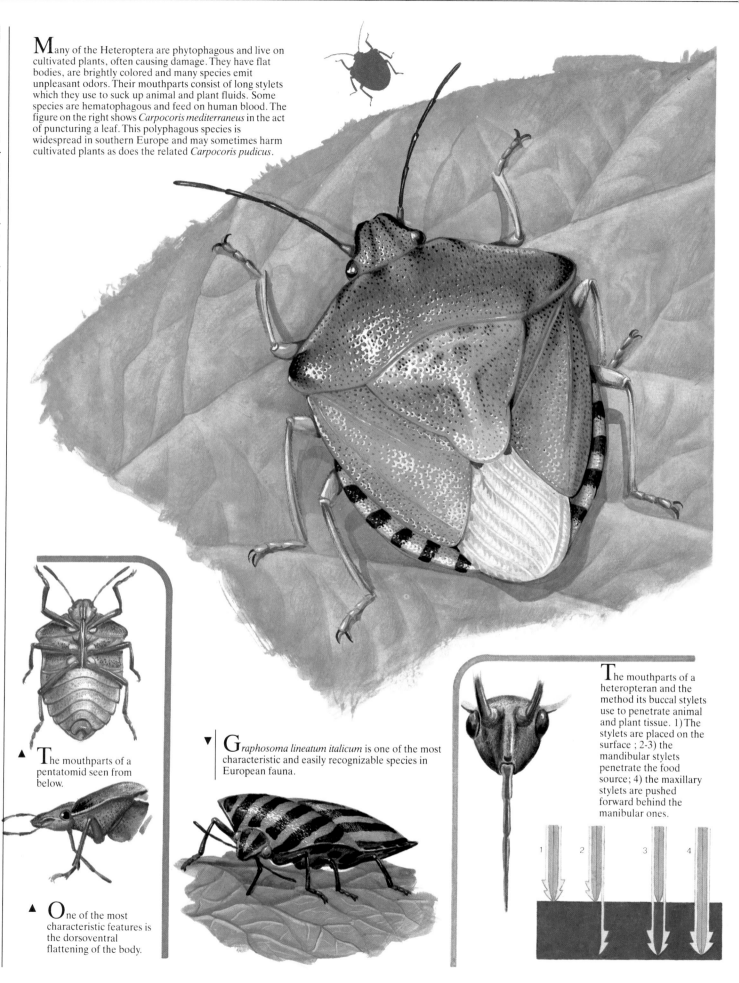

▲ The mouthparts of a pentatomid seen from below.

▲ One of the most characteristic features is the dorsoventral flattening of the body.

▼ *Graphosoma lineatum italicum* is one of the most characteristic and easily recognizable species in European fauna.

The mouthparts of a heteropteran and the method its buccal stylets use to penetrate animal and plant tissue. 1) The stylets are placed on the surface ; 2-3) the mandibular stylets penetrate the food source; 4) the maxillary stylets are pushed forward behind the manibular ones.

1   2   3   4

These bugs often bite their victims repeatedly and inject an irritant saliva either because they are searching for capillaries or veins or because their meal is interrupted by the unconscious movements of their victims. Following the bite, a red-white swelling forms. This is painful at first and then very itchy and its size varies depending upon the individual's sensitivity.

Man has carried *Cimex lectularius* throughout the world – it seems certain that it was not present in the Americas before the arrival of the Europeans – and in many countries its presence is a real calamity. Although it may not be a vector of diseases, it should be considered in instances of infectious disease; a tropical species, *Cimex rotundatus*, is a carrier of bubonic plague.

The Reduviidae are a family much more numerous than the previous one, containing about 3,000 described species. It includes many of the most active predators in the entire order. Tropical species are particularly numerous.

Reduviids are mainly nocturnal and the bite of many of them is nearly always extremely painful. The only exceptions are the habitually hematophagous species, whose saliva probably contains anesthetizing substances.

Some reduviids capture their prey by remaining motionless in ambush and seizing it as it passes nearby. Others hunt actively. When feeding they are capable of sucking up a considerable volume of animal juices in a single sitting and the larvae of *Rhodnius prolixus* can increase their weight ten or twelvefold. Some species produce oöthecae while others, such as *Rhinocoris albopilosus*, display parental care. Reduviids are useful to man when they kill harmful insects; they are pests when they transmit diseases, as frequently happens with the Triatominae.

With more than 6,000 species, the Pentatomidae constitute perhaps the largest and best-known heteropteran family. Its members are characterized by the pentagonal outline of their body, their five-jointed antennae, their bright coloration and, in some forms, the considerable development of the scutellum. It contains both phyto – and zoophagous species and many are of considerable biological and economic interest.

◀ G*raphosoma lineatum italicum*. a plant-eating species which lives by preference on wild Umbelliferae of the genus *Daucus*, in the act of piercing a stem.

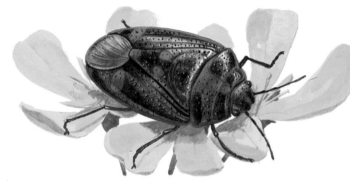

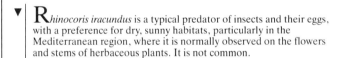

▲ E*urydema oleraceum* is a pentatomid which shows a preference for wild or cultivated Cruciferae but which can also feed on Solanaceae and the eggs of insects.

▼ R*hinocoris iracundus* is a typical predator of insects and their eggs, with a preference for dry, sunny habitats, particularly in the Mediterranean region, where it is normally observed on the flowers and stems of herbaceous plants. It is not common.

C*imex lectularius* will bite greedily not only man but any other animal which lives in the house. It hates light and hides during the day, only moving in darkness, unless forced by hunger to search for prey in natural or artificial light. A red-white swelling forms after the victim is bitten, the size of which depends on the individual's sensitivity. It is painful at first and then very itchy. *Cimex lectularius* has been spread throughout the world by man and its presence in some countries represents a real calamity. Although it may not be a vector of diseases, it should be considered in instances of infectious illness. A tropical species, *Cimex rotundatus* appears to be a carrier of bubonic plague.

▲ S*tephanitis rhododendri* is a species from the Far East which was introduced to Europe about eighty years ago. It attacks rhododendrons, particularly in greenhouses. It is very similar to *Stephanitis pyri*, a European species which once caused great harm to pears and apples.

◀ E*lasmucha grisea* is set apart from the others in the genus by the care which the mother lavishes on the eggs and the larvae. In the late spring the female lays her eggs, in groups of 30-40 on leaves and shrubs. She then sits on them by stationing herself above them with her body raised and her legs stretched apart. This lasts for about a week, and when the eggs hatch she remains with the larvae; it is only once her parental duties are over that the female departs to begin a new cycle the following year.

CICADAS AND ALLIES

Homoptera, Auchenorrhyncha

The members of the large insect order Homoptera have piercing-sucking mouthparts, like the Heteroptera or bugs, but their forewings are not modified into hemielytra. They are all phytophagous and include well-known agricultural pests such as aphids and coccids.

The order comprises two suborders, Sternorrhyncha (aphids and allies) and Auchenorrhyncha. We deal here with the latter.

The Auchenorrhyncha is a suborder of the Homoptera whose members are known as cicadas because of the appearance of the adults of the winged species. They are of small, medium or large size and feed by eating plants or sucking up their fluids. Their rostrum or labium arises in front of the forelegs whereas in the Sternorrhyncha its base is between the front legs. They have saltatory hindlegs and as a result are known by such names as leafhoppers, planthoppers, treehoppers, and froghoppers.

True cicadas (Cicadidae) form a family containing about 1,500 species known around the world for the noise of the males during sunny summer days. In the adults, the head bears three prominent ocelli arranged in a triangle, large projecting eyes, and a large ventrally disposed rostrum. The anterior femurs are enlarged and dentate. Both the fore and hind wings are generally transparent, membranous and have robust veins. In the females the abdomen bears a strong sawtoothed ovipositor and in the males a special sound-producing organ. The nymphs have fossorial forelegs and live in the soil, piercing roots to suck up the sap. The Cicadidae are particularly widespread in the tropics and subtropics and the adults vary in length from the less than ½ in (1.5 cm) of the European *Cicadetta brullei* to the 3 in (8 cm) of *Pomponia adusta* from Java. They are mainly gray or ocher in color with black spots but there are brightly colored species.

The sound-producing organ for which cicadas are universally famous is typical of male cicadids. It consists of two structures on either side of the first abdominal sternite. The sound is

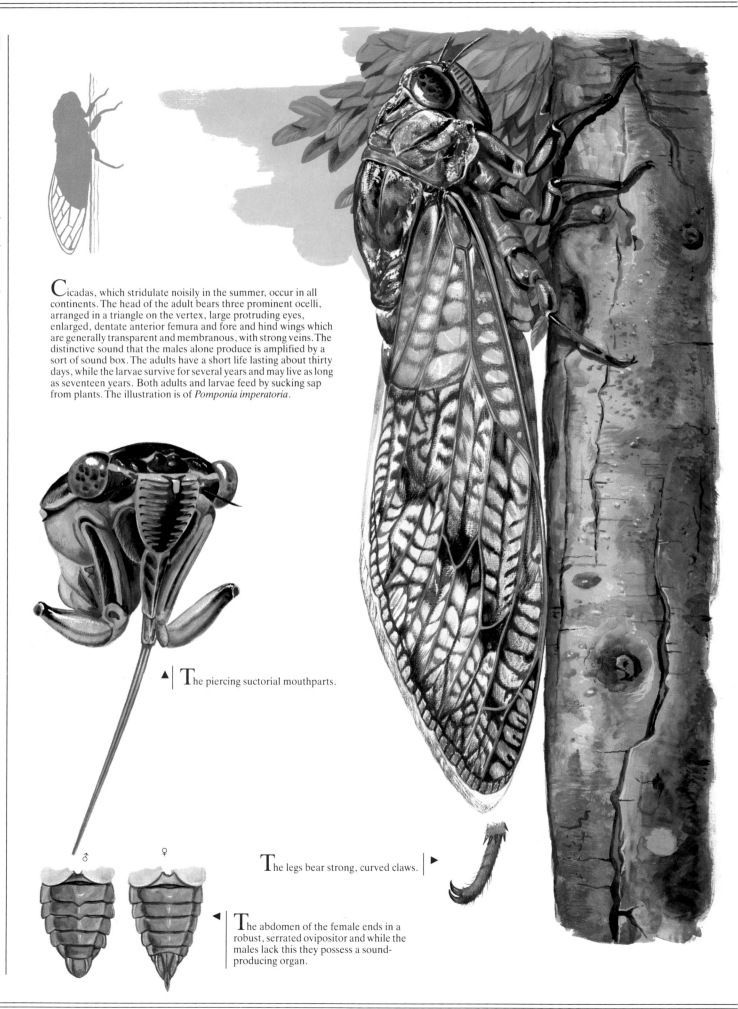

Cicadas, which stridulate noisily in the summer, occur in all continents. The head of the adult bears three prominent ocelli, arranged in a triangle on the vertex, large protruding eyes, enlarged, dentate anterior femura and fore and hind wings which are generally transparent and membranous, with strong veins. The distinctive sound that the males alone produce is amplified by a sort of sound box. The adults have a short life lasting about thirty days, while the larvae survive for several years and may live as long as seventeen years. Both adults and larvae feed by sucking sap from plants. The illustration is of *Pomponia imperatoria*.

▲ The piercing suctorial mouthparts.

The legs bear strong, curved claws. ▶

◀ The abdomen of the female ends in a robust, serrated ovipositor and while the males lack this they possess a sound-producing organ.

produced by the vibration of a prominent integumental membrane, known as the tymbal, on each side. From the outside each tymbal is convex and is crossed by elastic thickenings. Internally it is attached to a powerful muscle, and it is the rhythmic contraction of this that causes the tymbal to vibrate. It produces a crackling sound which can acoustically or mechanically be compared to the crackling produced when a convex tin cap is rapidly pushed in and out.

The males of each of the hundreds of cicada species produces a prenuptial song and the female is aroused and attracted by it. She detects the specific frequency by means of the tympanal organs, which lie in the second abdominal segment. The well-known, seemingly monotonous sound of cicadas in fact varies from species to species.

Each female lays several hundred elongated, fusiform eggs in the living tissues of tree branches. The nymphs usually hatch in the summer months, often when it is raining or when there is a heavy dew. They drop to the ground and dig into the soil, using their strong, typically fossorial forelegs. The length of the larval stage is known for only relatively few species but in general it is two, three or more years. In the North American *Magicicada septemdecim*, known as the periodical cicada because of the regular rhythm of its life cycle, the larval stage is known with certainty to last seventeen years.

The entire larval stage is spent underground. At the end of this period the nymphs move toward the surface and build chambers in which they wait for varying periods of time until the conditions above ground are suitable for their emergence. The appearance of the adults of a single species is usually almost simultaneous and it can sometimes be a striking event. Thousands of white nymphs will emerge in the morning or evening (depending upon the species) from a few square meters of ground and within minutes the bushes and trees will be covered by them.

The 1,500 members of family Cercopidae are mainly thermophile. Their larvae surround themselves in masses of froth which they produce, a habit which has earned them such names as spittlebugs or froghoppers. The adults are between 0.2 – 0.4 in (0.5 – 1 cm) long and have cicada-like bodies.

Adult of *Philaenus spumarius*.

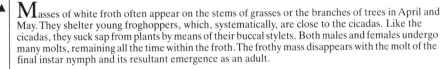

▲ Masses of white froth often appear on the stems of grasses or the branches of trees in April and May. They shelter young froghoppers, which, systematically, are close to the cicadas. Like the cicadas, they suck sap from plants by means of their buccal stylets. Both males and females undergo many molts, remaining all the time within the froth. The frothy mass disappears with the molt of the final instar nymph and its resultant emergence as an adult.

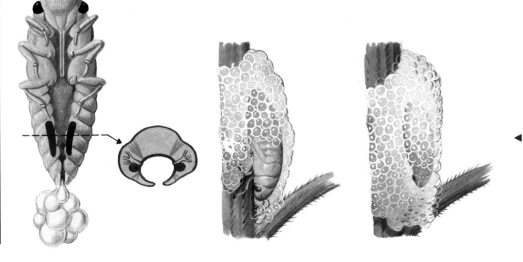

◄ A young froghopper seen ventrally and schematically in transverse section. The white froth is produced by mixing clear, slightly viscous excrement with air blown through an abdominal respiratory pseudo-tube, and it gradually covers the whole body of the animal.

NEUROPTERA

The Neuroptera are insects with well-developed wings, mostly with a complex network of veins. This order is quite heterogeneous. We deal here with two main subgroups, the Raphidioidea and the Planipennia.

The Raphidioidea are modest in size. The adults have a highly elongated prothorax and a distinct pterostigma on their wings. The females have long ovipositors. They live in forests. The elongated and flattened larvae are agile and, like the adults, predatory.

The suborder Planipennia comprises minute insects (wingspan 0.2 in/5 mm) together with medium-sized and even very large ones (wingspan up to 6½ in/16 cm). The larvae have characteristic piercing-sucking mouthparts, consisting of a pair of pincers. Metamorphosis takes place within a silky cocoon.

The members of the Mantispidae are reasonably large, with a highly elongated prothorax and raptorial forelegs, like those of a praying mantis. The larvae of the genus *Mantispa* develop at the expense of the eggs and sometimes the young spiders.

The members of the Chrysopidae are common, widely distributed medium-sized insects which are found in almost every part of the world. They are yellow-brown, reddish-brown or, more often, green in color and sometimes bear characteristic black spots. The eggs are generally elongated and are usually borne on a pedicel of varying length. The suctorial pincers of the young are elongated and curved to varying degrees. They feed on other insects and on mites.

The members of the Myrmeleontidae are medium to large in size, with wingspans of up to 6½ in (16 cm). They are known as ant lion flies because the larvae of some species feed on ants. They are widely distributed but are more frequent in warm, dry areas. The larvae have shortened, slightly broadened abdomens and feed on insects and other small arthropods. In order to catch their prey, the larvae of some genera use special techniques to dig the well-known funnel traps. They conceal themselves at the bottom of these with only their suctorial pincers protruding and seize any prey that slides into the pit, paralyzing it and then sucking out its contents.

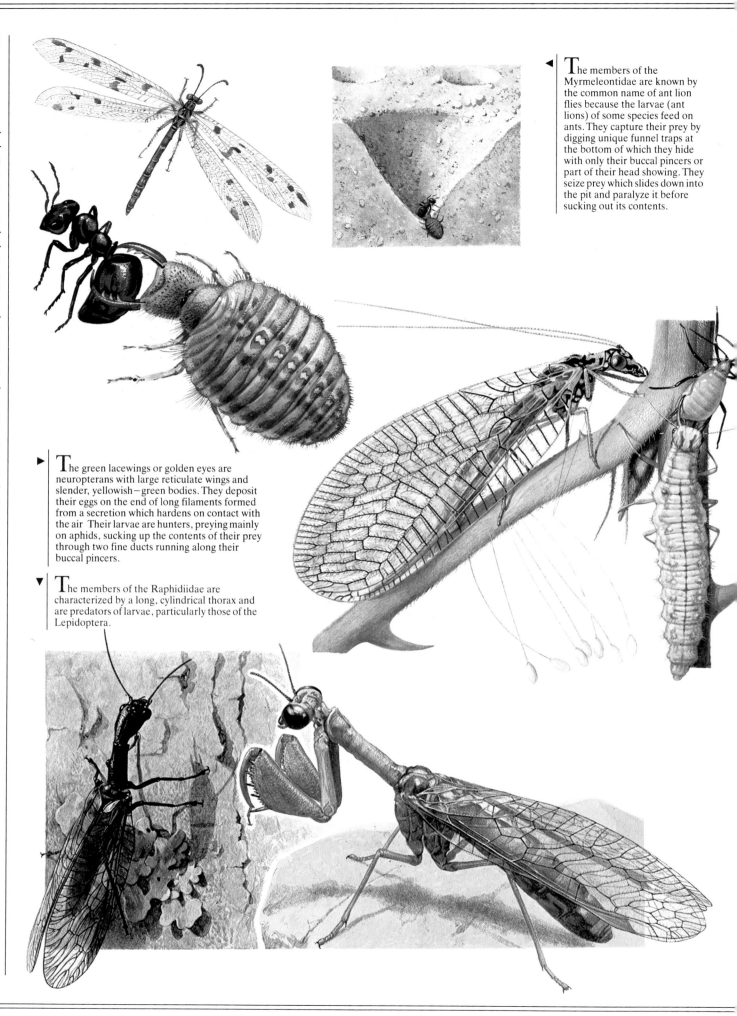

The members of the Myrmeleontidae are known by the common name of ant lion flies because the larvae (ant lions) of some species feed on ants. They capture their prey by digging unique funnel traps at the bottom of which they hide with only their buccal pincers or part of their head showing. They seize prey which slides down into the pit and paralyze it before sucking out its contents.

The green lacewings or golden eyes are neuropterans with large reticulate wings and slender, yellowish–green bodies. They deposit their eggs on the end of long filaments formed from a secretion which hardens on contact with the air. Their larvae are hunters, preying mainly on aphids, sucking up the contents of their prey through two fine ducts running along their buccal pincers.

The members of the Raphidiidae are characterized by a long, cylindrical thorax and are predators of larvae, particularly those of the Lepidoptera.

CADDIS FLIES
Trichoptera

Adult caddis flies (Trichoptera) are of small or medium-size. They have small heads with well-developed eyes and filiform antennae. Their four well-developed, membranous wings are covered by a more or less dense pubescence, and it is from this that the order takes its name, Trichoptera meaning hairy wings. There are, however, forms with few hairs or none at all (Macronematidae). The wings are dull yellows, browns, grays or black in color and few display metallic highlights or variegation. The adults rarely feed. They usually spend the day hidden among vegetation on the bank of the stream or lake where they have previously lived as aquatic larvae. The adults are predominantly crepuscular or nocturnal, and several species are attracted by artificial light. Highland rivers are rich in species; there are also species typical of still water.

Oviposition may occur in three ways. Some species deposit their eggs directly on underwater stones, others fix them to stones, wood or plants on the bottom with a glue that does not swell in the water. In both cases the females use their expanded middle pair of legs to help them swim underwater. In the third method of oviposition the eggs are surrounded by a gelatinous mass and are attached to the leaves of plants on the banks or dropped into the water during flight. The larvae of the Trichoptera are aquatic. They are divided into campodeiform larvae, which do not build moveable cases, and eruciform ones, which do.

The ability of trichopteran larvae to build their cases is the most striking feature of the order. Some larvae build a moveable, soft case of sand, shaped like a coffee bean, which is pierced by tiny holes or has ducts for the circulation of water. Other forms weave variously shaped nets between underwater plants and stones, with which they trap algae and small animals carried along by the water. The best known and most characteristic structures are the tubes which the larvae use to protect their fat, soft abdomens. These shelters are portable so that the larvae can shelter in them at the slightest hint of danger.

At rest the antennae and forelegs of a trichopteran are held pointing forward whilst the long wings are held rooflike over the abdomen. *Stenophylax* is rust-colored and its wings are not covered by a dense pubescence, with the result that its veins appear prominent. This genus frequents caves during the summer and does not feed.

Limnephilus rhombicus is characterized by the presence of a diagonal transparent patch on the forewings. This pair of wings is narrower than the hind ones and its margin is cut off at an angle. The adults fly over ponds at night. The larvae lack a case and their soft, fat abdomen with its tracheal gills is exposed whilst their dark head and thorax are sclerotized.

The larva of *Potamophylax cingulatus*, protected by its case of pebbles, nibbling leaves on the bottom of a watercourse before fixing itself to a stone in order to prepare for pupation.

In running waters the larvae of *Hydropsyche* hide in a fishing net woven with silk between vegetation and stones on the bottom, and catch small animals and algae which become entrapped in the mesh.

The larvae weave highly efficient fishing nets and capture huge quantities of small aquatic animals. The traps which they construct may be horn-shaped (1: *Neureclipsis bimaculata*), bowl-shaped (2: *Polycentropus flavomaculatus*), or consist of a series of tunnels side by side (3: *Hydropsyche angustipennis*). Other larvae build themselves underwater structures using spirally arranged cut fragments of leaves (4: *Phryganea grandis*), small shells and pieces of reed (5: *Limnephilus rhombicus*), which serve as curious and elegant protective cases.

BUTTERFLIES AND MOTHS

Lepidoptera

The butterflies and moths which make up the order Lepidoptera are insects which undergo a complete metamorphosis (holometabolous). They have masticatory mouthparts as larvae and, with few exceptions, licking-suctorial ones as adults. The wings are covered by small scales which overlap in the same way as do tiles on a roof, and the order takes its name from this feature, Lepidoptera meaning wings with scales. Butterfly antennae may be filiform, dentate, pectinate or feathery in appearance.

The wings of butterflies are covered by small, flat scales which are in fact modified hairs and it is these scales which are responsible for the patterning and coloration of the wings. The mouthparts are highly specialized and are usually of the licking-suctorial rather than the piercing type. This specialized organ is known as a proboscis and it enables butterflies to feed on sugary liquids. At rest it is coiled up in a spiral beneath the head but when it is extended it may be even longer than the insect itself, reaching 10 in (25 cm) in some Sphingidae.

The life cycle consists of four stages: egg, larva, chrysalis, and imago or adult insect. The egg is enclosed in a capsule with rigid, impermeable walls and it gives rise to a larva or caterpillar. Butterfly eggs are very variable in shape and they may be fusiform, spherical or flattened.

Butterfly larvae are commonly known as caterpillars and they usually have cylindrical bodies composed of a head and a series of segments bearing the spiracles on their sides. The mouthparts are masticatory and have large mandibles. The thoracic segments bear three pairs of jointed legs, corresponding to the adult ones. Some abdominal segments, usually the first four and the last one, possess unjointed, fleshy, tubular legs, the so-called prolegs, which bear small hooks. Caterpillars are normally phytophagous.

The exoskeleton of a caterpillar consists of a hard, rigid cuticle which is flexible at the joints. Molting occurs periodically when the rigid cuticular shell is no longer able to allow further

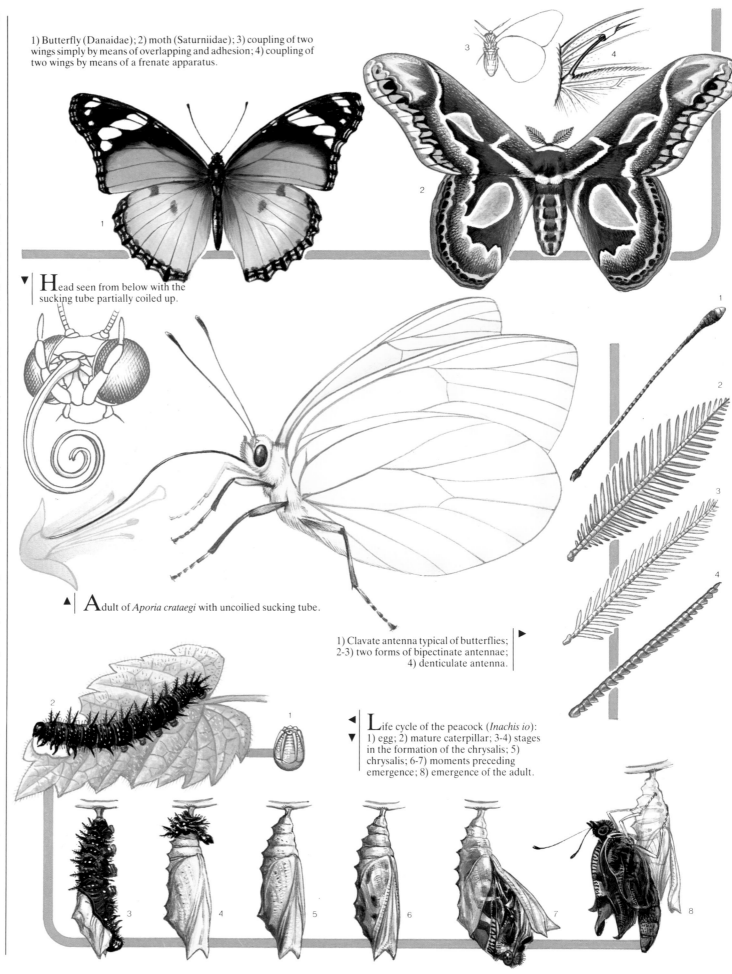

1) Butterfly (Danaidae); 2) moth (Saturniidae); 3) coupling of two wings simply by means of overlapping and adhesion; 4) coupling of two wings by means of a frenate apparatus.

▼ Head seen from below with the sucking tube partially coiled up.

▲ Adult of *Aporia crataegi* with uncoiled sucking tube.

► 1) Clavate antenna typical of butterflies; 2-3) two forms of bipectinate antennae; 4) denticulate antenna.

◄ ▼ Life cycle of the peacock (*Inachis io*): 1) egg; 2) mature caterpillar; 3-4) stages in the formation of the chrysalis; 5) chrysalis; 6-7) moments preceding emergence; 8) emergence of the adult.

growth of the larva. Once growth is complete, the caterpillar molts for the final time and forms a chrysalis. At the moment of pupation, the larval cuticle is split dorsally by the expansion and flexing of the thoracic segments. Some chrysalides, such as those of vanessid butterflies, attach themselves to a support while others, noctuid chrysalides for example, lie free on the ground. Others still, such as silkworms, form their chrysalides inside large cocoons.

After about a month or sometimes several months as a chrysalis, the adult begins to emerge under the influence of hormones (ecdysone). In order to break through the pupal cuticle the emerging adult forces its body fluids into its head and thorax and these, as they swell, split the anterior portion of the chrysalis cuticle. The adult emerges, extracting first its legs, then its abdomen and finally it excretes its metabolic waste products in the form of droplets. At this stage the butterfly is still wet and hangs itself from a support with wings hanging downward so as to help them unfold.

With the exception of some brachypterous females, butterflies have well-developed wings and are good fliers.

The order Lepidoptera is divided into two suborders, Homoneura and Heteroneura. The Homoneura contains primitive butterflies with similar venation on the two pairs of wings and forewings which are the same size as the hind ones. The Heteroneura comprises more highly evolved butterflies whose wings differ in their venation and whose forewings are larger than their hind ones.

The Heteroneura is further subdivided into the Monotrysia and the Ditrysia. In the Ditrysia, which includes the majority of butterflies, the females have two genital openings, one for mating and the other for oviposition, while in the Monotrysia they have just one such opening. The species belonging to some families, whose members have wingspans of a few millimeters, are commonly known as the Microlepidoptera, as opposed to the Macrolepidoptera, which contains all the larger forms. Although this distinction is used, it is not based on rigorously scientific grounds but on subjective opinion and hence it is liable to varying interpretations.

Another much used classification is the distinction between butterflies (Rhopalocera) and moths (Heterocera). At rest, butterflies hold their

▼| Various types of ordinary scales enlarged.

▲ An adult peacock (*Inachis io*). The vanessids (Nymphalinae) are the most beautiful and gaily colored group in the Nymphalidae. This is the largest family belonging to the Rhopalocera, containing more than 2,500 species. The vanessids have wings which are angular or which have dentate margins. Their upper surface is strikingly colored and the grayish brown undersurface is finely striped. When at rest, the butterfly closes its wings like a book and vanishes from sight, taking on the coloration of a dried-up leaf. The peacock is regarded as the most magnificent of European species due to its large, gaily colored eye spots. It is common in the mountains and lives mainly on nettles.

wings at right angles to their body axis while moths fold them at an angle. Butterflies have clavate antennae ending in a rounded, scale-covered swelling whereas the members of the Heterocera possess a variety of antennae. In the males these are often bulky and the antennal joints bear lateral expansions.

The most important butterfly families are the following: Hesperiidae (skippers), Papilionidae (swallowtails, apollos), Pieridae (whites, yellows), Lycaenidae (blues, coppers, hairstreaks), Nymphalidae (fritillaries, admirals, emperors, tortoiseshells), Satyridae (browns, ringlets) and Danaidae (monarchs).

Among the moths there are the Sphingidae (hawkmoths), the Lymantriidae (tussocks), the Arctiidae (tiger moths, ermines), the Noctuidae (noctuid moths), the Zygaenidae (burnets), the Lasyocampidae (eggars, lappets) as well as the four families briefly examined in the following lines.

The moths belonging to the family Saturniidae are among the giants of the insect world. Almost all saturniids are medium to large moths and some tropical species reach wingspans of 10 in (25 cm). The antennae are more highly developed in the males. The females of many Saturniids have special glands at the tips of their abdomens from which they secrete odorous substances (pheromones) that attract males from some distance. The receptor cells for this olfactory stimulus lie on the large antennae of the males.

Large, striking non-European Saturniids include *Platysamia cecropia* from North America, *Coscinoscera hercules*, a powerfully built moth whose hind wings end in a rather broad, rudimentary tail, and *Attacus atlas* (the atlas moth), a large Saturniid from eastern Asia which, with its wingspan of about 10 in (25 cm) is considered a giant among insects. *Rothschildia morana* is similar to the Atlas moth but smaller in size. A number of saturniids, for example *Actias selene* from eastern Asia and *Argema mittrei* from Madagascar, have their hind wings ending in a long, narrow tail.

Psychids are small moths with generally dark or dull wings, atrophied mouthparts – the adult does not feed – and marked sexual dimorphism. The males generally have pectinate antennae and functional wings, while the females have reduced wings or even none at all. They also lack eyes,

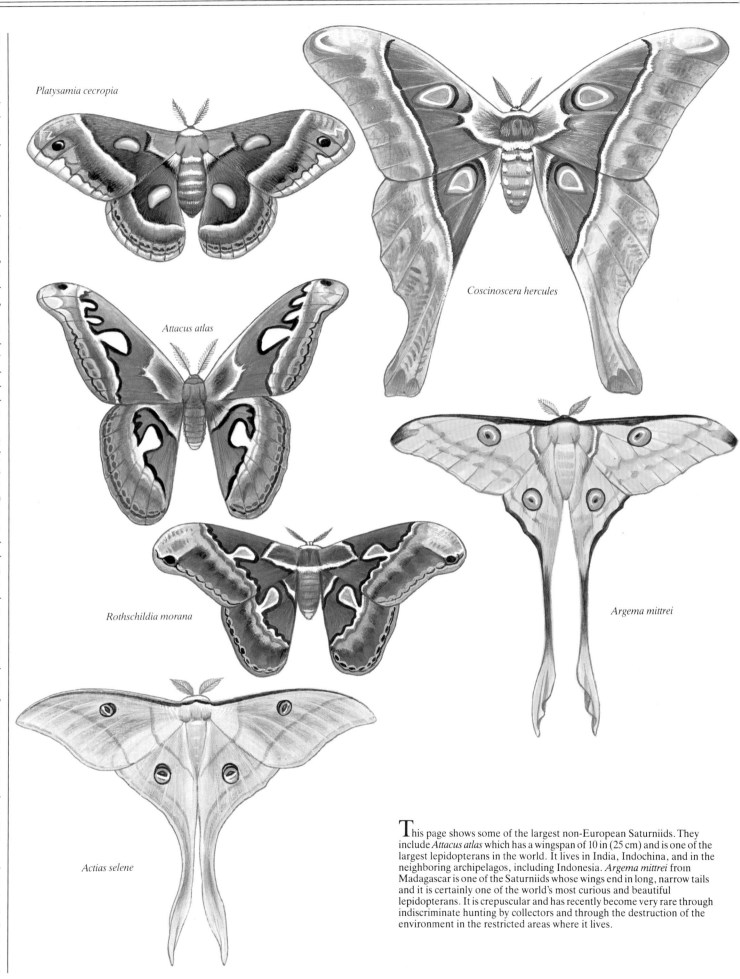

Platysamia cecropia

Coscinoscera hercules

Attacus atlas

Argema mittrei

Rothschildia morana

Actias selene

This page shows some of the largest non-European Saturniids. They include *Attacus atlas* which has a wingspan of 10 in (25 cm) and is one of the largest lepidopterans in the world. It lives in India, Indochina, and in the neighboring archipelagos, including Indonesia. *Argema mittrei* from Madagascar is one of the Saturniids whose wings end in long, narrow tails and it is certainly one of the world's most curious and beautiful lepidopterans. It is crepuscular and has recently become very rare through indiscriminate hunting by collectors and through the destruction of the environment in the restricted areas where it lives.

antennae, and sometimes legs, and they generally live inside the larval case, which is never abandoned, even for mating. These cases are built from a variety of material – such as bits of leaves, dried grass, earth, and fine sand – as external ornaments , holding the pieces together with filaments of silk. These are cryptic structures which allow the larvae to merge into their surrounding (homomorphism), providing protection in certain circumstances and reducing the losses due to predators. Psychids are generally crepuscular or nocturnal in habit, although they may sometimes be observed during the day. Their flight is slow and unsteady – even a breath of wind is enough to stop them.

The best-known representative of the family Bombycidae is undoubtedly the silkworm moth. It was introduced into Europe from China in about 552 AD in order to obtain silk from its cocoons and it is at present unknown in the wild although it is bred in almost every part of the world. The adult silkmoths are modest in size, with a wingspan of 1½ in (3.5 cm). They have yellowish wings and show little sexual dimorphism – both sexes have pectinate antennae. They lack a proboscis. Both sexes are poor flyers and, although the males especially beat their wings vigorously, they are unable to cover long distances.

The Geometridae is a family of small to medium-size moths whose wings are not generally very striking, grays and other dull shades predominating. The mouthparts are functional and the adults feed off sugary liquids. Geometrids are crepuscular or nocturnal in habit and they are attracted, sometimes in large numbers, by lights. Their larvae have only two pairs of abdominal prolegs, the anal and preanal pairs. When they move they grip the support firmly with their thoracic legs. The body is then arched strongly and the anal prolegs are moved forward and grip the support. Next the forelegs relax their grip and the anterior part of the body is moved forward. This curious method of movement, in which they appear to be measuring the ground, has earned them the names of measuring larvae, geometers or loopers and is also the reason for the family being known as the Geometridae.

◀ An adult of *Conephora unicolor* (on the left), one of the commonest Italian psychids, and a case with a chrysalis of the same species (on the right).

◀ A psychid larva with its protective case.

▼ Types of cases with ordered arrangement of components.

◀ An adult and larvae of the silk moth. It has been bred by man for about 5,000 years and has lost the ability to fly. It is thought to be derived, through a process of selection which the Chinese have carried out for many centuries, from the related *Theophila mandarina*, individuals of which still live in the wild in China.

▼ The cocoon of the silkworm is about 1½ in (3.5 cm) long and is ovoidal in shape with a slight constriction in the middle. The cocoons from which the males emerge are richer in silk than the female ones since the female silkworms are heavier and more bulky. Therefore, since they take up more space, the amount of silk secreted in cocoons of the same size will be smaller.

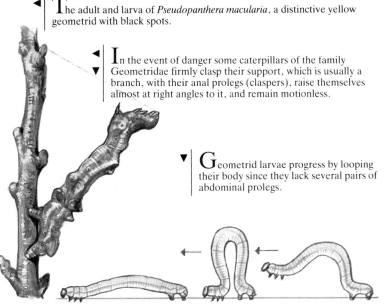

◀ The adult and larva of *Pseudopanthera macularia*, a distinctive yellow geometrid with black spots.

◀▼ In the event of danger some caterpillars of the family Geometridae firmly clasp their support, which is usually a branch, with their anal prolegs (claspers), raise themselves almost at right angles to it, and remain motionless.

▼ Geometrid larvae progress by looping their body since they lack several pairs of abdominal prolegs.

MOSQUITOES

Culicidae

The name mosquito is taken from the Spanish, meaning "small fly," and is used for the bloodsucking flies of the Culicidae family. The mosquitoes' main importance lies in the fact that the female can bite several humans in succession, acting as a carrier of some of mankind's most dreaded diseases. Their harm is enhanced by the ability of mosquito larvae to grow in small, often temporary pools of water.

Adult mosquitoes are slender, fragile insects, with long antennae. They are characterized by scales along their wing veins and other parts of the body and by a long proboscis. The scales are modified hairs which form bands or spots of color on the body.

Mosquitoes are insects of the night, or in many cases of twilight. There are some diurnal species, however, which inhabit forest. In subtropical zones these species are more commonly found above the tree-canopy, where they live off monkeys and birds.

Bloodsucking is a physiological necessity for the majority of mosquito females, bringing them the animal protein they need for their eggs to mature, though some are capable of going for years at time on a purely vegetarian diet, without taking a meal of blood.

Mosquito larvae are aquatic organisms of a special type, exploiting the particular conditions at the water's surface. This allows them to breathe in the air, while at the same time using the water to prevent themselves drying out and to provide the food they need. The larvae of some species however, are capable of surviving for long periods on the bottom.

Mosquito larvae feed off tiny prey such as diatoms, protozoans, and so forth. Because of the minute size of their prey they are known as filter-feeders. Their mouthparts are of the primitive, chewing type, and the mandibles have a horizontal motion; they have specially adapted mouth-brushes to push floating particles toward the mouth. The larvae of *Megarhinus* attack larger aquatic animals than the other species and even attack the larvae of other mosquitoes.

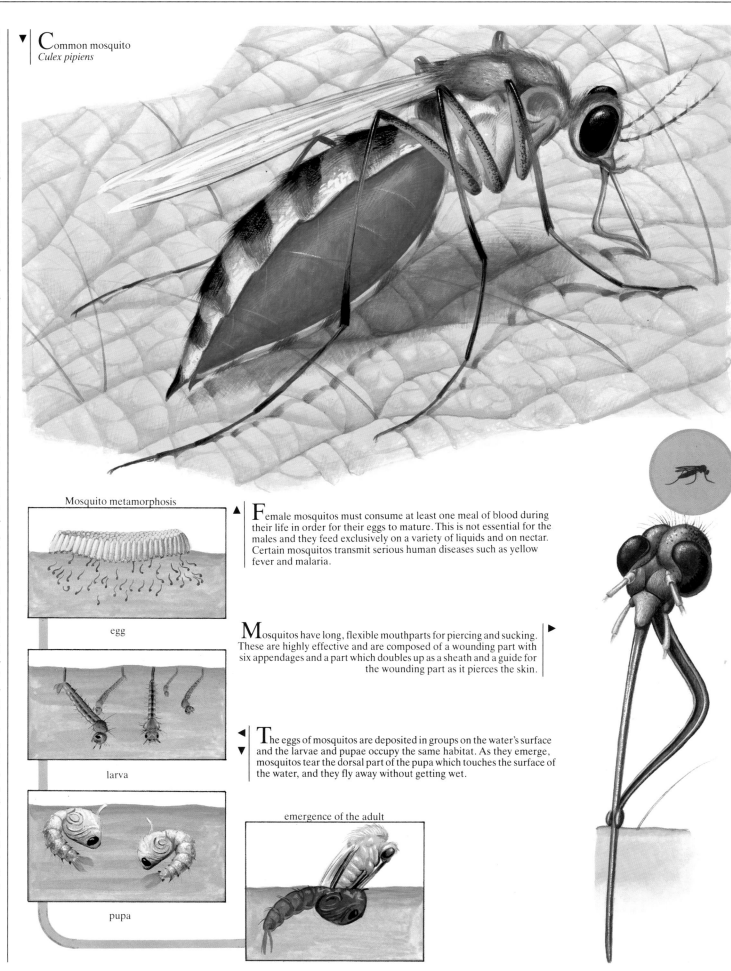

▼ Common mosquito
Culex pipiens

Mosquito metamorphosis

egg

larva

pupa

emergence of the adult

▲ **F**emale mosquitos must consume at least one meal of blood during their life in order for their eggs to mature. This is not essential for the males and they feed exclusively on a variety of liquids and on nectar. Certain mosquitos transmit serious human diseases such as yellow fever and malaria.

Mosquitos have long, flexible mouthparts for piercing and sucking. These are highly effective and are composed of a wounding part with six appendages and a part which doubles up as a sheath and a guide for the wounding part as it pierces the skin. ▶

◀ **T**he eggs of mosquitos are deposited in groups on the water's surface
▼ and the larvae and pupae occupy the same habitat. As they emerge, mosquitos tear the dorsal part of the pupa which touches the surface of the water, and they fly away without getting wet.

FLIES

Diptera

The true flies are among the most highly evolved of the Diptera, the two-winged insects. Of these the housefly is for millions of people the best-known representative. This fly does not bite, but feeds off all kinds of liquids and other substances, such as sugar, which it can dissolve with the substances it regurgitates. It is particularly fond of strong-smelling produce such as vegetables and meat just beginning to rot, and is also attracted by sores and running wounds in animals and men.

In the countryside housefly larvae prefer the excrement of pigs, horses, and humans, but in or near houses they live in rotting vegetable and animal matter and other kinds of household garbage found in bins. Houses thus provide all the requirements for several generations of flies to breed during the summer, so that the name of housefly is well deserved. The same reasons mean that it is suspected of transmitting a number of diseases to mankind.

The housefly is proverbial for its fertility. The female can lay up to 1,000 eggs separately or in batches of several dozen, at a rate of up to 100 a day. At 65°F (18°C) the larva completes its development within some 25 days. The female is ready to lay six to ten days after emerging from her pupa. Houseflies usually shun the sun, preferring the shade. In houses they are to be found in dark, damp rooms, in larders, etc. Huge numbers are also found in the country, where they infest stables and byres, carpeting the walls in seething masses.

Houseflies disappear in temperate and cold zones with the onset of winter, reappearing with the spring. It is not properly understood how they survive the winter, but it is known that they do so in very small numbers, and that most die of cold. The housefly is a truly cosmopolitan species, found in every continent and every climate in the world.

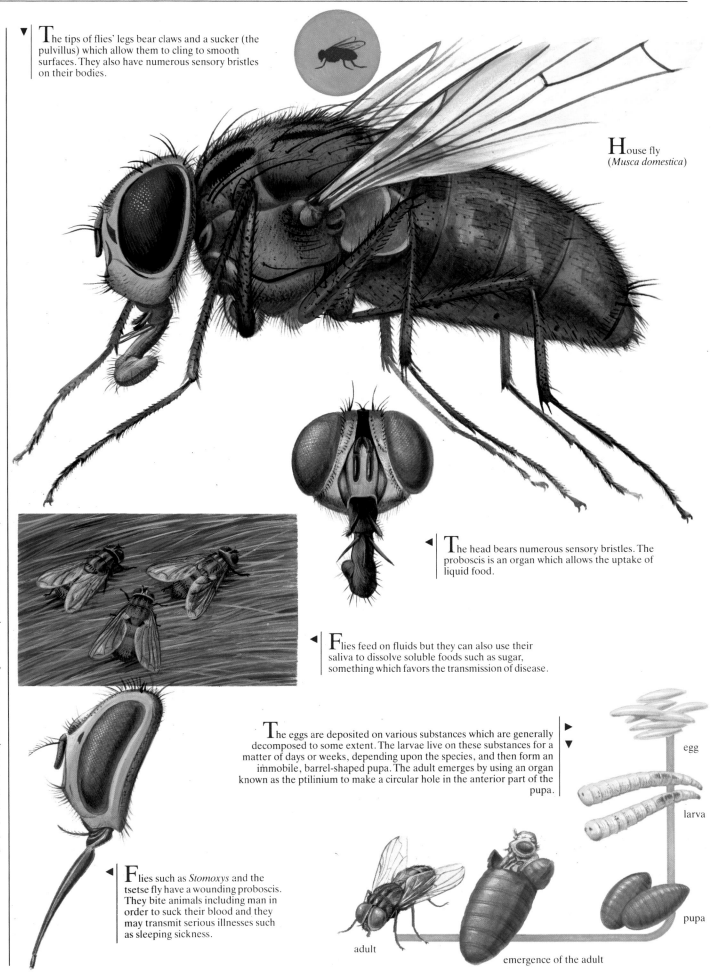

The tips of flies' legs bear claws and a sucker (the pulvillus) which allow them to cling to smooth surfaces. They also have numerous sensory bristles on their bodies.

House fly
(*Musca domestica*)

The head bears numerous sensory bristles. The proboscis is an organ which allows the uptake of liquid food.

Flies feed on fluids but they can also use their saliva to dissolve soluble foods such as sugar, something which favors the transmission of disease.

The eggs are deposited on various substances which are generally decomposed to some extent. The larvae live on these substances for a matter of days or weeks, depending upon the species, and then form an immobile, barrel-shaped pupa. The adult emerges by using an organ known as the ptilinium to make a circular hole in the anterior part of the pupa.

egg

larva

pupa

adult

emergence of the adult

Flies such as *Stomoxys* and the tsetse fly have a wounding proboscis. They bite animals including man in order to suck their blood and they may transmit serious illnesses such as sleeping sickness.

BEETLES
Coleoptera

The Coleoptera are essentially terrestrial animals, living on, in or under the soil, on or in trees, on or in leaves, on flowers and in fungi. They may be primary, secondary or tertiary consumers, phytophagous or xylophagous predatory, saprophagous or parasitic. There are also many aquatic forms.

They range in size from the tiny members of such families as the Corylophidae and the Trichopterygidae, of less than 0.02 in (0.5 mm) in length to some Scarabaeids and Cerambycids which are among the largest of all insects, over 6 in (16 cm) long.

The most obvious distinguishing feature shared by all the tens of thousands of different species is the fact their forewings have been transformed into rigid, more or less sclerotized cases known as elytra. The mouthparts point forward or downward and are typically masticatory. The elytra vary in form. In a number of cases they are reduced and are shorter than the abdomen, leaving some segments, usually two or three, uncovered. The membranous second pair of wings lie underneath the elytra and are usually completely hidden by them. Often, however, the wings are more or less reduced.

Coleopteran eggs are simple in form and lack any surface ornamentation. The larvae themselves vary in form and grow through a series of molts. Normally there are three of these but there may be four, six or more, separating the various larval instars. The larva is followed by the pupa, an immobile stage which does not feed and in which all the transformations leading to the adult take place.

The Coleoptera includes more than 100 families but only some of the principal ones will be mentioned here.

The family Cicindelidae, often regarded as a subfamily of the Carabidae, contains about 1,500 species found throughout the temperate and tropical regions of the globe. Most are very similar in appearance, usually being between ½ – ¾ in (1 – 2 cm) long and vividly and brilliantly colored, often with metallic colors and white spots. Their legs are long and slender, enabling them to run fast when not making brief, rapid flights.

They are voracious and highly effective predators, have large, sickle-

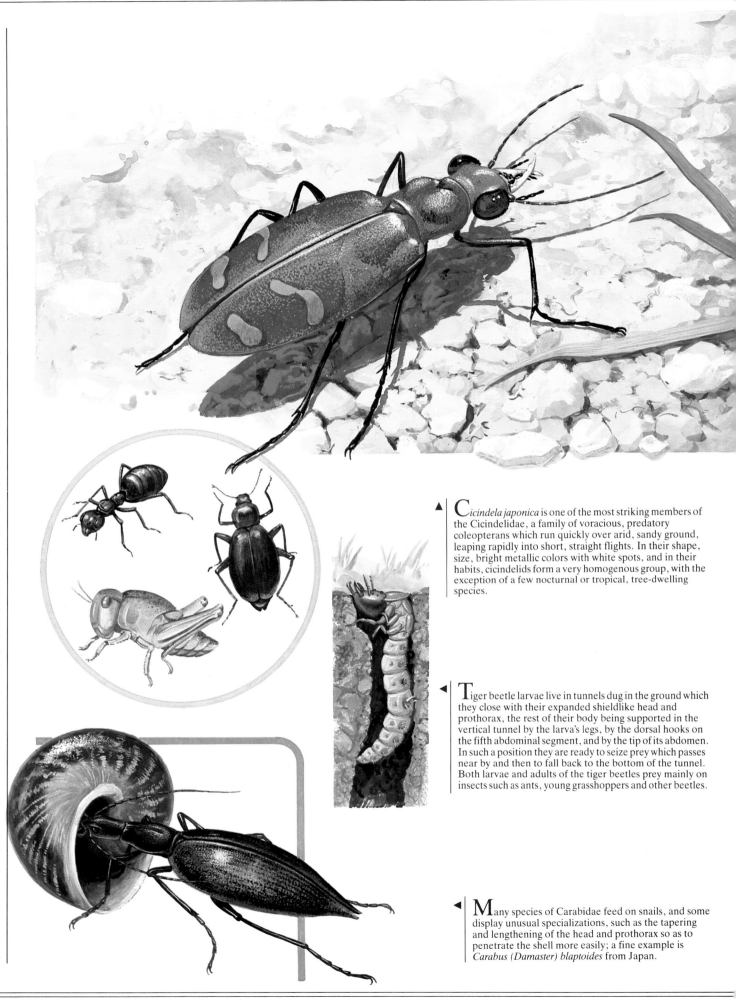

▲ *Cicindela japonica* is one of the most striking members of the Cicindelidae, a family of voracious, predatory coleopterans which run quickly over arid, sandy ground, leaping rapidly into short, straight flights. In their shape, size, bright metallic colors with white spots, and in their habits, cicindelids form a very homogenous group, with the exception of a few nocturnal or tropical, tree-dwelling species.

◄ Tiger beetle larvae live in tunnels dug in the ground which they close with their expanded shieldlike head and prothorax, the rest of their body being supported in the vertical tunnel by the larva's legs, by the dorsal hooks on the fifth abdominal segment, and by the tip of its abdomen. In such a position they are ready to seize prey which passes near by and then to fall back to the bottom of the tunnel. Both larvae and adults of the tiger beetles prey mainly on insects such as ants, young grasshoppers and other beetles.

◄ Many species of Carabidae feed on snails, and some display unusual specializations, such as the tapering and lengthening of the head and prothorax so as to penetrate the shell more easily; a fine example is *Carabus (Damaster) blaptoides* from Japan.

shaped and dentate mandibles and normally live in dry, sandy environments, along rivers, ponds, and the sea, or on hot, sunny plains.

Cicindelids generally prey on other insects such as small orthopterans, coleopterans, and ants, as well as spiders and crustaceans, which are captured with great speed and devoured voraciously.

The larvae are very distinctive and display specialized behavior. The head is bulky, very robust and sclerotized. It has large sickle-shaped mandibles and ocelli pointed in various directions so that the whole horizon can be scanned. The prothorax is also very robust and takes the form of a sclerotized plate. These curious larvae live in the same environments as the adults but in tunnels dug in the ground or in cracks in rocks, bark or wood.

A few Carabidae feed on seeds and plant matter but almost all the members of this enormous family of Coleoptera are typically predatory carnivores. They occur all round the world, at all altitudes, in the soil and in caves. They are much more varied in appearance than the preceding group and though they are usually fast runners they are only rarely winged, often having fused elytra. Unlike cicindelids, they are mostly nocturnal. They are usually black, although they often have brilliant metallic highlights.

The Carabinae, with the genera *Calosoma*, *Carabus*, and *Cychrus*, is the group containing the largest and the most striking species. *Calosoma sycophanta* is one of the best-known species. It is found throughout Europe and Asia and has also been introduced into North America as a means of controlling caterpillars which were harmful to forests. The large genus *Carabus* contains about 600 species of large predators. These all hunt living prey but they may also feed off various rotting or sugary organic substances. Their prey includes orthopterans, coleopterans, and lepidopterans and dipteran larvae, but principally it consists of earthworms and mollusks. Some subgenera have enlarged heads and break the shells with their strong mandibles while others, the subgenera *Procerus* and above all *Damaster*, have a long, thin prothorax, head and mouthparts and push their head and prothorax into the shell.

The Hydroadephaga comprises approximately 3,500 species of aquatic predators grouped into five or six

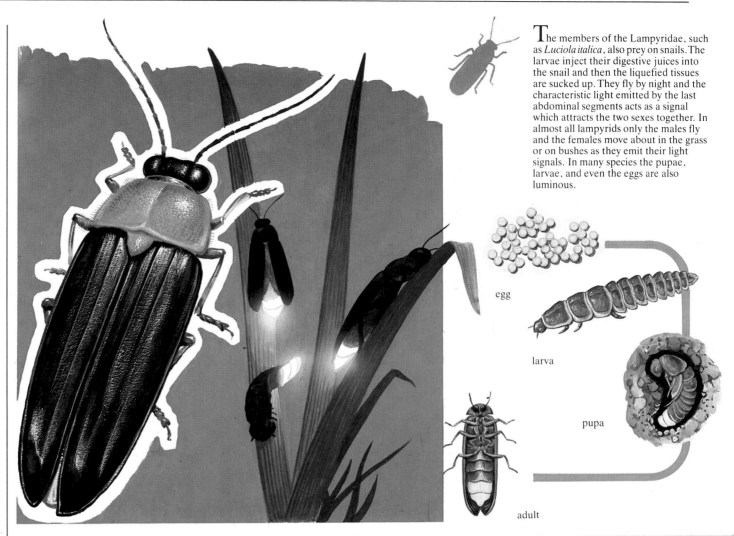

The members of the Lampyridae, such as *Luciola italica*, also prey on snails. The larvae inject their digestive juices into the snail and then the liquefied tissues are sucked up. They fly by night and the characteristic light emitted by the last abdominal segments acts as a signal which attracts the two sexes together. In almost all lampyrids only the males fly and the females move about in the grass or on bushes as they emit their light signals. In many species the pupae, larvae, and even the eggs are also luminous.

egg

larva

pupa

adult

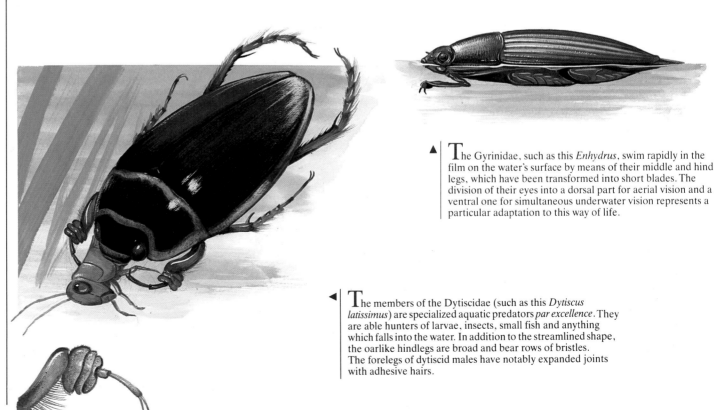

▲ The Gyrinidae, such as this *Enhydrus*, swim rapidly in the film on the water's surface by means of their middle and hind legs, which have been transformed into short blades. The division of their eyes into a dorsal part for aerial vision and a ventral one for simultaneous underwater vision represents a particular adaptation to this way of life.

◄ The members of the Dytiscidae (such as this *Dytiscus latissimus*) are specialized aquatic predators *par excellence*. They are able hunters of larvae, insects, small fish and anything which falls into the water. In addition to the streamlined shape, the oarlike hindlegs are broad and bear rows of bristles. The forelegs of dytiscid males have notably expanded joints with adhesive hairs.

families, of which the Dytiscidae and the Gyrinidae are the principal ones. They are caraboids adapted for an aquatic way of life, having streamlined, compact, fusiform, boatlike bodies with legs which, to varying extents, are transformed into oars. They are beetles living under the water both as larvae and as adults but the pupa metamorphose on land, in chambers dug in the ground or among the plants on the bank.

The Dytiscidae is the most numerous group. It is found throughout the world but principally in the northern hemisphere. Its members range in size from 0.04 in (1 mm) to 1½ in (4 cm), and they have rather flattened, sometimes discoidal bodies. They can be found in any fresh or brackish water from thermal springs to alpine streams, lakes, rivers, ponds or temporary pools and they are particularly common in small pools rich in vegetation, moving from one pool to another by flight.

The Gyrinidae are also aquatic predators, both as larvae and as adults, but they can immediately be distinguished from the previous family by their very short antennae, their quite elongated forelegs and their short middle and hind legs, which are radically modified to form short stout blades. A highly unusual character is the specialization of their eyes, which are divided into dorsal and ventral parts so that they can see both above and below the water's surface at the same time. The larvae are aquatic in the normal way but the adults swim on the surface of still or slowly moving waters in particular. Their backs are glossy, shining in the sunlight and they often swim in large groups, constantly moving in rapid circles or zigzags.

The Lampyridae are well removed systematically from the groups discussed here. However, all lampyrid larvae feed on gastropods and their behavior is therefore similar to that observed in carabid beetles. Lampyrid larvae inject a fluid into their prey through a duct in their mandibles which paralyzes it and digests its tissues.

They are nocturnal, medium-sized insects. The males are nearly always winged while the females are micropterous or apterous, and often vermiform. The males generally have large eyes and large antennae whereas the females usually have reduced eyes and short antennae. The final abdominal segments of the adult males and, to an

◄ *Cetonia aurata* is a flower-dwelling scarabaeid which is common throughout the Palearctic region.

▲▼ The cockchafer, *Melolontha melolontha*, is a scarabaeid which is well known for the harm it can cause to crops. The adult feeds on leaves and frequently attacks fruit trees. Every three or four years cockchafers appear in very large numbers which not even their most relentless predators, such as starlings, can control properly. Cockchafer larvae live in the ground and feed on the roots of plants, doing serious damage to vegetables and forage plants.

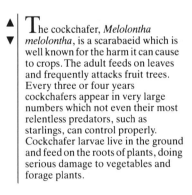

◄ The Cetoniinae are attracted by fluids emitted by plants during warm months or as a result of wounds.

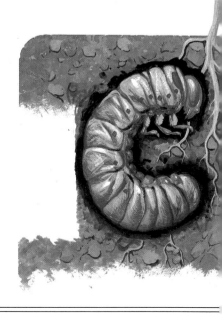

even greater extent, the adult females display a characteristic luminescene but this is often also present in the larvae and even the eggs. This light and in particular the frequency of the flashes helps in sex recognition and signals availability for mating.

The Lucanidae is a worldwide family of about 750 scarabaeoid beetles which is related to the Scarabaeidae. They are characterized by the enormous development of the males' mandibles. The stag beetle *Lucanus cervus*, so-called because of the gigantic, hornlike mandibles, is the largest and most spectacular of European beetles, reaching 3 in (8 cm) in length. It lives in broadleaved woods (oaks, chestnuts, maples, etc.) where it is possible to observe it in flight on warm summer evenings.

Numerous scarabaeid beetles bear striking, rigid exoskeletal processes on the clypeus and the pronotum which have always attracted the attention of experts, collectors, and the natives themselves. These features are usually only present in the male and if females do display them they are much more modest and less conspicuous (sexual dimorphism). They are often of large size with a bright metallic coloration.

The Cetoniinea is a numerous subfamily of scarabaeids which contains the large African goliath beetles. The heads of these beetles bear raised processes in the form of small horns. The legs are long and powerful, since they have to support the weight of these bulky animals, (which are among the largest of living insects), when they climb the trunks of trees. The larvae live on decomposing plant matter such as rotting wood on the floor of tropical forests. *Goliathus goliathus*, from western and central Africa, is the largest species, exceeding 4 in (10 cm) in length.

The subfamily Scarabaeinae contains one of the best-known groups of scarabaeids, the 90 or so members of the Phanaeini, which are typical of the New World. Their striking appearance, with the males bearing a frontal horn and more or less well-developed pronotal processes, and their myriad brilliant, metallic shades of gold, blue and green, have always attracted the interest of collectors. These forms occur in the southernmost part of the eastern part of the United States – where only a handful of species are found – and the whole of South America, with the exception of the

The stag beetle, *Lucanus cervus*, displays marked sexual dimorphism. The males bear enormous mandibles which they use in battles during mating. The winning male, after he has seized his rival, flings him down from the tree. Lucanid larvae develop in the wood of old trees and take several years to complete their cycle.

The coprophagous beetles of the genus *Scarabaeus* form bulky balls of dung which they transport by using their hindlegs to turn it, subsequently burying and devouring it. This is an adaptive strategy to avoid ecological competition from other coprophagous scarabaeids which feed directly on dung. In ancient Mediterranean civilizations such as the Egyptian, Etruscan and Phoenician ones, scarabs represent the symbol of the creative force of nature, of the rising and setting of the sun, and of resurrection. Images of scarabs were present at investitures and funeral ceremonies and on the seals of high state and religious officials.

extreme south. Although their coloration is magnificent, their diets appear repugnant to us. *Coprophanaeus lancifer*, for example, is a species from the tropical forests of Amazonia which Edmonds mentions having collected in large numbers from carrion bait. Several members of the genus *Coprophanaeus* are necrophagous, being attracted to fresh carcasses, and are nocturnal in habit. However, the majority of the Phanaeini (the genera *Phanaeus*, *Oxysternon*, *Diabroctis* and so on) retain a coprophagous diet.

The members of the Cerambycidae are highly distinctive beetles with elongated antennae, a fact which has earned them the name of Longicornia. The antennae vary greatly in length but are normally about as long as the body and are slightly shorter in the females than in the males. Sometimes, however, they are exceptionally long and in the males of *Acanthocinus aedilis* they are more than four times as long as the body.

In the males of *Cerambyx cerdo* the antennae are about twice as long as the body. This is a large species, almost 2 in (5 cm) long with a glossy brown-black coloration, a wrinkled prothorax, and two lateral pointed processes.

The Clytinae is a Cerambycid group which includes among others the genera *Clytus*, *Clytanthus*, and *Plagionotus*, all of which are medium to small in size, with bright and varied coloration and patterning, often consisting of yellow oblong spots on a black background or vice versa. The adults feed on flowers while the larvae live in dead wood or in herbaceous plants or shrubs.

The most striking and distinctive of the necrophilic beetles are undoubtedly the Silphidae, medium to large-sized elongated insects with robust legs and clavate antennae. Their coloration may be uniform or they may have black elytra with yellow-red spots. In addition to decomposing animal matter, *Silpha* sp. may also eat healthy or rotting plants. *Ablattaria laevigata* preys heavily on snails (gastropod mollusks), biting into them and secreting a liquid to dissolve their tissues. The snail withdraws into its shell and secretes froth. This, however, is dissolved by the liquid emitted by the silphid and at this point *Ablattaria* works its way into the shell and begins to eat the gastropod.

Other silphids feed on vertebrate carrion, other arthropods and on

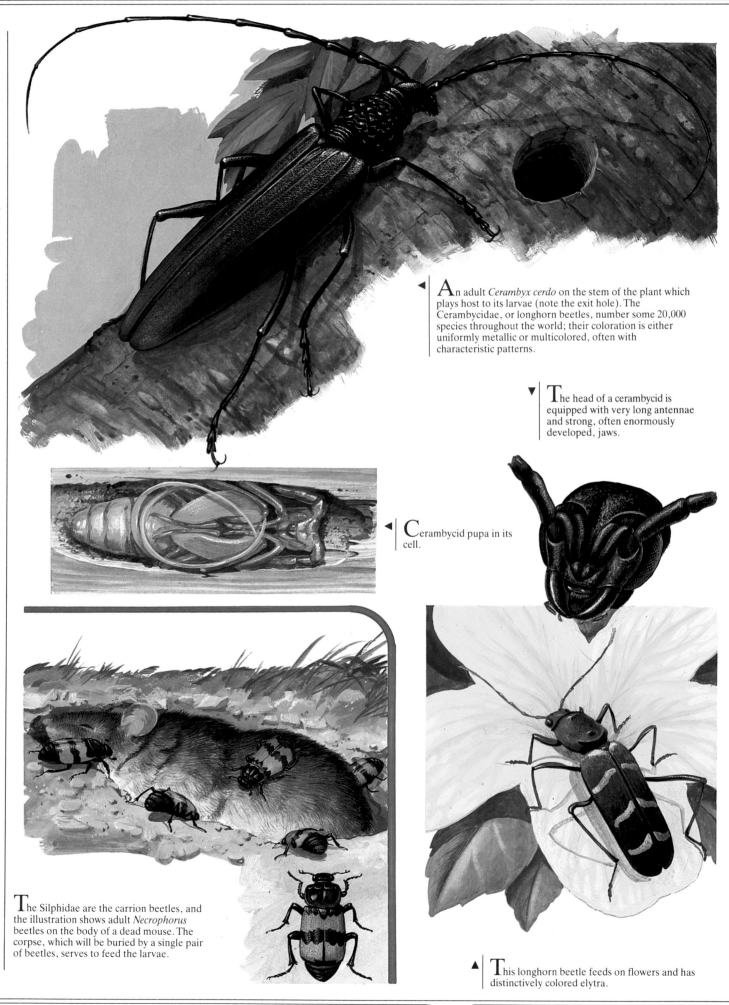

◀ An adult *Cerambyx cerdo* on the stem of the plant which plays host to its larvae (note the exit hole). The Cerambycidae, or longhorn beetles, number some 20,000 species throughout the world; their coloration is either uniformly metallic or multicolored, often with characteristic patterns.

▼ The head of a cerambycid is equipped with very long antennae and strong, often enormously developed, jaws.

◀ Cerambycid pupa in its cell.

The Silphidae are the carrion beetles, and the illustration shows adult *Necrophorus* beetles on the body of a dead mouse. The corpse, which will be buried by a single pair of beetles, serves to feed the larvae.

▲ This longhorn beetle feeds on flowers and has distinctively colored elytra.

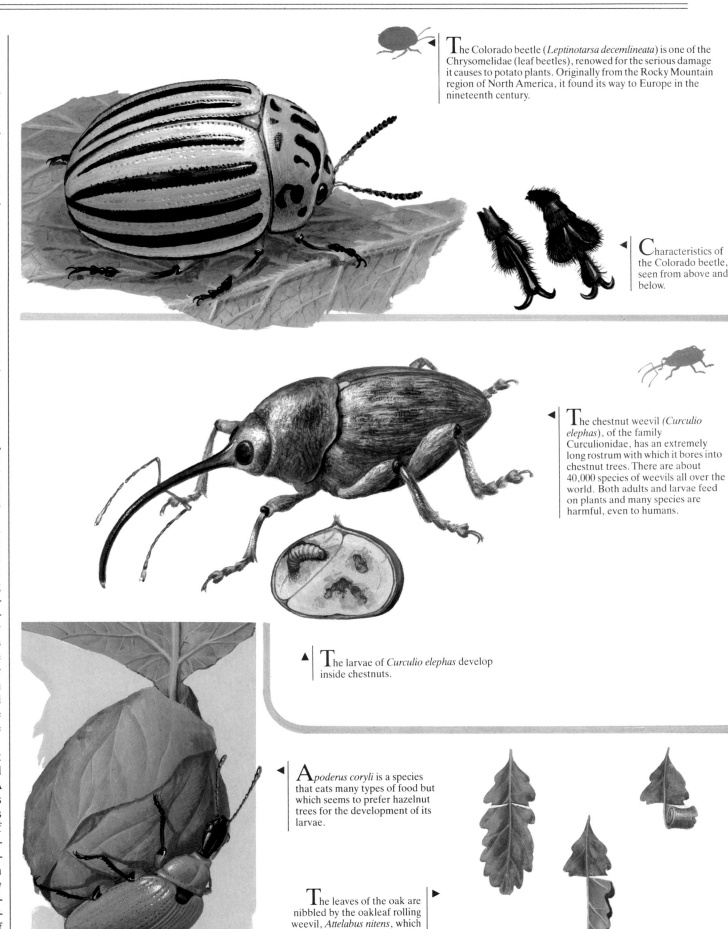

worms. The adults of *Necrophorus* have a highly developed sense of smell, allowing them to detect the body of a small vertebrate and they gather around it in great numbers. The members of each sex fight over the carcass until eventually only a single pair remains. This pair will then carry the body to a suitable place and bury it. Mating usually takes place underground, but first the carcass is reduced by the beetle's powerful mandibles to a rounded mass and is stripped of its hair or feathers.

Before laying her eggs, the female digs a gallery running off the crypt and then deposits the eggs individually in chambers situated along the gallery. She then returns to the crypt, chases off the male and feeds off the ball (made from the decomposing body) throughout the incubation period of the larvae. When the larvae hatch they move toward the ball of rotting flesh and begin to feed, although for their first few hours they are fed by their mother, who regurgitates food. This, therefore, is not just an example of the building of a nest, as happens in other coleopteran families, but it also involves true parental care, something which is rare among the insects.

The Chrysomelidae is an enormous family of phytophagous beetles with about 33,000 members, distributed around the world. Virtually all chrysomelids display glossy striking coloration. One species which is unfortunately now well known is *Leptinotarsa decemlineata*, commonly known as the Colorado beetle. This species is renowned for the damage which it causes to potatoes. It has only recently spread from its place of origin – the western states of the USA and Mexico, where it lived on plants of the genus *Solanum* – to the rest of the world.

The adult overwinters in the soil at depths of about 20 in (50 cm) and becomes active again in the spring. A female may lay as many as 2,000 eggs in the course of her life and deposits them in groups on the underside of leaves. After a week the orange-yellow larvae hatch and feed on the tissues of the leaves. They pass through four instars in a period of about twenty days. They then pupate in an underground chamber and their metamorphosis is complete in a couple of weeks.

The Colorado beetle (*Leptinotarsa decemlineata*) is one of the Chrysomelidae (leaf beetles), renowned for the serious damage it causes to potato plants. Originally from the Rocky Mountain region of North America, it found its way to Europe in the nineteenth century.

Characteristics of the Colorado beetle, seen from above and below.

The chestnut weevil (*Curculio elephas*), of the family Curculionidae, has an extremely long rostrum with which it bores into chestnut trees. There are about 40,000 species of weevils all over the world. Both adults and larvae feed on plants and many species are harmful, even to humans.

The larvae of *Curculio elephas* develop inside chestnuts.

Apoderus coryli is a species that eats many types of food but which seems to prefer hazelnut trees for the development of its larvae.

The leaves of the oak are nibbled by the oakleaf rolling weevil, *Attelabus nitens*, which uses a highly specialized technique to construct characteristic cigar-shaped nests for its larvae.

HYMENOPTERA
Terebrantia

The Terebrantia or Parasitica is a vast group of insects belonging to the order Hymenoptera. The females of these species vary in size from a few tenths of a millimeter to the 3½ in (9 cm) of *Rhyssa persuasoria*. Their abdomen bears an ovipositor, which is known as the terebra. It enables the hymenopteran to deposit eggs deep inside plant tissues or the bodies of its hosts. In some species it is very short, while in others which attack hosts living in galls, branches, fruit and so on it may be several centimeters long – 2 in (5 cm) in *Rhyssa persuasoria*.

The great majority of terebrants are parasites of other insects, but the group does include species whose larvae feed on plants, the small and curious agaonid chalcidoids being examples of this: they develop in the flowers of plants of the genus *Ficus* which have been transformed into galls. Various torymids, eurytomids, and eulophids develop in seeds, fruits, and other parts of plants.

The largest superfamilies are the Ichneumonoidea, the Proctotrupoidea, the Cinipoidea, and the Chalcidoidea. The Ichneumonoidea parasitize insects from numerous orders, and araneids. The Rhyssini is a tribe of large elegant ichneumonids whose larvae are external parasites of the larvae of various xylophagous insects (Coleoptera, Hymenoptera). The females of these species have a long ovipositor which reaches 1½ – 2½ in (4 – 6 cm) in *Rhyssa persuasoria*, a species which is a well-known parasite of the woodboring larvae of the siricid hymenopteran *Urocerus gigas*.

Another important group of Ichneumonoidea is the Braconidae, solitary or gregarious primary parasites of lepidopterans, coleopterans, dipterans, hymenopterans, and hemipterans. *Apanteles* is a typical genus of endophagous parasites of lepidopterans. The females of these parasites lay their egg or eggs in the juvenile stages of their victims, where they develop and give rise to larvae. When the latter are mature they emerge from their victim and weave a silken cocoon, a cocoon which may vary in structure and coloration, and in which the transformation into an adult takes place.

◄ *Blastophaga psenes*. Top, the winged female; left, the apterous male in the act of fertilizing a female still enclosed within the gall (the flower of a caprifig transformed into a gall) inside which it developed.

▲ The braconid parasite *Apanteles glomeratus* and, on the right, the dead body of a cabbage white caterpillar from which the cocooned larvae of the hymenopteran have emerged.

▶ Female of the ichneumonid *Rhyssa persuasoria* has a strong ovipostor some 1½-2½ in (4-6cm) long, and the figure shows the insect using it to lay an egg in a larva of *Urocerus gigas* which is housed in the trunk of a conifer.

◄ Some of the kinds of gall induced by cynipid hymenopterans, their formation being the result of a fluid released inside the plant by the female at the same time as she lays her eggs. Above, the gall of *Rhodites rosae* on a rose; left, those of *Cynips kollari* on an oak, and *Cynips quercustozae*, again on an oak.

BEES

Hymenoptera

Bees are highly evolved insects, often exhibiting very complex patterns of social life.

Bumblebees (genus *Bombus*) are large, hairy and noisy insects which can be seen flying everywhere but particularly in temperate regions. About 200 species are known and all are good pollinators of forage plants. Each colony is founded by a female who was fertilized the previous fall and who has spent the winter in a site found by chance or in an underground chamber specially dug by herself. The following spring she explores land and searches for a natural cavity which would be suitable for nesting. Then she builds the first breeding cells with wax secreted by her abdominal glands.

While the eggs are being incubated, and also for long periods during the development of the larvae, the female rests above the breeding cells and does not emerge from the nest. The mother assists her daughters as they emerge and it is at this point that social life begins, with the newly emerged females working inside the nest and foraging, and the queen laying eggs. In this way the colony grows continuously throughout the summer and may sometimes number several hundred individuals. It is not until late in the season that fertile females and males appear. These mate on flowers and after they have done so the society gradually dissolves.

Another group of bees are the carpenter bees, medium-sized or large hymenopterans with extremely hairy bodies and often displaying intense metallic colors. They are concentrated in the warm and temperate regions of the world. About 800 species are known and they are grouped in three genera *Lestis*, *Proxylocopa*, and *Xylocopa*. Most species nest in dried stems or hardwood. Living plants are only used occasionally. In temperate regions they have only one generation a year but in warm ones there are up to four.

The fertilized female of a typical solitary species overwinters in a temporary shelter or in the same nest in which she emerged. The following spring she prepares her own nest by digging a gallery with her mandibles and building a row of cells. Each cell is separated from the next by partitions of wood

▼ Bumblebees normally nest in holes in the ground, where they build cells made of wax and earth. They raise several larvae in each of these or use them for storing food.

▲ Bumblebees are hairy, variously colored, honey-producing hymenopterans and are the largest of the honey bees. They can be seen flying from one flower to another, sucking up the nectar and gathering the pollen with which they feed their young. Consequently, they are extremely important as pollinators of seeds and plants. They form eusocial colonies which are less advanced than those of honey bees.

▼ Carpenter bees are sometimes large in size and build their nests in galleries which are often specially excavated in wood. Many species are solitary while others are social.

▼ Carpenter bees build a certain number of breeding cells in each gallery. The cells are separated from one another by partitions made from chewed wood pulp which is arranged in a spiral pattern. A paste of pollen and nectar is placed in each cell and a single egg is deposited on the mixture. Adults frequently emerge from the outer cells of the nest before those from the inner cells, even though they are younger.

paste and the cells are frequently arranged in spirals. She provisions each of the cells with a mixture of pollen and nectar and lays an egg on top of the paste. Once she has done this, she abandons her work and dies. After the eggs have hatched, the newborn larvae consume the food which was left for them, pupate and then metamorphose into adults of both sexes. After mating, the females who have survived the winter begin to nest in their turn the following spring.

Among the honey bees (*Apis mellifica*), each hive contains a female known as the queen, a variable number of workers (between 30 and 60,000 or more) and at certain times during the year a small number of males or drones. The queen is the mother of all members of the colony while the workers are responsible for construction of the combs, for cleaning the nest, for collecting nectar and pollen, for raising the young and for defending the nest. There are a number of ways in which the queen clearly differs from the workers. She is larger than them and although she resembles them in having a sting she differs in lacking a pollen-collecting apparatus (combs and baskets on the hind legs).

The queen mates with several males during a series of flights and whereas the workers die after a few months she lives for four or five years. During good weather she is capable of laying up to 2,000 eggs in the space of 24 hours. These eggs will hatch into workers (sterile females), males or, from time to time, queens (fertile females) depending upon the size of the cell in which they were laid. The size of the cell appears to control the sex of the embryo by inducing the queen to lay a fertilized egg which will give rise to a female, or an unfertilized one, which will give rise to a male. The kind and amount of food with which a larva is fed determines whether its gonads will be sterile or not. Some 2 – 3 mg of royal jelly and a large amount of poorer-quality food will suffice for a worker, while to develop into a queen a larva requires 100 – 300 mg of royal jelly and nothing else.

Bee communities survive for years and multiply by swarming. This involves the old queen and about half the workers departing and establishing themselves in a new locality which has been found by scouts. The queen stores the sperm which she has

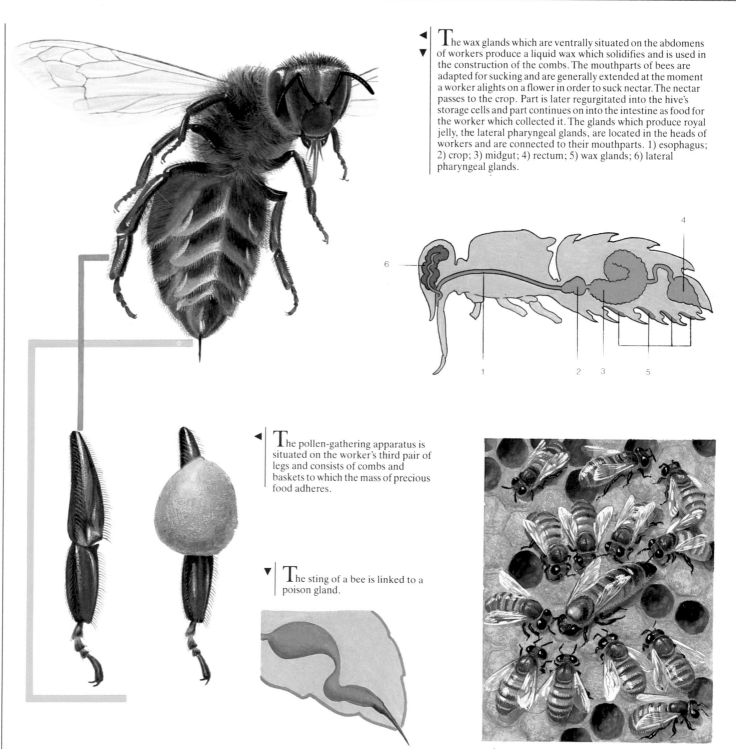

The wax glands which are ventrally situated on the abdomens of workers produce a liquid wax which solidifies and is used in the construction of the combs. The mouthparts of bees are adapted for sucking and are generally extended at the moment a worker alights on a flower in order to suck nectar. The nectar passes to the crop. Part is later regurgitated into the hive's storage cells and part continues on into the intestine as food for the worker which collected it. The glands which produce royal jelly, the lateral pharyngeal glands, are located in the heads of workers and are connected to their mouthparts. 1) esophagus; 2) crop; 3) midgut; 4) rectum; 5) wax glands; 6) lateral pharyngeal glands.

The pollen-gathering apparatus is situated on the worker's third pair of legs and consists of combs and baskets to which the mass of precious food adheres.

The sting of a bee is linked to a poison gland.

A queen bee surrounded by workers inside the hive.

honey queen bee   worker   male or drone

received from the males during mating in a spermatheca situated in her abdomen and connected to her oviduct. The seminal fluid which she stores in this way is sufficient to fertilize eggs over a period of years.

The queen, who is the only fertile female in a bee colony and the only one who has been fertilized, exercises an extraordinary degree of control over its other members. The persistent chemicals exerting this control produce "group effects" which are of great importance to the economy of the hive. A range of pheromones capable of eliciting various reactions are emitted by the queen's body.

There are no morphological differences between the workers but a division of labor has been clearly established between individuals on the basis of age and the needs of the family. Although tasks are not strictly tied to age, the workers normally perform them in a certain sequence. They live for about a month or a little longer and for their first few days they clean the cells. Then they turn to feeding the young larvae and providing them with the royal jelly secreted by their glands at this period. Next they feed the larvae which are almost mature with honey and pollen. At around ten days of age the royal jelly glands regress and the ones which produce wax develop. As this happens, the worker changes its occupation and concentrates on building combs, storing food in cells, removing left-over wax, or cleaning the hive and getting rid of waste. At the same time it makes exploratory flights outside the hive so as to learn about its surroundings. Once a worker has found a plant with plenty of food and has learnt its scent, it is capable of recognizing the same scent again and, obviously, the plant from which it came. When it is about twenty days old, a worker becomes a hive guardian, intercepting individuals as they leave or enter in order to check that they are not intruders.

One of the most significant and amazing scientific discoveries of the present century has been the proof that bees communicate and exchange information of considerable importance for the proper functioning of their families. A few years ago the German zoologist Karl von Frisch was awarded the Nobel Prize after years of study devoted to the bee.

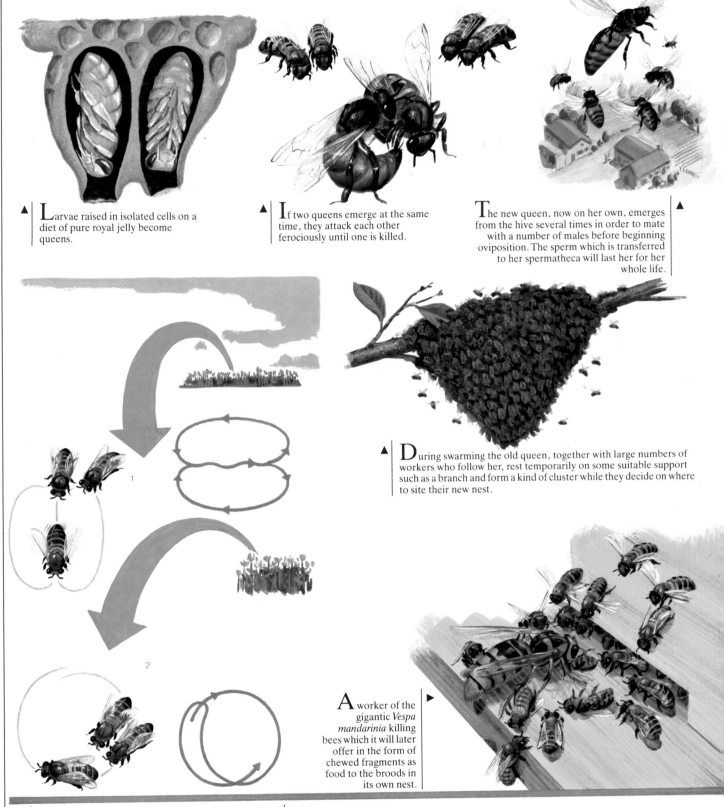

▲ Larvae raised in isolated cells on a diet of pure royal jelly become queens.

▲ If two queens emerge at the same time, they attack each other ferociously until one is killed.

▲ The new queen, now on her own, emerges from the hive several times in order to mate with a number of males before beginning oviposition. The sperm which is transferred to her spermatheca will last her for her whole life.

▲ During swarming the old queen, together with large numbers of workers who follow her, rest temporarily on some suitable support such as a branch and form a kind of cluster while they decide on where to site their new nest.

▶ A worker of the gigantic *Vespa mandarinia* killing bees which it will later offer in the form of chewed fragments as food to the broods in its own nest.

◀ Combs in beehives are composed of large numbers of cells which are used for rearing the broods and storing nectar and pollen. The queen is the only individual who lays eggs, and the workers, depending upon their ages, clean the nest, raise the young, build new cells, gather food, defend the hive, and ventilate it when the temperature is too high.

▲ Bees returning from a flight indicate the location of the food which has been discovered by dancing on the combs. In the round dance (2) the bee describes a sort of circle and changes direction frequently, telling the other bees that the nectar lies within a radius of about 100 yards (100m) . In the waggle dance the bee describes a figure-of-eight or two adjacent circles linked by a straight line. This tells its sisters that the source of food is more than 100 yards from the hive. The precise distance is apparent from the speed of the dance on the combs; the slower the dance, the farther away the food. The direction is indicated by whether the straight line between the two semicircles is vertical or at an angle. If the source of food lies in the same direction as the sun, the bee dances this straight line from the bottom to the top, whereas it lies in the opposite direction, the bee moves from top to bottom. If the source lies to the left of the sun, the bee angles the straight line to the left, and if the food lies to the right, the line is angled to the right.

WASPS
Vespoidea

Wasps are hymenopterous insects of the superfamily Vespoidea which possess a peculiar feature, the ability to fold the first pair of wings longitudinally. They are also known as the Diploptera. About 15,000 species have been described.

The subfamily Vespinae contains the largest forms, such as *Vespa* and *Vespula*. Their nests are easily recognizable since the cluster of combs is covered by a protective casing. Vespines are eusocial and form annual monogynous societies whose level of organization is slightly higher than that of bumblebees. Some members of this family, *Vespula austriaca* being one example, are social parasites.

In the above species the nest is found in the spring by a single fertile female who was fertilized the previous fall and who then remained inactive throughout the winter in some sheltered spot. After feeding on flowers she goes in search of a suitable place to nest. This might be a hollow trunk, a crack among rocks, an abandoned building (*Vespa crabro*, the hornet) or a branch, the ceiling of a dark room or a cave (*Vespula germanica* and *V. vulgaris*, *Dolichovespula media* and *D. saxonica*).

Having selected and possibly adapted the site, the female builds the first small comb of a few cells. This is supported by a stalk and its top is covered by only a single layered covering. The wasp uses a grayish, paperlike substance which it obtains by chewing dry wood or plant fibers. The female sticks an egg to the bottom of each hexagonal cell. On hatching, the first few larvae are fed on freshly caught insects, chewed to a pulp by their mother. When they reach maturity, the larvae spin a cocoon inside their cell and metamorphose. Then, with the appearance of workers, the queen ceases all other activity and concentrates on laying eggs. Meanwhile her daughters extend the nest, complete its covering, collect nectar, and hunt insect larvae, the genus *Vespa* preferring honey bees.

As the colony gradually expands, the combs are enlarged and increase in number, and the multilayered coverings which surround them are destroyed and rebuilt as necessary. Unlike those of bees, wasp combs

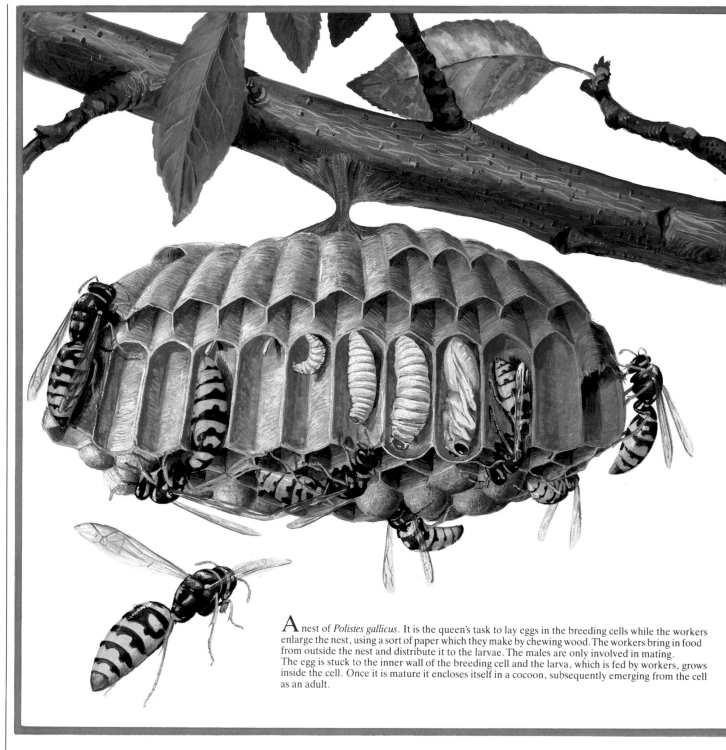

A nest of *Polistes gallicus*. It is the queen's task to lay eggs in the breeding cells while the workers enlarge the nest, using a sort of paper which they make by chewing wood. The workers bring in food from outside the nest and distribute it to the larvae. The males are only involved in mating. The egg is stuck to the inner wall of the breeding cell and the larva, which is fed by workers, grows inside the cell. Once it is mature it encloses itself in a cocoon, subsequently emerging from the cell as an adult.

The workers hunt insects, cut them into pieces with their mandibles, and offer them as balls of food to the larvae.

The adults feed on sugary substances which they generally suck from flowers or from the flesh of fruits.

have only a single layer of combs and their openings are directed downwards. These combs run horizontally and hang from pillars of paper which connect them together.

Caste dimorphism is well defined in vespine societies and probably results from a difference in diet. Those larvae which are destined to be queens are raised in larger cells and fed larger amounts of food than those which will become workers. Qualitatively, however, their diets are similar and are composed mainly of chewed insects, nectar, and the pulp of fruit. The division of labor in these colonies is probably very elementary. It appears that for at least the first few days after they have emerged, the workers concentrate on building the nest rather than on collecting nectar and feeding the young, and it is the slightly larger workers which collect the nectar.

The majority of wasps belong to the subfamily Polistinae. The genus *Polistes* is cosmopolitan. In many *Polistes* species the nests may be founded by one or more females who set to work in the spring. The nests of paper consist of just a single flat or slightly convex comb attached by means of a strong pedicel to a horizontal or angled support such as a rock, a tree, or a wall. Although these nests always remain modest in size, they may subsequently be enlarged. After several months of activity the colony breaks up in the fall, as it does in the Vespinae. The fertilized females and sometimes a few workers survive by passing the winter in a well-sheltered hiding place.

In the colonies of *Polistes gallicus* one of the group of females living together acts as queen, inhibiting ovarian development in the others by her aggressive behavior and forcing them to act as workers. *Polistes* sp., like vespines, initially raise their young on sugary fluids or on eggs deposited in their cells and then move on to animal matter (insects, spiders, etc.) which has been reduced to a pulp, ingested, and regurgitated or offered as solid, unregurgitated food. When the comb gets too hot, *Polistes* sp., like all wasps, reduce the temperature by beating their wings to produce a flow of air or by spraying drops of water over it. Another similarity with the vespinae is the occurence of cannibalism and the exchange of food.

The members of the genera *Vespa* and *Vespula* are often extremely aggressive both towards other insects, which they feed to their larvae, and towards other animals, including man. Their stings can often do considerable harm, and *Vespa mandarinia* from Asia is particularly dangerous. This species is first and foremost a scourge of honey bees, on which it feeds its broods.

The nests of *Vespa* and *Vespula*, unlike those of *Polistes*, are composed of several combs covered by a multilayered envelope of paper, and they are constructed both in the subsoil and in the open. The horizontal combs are linked together by columns of paper. The size of these nests depends upon the age of the colony.

The head of a wasp, showing its formidable mandibles.

ANTS
Formicidae

Ants (Formicidae) occur in all parts of
the world and in many respects may be
regarded as the most important eusocial insects, both in terms of the numbers of individuals and the number of
species (over 7,000). They have highly
specialized diets and large numbers of
insects are preyed upon. Other ants
prefer the seeds of plants, and some
are tied to termites, springtails, or the
eggs of various arthropods. A number
live at the expense of other ants and
some feed on the honeydew produced
by aphids. Yet others cultivate and eat
fungi. Some tropical ants, such as the
Attini, eat fungi cultivated by placing
the mycelia on spongy masses formed
from the chewed-up fragments of
various plants.

The great majority of ants build
their nests in the subsoil but others
nest in trees and establish such close
relationships with their host plants
that the latter are incapable of surviving without them. All ants live in eusocial colonies or are social parasites.
Their societies are permanent,
homogeneous or heterogeneous, and
may contain one or more females. Colonies may be founded independently
of other species or they may require
their help, leading to the establish-
ment of symbiotic relationships of varying degrees of intimacy which may
even be harmful or damaging for one
of the parties.

Certain ants nest in sacs of silk
woven by themselves or composed of
such matter as leaves or plant detritus
held together by silk threads taken
from spiders' webs or produced by
their own larvae, as in *Oecophylla
smaragdina*. These larvae are used as
shuttles by the workers, who grip them
halfway along their bodies with their
mandibles and force them to emit the
threads with which they tie the pieces
of leaves together, while other workers hold the pieces next to each other.
The end result is a kind of sac in which
the colony establishes itself.

Aphids feed on the sap of plants and
they take sugary fluids up into their
intestines which they later excrete in a
slightly altered form as a substance
known as honeydew. This is secreted in
large quantities and is much prized by
various species of higher ants, including
the Myrmicinae and the Formicinae,

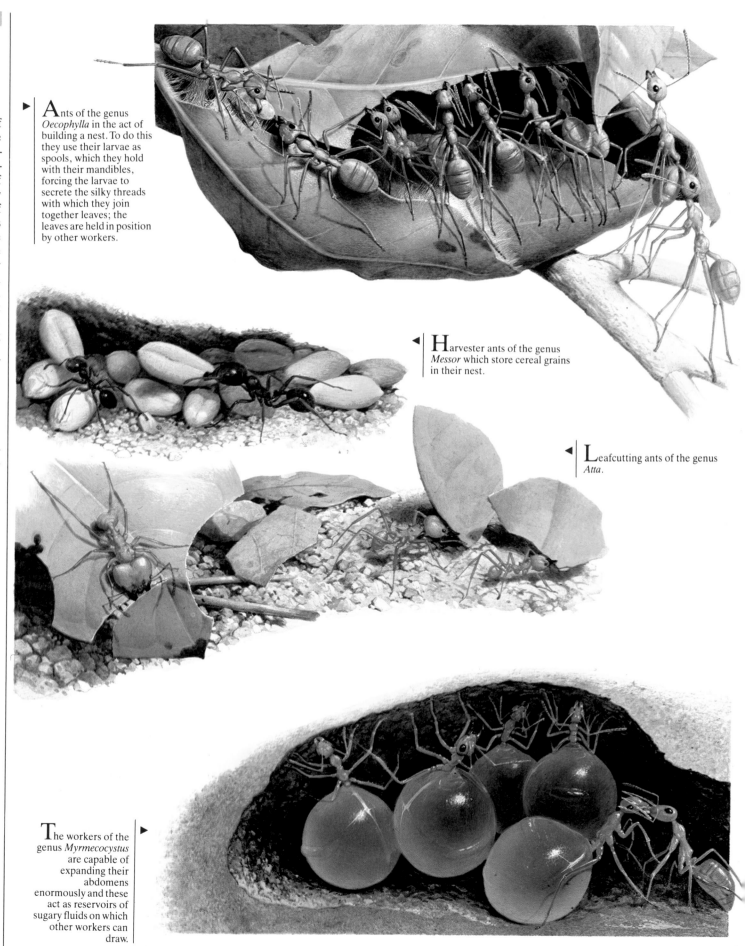

Ants of the genus *Oecophylla* in the act of building a nest. To do this they use their larvae as spools, which they hold with their mandibles, forcing the larvae to secrete the silky threads with which they join together leaves; the leaves are held in position by other workers.

Harvester ants of the genus *Messor* which store cereal grains in their nest.

Leafcutting ants of the genus *Atta*.

The workers of the genus *Myrmecocystus* are capable of expanding their abdomens enormously and these act as reservoirs of sugary fluids on which other workers can draw.

which collect it from the ground, from leaves, or even from the producers themselves, soliciting them directly. In *Formica rufa*, for example, honeydew constitutes more than half of its food intake while in other species it may only be eaten occasionally. Dependence on honeydew reaches a peak in certain American ants which depend exclusively on aphids, raising and caring for enough aphids to meet their needs in the same way as farmers tend their livestock. The care lavished by many ants on these trophobionts deserves fuller treatment.

Like all social insects, ants have developed stable castes within a single sex but, unlike other hymenopterans, they have three, namely the fertile females or queens, the workers, and the soldiers. In some species the workers have disappeared while in others the queens have been replaced by forms similar to workers.

The function of a queen in an ants' nest varies with age. If she is still a virgin her social behavior is resticted to exchanging food. After mating, she is involved in founding a new nest and fulfils all the tasks which will subsequently be undertaken by the workers. Later, she confines her activity to laying eggs and to feeding, either by regurgitation or by eating eggs. In some cases this process of change can be reversible.

The role of the soldier is specifically that of defense and the members of this caste possess mandibles suitable for cutting, piercing or blocking. Sometimes they can perform other duties such as collecting food or transforming themselves into living receptacles, for the benefit of the other members of the nest.

All the tasks about the nest are performed by the workers and their size is often related to the work that they undertake, the small workers frequently acting as foragers while the larger workers work inside the nest. Occasionally, as in *Oecophylla longinoda*, the position is reversed. The younger workers normally remain inside the nest whereas the older ones spend more time outside. Trophallaxis plays an important part in social organization involving a unilateral or reciprocal exchange of food between adults and an indirect or direct one between adults and larvae.

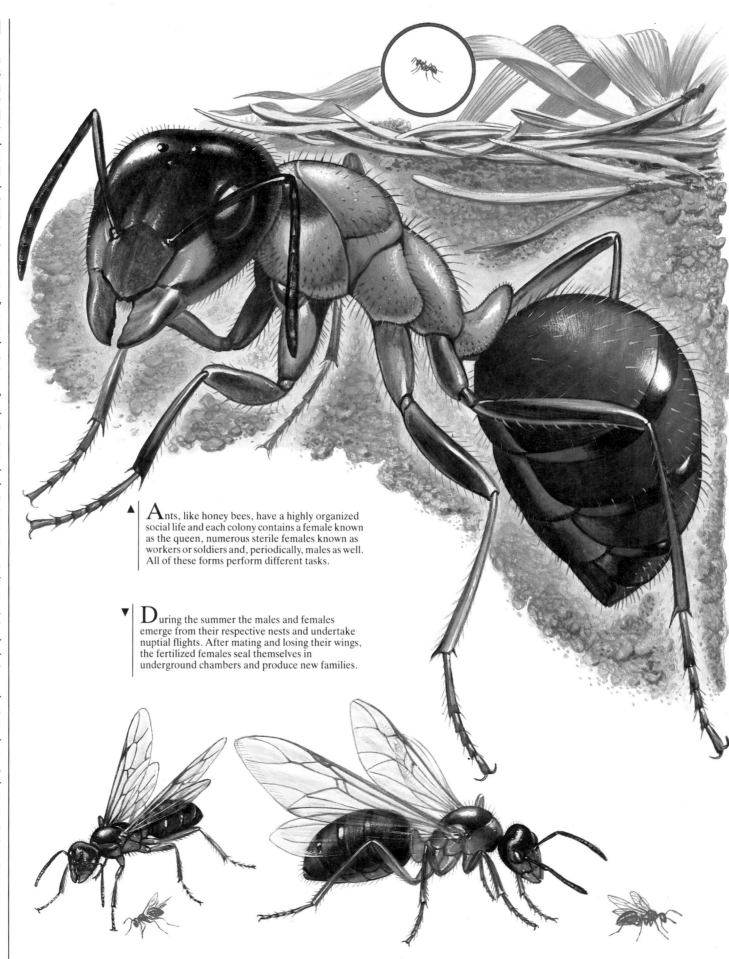

▲ Ants, like honey bees, have a highly organized social life and each colony contains a female known as the queen, numerous sterile females known as workers or soldiers and, periodically, males as well. All of these forms perform different tasks.

▼ During the summer the males and females emerge from their respective nests and undertake nuptial flights. After mating and losing their wings, the fertilized females seal themselves in underground chambers and produce new families.

MOLLUSKS

Mollusca

The Mollusca is one of the most important as well as one of the largest phyla in the animal kingdom and with over 100,000 species it is second only to the Arthropoda. It is also one of the most varied, since in the course of their evolution its members have diversified into an infinity of forms.

Mollusk bodies can be divided into five main parts: the foot, the head, the visceral mass, the mantle, and the shell. The foot is essentially a muscular organ used by the mollusk for locomotion. Its form varies in different mollusk groups since it is adapted to the various different substrates over which they move and the way in which they do so. In some cases – for example, the snail – there is a head in front of the foot. This often has two tentacles and these in turn bear eyes – at their base, somewhere along their length or at their tips.

Dorsal to the foot there is a sac, known as the visceral mass, containing the digestive, excretory, circulatory, and genital systems. This sac is covered by a layer of epithelial cells extending around the base of the sac as a marginal fold, the mantle or pallium. This epidermal fold encloses the head and body, together with a space known as the mantle cavity or pallial cavity lying between the mantle and the rest of the body. As will be seen later on, the relationship between a mollusk and its surroundings depends to a large degree on this cavity or rather on the organs lying in it.

Respiration takes place across a pair of gills or ctenidia situated in the mantle cavity. The bipectinate ctenidium is the most primitive type of gill. It consists of a central axis on the opposite sides of which two rows of gill filaments are inserted like the barbs of a feather. Respiratory exchange occurs at the level of these filaments. The mantle is also responsible for producing the well-known calcareous shell possessed by many members of this phylum.

Mollusks may be hermaphrodites or they may have separate sexes, but it is clear that hermaphroditism, even if self-fertilization is not possible, is more profitable than gonochorism (separate sexes) since in theory every meeting between individuals in

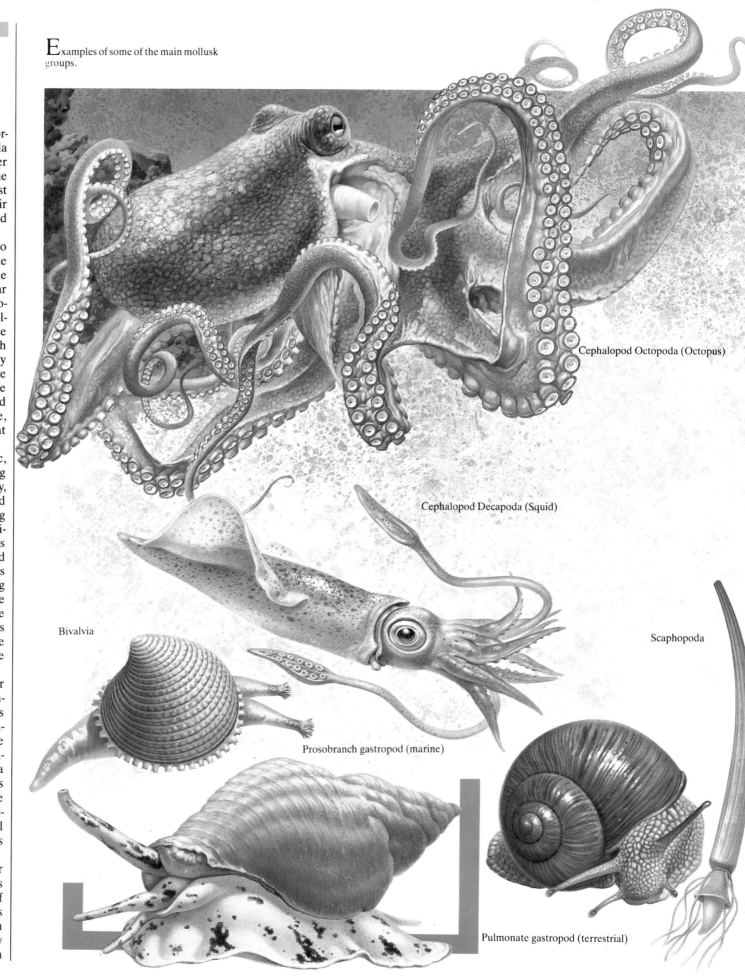

Examples of some of the main mollusk groups.

Cephalopod Octopoda (Octopus)

Cephalopod Decapoda (Squid)

Bivalvia

Scaphopoda

Prosobranch gastropod (marine)

Pulmonate gastropod (terrestrial)

breeding condition may result in fertilization, whereas when the sexes are separate an individual only has a 50 per cent chance of meeting one of the opposite sex. It should be pointed out that hermaphrodites rarely function as both sexes at the same time and that when gametes of the two sexes do mature simultaneously there are usually mechanisms to prevent self-fertilization. Sexual reproduction therefore requires two individuals

The egg develops inside its case and generally gives rise to a larva. This hatches and is carried far away from the spot in which it was laid. The most primitive larval form is the trochophore, which resembles the larval forms of annelids. The trochophore often remains within the egg case and gives rise to a second larval form, the veliger. This form is unique to the mollusk and frees itself from the egg case. It also already displays certain parts of the adult body, such as a foot, a mantle, a larval shell formed by a shell gland, and a sort of head consisting of two or more large lobes bearing tiny cilia which enable the larva to move and carry food particles suspended in the water to its mouth. Both these larval forms are adapted to living in the water and are found almost exclusively among marine mollusks, being supressed in all terrestrial mollusks and virtually all fresh-water ones.

The phylum Mollusca includes the classes Solenogastres, Caudofoveata, Polyplacophora, Monoplacophora, Gastropoda, Pelecypoda, Scaphopoda, and Cephalopoda.

Solenogastres and Caudofoveata are primitive, wormlike mollusks without a true shell. Polyplacophora, better known as chiton, are marine mollusks, mostly inhabiting the rocky shores. Monoplacophora are a small class of limpetlike animals.

Gastropoda is the most numerous and diverse of the mollusk classes, including both marine and fresh-water forms, as well as the terrestrial snails and slugs. Pelecypoda or Bivalvia are sedentary or little mobile mollusks, with a shell of two articulated pieces. Scaphopoda have toothlike, elongated conical shells and occur in sandy marine bottoms. Cephalopoda are the most evolved mollusks, often devoid of any shell and adapted to pelagic life in the sea.

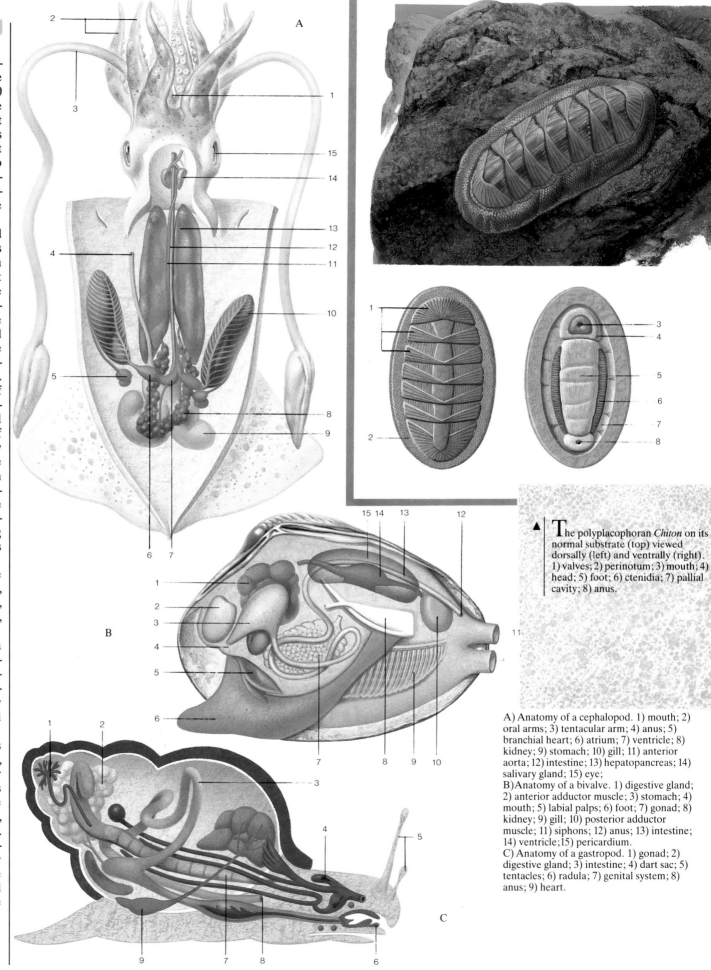

The polyplacophoran *Chiton* on its normal substrate (top) viewed dorsally (left) and ventrally (right). 1) valves; 2) perinotum; 3) mouth; 4) head; 5) foot; 6) ctenidia; 7) pallial cavity; 8) anus.

A) Anatomy of a cephalopod. 1) mouth; 2) oral arms; 3) tentacular arm; 4) anus; 5) branchial heart; 6) atrium; 7) ventricle; 8) kidney; 9) stomach; 10) gill; 11) anterior aorta; 12) intestine; 13) hepatopancreas; 14) salivary gland; 15) eye;
B) Anatomy of a bivalve. 1) digestive gland; 2) anterior adductor muscle; 3) stomach; 4) mouth; 5) labial palps; 6) foot; 7) gonad; 8) kidney; 9) gill; 10) posterior adductor muscle; 11) siphons; 12) anus; 13) intestine; 14) ventricle;15) pericardium.
C) Anatomy of a gastropod. 1) gonad; 2) digestive gland; 3) intestine; 4) dart sac; 5) tentacles; 6) radula; 7) genital system; 8) anus; 9) heart.

CEPHALOPODA

The modern Cephalopoda are mollusks in which the shell has been modifed to form a floating structure. Recent theories regard the cephalopods as direct descendants of the Monoplacophora, with an increased coiling of the shell. The apical region of the visceral mass of these primitive mollusks gradually withdrew, and the mantle covering it formed a series of calcareous internal septa, bounding gas-filled cavities. As a consequence of this, the cephalopods became progressively lighter as they were evolving until the volume of gas was sufficient to compensate for the weight of the shell and the body of the mollusk. At this point these animals acquired neutral buoyancy and were able to rise up effortlessly from the bottom to which they had previously been confined.

Another theory supposes that during their early evolutionary stages the herbivorous cephalopods became carnivores, the head bearing tentacular structures adapted to the capture of food. While these tentacular lobes were developing the foot was reduced. Once cephalopods had achieved neutral buoyancy, there still remained the problem of how to move about once they had risen off the bottom. It was the foot, the simplest and most versatile of mollusk organs, which acquired a new form and function. Since it was no longer needed for creeping over the bottom, it was reduced to a pair of mobile folds which partially overlap and can curl over to form a tube at the entrance to the mantle cavity. The rhythmical contraction of the musculature of these folds can move the animal in a fairly coordinated fashion as well as helping to circulate water through the deep mantle cavity.

The shell, which played an essential role in the evolution of the cephalopoda has in the modern forms tended to disappear completely in the Decapoda (squids and sepias) and is entirely absent in the Octopoda (octopuses). It is usually internal and considerably modified. The only living cephalopods with a well-developed external shell are the *Nautilus* of the western Indopacific waters.

Food is captured in various ways. Cuttlefish, for example, hover close to the bottom in coastal waters where

▲ The well-known octopod *Octopus vulgaris* with its funnel clearly visible.

◀ All cephalopods live in the sea. Some are benthic, others, such as squids, are able swimmers. They are all carnivores and use their oral or tentacular arms to catch food.

▼ Detail of a cuttlefish's mouth, showing the prominent mandibles that resemble a parrot's beak.

they catch shrimps and small fish. They use gentle jets of water from their funnels to blow prey off the sand. Then, as soon as it is within reach, the tentacular arms are shot out from pouches on either side of the mouth (the pouches themselves lie inside the ring of eight oral arms) to grasp the victim. These mechanisms of attack are innate and young cuttlefish begin by attacking small crustaceans before going on to take larger ones and fishes. However, it is only with age and experience that they learn how to approach different kinds of prey.

Octopuses, which are also predators of crustaceans, capture their food by striking rapidly from above with their arms. The prey is grasped by the jaws and killed or paralyzed with poison secreted by the salivary glands. It is then held by the arms coiled around it while being injected with the digestive enzymes. After a few hours, the prey, a crab for example, will be released apparently intact but in fact reduced to its exoskeleton, the flesh having been completely digested and sucked out – an example of what is known as extra-intestinal digestion.

The nervous system is both unusual and highly elaborate. The cerebral ganglia are more or less fused to form a brain enclosed within an extensively fenestrated cartilaginous capsule. This brain is connected laterally to the extremely large optic lobes where the enormous quantity of visual information is received. The cerebral mass consists of regions lying both above and beneath the esophagus, the former being the larger.

The sense organs are also extremely complex and refined. The eye is a large spherical structure, equalling the vertebrate eye in complexity. Unlike nearly all other mollusks, cephalopods recognize food or enemies primarily by sight and their sense of smell is reduced.

The sexes are separate in all cephalopods. The eggs are typically deposited in clusters and are usually attached to hard substrates. In some species they are cared for in any usual fashion. In *Octopus*, for example, the female cleans them with the tips of her arms or with jets of water. In *Argonauta* they are gathered together in a nidamental shell secreted by a pair of modified oral arms. The eggs are large, rich in yolk, and the embryos feed off a yolk sac.

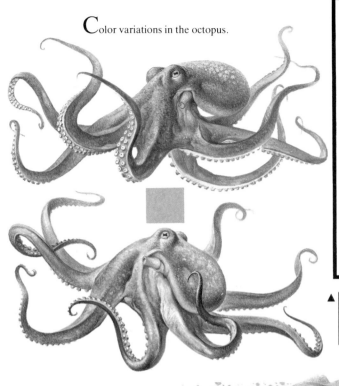

Color variations in the octopus.

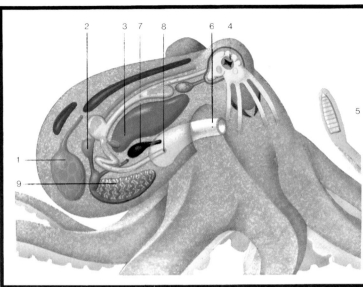

▲ Diagram of the anatomy of the octopus: 1) gonad; 2) heart; 3) liver; 4) eye; 5) hectocotylus arm; 6) funnel; 7) ink sac; 8) anus; 9) gill.
With the exception of *Nautilus*, all cephalopods are capabable of emitting a dense cloud of "ink" if disturbed. This is secreted by a special gland.

Sepia officinalis

Loligo vulgaris

cuttlefish bone

▼ Detail of suckers with a toothed horny ring on the oral arms of a decapod.

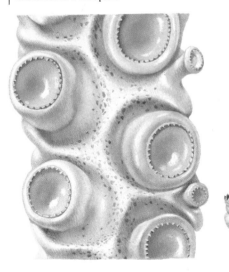

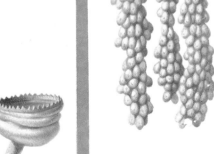

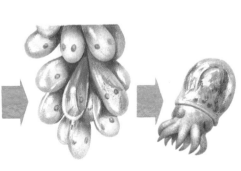

Diagram showing stages in the development of an octopus. The eggs are attached in strings to the roof of the animal's hole. The embryos develop inside the eggs and feed off a yolk sac, which is completely absorbed by the time the young individual hatches.

ECHINODERMATA

Starfish and sea urchins are the best-known representatives of the large group of Echinodermata, invertebrates whose members are to be found throughout the world seas from the shoreline to the deepest ocean depths. Their variety and beauty of form and coloration makes them some of the most attractive aquatic creatures.

Echinoderms are defined by three essential characteristics. Firstly, their bodies appear to have a spoked structure, the various parts being arranged around one main axis. As a result, they are radially symmetrical externally, although their internal organs are essentially bilaterally symmetrical and it is not possible to divide the body into radially arranged sections or actinomeres. Nevertheless, the majority of forms appear to display radial symmetry. The common, five-armed starfish are a particularly clear example. Their bodies can be divided into two symmetrical halves by drawing a line through any of their five arms and the opposite angle. Echinoderms are generally pentamerous since five radial and five interradial zones alternate around the central axis and this passes through the mouth.

A second notable feature of the echinoderms is their covering of calcareous plates. These are arranged in various ways and provide an armor which, while it is developed to varying degrees, is not external to the tissues of the body, since it is covered by an integument composed of an epithelium and part of the skin. The plates frequently bear granules, tubercles or spines, and these play a large part in shaping the animal's appearance.

The third feature is the presence of an internal water-vascular system consisting of fluid-filled canals. One canal circles the gut just behind the mouth and gives rise to canals that run along each radial zone. These canals are connected to numerous small and highly mobile hollow tentacles known as tube-feet or podia. The tube-feet often end in suckers and are arranged in two or more rows that run along each radial zone. The radial zones are in fact sometimes known as ambulacra, as opposed to the interambulacra lying between them. The circular canal of the water-vascular system also gives rise to a canal leading to the madreporite. This is

▲ The starfish *Luidia ciliaris* is an intense orange color and lives down to depths of 7,350 ft (400m) in the Mediterranean and the eastern Atlantic, preferring sandy bottoms.

Echinoid

◄ In the majority of starfish (Asteroidea) the body can be divided by five planes of symmetry which cross at the center, where the mouth lies.

Holothuroid

a perforated plate usually situated on the body's surface and it links the water-vascular system to the sea water outside. There may sometimes be more than one madreporite.

The body cavity, the coelom, varies in extent and contains a digestive system which may be tubular and sinuous, or saclike. In the latter case it may or may not possess diverticula. Similarly, there may or may not be an anus. There is no blood circulation but there is a system of fluid-filled cavities or lacunae. The nervous system is simple in structure, lacks ganglia, and is not associated with any well-developed or definite sense organs.

Echinoderms are extremely varied in size, ranging from species measuring only a few millimeters, while the snakelike bodies of *Synapta* reach several meters in length. No echinoderms are either colonial or parasitic. All species live in the sea and are a major component of the fauna and the biocoenoses of both tropical and polar seas. Numerous echinoderms are highly adapted to an abyssal life. They have a very varied diet. Starfish in particular are voracious predators and will even devour animals that match them in size. Their first line of defense consists of their dermal skeleton, a calcareous armor which in many cases bears a formidable array of spines.

The reproductive organs of echinoderms are very simple structures. As a rule the sexes are separate and there is no sexual dimorphism. The eggs are generally released into the water and then fertilized. They hatch into minute, bilaterally symmetrical larvae. Whereas the adults are typically benthic, i.e. bottom-living animals, the larvae are planktonic and swim about freely in the water by means of the beat of their numerous cilia. They continue to do so for a variable length of time, until, with the completion of their metamorphosis, they descend to the bottom and acquire their final adult form. It is an almost invariable rule that development is indirect, with a pelagic, bilaterally symmetrical larval phase and a benthic, adult phase which usually appears to be radially symmetrical. There are, however, instances of direct development, hermaphroditism, and species which brood their young.

The five modern echinoderm classes are the Crinoidea, Holothuroidea, Asteroidea, Ophiuroidea, and Echinoidea.

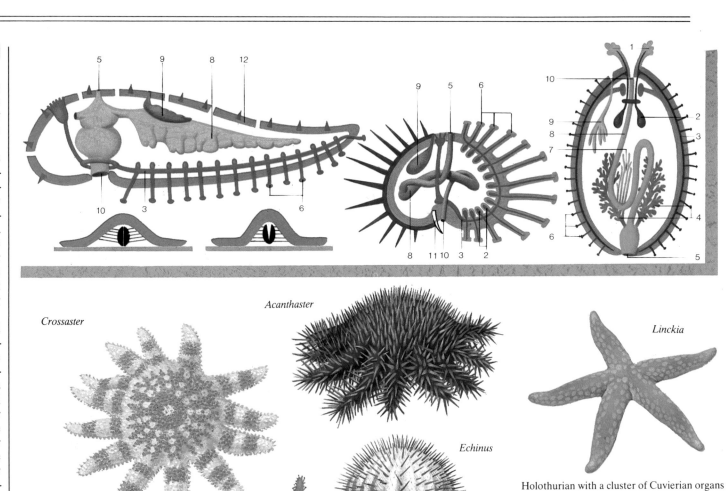

Acanthaster

Crossaster

Linckia

Echinus

Peltaster

Holothurian with a cluster of Cuvierian organs

Echinaster

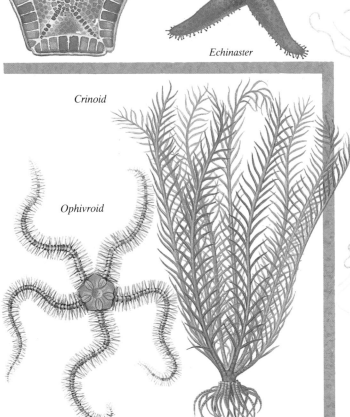

Crinoid

Ophivroid

Heterocentrotus

This plate shows some members of the large group Echinodermata, which in the variety and beauty of their forms, are among the most attractive of aquatic creatures.
Top: vertical section through an asteroid (A); the anatomy of an Echinoid (B); and a Holothuroid (C).
For all figures: 1) oral tentacles; 2) tentacle ampullae; 3) radial canal of the water-vascular system; 4) respiratory tree; 5) anus; 6) tube-feet; 7) Cuvierian organs; 8) intestine; 9) gonad; 10) mouth; 11) tooth; 12) skeletal plate with spine.
D-E) Two stages in the opening of a bivalve shell by a starfish using its tube-feet.

TUNICATA AND CEPHALOCHORDATA

Tunicata and Cephalochordata are two groups of marine animals closely related to vertebrates, together with which they form the phylum Chordata. This phylum includes organisms which for at least part of their lives possess a rigid and elastic chord of turgid cells enclosed in a sheath. This structure is known as the dorsal chord or notochord. It lies in the median sagittal plane beneath the neural tube and above the gut. However, this structural plan cannot easily be recognized in the various classes since, with the exception of the Cephalochordata, it may be lost in the course of development.

The Chordata is divided into three subphyla. The first is the Tunicata or Urochordata, in which the chord is only present in the tail of the larvae and in the tail of the adults, if they possess one. The second is the Acrania or Cephalochordata, in which the chord extends from one end of the animal to the other and persists throughout its life. The third is the Vertebrata or Hemicephalochordata, in which the chord is always present during embryonic development, when it extends from the mid-brain to the posterior end of the animal, but in adults it is generally replaced by the vertebrae.

Tunicata are all marine animals and are characterized by the possession of a test known as the house or tunic. This is composed of a cellulose-like substance and contains a scattering of cells. Unlike other chordates, they are unsegmented. There are three classes: Ascidiacea, Thaliacea, and Larvacea.

Ascidians are all sessile with a pelagic larval phase. Some are solitary while others are colonial. Their bodies are saclike, with two circular openings which are extended as short tubes, the oral and atrial siphons. The oral siphon leads to the saclike pharynx or branchial chamber whose walls are perforated by numerous branchial stigmata, a fact that results in it often being referred to as the branchial basket. Posteriorly, the branchial basket opens into the esophagus, which is followed by the stomach, a looped intestine, and the rectum. This opens into the peribranchial chamber or atrium and partially surrounds it. The atrium

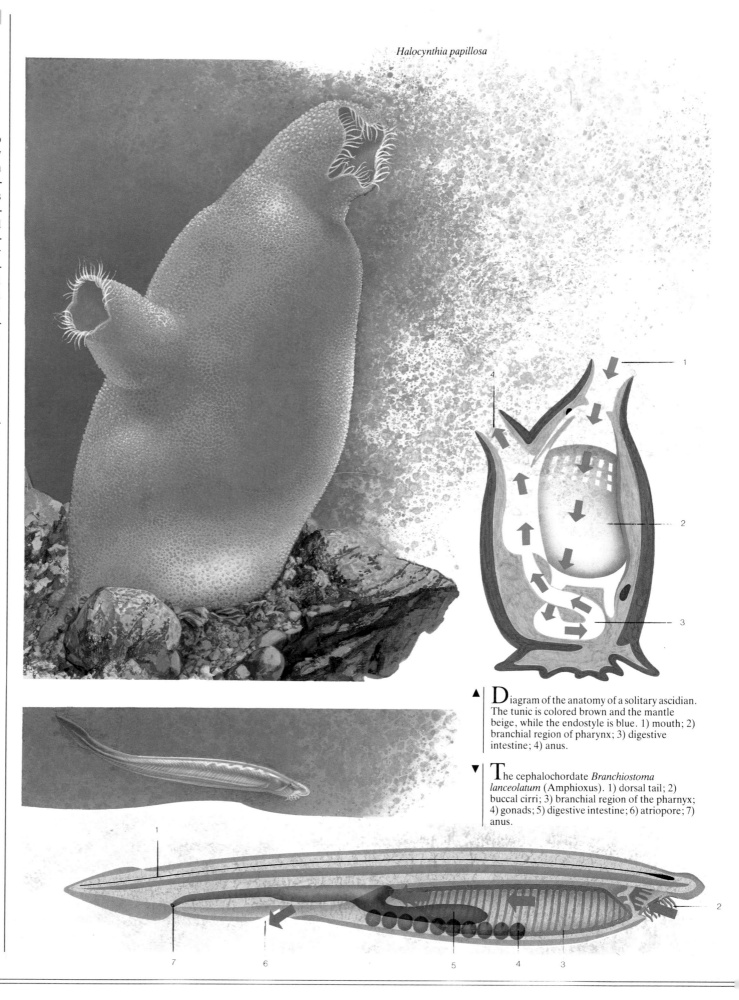

Halocynthia papillosa

▲ Diagram of the anatomy of a solitary ascidian. The tunic is colored brown and the mantle beige, while the endostyle is blue. 1) mouth; 2) branchial region of pharynx; 3) digestive intestine; 4) anus.

▼ The cephalochordate *Branchiostoma lanceolatum* (Amphioxus). 1) dorsal tail; 2) buccal cirri; 3) branchial region of the pharynx; 4) gonads; 5) digestive intestine; 6) atriopore; 7) anus.

opens to the outside through the atrial siphon.

Ascidians are filter feeders and water flows continuously through the oral siphon, into the branchial chamber and out through the stigmata and the atrial siphon. They are hermaphrodites. The larvae lead a pelagic life for a few hours and then attach themselves to a substrate, usually a hard one, and undergo metamorphosis. The tail, together with its contents, is reabsorbed and the juvenile siphons open. Ascidians are widely distributed in the coastal waters of all the world's seas.

The class Thaliacea is composed entirely of pelagic organisms very similar in structure to the ascidians. The tunic and entire body are generally transparent, with the exception of the visceral mass and the gonads. All forms display an alternation of asexual and sexual generations. The Thaliacea is divided into three orders, the Pyrosomidea, Doliolidea, and Salpidea.

The Pyrosomidea are colonial forms, strongly luminescent, as a result of two organs lying to the sides of the branchial region immediately beneath the oral siphon. The Doliolidea are small, barrel-shaped organisms a few millimeters or, exceptionally, centimeters in length. Like other members of the Thaliacea, the Salpidea (salps) are pelagic filter feeders with transparent bodies and an intensely colored visceral mass.

Finally, Larvacea or Appendicularia is a class of small pelagic tunicates in which the typical chordate structural plan persists throughout life. Their bodies are generally transparent and consist of an ovoidal trunk and a tail. As such, they resemble ascidian larvae, hence the name Larvacea.

Larvaceans are distributed throughout the world's seas but are particularly abundant in coastal waters (the neritic zone) where the phytoplankton is richest.

Cephalochordata are small, marine organisms about 2–3 in (5–7 cm) long and fishlike in appearance. Their name derives from the fact that the chord extends from the head to tail. This structure also persists in the adults. The body is nearly transparent and slightly compressed, giving it a lanceolate appearance. Only two genera are known. Cephalochordates live on soft bottoms in shallow waters. They feed by filtering small organic particles.

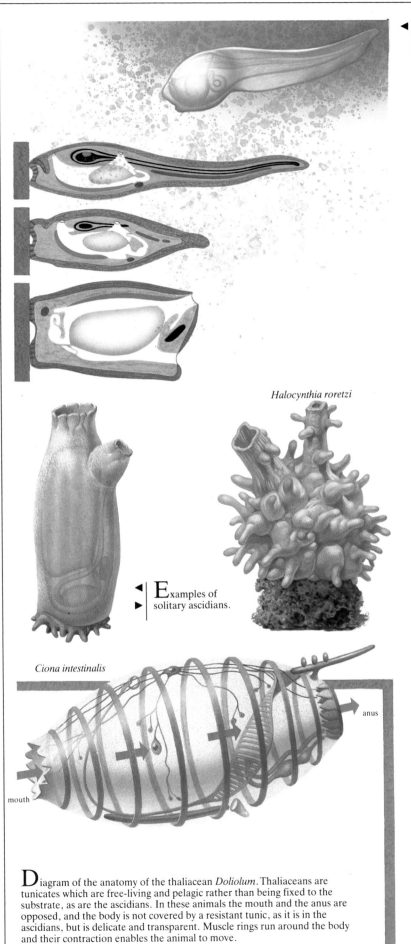

Stages in the metamorphosis of a larval ascidian. After it attaches itself to the substrate by its adhesive papillae, the larva, which to begin with resembles a tadpole, reabsorbs its tail. Meanwhile the developing internal organs rotate to reach their final positions.

Halocynthia roretzi

Examples of solitary ascidians.

Ciona intestinalis

mouth

anus

Diagram of the anatomy of the thaliacean Doliolum. Thaliaceans are tunicates which are free-living and pelagic rather than being fixed to the substrate, as are the ascidians. In these animals the mouth and the anus are opposed, and the body is not covered by a resistant tunic, as it is in the ascidians, but is delicate and transparent. Muscle rings run around the body and their contraction enables the animal to move.

An example of a colonial ascidian, Botryllus schlosseri. It is common and widespread in the North Sea. The tunics of the various individuals which form the colony join together to form a gelatinous mass. In the center of the colony there is a common, shared chamber, the atrium, into which the waste is emptied.

SEA LAMPREY

Petromyzon marinus

Class Cyclostomata
Order Petromyzontiformes
Family Petromyzonidae
Size Length 31 – 35 in (80 – 90 cm)
Weight 3 – 5½ lb (1.5 – 2.5 kg)
Distinctive features Mouth surrounded by suctorial funnel: no fins except for the caudal and dorsal which is divided in two in the adult
Coloration Dorsal and lateral regions whitish with black spots which sometimes meet to form a dorsal lattice in the adult; the young vary in color from light gray to yellow or shades of brown
Reproductive period Migrates to rivers in spring and reproduces in the following season from May to July
Eggs 20,000 – 240,000; 1mm in diameter
Sexual maturity 5 – 6 years of age

The sea lamprey is eel-like and the body is covered in a scaleless epidermis which is rich in mucous glands, making it highly viscous. The head terminates in an oral suctorial funnel with a series of horny teeth. The pharynx opens out in the center of the buccal funnel and the tongue also has pointed horny teeth which are used to pierce and break down the tissues of the victim. The compound eyes are well-developed, for sight is perhaps the most important sense to the survival of this form which can sometimes chase and attack a fish at surprising speeds.

The respiratory system consists of gill pouches ranged along the sides of the pharynx, each coming out through its own individual gill slit. The water that carries oxygen for respiration is not conducted to the gills through the mouth but through the seven apertures by rhythmic movements of the branchial "basket."

The larvae of the sea lamprey, the ammocoetes, take three to five years to develop. The metamorphosis takes about three months to complete. The young lamprey then migrates to the sea (or the Great Lakes in America) where it generally stays in the shallow coastal depths feeding on cod, mackerel, trout or salmon and also, at times, on sea mammals. After spending some three to five years in the sea, the lampreys reach sexual maturity and begin their migration up the rivers

▲ Lampreys spend a part of their lives in a marine environment where they feed on fish such as salmon. They attach their bodies firmly to the victim by means of the horny teeth on the buccal funnel, and break down the skin and tissues with their tongue, which also has pointed horny plates. In this way, they feed on the blood and the muscles but never the internal organs of the fish, which usually dies of the wounds inflicted, after the lamprey has gone.

▼ The most common victims of the lamprey, apart from salmon, are mackerel, cod, and sea trout.

▼ The dorsal fin is continuous on young lampreys just after metamorphosis and the gill slits do not appear completely separate.

at about the beginning of spring. They stop feeding during this period and the horny structures in their suctorial funnels tend to regress. While climbing the rivers, the males and females undergo a series of morphological changes: the dorsal fins of the female increase in size and cutaneous swellings appear in the anal region. The second dorsal fin also increases in size on the male and the anal papilla transforms into a copulatory organ.

The lampreys also show an active interest in light just before beginning their ascent of the rivers, and so leave the shaded areas where they spent their lives at sea. This change in their habits is essential in that mating takes place in rivers in areas which are exposed to sunlight. Once they have reached a suitable spot in which to lay their eggs, the so-called "grayling zone" where the water is not too cold but is clean and well oxygenated, the males choose a calm spot with a sandy or gravelly bottom where the water is about 30 – 48 in (80 – 120 cm) deep. There they begin to build their nest, digging a round ditch about 24 in (60 cm) in diameter, using the buccal funnel to move stones or other materials.

When the nest is complete, the female attaches to some object on the wall of the nest, such as a branch or a stone, etc., while the male fastens to her with his buccal funnel on the branchial region, and presses the abdomen of the female to aid the discharge of the eggs which are immediately fertilized before dropping into the nest. The female then moves off and mates with other males, while her partner covers the fertilized eggs as soon as they have been laid. The eggs take 10 to 20 days to develop, depending on the temperature of the water. As soon as they have emerged, the larvae absorb the yolk sac (a source of food in the earliest stages of life outside the egg) and then move to an area with a muddy bed where they dig small tunnels not much longer than their own bodies. Their anterior section projects from this tunnel with the buccal funnel pointing upstream to facilitate the entry of water containing small particles of food which are filtered by the fine branchial lamellae. The adults, which had undergone a regression of the hard buccal teeth while climbing the rivers to avoid injury during mating, can no longer feed, and so die after having laid the eggs.

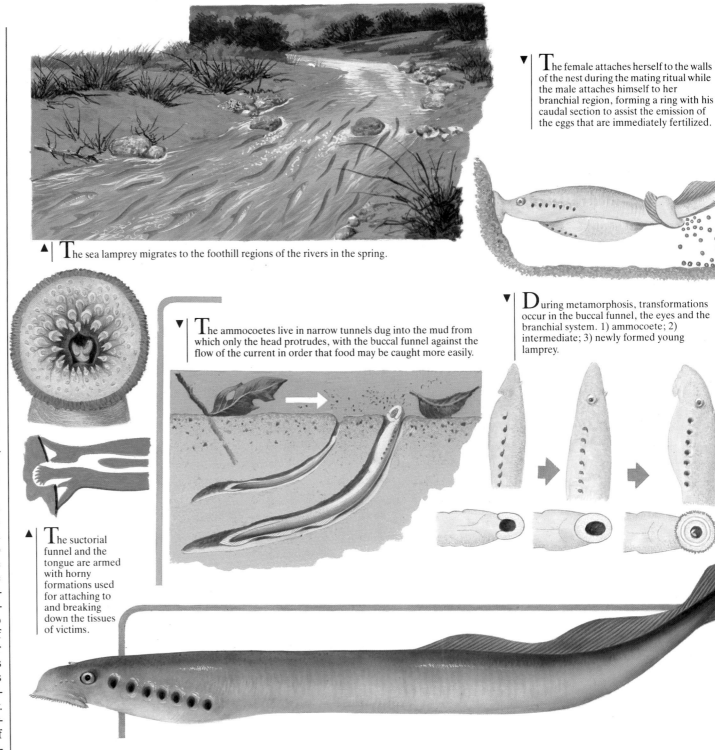

▲| The sea lamprey migrates to the foothill regions of the rivers in the spring.

▼| The female attaches herself to the walls of the nest during the mating ritual while the male attaches himself to her branchial region, forming a ring with his caudal section to assist the emission of the eggs that are immediately fertilized.

▼| The ammocoetes live in narrow tunnels dug into the mud from which only the head protrudes, with the buccal funnel against the flow of the current in order that food may be caught more easily.

▼| During metamorphosis, transformations occur in the buccal funnel, the eyes and the branchial system. 1) ammocoete; 2) intermediate; 3) newly formed young lamprey.

▲| The suctorial funnel and the tongue are armed with horny formations used for attaching to and breaking down the tissues of victims.

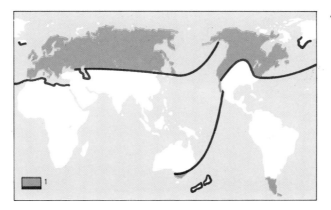

▲| All young lampreys are very similar to one another both in appearance and in coloring. They are classified on the basis of the arrangement of the horny teeth and buccal funnel.

◀| The family of Petromyzonidae has a scattered distribution area limited to cold and temperate regions of both hemispheres. This type of distribution is known as "bipolar." The black lines indicate the probable lines along which the primitive forms spread and penetrated the oceans in the Ice Ages. Lampreys are cold thermophiles and managed to cross the tropical and equatorial zones by taking advantage of cold currents in the ocean deep.

SHARKS
Squaliformes

The typical shark has a slender, graceful body which is slightly taller in the middle, with a pointed snout, two dorsal fins, and a sickle-shaped tail.

The snout is usually rather flat with ventral nostrils, each of which has a single aperture, in contrast to nearly all bony fish. The nostrils open into a largish sac whose walls are covered with numerous parallel folds. The nasal valves are also folds of skin of various shapes located near to the nostrils which sometimes connect with the upper edge of the mouth through a naso-oral groove. Because of the carnivorous diet, the teeth are highly developed and are ranged on both jaws in many rows. They can vary in shape, often directly related to the type of food the sharks eat, but are usually close together and have one or more points, with either smooth or serrated edges. In fact, they may even differ in shape from one jaw to the other. There are usually four to six rows of teeth, of which only the first few are usually functional, with replacement teeth in the rows behind lying on the back surface of the jaw. These only straighten up and become functional as the front teeth gradually wear and fall out. Fossilized sharks' teeth are often found in excellent condition, so accurate research can be done to establish the relationship between living species and those that formerly inhabited the seas. In fact, dental characteristics are very important for they are the major distinguishing factor between the species. Close examination of a shark's mouth shows the formation of more or less developed grooves in the skin at each corner; these are known as labial folds and contain small sensory pores that reach right up to the tip of the snout.

The more information is obtained about sharks as a whole, the more clearly they are differentiated from bony fish whose bodies are all covered in scales, having only one gill slit on each side, and whose fins are supported by clear rays like the spines of a fan; but there are also many other features (anatomical, physiological, and embryological) which distinguish bony fish and those of the subclass Actinopterygii in particular.

One of the biggest, most widely

The characteristic appearance of a large maneater such as *Carcharodon carcharias*.

distributed and most fearsome sharks is without a doubt the great white shark (*Carcharodon carcharias*), belonging to the family Isuridae. *Carcharodon* is one of the largest of the shark species, the maximum recorded size being 21 ft (6.4 m) found in a specimen caught near Cuba which weighed about 3¼ tons. It is a smooth-skinned shark with very small scales, each with three spines and with large, triangular and serrated teeth. There are two separate dorsal fins, the front one being very large, and a longitudinal ridge on either side at the base of the tail which is crescent-shaped because of the large lower lobe. It is gray or nearly black with a white belly. This enormous fish is found in the warm and temperate waters of all the oceans of the world, but never in great numbers. It lives in the open sea, but makes seasonal appearances near the coasts where it is unusual for it to be captured, although it happens occasionally in the Mediterranean and more often around the coasts of Australia.

Another animal worthy of special attention is the whale shark, not only for its exceptional size, but also because of a number of characteristics that are so unusual and unique that they set it apart as the sole representative of a clearly defined family, Rhincodontidae, named after the scientific name for this enormous fish, *Rhincodon typus*.

It has a long flat and rounded snout with a wide mouth at the tip, i.e. terminal instead of ventral, as with most sharks. The teeth are very small, with only one point, and are arranged in over 100 rows on each jaw, only the first dozen rows of which are functional. Even more interesting, perhaps, are the numerous fine horny appendages on each gill arch on the opposite side to the filaments facing the buccal pharyngeal cavity, which make up the filtering system by which the animal traps the organisms on which it feeds.

The whale shark is brown, dark gray or even black, with a large number of white or yellow patches. The belly is all white or yellow. It is the largest living fish which well deserves its popular name as it can grow up to 60 ft (18 m) in length and can weigh over 10 tons. It is mostly found in warm waters, but occasionally appears at higher latitudes, such as off New York.

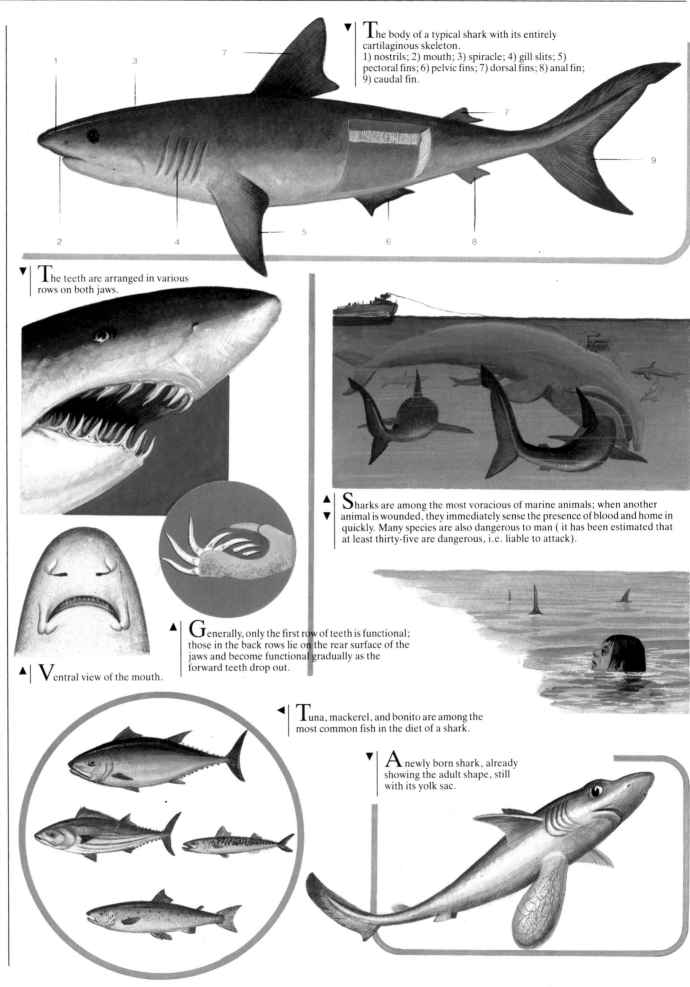

The body of a typical shark with its entirely cartilaginous skeleton.
1) nostrils; 2) mouth; 3) spiracle; 4) gill slits; 5) pectoral fins; 6) pelvic fins; 7) dorsal fins; 8) anal fin; 9) caudal fin.

The teeth are arranged in various rows on both jaws.

Sharks are among the most voracious of marine animals; when another animal is wounded, they immediately sense the presence of blood and home in quickly. Many species are also dangerous to man (it has been estimated that at least thirty-five are dangerous, i.e. liable to attack).

Ventral view of the mouth.

Generally, only the first row of teeth is functional; those in the back rows lie on the rear surface of the jaws and become functional gradually as the forward teeth drop out.

Tuna, mackerel, and bonito are among the most common fish in the diet of a shark.

A newly born shark, already showing the adult shape, still with its yolk sac.

RAYS

Rajiformes

There are many fish with cartilaginous skeletons living on the sea beds which are no less interesting in their own way than sharks, and rays are the classic example.

Rays, unlike sharks, always have five pairs of ventral gill slits, the spiracles are always present although they can vary in size, and they never have an anal fin.

Closely related to the true rays are some strange-looking animals, such as the sawfish (*Pristis*), the guitarfish (*Rhinobatos*) and the torpedo rays (*Torpedo*).

One of the best-known species is the huge manta. The word "manta" means a blanket or cover in Spanish, so the name becomes particularly appropriate for the enormous Rajiforme *Manta birostris* which presents certain similarities with another smaller species known as the devilfish (*Mobula mobular*), which is also found in the Mediterranean. Both species are particularly characterized by the two cephalic fins that jut out forward like horns on either side of their wide mouths. The manta can vary in color from brown, reddish or olive, to black on its dorsal side, whereas ventrally it is white. The mouth is terminal and measures just over half the width of the head, with large, rounded cephalic fins that can be rolled back. The body is wider than it is long because of the enormous pectoral fins. The manta can grow up to 23 ft (7 m) in width and weigh up to 1½ tons.

This great fish with its strange appearance is found in all the tropical seas and penetrates into temperate zones in summer. Mantas swim slowly, sometimes in small groups, and often have sucking fish attached. Their diet consists of small fish, crustaceans, and various types of planktonic organisms which are caught by the filtering appendages in its mouth. The manta is ovoviviparous, giving birth to only one offspring at each delivery, which can measure up to 5 ft (1.5 m) in width.

Other interesting members of the Rajiformes are the stingrays, i.e. the species of the genus *Dasyatis*, who have a sharp spine sticking out of their tails with which they can inflict incredibly painful wounds both because of the sting itself and also because of the

Dasyatis pastinaca

Stingrays are among the best-known members of the Rajiformes i.e. the cartilaginous fish which have to be classified as bottom dwellers because of their ecology. They are very reminiscent of rays in overall appearance and are distinguished mainly by the poisonous sting in their tails. This sting makes a formidable offensive and defensive weapon and is inserted into the dorsal section of the tail at varying distances between the base and the tip. Sometimes there are two of these stings, which are flat and covered in a fine layer of skin, with backward-pointing teeth on both edges (i.e. they point toward the base of the sting). It also has small muscles, which give it a certain degree of mobility, and parallel grooves that run along the whole lower surface. Between them lies the tissue that secretes the poison; this flows toward the far edge of the sting and is injected immediately. The serious effects were already known to the ancients, and more than one writer has made reference to them, not without his own imaginary additions and unusual comments. The disk of these animals is more or less quadrangular, but it can also be slightly rounded at the ends, and the tail is long and thin, with no terminal or dorsal fins, but often with longitudinal folds of skin. There are many small teeth.

powerful poison injected. The poison can cause gangrene and tetanus, with some fatal cases having been recorded. The fish periodically sheds its sting, growing a new one behind the old one, and it is not uncommon to find two or even three, one behind the other. Stingrays feed on both fish and invertebrates and are considered to be ovoviviparous. The classic example is the common stingray, *Dasyatis pastinaca*, which is very common in the Mediterranean, the Black Sea, and along the Atlantic coasts from Norway down to Angola. It is usually olive-colored on the back with a white stomach and gray-brown edges, often in irregular patches, and can measure at least 4½ ft (1.4 m) in length and weigh over 44 lb (20 kg).

Various stingrays are highly euryhaline, i.e. they adapt to different levels of salinity and so can penetrate inland waterways. There are also stingrays which are exclusively river fish, but they belong to another genus, *Potamotrygon*, which can grow up to very large sizes and live only in the regions of South America east of the Andes.

In a further group of Rajiformes, genus *Myliobatis*, generally known as eagle rays, the pectoral fins end sharply toward the head, leaving room for the eyes and the spiracles which are located on the sides instead of on the back, as with so many other Rajiformes. Instead of having the usual small teeth with one or more points, they often have grinding plates, one on each jaw, formed by the coalescence of flat and polygonal teeth ranged in rows. The tail is very slender, long and almost filamentlike at the end. There may be either a small dorsal fin or a poisonous caudal sting like that of the stingray. The best-known species include *Myliobatis aquila* (Mediterranean and eastern Atlantic) and *M. tobijei* (China, Korea, Japan). Both of these fish can grow to over 3 ft (1 m) in length and are a uniform brown color.

They are not strictly benthic for they swim rapidly, even at the surface, and are often seen to leap out of the water. They are often gregarious, forming very large groups, and feed mainly on mollusks, grinding the shells easily with their dental plates. Eagle rays are ovoviviparous.

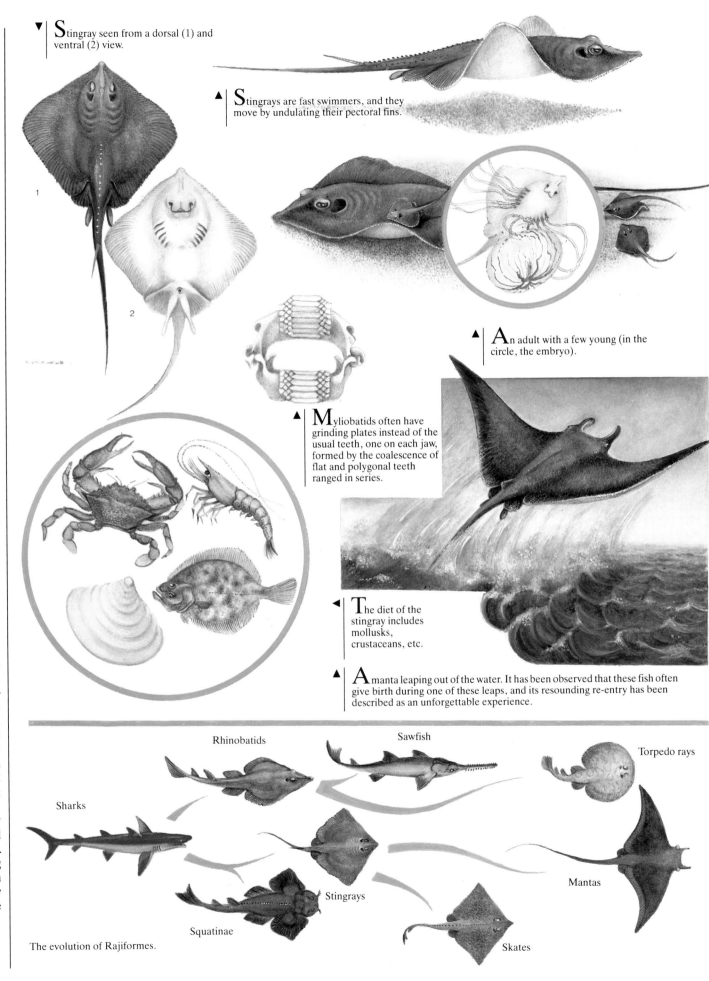

▼ Stingray seen from a dorsal (1) and ventral (2) view.

▲ Stingrays are fast swimmers, and they move by undulating their pectoral fins.

▲ An adult with a few young (in the circle, the embryo).

▲ Myliobatids often have grinding plates instead of the usual teeth, one on each jaw, formed by the coalescence of flat and polygonal teeth ranged in series.

◄ The diet of the stingray includes mollusks, crustaceans, etc.

▲ A manta leaping out of the water. It has been observed that these fish often give birth during one of these leaps, and its resounding re-entry has been described as an unforgettable experience.

Sharks

Rhinobatids

Sawfish

Torpedo rays

Squatinae

Stingrays

Skates

Mantas

The evolution of Rajiformes.

POLYPTERUS OR BICHIR

Polypterus senegalus

Order Polypteriformes
Family Polypteridae
Size Length up to 20 in (50 cm)
Weight Up to 2½ lb (1.17 kg)
Distinctive features Cylindrical body, 8 – 11 dorsal spines, 53 – 61 scales, arranged lengthwise, 14 – 21 predorsal scales, 33 – 40 around the body
Coloration Olive-gray, uniform in adults, belly whitish
Reproductive period During the rainy season, in flooded areas
Eggs 2,900 – 4,150 in individuals measuring 7 in (18.5 cm) and 9 in (23.2 cm) respectively
Sexual maturity At one year
Maximum age At least 6 years in the wild; longer in captivity

The family Polypteridae has just two genera: *Polypterus*, with eight species, and *Calamoichthys* (the reed-fish) with a single species. The species of the genus *Polypterus* can be identified and told apart by the shape of the body and the head; these are quite squat, and either cylindrical or flattish: other distinguishing features are the coloring, either uniform or with black speckling, the number of scales and dorsal pinnules, and the geographical distribution and preference for specific habitats.

The bichir (*Polypterus senegalus*) has an elongated, cylindrical body which is completely covered with bony, lozenge-shaped scales, joined together and covered with a layer of ganoin, a shiny substance not unlike enamel. The fairly small head is entirely covered with solid bony plates. The jugular plates, below the chin, are typical of the Polypteridae. On the whole the skeleton is comparable to that of other present-day fishes, but part of the inner skeleton remains cartilaginous in adults whereas the dermic skeleton forms a conspicuously ossified outer covering.

The dorsal fin consists of two parts: the frontmost part is split up into 8 – 11 pinnules or fin fragments, each consisting of a membrane supported by a strong bony spine; the rear part, which is not spiny, constitutes a part of the sharp tail (caudal) fin. The pectoral fins are roundish in shape, and formed

Congo bichir (*Polypterus ornatipinnis*)

The polypterus or bichir is mainly noctural. During the day it usually remains motionless near the surface, enjoying the heat from the sun's rays, or resting on the river-bed, supported on its pectoral fins which are held out like a fan. If not alarmed it moves about slowly, using just its pectoral fins, or by moving the hindquarters of its body. These fish are predators, as suggested by their wide mouth and strong jaws with small sharp teeth. They feed mainly on insect larvae and small invertebrates, and rarely on small fish. At irregular intervals they rise to the surface to breathe air directly from the atmosphere. When they do this they release an air bubble from the opercular (gill-cover) slit when the small bone which seals off the spiracle is raised. These breathing movements occur at a rate of 2-9 times per hour. Obviously the frequency increases when the polypterus becomes more active, and when there is little oxygen in the water. The sexes are equally distributed. The females grow faster than the males and reach an average length of 14-16 in (35-40 cm). The largest recorded specimen in the Chad basin, weighing 2.6 lbs (1.17 kg) and measuring 20 in (50 cm), was really an exception to the rule. A specimen caught in Mali in 1954 lived in an aquarium in Paris until 1974, thus reaching the ripe old age of 20.

by a series of radii coming from a lobe, the bony structure of which is one of the most noteworthy and important characteristics of the Polypteridae. The structure embracing the radii and the lobe is known as the brachiopterygium. The anal and ventral fins are normally developed.

The swim bladder, divided into two adjacent lobes, which are of different size, connects with the ventral region (not the dorsal region) of the esophagus. The walls, which are markedly vascularized, enable them to function like a rudimentary lung. There is also a functional spiracle which opens above the upper part of the head. The intestine has a spiral valve, as in the dipnoans, the coelacanths, and the cartilaginous fishes.

In the Sudanese and Sahelian regions where bichirs ordinarily live, reproduction takes place during the rainy season. When the level of the rivers rises, the animal can be seen swimming on the surface, near the bank, trying to make its way into inundated areas. In this period sexual dimorphism makes it easier to identify the two sexes. The males have a thicker and longer anal fin than the females, and their caudal peduncle is deformed and swollen on both sides. The female's abdomen is also enlarged. During mating, the male swims close to the female and leans against her flank with his anal fin folded over like a shell against his partner's belly. In captivity, egg-laying invariably takes place very early in the morning. The eggs are fertilized as they emerge and fall onto vegetation, to which they adhere rather precariously. They are spherical and about 0.9 mm in diameter. At 90°F (28°C) the eggs hatch after 60 hours. The larva, which cannot move at the outset, lies on the river bed and breathes with its external gills. On the lower part of the head, below both eyes, there are two organs designed for clinging. After eight days the 4-mm larva can start to feed, and it looks like a tadpole. At 15 days the young bichir becomes a voracious hunter of small prey but its unequal fins are still not differentiated and developed: the formation of the pinnules starts toward the end of the first month, beginning with the front ones. The external gills start to atrophy when the fish reaches a length of about 3 in (7.5 cm). They disappear altogether before the fish is a year old, as it approaches sexual maturity.

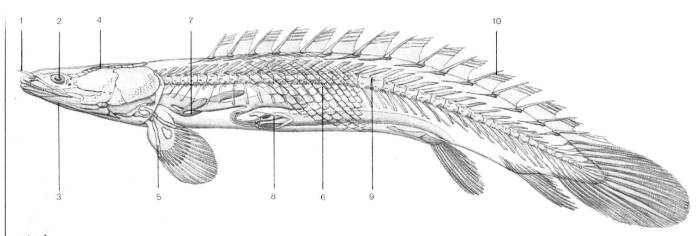

▲ Anatomy of the Polypteridae. 1) The polypterus has a tubular snout, and a very keen sense of smell; 2) the eyes, on the other hand, are small and have poor vision; 3) the jugular plates, beneath the chin, are a typical feature of the Polypteridae; 4) there is a functional spiracle which opens above the upper part of the head; 5) the pectoral fins are round in shape, formed by a series of radii coming from a lobe, the structure of which is one of the most prominent features of the Polypteridae; 6) the scales, which are bony and lozenge-shaped, are joined together and covered with a layer of ganoin; 7) the swim bladder is divided into two lobes of different size, but they are adjacent; 8) the intestine has a spiral valve; 9) the skeleton, broadly speaking, is comparable to that of other present-day fishes, but part of the internal skeleton remains cartilaginous; 10) the dorsal fin has two parts: the front part is divided into so many pinnules, or fin fragments, each consisting of a membrane supported by strong bony spines; the rear part, which is not spiny, is part of the sharp caudal or tail-fin.

▲ The polypterus usually stays in a static position, supporting its body with its pectoral fins; when in search of food, however, it edges its way forward, head outstretched, trying to sniff out what is ahead of it.

F in structure
1) spiny dorsal fin;
2) soft dorsal fin;
3) the tail is formed by a part of the dorsal fin and a section of the caudal fin.

► A polypterus in a swamp: it can breathe on dry land for a period of 3-4 hours.

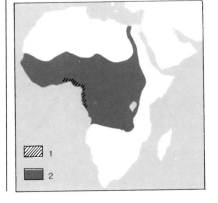

◄ L arva of the genus *Polypterus*.

◄ G eographical distribution of the Polypteridae:
1) genus *Calamoichthys* (reed fish);
2) genus *Polypterus*.

GAR PIKES
Lepisosteiformes

The fishes that belong to this family are elongated and almost cylindrical in shape. The very long snout, with the nasal apertures at the tip, looks like a form of beak.

Along the upper jaws there are 6–8 dermic bones with teeth, deriving from the preorbital structure. The teeth are pointed, and vary in size. The largest teeth are set in order on each jaw opposite gaps on the other jaw. These gaps consist at the base, of radiated folds of very small teeth.

Gar pikes are found at the present time only in North America, Mexico and Cuba, with seven species. *Lepisosteus oculatus*, found from the Great Lakes to the Mississippi valley and Mexico, and from Florida to Texas, has a head halfway in size between the long thin head of *L. osseus* – the longnosed gar – and the shorter, broader head of *L. spatula* – the alligator gar. *L. osseus* has a markedly longer and thinner snout. This species has the widest geographical distribution of the family in North America: from the St. Lawrence river to the Great Lakes, and from Florida to Texas. It can reach a length of 6 ft (1.5 m). It is the commonest species in the Mississippi valley in areas of still water, where there is mud; it likes warm, shallow water. Further to the north, on the other hand, it prefers the clear waters of lakes and rivers.

L. spatula – the alligator gar – is the largest member of the family. The record to date is a specimen measuring 10 ft (3 m) and weighing 304 lb (135 kg). The alligator is a voracious creature which feeds on all types of prey – dead or alive – which come its way.

L. osseus lays its eggs in late spring and early summer in shallow water. The green eggs have a diameter of ⅛ in (2 – 3 cm). Fertilization is external. After fertilization the parents scatter quickly, abandoning their offspring to fate. On the lower surface of the tip of the snout the larvae have suckers which enable them to hold on to any form of anchorage. They remain inactive until their vitelline reserves have been used up. These very young individuals then become extremely active and immediately behave like voracious predators.

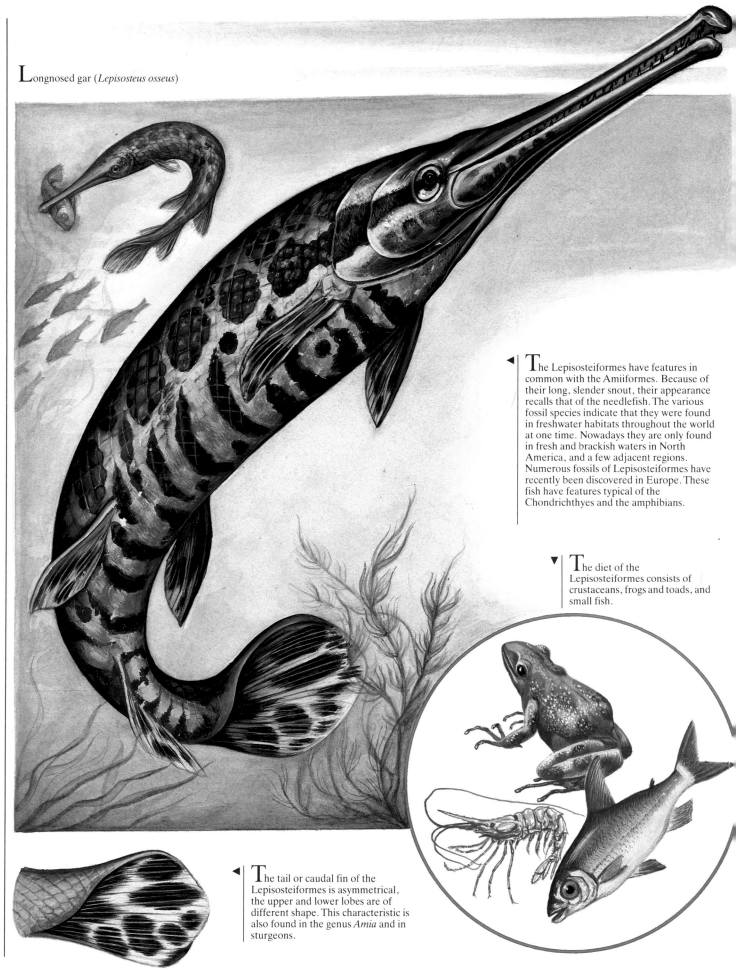

Longnosed gar (*Lepisosteus osseus*)

The Lepisosteiformes have features in common with the Amiiformes. Because of their long, slender snout, their appearance recalls that of the needlefish. The various fossil species indicate that they were found in freshwater habitats throughout the world at one time. Nowadays they are only found in fresh and brackish waters in North America, and a few adjacent regions. Numerous fossils of Lepisosteiformes have recently been discovered in Europe. These fish have features typical of the Chondrichthyes and the amphibians.

The diet of the Lepisosteiformes consists of crustaceans, frogs and toads, and small fish.

The tail or caudal fin of the Lepisosteiformes is asymmetrical, the upper and lower lobes are of different shape. This characteristic is also found in the genus *Amia* and in sturgeons.

BOWFIN

Amia calva

Order Amiiformes
Family Amiidae
Size Length 18 – 24 in (45 – 60 cm), in exceptional cases 3 ft (90 cm)
Weight Usually 2¼ – 3½ lb (1 – 1.5 kg) sometimes up to 7 lb (3 kg). The absolute record appears to be 15¼ lb (6.8 kg)
Reproductive period Late spring
Eggs 20,000 – 60,000 depending on the size of the female; hatching takes place after about 10 days
Sexual maturity 3 – 5 years
Maximum age In the wild, 12 years; in captivity between 25 – 30 years

The bowfin has an oblong, sturdy body with a massive head; it is scaleless. In the wild, at the present time, it is possible to see individuals measuring 18 – 24 in (45 – 60 cm) and weighing 2¼ – 3½ lb (1 – 1.5 kg).

The bowfin lives in still waters in North America, in particular in the eastern part of the continent from the Great Lakes to the St. Lawrence estuary, and from Virginia to Florida and Texas.

Amia calva is a very resistant fish, capable of living in oxygen-poor waters, thanks to the swim bladder which acts as a respiratory organ.

The bowfin reproduces in spring, from April to June depending on the latitude, moving south to north in waters with a temperature range of 60 – 66°F (16 – 19°C). During this period the males move into shallow waters where there is plenty of vegetation; they prepare a circular nest, measuring 12 – 36 in (30 – 90 cm) in diameter. The males defend the area around the nest from other males, raising their fins in an aggressive attitude. The female lays between 20,000 – 60,000 eggs with a diameter of about ⅛ in (2 – 3 mm). After egg-laying and fertilization the males mount a close watch on the eggs, "oxygenating" them every now and then with movements of their pectoral fins. The eggs hatch after 8 – 10 days; when hatched the fry are almost ⅜ in (8 mm) long; the males continue to watch carefully over their offspring.

Amia calva is a predatory fish which feeds on aquatic insects, fishes, amphibians, and freshwater crustaceans, etc.

Bowfin (*Amia calva*)

▶ The Amiidae enjoyed their heyday 100,000,000 or so years ago in the Jurassic and Cretaceous periods. At the present time there is just one species representing this family: *Amia calva*, which is nothing less than a living fossil. The bowfin lives in marsh- and swamplands and in slow-flowing rivers in the central and southern regions of North America.

EELS

Anguilliformes

There are sixteen species of eels (*Anguilla*). The best-known are the following ones: the European eel, *Anguilla anguilla*, widespread throughout Europe, from Iceland to North Africa, from the Canary Islands to the Black Sea; the American eel, *Anguilla rostrata*, that is found from the northern part of South America and the Caribbean islands throughout most of the United States and Canada to southern Greenland; and the Japanese eel, *Anguilla japonica*, living in rivers in eastern China, Japan, and adjacent offshore islands.

The breeding behavior and the life history are among the most interesting attributes of the eel. Different species have different breeding grounds but, where known, the behavior and life histories are similar. To illustrate the general principles, the European eel will serve as an example.

For many centuries eels have been an important source of food. During those centuries countless millions of eels had been gutted for the table. Yet no eel had been found with ovaries or testes. This situation changed in 1777 when Professor Mondini of the University of Bologna identified, in a female eel, developing ovaries. The ovaries had frilled edges, immature eggs, and lay along the top of the abdominal cavity. A century later, in 1874, a Polish scientist, Syrsti, found testes in a medium-sized eel. The matter was settled in 1897 when the Italians Grassi and Calundruccio caught a sexually mature female eel in the Straits of Messina and confirmed Mondini's correct identification of the organs with the frilled edges. Six years later, in 1903, a mature male eel was caught off Norway. It was obvious that the eggs must be laid in the sea, but what happened between the eggs hatching and the larvae growing to some 6 in (15 cm) long was unknown.

Actually, the larva of the eel had already been described. In 1763 Theodore Gronovius published a description, and a figure, of a small, transparent leaflike fish which he called *Leptocephalus*. Its true nature, however, was not realized. Grassi and Calundruccio in 1896 had the good fortune to catch two leptocephali alive in the Straits of Messina. They kept these

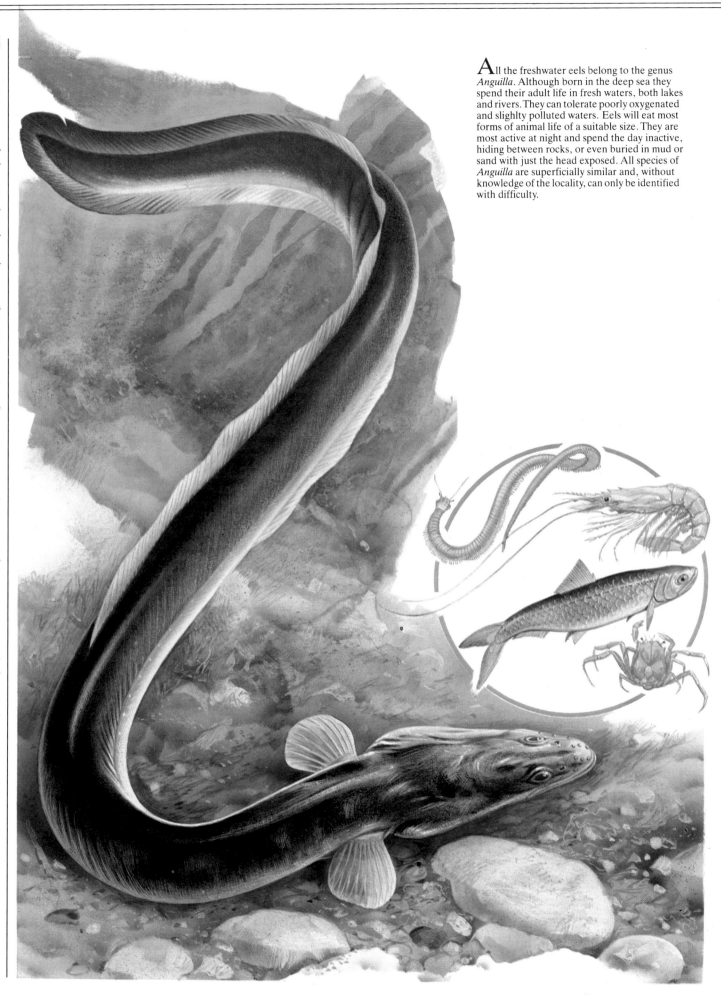

All the freshwater eels belong to the genus *Anguilla*. Although born in the deep sea they spend their adult life in fresh waters, both lakes and rivers. They can tolerate poorly oxygenated and slighlty polluted waters. Eels will eat most forms of animal life of a suitable size. They are most active at night and spend the day inactive, hiding between rocks, or even buried in mud or sand with just the head exposed. All species of *Anguilla* are superficially similar and, without knowledge of the locality, can only be identified with difficulty.

alive in an aquarium and much to their astonishment the leptocephali soon changed shape and became recognizable as young eels.

A major problem remained. Where did they breed? The answer was soon found. Ships sailing across the Atlantic and Mediterranean had been taking samples of the animal life at various points. It was noticed that the smallest Mediterranean leptocephali were in the west, the largest in the east. This pointed to the Atlantic as the breeding ground. Johannes Schmidt studied the samples and found that the size of the leptocephalus diminished westward. Following this process, he gained the credit for the discovery of the breeding ground in the Sargasso Sea between 20° and 30°N, 48° and 65°W. Here, the smallest leptocephali about ⅜ in (10 mm) long, were found near the surface.

We now know that both the European and the American eel breed in this region. However, no sexually mature adult has been caught there, nor eggs that unquestionably belong to the eel, so the depth of the spawning grounds is unknown. It is reasonable to assume, though, that this is at some depth because the eyes of adult eels enlarge as they go to sea, eels caught at sea travel at some depth and the youngest larvae have been taken at greater depths than larger larvae.

On the basis of laboratory experiments on the sexual maturity of eels, it seems likely that eels spawn at moderate depths and at temperatures of about 68°F (20°C). The Sargasso Sea is one of the few places in the world that provides these conditions because it is nearly a basin and high temperatures extend much deeper than is usual. A look back at the list of species of *Anguilla* and their distribution will show that they are absent from regions surrounding the south Atlantic and eastern Pacific, regions in which there are no warm, deep waters.

After hatching, the leptocephali drift back along the Gulf Stream, taking about three years to reach the European shores. There, in the shallow, colder and less saline waters, they change into elvers and move into rivers and streams where they feed and grow until they are ready to undertake the 3,750 miles (6,000 km) migration. As far as is known, adult eels die after spawning.

1) The adult eels migrate from rivers and lakes once a year into the sea to begin their journey to the Sargasso Sea.
2) In the depths of the Sargasso Sea, the eggs hatch into transparent willow-leaflike leptocephalus larvae. These larvae grow until they approach the coasts of Europe. In the shallow, less saline coastal waters they shrink and change into depigmented small imitations of the adults. These are called glass eels.
3) Glass eels move upstream and develop pigment as they do so.
4) Elvers. By now they are just like miniature versions of the adults and swim upstream in large swarms. Before rivers became so polluted, the number of elvers swimming upstream was so large and they were so densely packed that they could be easily caught and used as fertilizer on fields as well as food for humans.

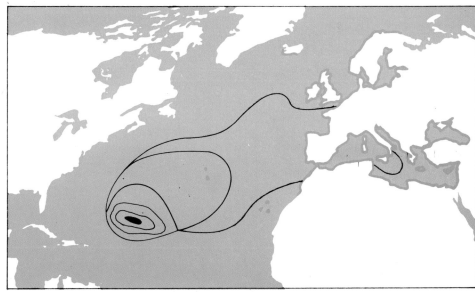

▲ The spawning ground and diffusion of the European eel.

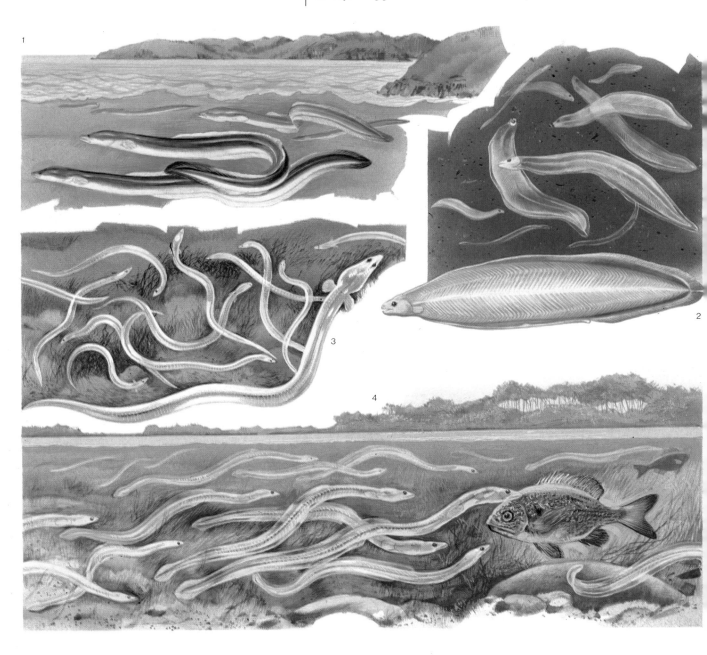

DEEP SEA SPINYEELS

Notacanthiformes

Three families of these bizarre deep sea fishes are known, Monognathidae, Saccopharyngidae, and Eurypharyngidae; it is, however, very likely that the monognathids may not be a distinct group of species but juveniles of the saccopharyngids.

Saccopharyngids are deep sea eels with very large mouths, distensible stomachs, long, tapering whiplike tails and teeth on the jaws. They lack scales, swim bladders and pelvic girdles. Individuals may grow to 6½ ft (2 m) in length, making them giants among deep sea fishes, but a great proportion of their length is the tail. The development of the huge mouth has resulted in some peculiar anatomical features. The gill elements, for example, are a long way behind the skull and are not attached to it. Each half of the gill arches is separate from its fellow. There are no opercular bones and the gill chambers are only partly covered by skin. Its breathing mechanism is, therefore, quite different from that of all other fishes.

There are probably four species of *Saccopharynx*. The body is jet-black and the first one caught – 50 in (128 cm) long – was described as an "elongated black sausage, due to a large sized fish which was still undigested in its stomach." Although it was caught in 5,600 ft (1700 m) of water, it was still alive at the surface, largely due to the fact that it had been caught by its teeth becoming entangled in the neck of the net, so it was not crushed by the weight of the other fishes.

In the upper jaw there are two rows of teeth, both curved and straight. On the lower jaw there is a single row with alternate large and small teeth. The largest tooth is about 2.5 mm long.

In all saccopharyngids there is a complex, luminous tail organ. This organ, and the general arrangement of the luminous tissue, is intriguing. Starting on the top of the head are two troughs with raised edges that run back to within 20 in (50 cm) of the tail tip. Along the back they are closer together, but they separate toward the tail as the dorsal fin comes between them. Each trough is filled with a white, luminous substance which, at

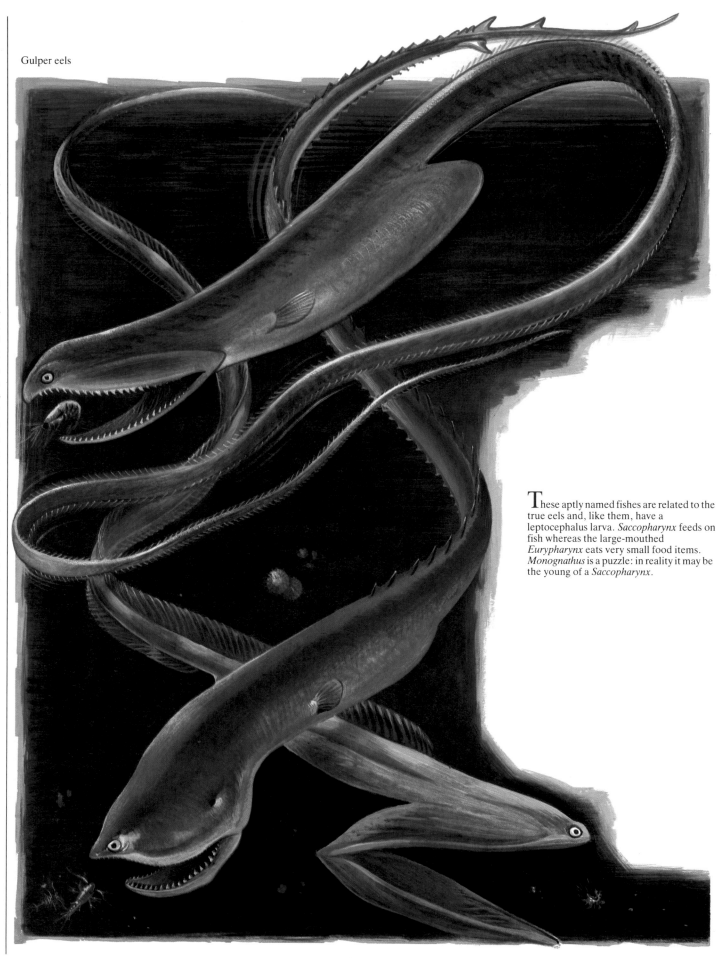

Gulper eels

These aptly named fishes are related to the true eels and, like them, have a leptocephalus larva. *Saccopharynx* feeds on fish whereas the large-mouthed *Eurypharynx* eats very small food items. *Monognathus* is a puzzle: in reality it may be the young of a *Saccopharynx*.

least along the anterior part of the troughs, glows with a pale light. Each dorsal fin ray is associated with a pair of oblique slashes, each of which also contains a white substance.

The tail organ starts about 6 in (15 cm) before the tip of the tail. A long way behind the last fin ray is a single pink tentacle, an elongated spindle with an enlarged head arising ventrally. The fish is shallowest at this point, only 2 mm deep, because the tail is depressed here. About 2¼ in (6 cm) further back the tail becomes rounded and broader, and from its dorsal and ventral edges arise 13 scarlet papillae (6 dorsal and 7 ventral) on the summit of depigmented bumps. Still further back is the main luminous organ. This is a compressed, leaflike, transparent zone with a substantial network of blood vessels.

What purpose this organ serves can only be hypothesized – *Saccopharynx* eats fairly large fish. Two specimens, each nearly 12 in (30 cm) long, were found in the stomach of *S. harrisoni*. It seems unlikely that the organ is used as a lure to catch prey. Despite the long, thin tail, the fish would need to severely contort itself, or swim round in circles, if the tail organ were used as a lure.

The family Eurypharyngidae (gulper eels) contains only one species, *Eurypharynx pelecanoides*, found in all tropical and subtropical seas at depths down to 27,000 ft (8000 m). The largest known specimens are nearly 3 ft (1 m) long. The mouth is enormous, and the jaws are about one-quarter the length of the entire body. There is an elastic membrane between each half of the lower jaw and at the back of the sides of the mouth. There are minute, irregularly arranged teeth on the jawbones. A very small pectoral fin is present some way behind the head. The body is velvety black save for a white groove running along each side of the base of the dorsal fin for its whole length. A small caudal organ is present but it is not known if it is luminous. Very little is known about the eel's habits. It probably feeds on plankton and small fishes.

A further related family is that of giganturoids (Giganturidae). There are two genera of these midwater fishes, *Bathyleptus* with three species, one in each of the tropical oceans, and *Gigantura* with two species from the tropical Atlantic.

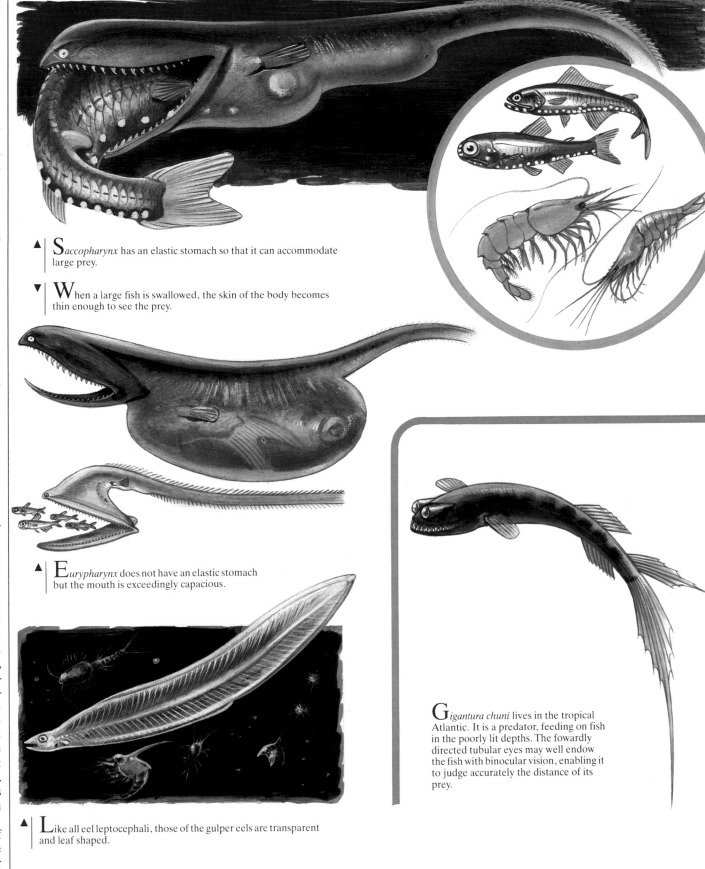

▲ *Saccopharynx* has an elastic stomach so that it can accommodate large prey.

▼ When a large fish is swallowed, the skin of the body becomes thin enough to see the prey.

▲ *Eurypharynx* does not have an elastic stomach but the mouth is exceedingly capacious.

▲ Like all eel leptocephali, those of the gulper eels are transparent and leaf shaped.

Gigantura chuni lives in the tropical Atlantic. It is a predator, feeding on fish in the poorly lit depths. The fowardly directed tubular eyes may well endow the fish with binocular vision, enabling it to judge accurately the distance of its prey.

SALMON

Genera *Oncorhynchus* and *Salmo*

Salmon are limited to the cold zones of the northern hemisphere and are divided into two genera: *Oncorhynchus* and *Salmo*.

The Pacific salmon (genus *Oncorhynchus*) includes six species distributed over both sides of the northern Pacific. Another species occupies an area between the river Amur in Siberia and the island of Formosa.

The Chinook, king or tyee salmon (*Oncorhynchus tshawytscha*) is the biggest of the Pacific salmon and can grow to 5 ft (1.5 m) in length and weigh up to 100 lb (45 kg). The marine adults generally stay in the central areas of the Pacific ocean and rarely go beyond the Bering Sea in the north and the Sea of Japan in the south.

The pink salmon (*Oncorhynchus gorbusha*) rarely grows above 24 – 28 in (60 – 70 cm) in length and weights of 11 – 15 lb (5 – 7 kg). At sea, the adults are found both in Arctic waters and in the Pacific and the Sea of Japan.

The chum or dog salmon (*Oncorhynchus keta*), like the previous species, has a somewhat modest commercial importance. It is also comparable in size and weight to the above. The distribution of this species at sea covers an area from the Arctic seas, roughly from the mouth of the river Lena in Siberia and the Mackenzie in Alaska in the north down to the Sea of Japan and the Sacramento River in California to the south.

The coho or silver salmon (*Oncorhynchus kisutch*) is the most important species from a commercial point of view. It rarely exceeds 32 in (80 cm) in length and weights of 4½ – 6½ lb (2 – 3 kg). The original distribution area of this species includes the seas and tributaries of the central Pacific area south of the Bering Straits and the southern limit goes no further than California on the North American coast and the Sea of Japan on the Asian side.

The sockeye or red salmon (*Oncorhynchus nerka*) appears under two different ecotypes: one anadromous migratory form and one living permanently in fresh water. They grow to quite modest sizes and the adults generally stay at around 24 in (60 cm) in length and 4½ – 6½ lb (2 – 3 kg) in weight when they return to fresh water.

The dog salmon (*Oncorhynchus keta*) is one of the species of "Pacific salmon" which shows the greatest homing instinct. After a period of three or four years at sea, the adults begin to make their way back to spawn and do not eat throughout the whole journey. They also undergo great morphological and physiological changes during the migration. The jaws of the males tend to curve and elongate until they cannot close their mouth. They can overcome rapids and waterfalls in the course of their journey, leaping out of the water sometimes up to 10 ft (3 m) in the air and over 26 ft (8 m) in distance, and can travel distances of over 1,250 miles (2,000 km) at a rate of about 25-30 miles (40-50 km) per day.

The non-migratory freshwater forms do not even grow to 16 in (40 cm). Both forms are found in overlapping areas from Hope Point in Alaska down to the Klamat River in California and from Northern Hokkaido in Japan down to the Anadyr River in Siberia.

The masu salmon (*Oncorhynchus masou*) is generally anadromous and can adapt to permanent life in inland waters. Maximum dimensions do not exceed 28 in (70 cm) and rarely go above 15½ – 17½ lb (7 – 8 kg) in weight.

The genus *Salmo* includes species which are mainly found in the Atlantic and connecting seas. The only migratory form in this area is the Atlantic salmon (*Salmo salar*). Like other salmon, trout and char, the Atlantic salmon has an anadromous and a non-migratory freshwater form. The latter does not grow to the same size as the anadromous form, whose average weight is 9 – 11 lb (4 – 5 kg), a little less for the lake forms.

Salmon are born in the headwaters of the rivers, where they spend the early part of their lives before beginning their migration to the sea. After a period of growth lasting a few years they find their way back to the exact place where they were born.

The mating behavior of *Oncorhynchus* and the Atlantic salmon is quite similar, for after returning to their place of birth, whether after a long migration that began in the ocean or just from a lake, the adults choose a suitable area to lay their eggs and fertilize them. In all cases, they choose stretches of the basin where the bottom is sandy or gravelly. Once they have reached a suitable spot, the females begin to build a nest (known as a redd). The construction of the redd is done exclusively by the female, while the males make their contribution by keeping any possible intruders at bay. When the redd is complete, the female settles herself in the center and only then is she approached by the dominant male who settles alongside her. The gametes are laid by both partners vibrating their bodies violently. The fertilized eggs laid on the bottom of the redd are covered with sand and gravel by the female. The eggs can be up to 7 mm in the case of the king salmon and 4 – 5 mm in the smaller species.

▲ The young of the dog salmon migrate immediately to the sea as soon as they leave the redds, retracing the route followed by their parents. Once they reach the sea they stay along the coasts for a few months and then move on to the open sea when they reach the smolt stage.

▼ During their life at sea, the dog salmon becomes a great predator, feeding off other fish.

▲ The lake becomes an alternative to the marine environment and the adults then migrate to the rivers in the same way, undergoing the same physiological changes as the marine forms.

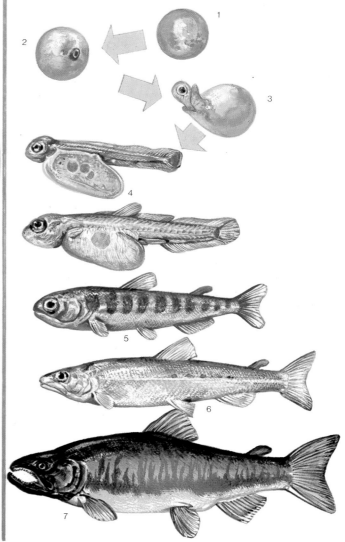

Development: 1) fertilized egg; 2) the eye appears early in the embryo and at this stage the eggs are highly resistant and can withstand movement; 3) hatching; 4) pre-larval stages with the yolk sac in various stages of reabsorption; 5) "parr"; 6) "smolt"; 7) adult male in mating colors.

ARAPAIMA OR PIRARUCU

Arapaima gigas

Order Osteoglossiformes
Family Osteoglossidae
Size Length up to 7½ ft (2.32 m)
Weight Up to 300 lb (133 kg)
Distinctive features The body is massive, covered with large thick scales; tail fin is small and round; dorsal and anal fins account for the rear third of the body
Coloration Front of the dorsal region and the sides are steel-gray with bluish highlights; from halfway down the body the scales have a red margin which becomes increasingly wide towards the tail
Breeding period When the water-level rises
Eggs 40,000 – 50,000 at each laying
Sexual maturity 4 – 5 years in a fish measuring 5½ ft (1.7 m) and weighing 90 – 100 lb (40 – 45 kg)

The arapaima is known more or less throughout the Amazon basin below an altitude of 650 ft (200 m). It is a predator which attacks all types of living prey. It has a sturdy, elongated body, covered with large thick scales. The scaleless head is covered with a very conspicuous dermic bone. The color of this fish is steel-gray with bluish highlights. The scales of the rear half of the body are edged with red, becoming brighter in hue as they near the tail.

The mouth is wide and the jaws have small conical teeth. The swim bladder acts as a lung and enables the fish to breathe both in and out of water. The length of the arapaima can reach about 7½ ft (2.32 m) overall, with a total weight of 300 lb (133 kg).

When the water level rises, after the first rains, the arapaima prepares its nest, a circular hole 8 in (20 cm) deep, which is carefully cleaned. When they hatch, the larvae measure nearly ½ in (11.6 mm) in length. They are equipped with a vitelline sac of considerable size and cannot move for the first 4 – 5 days. From the ninth day they start to breathe air on the surface, rising up every 4 – 7 minutes. Throughout its life the arapaima retains the habit of rising to the surface to breathe. Adults do so on average every 10 – 15 minutes: as they inhale there is a characteristic noise.

Arapaima (*Arapaima gigas*)

Among the fish found in Amazonia, in South America, the arapaima is undoubtedly one of the largest freshwater species, but it has now become a rarity. The arawana or arowana, on the other hand, is smaller, and more common. Members of the same family live in Africa, Southeast Asia and Australia. This distribution, which is like that of the Dipnoi, is an argument in favor of the theory of continental drift – the theory which holds that the land in the southern hemisphere was originally joined together to form a single continent: Gondwana.

Arawana or arowana
(*Osteoglossum bicirrhosum*) ₁)

SERRASALMIDAE

The Serrasalmids are Neotropical freshwater fish known to science and also to the general public because of the legendary ferocity of the predacious species known as the piranha. In fact, the family covers a large number of harmless species and can be subdivided into three subfamilies on the basis of their feeding habits.

The subfamily Serrasalminae comprises the true piranha, all grouped under the single genus *Serrasalmus*, whose mouths have a dense series of pointed pluricuspid teeth capable of removing pieces of flesh from the victims on which they feed. The genus include the dangerous true piranha *Serrasalmus piraya*, which is found only in the basin of the São Francisco river; *Serrasalmus ternetzi*, found in the Paraguay River; and the red piranha or natterer piranha (*Serrasalmus nattereri*), common to the Amazon and Orinoco.

They are basically gregarious and the various groups they form can include different species. The predacious forms can be found at all points of the rivers, but they prefer to stay close to the banks near wide bends. Their diet is made up almost exclusively of other fish, but if there are none available, they can turn to other sources such as small mammals, amphibians, and, in exceptional cases, humans or other large mammals bathing in the rivers.

The aggression of the group in these last two cases depends very much on the health of the victim and its ability to react to the first attack. With healthy subjects, the wounds are light because the victim's reaction disorientates the group, but its action becomes much more effective when the victim is sick, wounded or drowned and in this case, the victim is literally stripped to the bone. These habits of the piranha are well known to some indigenous tribes in the Amazon and Orinoco areas, who cannot give their dead a proper burial because of the marshy nature of the areas where they live, so they give them to the piranha to be stripped of the flesh; then they adorn the remaining bones with various knickknacks and ornaments before putting them on the high burial sites.

▲
◄ *Serrasalmus (Pygocentrus) piraya* is one of the three species of the true piranha found in the basin of the São Francisco river in Brazil. They are gregarious and tend to occupy the shore areas of the river and its tributaries where there is abundant vegetation and where they find their food, which mainly comprises other species of fish. In special circumstances, they can also eat other vertebrates such as aquatic rodents.

◄ The mouth of the piranha is armed with tricuspid teeth ranged in one row on their jawbones. There are also teeth on the palate bones.

▼ The piranha of the São Francisco river are sadly well-known for their aggressive nature, not only against large herbivores that fall into the water, but also against humans.

▼ The piranha take care of and protect their young after they hatch.

THE BLIND CHARACID OF MEXICO

The name "tetra" is commonly used for the members of the species which belong to the subfamily of the Tetragonopterinae, one of the twelve in the vast family of Characidae. The basic diagnostic feature distinguishing the tetra is the presence of a double row of teeth on the upper maxillary arches for there are generally one or three rows in the other subfamilies, and the fact that the predorsal spine is nearly always missing. The body is generally elongated and spindle-shaped, but tends to extend downward in the ventral region, producing more or less rounded shapes. The anal fin is quite large in many species, but this is rarely the case with the dorsal fin.

Among the most famous species of tetra are those which belong to the genus *Hyphessobrycon*, with the pink tetra (*H. rosaceus*), the red tetra (*H. flammeus*), the flag tetra (*H. heterorhabdus*) etc., as well as others such as the shining tetra (*Hemigrammus erythrozonus*), the diamond tetra (*Moenkhausia pittieri*) and the neon tetra.

The only characids to have succeeded in making their way beyond Central America to Mexico are *Astyanax* and the blind forms derived from it. These Mexican Characidae found themselves in areas subject to profound karst phenomena leading to the deepening and subsequent movement of certain underground rivers. Some stocks of *Astyanax* moved underground progressively with the rivers, and when the basins dried up, were forced to adapt to a subterranean environment. The evolution of these forms in surroundings with no light and where food supplies were quite scarce led to the gradual loss of body pigmentation and certain organs such as the eyes.

The first blind form, *Anoptichthys jordani*, was discovered in the Cueva Chica. Other forms, more or less adapted to a cave environment, were subsequently discovered in many other areas in some thirty grottoes all within an area of about 2,700 sq. miles (7,000 km²) over the Sierra del Guatemala, the Sierra de Nicolas Perez, the Sierra de Colmena, and the Sierra de El Abra.

Anoptichthys jordani

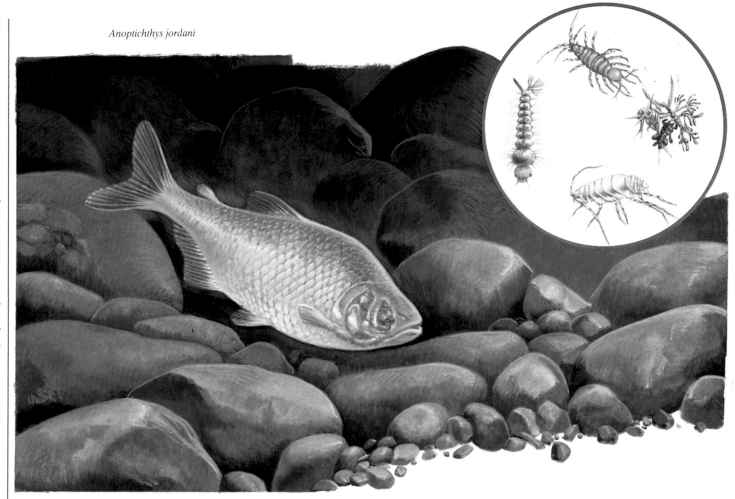

Astyanax fasciatus mexicanus

The Mexican blind tetra (*Anoptichthys jordani*) is no longer considered to be a valid species in that it can cross with the epigeal form *Astyanax fasciatus mexicanus*, from which it is derived. The gradual disappearance of the eyes which are actually present in the early stages of its life has led to the sharpening of its other senses, e.g. touch and smell, which are much more useful in environments where there is no light. The diet of the blind form is made up of various occasional elements, whereas the surface form feeds exclusively on zoo-organisms.

1) The Mexican blind tetra is found in the subterranean river systems in an area of about 2,700 sq. miles (7,000 sq. km) in South Mexico.
2) The true piranha is widely found in the main rivers of tropical South America, but not west of the Andes.

ELECTRIC EEL

Electrophorus electricus

The electric eel, known in Brazil as the Poraque, is found in the tropical regions of South America, especially in the basins of the Orinoco and the Amazon. Its ability to emit very powerful electric charges has made this fish famous since the eighteenth century, but the charging and discharging systems of the electric cells were only explained in 1953 by Keynes, Martins-Ferreira, and Altamirano. The electric eel can give out two types of electric impulse, one of low intensity (never more than 5 – 10V) which is very important to its sensory perception, and the other of a high voltage, (100V in specimens of about 4 in/10 cm and 500V in those over 3 ft/1 m); it uses the latter for defense and to stun its prey.

Its general morphology is reminiscent of the eel because of its elongated shape and the absence of pelvic fins, but its internal morphology is quite different. The electric organs are located in the tail which makes up about four-fifths of the total length of the animal, whereas the general body cavity, with the exclusion of the swim bladder (the only organ that extends into the tail) is positioned very much further forward, and the anal aperture is positioned near and immediately behind the pectoral fins. It has no dorsal fin and the caudal fin appears to run into the anal fin.

The tail is self-generating and reforms quite rapidly, even if almost completely removed, a characteristic that is relatively common to all other Gymnotoidei, although unlike the electric eel, the others cannot produce defensive electricity. They do actually have electric cells, although with impulses of only up to 1 – 2V, which are important in their daily life. The electric eel has, in fact, no enemies, as it defends itself very successfully with its extremely powerful electric charge and so it is very rare for it to suffer injury.

A related species, widely distributed in South America, is the carapus (*Gymnotus carapus*) which has great affinities with the electric eel, as can be seen in the shape of the head and the presence of large caniniform teeth: but it does differ in that its body is covered in scales and has a small caudal fin.

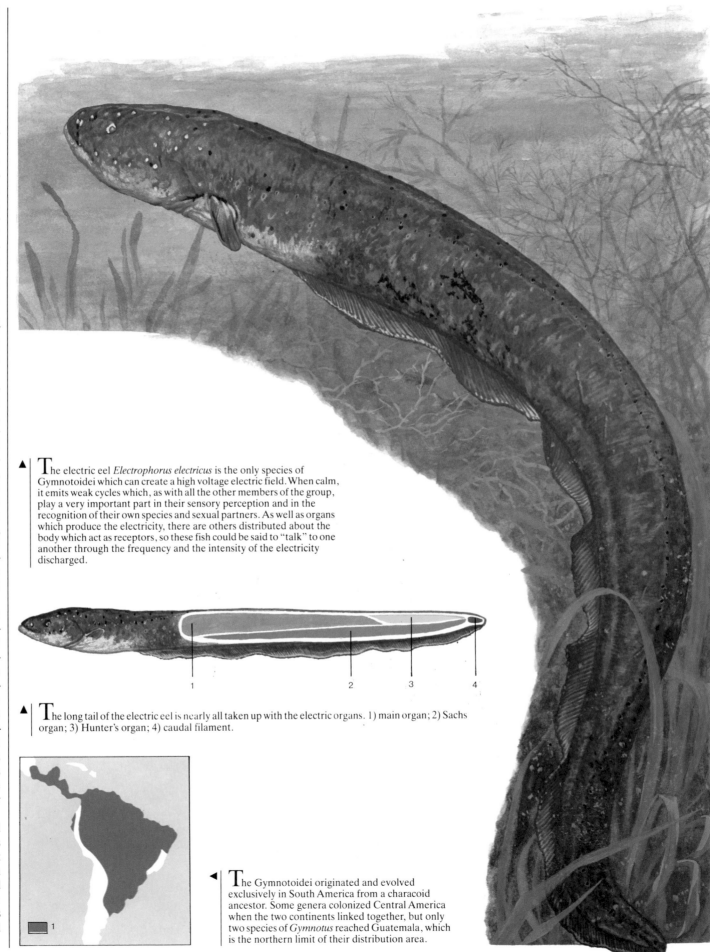

The electric eel *Electrophorus electricus* is the only species of Gymnotoidei which can create a high voltage electric field. When calm, it emits weak cycles which, as with all the other members of the group, play a very important part in their sensory perception and in the recognition of their own species and sexual partners. As well as organs which produce the electricity, there are others distributed about the body which act as receptors, so these fish could be said to "talk" to one another through the frequency and the intensity of the electricity discharged.

The long tail of the electric eel is nearly all taken up with the electric organs. 1) main organ; 2) Sachs organ; 3) Hunter's organ; 4) caudal filament.

The Gymnotoidei originated and evolved exclusively in South America from a characoid ancestor. Some genera colonized Central America when the two continents linked together, but only two species of *Gymnotus* reached Guatemala, which is the northern limit of their distribution area.

FROGFISHES
Antennariidae

The family Antennariidae or frogfishes is made up of fishes living in tropical seas in coral formations or floating gulfweed. Their remarkable camouflage enables them to blend in with their surroundings with their very variable and often beautiful and bright coloring. The body is bulky, spherical and fairly compressed; the head is broad, the mouth is diagonal in shape, and the lower jaw or mandible can project forward to seize prey. The skin is scaleless in *Histrio* and *Histiophryne*, or covered with tiny spines (in the *Phrynelox* and *Fowlerichthys*) which give it a rough appearance, or velvety in *Antennarius*.

There are numerous cutaneous arborescences or branchlike growths situated along the mucous ducts, around the mouth and on the rays of the vertex. Over the mouth protrudes an appendage, the so-called illicium, supporting a lure which has a particular form in each genus; after it come two separate rays which are thick and heavy, and support a membrane toward the rear; these rays are accentuated in *Antennarius* and inconspicuous in *Histiophryne*; they can be erected like a rhinoceros's horn in *Histrio*, and are sheathed with cutaneous arborescences.

The Antennariidae can puff themselves up by means of superimposed subcutaneous muscular tunics, one with lengthwise fibers, the other with star-shaped fibers. A reinforcing band of muscle between the pectoral and pelvic fins stops the tightened tissues from tearing when large prey are being swallowed.

The frogfishes lead a littoral or coastal existence in shallow water in warm seas where coral formations act as host. Their remarkable camouflage enables them to blend in perfectly with their surroundings. They spend much of their time motionless, trying to attract small fishes, mollusks or crustaceans with the undulating, swaying movements of the illicium.

The Antennariidae show marked sexual dimorphism, especially where their coloring is concerned: the males are light-colored with a large number of markings or colored ramifications; the females are dark-colored, often black, with a few markings.

▲ *Phrynelox tridens* belongs to the Antennariidae (frogfishes) in the order Pediculati, and shows more primitive characteristics than others in the order. Highly mimetic, it can blend with its surroundings, especially seaweed. The species shows marked sexual dimorphism, the female being darker in color. *Phrynelox* attracts small fishes or crustaceans living in the coral reef by waving its fishing filament as bait. It spends its life motionless but can walk 'on all fours' over rocks by moving forward alternately on its pectoral and ventral fins.

◀ To attract prey, the fish gently waves the vexillum of the illicium which serves as a lure; when a fish approaches, it lowers the filament horizontally, then springs from its hiding place and swallows the victim. In the course of digestion it folds the spine back in the resting position.

FLYING FISHES

Exocoetidea

The flying fishes are easily identifiable by the conspicuous development of the pectoral fins, but also of the lower lobe of the caudal fin and the ventral fins, enabling them to glide above the surface of the sea. Many different species of flying fishes are known belonging to six main genera. They are found in surface waters in the equatorial regions, and in the tropical and subtropical regions of all the oceans.

Flying fishes glide across the sea's surface. They can be divided into two categories: the first, known as the "monoplane" type, includes the species which have just one pair of wings, the pectoral fins. The second category, known as the "biplane" type, includes the species which have two pairs of wings, the pectoral and the ventral fins. Let us therefore follow the flight of a flying fish of the biplane type such as *Cypselurus*.

To start with, the fish swims fast, close to the surface of the water, with its pectoral and ventral fins folded in against its tapering body. Having reached a certain speed, the fish lifts its body out of the water, spreading out its pectoral fins and keeping them stiff. The caudal fin now beats very fast until the fish's speed increases to about 65 ft (20 m) per second or 45 mph (72 kmh). In this phase only the caudal fin is still submerged in the water. When a sufficient speed has been reached, the fish also stretches out its ventral fins, just as the tail leaves the water at precisely the same moment. The fish is now completely airborne. Then the speed gradually drops until it becomes insufficient for the fish to maintain height.

The eggs are laid on the surface. Some float, like those of the genus *Exocoetus*: these are pelagic species. The eggs are enveloped in a smooth membrane, with no filament, and measure 1.7 – 2.9 mm in diameter. Other eggs sink to the bottom; these are smaller than the pelagic eggs and often possess filaments.

The diet of the flying fishes consists of small crustaceans and fish larvae. At night the neritic species go to feed close to the coast and return to the open sea toward dawn, where they scatter during the daylight hours.

▲ Flying-fishes do not in fact fly, as their name suggests, but rather glide above the water. They live close to the surface in warm seas, and are found in all the oceans. If a predator or a ship approaches, they leave the water and glide through the air. Some species, like *Cypselurus*, are capable of covering distances of 1,350 ft (400 m), and can glide along up to 16-20 ft (5-6 m) above the waves.

▼ The flying-fish (*Exocoetus*) which has a single pair of "wings" – i.e. the pectoral fins – takes to the air as shown below: the tail fin, which acts as a "motor," starts to beat very fast from left to right; the fish then launches itself straight out of the water and as soon as its body is free of the water it stretches its wings fully, and keeps them in that rigid position. Having done this, it glides for a while over the waves before dropping back into the sea.

▲ The diet is based on zooplankton.

▶ Unlike the genus *Exocoetus*, the species shown on the right has two pairs of wings, the pectoral fins and the pelvic fins. It also has a streamlined, tapering body, and really does look like a glider.

Linophryne arborifer

ANGLERFISHES
Ceratioidea

Within this suborder of deep-sea fishes, related to the common anglerfishes (*Lophius* spp.) of shallow water, are to be found some of the most remarkable modifications known among vertebrates. One characteristic feature of this suborder is present in a more easily recognizable form in its shallow-water relatives. The first three rays of the dorsal fin have become separated from the rest of the fin and, in the course of time, have moved forward. The first ray has become elongated and its tip elaborate and fleshy. Muscles have been developed to make this first ray extremely mobile and it is used as a fishing rod. The fleshy end is moved about near the mouth in the usually optimistic assumption that some passing fish will mistake the tip for food. The bait is brought nearer the mouth and the prey is swallowed.

This fishing rod-like dorsal fin ray is called the illicium and the bait, the esca. But in the deep sea there is no light, so an esca just shaped like a tasty morsel or a small fish would not be seen and would therefore be of no use whatsoever. This apparent drawback has been overcome by making the esca luminous. Some species have, in addition, highly mobile, variously branched barbels on the chin, the tips of which, in a few species at least, are luminous. These are also thought to act as lures.

Once the prey has been lured toward the esca, the whole illicium is retracted or otherwise moved to bring the prey as close to the mouth as possible. Then there is either a sudden lunge or possibly some suction pressure and the fish is in the mouth. Large, sharply pointed teeth prevent its escape and the fish is swallowed. The stomach of anglers, as in many deep-sea fishes is extremely elastic so that fish larger than the captor can be accommodated.

Anglers do not necessarily limit themselves to fishes. Analyses of the contents of anglerfish stomachs have revealed the presence of squids, deep-sea crustaceans of many sorts, arrow worms and innumerable other forms of deep-sea fishes.

The deep sea anglerfishes are scaleless although in a few species (e.g. *Himantolophus* and *Ceratias*) there are

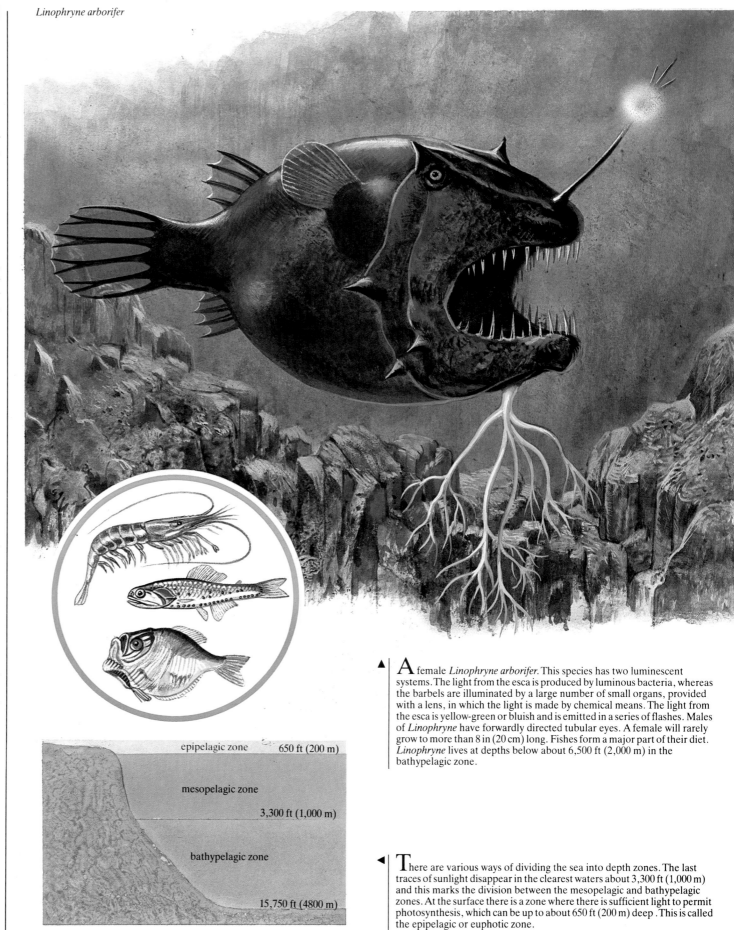

▲ A female *Linophryne arborifer*. This species has two luminescent systems. The light from the esca is produced by luminous bacteria, whereas the barbels are illuminated by a large number of small organs, provided with a lens, in which the light is made by chemical means. The light from the esca is yellow-green or bluish and is emitted in a series of flashes. Males of *Linophryne* have forwardly directed tubular eyes. A female will rarely grow to more than 8 in (20 cm) long. Fishes form a major part of their diet. *Linophryne* lives at depths below about 6,500 ft (2,000 m) in the bathypelagic zone.

epipelagic zone	650 ft (200 m)
mesopelagic zone	3,300 ft (1,000 m)
bathypelagic zone	15,750 ft (4800 m)

◄ There are various ways of dividing the sea into depth zones. The last traces of sunlight disappear in the clearest waters about 3,300 ft (1,000 m) and this marks the division between the mesopelagic and bathypelagic zones. At the surface there is a zone where there is sufficient light to permit photosynthesis, which can be up to about 650 ft (200 m) deep. This is called the epipelagic or euphotic zone.

nodules in the skin. In the oneirodid genus *Spiniphryne* the skin is covered with numerous small close-set spines which even cover the bases of the fins. The dorsal and anal fins are placed opposite one another and contain very few rays. The tail fin is fan-shaped with few, widely spaced, conspicuous thick rays. The pectoral fins are variously developed but, again, contain relatively few, rather thick rays. In some species the pectoral fin is mounted on a small raised base. Pelvic fins are absent, but in some species the pelvic bones are still present beneath the skin. The eyes of the adult female are very small. In most species the adult males have relatively large, sometimes tubular eyes, but males of *Gigantactis* have small eyes. The skeleton of all species is greatly reduced. Bones are poorly calcified, much cartilage is present and many bones are reduced in size to struts. The operculum (gill-cover) in most fishes is a fan-shaped bone but in oneirodid anglerfishes it is reduced to a V-shape. Although the jaw bones are well developed in comparison to other skull bones, they are fragile compared to those in many other fishes. Most species are deep brown or black in color.

Except for *Neoceratias*, all adult female anglerfishes have an illicium with an esca at the end. Except in *Caulophryne* this esca is luminous. The light comes from colonies of luminous bacteria living within the escal bulb.

The reproductive strategies within the ceratioid anglers vary between that generally practiced among midwater fishes to the strangest among all vertebrates – the adult males becoming parasitic on the females. The female develops a functional illicium lacked by the male. It is thought that after metamorphosis the females may take several years to reach sexual maturity. It is in the subsequent fate of the males that we see the most striking differences. After metamorphosis, the males are most inadequately adapted for feeding, so they must find a mate quickly. In free-living males the testes are already well developed before metamorphosis. After metamorphosis they develop pincerlike jaws thought to be for nipping the skin of the female during fertilization rather than for catching food. Often the body of the dwarf male literally fuses with the females; thereafter, the male lives as a parasite or as a simple body appendage of his partner.

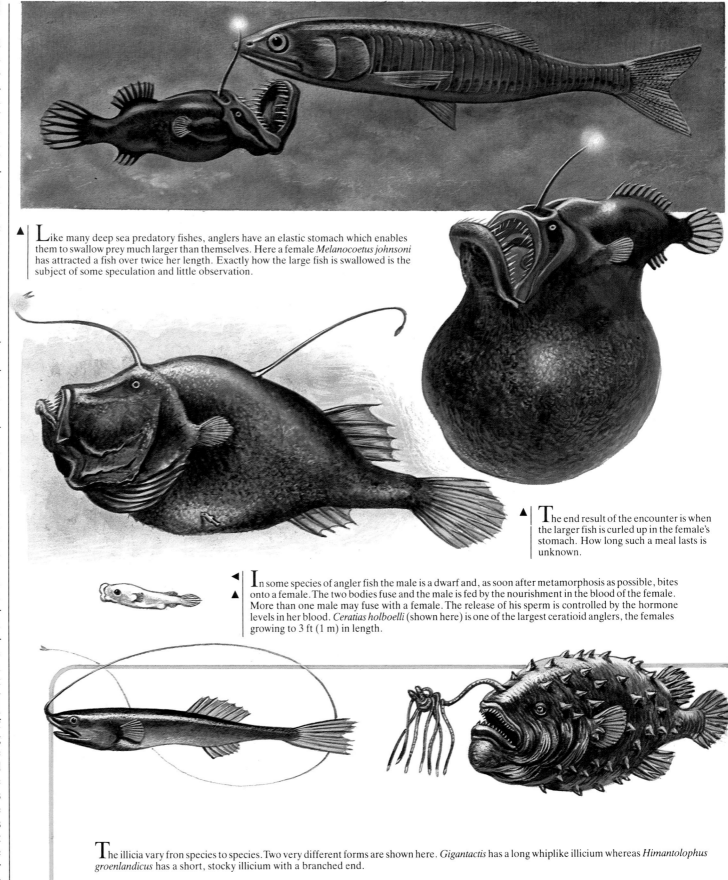

▲ Like many deep sea predatory fishes, anglers have an elastic stomach which enables them to swallow prey much larger than themselves. Here a female *Melanocoetus johnsoni* has attracted a fish over twice her length. Exactly how the large fish is swallowed is the subject of some speculation and little observation.

▲ The end result of the encounter is when the larger fish is curled up in the female's stomach. How long such a meal lasts is unknown.

◄ In some species of angler fish the male is a dwarf and, as soon after metamorphosis as possible, bites onto a female. The two bodies fuse and the male is fed by the nourishment in the blood of the female. More than one male may fuse with a female. The release of his sperm is controlled by the hormone levels in her blood. *Ceratias holboelli* (shown here) is one of the largest ceratioid anglers, the females growing to 3 ft (1 m) in length.

The illicia vary from species to species. Two very different forms are shown here. *Gigantactis* has a long whiplike illicium whereas *Himantolophus groenlandicus* has a short, stocky illicium with a branched end.

KILLIFISHES

Cyprinodontidae

The suborder Cyprinodontidae inclu-des smallish fishes similar in appear-ance to the Cyprinidae (the family of carps, barbels, goldfishes, etc.). The seven families with about 100 genera and 500 species are found in every con-tinent, with the exceptions of Australia, and the Arctic and Antarctic regions. Cyprinodontidae, Poeciliidae and Anablepidae are the most interesting families.

Killifishes have a dorsal fin sup-ported solely by soft rays, and situated about halfway down the back. The mouth is terminal, protactile and often upward-turned; the jaws, like certain bones of the palate and pharynx, have small conical or pluri-cuspidate teeth. The body is elongated and fairly com-pressed at the sides; the head is depre-ssed and flattened on the top. A large number of species show marked sex-ual dimorphism, especially in the case of the males, which have brightly col-ored liveries, unlike the females which have rather inconspicuous coloring.

Killifishes are small, rarely more than 4 in (10 cm) in length, and some-times quite aggressive. Of the roughly 60 genera known, most are found in the tropical areas of the Old and New Worlds, both in freshwater and brac-kish habitats.

Reproduction takes place from spring to late fall, and begins when the males break away from the groups and acquire their own territory. The females, ready for mating, separate from the group and tend to move toward the territory of a male, who invites them to mate. The female releases a single egg which is fertilized by the male, and sinks to the bottom. The eggs take a few days to develop and the newborn young measure 3 – 4 mm in length.

In some South American species belonging to the genera *Austrofundulus*, *Cynolebias* and *Rivulus* the lifespan only lasts for one season. These are the so-called "annual" Cyprinodontidae which live in pools that are liable to dry up in the summer and which manage to ensure the survival of the next genera-tion by laying "summering" eggs, covered in a thick shell, on the bottom of temporary pools. When the dry sea-son arrives, these eggs remain in the ground and can withstand dehydration

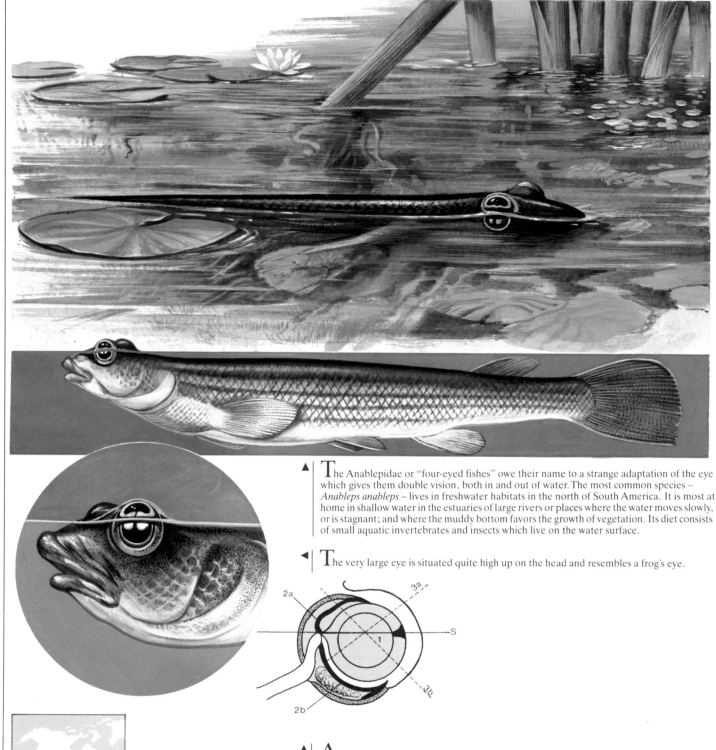

▲ The Anablepidae or "four-eyed fishes" owe their name to a strange adaptation of the eye which gives them double vision, both in and out of water. The most common species – *Anableps anableps* – lives in freshwater habitats in the north of South America. It is most at home in shallow water in the estuaries of large rivers or places where the water moves slowly, or is stagnant; and where the muddy bottom favors the growth of vegetation. Its diet consists of small aquatic invertebrates and insects which live on the water surface.

◄ The very large eye is situated quite high up on the head and resembles a frog's eye.

▲ A cross-section of the eye showing the method of double vision: 1) the crystalline lens; 2a) and 2b) the two different parts of the retina reached by the image; 3a) the direction of the images out of water; 3b) the direction of the images in water; s) water surface.

◄ The family Anablepidae has only formed relatively recently, insomuch as we have fossils which cannot be dated before the Pleistocene. It seems very probable that the family actually originated in Central America, from where it then spread out into the northern parts of South America.

as well as quite considerable mechanical stresses in some cases. But the embryo starts to develop almost as soon as the egg is laid, and it will often be some months before it has its "rendezvous" with the rainy season. As a result growth has to cease at a certain stage to prevent the young fish from emerging "out-of-season." As soon as the rains refill the temporary pool, the egg opens, the young fish emerges and starts to grow quickly.

After the Cyprinodontidae, the other family with a large number of species is the Poeciliidae, known in the United States as the livebearers, because of the viviparous reproductive habits of its members.

The Poeciliidae have evolved in Central America, from where they have subsequently dispersed toward the southern and northern parts of the New World. They make up a group of dominant fishes in fresh – and brackish water habitats. Members of the Poeciliidae are smallish in size, rarely exceeding 4 – 6 in (10 – 15 cm) in overall length. Some may be brightly colored, quite sturdy and easy to breed. Their reproductive system is exclusively viviparous. Among the species of this group are *Poecilia reticulata*, the true guppy, and the mollies, of which the best known are the Amazon molly (*Poecilia formosa*) and the sail-finned molly (*P. latipinna*).

Another fairly common genus is *Xiphophorus* which includes various species of platyfishes and swordtails. Among them are the platy (*Xiphophorus maculatus*), found in coastal basins in the Atlantic seaboard from Mexico to Honduras, and one of the most popular swordtails, *Xiphophorus helleri*. At the northern limit of the distribution area of this family we find the genus *Gambusia* with 34 species, found along the Atlantic seaboard of the United States, and throughout Central America. In America *G. affinis* is known as the mosquito fish, because of its ubiquitous nature. This species uses all types of habitat and can catch the larvae on which it feeds in very shallow water or even in the midst of dense aquatic vegetation.

The Anablepidae are a very small family, made up of the one genus *Anableps* with 5 or 6 species. These fishes, which are viviparous, have distinctively adapted their eyes to seeing both underwater and on the surface.

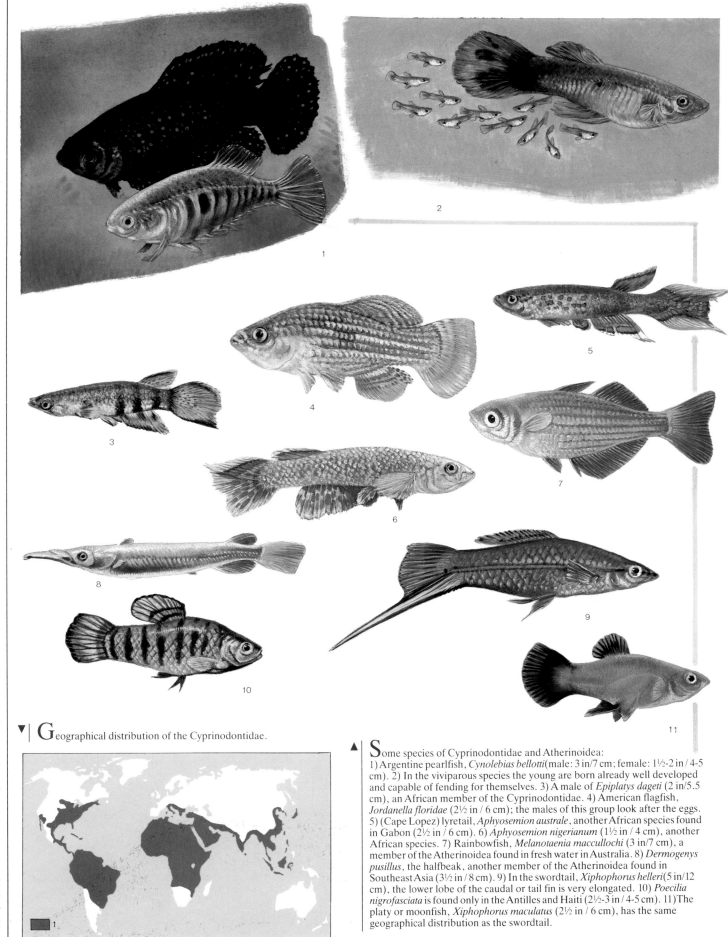

▼ | Geographical distribution of the Cyprinodontidae.

▲ | Some species of Cyprinodontidae and Atherinoidea:
1) Argentine pearlfish, *Cynolebias bellotti* (male: 3 in/7 cm; female: 1½-2 in / 4-5 cm). 2) In the viviparous species the young are born already well developed and capable of fending for themselves. 3) A male of *Epiplatys dageti* (2 in/5.5 cm), an African member of the Cyprinodontidae. 4) American flagfish, *Jordanella floridae* (2½ in / 6 cm); the males of this group look after the eggs. 5) (Cape Lopez) lyretail, *Aphyosemion australe*, another African species found in Gabon (2½ in / 6 cm). 6) *Aphyosemion nigerianum* (1½ in / 4 cm), another African species. 7) Rainbowfish, *Melanotaenia maccullochi* (3 in/7 cm), a member of the Atherinoidea found in fresh water in Australia. 8) *Dermogenys pusillus*, the halfbeak, another member of the Atherinoidea found in Southeast Asia (3½ in / 8 cm). 9) In the swordtail, *Xiphophorus helleri* (5 in/12 cm), the lower lobe of the caudal or tail fin is very elongated. 10) *Poecilia nigrofasciata* is found only in the Antilles and Haiti (2½-3 in / 4-5 cm). 11) The platy or moonfish, *Xiphophorus maculatus* (2½ in / 6 cm), has the same geographical distribution as the swordtail.

KING HERRING

Regalecus glesne

The carfish (Regalecidae) includes fishes with a ribbon-shaped, scaleless body. The dorsal fin is as long as the body, while the anal and caudal fins are almost invariably missing. The first rays of the dorsal fin are distinctively long and erectile, and look like a crest or mane.

The best-known member of the family is undoubtedly the king herring (*Regalecus glesne*) which has probably provided much of the fodder for man's belief in terrible serpentlike sea-monsters, living in the bowels of the ocean, which would certainly endanger the lives of the entire crews if they ever came to the surface – as it is claimed they have, now and then. The king herring can reach a length of more than 23 ft (7 m) and this is enough to explain how a creature of such a size might not readily be regarded as a mere fish: hence the intricate legend surrounding it.

This species ranges worldwide, although the largest number of sightings has been made in the North Atlantic.

Its name derives from the fact that it was frequently sighted by fishermen near large shoals of herring: it did not take long for it to be baptized as "king herring," and for it to be attributed with tasks such as showing the herring their way on their migrations.

The body of *Regalecus glesne* is very long and laterally compressed. The coloring is silvery with scarlet-red fins. The head is relatively small with a protactile mouth which is almost vertical and completely toothless. The eyes are large and round. On top of the head there is a brightly colored plume formed by the first rays of the dorsal fin.

This is a very rare species and most of the specimens taken have been found dead on beaches, or nearing the end of their life in shallow coastal waters.

Very little is known about its biological cycle: eggs and larval stages of the species are found near the surface in the Straits of Messina between July and December.

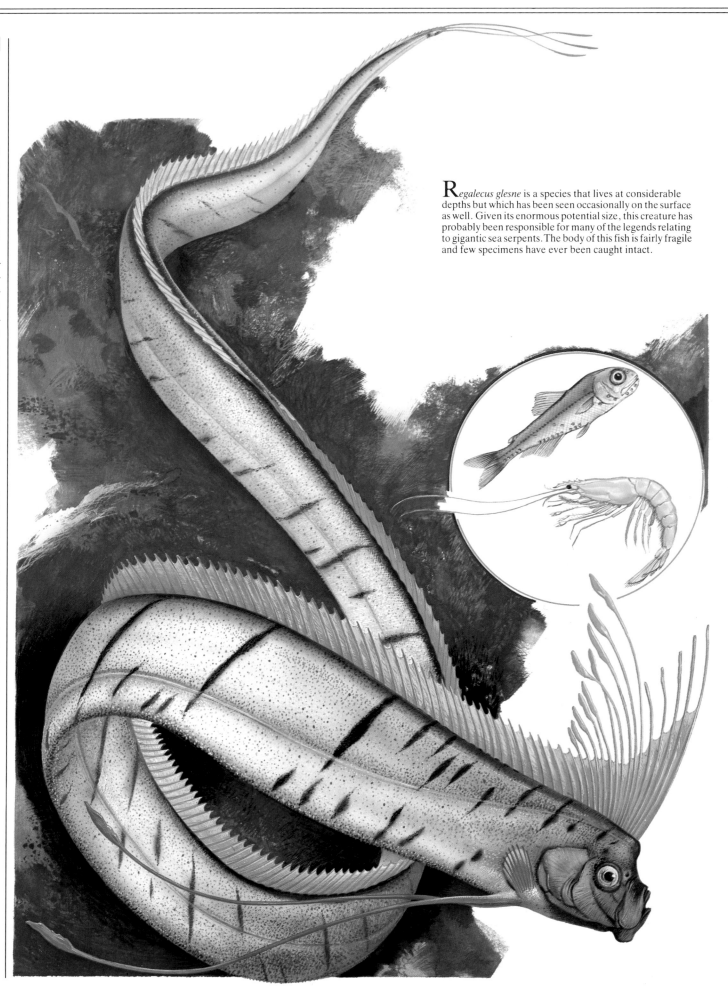

R*egalecus glesne* is a species that lives at considerable depths but which has been seen occasionally on the surface as well. Given its enormous potential size, this creature has probably been responsible for many of the legends relating to gigantic sea serpents. The body of this fish is fairly fragile and few specimens have ever been caught intact.

SEA HORSES
Syngnathidae

Fish belonging to the order Syngnathiformes have a tubular bony snout; they use it like a pipette, sucking in food together with water. The body is wholly or partly covered with bony plates; in the Syngnathidae (sea horses and relatives) these form a completely ossified body armor, arranged in rings around the body and tail.

The body of the sea horse (*Hippocampus hippocampus*) is covered with 11 rings, the tail with 34–35 rings. The dorsal fin is located on two body rings and one tail ring, and has 17 rays. The pectoral fin has 14–15 rays. The length of the snout makes up 40 per cent of the length of the head; the animal may be as much as 6½ in (16 cm) long overall. The body plates have sharp points which can benumb the part struck by them. The hump ('corona') is slightly oblique. The body coloration is blackish or dark brown with white patches or spots. There are no teeth in the mouth.

These fish are found off the Mediterranean and Atlantic coasts of Europe as far south as Algeria, living on beds of sand or detritus at depths of 25–150 ft (8–45 m). They prefer to live in fields of the seaweed *Posidonia* or of algae, which they cling to with their prehensile tails. The eyes can be moved to follow the movements of their prey, which they stalk very slowly. If they want to swim fast they take up a horizontal position, with the dorsal fin pointing upward. They can also swim in a vertical position, with the head either up or down, or coiled up. The various positions are controlled by movements of the gas in the swim bladder.

Reproduction takes place between May and August. From 318 to 500 eggs are laid in the male's brood pouch, and incubation takes place from June to July. The young are hatched between August and September. Sexual maturity is reached at about one year; young fish hatched in September can copulate the following May. The majority of individuals die after spawning for the first time; only a few survive to spawn again.

Many related species live in temperate and warm waters.

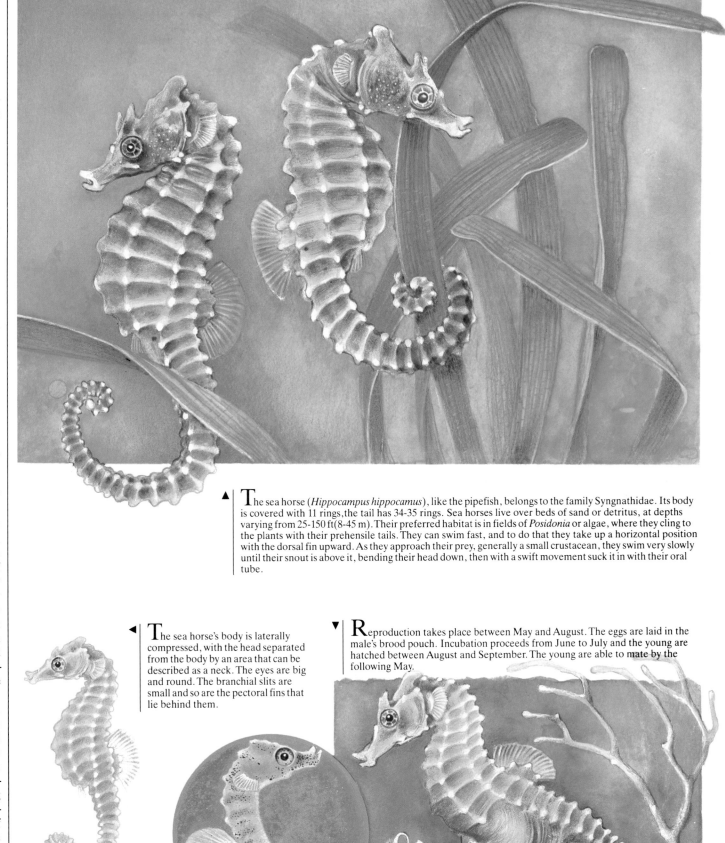

◀ The sea horse (*Hippocampus hippocamus*), like the pipefish, belongs to the family Syngnathidae. Its body is covered with 11 rings, the tail has 34-35 rings. Sea horses live over beds of sand or detritus, at depths varying from 25-150 ft (8-45 m). Their preferred habitat is in fields of *Posidonia* or algae, where they cling to the plants with their prehensile tails. They can swim fast, and to do that they take up a horizontal position with the dorsal fin upward. As they approach their prey, generally a small crustacean, they swim very slowly until their snout is above it, bending their head down, then with a swift movement suck it in with their oral tube.

◀ The sea horse's body is laterally compressed, with the head separated from the body by an area that can be described as a neck. The eyes are big and round. The branchial slits are small and so are the pectoral fins that lie behind them.

▼ Reproduction takes place between May and August. The eggs are laid in the male's brood pouch. Incubation proceeds from June to July and the young are hatched between August and September. The young are able to mate by the following May.

REMORAS
Echeneidae

The fishes belonging to this family have an elongated, spindle-shaped body. The head has a long adhesive apparatus on the top of it – a sort of long sucker formed by a double row of lamellae – by means of which these medium-sized fishes attach themselves to other fishes.

The Echeneidae have a distinctive coloration: the back is whitish and silvery, while the belly is colored. The most usual colors found on the belly and sides of the body are brown or blue, in quite dark shades. There are four distinct genera: *Echeneis*, *Phteirichthys*, *Remora*, and *Remorina*. These differ from one another mainly in the shape of the body, in the shape of the pectoral fins, which may be rounded or pointed, the way in which the lower jaw ends at the front, and the number of lamellae which form the cephalic disk.

The Echeneidae lay spherical, transparent eggs with a droplet of oil at the vegetative pole. The diameter of the egg is about 2.5 mm, in the sharksucker (*Echeneis naucrates*), the larvae of which hatch out on the third day of the incubation period.

Numerous observations confirm the role of "cleaner" carried out very efficiently by the remoras in relation to their hosts. Examination of stomach contents has revealed a large proportion of parasitic crustaceans, as well as fishes, in particular pilot fishes. The diet of these creatures must be quite varied, because the size of the various remoras differs from species to species. In fact, while the sharksucker (*Echeneis naucrates*) may exceed 24 in (60 cm) in length, the black remora (*Remora remora*) is never more than 14 in (35 cm) long.

Somewhat surprisingly, fishes belonging to the Echenidae have been seen affixed to the palate or to the gills of large bony or cartilaginous fishes. Various species have become the remora's favorite host. So we find the black remora (*Remora remora*) mainly on sharks; *R. brachyptera* and *R. osteochir* show a preference for the Histiophoridae (marine scombroids) and the Xiphiidae (swordfishes, etc.); *Remorina albescens* tend to select large members of the genus *Manta*, the manta rays.

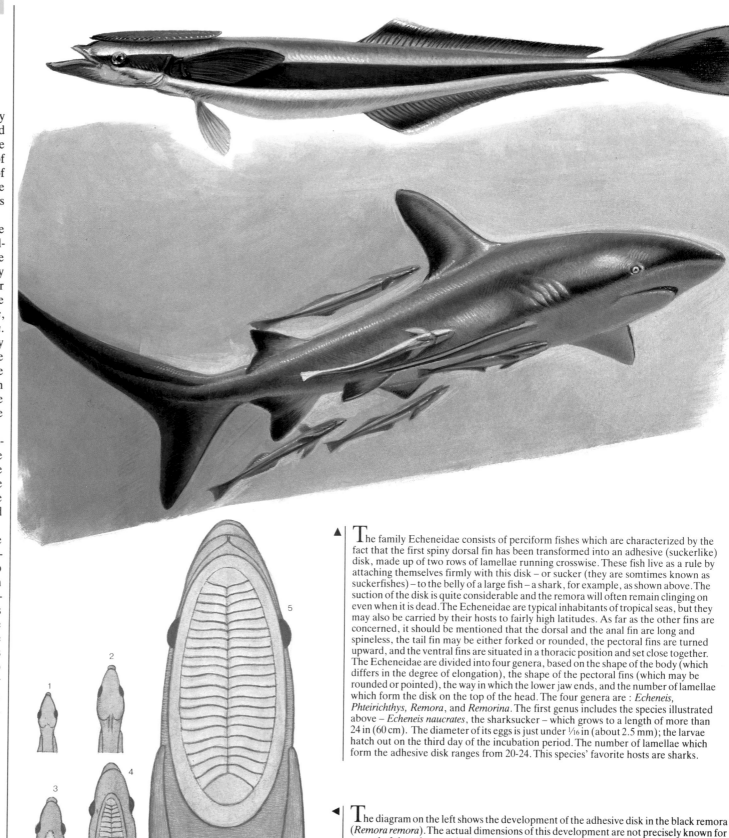

▲ The family Echeneidae consists of perciform fishes which are characterized by the fact that the first spiny dorsal fin has been transformed into an adhesive (suckerlike) disk, made up of two rows of lamellae running crosswise. These fish live as a rule by attaching themselves firmly with this disk – or sucker (they are somtimes known as suckerfishes) – to the belly of a large fish – a shark, for example, as shown above. The suction of the disk is quite considerable and the remora will often remain clinging on even when it is dead. The Echeneidae are typical inhabitants of tropical seas, but they may also be carried by their hosts to fairly high latitudes. As far as the other fins are concerned, it should be mentioned that the dorsal and the anal fin are long and spineless, the tail fin may be either forked or rounded, the pectoral fins are turned upward, and the ventral fins are situated in a thoracic position and set close together. The Echeneidae are divided into four genera, based on the shape of the body (which differs in the degree of elongation), the shape of the pectoral fins (which may be rounded or pointed), the way in which the lower jaw ends, and the number of lamellae which form the disk on the top of the head. The four genera are : *Echeneis*, *Phteirichthys*, *Remora*, and *Remorina*. The first genus includes the species illustrated above – *Echeneis naucrates*, the sharksucker – which grows to a length of more than 24 in (60 cm). The diameter of its eggs is just under ¹⁄₁₆ in (about 2.5 mm); the larvae hatch out on the third day of the incubation period. The number of lamellae which form the adhesive disk ranges from 20-24. This species' favorite hosts are sharks.

◄ The diagram on the left shows the development of the adhesive disk in the black remora (*Remora remora*). The actual dimensions of this development are not precisely known for several of the other species in the family. 1) At a length of ¼ in (6.5 mm) there is still no sign of a sucker at all; 2) at ⅜in (9.8 mm) an oval form appears behind the head; 3) at ½in (12 mm) it becomes more conspicuous, but there are still no visible lamellae; 4) at ¾in (18 mm) the development of the disk is already quite advanced; 5) at 1 in (25 mm) the adhesive disk is more or less perfectly formed.

ARCHERFISHES

Toxotidae

The six known species of archerfishes are well known because of their extraordinary way of hunting their prey, using their mouth structure like a blowgun – or peashooter. They have an elongated body which is fairly compressed laterally. The eyes are well developed, situated at the sides of the head, and set quite well forward.

These smallish fishes, which measure 4½ – 11 in (11.5 – 27 cm) overall, live in coastal waters with low salinity, in the brackish waters of estuaries and in rivers. They are found in eastern Asia, the Indo-Malayan archipelago, off the shores of Australia, the Philippine islands, the northern regions of Australia in particular, the Solomon Islands, and the New Hebrides.

By far the most widespread species is *Toxotes jaculator*, the archerfish or sumpit. Its favorite habitats are brackish estuaries and mangrove swamps. Apart from its hunting techniques, which will be discussed below, and about which a great deal is now known, almost nothing is known about this fish's biology.

The most interesting feature of the archerfishes is their ability to hunt for prey out of the water by using a powerful jet of water which is squirted from the mouth.

During the daylight hours the archerfishes like to stay just beneath the surface of the water from where they keep an eagle eye on the environment outside, taking on a typical "slanting" hunting posture, and waiting for a likely prey – probably an insect or a spider which has had the ill-fated idea of spinning its web near the water. Once the prey has been singled out, the fish takes aim, noiselessly moving back and forth, with the tip of its snout just above the water surface; then it squirts the fatal jet of water which will inevitably strike the target and knock it into the water, where it is swiftly gobbled up. As a rule, the archerfish never misses the bullseye; if the prey is some way off, it may fail to hit it at the first try, but the second shot never fails to strike home. However, this astonishing behavior does not occur in young individuals, which require a period of firing-practice before they achieve the accuracy of adults.

▲ The family Toxotidae – the archerfishes – consists of 6 species, all belonging to a single genus, *Toxotes*. These fish have the extraordinary ability to catch prey outside the water by squirting jets of water by means of special modifications in the mouth structure. The species illustrated here is the most widespread and the best-known, the archerfish or sumpit, *Toxotes jaculator*.

▼ By darting swiftly out of the water, the archerfishes can catch prey resting on the surface, or flying close to it.

▶ The buccal cavity of the members of the genus *Toxotes* is long and narrow. The tongue is large and fleshy at the base, and not mobile; but it is extremely slender at the tip.

◀ The distribution of the archerfishes covers a large area in the Indo-Pacific region. These fishes live in coastal waters with low salinity, the brackish waters of estuaries, and in rivers. In these habitats the archerfish lies in wait just beneath the surface of the water, waiting for a likely prey to be struck down with a jet of water. The mechanism which enables the archerfish to squirt these jets of water is very similar to that of a water-pistol: the water collected in the mouth (the water-pistol's reservoir) is subjected to pressure by means of contractions of the gill-covers and the floor of the mouth (the pistol's plunger). On the roof of the mouth there is a small groove about ¹⁄₁₆ in (2 mm) in diameter, which channels the pressurized water (i.e. the barrel) and causes it to leave the mouth in a powerful jet through a small aperture delimited by maxillary symphyses when the mouth is shut (the pistol's muzzle). The duration and the force of the jet (equivalent to the time and pressure on the trigger) can be varied as the fish wishes.

CLEANER FISH

Labroides dimidiatus

Order Perciformes
Family Labridae
Size Length 3 – 4 in (8 – 10 cm)
Weight ½ oz (10 – 15 g)
Distinctive features Proterogynous hermaphrodite. Possesses 52 – 53 scales along lateral line
Coloration Blue, merging to white in ventral region. The body is crossed from head to tail by a broad black band
Reproductive period Throughout year

The cleaner fish is the best known of all the fish species which perform the delicate task of keeping the bodies of other fishes free of parasites.

In this species, both sexes look alike; the basic color is blue, merging to white in the ventral region. The whole body, from head to tail, is crossed by a broad black band. When the female is spawning, a second, pinkish–brown band appears on the head.

The cleaner fish is to be found in all the world's tropical waters, including the Atlantic and Pacific, but is especially abundant along the coasts of the Indian Ocean and the Red Sea. Its preferred habitat is constituted by the walls of coral reefs, full of fissures and natural cavities, where it can establish a burrow. It has a liking for surface waters, but it is not rare to find it deeper, down to 165 ft (50 m), particularly in those zones where climatic variations during the year compel it to dive to such levels to find more favorable conditions.

Often a certain number of these small fishes establish private territories in neighboring zones, making up crowds of what experts describe as "cleaning stations," regularly frequented by large numbers of other species who congregate there in order to be carefully tended by the little cleaner fishes.

The social organization of *Labroides dimidiatus* is centered on harems which remain stable for several years; each is made up of one male and 6 – 7 adult females. Links between individuals of the group are controlled by a precise hierarchial structure, with the bigger fishes occupying higher-ranking positions. Each female possesses her own territory, inside which she performs all cleaning activities, chasing off all smaller and thus lower-ranking

▼ The cleaner fish (*Labroides dimidiatus*) is probably the best known of species performing these special cleaning functions, carrying out the delicate task of removing parasites from the body of many fish.

▼ Small copepods which burrow into the skin and settle in the gills of many fishes are the main food items of the cleaner fish.

▲
◄ The small cleaner fish has a single fin on the back, a truncated, rounded caudal fin, a terminally positioned mouth and well-developed lips. It seems to have no fear of approaching fish that are much larger than itself, such as stonebasses and cod. The latter stay still as the little cleaner explores their entire body, searching for small parasitic crustaceans which it eats. The favorite habitat is the wall of a coral reef with plenty of clefts and natural cavities, in which it can burrow.

▼ In the mouth of *Labroides dimidiatus* are four canine-like teeth. They constitute the specialized instruments whereby the cleaner fish extracts parasites from the body of its hosts.

females. The male dominates the whole group and, apart from owning his own piece of territory, may penetrate those belonging to the females of his harem.

Like many other representatives of the family Labridae, the cleaner fish is a proterogynous hermaphrodite; but in this instance sexual inversion, typical of such individuals, is regulated by the group's hierarchy.

When the male dies, the largest female, occupying the highest rank, undergoes sexual inversion and assumes the leading male's role in the group.

The eggs are planktonic and the larvae that hatch from them spend their period of development in open waters.

The relationship between the cleaner fishes and their hosts is defined by students of animal behavior as the process of "cleaning symbiosis"; it is one that has advantages for both individuals, the cleaner fish obtaining food and the host fish being freed of parasites. The cleaner fish attracts its customers with a series of movements which make up a so-called "cleaning dance"; the hosts, in their turn, invite the cleaner by assuming certain positions, varying according to species, some of them placing themselves in front of the smaller fish, remaining motionless and head downward, some opening their mouths wide, others exhibiting their flanks.

The cleaner fishes do not only attend to the needs of those species that frequent the zones where they themselves live; many species that normally live in open waters pay regular visits to the cleaning stations, and shoals of fishes can often be seen nearby, "queuing" for their turn.

Another fish, the small blenny *Aspidontus taeniatus*, is surprisingly similar in appearance to *Labroides dimidiatus* even though it belongs to a completely different family. This mimicry is so perfect that *Aspidontus taeniatus* imitates the cleaner fish, also in movement and behavior, tricking fishes, to allow it access; yet the blenny is not a cleaner, and will attack the fish thus approached, ripping off shreds of fin and flesh for eating.

Aspidontius taeniatus

▲ *Labroides dimidiatus* penetrates the gill openings of many fish. These cavities are very often the sites of large-scale infestations by parasites.

This small blenny gives an astonishing imitation of the appearance and behavior of *Labroides dimidiatus*. In this way it manages to approach unsuspecting fish and rips away shreds of fins, on which it feeds.

▲
▼ The cleaner fish, as shown in the illustrations, displays no fear even when venturing between the jaws of huge predators.

It would appear that the cleaner fish and its host can recognize each other ▲ at close quarters. Indeed, preliminary signals, such as the cleaner fish's dance, are less frequently needed if the two individuals have already had similar cleaning encounters.

◄ This picture might seem to show the end of one cleaner fish, but this is not so. The smaller fish, in fact, is in no danger, for it is extremely difficult for the host fish to attack and injure it. The host communicates its intentions of breaking off contact by shaking its head or half-closing its mouth and gill openings repeatedly.

ANEMONE FISHES

Genus Amphiprion

The small anemone fishes are inhabitants of coral reefs. They do not like swimming in the open sea and are always found near sea anemones, living in association with them and taking refuge inside them if danger threatens, without being harmed by the sting cells of their hosts.

The coloration is conspicuous, and there are usually broad vertical white stripes, edged with black, which contrast vividly with the rest of the body, normally orange.

There are some 25 species of anemone fishes, all inhabitants of warm seas and coral reefs. They are to be found from the western coasts of Africa to the Pacific, most living, however, in the zone extending from Indonesia to Australia and Micronesia.

Some species of anemone fish maintain the closest links with a particular genus of anemone (in many cases *Stoichactis*) while others can live in association with different genera.

In the breeding season each pair marks out its territory and often shows aggressive intentions toward others of the species. The eggs are laid on a spot close to an anemone. The parents, particularly the father, incubate the eggs until the young are born.

It has been suggested that this form of association is accepted in the interest of both parties, the fish helping to supply food for its host. The fish does indeed bring food but apparently it is limited to overlarge chunks, which have to be seized by the anemone to be broken into small fragments.

It has also been claimed that the anemone fish defends its host against predatory fishes, repelling, for example, butterfly fishes, which eat anemones.

► The fishes that belong to the genus *Amphiprion* are commonly known as anemone fishes. They are well known for the fact that they generally take refuge among the tentacles of sea anemones. The poisonous sting cells of certain anemones constitute a mortal danger to all fishes apart from those of the genus *Amphiprion*. It has, in fact, been proved that anemone fishes are not harmed by sting venom. It is also believed that they smear over their skin, as a kind of defense, a layer of mucus from the anemone itself. The genus *Amphiprion* belongs to the family Pomacentridae, attached to the suborder Percoidei of the Perciformes. They are brightly colored species of small size, very common along coral reefs and firm favorites of aquarists.

The members of the genus *Premnas*, which much resemble those of the genus *Amphiprion*, but differ from them by having two spines below the eyes and possessing smaller scales, are also known as anemone fishes. The *Amphiprion* species, because so small and difficult to catch in large quantities, are not fished commercially, although they are edible. But they are exported live for keeping in aquariums.

◄ The sea anemone possesses venomous sting cells on its tentacles. The poison paralyzes the victim and enables it to be conducted toward the mouth, there to be consumed. It will even eat anemone fishes if they are injured or when they are not smeared with its mucus; in other circumstances the anemone will accept the fishes and leave them unharmed.

BLUE PARROTFISH
Scarus coeruleus

Order Perciformes
Family Scaridae
Size Length usually about 12 in (30 cm)
Distinctive features Teeth fused to form dentary plates. Non-protractile mouth. Discontinuous lateral line; 22 longitudinal rows of cycloid scales
Coloration Blue, varying according to age

In the blue parrotfish, as in all Scaridae, the teeth of the upper and lower jaws are fused into two dentary plates, forming a "beak." The upper plate slightly overlaps the lower one when the mouth is closed; the latter, as in all the Scaridae, is not protractile.

The blue parrotfish is generally found along the western Atlantic shores of America, together with 20 or so related species. It also lives along the coasts of Florida and Brazil, and in the coral reefs surrounding the islands of the Caribbean.

It is easy to observe young individuals in the shallow waters normally inhabited by parrotfishes; but adults are harder to spot because they tend to live deeper.

During the night the blue parrotfish, like others of its family, surrounds itself with a spherical capsule of secreted mucus. The fish needs about 30 minutes to construct this capsule. The cocoon probably prevents the odor of the parrotfish reaching the nostrils of predators, but its precise role is still unknown. The blue parrotfish sleeps on the seabed or on rocks. In the morning it abandons its "nightshirt" but for a while its movements are uncoordinated: the fish collides with objects in its path and swims awkwardly. Should it be too disturbed by such interference, the fish will go to sleep again.

Like other representatives of the family, the blue parrotfish browses on coral but also feeds on small animals such as mollusks, crustaceans, sea urchins, and also algae; so its diet is virtually omnivorous.

The blue parrotfish (*Scarus coeruleus*) is an inhabitant of the coral reefs of the western Atlantic tropical and subtropical regions. The teeth are fused into two dentary plates, with a visible central suture: this apparatus constitutes its "beak." By reason of this anatomical pecularity and coloration, this and other related species have come to be called parrotfishes. Sexual dimorphism is quite frequent: adult males, but not females, have a frontal protuberance. The Scaridae feed by nibbling pieces of coral and also the shells of sea-urchins: in addition, their diet includes algae and marine plants.

MUDSKIPPERS

Periophthalminae

The mudskippers are fairly modest-sized fishes, presenting a certain number of individual characteristics, due to the fact that they are specialized for life out of water. The body is elongated, very thick at the front and slightly compressed at the rear. The head is large and the facial profile is almost straight. The big snout is a little flattened at the front. As in the majority of gobies, the ventral fins are linked to form an adhesive sucker.

The habit of spending long periods out of water is associated with various modifications and adaptations in the morphology of the fins. The pectorals, which enable the fishes to move about underground and support the weight of the whole body, are strong and pedunculate, formed by a kind of stump lengthened into a paddlelike fin. It operates like a small arm which terminates in a broad palmated "hand." The fin base of the mudskipper is supported by a bone structure that is stronger and more developed than that of other gobies, and is rendered more mobile, and suitable for a wide variety of movements, by the presence of very large, separated adductor and abductor muscles, situated on the inner and outer fin surfaces.

The subaerial habitat of mudskippers is reflected in other specific features, as, for example, the morphology of the eyes and respiratory tracts which have to perform their functions in an unaccustomed environment. The eyes are very peculiar and bear some resemblance to the eyes of amphibians. They are placed close together and bulge out; strikingly mobile, they are mounted on a kind of optical turret, and can be popped out, like the eyes of flatfishes, to operate as a periscope. They can, when necessary, be retracted into their sockets. In such a situation they are almost completely covered by protective folds of skin.

Mudskippers are able to breathe atmospheric oxygen for long periods thanks to the fact, that the mucus of mouth and pharynx is furnished with many blood vessels and the gill surface is relatively small. The gills must be kept moist at all times. The fishes can moreover greatly expand their gill cavities, so increasing the surface for

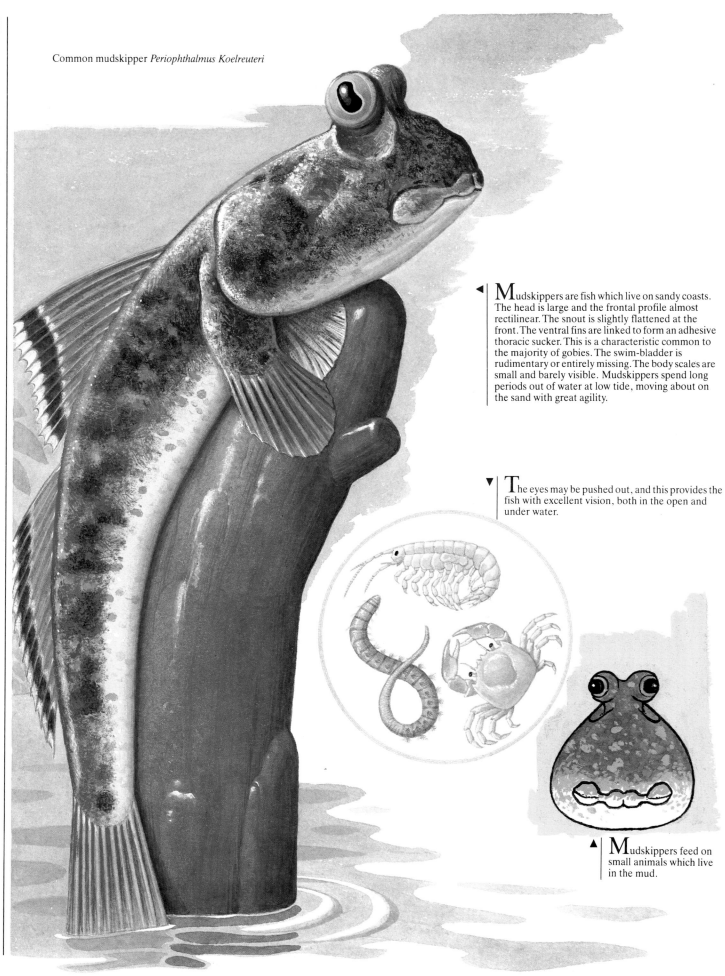

Common mudskipper *Periophthalmus Koelreuteri*

Mudskippers are fish which live on sandy coasts. The head is large and the frontal profile almost rectilinear. The snout is slightly flattened at the front. The ventral fins are linked to form an adhesive thoracic sucker. This is a characteristic common to the majority of gobies. The swim-bladder is rudimentary or entirely missing. The body scales are small and barely visible. Mudskippers spend long periods out of water at low tide, moving about on the sand with great agility.

The eyes may be pushed out, and this provides the fish with excellent vision, both in the open and under water.

Mudskippers feed on small animals which live in the mud.

gaseous exchanges and closing the gill openings.

This system of breathing has become so normal for these fishes that it is used, at least partially, even when they are in water. In fact, when under water, mudskippers habitually assume a sloping position, with the head higher than the rest of the body; they strongly dilate the gill cavities (the rear portion of which contains water) so that water thoroughly wets the back gills, while air is stored in the front part. As a result the front gills are only moistened by a small amount of water, retained by the capillaries.

The mudskippers inhabit the equatorial and tropical zones of Africa, both west and east, including Madagascar, and the same zones in Asia, extending as far as Australia. Where suitable habitats exist, they are common and plentiful; they particularly like mangrove swamps or sandy areas left exposed at low tide and frequent beaches, the shores of lagoons and marshes, and pools of salt water that form at low tide round the mouths of rivers. The fishes are, in fact, capable of withstanding considerable variations of salinity.

After digging a more or less complex burrow in soft ground, utilizing the excavated material to build a circular ledge round the opening, mudskippers retire inside. At other times, they may be found in the open, supported on the pectoral fins and the sucker, with head raised and eyes rolling comically round the sockets; this behavior undoubtedly helps to moisten the mucus and prevents it drying out in the air.

When not resting, mudskippers move around with an agility surprising for a fish. At low tide they lead a very active life, like that of land animals, and often assemble in small groups, often quarreling and fighting among themselves.

Food consists of small animals living in mud, but they may also eat flying insects, especially spiders.

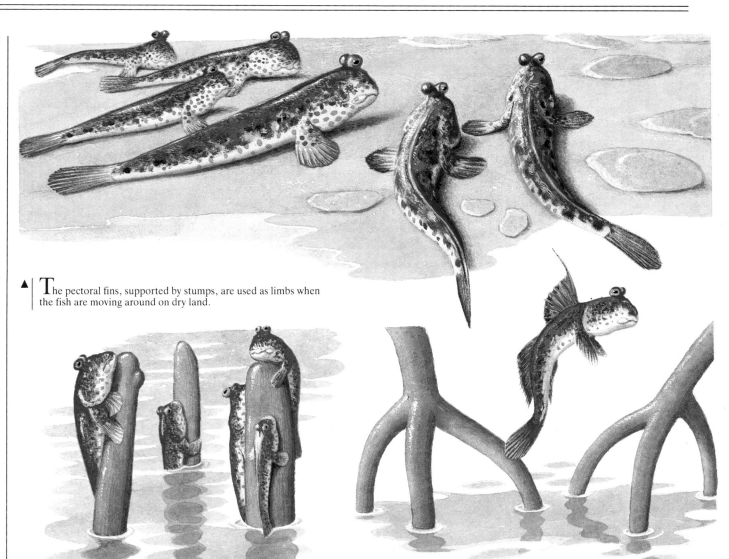

▲ The pectoral fins, supported by stumps, are used as limbs when the fish are moving around on dry land.

▲ Mudskippers prefer resting in an upright position, the front of the body out of the water and the caudal fin submerged.

▲ These animals are capable of making jumps and clambering over rocks and aerial mangrove roots.

The burrow that mudskippers dig in the ground may be of varying complexity: it always has a circular mound around the opening which is constructed by the fish themselves from the excavated material. ▶

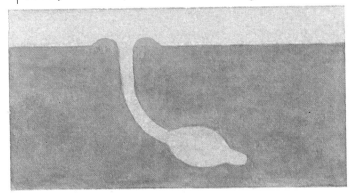

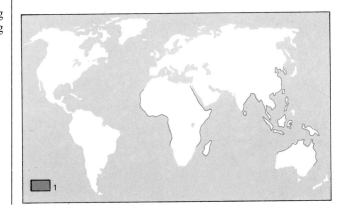

◀ 1) Mudskippers populate the equatorial and tropical zones of Africa, both east and west, and including Madagascar, as well as similar zones in Asia and as far east as Australia. They are very common and abundant in their favorite habitats, mangrove swamps or sandy soils, where they stay hidden at low tide. The fish will venture into river basins wherever the water is tidal.

SWORDFISH

Xiphias gladius

Order Perciformes
Family Xiphiidae
Size Length over 13 ft (4 m)
Weight Up to 1,100 lb (500 kg) or more
Distinctive features Elongated upper jaw forming a flattened, sharp rostrum
Coloration Gray-black on back, white on belly
Reproductive period From spring to summer
Eggs On average 16 million

The swordfish is one of the largest existing teleosts, characterized by its flattened rostrum, which is a third of the total length of its body, with a sharp point and cutting edges. This "sword" stems from the overdevelopment of the upper jaw; the lower jaw is much shorter but is also well-developed and terminates in a point. The mouth is large and the adults have no teeth. The coloration is uniform, gray-black on the back, white on the abdomen.

The swordfish is a cosmopolitan species, inhabiting virtually all the world's temperate and tropical seas: in the Atlantic, for example, it lives off all coasts and heads north at the end of summer and early fall, at which times it has been caught off the shores of Britain and in the North Sea. It is abundantly present off both coasts of the United States, but not fished commercially: it is, nevertheless, a favorite game fish. In the seas of Japan, on the other hand, it is of considerable economic importance, as it is in the Mediterranean, where it has a fairly wide distribution and where it has been fished traditionally since ancient times.

It is a pelagic, migratory fish, but it does not assemble in compact shoals even in the spawning season; at such times it often makes long journeys along fixed routes, yet still keeping a fair distance from others of its species. This behavior is derived from its solitary, aggressive nature, typical of many large predators, which prevents it making contact either with other individuals of its own kind or with other fishes that could be potential competitors.

There have been many examples of whales and other big cetaceans which have been killed with fragments of a

Swordfish
(*Xiphias gladius*)

The swordfish is a large fish inhabiting the world's tropical and temperate seas. It is notable for its long, flattened, pointed snout, resulting from the overdevelopment of the upper jaw. This species may grow to a length of more than 13 ft (4 m), a third of which is represented by its "sword." Despite its size, the swordfish is an agile and speedy swimmer, and is considered, in fact, to be one of the fastest of all sea animals. The body is powerful and streamlined, almost circular in cross-section. Females are generally larger than the males. The mouth is large and lacks teeth. There is a lateral line, although not clearly visible. The coloration is uniform, shaded gray-black on the back and dirty white on the abdomen. The dorsal fin is high, but its base is much shorter than is the case among the related Istiophoridae. The caudal peduncle has a single but strong keel on either side. The caudal fin is in a half-moon shape. There are no scales. The swordfish is a solitary, aggressive creature, typical of all large predators. This prevents it making contact with other members of its own or different species, the former being, in a sense, competitors. The only exception to this secluded life is during the spawning period. Partners form close links, so much so that if one is caught by fishermen the other stays circling around the vessel, as if searching for its mate.

swordfish's rostrum embedded in their muscles; and this seems to prove the truth of many legends relating the deep hostility between these two giants and the violent battles that take place between them.

Undoubtedly, therefore, the terrible weapon of the swordfish is far from merely decorative and is actively employed in the daily search for food: once it has come to grips with one or more animals, the swordfish strikes out with powerful lateral blows, killing or stunning its victim before grabbing it in the mouth. It hunts both by day and by night, showing a preference, according to circumstances, for mollusks, cephalopods, and pelagic fishes such as sardines, mackerels, etc.

The only exception to this unsociability is when the time comes for spawning: then the link with the partner is very strong, and it is not uncommon to see pairs of swordfish swimming close together in surface waters.

Observations of horizontal movements have established that it reaches quite considerable speeds in the water: it can, in fact swim at about 60 mph (100 kmh), making it one of the fastest animals in the oceans.

The spawning period of the swordfish extends from the end of spring and throughout the summer; and the female ejects eggs several times. The number of eggs emitted by an adult varies, according to her size, from 10 to 20 million; each egg is pelagic and measures 1.6 to 1.8 mm in diameter. After two and a half days from fertilization a larva, slightly over 4 mm long, hatches, and when it is four days old it begins to open its mouth and soon afterward to feed.

In these early stages the general structure is entirely different from that of the adult, and only later, as both jaws develop into a kind of beak, does the animal begin to take on its definitive appearance. Nevertheless, there are still many differences, such as the unified dorsal and anal fins, the presence of teeth in both jaws, and small scales on the body. As the fish grows, the scales and teeth disappear, only the upper jaw continues to develop, and the two dorsal fins and anal fins become separated.

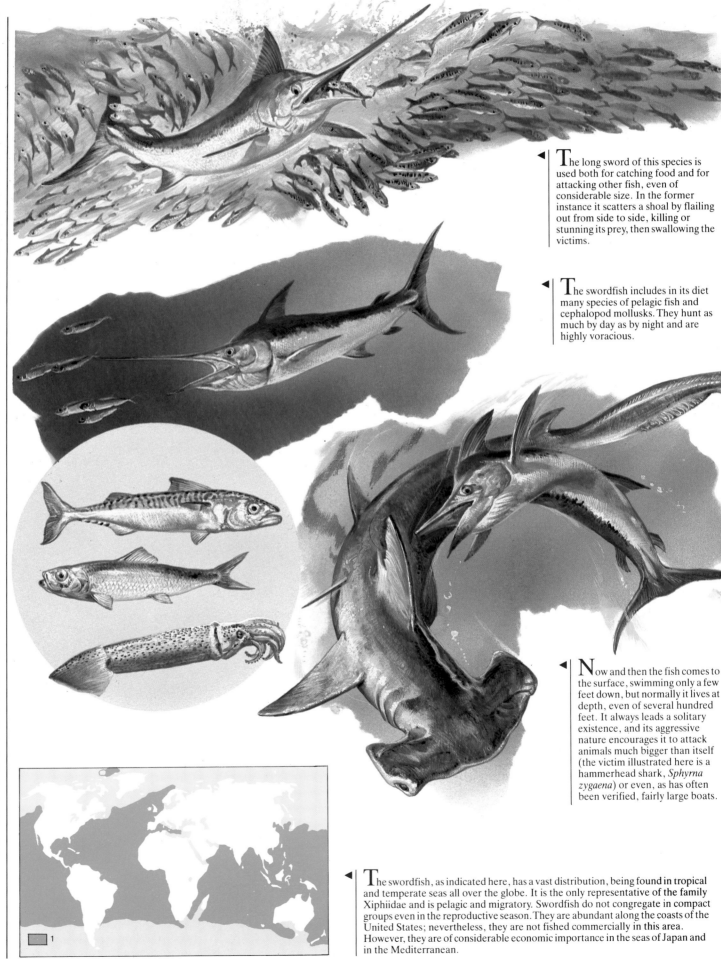

The long sword of this species is used both for catching food and for attacking other fish, even of considerable size. In the former instance it scatters a shoal by flailing out from side to side, killing or stunning its prey, then swallowing the victims.

The swordfish includes in its diet many species of pelagic fish and cephalopod mollusks. They hunt as much by day as by night and are highly voracious.

Now and then the fish comes to the surface, swimming only a few feet down, but normally it lives at depth, even of several hundred feet. It always leads a solitary existence, and its aggressive nature encourages it to attack animals much bigger than itself (the victim illustrated here is a hammerhead shark, *Sphyrna zygaena*) or even, as has often been verified, fairly large boats.

The swordfish, as indicated here, has a vast distribution, being found in tropical and temperate seas all over the globe. It is the only representative of the family Xiphiidae and is pelagic and migratory. Swordfish do not congregate in compact groups even in the reproductive season. They are abundant along the coasts of the United States; nevertheless, they are not fished commercially in this area. However, they are of considerable economic importance in the seas of Japan and in the Mediterranean.

BLUE MARLIN
Makaira nigricans

The sailfishes and marlins which belong to the family Istiophoridae are notable for their upper jaw, transformed into a long bony, lance-shaped snout.

These are pelagic species, found in all oceans and in the Mediterranean. They live in surface waters, especially on the high seas, though some species freely approach the coasts. They require warmth, and some make directly for the warmest waters of the equatorial zone; others, however, can stand or deliberately seek out somewhat more temperate waters.

The long, tapering, hydrodynamic body, allied to other morphological features, ensure that these fishes are speedy and tireless swimmers. They are continually on the move, in pursuit of shoals. They can perform spectacular leaps out of the water and sometimes launch attacks, for no obvious reason, on swimmers or vessels, penetrating very deeply with their sharp snout.

In the blue marlin, the blue back and silver belly are clearly divided by a line that runs along the flanks. It may often bear vertical stripes which resemble those of the striped marlin, but they are far less conspicuous and vanish rapidly after death. The body, furthermore, is stocky, the forward lobe of the dorsal fin is more pointed, and this fin becomes markedly lower in its rear portion. The snout is elongated and fairly sharp.

This is a fish of the open seas, rarely approaching the coast, and feeds freely on bonitos. It is the most tropical of all marlins, having a preference for very warm waters, causing it to cross the equator to take advantage of two summer seasons, in north and south. In addition to such journeys in quest of warmth, the blue marlin migrates to spawning grounds, which appear to be well defined.

The blue marlin may grow very large, its maximum length thought to be in the region of 18½ ft (5.5 m) for a weight of 1,550 lb (700 kg). However, because they are victims of over-intensive fishing, such large-sized individuals are seldom seen, and the average weight is around 220 lb (100 kg). The males are larger than the females.

The blue marlin (*Makaira nigricans*) belongs to the family Istiophoridae. It is a particularly popular game fish. The marlin much resembles the swordfish in various ways. It differs, however, in the shape of its bill, which is circular, not flattened, and also by the presence of two ventral fins.

CLIMBING PERCH

Anabas testudineus

Order Perciformes
Family Anabantidae
Size Length up to 9 – 10 in (23 – 25 cm) in wild; less in aquarium
Distinctive features Long dorsal and anal fins, the former composed of 16 – 19 spines, the latter of 9 – 11 spines, both accompanied by soft rays. Rounded caudal fin
Coloration Adults uniformly brownish-gray or greenish with paler or silvery belly; young have eye-spot on caudal peduncle
Reproductive period During rainy season, June – July in India
Sexual maturity 8 – 9 months in aquarium, 1 year in wild

The body of the climbing perch is laterally compressed, especially in the tail region. The dorsal and anal fins are made up of a spinous part, followed by a portion with soft rays, the former being longer than the latter. The caudal fin is rounded. Body and head are covered with ctenoid scales. The mouth is big and the jaws have small conical teeth. The operculum and sub-operculum have edges with strong spines. Above the first gill arch is a labyrinthine organ, formed of bony plates covered by a well vascularized layer of skin, which permits the fish to breathe atmospheric oxygen.

The climbing perch can live for long periods out of water because of their special breathing organs and are renowned chiefly for their ability to move about on land. This they do by means of their opercular spines which grip the ground or any other solid object. They then bend the body, supporting themselves on the tail, fix the spines a little farther on, and repeat the procedure as necessary. By half leaning or stretching out on one side they manage in this fashion to move along quite rapidly.

The climbing perch inhabits southern China, Vietnam, Cambodia, Thailand, Burma, India, Malaysia, Indonesia, the Philippines, etc. It lives both in fresh and brackish water, in rivers and especially stagnant waters with plenty of aquatic vegetation.

Climbing perch
(*Anabas testudineus*)

▼ The climbing perch hides in the mud or wet soil during the dry season. It waits there, its life processes slowed down, until the first rains arrive.

▼ 1) Distribution area of the climbing perch (*Anabas testudineus*).

▲ The climbing perch is a member of the family Anabantidae, which comprises, in addition to the eastern Asiatic genus *Anabas*, the two genera *Ctenopoma* and *Sandelia* from Africa. *Anabas testudineus* has an elongated, laterally compressed body, especially flat in the tail region. The coloration of the adults is drab, uniform gray-brown or green, the abdomen being paler or silvery. The young have a pale yellow bordered black spot on the caudal peduncle, and sometimes a black patch on the operculum. Because of their size, abundance and tasty flesh, they are in much demand as human food wherever they are found, being sturdy enough to be transported live for long distances in jars and baskets. They are widely sold in markets in the Far East, but sellers have to sprinkle them with water to prevent them from dying of desiccation, and must also watch them so that they do not escape and get lost. In many places, fishermen have a habit, when catching a climbing perch, of breaking its neck with a bite to prevent it getting away; yet there is a risk that the fish, as it struggles to get loose, may stick in the fisherman's throat, and be difficult to extract because of its opercular spines. Unless there is immediate surgical attention, death may result from suffocation. Such incidents have often been reported in adults and children from India and Thailand.

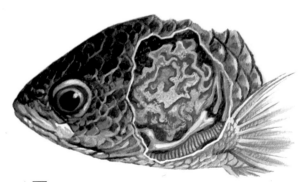

▲ The climbing perch can travel several hundred yards over dry land to get from one water hole to another. It supports itself on its pectoral fins and moves forward by wriggling its tail. It can live for some hours out of water thanks to the structure of an additional breathing organ called the labyrinth, which absorbs atmospheric oxygen. The labyrinth is situated in a cavity above the gills. The walls are covered by a highly vascularized layer of skin.

PLEURONECTIFORMES

Among the bony fishes, the Pleuronectiformes, commonly known as flatfishes, are the only fishes to be flattened on one side, the blind side (almost always colorless), and to have two eyes on the other side (usually pigmented). However, as we shall see when we come to consider the development of flatfishes, the larva is normal with one eye on either side of the head, becoming asymmetrical only in the course of metamorphosis.

Pleuronectiformes are found in all oceans, apart from the Arctic (into which the black halibut strays). Many of them, are so well concealed as they lie flat on a mottled surface, that only a photograph can distinguish the animal's outline. Not only does it imitate the coloration of the seabed, but it also faithfully reproduces the exact marks and patterns of the surrounding gravel. It is interesting to analyze the mechanisms of this phenomenon.

There are special cells in the skin of fishes, known as chromatophores, each of which contains pigment granules – erythrophores for red, xanthophores for yellow, melanophores for black, and leucophores for white. These cells are responsible for the colors and total variations of fishes. These star-shaped, branching cells never alter shape. Only the pigment granules change their position in the cell and thus affect coloration. The chromatophores respond to a dual command, nervous and hormonal.

Although flatfishes are able to change their color, each species has its own specific garb, used for identification. Studies of certain Pleuronectiformes (*Pleuronectes*, *Microstomus*, *Arnoglossus*, *Zeugopterus*, *Psetta*, *Solea*, etc.) have shown that the pigmentation of these fishes is similarly distributed. Some species, such as *Limanda limanda*, come very close to the general pattern. Others, however, differ in varying measure by virtue of the presence or absence of certain markings, distinctive patterns, etc. It is also worth noting that not all flatfishes have the same mimetic capacities. The plaice, for example, compensates for its imperfect camouflage by covering itself with a thin layer of sand, fanned over with the fins. Only the eyes peer out, attentive for a prey victim.

The larva of the flatfishes is similar

The fishes belonging to the order Pleuronectiformes, commonly called flatfish, are found in oceans almost the world over. They are distinguished clearly from other fishes by the shape of their body. They are, in fact, the only fishes to be flattened on one side (the blind side, unpigmented) and to possess two eyes on the other side, the ocular side, which is pigmented. According to group, the eyes may be either on the right side (Pleuronectidae and Soleidae), or on the left side (Bothidae and Cynoglossidae), or indifferently on one side or the other (Psettodidae). All these fishes are carnivorous, feeding, among other things, on crayfish, squids and marine invertebrates.

When hatched, the flatfish larva is identical in shape to the larvae of other fishes (above) and lives like them. In fact, it has an eye on both sides and swims belly downwards . Subsequently (as the drawings from top to bottom, show), it undergoes metamorphosis, the most spectacular phenomenon of which is the migration of one of the eyes to the opposite side, right or left depending on the family concerned. The flatfish, which until then has led a pelagic life, now drops to the bottom, coming to rest on its blind side.

in shape to that of other fishes. During the larval development it is possible to make out a number of stages: embryo, prelarva, larva, postlarva, and imago. In the last phase the animal shows all the charateristics of the adult.

The embryo, prelarva and larva all develop like those of most other fishes with an eye on either side and normal bilateral symmetry. It is pelagic and lives, depending on species, either close to the surface or at a greater depth, but always some distance from the bottom.

At the conclusion of the larval phase, during the postlarval stage, metamorphosis commences; the main effect of this is the migration of the eye, which travels round from the side on which the fish is lying to the side turned toward the surface; this may be either the left or the right side, depending on the family concerned. Before the eye begins its journey, its course is determined by the disappearance of the cranial cartilage. The movement may take place in different ways, according to the position of the origin of the dorsal fin. If, at the moment migration starts, the fin's origin is situated behind the eyes, the eye of what will later be the blind side travels across the back of the head to reach the ocular side. If, however, the dorsal fin is at that point situated above or in front of the eyes, the eye concerned will pass through the tissues of the cranium and the fin. After the transference, the dorsal fin's origin, especially in the former instance, will shift forward to reach its definitive position. The movement of the eye from one side to the other brings about deep and complex anatomical changes, which cannot be analyzed here. Briefly, however, they affect the nerves of the eye (the optic chiasm) and the orbit, with the formation of an orbital groove for the migrating eye. The eye movement is subsequently accompanied by the movement of a nostril, the deformation of the mouth and the development of pigments, but only on the ocular side. Metamorphosis is of short duration, particularly in relation to the length of the larval pelagic phase, which lasts many months, sometimes even a year. In the course of metamorphosis, the fish abandons the pelagic existence led during the larval stage, and becomes benthonic.

▲
▶ Flatfish generally live on shifting beds of sand or mud. They use their fins to cover themselves with sediment, from which only the head juts out (above). There they wait, motionless, until a prey (such as a fish, shown on the right) comes near. It then leaps out and swallows it, immediately burying itself once more in the sand or mud.

Growth of a flatfish.

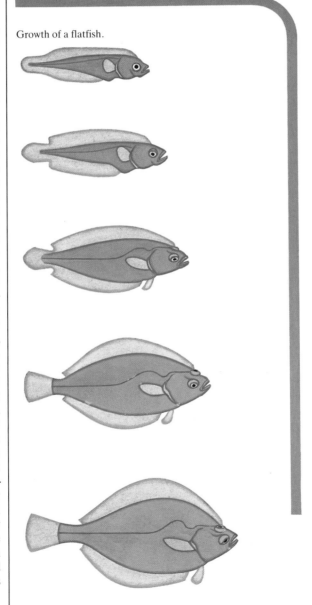

Imitative capacity of a flatfish.

▲ The Pleuronectiformes almost all have remarkable capacities for mimicry. Indeed, the coloration of the ocular side perfectly imitates the substratum. Thus, when a flatfish lying on a sandy floor (top) leaves it to settle on gravel (bottom), the light markings on the back get larger. Not only do these marks reproduce the size of the individual pieces of gravel or pebble seen by the fish, but also the shape. It has been verified, as a result of experiments carried out with certain species, that these fish, placed on artificial backgrounds colored black and white, are able to adopt similar colors and to cover themselves in white spots, equivalent in size and shape to those chosen for the test, within about a half an hour.

TRIGGERFISHES
Balistidae

In the fascinating fishes of the family Balistidae, the body is oval or oblong, covered with thick scales roughened by spines or small tubercles. The conical, incisorlike teeth are few in number and arranged in one or two rows on the jaws. The head has a characteristic appearance because of the position of the eyes, these being situated high and well removed from the small mouth. The first dorsal fin bears two or three strong spiniform rays.

The many species of Balistidae are collectively known as triggerfishes. This strange name is derived from the singular functioning of the spiniform dorsal rays. The first of these can take on an erect position thanks to a mechanism at the base of the second ray; only when this mechanism is released, by being lowered behind the second ray, can the first regain its mobility or again be bent. In fact, the fish, by straightening the forward dorsal fin, manages to anchor itself firmly in crevices of rock or coral, from which it is not easily removed.

Many species of triggerfish are adorned with brilliant colors and patterns which are an aid to identification; all are marine and littoral, with various ecological characteristics: some prefer open waters, others stay close to rocks or are associated with coral reefs. As a rule they are solitary fishes, swimming slowly by flapping the second dorsal and the anal fin, but lashing the tail from side to side if speed is required. The diet is carnivorous or herbivorous; some tropical species, like the large *Pseudobalistes flavimarginatus* – common in the Red Sea and many other Indo-Pacific regions – also consume long-spined sea urchins (*Diadema* sp.): they turn the animals over and break the abdominal shell with their strong jaws and teeth, swallowing the contents. The fishes also have the remarkable capacity of making sounds by contracting their swim-bladder; these are audible murmurs when they are removed from the water. Equally fascinating is their habit of rolling the eyes, each independently of the other, like chameleons.

The Balistidae are usually regarded as having little commercial importance; indeed, the flesh is considered

The family Balistidae, or triggerfishes, prototype of the Balistoidea, belongs to the order Tetraodontiformes. The triggerfish has an oval, oblong body, covered with thick scales. The shape of the head is unusual, due to the position of the eyes, situated very high and well separated from the mouth. *Balistoides conspicillum*, shown here, is one of the most easily recognizable members of the family, and also one of the most handsome. For this reason it changes hands in the trade at high prices, although it has difficulty in adapting to life in captivity. Its maximum length is 20 in (50 cm).

Balistoides conspicillum is found in the Indian and Pacific Oceans. It lives close to the barrier reefs and feeds on various invertebrates, caught on the ocean bed. It is a solitary species and, like other members of the Balistidae, tends to be sedentary. With respect to food, it is interesting to note that this fish nibbles, with its powerful jaws, both coral and calcareous algae, digesting the organic part.

poisonous. Yet certain species are eaten and much valued as food.

One of the most easily recognizable triggerfishes is *Balistoides conspicillum*, measuring about 20 in (50 cm) at most. It has the typical triggerfish shape, and is covered with thick, rough scales similar to plates. In front of the eye is a groove, while other small bony plates are to be found behind the gill openings. Along the caudal peduncle are two and a half rows of tubercles, which reinforce the animal's natural protection. The first dorsal fin consists of three spiniform rays, the third of which is not rudimentary, as in other triggerfishes. The second dorsal and anal fin are not raised at the front; the tail has a straight edge. Some of these characteristics are also found in other members of the family, but the same is untrue of the coloration, which is highly specific and makes this fish unmistakable. It is because of its multicolored livery, with its unique pattern, that some have described the species as the most beautiful fish in the world, and for that reason it has often been illustrated.

B. conspicillum possesses "somatolithic" coloration because it appears to interrupt the continuity of the various parts of the body. It is an inhabitant of coral reefs, and spends its life in close association with coral. It lives secluded and, like other triggerfishes, has markedly sedentary habits. If frightened, it often squeezes into a hole from which it cannot easily be removed, so firmly does it attach itself with the mechanism of the dorsal fin already described.

This fish is essentially zoophagous, feeding on sponges, hydroids, bryozoans, and other invertebrates: it also uses its strong jaws to nibble at coral and to chew calcareous algae, consuming the organic parts and expelling the mineral contents which are deposited on the bottom, there to mingle with the fine white powder that for the same reason is ejected from the anal opening of parrotfishes. The Balistidae are therefore devourers of coral who are not content to take only polyps, as other fishes do, but also swallow pieces of the polypary, or supporting structure.

The area of distribution is vast, embracing a large part of the Indian Ocean and warm zones of the Pacific; from the coasts of South Africa (Natal) it extends to Japan and the Fiji Islands (Polynesia).

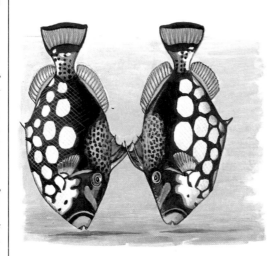

▲ While searching for food, *Balistoides conspicillum* often assumes a vertical position.

S tructure and function of the forward dorsal fin.

In the Balistidae, the forward dorsal fin consists of three spiniform rays. They are erectile, as the sequence of pictures shows, enabling the fishes to anchor themselves in rock clefts.

▲ If frightened, *Balistoides conspicillum* frequently hides inside a cavity, from which it is extracted only with difficulty because it attaches itself to the walls by means of its dorsal fin.

▲ Along with other species, these fish swim close to the bottom. They move slowly, undulating the second dorsal and anal fin. If they want to go faster, they flick their tail sideways.

▲ *Balistoides conspicillum* rests by lying down on the bottom, in the spaces between clumps of coral. The coloration of the species breaks up the continuity of the various parts of the body.

SUNFISHES
Molidae

Among the large fishes which, when caught, are often considered newsworthy, are the so-called sunfishes of the family Molidae. Among the most obvious features of these fishes is the large size, so much so that the Molidae can claim to be among the most spectacular of all marine animals. The body is round and oblong, flattened, and oddly truncated at the rear: it seems to consist only of the head, and indeed an alternative vernacular name is head-fish. The entire rear edge of the body is equipped with a fin which it would be natural to assume is the tail. However, this is a special structure originating from the fact that in the course of growth the primitive tail disappears and is replaced by a pseudo-tail deriving from the fusion, at the back, of the dorsal and anal fins; the rays of the upper part are dorsal, and those of the lower part anal. This pseudo-tail is called the clavus. Naturally, there is no caudal peduncle. The skin is rough by reason of the presence of spinules or small plates. The mouth is small, and neither of the jaws carry teeth, but do bear very strong plates which together form a beak similar to that of the porcupine fishes, since the dentary plate of each jaw (fairly large) has no median suture; so this is a two-part apparatus. The gill openings are small and the opercular processes are somewhat reduced and concealed under the skin.

The single dorsal and anal fins are especially worthy of note. Both are very tall; they are, in fact, raised and straight, similar and opposed, inserted in the rear of the body immediately in front of the clavus. There are no ventral fins and no pelvic girdle.

The skeleton is composed mainly of cartilage. The skull is fairly short and broad, with the upper part mostly occupied by the frontal bones, which extend some distance sideways. In keeping with the shortness of the body, there are few vertebrae, 16-20, of which 8 are precaudal; in the first of these the neurospines are bifid. The muscles are clearly related to the odd methods of locomotion employed by these curious fishes; the longitudinal muscles, which normally give an animal flexibility, are atrophied, but in compensation there are heavy

The Molidae, or sunfishes, are regarded as the most highly evolved and specialized of all the Tetraodontiformes. Their outline is unmistakable. The body appears to be cut off behind, where a pseudocaudal fin forms a clearly visible edge. The dorsal and anal fins, similar and opposed, serve for propulsion. *Mola mola*, the species illustrated here, is the best known of the few members of the family.

Ocean sunfish
(*Mola mola*)

bunches of muscle serving to raise and lower the dorsal and anal fins. There is no swim-bladder. The anal and urogenital openings are situated immediately in front of the anal fin.

Nowadays there are three genera, each represented by a single species: *Mola mola*, *Masturus lanceolatus*, and *Ranzania laevis*. All sunfishes are pelagic and are to be found both out at sea and near the shores; it is interesting to note that all three species are widely distributed in the temperate and warm regions of the world's oceans, and may therefore be called cosmopolitan. *Mola* and *Ranzania* are also present in the Mediterranean. These fishes are mainly found near the surface, although they also descend to depths of a few hundred meters, probably no more. They swim slowly with sideways flaps of the dorsal and anal fins, while the body stays stiff. They feed on various organisms, especially plankton, and also plant matter.

The classic representative of the Molidae is *Mola mola*, and this species is commonly taken as the prototype of the entire family. It is one of the most enormous fishes anywhere, its maximum length being almost 11 ft (3.3 m) and its weight nearly 2 tonnes. The body is rounded, silvery gray or olive-brown in color; in young individuals there are often circular black spots at the rear of the flanks. There are 16 – 20 rays in the dorsal fin, 14 – 18 in the anal fin. The pectoral fins are rounded. The intestine is fairly long.

This species is highly prolific; a female will carry at least 300 million immature eggs. When it hatches, the tiny larva (1.05 – 1.1 mm) looks like a pufferfish; the head is large and the rear part of the body is adorned by a continuous, primordial fin. The second larval stage is the so-called "ostracioniform" phase; the body is shorter and exhibits large, hornlike projections, together with a rear fin which gradually changes to the clavus. Finally there is a postlarval stage, corresponding to what was once assumed to be a genus called *Molacanthus*; it is still known by this name. The animal measures up to 2 in (1.5 cm); its body is shortened, high and very compressed, the rear part being atrophied and the skin covered with tiny bony plates, unequal in size and spaced apart, each bearing a short, conical spine. From the postlarval stage, it gradually takes on the adult appearance.

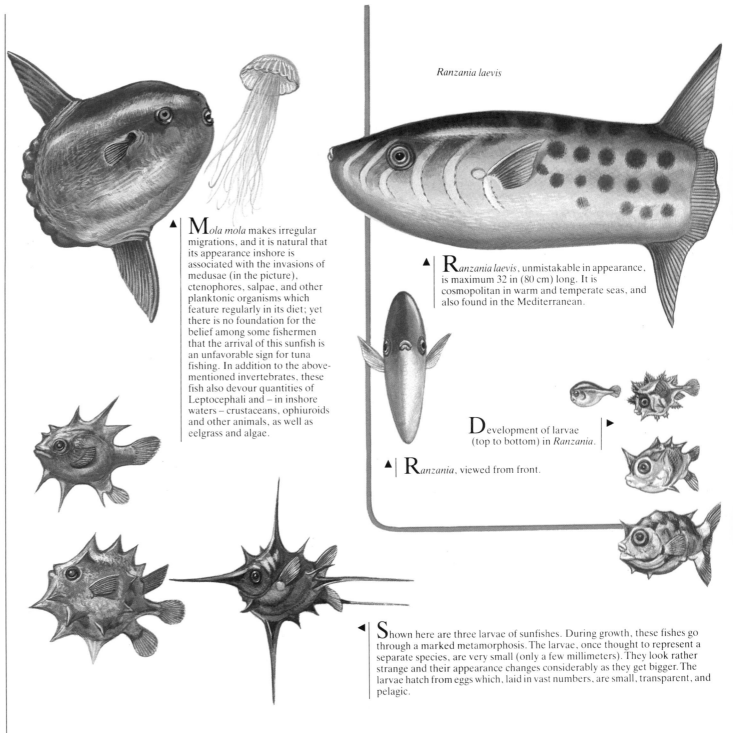

Ranzania laevis

▲ **M**ola mola makes irregular migrations, and it is natural that its appearance inshore is associated with the invasions of medusae (in the picture), ctenophores, salpae, and other planktonic organisms which feature regularly in its diet; yet there is no foundation for the belief among some fishermen that the arrival of this sunfish is an unfavorable sign for tuna fishing. In addition to the above-mentioned invertebrates, these fish also devour quantities of Leptocephali and – in inshore waters – crustaceans, ophiuroids and other animals, as well as eelgrass and algae.

▲ **R**anzania laevis, unmistakable in appearance, is maximum 32 in (80 cm) long. It is cosmopolitan in warm and temperate seas, and also found in the Mediterranean.

Development of larvae (top to bottom) in *Ranzania*. ▶

▲ **R**anzania, viewed from front.

◀ **S**hown here are three larvae of sunfishes. During growth, these fishes go through a marked metamorphosis. The larvae, once thought to represent a separate species, are very small (only a few millimeters). They look rather strange and their appearance changes considerably as they get bigger. The larvae hatch from eggs which, laid in vast numbers, are small, transparent, and pelagic.

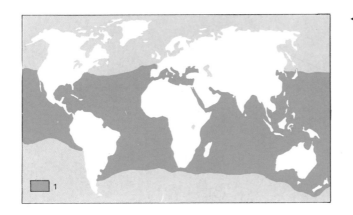

◀ **I**n giving *Mola* its first scientific name, Linnaeus mentioned it as inhabiting the Mediterranean, understandable because this fish is rare in the seas of northern Europe; occasionally it appears in the Skagerrak, off the coasts of Norway, and near Iceland. It can, however, be regarded as common in the Mediterranean. The catch consists mainly of young individuals, which are more gregarious, and often gather in large numbers inshore; but sometimes adults of considerable size are caught, which is a noteworthy occurrence. It is an indolent animal which is in the habit of staying immobile both on the surface, sometimes with its dorsal fin sticking out of the water, and deeper down near the bottom, where underwater divers are likely to see it suspended head downward. *Mola* is regarded as a surface fish but descends to a depth of at least 1,000 ft (300 m). 1) Distribution of the genus *Mola*.

CROSSOPTERYGII

During the very remote Devonian period of the Paleozoic era, the lands and seas of our globe were distributed in a very different manner from today. No less diverse were the fishes. Crossopterygii are among the fishes most accurately studied by paleontologists, who also assign to the same group numerous species found in more recent geological strata, namely Mesozoic. For a long time it was thought that the end of the Mesozoic era also signaled the end of this group of fishes. But in 1939 it was reported that a strange fish had been caught in the sea off South Africa, and that it was certainly a crossopterygian.

In December 1938 a fishing vessel off the shores of South Africa, near the mouth of the Chalumna River around East London, caught a fish which, by reason of its unusual appearance, was dispatched to that city's museum. The museum director, Latimer, was immediately aware of its importance, and sought the advice of the ichthyologist J.L.B. Smith; the latter realised that this was a novelty, and named the animal *Latimeria chalumnae*, publishing a description in 1939.

Latimeria chalumnae or the coelacanth is a massive fish of unmistakable appearance and is truly unique, among living species. The length may be up to 6 ft (1.8 m) and the weight up to 175 lb (80 kg). Females are bigger than males. While the rest of the body exhibits a normal fishlike outline, the characteristic tail immediately commands attention; the caudal fin does not appear to be preceded by a peduncle.

The color is gray-blue, varying in brightness, with irregular scattered spots on the flanks; they are lighter than the remaining body tint or even white.

The maximum height of the body is slightly less than the length of the head, which is just under one-third of the whole body length. The mouth is relatively large. There are neither premaxillary nor maxillary bones (the former being replaced by a few small dentary plates) but there is a series of strong, sharp, conical teeth; smaller teeth are present in the vomer and palate. There are also some larger front teeth, and some more smaller teeth, in the lower jaw. There are two nasal

Latimeria chalumnae is one of the most interesting fish in existence, being the sole representative to survive of the order Coelacanthiformes, belonging to the Crossopterygii. It was discovered off the coast of South Africa at the end of 1938, near East London. A series of studies showed that its structure is very different from that of other fish. Its length is up to 6 ft (1.80 m) and its weight 175 pounds (80 kg). Females are slightly bigger than males.

openings, both external, for *Latimera* lacks coanae.

The two dorsal fins are well separated, the front one being the larger, comprising eight strong rays which bear many short spines on their surface; the rear fin is propped by a short, fleshy lobe and has softer rays. The anal fin is similar to the second dorsal, to which it is opposed. The other fins are of greater interest because it is they that provide the fish with its strange appearance.

The caudal fin displays the typical structure of Coelacanthiformes, namely the division into three parts which make the whole fin very large. The upper and lower parts, similar and opposed to each other, are the biggest; to the rear they are in contact with the median lobe, which is the portion of the fin which has a rounded edge and is supported by a prominent fleshy lobe. The latter is connected to a raised linear zone running along the back and central parts of either flank; the backbone terminates horizontally inside this lobe. At first sight the small median portion of the tail appears to represent the whole fin, although it actually forms the terminal section.

The paired fins consist mainly of a fleshy part, namely a lobe which stems from the body surface and is covered with scales that are much smaller than those of the flanks; inside it is supported by a series of cartilaginous processes. The rays are arranged inside the lobe, except for the basal part. The large pectorals are inserted low down, immediately behind the lower section of the gill aperture. The ventrals are rather smaller and their base is situated almost at the level of the tip of the pectorals. Between the two bases is the cloacal opening.

The first dorsal fin with its spinous rays, the perfectly symmetrical, three-sectioned tail, and the other pedunculate fins combine to give the fish its particular physiognomy, very different from that of better known fishes.

As far as is known today, *Latimeria* is restricted to a limited area of the Indian Ocean, close to the Comoro group of islands; but it may appear occasionally outside this zone, as its original discovery in South Africa showed. Individuals have been caught mainly between 230 and 1,000 ft (70 and 300 m), but the fish has also been caught at greater depths, up to 2,000 ft (600 m). It lives a solitary existence, where the bottom is rocky, and shuns the light.

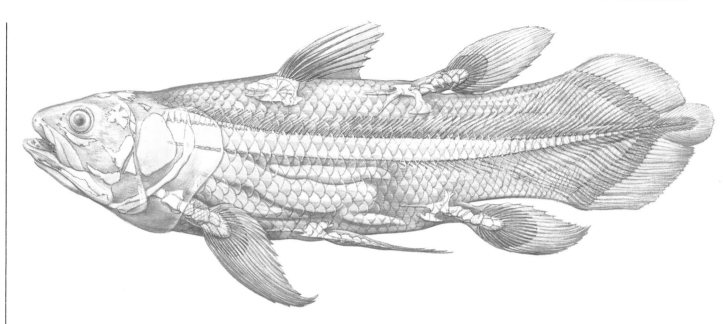

▼ Structure of the pectoral fin and its skeletal support in *Latimeria chalumnae*.

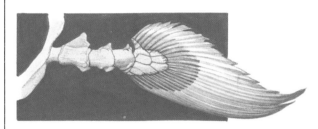

▲ The anatomical study of *Latimeria* has revealed a series of characteristics which are not only unique among present-day fish but also enable scientists to get a better understanding of fossil forms. The skeleton is largly cartilaginous and thus shows a measure of regression compared with the coelacanthus that once lived and had more bones in their skeleton. As in all crossopterygians, the skull is divided into two parts, front and back; they are not very mobile in relation to each other, either horizontally or vertically, and they articulate by means of special muscles. The snout region is short. There are five gill arches, the last being very small. The spine is similar to a large tube with consistent, fibrous and elastic walls; it is full of liquid and is unrestricted. There is, in fact, no trace of vertebral centers, but there is a series of cartilaginous neural arches with associated neurospines. There are no ribs. The encephalus is very small (in a specimen of 90 pounds or 40 kg it weighs less than 3 g!) and occupies only a small rear portion of the cranial cavity, the rest of which is filled with fat. The hypophysis is long and arranged horizontally; its glandular section contains a cavity which continues and has its outlet in the roof of the mouth. As regards the sensory organs, there is little of special mention concerning the eyes or nostrils, except to note that the latter are not accompanied by coanae, internal processes which are found in many crossopterygians but not coelacanths. The stomach is large and the intestine terminates in a cloaca, the outlet of which is situated betwen the ventral fins. *Latimeria*, like sharks and related fish, has a spiral valve in the intestine and a fair quantity of urea in the blood. The swim-bladder is degenerate, appearing as a large mass of fat contained in the visceral cavity. The reproductive apparatus is assymetrical, especially in the female, where there is virtually only the right ovary present; also the right testicle of the male is much larger than the other. Reproduction is ovoviviparous. A large female may carry 20 eggs with a diameter of 3½ in (9 cm). Gestation lasts about 13 months and births occur usually in February. Because the length of the embryos at birth is some 13 in (32 cm) the newborn individuals may be quite large.

◀ Shown here are some of the very ancient vertebrates representing various stages in the long evolutionary history of this large zoological group. Top to bottom: a primitive shark, a coelacanthiform, *Ichthyostega*, *Eryops*. The last two are amphibians.

LUNGFISHES
Dipnoi

These fishes commonly known as lungfishes, are capable of breathing atmospheric oxygen, in addition to the oxygen dissolved in the water. All the Dipnoi live in the water.

The six living species, all of which live in fresh water, are divided into two distinct families, Ceratodidae and Lepidosirenidae. The former contains the genus *Ceratodus*, with one Australian species, the latter the genus *Protopterus*, with four African species, and *Lepidosiren*, with one South American species.

Lungfishes have a somewhat elongated body, sometimes markedly eel-like, covered with soft, cycloid scales. The skeleton is largely cartilaginous. Instead of teeth, the jaws have two large upper plates for chewing, and two lower plates with crests. All the unpaired fins are linked, so as to form a single, continuous flap surrounding the body, from back to abdomen.

The paired fins are more unusual in structure. The fundamental support is given by a series of small skeletal pieces stretching all along the central axis to the tip. On both sides thin rays are arranged like barbs of a feather; they are very short and sometimes absent.

The most significant characteristic is the capacity to breathe air through a ventral lung. This is a large sac situated in the ventral region, as long as the visceral cavity, with its outlet at the beginning of the esophagus. The walls are alveolar and richly furnished with blood vessels. When a lungfish is submerged, both the lung and gills function; when the fish is on land, only the lung is used for breathing.

The Australian species *Neoceratodus forsteri*, differs from all the others by having an undivided pulmonary sac from which one vein takes blood to the heart. It lives permanently submerged, breathing air as well as water, but not exclusively the former. The color is silvery gray and the length is up to 6 ft (1.8 m). This fish is found in some Queensland rivers, moving slowly and keeping close to the bottom. It swallows a quantity of aquatic grasses, but mainly to extract the tiny animals on which it feeds. Spawning occurs in August and September. The embryonic development takes 10 days; there are no larval phases.

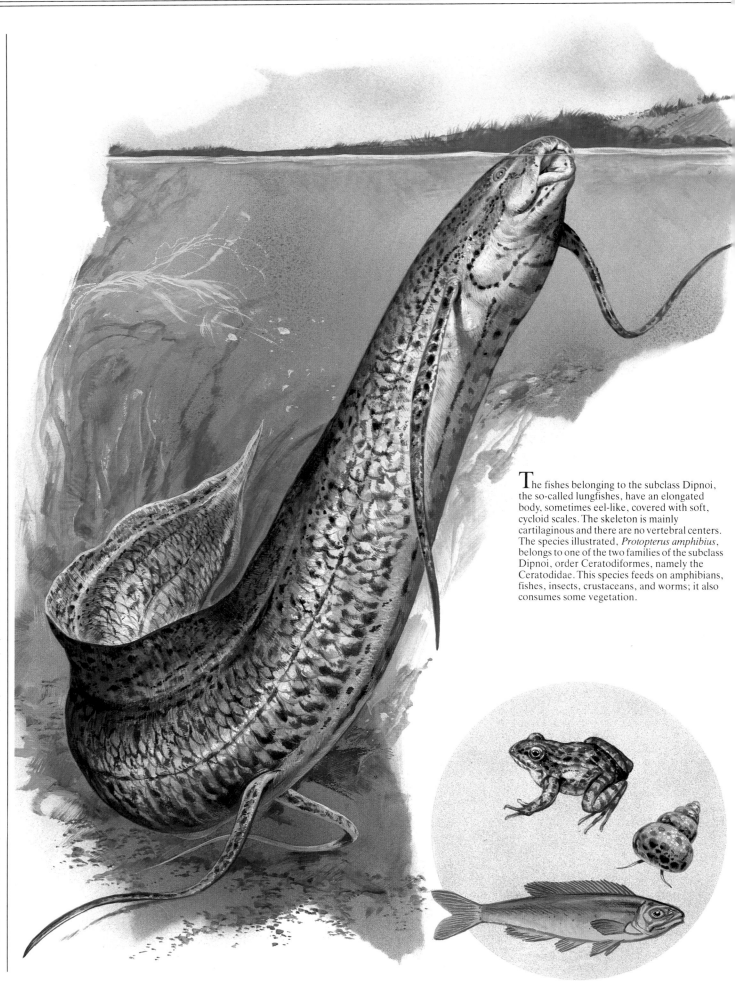

The fishes belonging to the subclass Dipnoi, the so-called lungfishes, have an elongated body, sometimes eel-like, covered with soft, cycloid scales. The skeleton is mainly cartilaginous and there are no vertebral centers. The species illustrated, *Protopterus amphibius*, belongs to one of the two families of the subclass Dipnoi, order Ceratodiformes, namely the Ceratodidae. This species feeds on amphibians, fishes, insects, crustaceans, and worms; it also consumes some vegetation.

The other Dipnoi (family Lepidosirenidae) have a very long body covered with small scales that are more or less hidden in the skin; the paired fins are soft. The lung is virtually divided in two, being formed of two parallel sacs that taper toward the rear. All species spend part of the year in water, but during the other months are found on dry land, where they hibernate, in the ground, breathing only atmospheric oxygen. The two genera are *Protopterus* and *Lepidosiren*.

The *Protopterus* species are among the most interesting African fishes, being widely distributed in equatorial regions. They live in swamps, in areas that are periodically flooded, and in lakes. The paired fins consist of one fundamental fleshy part, long and narrow, and a flap behind which contains thin rays. The bones are sometimes green.

These fish inhabit African waters from inland to coastal zones, where the eastern limits are from Somalia to Mozambique (Zambezi basin) and the western from Senegal (Gambia basin) to Zaire (Congo basin).

The same family contains the American lungfish *Lepidosiren paradoxa*. It differs from the *Protopterus* species by having a slender, elongated, serpentiform body, paired fins that are more threadlike and totally lack rays, and with no rudimentary gills in the adults. The color is yellowish-gray with black spots, and the length is up to about 3 ft (1 m). This lungfish lives in swamps with plenty of vegetation, and its range includes a large part of South America. Food consists mainly of aquatic gastropods, but also algae, especially during the juvenile phase. This fish, like the *Protopterus* species, hibernates throughout the dry season, hidden in a tubular hole which it digs in the mud. The entrance is sealed by a plug of mud with a few holes. The animal is wrapped round itself, head upward.

Soon after it wakes spawning begins. The eggs are laid in a nest consisting of a hollow measuring up to 1¾ ft (1.5 m) in diameter. The males watch over the eggs and newly hatched larvae, oxygenating the water by means of a number of cutaneous filaments that form temporarily on the ventral fins, and from which escape bubbles of gas.

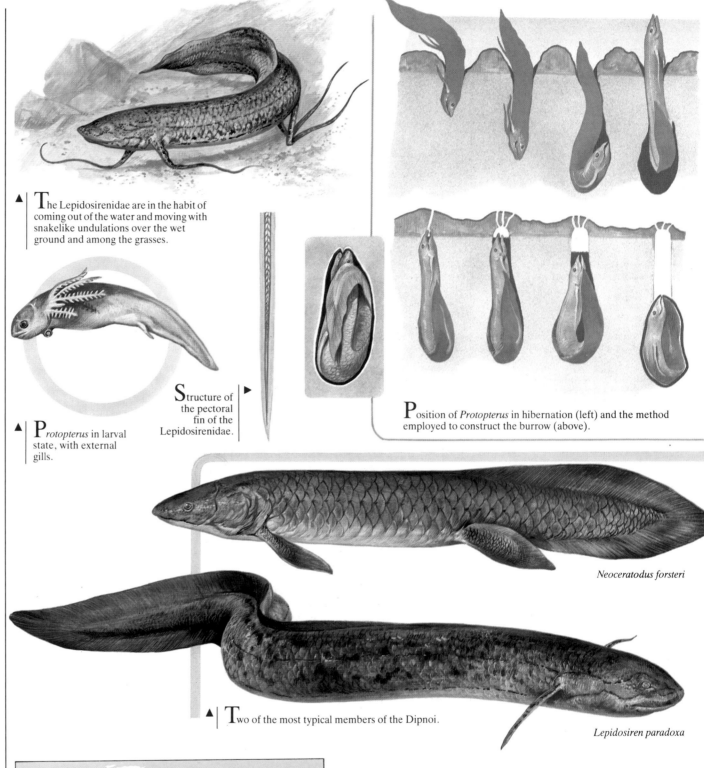

▲ The Lepidosirenidae are in the habit of coming out of the water and moving with snakelike undulations over the wet ground and among the grasses.

▲ *Protopterus* in larval state, with external gills.

▶ Structure of the pectoral fin of the Lepidosirenidae.

Position of *Protopterus* in hibernation (left) and the method employed to construct the burrow (above).

Neoceratodus forsteri

▲ Two of the most typical members of the Dipnoi.

Lepidosiren paradoxa

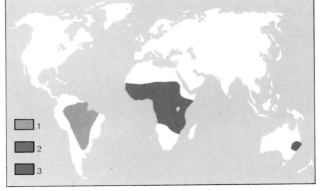

◀ The Dipnoi live in waters where oxygen may be very scarce, compelling the animal to rise frequently to the surface, where it inhales and exhales through the mouth. One of the most interesting features of lungfish biology is their periodic hibernation. When water is scarce, with the arrival of the dry season, they build a burrow in the muddy bottom and stay there, folded up. The snout is turned upward, toward the opening, so that regular breathing can take place through the lungs alone. The walls of the cavity are covered with hardened mucus, secreted by the animal's cutaneous glands. The fat accumulated around the kidneys and gonads serve as food, and to this end some of the muscles show fatty degeneration. 1) *Lepidosiren*; 2) *Protopterus*; 3) *Neoceratodus*.

JAPANESE GIANT SALAMANDER

Megalobatrachus japonicus

Order Urodela
Family Cryptobranchidae
Size Length 4¾ ft (1.44 m) max.
Weight Over 50 lb (23 kg) max.
Reproductive period Once a year, from the end of August to September
Number of eggs laid 800 – 1,000
Larval period About 3 years
Sexual maturity 5 – 6 years
Maximum age About 80 years

Japanese giant salamanders are large, grotesque amphibians who spend their entire lives in the mountain streams of western Japan. They have a large head, are quite flat dorso-ventrally, and are round at the snout. The outer nostrils are small, opening at the end of the snout, just above the upper lip. The eyes are extremely small, lacking eyelids. The mouth is large, extending far backward; the mouth cavity is furnished with many denticles on both the upper and lower jaws. The limbs are short, thick and flat. The forelimbs have four digits, the hindlimbs five toes. The tail is much shorter than the trunk and its hind half becomes laterally flat, thus presenting a finlike appearance. The back is dark fuscous, scattered with dark spots, small or large. The belly is more faintly colored.

The habitats of the giant salamander are situated between 1,000 – 3,300 ft (300 – 1,000 m) in altitude, existing in rivers 100 ft (30 m) wide down to small streams about 3 ft (1 m) in width.

The animals are rarely to be seen during the day time except during rainfall. They remain hidden in their nests during the day and at night they come out and wander on the riverbed in search of food. The nests are mostly made in holes in the soil of the banks or in hollows under bare rocks. Some nests have only one water inlet/outlet, others two. The surrounding area is tree-covered, their branches and other plants hanging over the water surface; a network of small roots hang down into the nests. The entrance is narrow, usually 4 in (10 cm) in diameter and the nest itself consists of a passage and a living space; the former 6 – 10 ft (2 – 3 m) long, from the stream to the latter. The living space measures about

Japanese giant salamander
(*Megalobatrachus japonicus*)

Japanese giant salamanders, closely resembling the European giant salamander of the Tertiary period, are world-famous as "living fossils." They spend their whole lives in the water. Usually living in clean mountain streams, they are sometimes seen in urban ditches after a flood. They can live for some 80 years.

3 ft (1 m) in diameter, the center or one side being deeper than the rest. The entrance is so made that running water rushes into it together with animals which might serve as their food. If the nest has two openings, one for the incoming water and the other for outgoing water, the salamanders themselves usually come in and go out of the nest through the latter.

The Japanese giant salamander leads a solitary life and is rarely found in groups of two or three. From late fall to winter they spend their time deep in their nests. In spring and summer, although they dwell in their nests and find food there, they do not necessarily settle in one nest, often moving to another after wandering along the riverbed. The animals do not like to be exposed to the light and have a tendency to hide in shade.

Sensing the food is done with the aid of tactile and smelling senses. Food approaching the mouth is drawn into it at lightning speed. Examination of stomach contents reveals that a kind of small crab (*Potamon dehaani*) constitutes 80 per cent, the rest consisting of small fish, frogs, insects, snails, and earthworms. They eat not only living animals but also dead frogs and fish.

Japanese giant salamanders are voracious omnivores, even preying on each other, the larger individuals swallowing the smaller ones and wounding those of similar size by biting on the limbs or tail. Having once bitten a victim, they will not let go easily. If necessary they can endure starvation and do without food for several months.

The eggs of Japanese gaint salamanders are about ⅕ in (5 mm) in diameter. Each female lays about 800–1,000 eggs in two gelatinous strings. She leaves the cave when the egg-laying is over, while the male remains there to guard the eggs. The male's movements cause the eggs to tangle into a ball-like mass. He remains with the egg-mass, protecting it from such enemies as newts, and ensuring that a constant flow of fresh water passes over the eggs. The eggs hatch after some 50 days. The larvae immediately after incubation are 1 in (2.5 cm) in length; they undergo metamorphosis when they are about 8 in (20 cm) long, 3 years after hatching, and reach maturity when they are 5 or 6 years old and about 22 in (55 cm) in length.

◀ Giant salamanders stay quietly in their nests in the banks of clean streams during the day. At night they go out wandering on the river bed. They will bite anything that approaches the mouth.

A Japanese giant salamander swallowing a frog. ▶

Chinese giant salamander (*Megalobatrachus davidianus*)

▲ The egg-mass is in the form of beads connected by gelatinous matter. They hatch after about 50 days. The larvae await metamorphosis, breathing through external gills.

Alligator salamander (*Cryptobranchus alleganiensis*)

◀ The area of distribution of the family Crytobranchidae includes isolated areas in the United States and eastern Asia.

AMPHIUMIDAE, PROTEIDAE, AND SIRENIDAE

The Amphiumidae have a long, cylindrical body like that of an eel. Their limbs are extremely small and rudimentary, the feet slender, with reduced digits. Their snout is pointed, their eyes minute, with no eyelids, and they have no tongue, but they possess lungs, reaching the adult stage by way of an incomplete metamorphosis. The adults have no external gills.

There is only one genus in the family *Amphiuma*, with three fairly similar species 12 – 40 in (30 – 100 cm) long. These eel-like creatures, which retain certain larval features even as adults, are colored brown or gray on the back, fading on the flanks and belly. They are endemic to the southeastern United States, and live in marshes and in bogs.

Reproduction takes place from January to May. The 350 eggs are laid in holes or under tree-stumps where the female watches over them continually. The larvae emerge after 5 months, they are 1½ – 2¼ in (4 – 6 cm) long and already have limbs and gills.

The family Proteidae have an elongated body, no eyelids small limbs, external gills and lungs. The family comprises two genera, *Proteus* and *Necturus*, distinguished mainly by the eyes, atrophied and hidden under the skin in *Proteus* and well developed, although still beneath the skin, in *Necturus*.

There is only one species of the genus *Proteus*; whereas the genus *Necturus* has 3 – 5 species. The adult proteus or olm (*Proteus anguinus*) has a body like an eel's, rudimentary eyes hidden under the skin, three digits on the forefeet and two on the hind; gills are still present. It is generally whitish in color and 8 – 12 in (20 – 30 cm) long.

As a rule the proteus is oviparous. Two or three days before laying her eggs the female chooses an area 6 – 12 in (15 – 30 cm) across the inside wall of a vertical rock and there, in the course of 3 – 4 weeks, lays 10 – 70 white, spherical eggs, with a diameter of about 0.2 in (4 – 5 mm). Both male and female exercise protective care over the eggs. The larvae emerge after 13 – 20 weeks.

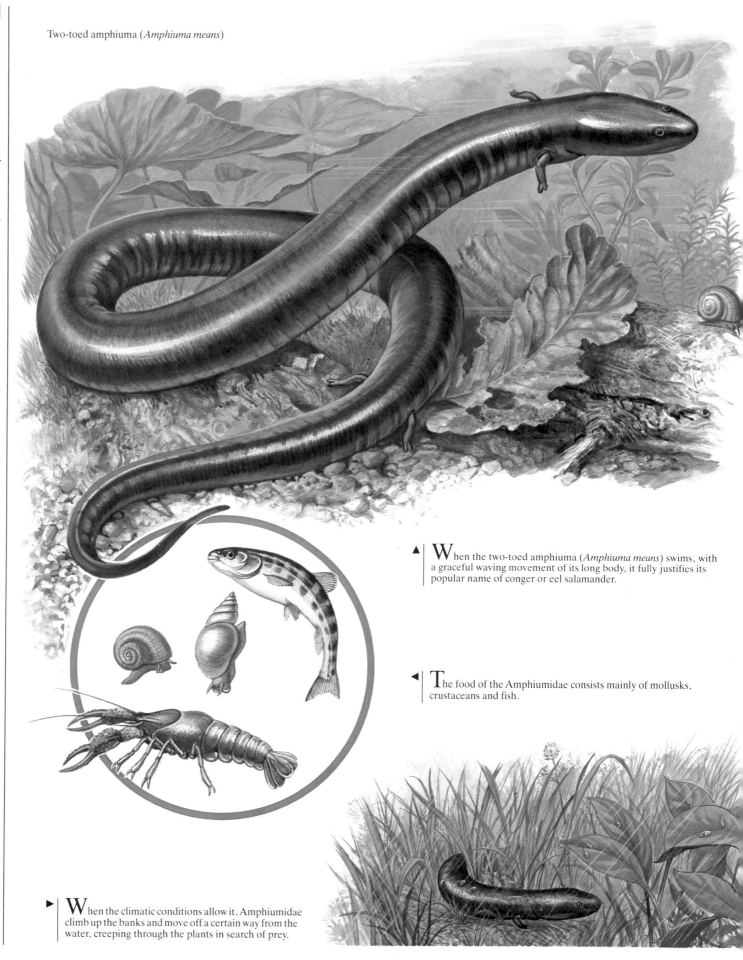

Two-toed amphiuma (*Amphiuma means*)

▲ When the two-toed amphiuma (*Amphiuma means*) swims, with a graceful waving movement of its long body, it fully justifies its popular name of conger or eel salamander.

◄ The food of the Amphiumidae consists mainly of mollusks, crustaceans and fish.

► When the climatic conditions allow it, Amphiumidae climb up the banks and move off a certain way from the water, creeping through the plants in search of prey.

The best-known species of *Necturus* is the mudpuppy (*Necturus maculosus*). The members of the genus grow to a maximum length of 12 – 17 in (30 – 43 cm). The snout is squared off and wedge-shaped, and the long, flat body has one spinal groove and 15 pairs of costal grooves: the tail is compressed and laterally flattened toward the tip. The four limbs are short and thick and each has four digits. The mudpuppy spends almost the whole day hidden in vegetation at the bottom of its pool or in the mud, and only becomes active in the evening and at night. The sexes normally live separate lives, but in fall they get together for reproduction. Between May and June the female lays a number of eggs, pale yellow and about ¼ in (5 – 6 mm) across, among the stones, under pebbles, or at the base of tree trunks or submerged stumps, and carefully attach them to one another. The females watch over the eggs during the incubation period and sometimes even stay with the eggs for several days after the larvae have been hatched.

The Sirenidae are another family of caudate amphibians that retain some of their larval features in the adult state. They have a long, thin body and no hind legs, only forelimbs, which are very small and have 3 – 4 digits. Their eyes are minute, with no eyelids, and even in the adult state they have bunches of external gills. There are two genera in the family, *Siren* with two species and *pseudobranchus* with only one.

The greater siren or mud-eel (*Siren lacertina*), 28 – 40 in (70 – 100 cm) long, is the giant of the family. It is characterized by three pairs of branchial apertures, by tetradactyl limbs and by the fact that only the skin goes through a complete metamorphosis.

Sirens spend the day in water, in places where there are luxuriant underwater plants, but at night they come out on to the land, though they generally stay near the banks. The females lay up to 300 pale-colored eggs, which they attach to aquatic plants or submerged roots.

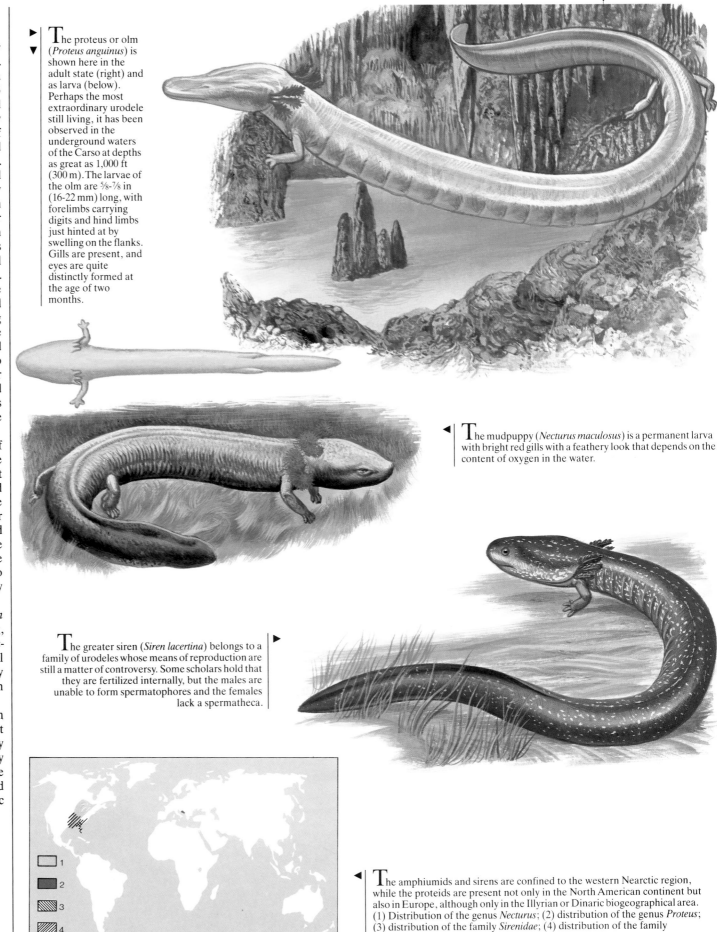

The proteus or olm (*Proteus anguinus*) is shown here in the adult state (right) and as larva (below). Perhaps the most extraordinary urodele still living, it has been observed in the underground waters of the Carso at depths as great as 1,000 ft (300 m). The larvae of the olm are ⅝-⅞ in (16-22 mm) long, with forelimbs carrying digits and hind limbs just hinted at by swelling on the flanks. Gills are present, and eyes are quite distinctly formed at the age of two months.

The mudpuppy (*Necturus maculosus*) is a permanent larva with bright red gills with a feathery look that depends on the content of oxygen in the water.

The greater siren (*Siren lacertina*) belongs to a family of urodeles whose means of reproduction are still a matter of controversy. Some scholars hold that they are fertilized internally, but the males are unable to form spermatophores and the females lack a spermatheca.

The amphiumids and sirens are confined to the western Nearctic region, while the proteids are present not only in the North American continent but also in Europe, although only in the Illyrian or Dinaric biogeographical area. (1) Distribution of the genus *Necturus*; (2) distribution of the genus *Proteus*; (3) distribution of the family *Sirenidae*; (4) distribution of the family *Amphiumidae*.

SALAMANDERS

Ambystomatidae

The best known of the various species of ambystomiols is the tiger salamander, *Ambystoma tigrinum*. This amphibian grows to a length of 8 – 13 in (19 – 33 cm) and is a urodele of robust habits, with highly variable coloration. The neotenic larvae are found in Lake Xochimilco, 12 miles (20 km) southeast of Mexico City.

Other members of the genus include the salt salamander (*A. subsalsum*), found only in the lake of Alchichica, near Orizaba (Puebla, Mexico); the mole salamander (*A. talpoideum*), from the southeastern United States: the opaque salamander (*A. opacum*), from the eastern United States; the Lake Superior salamander (*A. laterale*), long thought to be identical with Jefferson's salamander (*A. jeffersonianum*), which occurs in the central eastern United States from Pennsylvania and Virginia as far as Missouri and Alabama: the speckled salamander (*A. maculatum*) from southeast Canada and the eastern United States; the girdled salamander (*A. cingulatum*) from South Carolina, Florida, and Alabama; the graceful salamander (*A. gracile*), found from northern California to British Colombia; the Texas salamander (*A. texanum*), distributed in central and central southern United States; and the large-toed salamander (*A. macrodactylum*), which occurs in the Pacific coast States and as far east as Idaho and Montana.

The great Pacific salamander (*Dicamptodon ensatus*), is found in the rainforests of the western United States. The Olympic salamander (*Rhyacotriton olympicus*) is found only in the Pacific coastal areas of the United States, from the southern Olympic Mountains to Humboldt County (California) in the south.

The majority of these species usually live on land, hidden in underground refuges of various kinds; it is only during the mating season, winter and spring for the types that live at low altitudes, summer for the mountain types, that they temporarily take to the water. They may occasionaly venture into the open outside the spawning season, but only in rainy weather. This refers of course only to metamorphosed specimens; the larvae can be seen in water at practically any

Tiger salamander
(*Ambystoma tigrinum*)

The tiger salamander (*Ambystoma tigrinum*), seen above in the larval stage and below after metamorphosis, feeds mostly on the larvae of insects and anuran amphibians, and on earthworms. This urodele, on the basis of complex physiological relations in which the secretions by the pituitary and thyroid glands play a principal role, can either reach sexual maturity through metamorphosis or develop retaining the larval habits and characteristics unchanged (neoteny), according to the bioclimatic attributes of its habitat.

time of the year. Depending on the species and on the bioclimatic characteristics of their biotope, these larvae metamorphose after one year of life, after two years in mountain habitats or localities in the northern part of their area of distribution, or reach sexual maturity while still remaining in the larval stage, a phenomenon known as neoteny.

One of the species of this family that has been best studied, is the speckled salamander (*Ambystoma maculatum*). This species, which seems not to exceed a length of 9¼ in (23 cm), migrates by night from its hiding place to the water where it reproduces, and there in the course of a few days it mates and lays its eggs; as soon as spawning is complete, the females, always in a group, return to their hiding place by the same route over which they moved out.

Rain and cold drive the mole salamander (*A. talpoideum*) to migrate in large numbers, always at night, toward the sheets of water where they reproduce. When they get there both sexes spend the daytime hidden on the bottom of the pools, and it is not until darkness falls that, following one another round in circles, they start on the courtship ceremony. The eggs, up to 400 of them joined in bunches, are generally laid at night.

The opaque salamander (*A. opacum*) also mates and reproduces in the fall but lays its eggs on the bottom of dry ponds and puddles; the larvae emerge from the eggs as soon as they are covered by rainwater and the water level rises. The larvae already have gills, adhesive filaments and hind legs when they emerge from the eggs; in August – September, when they measure 1½ – 3 in (4 – 7.5 cm), metamorphosis begins, and they will be sexually receptive by the next spring.

Most members of the genus *Ambystoma* normally reach the adult stage through metamorphosis, with the exception of the tiger salamander, many populations of which are known of individuals that remain, and actually reproduce, in the larval stage, developing much more quickly than the "normal" individuals.

Like many other urodeles, the species of the genus *Ambystoma* adopt a characteristic defense posture when threatened or violently excited; the young of Jefferson's salamander, for instance, roll their tail on to their back.

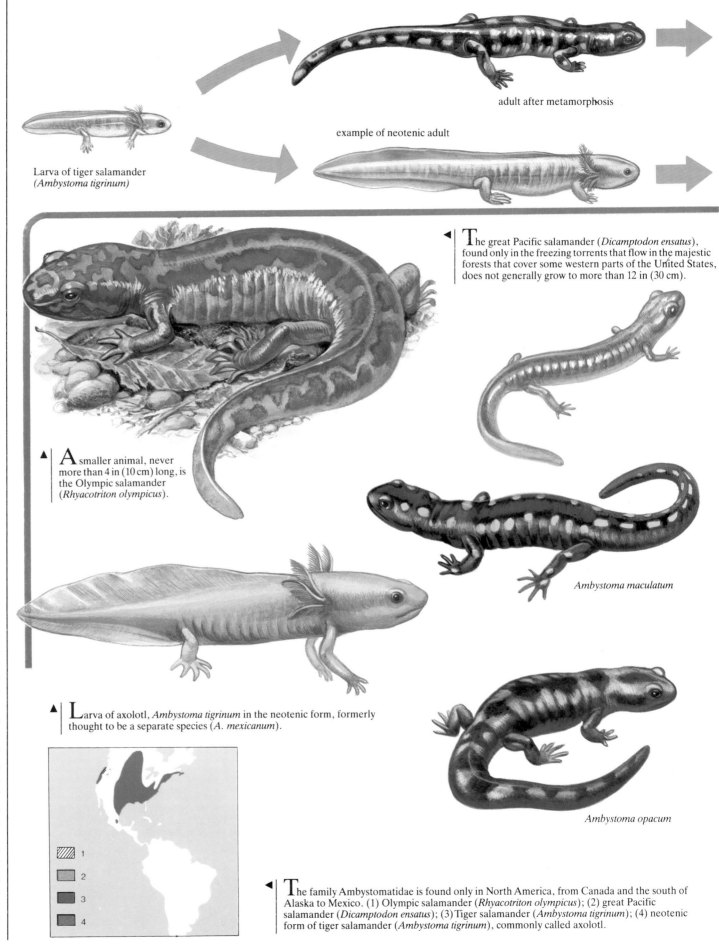

adult after metamorphosis

example of neotenic adult

Larva of tiger salamander (*Ambystoma tigrinum*)

◀ The great Pacific salamander (*Dicamptodon ensatus*), found only in the freezing torrents that flow in the majestic forests that cover some western parts of the United States, does not generally grow to more than 12 in (30 cm).

▲ ◀ A smaller animal, never more than 4 in (10 cm) long, is the Olympic salamander (*Rhyacotriton olympicus*).

Ambystoma maculatum

▲ ◀ Larva of axolotl, *Ambystoma tigrinum* in the neotenic form, formerly thought to be a separate species (*A. mexicanum*).

Ambystoma opacum

◀ The family Ambystomatidae is found only in North America, from Canada and the south of Alaska to Mexico. (1) Olympic salamander (*Rhyacotriton olympicus*); (2) great Pacific salamander (*Dicamptodon ensatus*); (3) Tiger salamander (*Ambystoma tigrinum*); (4) neotenic form of tiger salamander (*Ambystoma tigrinum*), commonly called axolotl.

LUNGLESS SALAMANDERS

Plethodontidae

The lungless salamanders of the family Plethodontidae, with about 23 genera and over 180 species, make up 60 per cent of all living urodeles. Measuring 1½ in (4 cm) to over 8 in (20 cm) long, most species have a slender body and tail; the limbs are little developed or greatly reduced, having four digits on the forelimbs and either four or five on the hind. Adult animals may rarely gills. The tongue is small, free and attached at the front. These urodeles generally have fairly bright basic colors with a very faint pattern.

The family is widely distributed in North America, also in South America as far as latitude 20°S and, to a lesser extent, in southern Europe – in the Maritime Alps, the northern and central Apennines, and central southern Sardinia. Some forms are essentially aquatic, others are terrestrial; some live in caves.

The Plethodontidae breathe through their skin and the mucous lining of their oral cavity. The species in the family which are ethologically most primitive live in water, retaining their gills, for the whole of their life (neotenic forms). The cave-dwelling species are so well accustomed to darkness that if they are kept in a lighted tank they need 4 – 5 weeks of acclimatization before they develop their normal activity.

The species of the genus *Plethodon*, mostly live in damp woods, where they pass the day under bark, moss, and branches, or in rotting trunks; they generally move about at night or in wet weather. On the upper side of their tails they have poison glands that can secrete a milky, sticky substance, giving them an effective means of defense against regular or casual predators. When alarmed or disturbed, the members of the genus *Plethodon* sometimes assume a typical threatening posture, stretching out their hindlegs with the toes straight and stiff and at the same time carrying their head in a horizontal position, arching their body downward and curving the tail upward, shaking it toward the attacker; in some cases they may shed their tail, leaving it in the attacker's mouth and taking advantage of its surprise to make their escape.

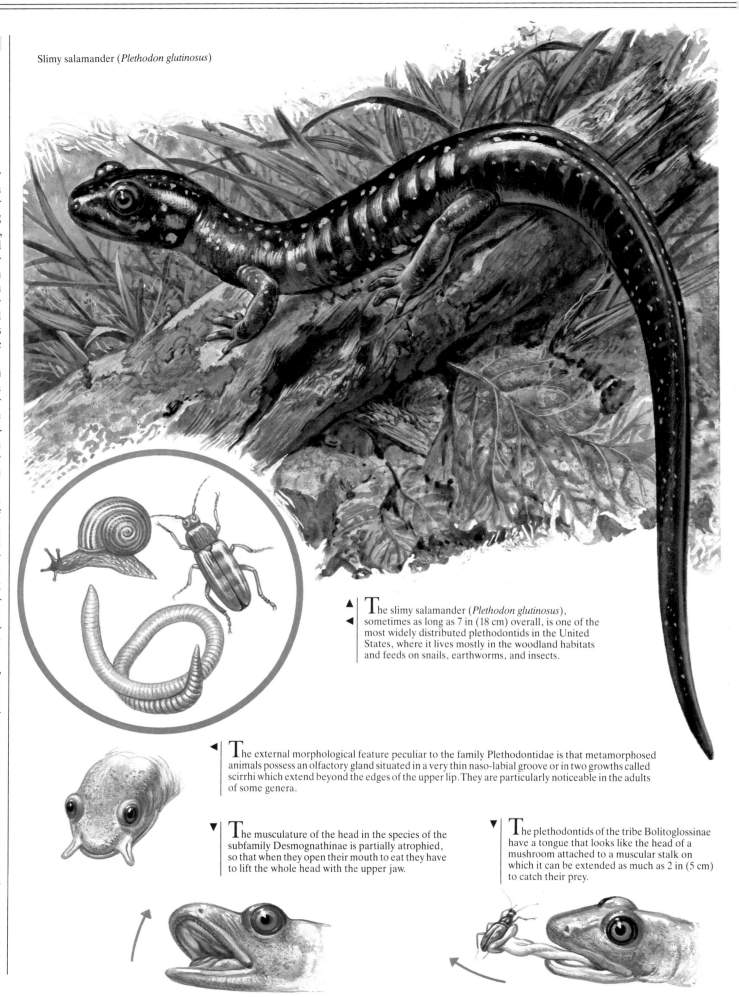

Slimy salamander (*Plethodon glutinosus*)

▲
◄ The slimy salamander (*Plethodon glutinosus*), sometimes as long as 7 in (18 cm) overall, is one of the most widely distributed plethodontids in the United States, where it lives mostly in the woodland habitats and feeds on snails, earthworms, and insects.

◄ The external morphological feature peculiar to the family Plethodontidae is that metamorphosed animals possess an olfactory gland situated in a very thin naso-labial groove or in two growths called scirrhi which extend beyond the edges of the upper lip. They are particularly noticeable in the adults of some genera.

▼ The musculature of the head in the species of the subfamily Desmognathinae is partially atrophied, so that when they open their mouth to eat they have to lift the whole head with the upper jaw.

▼ The plethodontids of the tribe Bolitoglossinae have a tongue that looks like the head of a mushroom attached to a muscular stalk on which it can be extended as much as 2 in (5 cm) to catch their prey.

The species of the genus *Aneides* generally live near watercourses, but are very good climbers and may climb trees 30 – 65 ft (10 – 20 m) or more in order to catch insects; these salamanders can also jump and can run quite fast. If threatened they assume a posture similar to the genera *Plethodon* and *Ensatina*, and squeak. They also defend themselves by biting.

From a biogeographical point of view the most interesting genus is *Hydromantes*, which has three species in California and a few others in Sardinia and continental Italy, in the Maritime Alps, and the northern and central Apennines. The members of the genus *Hydromantes* almost always live in caves, from which they emerge when it rains or when the atmospheric humidity is high. (As an exception, *Hydromantes italicus* and *H. genei* may sometimes be found in water.) They lay eggs to which the females devote great parental care; they are slow movers but can climb up rocks and walls with the aid of their prehensile tails.

The members of the species *Batrachoseps* are also primitive lungless salamanders, passing most of their life underground and active on the surface only during the rainy season. They are often gregarious, almost certainly not territorial, and seem never to venture more than 60 ft (20 m) from their regular refuges. If molested or frightened they squeeze together to form an almost spherical mass or a sort of spiral, emit uric acid from the cloaca and try to anchor themselves to any available support with their tails.

The courtship ceremony and coupling, based on scent and touch stimuli, are fairly similar in the species of different genera. Not more than 12 – 22 eggs are usually laid at a time, and the young emerge from them completely formed. The eggs are mostly laid in holes in the ground or in rotting tree-trunks and are almost always watched over by the female. If not given this parental care the brood often fails to develop; in some species, *Plethodon cinereus* for instance, the nest is actually defended. The young may be born after 1 – 12 months, depending on the species and the bioclimatic nature of their habitat, and become sexually mature at 2 years.

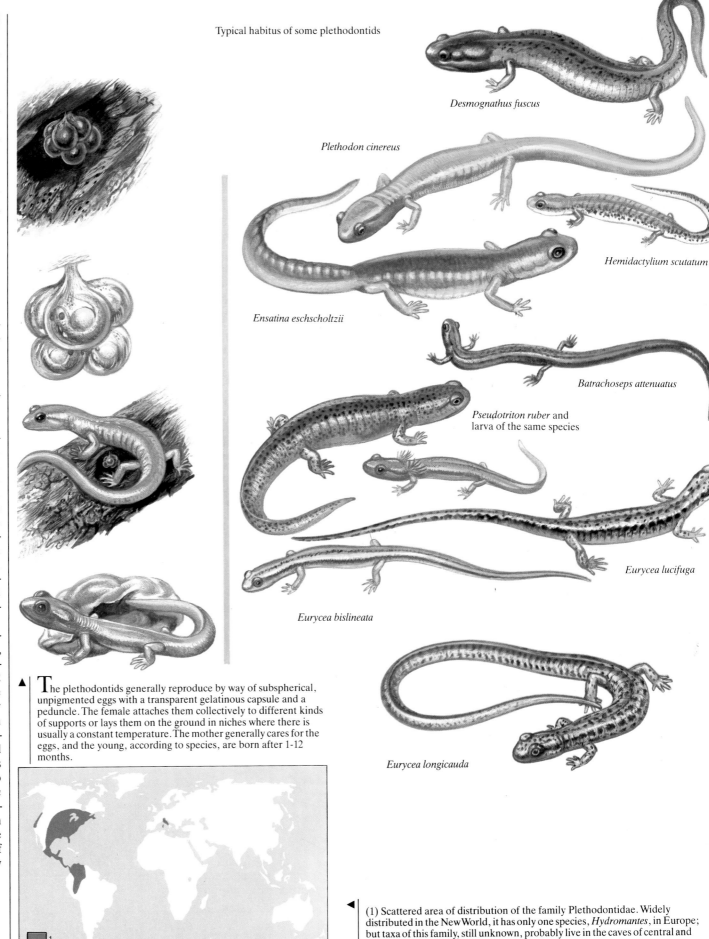

Typical habitus of some plethodontids

Desmognathus fuscus

Plethodon cinereus

Hemidactylium scutatum

Ensatina eschscholtzii

Batrachoseps attenuatus

Pseudotriton ruber and larva of the same species

Eurycea lucifuga

Eurycea bislineata

Eurycea longicauda

▲ The plethodontids generally reproduce by way of subspherical, unpigmented eggs with a transparent gelatinous capsule and a peduncle. The female attaches them collectively to different kinds of supports or lays them on the ground in niches where there is usually a constant temperature. The mother generally cares for the eggs, and the young, according to species, are born after 1-12 months.

◄ (1) Scattered area of distribution of the family Plethodontidae. Widely distributed in the New World, it has only one species, *Hydromantes*, in Europe; but taxa of this family, still unknown, probably live in the caves of central and eastern Asia.

ANURANS

Anura

The tailless amphibians or anurans, no less than the urodeles, are to a considerable extent dependent on water, but unlike them they have developed from a fishlike structure. Adult anurans have gone over to a hopping motion, and even when, like the toads, they have returned to walking, they no longer move with the serpentine motion of the urodeles.

As this development took place, the body of the anurans was much shortened and the tail was lost, so that any layman can immediately tell an anuran from a urodele. Only the juvenile forms of anurans have tails, which the larvae (tadpoles) use to help them swim like fish.

As might be expected from the build of the rest of their bodies, the limbs of anurans play a much more important part in their locomotion than do those of urodeles, and so have to be more powerful, especially the hindlegs, which are much longer than the forelegs. In some of the hopping species the total length of the hindlegs is actually greater than that of the head and body together.

All water lost from the body has to be replaced. Anurans do not drink; they have to go into water and absorb it through their skin.

Respiration takes place largely through the outer surface of the skin. Frogs' lungs, therefore have only as many lung vesicles as are necessary to carry out this exchange of gases. Frogs have no ribs, so they cannot breathe in and out and have literally to pump air into their lungs by the use of the suprahyoid muscles and let it out again after several strokes of the pump. When frogs are at rest it can be seen that only the throat pulsates; it is not until they become more active that for every two pulsations of the throat, there is one for the lungs. With breathing so little centralized, it is not necessary for large amounts of the respiratory gases to be carried by the blood from the lungs to the consuming tissues, nor indeed for a particularly efficient blood circulation system.

The intestine in the digestive apparatus of the adult anurans is relatively short, a typical feature in predatory animals. The tadpoles of the anurans, however, have a long intestine, typical of vegetarian animals.

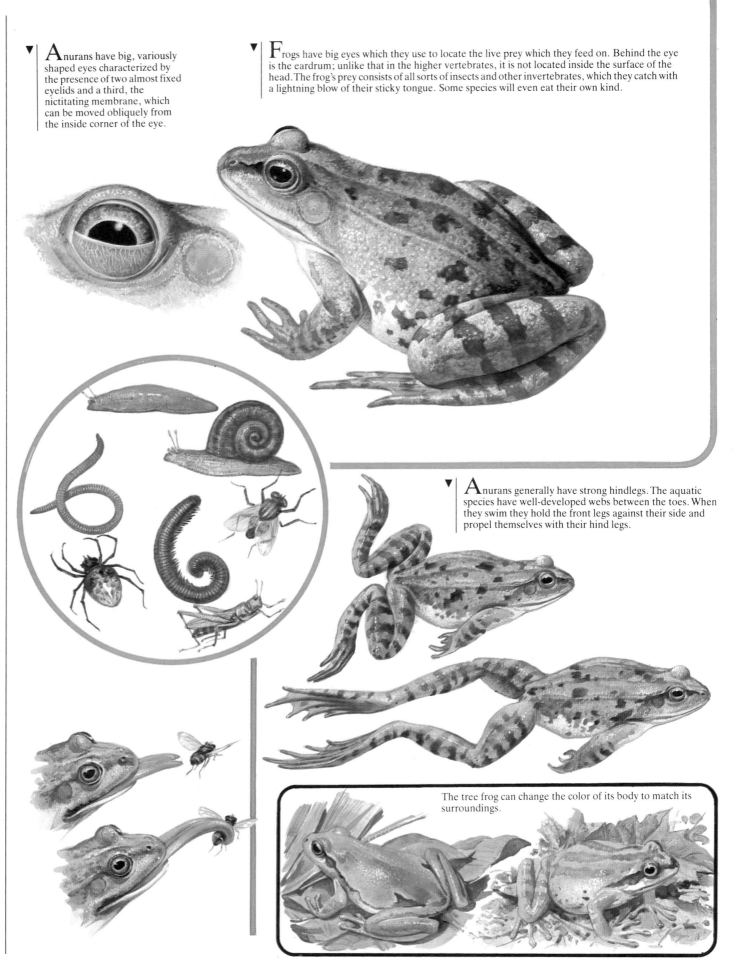

▼ Anurans have big, variously shaped eyes characterized by the presence of two almost fixed eyelids and a third, the nictitating membrane, which can be moved obliquely from the inside corner of the eye.

▼ Frogs have big eyes which they use to locate the live prey which they feed on. Behind the eye is the eardrum; unlike that in the higher vertebrates, it is not located inside the surface of the head. The frog's prey consists of all sorts of insects and other invertebrates, which they catch with a lightning blow of their sticky tongue. Some species will even eat their own kind.

▼ Anurans generally have strong hindlegs. The aquatic species have well-developed webs between the toes. When they swim they hold the front legs against their side and propel themselves with their hind legs.

The tree frog can change the color of its body to match its surroundings.

In most species of frog the tongue is attached at the front of the mouth and the free end is folded backward when at rest. When a frog sees a small insect or other little creature moving, the sticky tongue is flicked out like lightning, seizes the prey and then is drawn back just as quickly into the mouth. In seeking their prey anurans are guided mainly by sight, although they are also attracted by sound and scent.

The males of most species of frogs, and sometimes also the females, are able to make vocal sounds. The male's voice can attract other individuals of the same species to the spawning area, and other males may be induced to join in the chorus. The sound may also have some territorial significance: it makes sure that other individuals stay at a distance – a distance differing from one species to another. This is true also of females when they hear the call: they only go straight to the male if they are nearly ready to spawn.

When the male sees the female, he leaps on to her back and after a little time she begins to lay her eggs. Unlike urodeles' eggs, the eggs of anurans are fertilized externally, with the single exception of *Ascaphus*. The eggs are transparent, so that the division of the cells can be seen very clearly. The embryo generally emerges from the egg while it still has external gills, but these are soon absorbed in the branchial cavities and the larva takes on the typical form of the tadpole, with internal gills, a highly specialized mouth, and a spirally twisted intestine.

Frog tadpoles feed very differently from mature frogs. Either they have a gill-trap adapted to filter plankton, or – in the majority of cases – they have a highly specialized mouth structure with rows of little horny teeth and a horny beak, which they use to tear through algae and organic matter. They locate their food by touch, scent, and sight.

Within about a week a mature tadpole turns into a juvenile frog. Jaws, mouth, and intestines are completely restructured, the gills atrophy and the forelegs grow out through the gill chambers. Moreover, the former comprehensive and adaptable feeding habit of the tadpole gives way to a highly specialized predatory behavior.

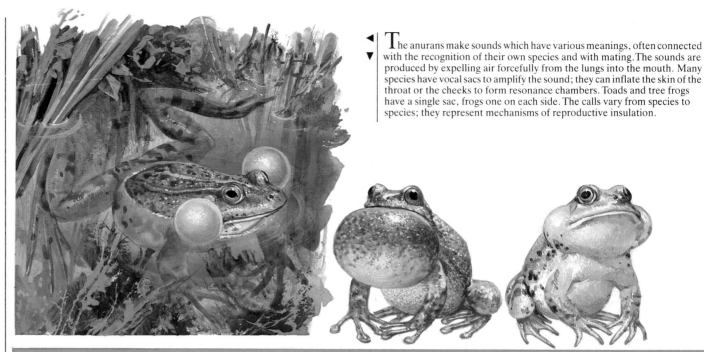

The anurans make sounds which have various meanings, often connected with the recognition of their own species and with mating. The sounds are produced by expelling air forcefully from the lungs into the mouth. Many species have vocal sacs to amplify the sound; they can inflate the skin of the throat or the cheeks to form resonance chambers. Toads and tree frogs have a single sac, frogs one on each side. The calls vary from species to species; they represent mechanisms of reproductive insulation.

While the female lays the eggs, the male grasps her firmly with its forelimbs and fertilizes them (external fertilization).

Phases of the frog's development. When the tadpoles emerge from the eggs they still have external gills and are stuck to the underwater plants. Only when the mouth has developed and the gills have retreated into the branchial cavities are they able to swim and feed freely.

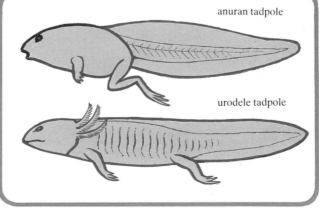

anuran tadpole

urodele tadpole

PIPIDAE, ASCAPHIDAE AND LEIOPELMATIDAE

The pipids (family Pipidae) are aquatic anurans whose tongue is completely attached to the floor of the mouth. Their larvae are very characteristic. During metamorphosis their forelegs may appear through the spiracles, greatly interfering with their breathing; in any case they acquire functional lungs very early – in the larvae of *Pipa carvalhoi* as soon as they emerge from the skin of their mother's back.

The honeycomb toads of the genus *Pipa* can be divided into two groups. Two large species lay very big eggs rich in yolk, from which the frogs emerge fully developed. The three smaller species lay eggs containing rather less yolk, and these, unlike those of their bigger relatives, sink completely into the female's skin. The larvae emerge from them as filter larvae, very much like the larvae of the genus *Xenopus* in appearance but without the stiff tentacles at the corners of the mouth.

The genus *Xenopus* lives in Africa south of the Sahara in almost every biotope, though preferably in water. If the water dries up, the savanna species either migrate overland to some other standing water nearby or dig into the mud or under some solid object and wait there for the next rain.

The family Ascaphidae contains only one genus with one species, *Ascaphus truei*, which lives in mountain streams in the Rockies. Both frogs and tadpoles live there. On account of the endless noise of the water as it flows and falls, *Ascaphus* is one of the few frogs whose voice plays no part in mating, and the species is almost dumb. The larva is remarkable for its overdeveloped suction apparatus and its extreme flatness.

In the family Leiopelmatidae there are only three surviving species of the genus *Leiopelma*. The eggs are laid in turf in the absence of standing water.

Ascaphus and *Leiopelma* have many features in common; they are the most primitive of all frogs and can be recognized by their peculiar vertebrae.

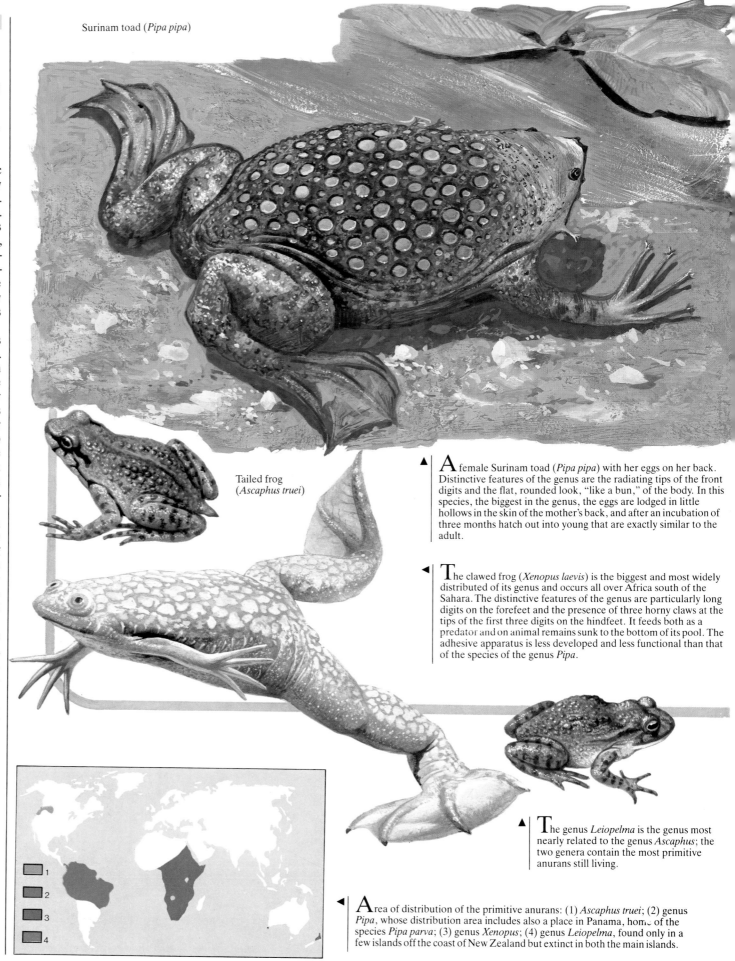

Surinam toad (*Pipa pipa*)

Tailed frog (*Ascaphus truei*)

▲ A female Surinam toad (*Pipa pipa*) with her eggs on her back. Distinctive features of the genus are the radiating tips of the front digits and the flat, rounded look, "like a bun," of the body. In this species, the biggest in the genus, the eggs are lodged in little hollows in the skin of the mother's back, and after an incubation of three months hatch out into young that are exactly similar to the adult.

◄ The clawed frog (*Xenopus laevis*) is the biggest and most widely distributed of its genus and occurs all over Africa south of the Sahara. The distinctive features of the genus are particularly long digits on the forefeet and the presence of three horny claws at the tips of the first three digits on the hindfeet. It feeds both as a predator and on animal remains sunk to the bottom of its pool. The adhesive apparatus is less developed and less functional than that of the species of the genus *Pipa*.

▲ The genus *Leiopelma* is the genus most nearly related to the genus *Ascaphus*; the two genera contain the most primitive anurans still living.

◄ Area of distribution of the primitive anurans: (1) *Ascaphus truei*; (2) genus *Pipa*, whose distribution area includes also a place in Panama, home of the species *Pipa parva*; (3) genus *Xenopus*; (4) genus *Leiopelma*, found only in a few islands off the coast of New Zealand but extinct in both the main islands.

RANID FROGS
Ranidae

The ranid frogs are one of the most numerous groups of anurans, both in the number of their species and also in the number of individuals. There are species living almost everywhere in Eurasia, Africa, and North and Central America.

Ranids have highly varied living habits, some species being entirely aquatic, others only entering the water for a short time to couple and passing the rest of their lives away from it. The main development of the family has taken place in Africa, where the most numerous forms live, but the center of origin certainly lies in southern Asia.

Species of the subfamily Astylosterninae live in the West African rainforest. One of this group is the hairy frog (*Astylosternus robustus*) with its long, thin filaments of skin on the flanks and thighs, well supplied with blood vessels. This is one of the forms that has sharp ends to the toes, and it can draw blood from the hand of anyone who tries to hold it. Its tadpoles are streamlined and swim well in flowing water: they have a powerful sucking apparatus at the mouth, though after metamorphosis they feed on land.

The genus *Rana* is distinguished by horizontal pupils, a tongue attached at the point of the lower jaw, free fingers on the forefeet, and webs, which may be large or small, between the toes of the hindfeet. Over 200 species of *Rana* are known; they live all over the world except for southern South America, central and southern Australia, New Zealand, and some of the Pacific islands, but they are not found in deserts or in regions of permanent ice. Almost all species can jump very well and live in very wet habitats, but many never leave the water, or the banks bordering it, and they always have to return to it when they lay their eggs. The central and southern European species are usually divided into two groups, the aquatic species, generally green in color, and the brown species that live in woods or fields and only return to the water to spawn. A representative of the brown frogs in North America is the wood frog, *Rana sylvatica*.

Some of the ranid frogs

Edible frog (*Rana esculenta*)

Wood frog (*Rana sylvatica*)

Swamp frog (*Rana arvalis*)

Meadow frog or leopard frog (*Rana pipiens*)

Hairy frog (*Astylosternus robustus*)

Rana hosii

American bullfrog (*Rana catesbeiana*)

Marsh frog (*Rana ridibunda*)

Rana erythraea

Goliath frog (*Conraua goliath*)

DENDROBATES SILVERSTONEI

Order Anura
Family Dendrobatidae
Size Length, female 1½ – 1¾ in (3.6 – 4.2 cm); male a little smaller
Number of eggs Up to 30
Larval period 2 months, including some days on the male's back
Sexual maturity 1 year (?)

Dendrobates silverstonei is a brilliantly colored frog living in the eastern part of the Peruvian Andes. It prefers altitudes between 4,200 and 6,000 ft (1,300 and 1,800 m) and is found more often at the edge of the forest than deep within it, spending most of its time on the floor of the forest and, unlike other members of the genus, hardly ever climbing trees. The animals sit on the ground in the open, catching small insects; they are quite ready to eat ants.

The eggs are laid in the shelter of fallen leaves and treetrunks. Typical of the Dendrobatidae is the male's habit of staying with the eggs: the tadpoles climb up and stay on the male's back. It is not known how they feed at this stage. Probably their ride on the male's back is simply a way of reaching water where they can continue to develop and grow until metamorphosis.

A related species, the mouth-breeding frog or Darwin's frog (*Rhinoderma darwini*) is small, about 1 in (2.6 cm) and rather slender, with a triangular head and an excrescence of skin on the tip of its snout that gives it a tip-tilted look. It lives in the rainforest of Chile and Argentina, mainly in the undergrowth near small watercourses.

In the warmer season the males of *Rhinoderma* congregate at certain places from which their piping can be heard, and this attracts the females. These lay their eggs on wet ground or on moss, then disappear again, and the males stay with the eggs. When the embryos have developed so far that they can be seen moving through the gelatinous envelopes of the eggs, they are snapped up by the waiting males. The eggs do not reach the stomach but remain in the father's – or stepfather's – vocal sac, where they continue to develop, feeding on scraps from inside of the vocal sac, until they metamorphose.

▲
◄ *Dendrobates silverstonei* is more adapted to life on the ground than others of the family. The male guards the eggs until the tadpoles are hatched, and the tadpoles then climb on to the male's back. After carrying them around for a few days the father puts them down in a pool to complete their development. The tadpoles are well protected on the male's backs by the presence of poisonous substances in the adult male's skin. The main function of this poisonous secretion is defense against microscopic organisms which might infest the damp skin and cause harm to the host.

► The mouth-breeding frog or Darwin's frog (*Rhinoderma darwini*) lives in the damp, somewhat cooler forests of southern South America. These males, too, mount guard over the eggs. As soon as the tadpoles begin to move inside the eggs the fathers suck them up into their vocal sacs and "bring them up" there until they are fully developed. The genus *Rhinoderma* used to be included in the family Dendrobatidae, and in fact is closely related to that family. Nowadays the genus is recognized as a family on its own, whose characteristics include the presence of a firmisternal shoulder girdle, the absence of palatine teeth and a tendency for the vertebrae to be fused.

MALAYAN FLYING FROG

Rhacophorus reinwardti

Order Anura
Family Rhacophoridae
Size Length , female up to 3 in (8 cm),
male a little smaller

This rhacophorid has a flat but rather broad head, big eyes with horizontal pupils, and a slender body with long hindlegs. There are big adhesive disks on the tips of the digits. What is particularly remarkable is the presence of membranes that fill almost the whole space between the fingers and the toes. There is another membrane on the outer side of the forearm and a small fold of skin from the heel to just above the anus. The coloring varies but is mostly green above and yellowish underneath. There are blue patches on the shoulders and on the membranes on the feet..

Rhacophorus reinwardti lives in the islands of Sumatra, Banka, and Java, in the trees and bamboo thickets of the wet warm forests.

It is rather an exaggeration to call this animal a flying frog, for it cannot fly in the true sense of the word, even if it does exhibit some rudimentary capacity in that field. The membranes on its feet and the flat shape of its body do enable it to glide, and it can change direction while gliding in order to move from one branch to another.

Rhacophorus reinwardti lays its eggs in a way that is common among rhacophorids. The male embraces the female around the shoulders and, as the female produces the eggs wrapped in a gelatinous slime, the male beats this slime into froth with its hindlegs. The eggs are laid on the leaves of plants that overhang the water. When coupling is finished the animals free themselves from the froth and leave it behind with the eggs contained in it. The froth forms a crust on the outside and turns brownish, thus protecting the embryos from being dried out. When tadpoles develop from the embryos, they emerge from the froth nest and fall into the water below them, where they can continue their development until metamorphosis.

◄
▼ The Malayan flying frog (*Rhacophorus reinwardti*) is a typical arboreal species, even more adapted to such a life than other species. Its fore– and hind legs not only enable it to climb, but also, thanks to the presence of extensible membranes, to glide from branch to branch. The rhacophorids resemble the Hylidae but also have some similarities to the true frogs (family Ranidae).

▲ Gliding flight is found not only in the rhacophorids (3) but also in other species in the animal kingdom, such as the flying dragon (*Draco volans*) (1), in which the aerial membranes are supported by the ribs. Some of the geckos (2) are also able to glide, for example the genus *Ptychozoon*.

◄ The family Rhacophoridae is distributed throughout Southeast Asia, in the Philippines, Japan, almost all of Africa, and in Madagascar. It includes aquatic and terrestrial forms, but the majority of the species seems to be adapted to an arboreal existence. (1) *Rhacophorus pardalis*; (2) *Rhacophorus reinwardti*; (3) *Rhacophorus nigropalmatus*; (4) *Rhacophorus schlegeli*.

TURTLES AND TORTOISES

Testudines (Chelonia)

The Chelonia – turtles, tortoises and terrapins – have their body enclosed in a shell which may take a number of different forms and from which their head and forelimbs emerge at the front and their tail and hindlimbs at the back. The shell is formed by the bones of the skeleton, but mostly by the flat, wide bones formed by ossification of the dermis, which are generally fused with the bones of the skeleton. The external surface of the shell is generally covered by horny laminae.

The shell of the chelonians is in two parts, one dorsal, the carapace, and one ventral, the plastron; these two parts may either be fused together, and thus fixed, or joined by elastic ligaments and so relatively movable. The carapace and plastron are covered with horny plates, generally side by side but occasionally overlapping.

Teeth are missing in both the upper and lower jaw; the jaws have sharp ridges and are enclosed in a horny beak. In turtles particularly, but also to some extent in certain tortoises, the head, neck, feet, and tail cannot be wholly or partly retracted. In most tortoises, however, the neck can be retracted, either by a movement in the vertical plane (which leaves the snout still turned to the front) or by turning in the horizontal plane, so that when the head is at rest, the snout is turned to right or left. The tongue is soft, fleshy and usually not protractile.

The respiratory system is particularly interesting. In land tortoises the lungs are filled and emptied by a piston-like movement of the neck and forelimbs helped by the hyoid system and the pharynx; in aquatic tortoises and in turtles, respiration takes place by means of two sacs at the sides of the cloaca.

The Chelonia reproduce by means of spherical or ellipsoidal eggs which the female lays, some species by day and some by night, in holes dug in sand or soft earth; the number of eggs varies with ecological characteristics of the species and in turtles may be more than a hundred. Incubation is generally left to the warmth of the surrounding earth.

Chelonians are probably the longest-lived of all vertebrates and may live over 200 years.

The green turtle, possibly the best known species, resembles other turtles in that it lives entirely in the sea but makes its nest on land. In the water its limbs, shaped like fins, enable it to swim fast and easily, but on land it moves very clumsily. This species feeds almost exclusively on algae, while other turtles are carnivorous, feeding mainly on crustaceans, coelenterates, cephalopods, mollusks, echinoderms and fish.

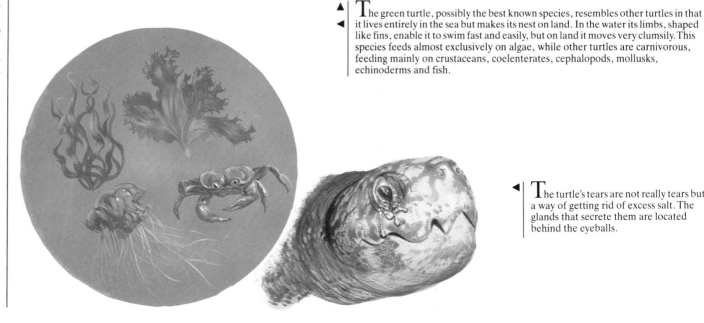

The turtle's tears are not really tears but a way of getting rid of excess salt. The glands that secrete them are located behind the eyeballs.

The best-known family of Chelonia are possibly the Testudinidae which have a convex greatly ossified shell and short, stout, columnar legs with the digits joined in a sort of stump, with only the claws protruding. The genus *Testudo*, the best known of the family and perhaps indeed of the whole order, contains about 30 species.

The common or Hermann's tortoise (*Testudo hermanni*) can be recognized at once; the tip of its tail is covered by a strong horny shield and generally it has two supercaudal shields. The length of this species is about 8 – 12 in (20 – 30 cm) and it weighs anything from 4½ to 10 lbs (2 to 4.5 kg).

Similar to this species is the Greek tortoise (*Testudo graeca*), which has no horny shield on its tail and only one supercaudal shield; it has a big conical nodule on each side of the tail and its carapace is yellowish or olive brown, with dark patches. *Testudo marginata* is larger – up to 14 in (35 cm) long – and heavier – up to 9 – 18 lb (4 – 8 kg). It has no horny shield on the tail and only one supercaudal shield. The carapace is elongated, and slightly flattened in the center. The carapace is olive or dark brown with yellowish areolae at the top of each shield; in old animals it becomes black, with the yellowish areolae very marked.

The family Testudinidae includes the majority of the species found in Africa south of the Sahara. The best known and most widespread species there is, is the leopard tortoise (*Testudo pardalis*), which may be up to 26 in (65 cm) long and lives mostly in the savannas and steppes. The semidesert regions of Central Africa are the home of *Testudo sulcata*, whose carapace has deep concentric incisions and may measure as much as 30 in (75 cm). A radial pattern made by lines starting symmetrically from the center of each plate in the shell is found on many southern African species and is particularly marked on *Testudo radiata*, a native of Madagascar.

Radial patterns are also found on several Testudinidae in southern Asia; best known is *Testudo elegans*, a mainly crepuscular species. In the wet forests of South America the genus *Testudo* is represented by species such as *T. carbonaria* and *T. denticulata*, which are up to 20 in (50 cm) long and active almost all day, while the arid regions of Argentina and Uruguay are the home of *T. chilensis*.

Successive phases of the nesting of turtles.

The female turtles use their hind paddles to dig holes about 16-30 in (40-75 cm) deep in the sand several feet above the highwater mark, and at intervals lay 60-200 eggs in them, each about as big as a mandarin. The young are born after 35-75 days, according to species, and immediately make for the sea.

As they try to reach the sea as quickly as possible, the young may be caught by different kinds of animals, both autochthonous and allochthonous.

The Galapagos tortoise (*T. elephantopus*), from the islands of the same name, is a giant form which may grow to a length of 44 in (110 cm). Today it is a protected species.

Other giant tortoises live in the Seychelles Islands. *T. gigantea* has a record length of 48 in (120 cm); this species once used to occur in many Indian Ocean islands, but has been wiped out there by human activities.

The genus *Testudo* does not occur in North America; its place is taken in the southern States and northern Mexico by the genus *Gopherus*. The most characteristic species is the desert tortoise (*Gopherus polyphemus*), a form up to 14 in (35 cm) long, with living habits remarkably like those of *Testudo horsfieldii*.

The tortoises of the genus *Kinixys*, found in central southern Africa, are better known as hinge tortoises; they have a sort of movable hinge on the rear of the carapace that enables them to lower the back of it.

Granite mountains and mountain pastures are the favorite habitat of the species of the genus *Homopus*, 4 – 8 in (10 – 20 cm) long, and confined to southern Africa.

The rocky slopes of central East Africa at altitudes above 3,000 ft (1,000 m) are the home of the soft-shelled tortoise (*Malacochersus tornieri*), a species up to 6 in (15 cm) long which has a carapace as flat as a table and only slightly ossified, so that it yields to the slightest pressure.

With some exceptions, the ecology of the Testudinidae is fairly uniform. For example, the daily activity cycle of Hermann's tortoise is mostly dependent on the temperature. In the warmest hours of the day it retires into the shade of the bushes, becoming active again halfway through the afternoon. Mating takes place between April and June. The male is territorial; he follows the female and when he reaches her bites her forefeet repeatedly, often drawing blood, and strikes her violently each time with his shell, to make her retract her head under her shell and move her feet so as to reveal her tail and cloaca. The male then climbs on to the back of the female's carapace. The female lays 2 – 12 ellipsoidal eggs with a white, chalky shell in holes which the animal digs at the base of some plant. This species lives on leaves, fruit, worms, excrement, etc.

▲
◄ The huge, extraordinary, archaic and strictly protected Galapagos tortoise (*Testudo elephantopus*), which is present in those islands in nine subspecies, carries out real migrations from the drier places to the xeric places and vice versa. It has become so specialized as a result of the habitat in which it lives that in the arid areas it lives almost entirely on cactus fruits.

MATAMATA
Chelys fimbriata

Order Testudines (Chelonia)
Family Chelidae
Size Length, 8 – 16 in (20 – 40 cm)
Weight About 1¼ – 3¼ lb
(600 – 1,500 g)
Nest Very probably on the ground
beside water

This tortoise has an oval carapace widening somewhat at the back and not greatly convex, on which both the vertebral and the costal horny plates are shaped like a base with a pyramid; the marginal plates are rough and bluntly pointed, with the points outward. The long, flat neck is covered with bare, rough warts. The head is triangular and very flat, the snout is long and thin, resembling a proboscis. The eyes are very small, partly hidden by the growths of skin; the jaws are weak and have no horny covering. In adults the carapace is a uniform dark brown, the plastron yellowish-brown with dark patches; the areas not covered by the shell are gray.

This fantastic tortoise is found in fresh water, especially stagnant water, in South America – Venezuela, Guyana, and central southern Brazil.

The reproduction process and the general way of life of this species are not very well known, at any rate in nature. The matamata generally lies hidden in the mud along the sides of stretches of water or amid the wet waterside vegetation during the day, with its head and neck and sometimes also its feet completely or partly hidden under the shell. It becomes active when darkness falls. It enters the water and starts to chase swiftly after fish, tadpoles, vertebrates without shells, and plants. But sometimes it lies in ambush; camouflaged against the muddy bottom of the stagnant water with its decaying plants, it waits until its prey passes near, then, as soon as it is within range, opens its mouth wide, causing a violent suction that, if well gauged, will practically bring the food into its mouth.

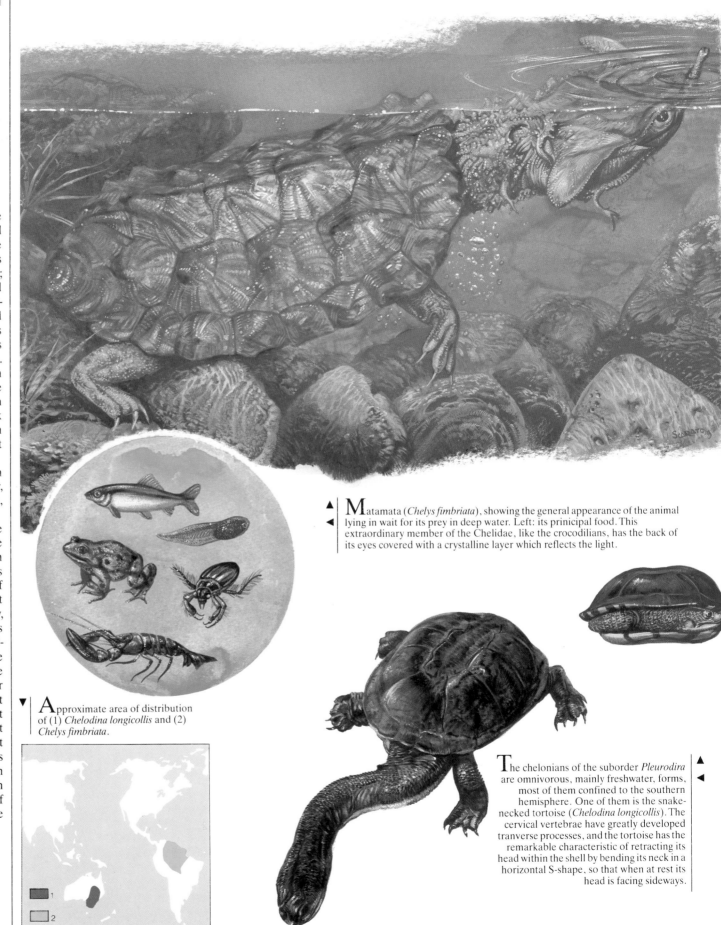

▲◀ Matamata (*Chelys fimbriata*), showing the general appearance of the animal lying in wait for its prey in deep water. Left: its prinicipal food. This extraordinary member of the Chelidae, like the crocodilians, has the back of its eyes covered with a crystalline layer which reflects the light.

▼ Approximate area of distribution of (1) *Chelodina longicollis* and (2) *Chelys fimbriata*.

1
2

▲◀ The chelonians of the suborder *Pleurodira* are omnivorous, mainly freshwater, forms, most of them confined to the southern hemisphere. One of them is the snake-necked tortoise (*Chelodina longicollis*). The cervical vertebrae have greatly developed tranverse processes, and the tortoise has the remarkable characteristic of retracting its head within the shell by bending its neck in a horizontal S-shape, so that when at rest its head is facing sideways.

SNAPPING TURTLES

Chelydridae

The snapping turtles are freshwater turtles with a comparatively small, flat carapace that only becomes ossified when the animals are old. The head cannot be fully retracted under the shell; it is very big and has one or two very small skin excrescences on the front and back. The snout looks like a beak. All digits are webbed and those on the forefeet have strong claws.

The snapper (*Chelydra serpentina*) is as much as 3 ft (1 m) long including the tail – although the carapace is not generally more than 16 – 19 in (40 – 47 cm) in length – and weighs a maximum of about 65 lbs (30 kg). It is the better known and more widespread species of the family, living in southern Canada, in the eastern United States east of the Cordillera and as far south as Florida, and in Mexico.

The snapper is prodigiously active. At night, or even by day if it is hungry it becomes the most tireless, voracious and aggressive predator in the river. Swiftly, but always watchfully, it moves off to the bays and creeks where the current is weakest and the fish generally most plentiful; then, with incredible speed, it darts out into the shoal and seizes as many fish as it can, or perhaps selects one special fish and chases it until it catches it. It will also find food on land, where, mostly at night, it will catch frogs, toads, snakes, any birds that nest on the ground or in trees with sloping trunks, and even small mammals, which it seizes, tears to pieces with its powerful beak and long claws, and then eats. It is generally afraid of humans, but that does not stop it coming near enough to houses to carry off geese and ducks.

The mating period lasts from April to October, according to the climate, and coupling takes place both in water and on land. After some days the female digs a hole 4 – 6 in (10 – 15 cm) deep in the sand or somewhere near the bank where the soil is soft enough, and there lays up to 30 almost spherical eggs about 1½ in (3 cm) in diameter with a soft, chalky shell, and immediately covers them with earth and leaves. The young are hatched out after 2½ months.

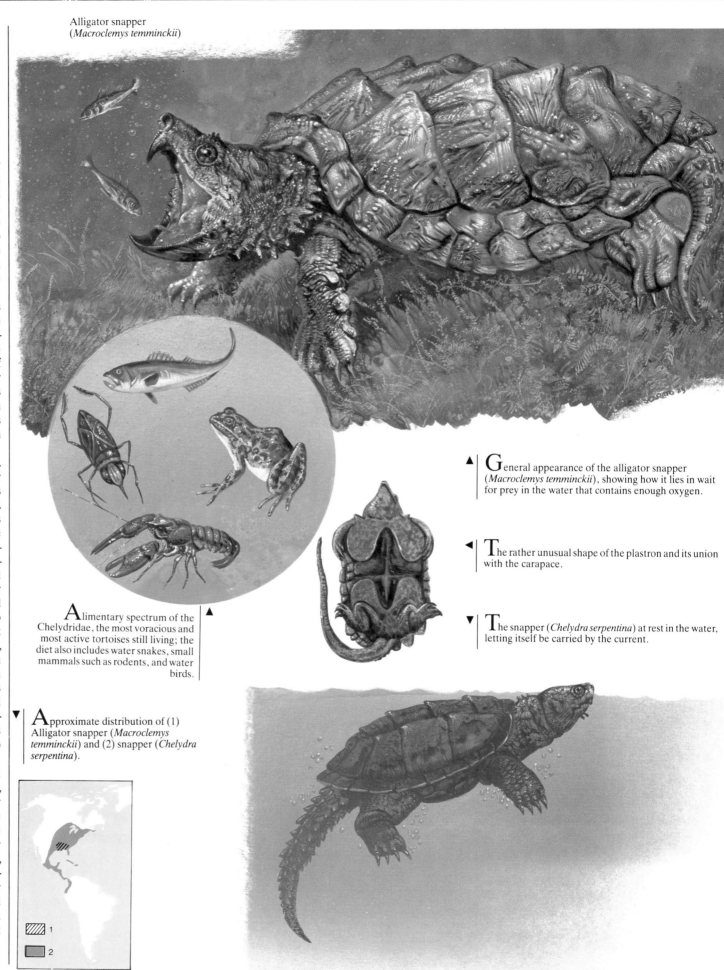

Alligator snapper
(*Macroclemys temminckii*)

Alimentary spectrum of the Chelydridae, the most voracious and most active tortoises still living; the diet also includes water snakes, small mammals such as rodents, and water birds.

General appearance of the alligator snapper (*Macroclemys temminckii*), showing how it lies in wait for prey in the water that contains enough oxygen.

The rather unusual shape of the plastron and its union with the carapace.

The snapper (*Chelydra serpentina*) at rest in the water, letting itself be carried by the current.

Approximate distribution of (1) Alligator snapper (*Macroclemys temminckii*) and (2) snapper (*Chelydra serpentina*).

1
2

TUATARA

Rhyncocephalia

The tuatara, only surviving species of the reptilion order Rhyncocephalia, grows to a length of up to 26 in (65 cm) and weighs not more than 2¼ lbs (1 kg), with a rather big, tall, powerful head in relation to its body. A crest of movable bony plates rises from the top of its head and continues along the line of the backbone as far as the tail. The eyes are black and highly developed, with a vertical pupil. There is no exterior opening to the ear. The body is stout and laterally compressed, supported on thick limbs with hands and feet whose five digits bear claws and are joined at the base by a small membrane. The upper parts, including the legs, are covered with little granular scales, the underparts with small plates arranged in transverse lines. The basic color of the upper parts is brown or grayish, with yellowish spots.

One of this reptile's most unusual features is the great development of the pineal gland, which is constructed rather like an eye – the third eye or pineal eye, with a lens and a retina and nervous elements connected with the brain, at least in young specimens. The function of this third eye is highly controversial. Some authorities hold that it actually functions as an eye, at any rate in young animals; others argue that since in adults relations between the brain and the retina are difficult and the thickness of the horny scale prevents any light from passing through it, the eye can have no visual function.

The tuatara is found in about 20 small islands off New Zealand. In the spring the females lay 2 – 15 eggs in burrows that they dig for themselves; the eggs have a parchmentlike skin and are flattened at the ends, barely 1¼ in (3 cm) in length and 0.1 – 0.2 oz (4 – 6 g) in weight. The mother ends by filling in the nest and covering it with earth and leaves that she has gathered in readiness; after that she pays no more attention to her eggs. They do not hatch for some 13 – 15 months; then the young use the tooth at the tip of their snouts to bite their way out of the eggs, and after 12 months have absorbed so much moisture that they look like little rubber balls.

Tuatara (*Sphenodon punctatus*)

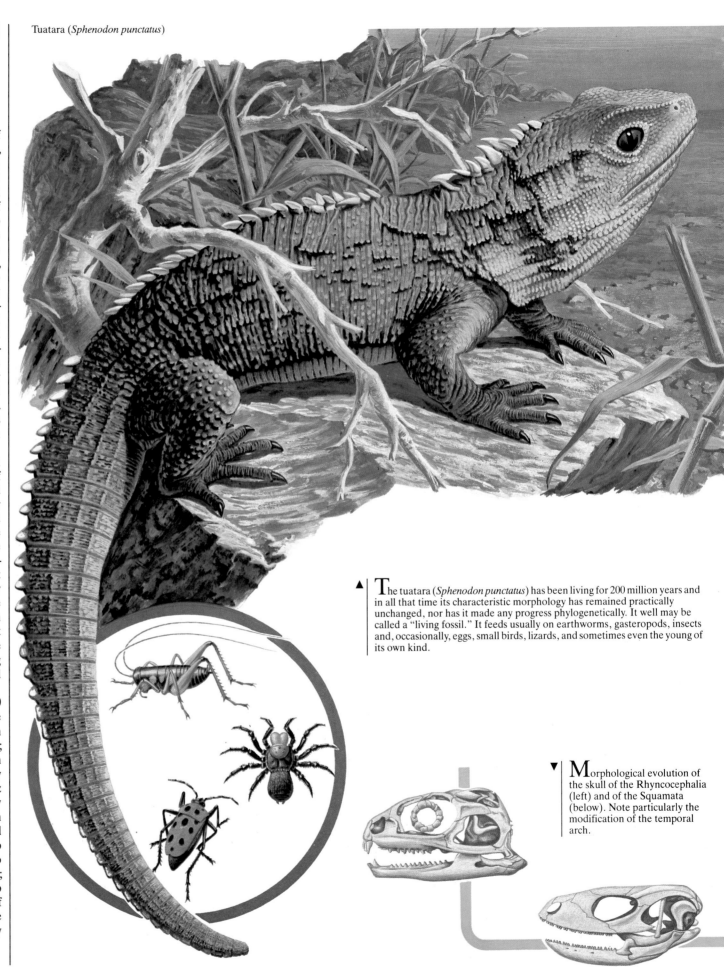

▲ The tuatara (*Sphenodon punctatus*) has been living for 200 million years and in all that time its characteristic morphology has remained practically unchanged, nor has it made any progress phylogenetically. It well may be called a "living fossil." It feeds usually on earthworms, gasteropods, insects and, occasionally, eggs, small birds, lizards, and sometimes even the young of its own kind.

▼ Morphological evolution of the skull of the Rhyncocephalia (left) and of the Squamata (below). Note particularly the modification of the temporal arch.

GREEN IGUANA

Iguana iguana

Order Squamata
Suborder Sauria
Family Iguanidae
Size Total length up to 87 in (220 cm), of which 60 in (150 cm) is the tail
Reproductive period In Central America October to December
Number of eggs 24 – 45
Period of incubation 90 days
Sexual maturity 2 years
Maximum age 10 years

The green iguana, the biggest of all lizards after the monitors, is strongly built, with powerful claws on its feet and a broad head. There is a crest of soft spines on the back and the long tail, and similar spines on the front of the dewlap, which is particularly conspicuous in males.

The reptile is found in the whole of the humid tropical region of Latin America, from southern Mexico to central Brazil. It is arboreal, climbing as high as 65 ft (20 m) in the branches, and is a good swimmer, preferring to live on the banks of rivers.

This giant lizard is solitary in habit. Only the newborn animals are thought to live together socially for a few days.

Males engage in ritual fights. Both contestants begin by nodding their heads, then the two males "dance" round each other, strike each other with their tails and bite each other in the neck. The weaker is always ready to give in, so they do not often hurt each other seriously.

The eggs are buried in the sand. The young, 10 in (25 cm) long, emerge after 3 months at the beginning of the rainy season. At first their diet consists largely of insects, worms, and snails, but when adult they are almost completely vegetarian.

The nearest relatives of the green iguana are various other big vegetarian iguanas which, oddly enough, all live on islands off South America.

The two giant lizards of the Galapagos Islands in the eastern Pacific are presumably descended from a common ancestor, which must have reached the islands by swimming or possibly by climbing on to pieces of driftwood. The land iguana (*Conolophus subcristatus*) was once numerous on the Galapagos Islands, but over hunting has now greatly reduced its numbers.

Green iguana (*Iguana iguana*)

▲
◀ The green iguana (*Iguana iguana*) is the biggest of the family Iguanidae, reaching a length of over 7 ft (2.2 m). It has a dorsal crest and a large jugular sac. It lives in the forests of South America, where it feeds mostly on plants and defends itself against enemies by powerful blows with its tail.

▼ The land iguana (*Conolophus subcristatus*) lives in the Galapagos Islands. Darwin made an intensive study of these animals and of the sea iguanas, which were very numerous at that time, and drew valid arguments from it for his theory of evolution. The land iguana feeds on plants, especially cactus, which it devours with all the spines.

The sea iguana (*Amblyrhynchus cristatus*) is the only lizard now living which is truly at home in the sea. It lives on the rocky coasts of the Galapagos Islands, sometimes in huge groups. At ebbtide these 5 ft (1.5 m) long iguanas enter the sea and swim off, propelling themselves with their laterally compressed tails, to graze from the algae on the rocks, both above and below the surface.

The Fiji iguana (*Brachylophus fasciatus*), an arboreal species threatened with extinction as a result of massive forest clearance, is found in Fiji and Tonga.

Similarly threatened by human encroachment is the rhinoceros iguana (*Cyclura cornuta*), found in Haiti, in the Caribbean. This terrestrial species lives in dry thornbush savannas. Only the males have horns on their noses. They use them as hooks in their territorial battles, in which each tries to turn the other over on its side.

The common basilisk (*Basiliscus basiliscus*) is a slender, medium-sized lizard with the flaps of the skin on the head, back and tail characteristic of the species.

The green anole (*Anolis carolinensis*) from the southeastern USA, is a member of the reptile genus of which there are 165 species with many geographical races. The greatest variety occurs in the West Indies, where some tiny islands have species of their own.

The most extraordinary members of the iguanids are the little "horned toads" (*Phrynosoma*), from the dry country in the west of North America. They are protected from their enemies by a spiny armor, and are also able to bury themselves in the sand at lightning speed. When attacked they can spray a jet of blood from their eyelid for as far as 3 ft (1 m). They live almost exclusively on ants.

The Colorado fringed-toed iguana (*Uma notata*), from the southwestern USA, is outstandingly well adapted to life in the sand dunes.

Another terrestrial iguanid from North America is the collared iguana (*Crotaphytus collaris*). Like the basilisk, it can run for short distances on its hindlegs. It can change color to a certain extent according to the temperature and the light and to its mood. This lizard, 16 in (40 cm) long, is an aggressive predator that can catch smaller lizards as well as insects.

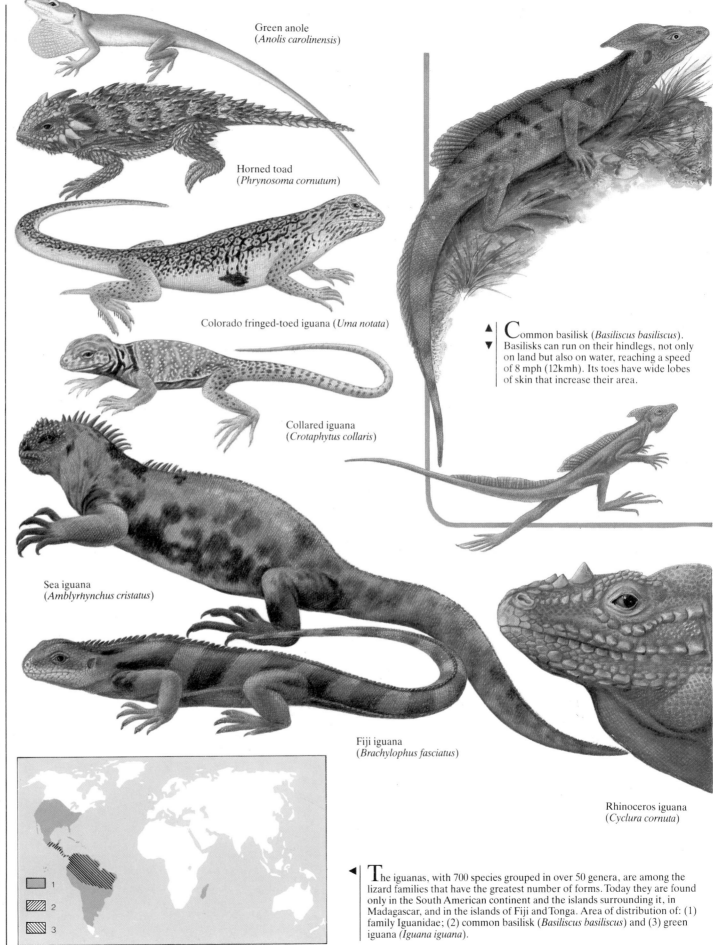

Green anole
(*Anolis carolinensis*)

Horned toad
(*Phrynosoma cornutum*)

Colorado fringed-toed iguana (*Uma notata*)

Collared iguana
(*Crotaphytus collaris*)

Sea iguana
(*Amblyrhynchus cristatus*)

Fiji iguana
(*Brachylophus fasciatus*)

▲ Common basilisk (*Basiliscus basiliscus*).
▼ Basilisks can run on their hindlegs, not only on land but also on water, reaching a speed of 8 mph (12kmh). Its toes have wide lobes of skin that increase their area.

Rhinoceros iguana
(*Cyclura cornuta*)

◄ The iguanas, with 700 species grouped in over 50 genera, are among the lizard families that have the greatest number of forms. Today they are found only in the South American continent and the islands surrounding it, in Madagascar, and in the islands of Fiji and Tonga. Area of distribution of: (1) family Iguanidae; (2) common basilisk (*Basiliscus basiliscus*) and (3) green iguana (*Iguana iguana*).

JACKSON'S CHAMELEON

Chamaeleo jacksoni

Order Squamata
Suborder Sauria
Family Chamaeleonidae
Size Total length 12½ in (32 cm), of which 6 in (15 cm) is the tail
Reproductive period Probably June
Gestation 6 – 8 months
Number of young 14 – 40
Sexual maturity 1 year
Maximum age 4 years

Most of the pecularities of chameleons are evidently adaptations to life in the trees. The body is laterally compressed and covered with irregularly arranged scales, some small, some larger. There is a low crest of skin on the back and tail. The head is protected by a casque of bony plates covered with scales, which extends backward over the neck with a central and two lateral extensions. There is no ear aperture. The eyes are protruding hemispheres, overgrown with skin except for the little pupils; they can turn in all directions completely independently of each other. Hidden behind the wide opening of the mouth is an extraordinarily elastic extensible tongue, which when stretched out is nearly as long as the body. The male Jackson's chameleon (*Chamaeleo jacksoni*) has three long horns on its forehead, made of horny skin with bases of bone. The feet are modified to form prehensile pincers. The tail forms a fifth prehensile limb; it can be coiled inward like an elephant's trunk and gives the animal a firm grasp on twigs.

Jackson's chameleon lives in temperate hill forests at altitudes of up to 10,000 ft (3,000 m) in the mountainous areas of Kenya and Tanzania.

Chameleons hunt insects on which they feed by means of a slow, stealthy ambush. The prey is caught by the sticky secretion covering the tongue's tip.

Chameleons are famous for their ability to change color. They are solitary animals, the most solitary of all lizards. It is only in the mating period that females will allow males to approach them. Like many upland chameleons, the Jackson's chameleon is ovoviviparous.

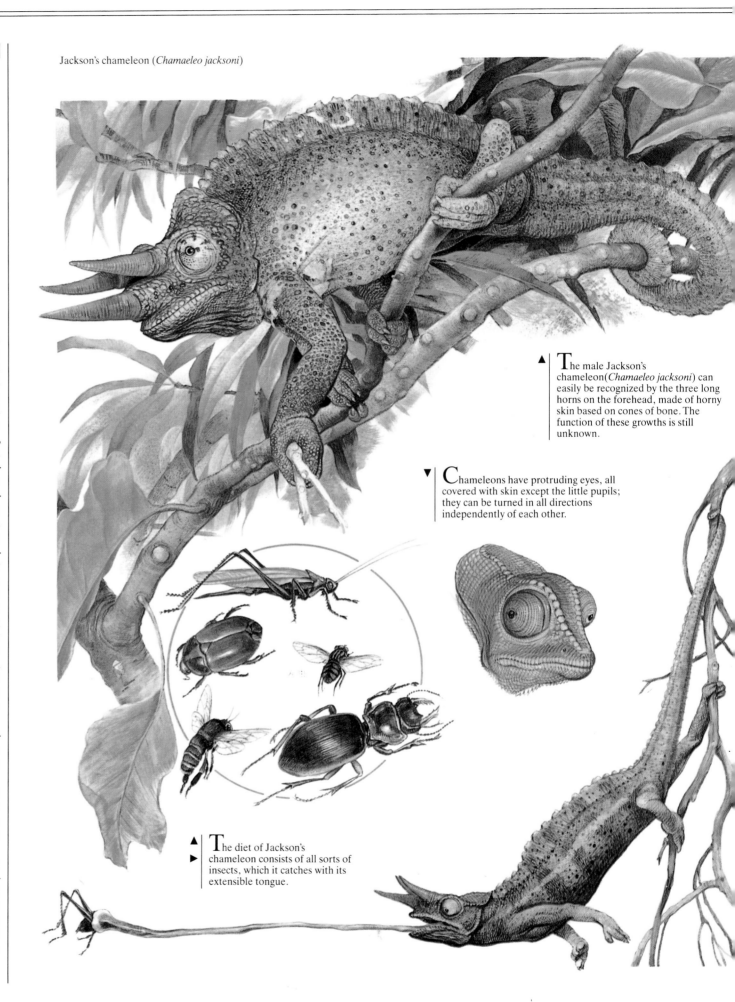

Jackson's chameleon (*Chamaeleo jacksoni*)

The male Jackson's chameleon(*Chamaeleo jacksoni*) can easily be recognized by the three long horns on the forehead, made of horny skin based on cones of bone. The function of these growths is still unknown.

Chameleons have protruding eyes, all covered with skin except the little pupils; they can be turned in all directions independently of each other.

The diet of Jackson's chameleon consists of all sorts of insects, which it catches with its extensible tongue.

FLYING DRAGON

Draco volans

Order Squamata
Suborder Sauria
Family Agamidae
Size Total length 9 in (22 cm), of which 6 in (14 cm) is the tail
Reproductive period All the year round
Number of eggs 2–5 (most commonly 4)
Period of incubation 1–2 months

Sitting on a tree trunk, the inconspicuous little flying dragon looks quite an ordinary lizard. But suddenly it springs into the air, and you think you are looking at a brilliant butterfly. The animal owes its ability to glide to flaps of skin on the side of its body, which are supported by extensions of the ribs and folded against the body when at rest.

The colors on these gliding flaps differ from one species to another; in *Draco volans* they are blue with black spots, in other species black with yellow or red. There are also flaplike appendages on each side of the head, patterned in black and white.

Draco volans lives in the rainforest in the Philippines, Malaysia, and Indonesia. Other species occur in Sri Lanka and southern India. Their habitat has the air saturated with humidity, no real dry season and a permanently high temperature.

The flying dragon spends its whole life in the trees except when it descends to lay its eggs. Its flight pattern is not active, effected by flapping the wings, but a passive glide, transforming the free fall into a controlled forward fall with the help of the cushion of air under outstretched flaps. The distance covered in a flight can be as much as 330 ft (100 m), but normally, in its home forests, the flying dragon does not glide more than about 65 ft (20 m) from one tree to another. The gliding flaps are not used only for flight; they are also used to frighten enemies and in mating. The diet consists almost exclusively of tree ants, which it licks up with its tongue.

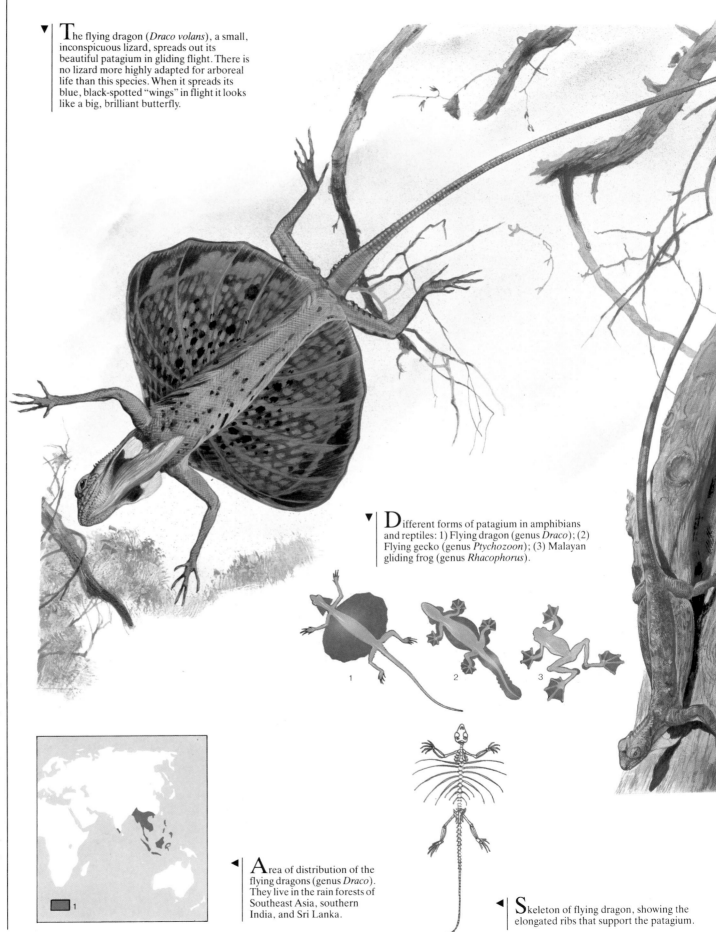

The flying dragon (*Draco volans*), a small, inconspicuous lizard, spreads out its beautiful patagium in gliding flight. There is no lizard more highly adapted for arboreal life than this species. When it spreads its blue, black-spotted "wings" in flight it looks like a big, brilliant butterfly.

Different forms of patagium in amphibians and reptiles: 1) Flying dragon (genus *Draco*); (2) Flying gecko (genus *Ptychozoon*); (3) Malayan gliding frog (genus *Rhacophorus*).

Area of distribution of the flying dragons (genus *Draco*). They live in the rain forests of Southeast Asia, southern India, and Sri Lanka.

Skeleton of flying dragon, showing the elongated ribs that support the patagium.

FRILLED LIZARD

Chlamydosaurus kingi

Order Squamata
Suborder Sauria
Family Agamidae
Size Total length 32 in (80 cm), of which 22 in (55 cm) is the tail

The special feature of this medium-sized agamid is the folds of skin behind its head; if excited, the animal can spread them, when they look like a collar 8 in (20 cm) across, decorated in many species with reddish, yellow, black or white spots. The collar is supported by cartilaginous extensions of the hyoid bone, so that it can be opened like an umbrella.

The tail of the frilled lizard is among the longest of all lizards, and the hindlegs are considerably more strongly developed than the forelegs. The coloring is a dull brown with a pattern like the bark of a tree.

The frilled lizard occurs in north and northwest Australia and in the south of New Guinea. It is arboreal, living in savannas and dry forests.

When a frilled lizard is disturbed by the approach of a bigger animal, a snake for example, or a human being, it assumes a characteristic defense posture. It tries to scare the aggressor with its mouth wide open and its collar erected, spitting and lashing its tail to and fro like a whip. The collar and the fierce behavior combine to make the harmless lizard look much bigger and more dangerous. If the aggressor still refuses to be driven off, the animal angrily springs at it and bites it. Then suddenly it turns round, jumps down from the tree and runs away on its hindlegs with a swinging gait, its head held straight up, its tail held at right angles to its body as a counterpoise and its forelegs pressed against its body.

The diet of the frilled lizard consists, among other things, of big beetles and spiders. Given the opportunity, it also eats birds' eggs and small mammals.

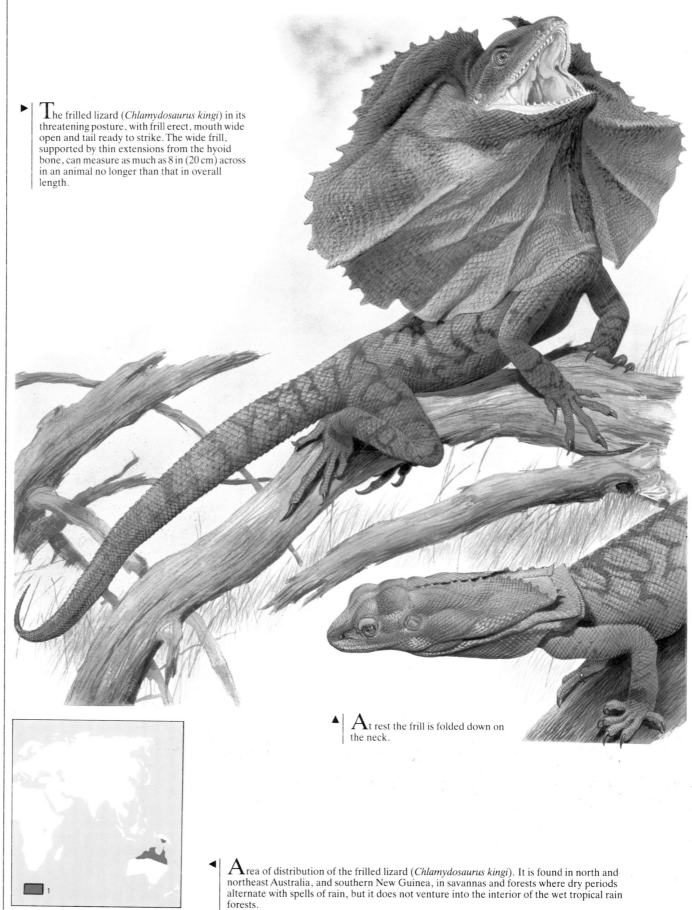

The frilled lizard (*Chlamydosaurus kingi*) in its threatening posture, with frill erect, mouth wide open and tail ready to strike. The wide frill, supported by thin extensions from the hyoid bone, can measure as much as 8 in (20 cm) across in an animal no longer than that in overall length.

At rest the frill is folded down on the neck.

Area of distribution of the frilled lizard (*Chlamydosaurus kingi*). It is found in north and northeast Australia, and southern New Guinea, in savannas and forests where dry periods alternate with spells of rain, but it does not venture into the interior of the wet tropical rain forests.

GILA MONSTER

Heloderma suspectum

Order Squamata
Suborder Sauria
Family Helodermatidae
Size Length up to 20 in (50 cm), occasionally more
Weight 2¼ – 3¼ lb (1 – 1.5 kg)
Reproductive period Winter and spring
Number of eggs Generally 2–6, sometimes up to 13
Maximum age Over 20 years

The most remarkable of all the New World lizards are the *Heloderma suspectum*, the Gila monster, and its relative *Heloderma horridum*, the only survivors of the horde of poisonous monsters that roamed the earth 30–40 million years ago. Gila monsters, with their plump body, the often clumsy-looking fat tail, and the black and orange or pink coloring, could never be confused with any other lizard.

The area of distribution of *Heloderma suspectum* extends across Utah, Nevada, Arizona, New Mexico, and northwest Mexico; it has also recently been discovered in the Providence Mountains in southeastern California. The natural habitat of the Gila monster includes the Sonora and Chihuahua deserts, and parts of the Mojave and Colorado deserts.

The brilliant coloring of these lizards seems to act as a warning. All heloderms are poisonous. The venom apparatus, which lies in the lower jaw and not in the upper jaw as in snakes, has a part to play in the digestive process as well as in defense; small mammals and birds bitten by the Gila monster decompose more quickly than others killed at the same time by other means.

Heloderms feed on baby rodents, small birds and, most of all, on eggs. There have not been very many cases of humans being bitten, and only very few of them have proved fatal.

Gila monsters prefer to live in flat desert country with low, domed knolls, living in burrows either dug by themselves or taken over from other animals. Their eggs, laid in late spring and early summer, take about 100 – 120 days to develop, and the young are about 6½ in (16 cm) long when they hatch. Given plenty of food, they grow quickly and by the age of 3 years are as big as the adults.

▲ An example of the Gila monster of the subspecies *Heloderma suspectum cinctum*, easily recognizable by its brilliant coloring, with the bright pink and black transverse stripes on the body and five broad broken bands on the tail. In the south of their distribution area the coloring of these animals is generally a less bright pale pink. These heloderms are mainly crepuscular; their eyes are small and their sight is not good. Their short, rather stout legs are used to burrow into hard earth and help them to dig their way out of the ground.

▼ The beaded lizard (*Heloderma horridum*) lives in Mexico, where there are three geographical races. Its body is narrower than that of the Gila monster, dark brown with a black head. There are roundish yellow patches on the body and yellow rings on the tail.

◄ (1) The area of distribution of the slowworm (*Anguis fragilis*) takes in almost the whole of Europe. There are three subspecies, one eastern, one western, and one found only in the Peloponnese. (2) The area of distribution of *Heloderma suspectum* covers the southwestern parts of the United States, while (3) *Heloderma horridum* is found in western Mexico.

KOMODO DRAGON

Varanus komodoensis

Order Squamata
Suborder Sauria
Family Varanidae
Size Male: total length 10 ft (3 m), of which 5¼ ft (1.6 m), is the tail; female: total length 6½ ft (2 m), of which 3¾ ft (1.1 m) is the tail
Weight Up to 350 lb (160 kg)
Reproductive period July – August (?)
Number of eggs 25
Period of incubation 6 – 8 weeks
Sexual maturity 3 – 5 years
Maximum age Over 25 years

The Komodo dragon (*Varanus komodoensis*), only discovered in 1912, is the biggest living lizard. It is true that the Papua monitor (*Varanus salvadori*) is longer – over 13 ft (4 m) – but it is much slimmer than the Komodo dragon and only half the weight; the Komodo dragon is unusually solidly and powerfully built for a lizard.

The body is covered with small scales; the neck is thick and the head broad and elongated. The huge mouth contains teeth ½ in (1 cm) long and a deeply cleft tongue 12 – 16 in (30 – 40 cm) long. The legs are well developed and there are long claws on the toes. The muscular tail has no fracture planes and is somewhat laterally compressed. The males vary in color from dark gray to brick red; the females, which are smaller, are olive-brown with yellow patches on the throat.

The Komodo dragon is the biggest predator on the islands where it lives. It hunts hog–deer, wild pig, macaques, and rats, and digs up the eggs of mound birds. Although it normally moves very slowly, constantly flicking out its tongue to right and left, it can run as fast as a man for short stretches. Smaller specimens are said to lurk in trees above tracks used by game and jump on to the backs of deer or pigs.

It uses its eyes to locate its prey, seeing moving objects very distinctly but easily overlooking those that do not move. It has only rudimentary hearing. It also makes eagerly for carrion, which it recognizes by scent, tearing big pieces off its prey with its sharp teeth and swallowing them without chewing, holding the carcass down with the claws of its forefeet. It takes

Komodo dragon (*Varanus komodoensis*)

▲ The Komodo dragon (*Varanus komodoensis*), at 10 ft (3 m) long the giant among the still surviving lizards, lives only in some small islands in Indonesia. Despite its great size it can move extremely quickly.

◄ It feeds mostly on small and medium-sized mammals and is quite ready to eat carrion. It uses its sharp teeth to tear great pieces of flesh off its dead prey, holding it down with its forefeet, and swallows them without chewing.

several days to digest its food. The males enforce a strict order of priority in feeding. The strongest male will not let weaker animals approach the prey until it has eaten enough, but females are allowed to eat unhindered and are tolerant of each other.

The Komodo dragon sleeps in a burrow that it digs for itself, with a narrow entry and a chamber inside 3–6 ft (1–2 m) wide. It may be active both by day and by night, and it finds its way in the dark by using its tongue, which is remarkably sensitive to taste and scent stimuli.

The males are territorial in habit. During the mating period they engage in "boxing matches" with each other, rearing up on their hindlegs, but they do not make use of their strong, dangerous weapons, their claws and teeth and their strong tail. Females bury their eggs, which have soft parchment shells. The eggs are 3–5 in (8–12 cm) long and 2½ in (6 cm) across, weighing about ½ lb (200 g).

All the other 31 species of monitor are included in the same genus, *Varanus*, since outwardly they all look very much alike. They are distributed everywhere in the tropical regions of the Old World, in every environment from deserts to mangrove swamps. Monitors can run, climb, dig and swim equally well, and so are able to occupy the most varied environments.

The other monitor species are not as powerfully built as the Komodo dragon. They have narrower heads and the neck and tail are substantially longer in proportion to the body, so that they cannot prey on such large animals.

The four monitors found in the south of Asia share the environment in the same way as the African species. One species lives in the desert, one in the steppes, one climbs trees and one, here too, is aquatic – the water monitor (*Varanus salvator*) which, like the Nile monitor, has a laterally compressed tail for swimming. Since it is quite ready to swim over arms of the sea, it has also spread to Sri Lanka and over all the Indonesian islands except New Guinea, so that several different subspecies have developed.

The great majority of monitors live in the Australian zoogeographical region (Australasia and New Guinea) and in the transitional region toward Asia – the islands of Timor, Flores and Celebes. The smallest species is only 8 in (20 cm) long.

▲ The monitor's tongue, forked like a snake's tongue, is its most important sense-organ. It is continuously flicked in and out and enables the animal to pick up tactile and olfactory stimuli.

The monitor is famed for its voracity, as A.E. Brehm records in his work *Illustriertes Tierleben* (Illustrated Life of the Animals): "Observing monitors in captivity, it is easy to see that they are predatory animals in the true sense of the word. They prefer live prey to any other kind of food, though they will eat raw meat and meat of dead animals with equal satisfaction. To bring them to life, it is enough to put a dozen living lizards or frogs in their cage; at once, forgetting their usual listlessness, they become alert, with a lively expression; their eyes shine and their remarkably long tongue appears and disappears with extraordinary speed. After a few moments they get on the warpath, as the saying goes, to catch one of their quarry. The lizards, mad with terror, run here and there in the cage, climb up and down and take the most fearsome leaps, and the frogs never stop hopping about. The eyes and tongue of the monitor lying in wait for them make it clear that the bold plunderer is just looking for the right moment to attack them. Suddenly, unexpectedly, it shoots out its head and with wonderful certainty seizes a frog or lizard, dispatches it with a bite that is clearly audible and devours it immediately. All wretched victims are killed in this way one after another, and the same thing would happen if, instead of one dozen, there were several dozen of them. If a few eggs are placed in the monitor's cage it can be seen at once that such appetizing food does not pass unobserved by the cunning reptile, which goes at once to examine one of the eggs with its tongue, then takes it in its mouth, raises its head, breaks it and happily gulps down the contents."

Nile monitor (*Varanus niloticus*)

Water monitor (*Varanus salvator*)

Perentie (*Varanus giganteus*)

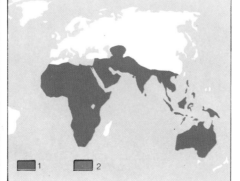

◄ The monitors (family Varanidae) are fairly widely distributed, in Africa, Southern Asia, the Malayan archipelago and Australia, but not in Europe or America. The family looks fairly uniform morphologically, but this outward similarity contrasts markedly with the variety of living habits met in the different species: there are arboreal monitors, others that live on the ground and others that are skillful swimmers. (1) Varanidae; (2) *Varanus komodoensis*.

BOA CONSTRICTOR

Boa constrictor

Order Squamata
Suborder Ophidia
Family Boidae
Size Length 10 – 13 ft (3 – 4 m)
Reproductive period Varies from region to region; in the tropics generally December to March
Number of young 20 – 50, occasionally over 50
Maximum age Rarely more than 40 years

Next to the anaconda (*Eunectes murinus*), the boa constrictor (*Boa constrictor*) is the best-known snake from the tropics and subtropics of South America. It has a triangular head and a massive, muscular body. The coloration of the body can vary immensely, even from one individual to another. The ground color of the body may be various shades of red, red-brown, gray-brown, yellow-brown or light leaden gray.

The boa constrictor lives in dry, hot places in open woodland and thick bush usually near water, flowing or still.

The boa feeds on birds and small mammals. Like other Boidae, it lies in wait for its prey, strikes it at lightning speed as it passes and strangles it by coiling round it.

The boa constrictor gives birth between May and August to up to 60 young, which are about 14 – 20 in (35 – 50 cm) long and can feed themselves on mice and small birds after their first slough.

A giant relative of the boa is the anaconda (*Eunectes murinus*). This huge snake has a longish head not greatly distinct from the neck. The body is exceedingly stocky and muscular. It is a native of tropical South America, found in Brazil, Colombia, Peru, Ecuador, Venezuela, Guyana, and Trinidad. An aquatic species which always stays in or beside water; it likes to sun itself on overhanging branches, on rocks or on warm sand. Often it lies in the water all day with only the tip of its snout above the surface. The anaconda will eat any kind of mammal – capybara, agouti, paca, – and also birds, fish and, on occasion, caimans and snakes. After a big meal it stretches

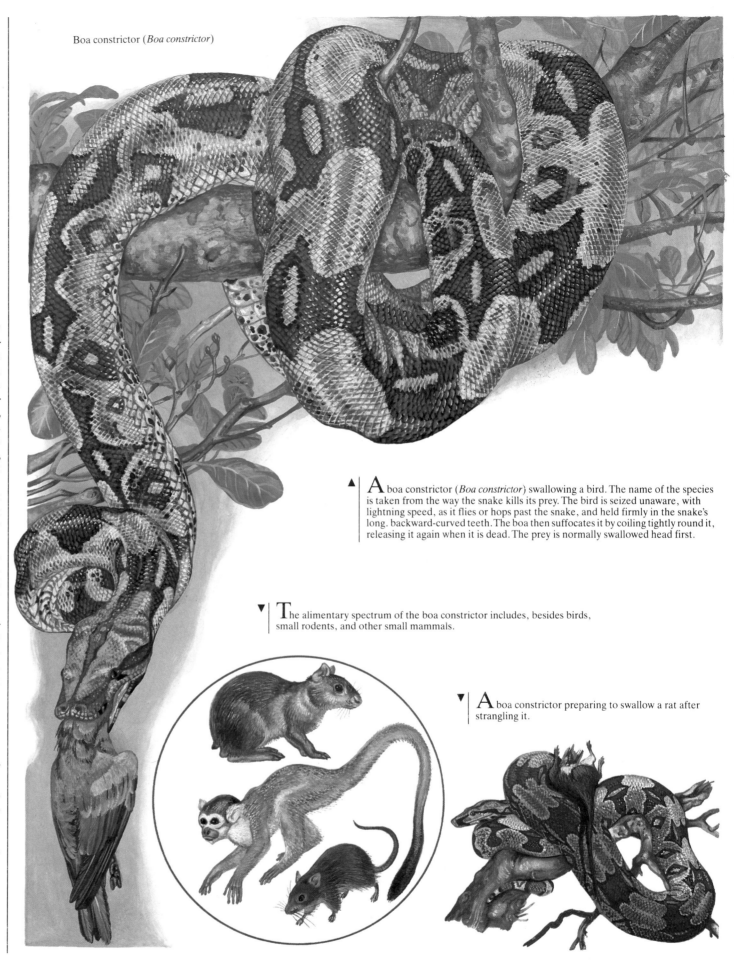

Boa constrictor (*Boa constrictor*)

▲ A boa constrictor (*Boa constrictor*) swallowing a bird. The name of the species is taken from the way the snake kills its prey. The bird is seized unaware, with lightning speed, as it flies or hops past the snake, and held firmly in the snake's long, backward-curved teeth. The boa then suffocates it by coiling tightly round it, releasing it again when it is dead. The prey is normally swallowed head first.

▼ The alimentary spectrum of the boa constrictor includes, besides birds, small rodents, and other small mammals.

▼ A boa constrictor preparing to swallow a rat after strangling it.

out, completely inert, to digest its food, and that may take several days.

One of the most beautiful of the South American Boidae is the emerald tree-boa (*Corallus caninus*). It bears a striking resemblance to the green tree-python (*Chondropython viridis*) of New Guinea and Australia, with which it is often confused. The emerald tree-boa has a pointed, wedge-shaped head clearly distinct from its neck and muscular body. It is a strictly arboreal snake and so has a well-developed prehensile tail. Its back and flanks are leaf-green, the lip scales and the belly bright yellow. A white stripe runs along the median line of the back, with white or yellow transverse stripes branching off at regular intervals. The young of this species are red. The emerald tree-boa has very distinct heat-sensitive organs on the upper and lower labial scales.

This great snake, 6½ – 10 ft (2 – 3 m) long, lives in the humid tropical forests of Guyana, Brazil, northern Bolivia, and eastern Peru. Its green coloring makes it hard to see in dense foliage. It twines round a branch with its head hidden in its coils and in this ostensibly restful position lies in wait for birds and mammals, which it generally catches from above and strangles with three coils of its body.

The rainbow boa (*Epicrates cenchria*) distributed from Costa Rica to Argentina, has a muscular but elongated body with a highly prehensile tail. It has no heat-sensitive organs on the scales of the upper lip. This snake, which grows up to 6½ ft (2 m) long, varies in color between yellow and rufous. It lives in rocky terrain or in woods and can sometimes be found on farmland, lying in wait for the small mammals and birds on which it preys. It may be met as often on the ground as in the branches of the trees, and is most active at night. Like the other Boidae, it is ovoviviparous.

The spotted-sand boa (*Eryx conicus*) is a species about 32 – 40 in (80 – 100 cm) long, with markedly keeled scales, especially on top of the tail, and a wedged-shaped head that stands out very little from the neck. The eye is small, the pupil narrowing to a vertical slit in bright light. The ground color is light brown, with big spots, dark brown bordered with black, on the back; they may combine to form a zigzag stripe. If seized, it reacts violently and bites hard. The female gives birth to 6 – 8 young.

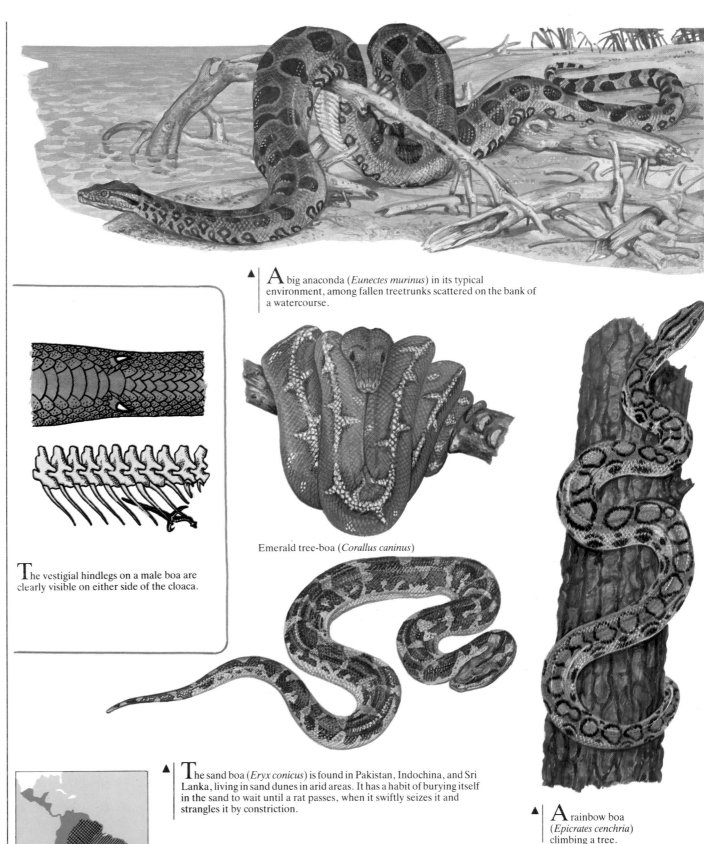

▲ A big anaconda (*Eunectes murinus*) in its typical environment, among fallen treetrunks scattered on the bank of a watercourse.

The vestigial hindlegs on a male boa are clearly visible on either side of the cloaca.

Emerald tree-boa (*Corallus caninus*)

▲ The sand boa (*Eryx conicus*) is found in Pakistan, Indochina, and Sri Lanka, living in sand dunes in arid areas. It has a habit of burying itself in the sand to wait until a rat passes, when it swiftly seizes it and strangles it by constriction.

▲ A rainbow boa (*Epicrates cenchria*) climbing a tree.

◄ Distribution area of the boas (subfamily Boinae). This group is mostly found in Central and South America, though some rare species occur in North America, southeast Europe, Madagascar, and New Guinea. (1) Area of distribution of the anaconda (*Eunectes murinus*); (2) distribution of the emerald tree-boa (*Corallus caninus*); (3) distribution of the boa constrictor (*Boa constrictor*).

1
2
3

COLUBRIDS
Colubridae

The colubrids, which are found in all the continents of the world in a great number of genera and species, are divided into two different groups. In the Aglypha, the teeth are generally round in cross-section. These snakes are nearly always harmless. In the Opisthoglypha, the teeth at the hinder end of the upper jaw, a long way back in the mouth, are grooved; all the opisthoglyphs have poison glands which are connected to these ducts in the teeth. The venom of these snakes is not generally particularly powerful, but there are exceptions, like the boomslang (*Dispholidus typus*), which is found in many parts of Africa, and the African vine snake (*Thelotornis kirtlandi*).

Many colubrids which live by or in water are excellent swimmers and divers. Most are oviparous. All colubrids feed on living animals – small mammals of all sorts, birds, reptiles, amphibians, and fish.

The tessellated water snake (*Natrix tessellata*) is about 5 ft (1.5 m) long. As an adaptation to an aquatic life, the snout is rather pointed and the nostrils are directed upward. The body coloring is subject to considerable variation, but is mostly brown or gray.

Natrix tessellata has an enormous area of distribution, extending from central and southern Europe eastward to northwest India and western China. It lives mostly beside still or slowly flowing water and occurs especially on banks overgrown with trees and bushes. The snake swims and dives very well and can stay under water for a long time without coming up for air. It is also very agile on land. It lives largely on fish, but will occasionally eat amphibians.

The viperine snake (*Natrix maura*) looks rather similar, with a flat head clearly standing out from the neck. Its coloring is very varied, gray, yellow or green. It is native to northwest Africa, Spain and Portugal, the south of France, Sardinia, and the Balearic Islands. A typical water snake, it is always found in the immediate vicinity of flowing or still water where there is abundant vegetation.

The common American water snake (*Natrix sipedon*), which is very similar in shape and coloring to the species

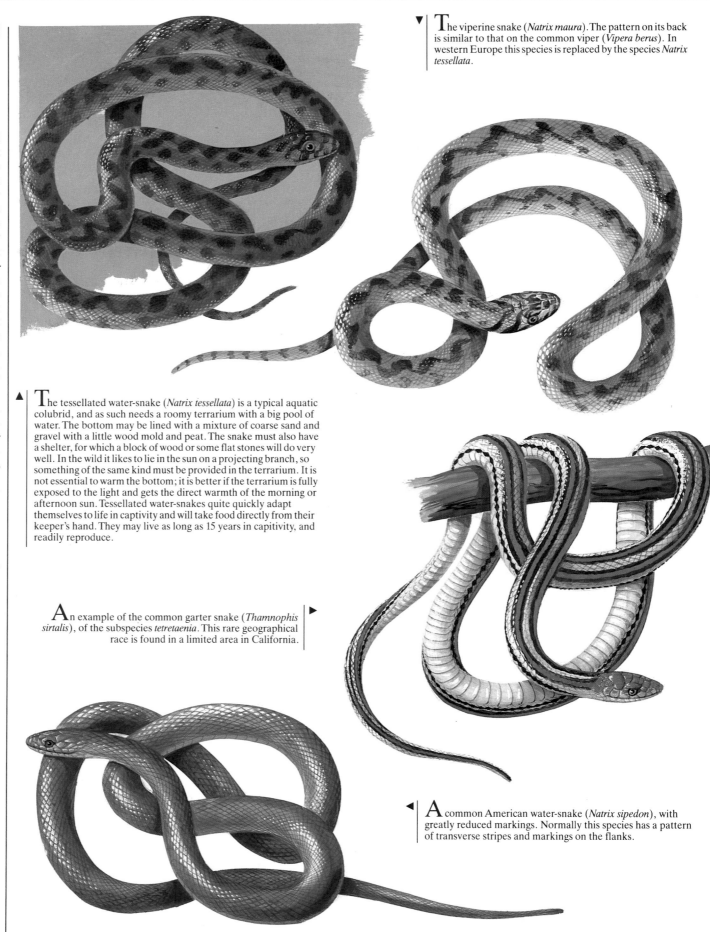

▼ The viperine snake (*Natrix maura*). The pattern on its back is similar to that on the common viper (*Vipera berus*). In western Europe this species is replaced by the species *Natrix tessellata*.

▲ The tessellated water-snake (*Natrix tessellata*) is a typical aquatic colubrid, and as such needs a roomy terrarium with a big pool of water. The bottom may be lined with a mixture of coarse sand and gravel with a little wood mold and peat. The snake must also have a shelter, for which a block of wood or some flat stones will do very well. In the wild it likes to lie in the sun on a projecting branch, so something of the same kind must be provided in the terrarium. It is not essential to warm the bottom; it is better if the terrarium is fully exposed to the light and gets the direct warmth of the morning or afternoon sun. Tessellated water-snakes quite quickly adapt themselves to life in captivity and will take food directly from their keeper's hand. They may live as long as 15 years in capitivity, and readily reproduce.

An example of the common garter snake (*Thamnophis sirtalis*), of the subspecies *tetretaenia*. This rare geographical race is found in a limited area in California. ▶

◀ A common American water-snake (*Natrix sipedon*), with greatly reduced markings. Normally this species has a pattern of transverse stripes and markings on the flanks.

Natrix fasciata, is the only big colubrid found in the north of America. It measures up to 54 in (135 cm), with a long head that does not greatly stand out from the body. It always lives near water, but moves just as freely on land as in water. It feeds on fish and amphibians, occasionally on mice. It is viviparous, and bears up to 46 young.

The common garter snake (*Thamnophis sirtalis*), which occurs in at least 13 subspecies, lives in the south of Canada, the greater part of the United States, and as far south as northern Mexico. There is considerable variety in both the coloring and the pattern of the different geographical races of this species; sometimes there are more stripes, sometimes more spots. Garter snakes have a slender body and a long, tapering tail. They occur in a wide variety of environments. For the most part they show a preference for damp places. These snakes feed on amphibians, fish, mice, insects, and earthworms.

Less well known is *Opisthotropis balteata*, an oviparous species that grows over 40 in (100 cm) long, found in Hainan, various places in China, Kampuchea, and Tonkin. This is a snake of low hill country, by or near rivers, where it hides under rocks or stones. It has one notable characteristic, very rare in snakes: it can shed its tail if it is seized. It feeds on small fish and amphibians.

The species *Rhabdophis tigrinus* has a head that does not stand out from the neck, a thin body and a long tail. This snake, seldom more than 40 in (100 cm) long, is native to Manchuria, Korea, Japan, and China, where it lives on the plains and up to 6,500 ft (2,000 m) in the mountains, in both wet and dry country. Its diet consists of frogs, toads, fish, mice, rats, birds, and grasshoppers.

The species *Xenodermus javanicus*, about 24 in (60 cm) long, is distributed from the south of Thailand and Tenasserim in Burma to the Malayan peninsula. It lives in wet country where the soil is soft – frequently in rice fields – and is wholly nocturnal. It is mostly found on the plains, but also occurs as far as 3,500 ft (1,100 m) or more up the mountains. It is not a very active animal, and lives entirely on frogs. The female lays 2 – 4 eggs.

The eastern hog-nosed snake (*Heterodon platyrrhinos*) is a clumsily built reptile with a thick body, short tail and broad head. Native to southern Canada and the central and eastern

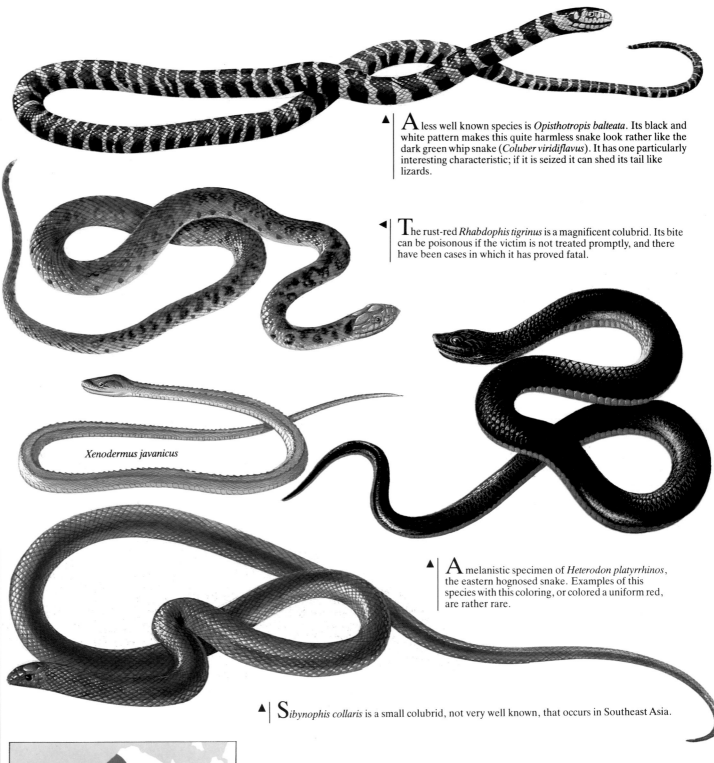

A less well known species is *Opisthotropis balteata*. Its black and white pattern makes this quite harmless snake look rather like the dark green whip snake (*Coluber viridiflavus*). It has one particularly interesting characteristic; if it is seized it can shed its tail like lizards.

The rust-red *Rhabdophis tigrinus* is a magnificent colubrid. Its bite can be poisonous if the victim is not treated promptly, and there have been cases in which it has proved fatal.

Xenodermus javanicus

A melanistic specimen of *Heterodon platyrrhinos*, the eastern hognosed snake. Examples of this species with this coloring, or colored a uniform red, are rather rare.

Sibynophis collaris is a small colubrid, not very well known, that occurs in Southeast Asia.

(1; Area of distribution of the grass snake (*Natrix natrix*). The nine geographical races of this species are distributed over a vast area taking in almost the whole of Europe, extending into Asia as far as Lake Baikal and reaching latitude 67°N. It does not occur in Ireland, the Balearic Islands, Malta, Crete, or some of the islands in the Cyclades.

United States, it is a clumsy-looking snake, mostly living in dry terrain where there are sand dunes, light woods, the dry edges of fields, and meadows and desert. It feeds mainly on toads, frogs, and salamanders. It hibernates for 4 – 6 months, mates in the spring and in June or July lays 6 – 42 eggs from which the eggs are hatched after 39 – 60 days, being then 6 – 8 in (15 – 20 cm) long.

The paradise tree-snake (*Chrysopelea paradisi*) has the long, graceful body characteristic of arboreal snakes. It can be found from the Kra isthmus in the south of Thailand to the Malayan peninsula, in the Greater Sunda Islands – and in Borneo, Celebes, and the Philippines. The snake eats lizards, birds, mice, and bats. Its venom is not very powerful. When it catches its prey it holds it in its jaws and kills it by constriction, finally releasing it from its jaws but not from its coils, and beginning to swallow it head first, even if it is still struggling.

This snake has one very special characteristic: its ability to "parachute." As it glides from one tree to another it stretches its body out sideways by opening its ribs, so that the belly is actually concave. The paradise tree-snake is oviparous.

The green whip-snake (*Oxybelis fulgidus*), whose distribution area extends from Mexico to Argentina, has a body structure and coloring highly adapted for life in trees and bushes, and moves in the branches with rare grace and agility. Generally it grows to a length of 5 – 6 ft (1.5 – 1.8 m). This snake is active by day and night, and never descends to the ground; it is found in plains and low hills up to 3,300 ft (1,000 m). It lies in loose coils on trees and bushes, its long, leaf-green body looking like a creeper and providing remarkable camouflage against its natural surroundings. Its food consists of lizards, nestlings, and frogs. Its venom is quickly effective, but these snakes are not a danger to humans and in fact seldom bite when disturbed. The female lays about 6 eggs in June.

The vine snake (*Thelotornis kirtlandi*) inhabits almost the whole of tropical Africa. It has an uncommonly thin body and tail and may grow to a length of 5¾ ft (1.7 m). Its habitat is in the bushes and trees, to which it is outstandingly well adapted by its shape and coloring. Resting in the trees, it looks like a liana.

▶ A so-called flying snake, the paradise tree-snake (*Chrysopelea paradisi*). By raising its ribs, this species (which is similar to the related species, *Chrysopelea ornata*) is able to flatten its body and arch the surface of the belly inward. In this way it can move from one tree to another by gliding through the air.

▼ Cross-section through the body in the normal position (left) and in the flattened position (right).

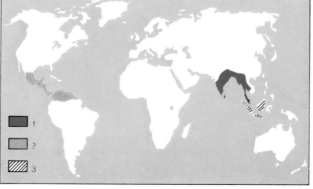

▲ The green whip-snake (*Oxybelis fulgidus*) is much like the Asian species *Ahaetulla prasina*, the green tree-snake, both in appearance and behavior. It can be easily distinguished by its round pupils.

▲ The slender, tapering form of the vine snake (*Thelotornis kirtlandii*) marks it out at once as an arboreal species. Unlike most opisthoglyph snakes, it produces a venom which is lethal to man.

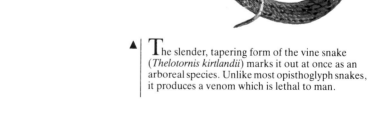

◀ Distribution area of some of the colubrids. (1) *Ahaetulla prasina* is distributed from Bengal and the eastern Himalayas to the whole of Indochina and the Malayan peninsula. (2) *Oxybelis fulgidus* is found in Central America, from Mexico to Amazonia. (3) *Chrysopelea paradisi* occurs from southern Thailand to the Malayan peninsula, the Sunda Islands, and the Philippines.

AFRICAN EGG-EATING SNAKE

Dasypeltis scabra

The common African egg-eating snake is 28 – 36 in (70 – 90 cm) long, with a small head only slightly distinct from its neck. Its eyes are small, with vertical pupils, and its snout is blunt. There are 3 – 9 very small teeth on each side of the upper jaw, and these have no function. The vertebrae exhibit a remarkable adaptation to the function of teeth. The lower vertebral processes are covered with a coating like the enamel on teeth, and penetrate the upper wall of the esophagus to form a kind of saw. The body scales are elongated and clearly keeled. The ground color of the egg-eating snake's body is gray, brown or yellow.

The snake has an enormous area of distribution from the south of Arabia and East and Central Africa to South Africa. The usual habitat is dry bush or forest, where the snake lives on the ground and in the trees. Its diet consists exclusively of birds' eggs, so it is no wonder that it is an excellent climber, often found near birds' nests. It is mainly nocturnal. An adult African egg-eating snake, with a head no thicker than a human finger, can without difficulty swallow a hen's egg. It traces birds' eggs by its sense of smell.

The snake is completely harmless, but it looks rather like the venomous night adder (*Causus rhombeatus*) and is often mistaken for it and killed. The female lays 12 – 15 eggs measuring 1½ × ¾ in (36 × 18 mm), in December or January and often again in April or May. The eggs are laid separately, not sticking together. After 3 – 4 months the young emerge, about 9 in (23 cm) long.

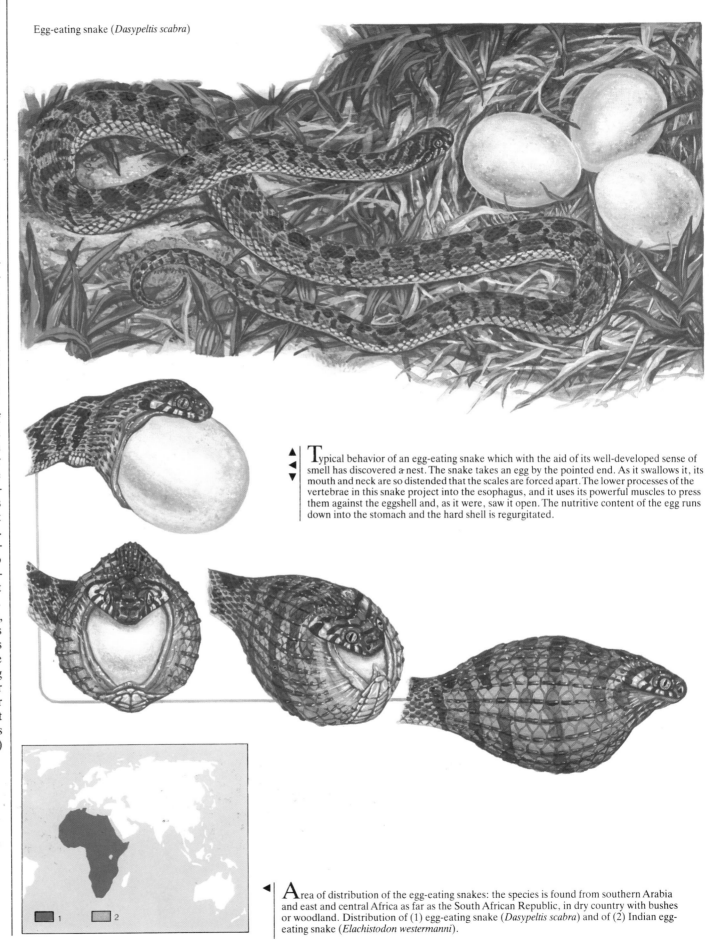

Egg-eating snake (*Dasypeltis scabra*)

▲◄▼ Typical behavior of an egg-eating snake which with the aid of its well-developed sense of smell has discovered a nest. The snake takes an egg by the pointed end. As it swallows it, its mouth and neck are so distended that the scales are forced apart. The lower processes of the vertebrae in this snake project into the esophagus, and it uses its powerful muscles to press them against the eggshell and, as it were, saw it open. The nutritive content of the egg runs down into the stomach and the hard shell is regurgitated.

◄ Area of distribution of the egg-eating snakes: the species is found from southern Arabia and east and central Africa as far as the South African Republic, in dry country with bushes or woodland. Distribution of (1) egg-eating snake (*Dasypeltis scabra*) and of (2) Indian egg-eating snake (*Elachistodon westermanni*).

INDIAN COBRA
Naja naja

Order Squamata
Suborder Ophidia
Family Elapidae
Size Length 60 – 80 in (180 – 200 cm) or a little more
Reproductive period January to July
Number of eggs 10 – 20, at most 45
Maximum age 20 years or more

The Indian cobra is the best known of the cobras. It has a short, flat head that does not stand out greatly from the neck. Overall size, as well as color and pattern on the body are subject to wide variation, according to the geographical races.

The Indian cobra is native to the southern Asian continent from east of the Caspian Sea to the East Indies, Hainan, and Taiwan. It is usually found near water, very often in ricefields, in neglected gardens, on plantations and, no less often, in the immediate vicinity of human residences. The cobra will sometimes find its way into houses, where it can be a danger to people, who may tread on it accidentally. It lives in the jungle, from sea level to an altitude of 8,000 ft (2,500 m). In point of fact, the cobra can be found wherever there is food and shelter for it. It likes best to lie up in termite-hills, in the mud walls of ricefields, in old buildings and under all sorts of old rubbish.

The Indian cobra is active by day, but more so at night. It is a shy creature which flees from humans; but if cornered it rears up the front part of its body and spreads the hood in the area of the neck like a shield. Some geographical races spit venom at their enemies. Cobras' venom is extremely powerful. It acts on the nervous system, and stops breathing. *Naja naja* takes a great variety of prey – small mammals, birds, frogs, toads, lizards, and snakes. The young cobras hatch after 69 – 84 days, when they are 10 – 12 in (25 – 30 cm) long.

◄ An Indian cobra of the subspecies *Naja naja naja* in the typical defensive position. When this species feels itself menaced, it erects the ribs and extends the skin of its neck, forming the characteristic hood with its pattern of spectacles.

▼ For its prey this snake prefers rodents, birds, and amphibians. In captivity, the young tend to feed mostly on amphibians, but as they grow will readily eat mice and other sorts of rodents.

HARLEQUIN CORAL SNAKE

Micrurus fulvius

Order Squamata
Suborder Ophidia
Family Elapidae
Size Length up to 48 in (120 cm)
Reproductive period April to June
Number of eggs From 3 to 22
Period of incubation About 3 months
Maximum age 10 years or more

The harlequin coral snake has a short, flat head not distinct from the neck, small eyes with round pupils, an elongated cylindrical body and a short tail. The brightly shining scales are all unkeeled. The body has black and red rings round it with narrower yellow rings between the black and the red. There are black spots on the red rings.

The snake inhabits the southern and southeastern United States and the northeast of Mexico, where it is mostly found in low-lying country. It occurs equally in dry and wet places.

Micrurus fulvius is a markedly nocturnal species, passing the day in holes in the ground, under fallen trees and branches, in piles of rotting twigs or under fallen leaves. It feeds on small snakes and lizards, which it holds between its jaws long enough for its powerful nerve poison to kill them.

One of the most beautiful coral snakes is the cobra coral snake, (*Micrurus frontalis*), found in southwestern Brazil, Uruguay, Paraguay, and Bolivia. This species, sometimes over 52 in (130 cm) long, looks much like the harlequin coral snake. It lives mainly in the forests. The snake is not aggressive but will bite dangerously if roughly handled.

One of the smallest, and one of the prettiest, of the coral snakes is the Arizona coral snake (*Micruroides euryxanthus*). This snake, which can reach a length of 20 in (50 cm) is extraordinarily beautifully colored. An inhabitant of the southwestern United States and northwestern Mexico, it is a small snake, preferring dry places overgrown with low bushes and sparsely growing trees.

Harlequin coral snake
(*Micrurus fulvius*)

◀ **A** medium-sized North American harlequin coral snake (*Micrurus fulvius*). When the animal is frightened it hides its head under its coils and shakes its body from side to side. Besides lizards and non-poisonous snakes this species also eats young rattlesnakes, crushing them between its jaws until they are dead. It is immune to their bite.

▲ **A**bove: two coral snakes in characteristic positions. Left, the Arizona coral snake (*Micruroides euryxanthus*); right, the cobra coral snake (*Micrurus frontalis*).

◀ **D**istribution of the coral snakes – there are about 50 species – in North, Central, and South America.

RATTLESNAKES
Crotalus

The rattlesnakes are among the most famous and most feared snakes in the world. People see them as fierce and cunning creatures; but like all other snakes, rattlesnakes are actually timid and nervous.

There are over 30 species of rattlesnakes, most of them native to Mexico and the southern United States. With the exception of the Santa Catalina rattlesnake (*Crotalus catalinensis*), all rattlesnakes have a so-called rattle on the end of their tails. It consists of a series of hollow rings of a horny substance, keratin – the same substance that our fingernails are made of – interconnected but not fixed to each other. Each time a rattlesnake sloughs its skin, a new ring appears at the end of its tail. Adult rattlesnakes molt three or four times a year. The rattle is extremely brittle and often gets broken. When a rattlesnake feels it is in danger or becomes excited, it shakes the rattle 40 – 60 times per second, making the characteristic sound that warns enemies and is meant to frighten them away.

Rattlesnakes are only dangerous if they are not seen and are accidentally trodden on or otherwise disturbed. Their bite is dangerous, especially to children, but seldom fatal. The snakes are virtually immune to their own venom. Their diet consists of small mammals, birds, and occasionally lizards and frogs.

There are two genera of rattlesnakes: *Crotalus* (true rattlesnakes) and *Sistrurus* (pygmy rattlesnakes).

The western diamondback (*Crotalus atrox*) has a broad, flat head clearly distinct from the neck. The body is stout and muscular and the scales markedly keeled. It is distributed over wide areas of the western United States and as far south as central Mexico. It is found in the plains and in the mountains, in deserts and canyons, in uncultivated and cultivated ground. The specific name *atrox* is certainly appropriate to this snake's life habits. At the least disturbance it coils its body up into a defensive spiral and rattles loudly and incessantly; it lowers its head a little, waiting for a chance to strike at the approaching enemy and bite it. In the USA it is responsible for the majority of cases of snakebite. The

On the pit-viper illustrated here the rattle is clearly visible, composed in this case of seven ring segments. These rings are hollow and loosely attached to each other, so as to produce the characteristic sound when the tail is vibrated. They are rather fragile and apt to get worn or broken, and the outside rings are periodically replaced. The number of rings in the majority of pit-vipers varies from seven to twelve.

The diagram on the left illustrates details of the structure of a rattle.

All pit-vipers of the genera *Crotalus* and *Sistrurus* have a pit between the eye and the nostril with a thin membrane at the base provided with a great number of nervous heat-receptors. This organ can detect the presence of bodies warmer than the surrounding temperature, and with its aid the snakes can locate warmblooded enemies or prey.

western diamondback feeds on mice, rats, rabbits, and other rodents.

The sidewinder (*Crotalus cerastes*) is a small species, 18 – 30 in (45 – 75 cm) long. It lives in the desert areas of eastern California, southern Nevada, southwestern Utah, Arizona, northeastern Baja California and northwest Mexico. Its home is in the sand dunes overgrown with ocotillos, mesquite and creosote bushes. The sidewinder is occasionally found in rocky deserts and even on cultivated land. It feeds mainly on lizards, and to a smaller extent on mice.

The prairie rattlesnake (*Crotalus viridis*) is the most widely distributed rattlesnake in the United States. The head is heart-shaped and flat, standing well out from the neck. It grows to anything from 24 to 62 in (60 to 155 cm). Its area of distribution extends from the south of Canada to the central and western states of the USA and as far south as northwest Mexico, where it can be found at altitudes from sea level to 12,000 ft (3,700 m). It occurs in a great variety of biotopes, living in pine and oak woods, on sand dunes near the coast, on mountain slopes where there are all sorts of loose stones and low vegetation, and in the open prairies. It is active by day and by night, feeding on a variety of small mammals and on birds, sometimes on lizards and even on toads and insects. The snake hibernates between 4 and 8 months, depending on the locality; large numbers of them often share the same shelter with members of their own species and with other snakes. The female gives birth to an average of 7 – 10 young, 10 in (25 cm) long, in a two-yearly cycle.

The cascabel (*Crotalus durissus*) has a long, triangular head standing out clearly from the slender neck. It is up to 6 ft (1.8 m) long, with a rather stout body, triangular in section. This snake, which occurs from the south of Mexico across Central America as far south as Argentina, prefers dry, stony places with a growth of low bushes, at altitudes up to 6,500 ft (2,000 m). It is a sluggish creature, peaceful rather than aggressive. During the day it generally lies in one place with its body coiled up. If disturbed it draws attention to itself by rattling loudly, but when roused it strikes swiftly and hard. It has the strongest venom of all the rattlesnakes and nearly 75 per cent of people who are bitten die if they do not receive quickly large quantities of serum.

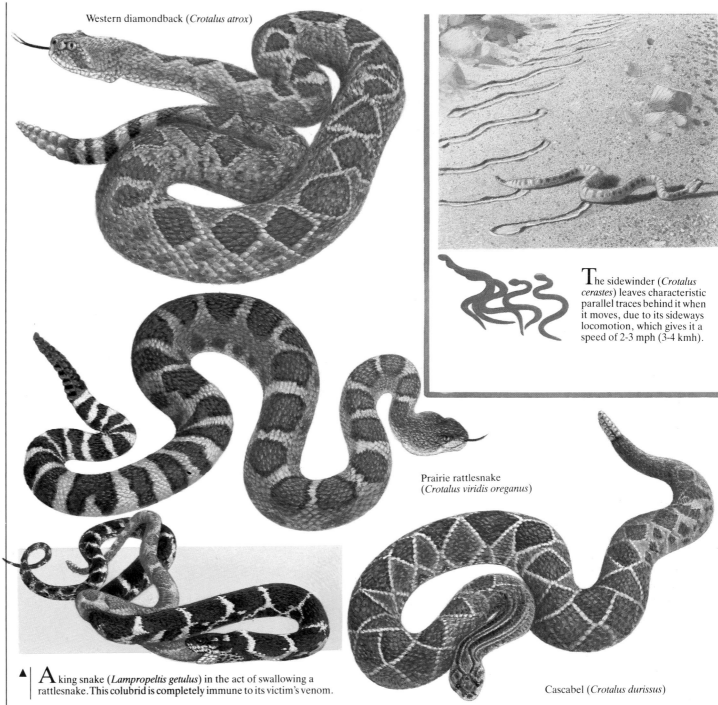

Western diamondback (*Crotalus atrox*)

The sidewinder (*Crotalus cerastes*) leaves characteristic parallel traces behind it when it moves, due to its sideways locomotion, which gives it a speed of 2-3 mph (3-4 kmh).

Prairie rattlesnake (*Crotalus viridis oreganus*)

▲ A king snake (*Lampropeltis getulus*) in the act of swallowing a rattlesnake. This colubrid is completely immune to its victim's venom.

Cascabel (*Crotalus durissus*)

◀ Area of distribution of the pit-vipers of the genera *Crotalus* and *Sistrurus*. In the first of these there are some 30 species, distributed from southern Canada to Brazil and the north of Argentina and concentrated particularly in North America. The second genus comprises three species, present in South and Central America. They occupy the most diverse of habitats, from swamps and equatorial rainforest through the stony, rugged woodlands of central eastern North America to the burning deserts of the southwestern United States.

CROCODILIANS
Crocodylia

All the crocodilians have a long body with a vertically compressed tail and four short legs. Their true habitat is the water; they are all rather awkward on land. There are five toes on the forelegs, four on the hindlegs, which are webbed to a varying extent. The skin is tough and leathery. The teeth, which differ in size and shape, lie in cavities in the jaw, called alveoli, and are renewed regularly.

Crocodilians have an obviously lizardlike shape. Among the crocodilians there are forms such as the smooth-fronted caiman (*Paleosuchus trigonatus*) which are no more than 4¾ ft (1.4 m) long, and giant forms such as the estuarine crocodile (*Crocodylus porosus*), which in exceptional cases can reach the immense length of 33 ft (10 m).

Crocodilians are predators, exclusively carnivorous. They not only hunt living animals but also eat carrion. When young they live on big water insects, crustaceans, tadpoles, frogs, and small fish. As they grow older they move on to bigger prey – water birds, cats and dogs, pigs, small antelope, monkeys, and even bigger animals like lions and the bigger species of antelope.

All crocodilians lay hard-shelled, white eggs, about the size of that of a goose. The female scrapes up a nest consisting of uprooted grass, reeds, leaves, twigs, branches and so on, into a round heap 3 – 6 ft (1 – 2 m) across and about 20 – 40 in (50 – 100 cm) high. The female guards the eggs until they hatch.

The Nile crocodile (*Crocodylus niloticus*) is about 16 ft (5 m) long, with a fairly long snout about one and a half or two times as long as it is broad at the base. It occurs in Africa south of the Sahara in Madagascar, the Comoro Islands, and Seychelles. The species lives in rivers, lakes, marshes, and swamps.

The smallest of the crocodilians is *Osteolaemus tetraspis*. This species has a comparatively short snout and looks rather like the South American smooth-fronted caimans of the genus *Paleosuchus*. This dwarf crocodile is found almost exclusively in the rainforest of tropical and equatorial Africa, living both in fast flowing and

Osteolaemus tetraspis

Marsh crocodile (*Crocodylus palustris*)

Estuarine crocodile (*Crocodylus porosus*)

American crocodile (*Crocodylus acutus*)

False gavial (*Tomistoma schlegelii*)

in sluggish waters: but it does also move into the waters in the savannas immediately on the edge of the rainforest.

The marsh crocodile or mugger (*Crocodylus palustris*) grows to a length of 19 ft (5.8 m). It lives in Pakistan, India, Bangladesh, and Sri Lanka. The reptile looks very much like the Nile crocodile. It lives on the land beside fresh water, though in Sri Lanka it is also found in brackish water in swamps. Its habitat is in marshes, lakes, and rivers, and its food consists of fish, frogs, birds, and mammals of a suitable size.

The American crocodile (*Crocodylus acutus*) has a notably long, pointed snout. Adult specimens are generally up to 13 ft (4 m) long, but exceptional specimens have reached a length of 25 ft (7.7 m). It has a wide area of distribution, extending from the south of Florida across Central America to northern parts of South America, living in coastal areas and spreading into major rivers, especially if they run through big swamps.

The American crocodile lives mainly on fish, but examination of the stomachs of dead specimens reveals that it also eats crustaceans, birds, and mammals. All the stomachs examined contained stones.

The false gavial (*Tomistoma schlegeli*) has an extremely long, thin snout, four and a half times as long as it is broad at the base. Unlike the gavial of the Ganges (*Gavialis gangeticus*), whose snout narrows suddenly near the base and continues to narrow to the tip, the false gavial has a snout that narrows more gradually from base to tip. The upper jaw has 20 – 21 teeth on each side, the lower jaw 18 – 19. In exceptional cases it reaches an overall length of 18 ft (5.6 m). It lives in Malaya, Sumatra, and Borneo, in lakes, morasses and rivers, where it generally stays near the banks.

The genus *Alligator* contains two species. The American alligator (*Alligator mississipiensis*), which is found in the southeastern United States, can in exceptional cases reach a length of 20 ft (6 m), while the Chinese alligator (*Alligator sinensis*) is not more than 7 ft (2.1 m) long. The latter species lives in the lower reaches of the Yang-tse Kiang in China.

Closely related to the alligators is the black caiman (*Melanosuchus niger*), which reaches a length of 15 ft (4.5 m).

American alligator
(*Alligator mississipiensis*)

Black caiman (*Melanosuchus niger*)

Indian gavial (*Gavialis gangeticus*)

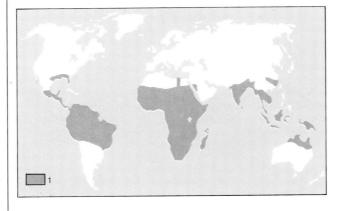

1) The distribution area of the crocodilians extends over nearly all the tropical regions of the Old and New World. They are all amphibians. While they are also active by day, they are much more lively and bellicose at night. As recently as the 1940s crocodiles were still remarkably frequent in many parts of their distribution area. Today, in consequence of the ruthless hunting to which they have been subjected, they have become rare all over the world and are almost in danger of extinction.

OSTRICH

Struthio camelus

Order Struthioniformes
Family Struthionidae
Size Height 8¼ ft (2.5 m); length 6 ft (1.8 m)
Weight 300 lb (136 kg)
Distribution Central, east and southern Africa
Eggs 10 – 25
Chicks Nidifugous

The ostrich is exceptionally well adapted to life in open surroundings where many predators roam. The head is small and virtually naked, with large eyes protected against dust and sandstorms by long lashes. The very long neck, functions as a periscope for surveying the surrounding terrain from on high, often rearing up above the low acacia bushes. The wings, despite not being used for flying, still retain long flight feathers, which will help the bird keep its balance when running. The numerous tail feathers serve only as distinct signals during various stages of social life.

The diet of leaves and shoots is extremely varied. When feeding, ostriches graze in scattered flocks of variable size, but one individual always stays on the alert, ready to spot any kind of danger and warn the others with deep alarm calls.

Ostriches are very speedy runners. At maximum speed an adult can touch 43 mph (70 kmh); and the bird's long strides can carry it along with leaps of up to 10 ft (3 m).

The ostrich normally leads a communal life. When the breeding season approaches, the males move about in groups of several dozens, while at the same time the females and young form considerably larger flocks. The ostrich is generally polygamous, each male coupling with two, three or even more females. In due course the male courts and copulates with all the females in his harem, and by this time he is looking around for a suitable place to build the nest. Once the nest is constructed, several females approach and lay their eggs. When all the egg-laying is completed, the dominant female will sometimes chase all the others away from the nesting site, remaining alone with the male and helping him with the duties of incubation.

▲ The evolutionary history of the ostrich began on the steppes of Asia, perhaps during the Eocene, when groups of small running birds broke off from the original branch of flying birds. These flightless birds soon adapted to their new ecological niche, successfully exploiting this environment. Indeed, during the Pliocene giant forms already existed, having extended their range as far as Mongolia in the north and the tip of Africa in the south.

The ostrich (*Struthio camelus*) is today the only bird to have mastered the conditions of the African savanna, where sheer speed is the basic key to survival both for predator and prey, the hunter and the hunted. The ostrich has developed to perfection the capacity for spotting, in good time, the danger posed by large predators such as lions and cheetahs, and of escaping on foot as rapidly as possible.

RHEA

Rhea americana

Order Rheiformes
Family Rheidae
Size Height 5½ ft (1.7 m); length 4¼ ft (1.3 m)
Weight 55 lb (25 kg)
Distribution South America
Eggs 15 – 20
Chicks Nidifugous

Not so powerful as the ostrich, the rhea has a relatively compact body, which, except for the almost naked legs, is uniformly brown. The wings are larger than in all other ratites, being used by the rhea to balance itself when running at speed. Frequently, while running, the rhea will suddenly stop and throw itself to the ground, somewhat like an ostrich, stretching its neck along the surface. The legs, very strong as in all running birds, are covered by a series of horny plates.

In the dry, flat expanses of the pampas the rhea feeds on the fruits of various species of crowberry (*Empetrum*) as well as cultivated fruits. An important part of the diet is additionally made up of the shoots and leaves of many leguminous and graminaceous plants, insects and lizards.

Rheas normally live in stable flocks outside the breeding season, but older males, which are markedly larger than the females, usually live on their own. With the approach of spring, when the days become longer and the temperature rises, the males turn decidedly territorial and engage in combat, often very violently, with rivals, dealing out powerful kicks and blows of the beak. Having won a portion of territory, each individual male starts courting females. One male may, within a short time, assemble a harem of 15 – 20 females inside his territory. Then, having chosen a patch of sandy ground well concealed by trees, he will dig a hole and proceed to line it with leaves and grass. He mates with the various females and they begin laying their eggs either in the principal nest or in any of the other holes dug by the male. As soon as the nest is full of eggs, he starts incubating them. After 35 days' incubation, the eggs start to hatch and the male stays on the nest for another 48 hours. The chicks grow very fast and within a couple of months are one-third the weight of the adults.

Although not so impressive in appearance, the rhea is very similar to the ostrich and plays the same role in South America as its counterpart does on the African savanna. This affinity suggests that they may have had a common ancestor, the progenitor of a group of birds which later became diversified when natural barriers appeared, isolating one from the other.

Incubation of eggs is the task of the male, who drives away the female when the nest is full. After the eggs hatch he remains on the nest for a further 48 hours. The chicks grow quickly and soon become independent.

Darwin's rhea (*Pterocnemia pennata*) is a somewhat smaller species, varying from its relative, too, in possessing a different number of horny plates on its powerful legs.

Distribution of the two South American rheas: 1) Darwin's rhea (*Pterocnemia pennata*); 2) Rhea (*Rhea americana*).

CASSOWARY

Casuarius casuarius

Order Casuariiformes
Family Casuariidae
Size Height 3¼ ft (1 m); length 5¼ ft (1.6 m)
Weight 187 lb (85 kg)
Distribution Northeast Australia, New Guinea
Eggs 3 – 6
Chicks Nidifugous

The cassowary is a large running bird adapted to the dense forest that still covers much of New Guinea. There are three distinct species, two of which are found exclusively in New Guinea and on the island of New Britain; the third, the common or Australian cassowary (*Casuarius casuarius*), is also an inhabitant of the Queensland peninsula in northeast Australia.

Although they stand up to 3¼ ft (1 m) high at the back, cassowaries give the impression of being extraordinarily stocky. The body, like that of the emu, is noticeably elongated and is supported by fairly short, though heavy, legs. The feet, broad and powerful, are those of an accomplished runner; they have three toes, the innermost one being short but furnished with a strong claw which constitutes a terrible weapon. The extremely thick plumage is glossy black with vivid blue reflections.

As is the case with the ostrich, a cassowary, as it runs through the forest, will extend its stumps of wings, not so much in order to maintain balance as to open gaps in the dense vegetation. The abundant, compact plumage is, furthermore, useful for lessening any pain or damage that the bird might sustain by colliding with branches or trunks as it runs through the trees.

It would seem that cassowaries are monogamous birds. Outside the breeding season it is usual to encounter only solitary individuals. Pairs form before August. The female lays 3 – 5 dark green eggs in a small hole on the ground, the nest being wadded with vegetation. Incubation is the responsibility of the male. At birth the chicks are covered with striped plumage and are nidifugous.

▼ The cassowary has an exceptionally robust build, its sturdy legs being covered by horny plates and the broad, heavy feet indicating that the bird is a powerful runner.

▲◄ The most spectacular feature of the cassowary (*Casuarius casuarius*) is the huge, horny growth jutting out, like a helmet, from the head. The shape and size of this casque vary from one species to another, and it has a very precise function; as the bird runs through the undergrowth at speeds of up to 31 mph (50 kmh) it stretches out its neck and head parallel to the ground, using the casque to prise open gaps in the vegetation without risk of injury.

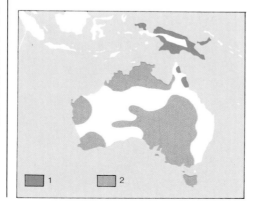

◄ 1) The cassowary lives in dense forests which cover a large part of New Guinea. The single-wattled cassowary (*Casuarius unappendiculatus*) and Bennett's cassowary (*C. bennetti*) are found only in New Guinea and on the island of New Britain, whereas the common or Australian cassowary (*C. casuarius*) is also an inhabitant of northeastern Australia, in the York Peninsula. The cassowary has no enemies apart from man; the natives hunt it for its flesh but this has never put its survival at risk. There is a greater potential threat in the progessive destruction of its forest habitats. 2) The emu has colonized the dry plains of the Australian continent. It, too, has been adversely affected by the indiscriminate hunting to which it was subjected until quite recently. Tens of thousands of birds were slaughtered every year, the incentive being a money reward offered by the governments to anyone bringing in an emu's beak.

KIWI

Apteryx australis

Order Apterygiformes
Family Apterygidae
Size Length 22 – 27 in (55 – 68 cm)
Weight Male about 4½ lb (2 kg);
female about 7 lb (3 kg)
Distribution New Zealand
Eggs 1 – 3
Chicks Nidicolous for about 3 – 4 days

The dense, luxuriant forests which still cover large areas of New Zealand harbor the kiwi, a strange bird quite unable to fly, its wings being reduced to two stumps into which the 13 remiges are inserted. Its plumage has an unusual consistency, rather like coarse hair. The tail has completely vanished, while the legs are very strong yet short, dark brown in color and partially covered by horny plates. Very remarkable is the bill, long and slightly curved downward, the upper jaw jutting out a little above the lower and the nostrils opening at the tip.

After spending the hours of daylight hidden in dark ravines or dense bush, the kiwi becomes very active as soon as night falls. Darting about, head lowered, it scratches at the ground in search of food, which consists in the main of insects and other invertebrates. The long beak probes into the moist forest soil for worms, myriapods, and larvae, digging them out so that they can be swiftly swallowed. It is likely that the kiwi makes use of its highly acute hearing to find this type of prey, for its ear openings are very large. Moving through the bracken and around the rotting trunks, it also catches spiders, snails, and many orthopterans. But when the climate is at its driest the bird turns largely vegetarian.

The kiwi seems to be monogamous; once the pair is formed, the male builds a rudimentary nest on the ground. The shiny white egg is remarkably large in relation to the female's body size – up to 14 per cent of her weight. Incubation is almost the exclusive responsibility of the male, who sits on the nest for about 84 days, except when he leaves it at night to look for food. At birth, the chicks are covered in soft brown down which is exactly like that of the adults.

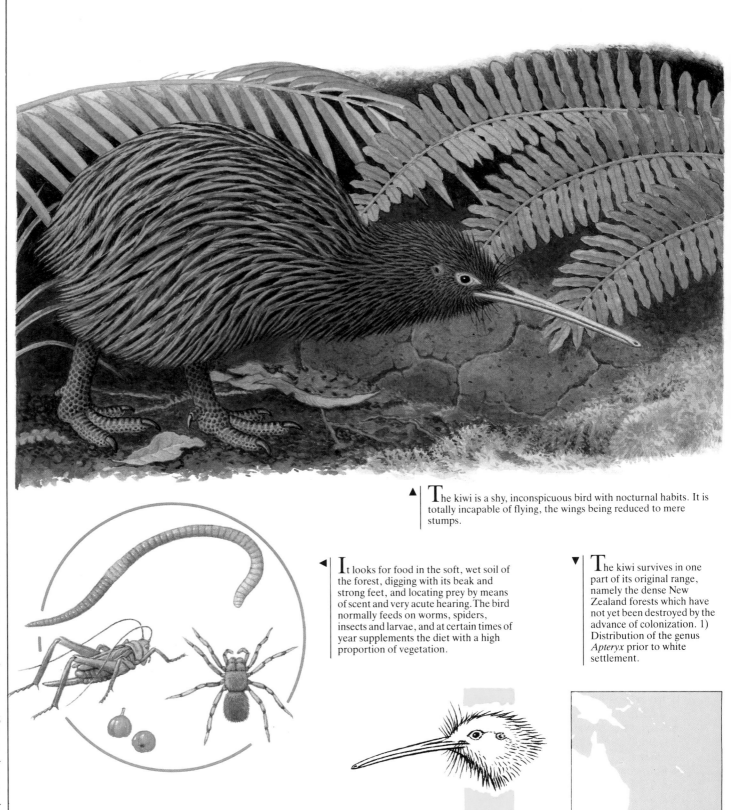

▲ The kiwi is a shy, inconspicuous bird with nocturnal habits. It is totally incapable of flying, the wings being reduced to mere stumps.

◄ It looks for food in the soft, wet soil of the forest, digging with its beak and strong feet, and locating prey by means of scent and very acute hearing. The bird normally feeds on worms, spiders, insects and larvae, and at certain times of year supplements the diet with a high proportion of vegetation.

▼ The kiwi survives in one part of its original range, namely the dense New Zealand forests which have not yet been destroyed by the advance of colonization. 1) Distribution of the genus *Apteryx* prior to white settlement.

► A characteristic feature of the kiwi is its bill, long, slightly curved downward and with nostrils that open at the tip. This last detail distinguishes the kiwi from the majority of other birds, whose nostrils are situated on the bottom of the beak, and it emphasizes the importance of scent in the search for food.

1

EMPEROR PENGUIN

Aptenodytes forsteri

Order Sphenisciformes
Family Spheniscidae
Size Length about 45 in (115 cm)
Weight About 65 lb (30 kg)
Distribution Antarctic continent
Eggs 1
Chicks Nidicolous

The coasts of the vast continent fringing the Antarctic Ocean are the home of the emperor penguin, the largest species of its order, which breeds here in enormous colonies.

In the emperor penguin, like other members of the family, the entire body is covered by dense plumage. The wings are very short in relation to the body, and the legs, completely feathered, terminate in comparatively small feet. The color of the plumage follows the general pattern found in most penguins; back, wings and head down to the throat are shiny black while the abdomen is white with yellow tints.

The emperor penguin feeds on many kinds of marine animals, particularly the shoals of squid that often inhabit these relatively deep waters.

The penguins begin to arrive at their breeding sites in small groups, the numbers steadily increasing the closer they get to the zone where the colony regularly assembles. The journey from the coast, which is already covered by pack-ice, entails a considerable expenditure of energy, because the areas selected for reproduction may be a long distance from the sea. Apparently the emperor penguin returns to the same site year after year.

The single egg is incubated beneath a fold of skin between the feet. Within 6 – 12 hours of laying the egg, the female passes it over to her mate, who places it between his feet, and goes off in search of food. The burden of incubation now falls exclusively on the male. The females arrive back at about the time when the eggs are almost ready to hatch, so that the newborn chicks can receive fresh food from their mothers. Once they have molted and aquired proper plumage, they quit the colony for the open sea, where there is now an abundance of food.

▲ The emperor penguin, largest of living Sphenisciformes, is particularly adapted for withstanding the terrible southern winter. It, too, forms huge colonies: the one on Coulman Island brings together more than 30,000 birds.

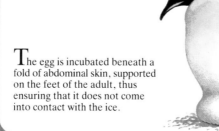

The egg is incubated beneath a fold of abdominal skin, supported on the feet of the adult, thus ensuring that it does not come into contact with the ice.

◄ The burden of incubation falls entirely on the male. Motionless in the freezing cold winter, he carries out the task which, when complete, will have forced him to go more than three months without food.

WANDERING ALBATROSS

Diomedea exulans

Order Procellariiformes
Family Diomedeidae
Size Length 28 – 48 in (71 – 122 cm)
Weight 13 – 18 lb (6 – 8 kg)
Distribution Southern hemisphere, North Pacific
Habits Gregarious; pelagic, transoceanic migrants
Nesting On ground
Reproductive period Autumn – winter or spring – summer
Eggs 1
Chicks Semi-inept
Sexual maturity 6 – 10 years
Maximum age About 40 years

The albatrosses are the largest known flying birds. A simple distinguishing feature is the huge bill made up of numerous horny plates. The nostrils, in the form of short tubes, are situated on either side of the central slab of the upper mandible.

Albatrosses are to be found in almost all of the world's oceans: nine species live in the southern hemisphere, three in the North Pacific and one in the tropics. They are exceptional fliers: the Laysan albatross nests in Hawaii and migrates regularly across the Pacific, sometimes reaching Kamchatka and New Zealand, and the wandering albatross, distributed throughout Oceania, spends approximately 12 – 13 months, the period between two successive breeding cycles, flying the world's oceans, sometimes reaching northern Europe.

No other bird can rival the albatross in remaining for hours on end suspended in the air, hardly ever moving its wings. They feed chiefly on squids, caught on the surface either in flight or when at rest.

The birds normally nest in colonies. The nests are situated in small holes scooped out with the beak or simply on the ground, and they consist of soil and mud. The birds are normally very regular in returning to the same nesting sites. The female lays one large egg, which is incubated for 60 – 80 days. Both parents take part in incubation. The newborn chick is fed by both parents for the first 3 – 5 weeks on pulpy food mixed with the oily secretions of the glandular stomach.

The albatrosses are the largest representatives of the order Procellariiformes. The wandering albatross (the drawing shows an adult and, on the right, an immature individual) is the largest of all marine birds. There are three species of albatross in the northern hemisphere and ten in the southern hemisphere. They are carried along by the strong sea winds, seldom flapping their wings; in flight they hold the bill downward, repeatedly skimming the waves.

The bill of the albatross, composed of horny plates, is very stout, the nostrils being situated on either side of the central plate of the upper mandible.

WHITE PELICAN

Pelecanus onocrotalus

Order Pelecaniformes
Family Pelicanidae
Size Length 43 – 70 in (110 – 178 cm)
Weight 15 – 31 lbs (7 – 14 kg)
Distribution Europe, Asia, Africa, America, and Australia
Habits Gregarious and migratory
Nesting In trees or on ground
Reproductive period Spring and summer
Incubation 30 – 42 days
Eggs 2 – 3
Chicks Inept
Sexual maturity 3 – 4 years

Pelicans are large birds, commonly associated with fresh or brackish water; their large, broad wings, spanning almost 10 ft (3 m), facilitate the characteristic gliding flight.

The bill is very large and the upper mandible terminates in a small hook. From the lower mandible hangs a voluminous, dilatable pouch, with a capacity of 2 gallons (13 liters) and this gives the bird its characteristic and easily recognizable appearance. The pouch not only stores fish but is used as a net to catch them. The plumage is white or dark gray in the adults.

Although pelicans occasionally feed on crustaceans, worms, and organic refuse, they are, first and foremost, fishing birds. Their technique for catching fish varies according to species. White pelicans indulge in communal fishing while the brown ones catch their prey by diving.

Thanks to the air sacs under the skin which help to buoy up their heavy body in water, pelicans are good swimmers. They are gregarious by nature and are often seen flying in a characteristic diagonal formation.

During the courtship period pelicans build a nest with reeds, twigs, and scraps of vegetation. The female lays 2 – 3 bluish or yellowish eggs with a dirty-white shell. The naked, chicks remain in the nest from 85 to 105 days.

The parent birds swallow the prey and reduce it to a consistent pulp inside the crop; then it is regurgitated into the expansible pouch beneath the lower mandible so that the chicks can thrust in the whole head for feeding.

White pelican (*Pelecanus onocrotalus*)

Pelicans, among the largest of all aquatic birds, are famous for the pouch of skin hanging from the lower mandible, which is used for netting fish. Their feet are webbed and this extends to the rear toe as well. There are white and brown pelicans, each with a different method of catching fish, their principal prey.

Foot of a pelican: all four toes are joined by a single web.

COMMON CORMORANT

Phalacrocorax carbo

Order Pelecaniformes
Family Phalacrocracidae
Size Length 18 – 36 in (48 – 92 cm)
Weight 1½ – 7½ lb (0.7 – 3.5 kg)
Distribution Worldwide, excluding polar regions
Habits Colonial; some species migratory
Nesting In trees and rocks
Reproductive period Spring – summer or winter – spring
Incubation 27 – 30 days
Eggs 2 – 4
Chicks Inept
Sexual maturity 3 years

There are 29 species of cormorants: eight live only in America, eleven in Europe, Asia and Africa, six in Australia and the remaining four virtually all over the globe.

They have long necks, fairly small, rounded wings and a distinctive skull structure which enables them to keep hold of prey. The plumage is generally dark, but species from the southern hemisphere also have white underparts. Because the plumage is not waterproof these birds can slip silently into the water but they have to expose their feathers to the air so as to dry off.

Among cormorants, the nesting site is chosen by the male who tries to attract the female with a special form of nuptial display, raising and lowering his wings repeatedly and folding the primary remiges behind the secondary and tertiary feathers.

Nest-building materials are assembled by the male but the female partner helps in the construction as soon as the eggs are laid. Both birds take it in turns to incubate, greeting each other every time they arrive or depart. Each species has its own ceremonial pattern of greeting, as does each breeding pair; in this way they manage to locate their nest among thousands of others.

Both partners take part in the rearing of the chicks. They defend the nest with threatening attitudes and raucous cries.

All species feed chiefly on fish but the diet may also include cephalopod mollusks, crustaceans, and amphibians.

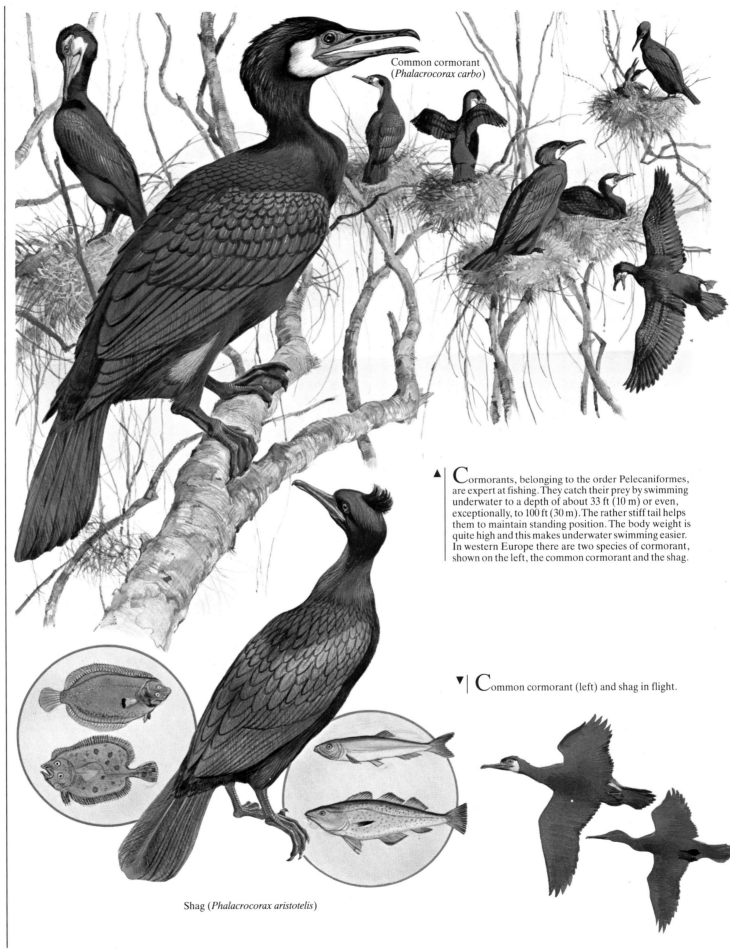

Common cormorant
(*Phalacrocorax carbo*)

▲ Cormorants, belonging to the order Pelecaniformes, are expert at fishing. They catch their prey by swimming underwater to a depth of about 33 ft (10 m) or even, exceptionally, to 100 ft (30 m). The rather stiff tail helps them to maintain standing position. The body weight is quite high and this makes underwater swimming easier. In western Europe there are two species of cormorant, shown on the left, the common cormorant and the shag.

▼ Common cormorant (left) and shag in flight.

Shag (*Phalacrocorax aristotelis*)

ANHINGA
Anhinga anhinga

Order Pelecaniformes
Family Anhingidae
Size Length 36 in (90 cm)
Distribution Tropical America
Habits Aquatic; gregarious in breeding season
Nesting In trees, sometimes on ground
Eggs 2 – 5
Chicks Nidicolous

There are two species of anhingas, water birds inhabiting tropical and subtropical regions all over the world: the anhinga (*Anhinga anhinga*) from America and the African darter (*A. rufa*).

Anhingas, also known as darters or snakebirds (because of their long, flexible neck) have an elongated body, a hooked bill and a very long, slender neck composed of 20 vertebrae; the eighth and ninth vertebrae possess a bony outgrowth, into which are inserted powerful muscles that allow the neck to fold into an S-shape and to be released like a spring. The feet are wholly webbed for easy movement through the water.

The American anhinga is widely distributed in the southern parts of the United States, extending its range to Central America and northern Argentina. It lives in lakes and freshwater swamps as well as river estuaries thickly planted with mangroves. The bird feeds on fish and other aquatic creatures (crustaceans, mollusks, and insects).

During the courtship display both birds face each other, tail raised, head resting on neck, beak down and holding a twig. The male then assembles branches and twigs for the nest and the female arranges them in the form of a platform.

The pale blue-green eggs have the same calcareous covering as those of cormorants and are incubated by both parents for 25 – 28 days. The chicks are fed by the parents with partially digested regurgitated pulp.

Anhingas or darters are able to expel all air from their plumage, enabling them to submerge completely and silently. Prey consist of fish, crustaceans, frogs, salamanders, aquatic insects, and larvae.

The birds spend many hours a day on a perch protruding from the water in order to dry their plumage, the open-winged posture being typical, too, of cormorants.

The drawing shows the perfect fishing technique of the anhinga. The S-shaped neck is thrust out and the bill impales the fish which is then tossed in the air to be swallowed, head first.

Anhingas inhabit the tropical, equatorial and subtropical regions of the world. According to some authors there are only two species: 1) Anhinga (*Anhinga anhinga*) from the New World; 2) African darter (*Anhinga rufa*) from the Old World.

MAGNIFICENT FRIGATE-BIRD

Fregata magnificens

Order Pelecaniformes
Family Fregatidae
Size Length 40 – 44 in (103 – 112 cm), head to tail
Wingspan About 7½ ft (2.3 m)
Weight 3 – 3¼ lb (1.4 – 1.5 kg)
Distribution Galapagos, Antilles and Cape Verde Islands
Habits Gregarious
Nesting In trees or on shrubs, sometimes on rocks
Eggs 1
Chicks Nidicolous

The frigate-birds are the best fliers in the order of Pelecaniformes. Their wings are very long and narrow with pointed tips, and the tail is forked.

The magnificent frigate-bird lives in tropical zones of the eastern Pacific and Atlantic Oceans.

In the air this bird is unrivaled for speed and grace, soaring and gliding for hours with occasional lazy flaps of its huge wings. It is noted for its parasitic habits, and because of its flying powers it manages to obtain much of its food by pursuing other birds such as gulls, cormorants, pelicans and, above all, boobies, harassing and tormenting them until they regurgitate the fish they have only recently swallowed.

This species tends to nest at any time of the year. The nest is situated on or near shore, generally in trees or low bushes.

Prior to mating, the birds indulge in courtship and nuptial displays. When a male sights a possible mate, he opens his wings, trembles and lets out excited cries; at the same time he shakes his head rhythmically from left to right and vice-versa, neck thrown back so as to give special prominence to the huge gular pouch of naked skin, now bright crimson and so taut and swollen with air that it seems about to burst. The pouch is a visual signal, serving both to attract the female and to mark each individual portion of territory. Incubation of a single egg lasts approximately 40 – 50 days and is undertaken by both parents, who also continue to collaborate in raising the young.

▲
◄ The magnificent frigate-bird, like other species belonging to the same family, is an excellent flier. The plumage of the males (shown here in flight) is shiny black with blue reflections; and the throat is adorned with a crimson pouch of naked skin. The female (shown perched) is duller in hue with a whitish patch on the breast. This species spends much of the time in the air, moving slowly and awkwardly on land: for this reason it usually perches or rests fairly high up, in trees or on rocks and cliffs, from which vantage points it can easily take wing.

▲ Because the species has such markedly aerial habits, the feet have adapted by losing most of the interdigital webbing that typifies other Pelecaniformes. The birds compensate for poor swimming and walking powers by the development of prehensile claws that are ideal for gripping branches and rocks.

▲ Food consists in the main of tiny marine creatures, especially flying fish, cuttlefish, small turtles, and jellyfish.

CICONIIFORMES

The most obvious characteristic of all the Ciconiiformes (storks, herons, ibises, etc.) are the long legs, designed for wading in shallow water, the equally long neck, necessary for reaching food at ground level in counterbalance to the legs, and the large, usually pointed bill, ideal for capturing live prey such as fish and aquatic insects. Body shape and size vary, of course, from one species to another, reflecting adaptations to different environments and individual modes of life; the beaks, in particular, sometimes assume very strange forms as in the shoebill stork or the spoonbill.

The color of the plumage is generally white, gray or black, often with metallic reflections; the naked parts, such as legs and neck, as well as the horny beak, may be red or bright yellow. The birds are medium-sized or large, the Indian marabou weighing 13 – 15 lb (6 – 7 kg). In flight, the true storks hold their long legs behind them, forming a straight line with the outstretched neck, so that the broad, voluminous wings create a cross-shaped silhouette; the herons, however, keep their neck folded and the head tucked between the shoulders.

The Ciconiiformes inhabit every continent, except for Arctic and Antarctic zones, most species being found in Africa and tropical Asia.

These birds mainly frequent zones of shallow water such as swamps and the edges of lakes and rivers, their distribution being determined by these surroundings; but some species, such as the white stork, are often found on steppes and cultivated grasslands, while the hermit ibis shows a preference for arid and desert habitats.

The species of Ciconiiformes that live in the higher latitudes are migratory, heading toward the equator in winter.

Ciconiiformes nest in groups or colonies of varying size, numbering up to several thousand pairs. The nests are situated in trees, among marsh vegetation or, more rarely, on rock ledges (hermit ibis). The most common type of nest is a huge pile of branches or interlaced reeds, slightly cup-shaped.

Oriental white stork
(*Ciconia boyciana*)

Black stork
(*Ciconia nigra*)

Hermit ibis
(*Geronticus eremita*)

Greater flamingo
(*Phoenicopterus ruber*)

Wood ibis
(*Ibis ibis*)

Gray heron
(*Ardea cinerea*)

Jabiru
(*Jabiru mycteria*)

Boat-billed heron
(*Cochlearius cochlearius*)

Indian open-billed stork
(*Anastomus oscitans*)

Shoebill stork
(*Balaeniceps rex*)

Hammerhead stork
(*Scopus umbretta*)

Saddle-billed stork
(*Ephippiorhynchus senegalensis*)

Marabou
(*Leptoptilos crumeniferus*)

There are about 113 species of birds belonging to the order Ciconiiformes. They are divided into six families: Ciconiidae (true storks), seven representatives of which are illustrated on the left: Ardeidae (represented above by the gray heron): Cochleariidae (boat-billed heron): Threskiornithidae (hermit ibis): Balaenicipitidae (shoebill stork): and Scopidae (hammerhead stork). The Phoenicopteridae (flamingos), formerly included among the Ciconiiformes, are, according to modern classification, allocated a seperate order, Phoenicopteriformes.

ROSEATE SPOONBILL

Ajaja ajaja

Order Ciconiiformes
Family Threskiornithidae
Size Length 26 – 31 in (68 – 81 cm)
Distribution Central and South America
Habits Aquatic; gregarious
Nesting On trees
Eggs 1 – 4, usually 2 or 3
Chicks Nidicolous

In the roseate spoonbill, the plumage of the adult is pink with scarlet-tinted wings. The neck is white, the legs red and the tail feathers yellow to orange. The naked skin of the head and the broad, flat-tipped bill are gray-green. The young bird's plumage, however, is completely white, while the bill and the head, which is wholly covered with feathers, are yellowish.

This species, the only American spoonbill, inhabits a few zones in the southern states of the USA (Texas, Florida, and Louisiana) and in Central and South America. Formerly common, the roseate spoonbill population has been systematically destroyed because of the commercial demand for its handsome feathers. The bird is mostly found in remote areas of swampland surrounded by dense concentrations of aquatic plants, and in mangrove woods close to the coasts.

The nests are built in colonies, often in company with those of other aquatic birds such as ibises, herons, and egrets, and comprise heaps of branches and plant stems with a lining of leaves and softer grass. The female lays 1 – 4 eggs, usually 2 or 3, which are white with brown spots. Incubation lasts 23 – 24 days and is shared by both parents. The chicks are able to fly within 40 days.

A related species is the European or white spoonbill (*Platalea leucorodia*), which has white, ocher-tinted plumage on the breast, a tuft of feathers on the head and a black bill with a yellow tip. Slightly larger than the roseate spoonbill, the species lives in southern and eastern Europe, in Asia and in a few parts of Africa. Breeding colonies are located in dense reedbeds surrounded by stretches of deep water that guarantee them protection from predatory mammals.

Roseate spoonbill
(*Ajaja ajaja*)

▲ Roseate spoonbills live on marshy terrain, in ponds and lakes with plenty of aquatic vegetation and bushes jutting straight out of the water, especially in remote areas where they feel secure and to which have retreated because of the intensive hunting that has practically wiped them out. It was only thanks to the National Audubon Society of America that an end was put to the capturing of these birds for their plumage, with sanctuaries established for them and for other marshland birds.

White spoonbill
(*Platalea leucorodia*)

▲ Both species feed on a wide range of small water creatures, such as crustaceans, insects and larvae, mollusks, amphibians, and small fish. They supplement this animal diet with aquatic plants and seeds.

▶ The European or white spoonbill, slightly larger than the roseate spoonbill, looks more slender and graceful and is further embellished by the crest of feathers on its head. It is an inhabitant of the Old World, found in Europe, Asia, and Africa.

ARDEIDAE

For the most part, the 64 species belonging to the family Ardeidae are of average size, slender in build, with long legs, a flexible neck and a pointed beak. Most of the Ardeidae are active by day but some species, such as the night herons, hunt at night. The two sexes are very similar and can only be distinguished visually by their behavior while breeding.

Certain species are entirely white (a feature of very few of the world's birds) and some wholly black. Others have plumage of various shades but always in a mixture of the same white, gray, black, and reddish-brown colors; a few are brown flecked with white.

The Ardeidae walk with ease through the water, supported by their long toes on the slimy bottom. They are capable of swimming but only venture into really deep water on rare occasions. They fly slowly, powerfully and majestically, with long, broad wingbeats. In flight the neck is folded in an S-shape, the head is tucked between the shoulders and the legs are stretched out backward.

The Ardeidae are represented in all the continents apart from Antarctica: although most numerous in the tropics, they are also widely distributed in temperate zones. Their diet of fish makes them dependent upon water for survival and they always live near swamps, lakes and rivers.

The majority of species migrate during the cold season to equatorial regions but those already living in warm latitudes, such as the goliath heron of Africa, confine themselves to short journeys in zones where the water contains plenty of fish.

With the exception of bitterns, which are always solitary by habit, the other Ardeidae are more or less gregarious, coming together to roost at night and to breed in colonies (known as heronries) which may contain thousands of nests. Pairs stay together only for one breeding season, and both sexes collaborate equally in the laborious task of incubating and raising the brood. The chicks are born unfeathered and incapable of doing anything, becoming self-sufficient between the ages of 40 and 60 days, according to the size of the species.

Little egret
(*Egretta garzetta*)

Cattle egret
(*Ardeola ibis*)

Reddish egret
(*Dichromanassa rufescens*)

Louisiana heron
(*Hydranassa tricolor*)

Goliath heron
(*Ardea goliath*)

Purple heron
(*Ardea purpurea*)

Great white heron
(*Casmerodius albus*)

Little bittern
(*Ixobrychus minutus*)

Japanese
night heron
(*Gorsachius
goisagi*)

Least bittern
(*Ixobrychus exilis*)

Bittern
(*Botaurus stellaris*)

Night heron
(*Nycticorax nycticorax*)

Black heron
(*Melanophoyx ardesiaca*)

FLAMINGOS

Order Phoenicopteriformes
Family Phoenicopteridae
Size Lesser and James' are the smallest species, having a total length of 31 – 39 in (95 – 100 cm) and a wingspan in the order of 37 – 39 in (95 – 100 cm). Greater/Caribbean is the largest and can reach a total length of 78 in (200 cm) with a wingspan of up to 70 in (187 cm)
Weight From about 3½ lb (1.6 kg) in the Lesser to over 9½ lb (4.4 kg) in large male Greaters
Incubation From 27 – 31 days
Eggs 1, exceptionally 2
Sexual maturity At least 2 – 3 years
Maximum age 27 years recorded in wild (Camargue) and up to 50 years in captivity (Basle Zoo).

Flamingos are among the most spectacular of birds, especially in flight, their neck and legs outstretched, wings flashing red and black, accompanied by gooselike honking calls.

There are six species of flamingo in the world: two in the Old World and four in the New. All have similar preference for areas of shallow brackish or salt water, varying in altitude throughout the world from sea-level to about 13,000 ft (4,000 m).

All species of flamingos are gregarious and sometimes congregate in flocks numbering thousands or even hundreds of thousands. Unusually high numbers assemble either as a result of the temporary drying out of some of the wetlands they frequent, because food is particularly abundant in a certain place, or for breeding.

Flamingos usually build a conical-shaped nest, using their bill to scrape up the mud from around the spot chosen for breeding. The single egg is laid in a shallow depression on top and the nests are densely grouped together. Incubation, by both sexes, takes from 27 to 31 days. On hatching the chick is dressed in a white down.

The bill of the flamingos is composed of a complex system of lamellae used as filters or retainers, distributed along both mandibles. The thick fleshy tongue is equipped with spines and lies in a groove of the lower mandible. It functions as a piston pumping 3 – 4 times per second, drawing in organic rich mud or water. Food particles are retained by the lamellae as the water is expelled.

Greater flamingos on their nests. The colony usually comprises thousands of pairs, generally on islands in inaccessible areas where the birds are safe from predatory mammals and from man.

GRAYLAG GOOSE

Anser anser

Order Anseriformes
Family Anatidae; subfamily Anserinae
Size Length 30 – 36 in (75 – 90 cm)
Wingspan 58 – 72 in (147 – 180 cm)
Weight 6¼ – 8¼ lb (2.9 – 3.7 kg)
Distribution Europe and Asia
Habits Gregarious, except during breeding season
Nesting On ground
Eggs 4 – 7, exceptionally up to 12
Chicks Nidifugous

The graylag goose is the best known, if not the most abundant, species of goose, one reason being that it is the ancestor of various domestic strains.

In the wild the bird is easy to identify because it is the only one of the "gray" geese to have a large, uniformly pink or orange bill (with a whitish hook). In flight the graylag goose displays the broad silvery zone on the upper wing which, from a distance, appears almost white. The upper parts of the body are gray-brown and the feather tips are whitish so that they form a series of thin white transverse stripes. These stripes are broader and clearer among birds of eastern populations, who thus have a lighter appearance overall. The underparts are more or less uniformly pale and the legs are flesh-colored. The short tail is blackish and makes a striking contrast with the white rump. Because the sexes are similar it is somewhat difficult to distinguish them in the wild; but sometimes this is possible by comparing the sizes (males are larger) and attitudes.

On the other hand, there is never any problem in recognizing the young of the year, for they are darker and more brownish than the adults, displaying fewer white stripes on the back.

This species at one time nested over a much wider area, both in Asia and in Europe. Nowadays there are large, well distributed populations in much of central Asia and European Russia, but the bird has practically disappeared as a nesting species from western and southern Europe.

The graylag goose has a preference for wet grasslands, often, but not invariably, near areas covered by swamps and lakes. Like many other

The family Anatidae (swans, geese, and ducks) comprises many species of aquatic birds, furnished with short but robust legs and capable of swimming and flying long distances. The graylag goose, like other geese, possesses long legs which are particularly suited for walking on dry land. They are easily distinguished from other species by the almost uniform pink or orange color of the bill and the gray-brown body.

Geese feed mainly on plants which they rip and chew with the tiny teeth or lamellae along both mandibles of the bill.

geese, it relies on water more for reasons of safety than for purposes of feeding. Indeed, without exception, when dusk approaches, flocks of geese that have been feeding in fields simultaneously take their departure for the places where they regularly spend the night; their "nocturnal quarters" are usually situated along low-lying shores, in muddy or sandy river estuaries or in lagoons, perhaps where a strip of land, surrounded by water, juts out.

The nest of the graylag goose is usually a somewhat rough-and-ready construction, formed mainly of scraps of vegetation heaped up on the ground into a cone which is then stuffed with feathers. During the breeding season the birds relinquish their gregarious habits and each pair defends its own small territory, not allowing any other members of the species to intrude. The young hatch after 25 days of incubation and are capable of embarking on their first flights after a couple of weeks. During this time they are attended and protected by both parents. In the second (or, more often, the third) year the geese mate, remaining loyal to their partner for the rest of their life.

The ethologist Konrad Lorenz, author of some of the first and most celebrated studies on the behavior of graylag geese, emphasizes that among geese monogamy is the rule, but that every rule has its exceptions. Of particular importance is the description of the phased learning process known as "imprinting," a phenomenon encountered among many animals, particularly those species with a measure of social organization. Lorenz has affirmed that a young goose, shortly after hatching, may learn to regard almost any animal or human, or even an object, as its parent, in the event of the latter moving close by and making occasional sounds that are similar, but not necessarily identical, to the "contact" call generally used by the species. In this way the young goose receives the imprint of its foster parent, which may be a hen, a turkey, a human being or even a self-propelled, sound-equipped cardboard box. The goose thus identifies with its adoptive parent, behaving in the latter's presence exactly as it would with one of its kind; having reached maturity, it may even attempt to mate with individuals or objects resembling its fosterparent, refusing other geese.

When they fly long distances, the geese adopt the typical V-formation used by all large, gregarious birds when they migrate.

Graylag geese usually feed in fields and grasslands, not necessarily in wet zones.

Young graylag goose shortly after hatching.

Position of graylag goose while asleep.

A female (who incubates alone) recovering an egg that has rolled out of the nest.

Graylag goslings may follow their mother around within a day of hatching.

During the days after hatching, should the mother not be available, baby geese will accept as a foster parent virtually any object or animal that happens to move nearby, including humans.

WHOOPER SWAN

Cygnus cygnus

Order Anseriformes
Family Anatidae
Size Length 58 – 64 in (145 – 160 cm)
Distribution Europe and Asia
Nesting At water's edge
Eggs 5 – 6, exceptionally 4 – 8
Chicks Nidifugous

Swans are birds of considerable size, larger than the biggest geese (wild). They have a very long neck and their plumage is white (among species of the northern hemisphere) or black or black-and-white (in southern hemisphere).

The birds spend much of their time swimming and find most forms of food in the water, straining the surface layers or submerging head and neck, to reach the plants growing on the bottom.

These birds need broad tracts of water, especially while they are growing, for the considerable weight of the body might hamper the development of the legs if the latter had to support the bird too frequently on dry land.

As a rule the bill of a swan is high at the base but fairly long. The cygnets are grayish or brownish, and this plumage distinguishes them immediately from the adults when they mingle in large flocks.

The five existing swan species are all classified in the genus *Cygnus* and do not differ much from one another. Contrary to what might be supposed, given their size, swans are excellent and powerful fliers, capable of migrating many hundreds of miles.

The whooper swan (*Cygnus cygnus*) is easily distinguished by the absence of a frontal knob; its body has a square appearance and the neck is held straight and rigid rather than elegantly folded. Its voice is deep and musical, similar to the sound of a trumpet. For this reason the American subspecies *C. c. buccinator* bears the vernacular name of trumpeter swan. It is the largest of all the swans and may weigh more than 33 lb (15 kg).

The whooper swan nests in Iceland, Norway, Sweden, Finland, Russia, Siberia as far as Kamchatka, Sakhalin, the Commander Islands, and Japan, as well as some zones of central Asia. It winters in the British Isles, Europe, North Africa, Asia Minor, Iran, northern India, China, and Japan. The

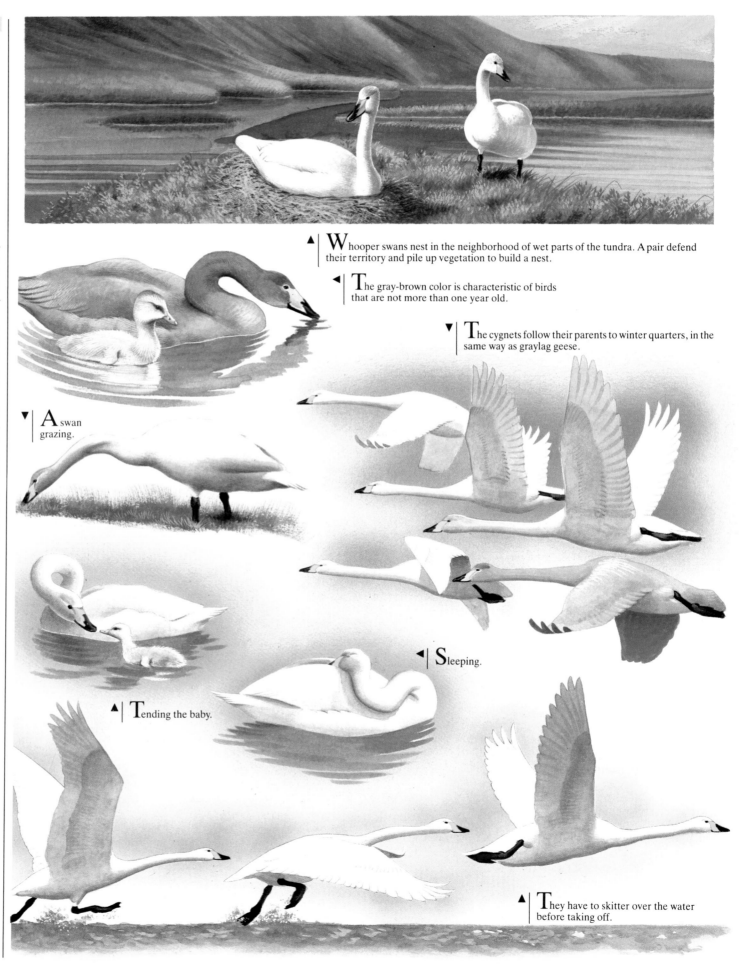

▲ Whooper swans nest in the neighborhood of wet parts of the tundra. A pair defend their territory and pile up vegetation to build a nest.

◄ The gray-brown color is characteristic of birds that are not more than one year old.

▼ The cygnets follow their parents to winter quarters, in the same way as graylag geese.

▼ A swan grazing.

◄ Sleeping.

▲ Tending the baby.

▲ They have to skitter over the water before taking off.

trumpeter swan once had a wide distribution in various parts of North America, but is nowadays restricted to a zone on the borders of Canada, the United States, and Alaska.

Whooper swans nest for preference close to lakes, in the tundra, on heathland or in swampy areas near the estuaries of arctic rivers. In winter they assemble in zones farther to the south because of ice and snow which, if extensive, prevent them obtaining food.

The mute swan (*C. olor*) may be distinguished from similar species by the color of its beak, which is almost wholly orange, with black edges and black knob on the base, connected to the forehead. The legs are also black (rarely fleshy or gray) and the pointed tail is fairly prominent.

The range of the mute swan includes Denmark, central and southern Sweden, northern Germany, Poland, Roumania, central Russia, Asia Minor, and central and eastern Asia to Mongolia and the Dagur province of northern Manchuria. In winter it migrates southward.

The nest of the mute swan is preferably situated on an islet in the water of a swamp, but semi-domesticated birds will build a nest anywhere close to water. Both birds help to build it and the male later stations himself nearby while his mate incubates. She lays 4–7 (exceptionally 12) eggs and incubates them for 36 days. The chicks are tended by the parents and are able to fly 120–150 days after hatching.

The whistling swan (*C. columbianus*) is in many respects similar to the whooper swan, with all the main characteristics of the latter except that it is a good deal smaller. The neck, in fact, is rather short and the body tends to be rounded rather than elongated; the voice is musical and resonant.

The best-known species from the southern hemisphere is undoubtedly the black swan (*C. atratus*), with elegant curly black plumage, and deep red bill barred with white at the tip.

The comparatively small black-necked swan (*C. melanocoryphus*) from South America, flies northward for winter migration. It has a white body, a deep, velvety black neck and a white stripe across the eye. The bill is gray, with a large, bilobate, flesh-pink frontal knob at the base.

The female has the odd habit of carrying her babies on her back when they go swimming.

Trumpeter swan
(*Cygnus cygnus buccinator*)

Black-necked swan
(*Cygnus melanocoryphus*)

Mute swan
(*Cygnus olor*)

Black swan
(*Cygnus atratus*)

▲ From left: the different bills of the mute swan. the whooper swan, and the whistling swan.

◄ Apart from the mute swan, which has a wide distribution almost everywhere, the other species require absolute and total protection because of their rarity and their exceptional ornamental value. 1) Whooper swan (*Cygnus cygnus*); 2) Mute swan (*Cygnus olor*); 3) Black swan (*Cygnus atratus*); 4) Whistling swan (*Cygnus columbianus*); 5) Black-necked swan (*Cygnus melanocoryphus*).

DUCKS

Ducks that normally feed on the surface without completely submerging their bodies in water, leaving at least the rear portion exposed, are generally known as dabbling ducks. Among these species the secondary remiges form a rectangular zone on the wings which is clearly defined and brightly colored, with metallic and often variously reflected tints; this patch is called the speculum.

The presence of this "wing mirror" is probably explained by the need of individual ducks to recognize others of their kind easily from a distance and while flying.

The so-called diving ducks mostly have black and white zones on their wings, or wings of uniform color. They are so named because they are in the habit of submerging their bodies entirely when looking for food, often diving to a depth of several feet.

The two groups, dabbling and diving ducks, differ as well in various general ways, consistent with the fact that the latter are more reliant on water. The dabbling ducks have smaller webs on their feet and fairly short toes, relative to body dimensions. The diving ducks, on the other hand, have feet that are broadly webbed so as to facilitate underwater swimming. The feet, furthermore, are positioned some way back on the body so that diving ducks tend to look more upright when on the surface.

Another distinction between the two groups is the shape of the bill, which varies according to the kind of food eaten. Dabbling ducks have bills suitable for filtering and chewing, namely flat and fairly long. Diving ducks, particularly those spending the winter on the seacoasts, have beaks that are fairly high at the base, and a large head. Those which stick to freshwater zones even in winter also have broad, flat bills, since much of their food consists of vegetation; but the marine species, such as the eiders and the old squaw, have bills narrowing at the tip, and the sea-dwelling mergansers, which feed almost wholly on fish, have exceptionally long and narrow beaks.

Ducks are classified into several tribes and genera.

The tribe of Tadornini comprises birds that, to some extent, bear some

Shelduck
(*Tadorna tadorna*)

Lesser whistling duck
(*Dendrocygna javanica*)

Egyptian goose
(*Alopochen aegyptiacus*)

Shoveler
(*Anas clypeata*)

Falcated teal
(*Anas falcata*)

American wigeon
(*Anas americana*)

Wigeon
(*Anas penelope*)

Garganey teal
(*Anas querquedula*)

Gadwell
(*Anas strepera*)

similarity to geese as well as to ducks. One of the most representative species of this tribe is the shelduck (*Tadorna tadorna*), a bird closely associated with broad tracts of salt water and so generally found along the seacoasts.

The tribe of Anatini comprises the dabbling ducks. The shoveler (*Anas clypeata*) is easily recognizable from the shape and size of its bill, which is adapted mainly for filtering water so that the duck can collect the plankton which constitutes an important part of its diet. This species is widespread over the entire Holarctic region.

The garganey teal (*A. querquedula*) is slightly smaller and easily distinguished from the shoveler by its much smaller bill and the peculiar colors of the male in his nuptial livery.

The falcated teal (*A. falcata*) is a handsome bird that ranges widely over northeast Asia and reaches China and Japan in the winter. Its name is derived from the sickle-shaped tertiary remiges, which are particularly long and curving in the males. Very similar in general body structure and behavior is the gadwall (*A .strepera*), whose area of distribution is, however, considerably more vast, comprising North America, Europe, and Asia.

The wigeon (*A. penelope*) has a wide range in Asia and Europe, while in America the species is replaced by two similar species, the American wigeon (*A. americana*) and the southern wigeon (*A. sibilatrix*), inhabiting northern and southern regions respectively. Their ideal habitat are the grasslands, close to water.

Almost the opposite, ecologically, of the wigeons are the pintails, who possess a long, narrow neck, head and bill, and an equally narrow tail that terminates in a point. The pintails, in fact, frequent the same types of habitat as do the wigeons, enjoying a similar diet and finding their food down to a depth of some 16 in (40 cm) without submerging their body entirely. The pintail (*A. acuta*) breeds in North America as well as in Europe and Asia, flying to Africa and the more southerly parts of Asia in the winter months.

The perching ducks (tribe Cairinini) includes the highly unusual mandarin duck (*Aix galericulata*) which is found in Japan, Sakhalin, Manchuria, northeastern China and the Ussuri-Amur region, wintering even farther south.

Pintail
(*Anas acuta*)

Spotbill duck
(*Anas poecilorhyncha*)

Teal
(*Anas crecca*)

Baikal teal
(*Anas formosa*)

Wood duck
(*Aix sponsa*)

Flightless steamer duck
(*Tachyeres pteneres*)

The steamer ducks are the only ducks that are unable to fly. They flee by running across the water, flapping their wings, and by swimming underwater, likewise using the wings.

Mandarin duck
(*Aix galericulata*)

Muscovy duck
(*Cairina moschata*)

FALCONIFORMES

The order Falconiformes comprises all diurnal birds of prey, notable for their particularly robust build, adapted to hunting and flying.

The mountain hawk-eagle (*Spizaëtus nipalensis*) belongs to the group of so-called "booted" eagles (family Accipitridae). The black bill is fairly solid. The legs are covered with feathers up to the joints; they are very strong and the feet are equipped with hooked black claws. The adult's overall length is about 27 – 35 in (66 – 86 cm). The bird performs rapid maneuvers among the trees of the forest when hunting prey, which includes young monkeys and other small to medium-sized mammals, as well as birds.

The mountain hawk-eagle lives in mountain forests at altitudes of 2,000 – 6,600 ft (600 – 2,000 m) and more in the Western Ghats, Sri Lanka, the Himalayas, Indochina, eastern China as far as the Yangtze-Kiang, the Korean peninsula, the Japanese islands, and Taiwan. Solitary by habit, it nests on trees. The female lays one egg, and the chicks are nidicolous.

The buzzard (*Buteo buteo*), also a member of the Accipitridae, measures 20 – 22 in (51 – 56 cm) in total length, has a wingspan of 46 – 56 in (115 – 140 cm) and weighs 1¼ – 3 lb (0.6 – 1.4 kg). This species is abundantly distributed in the wooded zones and taiga of the Palearctic region.

In many wooded areas bordering the cultivated steppes of central Europe, the buzzard is the commonest bird of prey. Although it nests in woods, it hunts in the open fields. The nest is generally situated in trees but also on rocks, especially in Mediterranean countries. The raptor feeds on small rodents and on other mammals up to the size of a small hare, on birds, reptiles, insects, and other invertebrates; nor does it refuse carrion in winter. One of its most typical hunting techniques is to perch in a tree or on a post, attentively watching for movement in the fields below. The buzzard has the ability to hover in midair, which greatly improves its hunting prospects.

The female usually lays 2 – 3 eggs, exceptionally 1 or 4 – 6. The chicks are nidicolous.

The osprey or fish hawk (*Pandion haliaëtus*) is the sole representative of

Mountain hawk-eagle
(*Spizaëtus nipalensis*)

Buzzard
(*Buteo buteo*)

Osprey
(*Pandion haliaëtus*)

Northern goshawk
(*Accipiter gentilis*)

Hen harrier
(*Circus cyaneus*)

Black kite
(*Milvus migrans*)

Secretary bird
(*Sagittarius serpentarius*)

Peregrine falcon
(*Falco peregrinus*)

Gray-faced
buzzard-eagle
(*Butastur indicu*

Andean condor
(*Vultur gryphus*)

the family Pandionidae. It is the only diurnal bird of prey with a reversible toe and with nostrils that can be closed, perhaps as an adaptation to its technique of catching fish (its exclusive food), namely by diving into water.

Its total length is 22 – 24 in (55 – 60 cm), the wingspan 58 – 66 in (145 – 165 cm) and the weight 2½ – 4½ lb (1.1 – 2 kg). The legs are naked and covered with scales, and the feet are powerful; the scaled toes have their lower parts, especially at the joints, covered by pointed horny plates which, together with the long, curving claws, enable the bird to take a firm grasp of slippery prey.

The osprey ranges widely over Eurasia, Africa, North America, and central and coastal regions of Australia. It is not found in the polar regions or in South America. In temperate latitudes the bird frequents lakes and ponds with plenty of fish, as well as major rivers, especially in Asia, while in tropical and subtropical climes it is commonest along the coasts.

The osprey is a solitary species and only locally gregarious. The female lays, on average, 3 eggs; the chicks are nidicolous.

Another member of the Accipitridae, the hen harrier (*Circus cyaneus*) has a total length of 17 – 22 in (43 – 55 cm), a wingspan of 41 – 50 in (102 – 125 cm) and a weight of 10 – 22½ oz (290 – 700 g). It ranges over large tracts of central and southern Europe, as well as North America from Alaska to California, inhabiting natural and cultivated steppe-land, moors, and swamps. Its prey consists of small mammals and birds, reptiles, and amphibians. The nest may be situated on moors, in reafforested zones, in cornfields or in swampy areas among reeds and rushes. The species lays 3 – 6 eggs and the chicks are some time in the nest.

The gray-faced buzzard-eagle (*Butastur indicus*) (family Accipitridae), has a wide distribution through India, Southeast Asia, and central Africa. This is another raptor of a good deal smaller and slimmer than the buzzard, which it otherwise resembles. Its total length is 16 – 18 in (40 – 45 cm) and its wingspan 36 – 44 in (90 – 110 cm). It inhabits cultivated areas and woodlands interspersed with open spaces. Diet and hunting technique are similar to those of the buzzard.

White-tailed sea eagle
(*Haliaëtus albicilla*)

Steller's sea eagle
(*Haliaëtus pelagicus*))

Bald eagle
(*Haliaëtus leucocephalus*)

Black vulture
(*Aegypius monachus*)

▲ | The golden eagle is the commonest and best known of all eagles. Once widely distributed throughout Europe, in North Africa and in enormous areas of Asia and North America, it has been exterminated in its European habitat and in eastern parts of the United States.
1) Golden eagle (*Aquila chrysaëtos*).

▼ | 1) The members of the order Falconiformes are found all over the world; 2) in these zones, however, they are exceptionally seen.

On these pages some representatives of all the families belonging to the order Falconiformes are illustrated. The most primitive family, the Cathartidae, contains the Andean condor. The Pandionidae are represented by the osprey, which is also the only surviving species of the family. The Accipitridae comprise the majority of all living birds of prey, and the drawings show three species of a sea eagle, the black vulture, the hen harrier, the northern goshawk, the gray-faced buzzard-eagle, the common buzzard and the mountain hawk-eagle. The family Sagittariidae is constituted of the sole species, the secretary bird. Finally, the peregrine falcon, representing the most highly evolved family, Falconidae.

ANDEAN CONDOR
Vultur gryphus

Order Falconiformes
Family Cathartidae
Size Length about 3¼ – 4 ft (1 – 1.16 m)
Wingspan 9 – 10¼ ft (2.75 – 3.15 m)
Weight 20 – 26½ lb (9 – 12 kg)
Distribution South America
Habits Gregarious
Nesting In rock cavities
Eggs 1 (?2)
Chicks Nidicolous

Apart from their impressive size, adult Andean condors may be recognized by the color of their plumage, black with metallic reflections, and the wholly or partially white secondary remiges and greater coverts. The head is completely naked, and the male condor has a characteristic fleshy crest, some 4 in (10 cm) long and 1¾ in (4.5 cm) high; the female lacks both this crest and the male's lobe-shaped wattles. The color of the iris varies, too, that of the male being light brown and the female's reddish-brown.

The bill is solid and quite powerful, enabling the condor to tear strips of flesh from the carcasses of fairly large land and marine mammals. There is a white collar of down, slightly narrower in the female, at the base of the long, featherless neck.

The range of the Andean condor extends from northern Colombia along the line of the Andes south to Tierra del Feugo and then northward along the Atlantic coast of Argentina to the mouth of the Rio Negro, but in many regions the species has become rare or is already extinct. In the Andes the bird lives at heights of 10,000 to 16,500 ft (3,000 to 5,000 m), but in the southern part of its range, along the Atlantic and Pacific coasts, it also nests on high sea cliffs.

The condor is a social species as far as its scavenging habits are concerned, but does not nest in large colonies. Immature birds as well as non-breeding adults gather every evening on particular roosts situated on rock ledges, these being visible from afar by the white of the bird's excrement. More than 20 condors may assemble here for the night. Late in the morning, when the sun's heat has created rising thermal currents, the condors take wing

An adult Andean condor about to take wing. This bird's size is greater than that of all other birds of prey. The naked head and neck, with the collar of soft down, are special adaptations to a diet of carrion, the same features being present in many other vultures of the Old and New Worlds.

A fleshy crest and a light brown iris distinguish the male Andean condor from the female, the latter also being smaller.

and begin to soar, scanning the vast spaces below with their exceptionally keen eyes for carrion which may already have been discovered by other scavengers such as turkey vultures and caracaras. Apparently there is a social hierarchy among condors which is observed while they feed. Dominant individuals accept the presence of sub-dominants and "candidates," and it is rare for aggressiveness to culminate in outright struggles to establish a new hierarchy.

One white egg is laid on the bare ground inside a small cave in the rock wall, at altitudes varying from sea level to over 13,000 ft (4,000 m). Often several pairs will nest in the same rock face, each defending the surroundings of their little cavity. The nests, therefore, are extremely difficult to locate, not only because of the site but also because the condors are highly secretive while nesting. Incubation is carried out mainly by the female, although the male sometimes relieves her for a few hours a day. The young hatch after about 2 months and then remain in the nest for a further 6 weeks, depending upon the parents for food even after they begin flying. The entire breeding cycle may thus take more than a year, with the result that an egg is laid only every other year.

A related species, the California condor (*Gymnogyps californianus*), has a total length of about 3¼ – 4 ft (1 – 1.15 m) and a weight varying from 20 – 30 lb (9 – 13.5 kg). It nests in a rock cavity, laying one egg. The nidicolous chick stays for several months in the nest.

The plumage is black with bluish metallic reflections. The white wing bars, visible from beneath, are a certain means of identification when the bird is in flight, as is the huge wingspan, equivalent to that of the Andean condor.

Today the California condor's range is limited to a small region north of Los Angeles. During the first half of the present century the condor population was about 60 individuals, now reduced to less than 40 in spite of the conservation attempts of biologists and the American authorities.

▼ Male Andean condor gliding. The bird's wingspan may reach about 10 ft (3.15 m). The long, broad wings make it possible for the condor to utilize every rising air current without having to waste energy on flapping flight.

▼ Like the Old World vultures, the Andean condor and other New World vultures feed principally on the carcasses of land and marine mammals.

▼ This aggressive behavior by two males is designed to establish a pecking order when feeding.

▼ Adult California condor, whose size is similar to that of the Andean condor. It is now one of the rarest birds in the world.

▲ The turkey vulture is the most abundant of all the New World vulture species.

► The king vulture is notable for the many vivid colors on its head.

◄ 1) The habitats of the king vulture (*Sarcorhamphus papa*) are savannas and the tropical forests extending from central Mexico to Paraguay and northern Argentina. 2) The Andean condor (*Vultur gryphus*) lives in northern Colombia along the range of the Andes southward to Tierra del Feugo, and along the Atlantic coast of Argentina to the mouth of the Rio Negro. 3) The California condor (*Gymnogyps californianus*) is today confined to a small area north of Los Angeles, represented by not more than 40 individuals.

1
2
3

GOLDEN EAGLE

Aquila chrysaëtos

Order Falconiformes
Family Accipitridae
Size Length 2½ – 3½ ft (75 – 90 cm)
Wingspan 6 – 7¼ ft (1.8 – 2.2 m)
Weight 6 – 15 lb (2.7 – 6.7 kg)
Distribution Europe, North Africa, Asia, North America
Habits Solitary
Nesting In rock cavities or trees
Eggs 1 – 3, normally 2
Chicks Nidicolous

The golden eagle may be distinguished from other eagles by its enormous size and its almost uniformly dark brown coloration, the nape and head of the adult tending towards golden-bronze or grayish. The bill is strong and fairly stout, tibia and tarsus are very large and "booted" to the joints. The toes are big and strong, with long hooked claws; the rear claw is far larger than the rear toe. In flight the golden eagle is easily recognized by its long but not unusually broad wings, narrower and trimmed toward the front, by the protracted head and by the long, slightly rounded tail.

Immature golden eagles are almost black with white spots on the wings and have a white tail terminating in a broad transverse black stripe. In the years following birth the white patterns on wing and tail gradually fade, disappearing completely in the fifth or sixth year of life as the bird attains sexual maturity. Except when in a family group, it is rare to see more than two golden eagles flying together.

This species was originally distributed all over Europe, in North Africa, over vast areas of Asia and in North America. In the course of history the species has been wiped out over much of its European range and in eastern parts of the United States as a result of human modification and transformation of the environment.

In central and southern Europe the species is relegated mainly to mountain regions with plenty of rocks and few trees, where there are deep gorges and inaccessible ledges for building the eyrie. In Scandinavia and the USSR, however, the bird also frequents areas of flat woodland devoid of human settlement. Here the nests

Immature golden eagle on a high vantage point, grasping a passerine in its claws. Of all present-day eagles, this is the most widely distributed and abundant.

are built chiefly in trees. Although the golden eagle has, in many regions, become a true mountain species, there are still zones where it breeds at low altitudes as in Scotland, Spain, Sardinia, and Crete. These are all hilly areas with broken terrain, very low population density and the minimum of human interference.

The density of the golden eagle population is restricted by the need for a large quantity of prey and the availability of suitable nesting sites. In places where human impact on the environment has been negligible, the species remains closely attached to its traditional habitats, utilizing the same sites from one generation to another.

Like many other large birds of prey, the golden eagle lives in couples, such pairs often being formed as early as the second year of life. During the "engagement" period until the attainment of sexual maturity in the fifth year, the two birds visit their chosen nesting site frequently, heaping up dry and leafy branches for the construction or repair of the nest. Each pair possesses several nests, often located on the same rock face or in the same wooded district. Some eyries are used for dozens of years and, according to the avaliable site, may be up to 10 ft (3 m) high and more than 6½ ft (2 m) across. Male and female share in the building or repair work.

During courtship, the golden eagle performs nuptial flights, including one particularly spectacular display in which the male nosedives toward the female and she suddenly turns in midair onto her back, so that their claws touch.

As a rule 2 eggs are laid at an interval of 2–3 days, this occurring towards the end of February in southern parts of the range and near the end of March in central and northern zones. Incubation commences as soon as the first egg is laid. It is undertaken chiefly by the female, who is fed by the male, he briefly taking her place on the eggs as she feeds.

Initially the male brings food for the eaglets, but as they grow the female joins him in this task. Until they are about a month old, the young are fed by the mother on strips of meat that she has torn from the carcass with her beak. In due course, and not without some effort, the eaglets begin feeding on their own. At the age of about 3 months the eaglets have normally made their first flight.

▼ The vast wing surface with its trimmed primary remiges enables the golden eagle to use warm air currents and glide on high with the least expenditure of energy.

▲ The element of surprise is essential to the golden eagle's hunting technique, and prey is generally killed on the ground. Crows, small raptors, ducks, and other birds may also be caught on the wing, however, as the eagle suddenly and swiftly turns to attack.

▼ After hatching, the eaglets are covered with thick whitish-gray down.

◄ The golden eagle feeds principally on small and medium-sized mammals such as rabbits, hares, marmots, mice, etc. as well as birds. But it will not refuse carrion, especially in winter.

It nests as a rule on rock faces, usually situated at a lower altitude than its hunting territory; this makes it easier to carry heavy prey back to the eyrie. ►

TETRAONIDAE

The family Tetraonidae (grouse and ptarmigans) is represented by 11 genera with 18 species.

The members of this family are distinguished from other Galliformes in several ways. Stock and compact in build, they are medium to large birds, the tail being average or long, the bill short and curved, with feathered nostrils. Over the eyes are bare patches of red skin (caruncles), more developed in the males and becoming stiffer and larger during the breeding season. The legs and sometimes the feet as well are covered by feathers; the rear toe is shorter and higher positioned than the other three and at the sides of the toes are comblike horny appendages.

In some species there are air-sacs on the neck, identical in texture to the caruncles; in others there are, instead, tufts of erectile feathers on neck or crown.

In the past, the Tetraonidae inhabited large tracts of moorland and woodland in the northern parts of the northern hemisphere. After the advance and retreat of the glaciations they extended their range southward and eventually colonized the mountain systems of central and southern Europe, of North America and of southern Siberia. Present-day forms have evolved from an ancestral group of monogamous Tetraonidae living in wooded areas, and have branched off in two directions.

Some species have maintained monogamous courtship behavior; these are the so-called solitarily displaying species and are therefore regarded as being less evolved. Among the representatives of this group are the hazel grouse (*Tetrastes bonasia*), the ptarmigan (*Lagopus mutus*), the willow grouse (*Lagopus lagopus*), the ruffed grouse (*Bonasa umbellus*), and many other species. As a rule the courting pair takes over a territory and will seldom abandon it. The male assists the female in incubation and sometimes distracts the attention of possible predators. The sexes generally look similar. Species living in woodland have a fairly long tail and other very mobile structures; and apart from giving clear visual signals they emit loud, repeated calls (this being particularly characteristic of the ruffed grouse).

Other more highly evolved species have developed gregarious behavior during the breeding period and are known as

▲ A group of ptarmigans in winter plumage toward the end of fall. In the foreground on the left is an adult male, and in the center a female who has not yet finished her molt.

▼ A pair of ptarmigans with their brood high up in the mountain pastures at the beginning of summer.

▼ The nostrils of the ptarmigans are covered with feathers and there are red caruncles over the eyes, the latter being especially notable in the male, together with a band of black feathers extending from the base of the bill to the rear of the eye. The tarsus and foot are covered in fine down which helps the bird to walk on snow; the rear toe is raised well above the level of the others.

collectively displaying species. Males tend to be fairly promiscuous, and each individual attempts, by displays, calls, and combats, to demonstrate his superiority over other rivals and thus earn the right to establish ownership of a domain for singing.

Belonging to this group are the black grouse (*Lyrurus tetrix*), the capercaillie (*Tetrao urogallus*), the prairie chicken (*Tympanuchus cupido*), the sage grouse (*Centrocercus urophasianus*), and other species from North America and eastern Asia. Normally these species display a striking sexual dimorphism and for much of the year the sexes live separately. They tend to live in fairly open habitats, though an exception to this rule is exhibited by the capercaillie which displays in clearings, among snowfields and slopes inside the area of occupied territory. Each male, day after day, takes up his position inside the communal display ground and fiercely defends his little piece of territory. Individual areas toward the center of the display ground tend to be quite small but those nearer the outside are more extensive and occupied only by young males. A central position gives the male a better chance of mating because the females, when the moment is ripe, always head for the part of the territory where the greatest number of suitors are assembled. Combats between males are grimly selective, and the bird which emerges at the end to claim the center of the display ground is surely the strongest and cleverest fighter, exploiting to the full his knowledge of the terrain.

In all species the male exhibits characteristic behavior in the breeding season, performing a succession of actions that culminate in copulation. The females, on the other hand, all behave in the same manner when confronted by a male; when ready for the sexual act they lie flat on the ground, spread their wings slightly and prepare to receive their mate.

▲ When winter snowfall is heavy and the cold intense, the ptarmigan shelters at night by digging a hole in the snow.

▲ Phase of the spring courtship.

▼ A brooding female.

▼ An egg (natural size).

◀ Male ptarmigan in winter (left) and summer plumage.

Greater prairie chicken
(*Tympanuchus cupido*)

Ruffed grouse
(*Bonasa umbellus*)

Red grouse
(*Lagopus lagopus scoticus*)

Black grouse
(*Lyrurus tetrix*)

Hazel grouse
(*Tetrastes bonasia*)

COMMON PEAFOWL

Pavo cristatus

Order Galliformes
Family Phasianidae
Size Length, adult male 44 – 48 in (110 – 120 cm); adult female 36 in (90 cm)
Distribution India and Sri Lanka
Habits Gregarious for most of the year
Nesting On ground
Eggs 4 – 8
Chicks Nidifugous

The common peafowl is the most spectacularly colored of all gallinaceous birds. The male's plumage is exceptionally brilliant. Head, neck and breast are blue-green and violet with metallic reflections. There is a patch of naked skin at the sides of the head around the eyes, and a crest of feathers with barbs only at the tip adorns the crown.

The fairly large beak is light brown and the iris of the eyes is also brown. The feathers of the back are greenish-gold with bronze edges, the tertiary wing coverts are white with closely ranged black bars, the secondary and primary coverts are blue-green with metallic tints, and both the remiges and rectrices are brown.

The upper tail feathers (of which there are 100 – 150) are very much longer than the rectrices and constitute the peacock's train. These feathers may grow to a length of 5 ft (1.6 m) – they continue growing up to the sixth year – but normally measure 4 – 4¼ ft (1.2 – 1.3 m). They possess long metallic-green barbs with blue and bronze reflections, and near the tips the barbs themselves merge to form an eyelike spot known as an ocellus, the bright blue center of which is surrounded by concentric brown, golden-yellow, and purple rings.

The peahen is smaller than the peacock. She has no train and her plumage is less gaudy.

The geographical range of the common peafowl comprises the whole of India and the island of Sri Lanka. It lives in forests and along river banks as well as on the edges of broad clearings, in warm, wet regions; and in the mountains of southern India it frequents open rainforests with sparse tree and shrub growth up to an altitude of 6,500 ft (2,000 m).

The common peafowl is a sedentary

During the breeding season, the peacock, in the presence of the hens, raises his tail, spreads out the magnificent, long upper tail feathers in a broad fan, and struts proudly in this display posture across his territory.

bird, living for the major part of the year in flocks of varying size. These large groups only disperse at the beginning of spring when each adult cock strays off, followed, as a rule, by 2 – 5 hens. The breeding period lasts throughout the spring. During the courtship parades, the male, watched by the females, raises the rectrices and spreads out the upper tail feathers like a fan. The hens in the group come running to his call and duly assume the postures that characteristically indicate readiness for mating, crouching on the ground in front of the male, wings half-open. At this signal the peacock quickly closes his magnificent train and mates with them in turn. After a while the hen prepares a rudimentary nest on the ground, usually high up in the shelter of a shrub or plant. In this crude nest she generally lays 4 – 5 eggs, but in the view of some authors there may be many more. When this activity is over she begins incubation, which lasts 28 – 30 days. In the wild, peafowl are omnivorous, feeding principally on vegetable substances (shoots, leaves, berries, seeds, etc.) but also on animals (snails, worms and, above all, insects).

Apart from the common peafowl, the subfamily Pavoninae comprises two other species, the green peacock (*Pavo muticus*), and the Congo peacock (*Afropavo congensis*).

The male green peacock is larger than his common relative. His plumage is predominantly green with metallic blue reflections and even more magnificent. The female, too, has bright green plumage but no train. The range of this species extends from Southeast Assam to Thailand and southern China, including the Malaysian peninsula and the island of Java.

The Congo peacock differs markedly from the two aforementioned species mainly by reason of its featherless neck and the absence of a train. The species was first described by the American ornithologist Chapin in 1936. He had seen, displayed in a case at the Congo Museum in Tervueren, Belgium, a pair of these stufffed Galliformes, wrongly described as young common peafowl. Having realized this classification error, Chapin planned to confirm the existence of a new species, and a year later, exploring the Ituri region of the Congo, succeeded in capturing seven specimens. The species was, in fact, known to the local population and to the whites living there.

◀ At night the bird takes refuge high up in the tree canopy.

◀ The peacock is essentially a grounddwelling species but can, if forced, fly quite easily.

▲ The peahen accompanies her chicks in order to find food and sometimes, during their first few days, feeds them herself.

Green peacock
(*Pavo muticus*)

Common peacock
(*Pavo cristatus*)

Congo peacock
(*Afropavo congensis*)

1) The congo peacock (*Afropavo congensis*) lives in a fairly restricted area of the former Belgian colony, in the tropical rain forests. It was only recently discovered, in 1936. 2) The common peafowl (*Pavo cristatus*) lives throughout India and on Sri Lanka, in hill and mountain zones up to 6,500 ft (2,000 m), notably in wet woodlands with many clearings. Easily domesticated, it has been known in Mediterranean countries since antiquity and is nowadays widely bred for ornamental purposes. 3) The green peacock (*Pavo muticus*) is found in Southeast Asia and on the island of Java.

1
2
3

RING-NECKED PHEASANT

Phasianus colchicus

Order Galliformes
Family Phasianidae
Size Length, adult male 30 – 36 in (75 – 90 cm); adult female 22 – 25 in (56 – 63 cm)
Weight Adult male 2½ – 3½ lb (1.15 – 1.5 kg); adult female 2 – 2½ lb (0.9 – 1.1 kg)
Nesting On ground
Eggs 7 – 14, brown to bright green or pale olive, fairly rounded in shape
Chicks Nidifugous

The ring-necked pheasant (*Phasianus colchicus*) is notable for its beautiful plumage and characteristic long, pointed tail. There is marked sexual dimorphism, both as regards dimensions and coloration. The female's plumage is very drab whereas that of the male is extremely showy.

Ring-necked pheasants live freely wherever they find open woodland, hedges, and scrub, on the fringes of uncultivated land.

In winter they come together to form groups either of cocks and hens alone. At the beginning of spring these groups disperse and the cocks wander off to find suitable territories. Once in occupation of his zone, each male reinforces his claim by singing, and sometimes confronts rivals penetrating his domain. The area chosen is usually thickly covered with bushes, on the edges of a wood, including some open areas close to meadows or paths. The courtship period is fairly prolonged and the first mating activities take place, depending on the zone, from April onward.

The hens subsequently retire to their chosen nesting sites and begin laying their eggs. The nest is a hollow in the ground, lined with stems of dry grass and a few feathers dropped by the female;it is situated in the midst of fallen leaves, between two mounds of earth, under the branches of a small bush, on the edges of a field or in a hedge. The clutch usually consists of some 10 pale olive-green eggs; laying begins after the middle of April and the duration of incubation is 23 – 24 days. Normally there is only one clutch annually. After the eggs hatch, the hens remain where they are until the

▲ Male ring-necked pheasant in spring, busy patrolling the territory he occupies during the breeding period. A female is perched on the dead branch.

◄ This bird feeds principally on vegetation (seeds, plant tops, and fruit); in summer and fall there is also a large amount of animal food included in the diet, especially of the young.

◄ Cock pheasants have feet equipped with spurs.

chicks are fledged. After 4 – 5 months the young pheasants wear plumage similar to that of the adults.

Food varies considerably from season to season, but fundamentally it consists of herbaceous vegetation, seeds of gramineous species and other plants, berries, various fruits, and also animal substances.

There are many further species of pheasants living wild in Asia. The copper pheasant (*Syrmaticus soemmerringii*) is an inhabitant of the mountain forests of the Japanese island of Kyushu, above a height of 4,000 ft (1,200 m). Its typical habitat is dense brushwood and undergrowth, with small clearings close to streams and rivers. The golden pheasant (*Chrysolophus pictus*) and Lady Amherst's pheasant (*C. amherstiae*) are undoubtedly the most colorful and resplendent of all Asiatic pheasants. The former lives in the densest brushwood of the mountains of central and western China, up to an altitude of 8,200 ft (2,500 m) feeding principally on the leaves and buds of various shrubs and of dwarf bamboos.

Lady Amherst's pheasant is decked out with even more colors than the golden pheasant; the tail is longer and in the course of display stands out all the more prominently, together with the brilliant hues of the nuptial garb. This bird lives on the rocky slopes of the mountains of southwest China between 7,000 and 12,000 ft (2,100 and 3,600 m), and usually hunts for food among shrubs and stands of bamboo, consuming mainly buds.

The silver pheasant (*Lophura nycthemera*) lives in pairs or small groups in the mountain forests of Southeast Asia at altitudes between 2,000 and 7,000 ft (600 and 2,100 m). The vast geographical range comprises the whole northeastern part of the Indochinese peninsula to the Gulf of Tonkin, and all southeastern China.

The Himalayan monal pheasant (*Lophophorus impeyanus*) also has an extremely colorful plumage. The distribution of this species is vast, from Afghanistan and across the mountains of southern Asia to Tibet and Bhutan. The pheasant normally inhabits open coniferous forests or mixed forests of conifers and deciduous trees, usually settling on rocky slopes or deep ravines at heights of between 9,000 and 12,000 ft (2,700 and 3,600 m).

▲| A brooding hen blends with her surroundings.

◄| The unexpected flushing of a cock pheasant in spring gives away the position of its song territory.

◄| Nuptial song of the male during spring.

◄| Chick aged a few days.

Copper pheasant (*Syrmaticus soemmerringii*)

Silver pheasant (*Lophura nycthemera*)

Golden pheasant (*Chrysolophus pictus*)

Himalayan monal pheasant (*Lophophorus impeyanus*)

Lady Amherst's pheasant (*Chrysolophus amherstiae*)

◄| Indigenous populations of the ring-necked pheasant are nowadays distributed over a discontinuous range from the southern and eastern shores of the Black Sea across central Asia to the east coasts of China. It was introduced in ancient times to Europe; it is not found in Iceland, northern Scandinavia, southern and western parts of the Iberian peninsula, the mainland of Italy, and southern Greece.
1) Distribution of ring-necked pheasant (*Phasianus colchicus*).

HOATZIN

Opisthocomus hoazin

Order Galliformes
Suborder Opisthocomi
Family Opisthocomidae
Size Length 24 in (60 cm)
Distribution South America
Habits Gregarious, arboreal
Nesting On branches low down on trees
Eggs 2 – 5, whitish with brown spots
Chicks Nidifugous and temporarily equipped with claws on tips of wings

The hoatzin has a fairly long body structure, and the upper-parts are mainly brown, with thin whitish streaks on the back; the feathers of the neck and breast are fawn, and the plumage of the abdomen, underparts, and remiges is reddish-brown.

It is interesting to note that the forelimbs (namely the wings) of newly hatched hoatzins are furnished with two well-developed, mobile claws, used for clambering about the branches. As the baby bird grows, these claws gradually atrophy and eventually disappear.

The hoatzin is distributed through the dense gallery forests and along streams and rivers in Colombia, Bolivia, Peru, and the Amazon basin. They are gregarious birds that live mainly in trees, where they find most of their food.

During the breeding season pairs do not move far apart and sometimes nest and brood quite close to one another in small groups. The nest is constructed on branches a little way above the ground or water surface; as a rule it takes the form of a large flattened basket, being made of interlaced sticks and dry scraps of vegetation. Both male and female collaborate in building the nest.

Incubation of the eggs is shared by both parents, and these hatch about 28 days after the last one is laid. At birth the chicks are totally naked but nevertheless able to move around quite nimbly, using their wing claws to climb, grip and transfer from branch to branch. During the first few days they are fed by the parents, but they grow very fast and soon become almost self-sufficient.

The most important sources of food for this species are the leaves of the arum plants and the fruits and leaves of other aquatic plants.

The hoatzin is basically an arboreal, gregarious member of the Galliformes. During the day it often lets out strong cries to keep in touch with other individuals of the group. It feeds on the leaves and fruits of various aquatic plants, but a large part of its diet is made up of the leaves of arum plants.

The forelimbs or wings of baby hoatzins are furnished with strong claws which help them to climb about in the trees.

The hoatzin is a South American species which lives in dense equatorial forests and along the banks of rivers in Bolivia, Colombia, Peru, and the Amazon basin.
1)*Opisthocomus hoazin*.

JACANAS
Jacanidae

Seven species of jacanas make up this most unusual family of waders. The one feature which immediately distinguishes them is extraordinary long toes, ending in a huge hind claw enabling them to walk on floating water plants. The legs too are long (a feature enhanced by bare tibia) but the bill is short, often with a fleshy frontal shield on the forehead and forecrown.

The pheasant-tailed jacana (*Hydrophasianus chirurgus*) is the only species with distinct winter and summer plumages. In its summer breeding dress it has a white forehead, face, throat, and neck bordered by a thin black line merging on the breast into the very dark brown underparts. The nape is a brilliant golden-yellow, contrasting with the brown back. The wings and most coverts are white. It has a long brown tail.

Living in watery areas they are quite capable of swimming well if needed. If threatened they will take refuge either by submerging among vegetation with just their bill showing or diving and remaining completely submerged for several minutes. Diving is only resorted to when the bird is injured or cannot fly well.

Jacanas eat a wide range of items and most species are thought to concentrate on invertebrates. The majority of individuals ingest some plant material, including seeds.

The breeding season is usually difficult to define since it varies annually with the timing of the rains. The peak of egg-laying takes place towards the end of the rainy season when water levels have reached the maximum and are relatively stable.

Jacanas are territorial in the breeding season. Territory disputes are frequent and are resolved by threat displays. The nest is a very poor structure. Usually it is constructed on floating weed and only a few extra strands of vegetation are included to prevent the eggs rolling over the side or falling through the bottom. The 4 eggs are incubated by the male alone. They are laid daily and incubation, which lasts for about 26 days, commences with the first egg. The chicks which are pale brownish above, are tended by the male.

The pheasant-tailed javana (*Hydrophasianus chirurgus*) is the only member of the family Jacanidae exhibiting two plumage color phases, one in winter and the other in summer; its tail may measure up to 12 in (30 cm). The bird lives in zones of quiet, shallow water, forming flocks of up to a hundred or so individuals.

The feet are particularly well adapted for walking on floating vegetation. As it moves, the bird raises its legs very high to shake off any grass that may be attached to them.

African jacana
(*Actophilornis africana*)

American jacana
(*Jacana spinosa*)

Bronze-winged jacana
(*Metopidius indicus*)

Most of these birds live in tropical regions. They have not been subjected to intensive hunting, so that the main problem facing them is one of habitat. Over their range a decrease in the area of suitable wetlands has been recorded, and although the change does not appear to be very dramatic, it is doubtful whether future prospects are too good. 1) Distribution of family Jacanidae.

GRUIFORMES

The order Gruiformes (or Ralliformes) comprises 11 or 12 families and approximately 200 living or recently extinct species, all sharing common anatomical features but differing notably from one another in morphology and biology. The Gruiformes possess long legs and are familiarly known as waders, as are the representatives of the order Ciconiiformes. Yet certain characteristics of the bill and the feet as well as the development of the chicks show that these two orders are, in fact, markedly differentiated.

The birds belonging to this order are of variable size, usually with short, rounded wings not too well adapted for flying (except in the case of the cranes) but almost always with long legs for running rapidly on the ground. As a rule the Gruiformes have four toes on either foot, but the large toe is generally smaller and higher positioned than the others; for this reason the birds find it very difficult to grasp branches, seldom and most unwillingly perching in trees. The feet are not webbed but the coots and finfoots have membranous flaps (lobate webs) on their toes. The plumage is not, as a rule, brightly colored. The bill is normally strong, and the chicks have a thick layer of down and are nidifugous.

The family Gruidae contains 14 species. The sexes are generally similar, the color of the wings and body ranging from white to gray, with black remiges. Some species have a naked, bright red patch on the head.

Many species perform characteristic dances which are not necessarily confined to the breeding season. Monogamy is the rule, both parents building the nest and incubating the two eggs. Because of the special structure of the trachea, cranes have powerful voices that can be heard for several miles.

The demoiselle crane (*Anthropoides virgo*) is the smallest member of the family, measuring 38 in (95 cm), and displays typical tufts of white feathers on either side of the head. The whooping crane (*G. americana*) was once abundant over its entire range, which extended to Canada. In 1941, in spite of severe protective measures, only 23 birds were counted in the Aransas Wildlife Refuge, its restricted wintering zone on the coast of the Gulf of Mexico.

Some representatives of the family Gruidae.

Japanese crane
(*Grus japonensis*)

Sarus crane
(*Grus antigone*)

Siberian crane
(*Grus leucogeranus*)

Whooping crane
(*Grus americana*)

Demoiselle crane
(*Anthropoides virgo*)

Hooded crane
(*Grus monacha*)

White-naped crane
(*Grus vipio*)

The family Eurypygidae is represented by a single species, the sun bittern (*Eurypyga helias*) from the forests of South America.

The trumpeters (family Psophiidae) are represented by three species with similar habits, living in the forests of Brazil.

The family Aramidae is made up of only one living species, the limpkin (*Aramus guarauna*). About 24 in (60 cm) long, this bird is found in the southern United States.

The two constituent species of the Cariamidae are the crested seriema (*Cariama cristata*) and Burmeister's seriema (*Chunga burmeisteri*), inhabitants of the steppes and sparse forests of the high plateau regions of Brazil, Paraguay, and northern Argentina.

The family Mesitornithidae contains three small species, measuring 10 in (25 cm) living in Madagascar.

There are 15 species of hemipodes, or Turnicidae, looking somewhat like the common quail.

The three species of finfoots (Heliornithidae) are essentially aquatic by habit, shy birds living on the shores of rivers and swamps of tropical forests. Peter's finfoot (*Podica senegalensis*) is the largest, measuring 24 in (60 cm) long.

The family Rallidae is the largest family of the entire order, containing some 132 species generally known as rails. Some are terrestrial, others aquatic, and all are medium to small in size, perfectly adapted to living in thick marsh vegetation and on the banks of lakes and rivers. Many of the birds are active mainly at night and some, though common, are known almost exclusively by their calls.

The family Rhynochetidae only comprises the kagu (*Rhynochetos jubatus*), an inhabitant of the dense forests of New Caledonia.

The family Otididae consists of 22 species, typically adapted to life at ground level, with long, sturdy legs. The bustards live in semidesert zones, grassy savannas, and prairies with scattered tree growth. Many of these large birds are furnished with ornamental feathers on head, neck, throat and nape, displaying them to full advantage in the courtship period or using them as warning signals. The best-known species is the great bustard (*Otis tarda*).

White-winged trumpeter
(*Psophia leucoptera*)

Bustard quail
(*Turnix suscitator*)

Great bustard
(*Otis tarda*)

Limpkin
(*Aramus guarauna*)

Kagu
(*Rhynochetos jubatus*)

Water rail
(*Rallus aquaticus*)

Peter's finfoot
(*Podica senegalensis*)

▲ The order Gruiformes is subdivided into 11 (or 12, in the view of some authors) families, with a total of some 200 species, either living or recently extinct. Above, from left to right and from top to bottom, are representatives of some of these families: Psophiidae, Turnicidae, Aramidae, Otididae, Rallidae, Rhynochetidae and Heliornithidae.

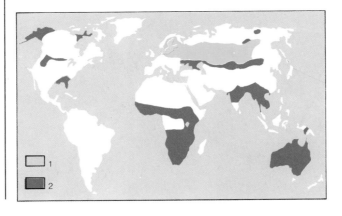

◀ The birds belonging to the family Gruidae are widely distributed throughout the world, except in South America, the Indo−Malaysian archipelago, New Zealand, and the Polynesian islands. The only species nesting in Europe is the common crane, which also ranges into Asia. 1) Common crane (*Grus grus*); 2) other members of the family Gruidae.

MOORHEN
Gallinula chloropus

Order Gruiformes
Family Rallidae
Size Length 12½ – 14 in (32 – 35 cm)
Weight About 12 oz (320 – 330 g)
Distribution Europe, Asia, Africa, and America
Reproductive period March to April, with 2, rarely 3, clutches
Incubation 20 – 21 days
Eggs 5 – 11
Chicks Nidifugous

The moorhen is a water bird roughly the size of a pigeon. The wings are short and rounded, the body flattened from side to side, and the short tail flicks rhythmically up and down, especially when the bird is frightened. Adults have white stripes on the flanks, the white rump is divided in half by a black band, and the yellow-tipped red bill is surmounted by a bright red frontal plate. The legs are greenish with an orange or red "garter" on the lower part of the tibia, and the iris is reddish-brown.

The moorhen may be sedentary, a bird of passage or migratory, depending upon climatic conditions prevailing in breeding grounds. It usually frequents the banks of rivers and lakes, ditches and canals, swamps, marshes and cultivated land, particularly water-meadows and rice-paddies.

Not as shy and secretive as other Rallidae, the moorhen may often be seen swimming in open water or reconnoitring the banks, scuttling into vegetation at the slightest noise. Indeed, if disturbed, the moorhen immediately skitters across the water, wings beating rapidly, to find safety. It is reluctant to fly and if forced to do so rises heavily into the air, legs dangling. Very often, to escape danger, it will dive under the water and perhaps stay there for a couple of minutes, attached by feet and bill to aquatic plants and using both feet and wings for swimming. The bird resorts to diving more as a means of defense than as a way of finding food. The nest is built on the water or very close by, but sometimes it may be placed in a tree or bush or even borrowed from a crow, a rook or a magpie. Both sexes help to build it, the male carrying the materials, the female arranging them. In addition to this nest, used for depositing the eggs, the

Moorhen
(*Gallinula chloropus*)

Coot
(*Fulica atra*)

▲ The moorhen is a familiar bird of different aquatic surroundings. The redbill and frontal shield distinguish it at a glance from other Rallidae such as the coot, which is bigger and has a white bill and frontal plate. Its food is varied, comprised chiefly of vegetation and, to a lesser extent, animal prey such as aquatic insects, worms, snails, and small fish.

The nest is built among reeds of interlaced water grasses. Sometimes it is situated so as to rise and fall with the water level. ▶

moorhen builds other, more rudimentary nests that play their part in various stages of the courtship and in raising the young. The female lays 5 – 11 eggs, which are grayish-white with reddish-brown spots. Incubation by both sexes lasts 20 – 21 days.

A common bird of ponds and marshes, closely related to the moorhen, is the coot (*Fulica atra*). The adult measuring 15 – 18 in (38 – 45 cm) and weighing 25 – 35 oz (700 – 1,000 g), is easily recognized by its bill and frontal shield, which are both white, and stand out against the predominantly slate-gray plumage and shining black head and neck. The coot nests almost all over Europe, in North Africa, and in central-southern Asia; in Australia and New Guinea it is represented by similar species. Like the moorhen, it may be sedentary, a bird of passage or migratory. The bird spends much of its time in the water and swims jerkily, moving its head to and fro. It is in the habit of diving for food, sometimes to a depth of 26 ft (8 m). Besides eating large quantities of aquatic plants, the coot also consumes various species of mollusks, insects, larvae and, less frequently, worms and small fish. Both sexes collaborate in building their nest, which is generally made of aquatic vegetation, so interwoven as to make a floating platform. Incubation of the 7 – 12 eggs lasts 21 – 25 days and is shared by both sexes. The chicks are capable of diving at the age of 5 – 6 days, and are easily distinguished by their orange-red head.

An elegant member of the family, unmistakable by its splendid plumage, is the larger purple gallinule (*Porphyrio porphyrio*). The upperparts of the body are dark purple-blue, the breast is pale blue with metallic tints, and the pure white rump contrasts with the black abdomen; the bill, the long legs and the broad frontal plate are bright red. Some 20 species exist in various parts of the world.

A last mention should be made of the takahe (*Notornis mantelli*), a large flightless rail with brillant blue-green plumage, a massive beak, red at the base and pink at the tip, and a vivid red frontal shield. Nowadays it is a protected species in danger of extinction. The nest is a kind of tunnel between tufts of grass, containing 1 – 2 opaque, creamy, brown-speckled eggs.

▲ To take off, the coot gets a lift by skittering over the water for a short distance.

▲ When disturbed, the coot dives and swims underwater with rhythmical foot movements.

▲ The coot's foot is provided with toes enveloped in membranous webs.

The takahé (*Notornis mantelli*) is a flightless rail from New Zealand which is about the same size as a turkey. Thought to be extinct around the middle of the ninteenth century, it was accidentally rediscovered in 1948, but is obviously an endangered species, even if protected.

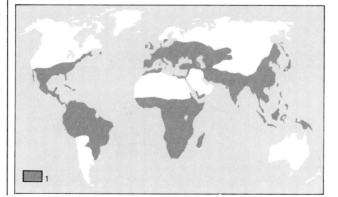

▲ Baby coot (orange-red head) and baby moorhen (red, yellow-tipped beak).

▲ Above, left to right: the rare crested coot (*Fulica cristata*) has characteristic fleshy red projections over its white forehead plate. The larger purple gallinule (*Porphyrio porphyrio*) has bright red legs, bill, and frontal shield, while the American purple gallinule (*P. martinica*) has its red, yellow-tipped bill surmounted by a light blue frontal plate, and pure yellow legs.

◀ The moorhen is distributed all over the world except for polar and desert regions; in Australia it is replaced by related species. Its habitats are wet places such as the banks of rivers, lakes, ditches and canals, swamps and marshes, water-meadows, and rice-paddies. 1) *Gallinula chloropus*.

COMMON TERN

Sterna hirundo

Order Charadriiformes
Family Laridae
Size Length 14½ in (36 cm)
Distribution Throughout northern hemisphere, with cosmopolitan range
Habits Gregarious
Nesting From end of May to early June
Eggs 2 – 3, blue or brown with dark spots
Chicks Covered in yellow-gray or speckled brown down; semi-nidifugous

In the breeding season adults of the common tern are completely black on top of the head, while in winter the crown is brown, streaked with white. The color of the bill also changes with the seasons: in summer it is a handsome orange-red with a black tip, and the black gradually spreads so that at the height of winter there are only faint traces of red visible at the base. The back, the top of the forked tail and the wings are gray, and the tips of the primary remiges are black. The rump and underparts are white; in summer the breast and abdomen are tinged light gray.

The common tern has a particularly wide distribution, its range embracing almost all continents apart from Antarctica. The environments selected as nesting zones tend to vary. Like all terns, they frequent sandy coastlines, dunes, brackish marshes, river estuaries and the like, but also nest in freshwater zones, on the banks of streams and rivers, along the shores of inland lakes.

It is undoubtedly in the air that terns show themselves to best advantage. Their flight pattern, with slow, regular wingbeats, is a picture of effortless grace. Much of their time has to be spent in hunting for food, and they may often be seen in groups, skimming slowly over the water, head lowered to catch the least sign of movement on or beneath the surface. Food consists in the main of small fish, crustaceans, and mollusks.

The common tern nests in crowded colonies causing bitter territorial rivalry. Between April and May the female lays 2 – 3 blue-green, brown-spotted eggs, which are incubated in turn by both sexes for about 3 weeks.

Although considered a marine bird, the common tern is not usually found out at sea, preferring to stick to the coasts, the mouths of rivers, and also inland waters. Large flocks are often encountered close to ports. This bird feeds principally on small surface fish but also consumes crustaceans and insects.

► Silhouettes of some sea birds in flight.

Shearwater   Skua   Gull   Tern

GREAT SKUA

Stercorarius skua

Order Charadriiformes
Family Stercorariidae
Size Length 23½ in (58 cm)
Distribution In the northern hemisphere it nests from the Scottish isles to Iceland. In the southern hemisphere it lives in the circumpolar regions of Antarctica. In the winter it ranges over the Atlantic to the tropic of Cancer.
Nesting End – May to early June. Single clutch
Eggs Usually 2, rarely 1, olive-brown or grayish-yellow with brown spots
Chicks Born with yellowish-brown down, paler on underparts. Semi-nidifugous

The great skua is completely brown, except at the base of the primary flight feathers where white patches are visible on both sides of the wings. It looks much like a brown gull but the wings are more rounded and less angular, the tail is shorter, and it is altogether heavier and more awkward on the ground.

The skuas are noticeably aggressive toward other sea birds, pursuing them relentlessly until they drop or even regurgitate their prey, this often being snatched up before it hits the water. Living principally by plunder, they feed on fish, rodents, insects, birds, carrion, and all kinds of refuse, and sometimes berries as well. All non-digestible parts of their prey, such as skin and bones, are subsequently regurgitated as small rounded pellets, as happens among most birds of prey.

Skuas live for most of the year at sea and settle on dry land only for breeding. The great skua usually nests close to the sea, on moors at varying altitudes, on bare ground or planted terrain, and in river estuaries. They normally nest in small colonies or isolated pairs. The nest is a small hollow dug in the ground by both members of the pair, who then line it with scraps of grass, moss, and other materials. Eggs are laid between the end of May and the early part of July and this is preceded by courtship parades; the male great skua struts in front of his partner, ruffling his neck feathers. Incubation by both parents begins as soon as the first egg is laid, and after 23 – 30 days the first chick hatches.

Like all its relatives, the great skua is a kleptoparasite, feeding on the fish it steals from other sea birds. This aggressive habit partly explains their family name of Stercorariidae; it used to be believed that they ate the excrement emitted by the terrified birds they were pursuing, but skuas actually feed on birds, carrion, eggs and chicks, lemmings, and, of course, fish.

The bill of skuas (below) is fairly similar to that of gulls (above) but more prominently hooked at the tip, in keeping with its predatory habits.

COMMON GUILLEMOT

Uria aalge

Order Charadriiformes
Family Alcidae
Size Length 16½ in (41 cm)
Distribution Northern coasts of the Atlantic and Pacific Oceans (North America, northern Europe, Greenland, Iceland)
Habits Marine, gregarious
Nesting In colonies on rocky islets and cliffs
Eggs 1, large and pear-shaped
Chicks Semi-nidicolous, venturing into sea before being able to fly

All the species in the family Alcidae have fairly similar plumage, black above and white below but sometimes completely black. Variation and contrast is effected by white patches and wing bands, distinctive patterns on the head (some species have tufts of colored feathers), naked skin on the beak and brightly colored legs and throat, all designed to help individuals of a species to communicate with one another. The basic black and white coloration clearly has a mimetic function. Aerial predators, especially sea eagles, are unable to pick out the black back of a bird floating on the dark sea surface, while underwater hunters such as whales and carnivorous fish cannot distinguish from below the bird's white belly against the dazzling light of the clear sky. Both sexes have similar plumage but may look very different at certain seasons; and both molt their wing feathers all together so that for a while thay are unable to fly. The sounds made by the birds are rudimentary, a blend of grunts, raucous cries, and whistles.

The alcids are ecological counterparts in the northern hemisphere of the penguins and diving petrels of the southern hemisphere. Auks and penguins represent a clear example of evolutionary convergence, that phenomenon whereby animals that are separately classified (penguins belong to the order Sphenisciformes and auks to the Charadriiformes) have come to look and behave alike because they live in the same environment and feed in the same way.

A typical representative of the family is the common guillemot (*Uria aalge*).

Guillemots nest on cliffs, crowding together on narrow rock ledges overlooking the sea. The clouds of birds wheeling over the cliffs as they return from fishing, the sharp, penetrating smell, the white excrement staining the rocks and the raucous cries emitted incessantly by adults and young, provide a spectacle of great beauty and animation.

Food consists of fish and, to a lesser extent, crustaceans, mollusks, and worms.

It looks much like a penguin, with its tapered body, long neck, conical and pointed bill, and feet positioned far back under the abdomen. The plumage is white on the belly, black or chocolate-brown on the back, head and neck. The feet and bill are black.

The guillemot is a sea bird which ventures onto dry land only for nesting; much of its life is spent on the high seas. It moves awkwardly on land and is forced to rest sitting upright on its tarsi. Nor is it notably versatile in the air; the short, narrow wings have to be kept fluttering rapidly to support the heavy body, the short tail precludes sudden changes of direction, and the webbed feet stick out widely from the sides of the body.

In the sea, however, the bird comes into its own, displaying its perfect adaptation to the element; the soft, thick plumage is covered by a layer of oil secreted by the uropygial gland and smeared over the feathers with the bill, protecting the body from the water and the cold. When the guillemot makes a brief dive underwater, it swims by beating its wings in paddlelike fashion and uses its feet as a rudder for changes in direction. It can dive to a depth of about 33 ft (10 m) and can go without breathing for more than a minute.

Toward the end of December the guillemots head for the shore, returning regularly to the sites used for breeding in the previous years. By April thousands of pairs have settled on the spots chosen for nest-building. The birds establish their colonies on the flat summits of rocky islands and on cliff ledges, precariously balanced as they defend the few square inches of space separating them from their neighbors. The egg is pale blue-green with brown and black marks; it is markedly pear-shaped so that if blown and buffeted by the wind it will roll about on the lighter pointed end and will be less likely to tumble off the narrow rock ledge. Both sexes share the incubation for 32 – 34 days.

By the time it is 3 weeks old the fledgling's plumage is already waterproof even though the feathers are hardly sprouting; urged on by the parents it hurls itself down from a few dozen feet into the sea, where it will learn to be an expert swimmer and diver before it can fly.

◄ Prey is usually caught underwater after an acrobatic chase; the guillemot uses its wings as paddles and its feet as a rudder.

Winter

Summer

Pigeon guillemot
(*Cepphus columba*)

Common puffin
(*Fratercula arctica*)

Razorbill
(*Alca torda*)

Little auk
(*Plautus alle*)

Crested auklet
(*Aethia cristatella*)

◄▼ The guillemot incubates its single egg by holding it between its feet, usually turning its body toward the rock face for protection against the wind. The egg is pear-shaped with a prominently pointed tip; in this way, if pushed, it will turn on its axis without falling.

▲ The alcids and penguins are similar in appearance and behavior although they belong to two distinct bird orders. However, they differ in size: the guillemot, on the left, is about 16½ in (41 cm) long, whereas the emperor penguin, on the right, measures about 48 in (120 cm).

▼ Common guillemot (*Uria aalge*) in winter plumage.

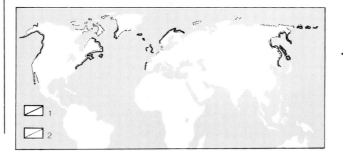

◄ The birds belonging to the family Alcidae are all marine species and are found in the cold zones of the northern hemisphere. After breeding they fly south into the Pacific and Atlantic: the guillemot's winter travels may take it as far as the Mediterranean, California, and northern Japan. 1) Family Alcidae; 2) Common guillemot (*Uria aalge*).

DOVES AND PIGEONS

Columbidae

There is no clear taxonomic distinction between doves and pigeons; both forms belong to the family Columbidae and are distributed almost everywhere, except in polar regions. Their sizes are very variable, some species being no bigger than a sparrow and others as large as a turkey; furthermore, the feeding habits of the 289 species of Columbidae range from those which are almost exclusively seed-eaters to those which feed basically on fruit. More than half these species live in the Indo-Malaysian regions or in Australia, while one small goup inhabits the warm latitudes of America; six species are found in Europe.

Certain species, such as the rock dove (common or wild pigeon) display similar plumage in male and female; others exhibit colors designed to attract the opposite sex for breeding purposes, and this results in marked sexual dimorphism. All the Columbidae are monogamous, proverbially "loving" and loyal to each other. The nest is generally a roughly assembled structure, containing, as a rule, a couple of eggs, usually built by both parents who also collaborate in rearing the brood, taking turns to incubate. The incubation period varies from 12 – 30 days. Other common features are the nasal cere and the so-called "pigeon's milk."

The largest subfamily is that of the Treroninae or fruit pigeons, with a limited distribution over the tropical zones of the Old World, especially the Indo-Malaysian regions. All are essentially fruit-eating species and the majority show marked sexual dimorphism, the colors of the males often being vivid and spectacular.

One of the most typical representatives of the subfamily is the white-bellied green pigeon (*Sphenurus sieboldii*), a bird of southern Asia and Indonesia; it is about the same size as a common pigeon, the body yellowish-green with chestnut-brown upper parts, the legs being crimson and the eyes encircled with blue. Like almost all fruit pigeons, it moves about in groups, visiting trees heavy with ripe fruit. To find this food the colony shifts from

The family Columbidae contains a large number of species that vary greatly in size and choice of food.

Stock dove
(*Columba oenas*)

European turtledove
(*Streptopelia turtur*)

EURASIA

Rufous turtledove
(*Streptopelia orientalis*)

Collared dove
(*Streptopelia decaoto*)

Wood pigeon
(*Columba palumbus*)

Japanese wood pigeon
(*Columba janthina*)

Green pigeon
(*Sphenurus sieboldii*)

Pallas's sand-grouse (*Syrrhaptes paradoxus*) belongs to the family Pteroclidae, which, together with the family Columbidae, makes up the order Columbiformes.

SOUTHERN ASIA AND AUSTRALIA

Plumed pigeon
(*Lophophaps plumifera*)

Large green pigeon
(*Treron capellei*)

Elegant imperial pigeon
(*Ducula concinna*)

Red-breasted fruit dove
(*Ptilinopus viridis*)

Emerald dove
(*Chalcophaps indica*)

Nicobar pigeon
(*Caloenas nicobarica*)

Bleeding heart pigeon
(*Gallicolumba luzonica*)

Yellow-bellied fruit pigeon
(*Leucotreon cinctatus*)

Green imperial pigeon
(*Ducula aenea*)

low-lying plains, where the fruit ripens earlier, to higher areas, so that each year there is a slow and gradual migration. Despite the bright colors, the bird is not easy to observe, because for most of the time it is well hidden high up in the fruit trees, capable of hanging upside-down, if need be, to reach the berries.

The largest group of Treroninae comprises the fruit doves of the genus *Ptilinopus*, the best known of which is the superb fruit dove (*P. superbus*), found in New Guinea, Tasmania, and Indonesia.

The imperial or nutmeg pigeons of the genus *Ducula* are notable for their brilliant metallic tints. One representative of the group is the green imperial pigeon (*D. aenea*), a very beautiful bird measuring almost 16 in (40 cm), with vivid metallic plumage.

The small subfamily Gourinae contains only three species, known as the crowned pigeons and occurring in New Guinea. Another important subfamily, the Columbinae, includes both seed-eating and fruit-eating species, along with some of the most markedly gregarious pigeons of the family.

The genus *Streptopelia* includes the African mourning dove (*S. decipiens*) and the European turtle-dove (*S. turtur*). Similar to them is the mourning dove (*Zenaidura macroura*) from Mexico and North America. About 12 in (30 cm) long, it has gray-brown plumage, the neck being a little darker with pink and violet tints on either side. It is the commonest American species, often nesting in cities.

One of the most decorative and vividly colored turtle-doves is the emerald dove (*Chalcophaps indica*), a bird with terrestrial habits, found in the Indo-Malaysian forests and in Australia.

The genus *Columba*, in addition to the common pigeon (*C. livia*), contains two other European species, the wood pigeon (*C. palumbus*) and the stock dove (*C. oenas*).

There are two families of birds closely related to Columbidae. The first is the Pteroclidae family, just comprising 16 species known as the sandgrouse, living in open and often desert regions of the Old World. The last family, the Rhaphidae, is presently extinct. It included a few flightless species, such as the dodo (*Raphus cucullatus*), which is now extinct. This was a gigantic flightless pigeon which measured more than 3 ft (1 m) in length.

AMERICA

Mourning dove (*Zeinadura macroura*)

The dodo (*Raphus cucullatus*) lived on the island of Mauritius and became extinct in 1680. It was as big as a turkey, with a plump body and a proportionately large head.

Blue-crowned pigeon (*Goura cristata*)

Magpie pouter

Fantail

Jacobin

Double-crested white trumpeter

1) The birds making up the family Columbidae live all over the world; about half of these species are concentrated in the Indo-Malaysian regions and the continent of Australia.
2) The Columbidae are very rare or absent in some areas, particularly the polar regions.

◀ Varieties of domestic pigeons.

PARROTS AND ALLIES
Psittaciformes

The strongly hooked beak, with both jaws markedly hinged, the feet with two toes turned forward and two backward, the striking colors, predominantly green, red, yellow and blue, and the distinctive cries, almost always loud and raucous, are just a few of the more obvious characteristics that make the parrots so easily identifiable.

Although the majority of parrots live in the tropical jungle, it is fair to say that there is hardly any habitat they do not occupy. Some species are found in grassy and wooded savannas, in semidesert and desert regions, in cultivated zones, in high mountains where the ground is covered by snow for most of the year, in mangrove swamps, on cliffs, and in salt lagoons along the seashore.

The largest representative of the order is the Hyacinthine macaw (*Anodorhynchus hyacinthinus*) from Brazil, which measures about 3 ft (1 m) in length and weighs 3 lb (1.5 kg), while the smallest is the buff-faced pygmy parrot (*Micropsitta pusio*) from New Guinea, which is barely 3½ in (8.5 cm) long and only weighs about ½ oz (15 g).

The principal and most striking aspect of the parrots, nevertheless, is their range of colors, usually very vivid, with a predominance of green. Sexual dimorphism, namely a difference in color between male and female, is fairly widespread among parrots from Australia, New Guinea, and Asia. Normally it is the male who boasts the more brilliant colors but the opposite is true of the eclectus parrot (*Eclectus roratus*) of New Guinea and neighboring regions, for the female is red and blue and the male mainly green. All cockatoos bear mobile crests of varying shapes. Crests are used for sending signals, especially during courtship.

In spite of a superficial resemblance to that of birds of prey and especially owls, a parrot's beak, as can easily be observed, functions in quite a different manner. While eating, the two parts of a parrot's bill operate somewhat like the jaws of ruminants, the cutting edges of the lower part moving rhythmically against the grooved roof

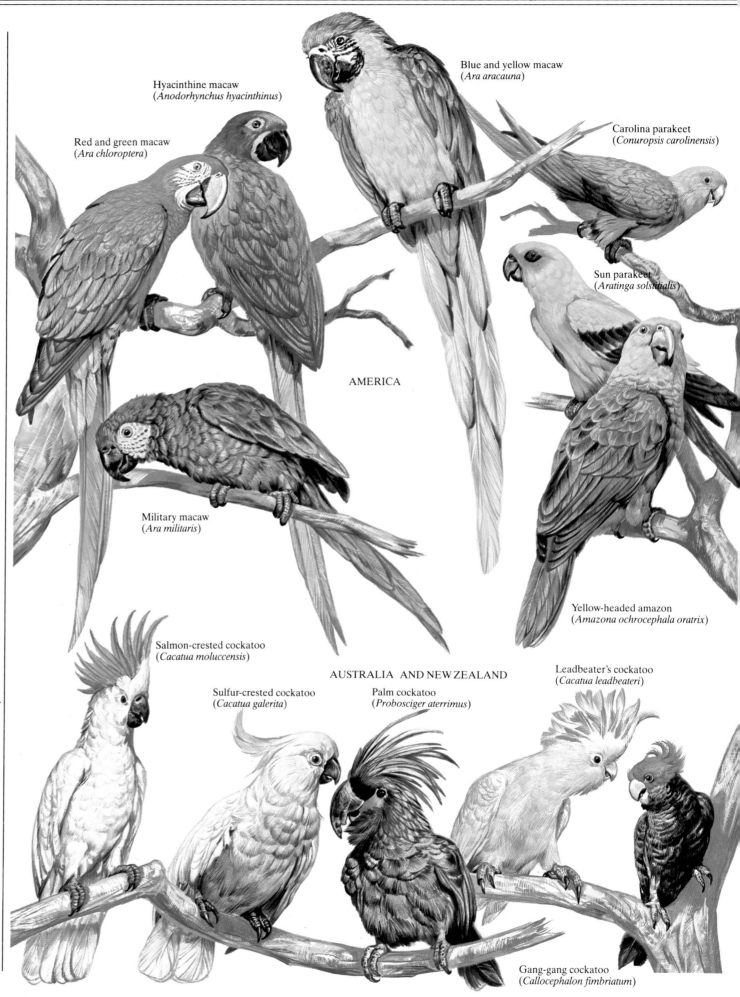

Hyacinthine macaw
(*Anodorhynchus hyacinthinus*)

Blue and yellow macaw
(*Ara aracauna*)

Red and green macaw
(*Ara chloroptera*)

Carolina parakeet
(*Conuropsis carolinensis*)

Sun parakeet
(*Aratinga solstitialis*)

AMERICA

Military macaw
(*Ara militaris*)

Yellow-headed amazon
(*Amazona ochrocephala oratrix*)

Salmon-crested cockatoo
(*Cacatua moluccensis*)

AUSTRALIA AND NEW ZEALAND

Leadbeater's cockatoo
(*Cacatua leadbeateri*)

Sulfur-crested cockatoo
(*Cacatua galerita*)

Palm cockatoo
(*Probosciger aterrimus*)

Gang-gang cockatoo
(*Callocephalon fimbriatum*)

of the upper part, shelling or grinding food with the aid of the tongue. In addition to eating, the beak is also used as an extra point of support as the parrot moves through the branches.

The majority of parrots feed on seeds, berries, grass, leaves, tender slivers of bark, shoots, buds, and roots. The strictly arboreal Loriini feed almost exclusively on nectar, pollen, and sweet pulps. Insects are included, to some extent, in the diet of almost all species, but some, such as the black cockatoos of the genus *Calyptorhynchus* and in particular the kaka or southern nestor (*Nestor meridionalis*), are markedly insectivorous and spend most of the time ripping away old bark to find larvae. It is possible that small vertebrates are also included in the diet of more parrot species than is generally believed. Among the mainly vegetarian species, some are highly specialized in cracking open nuts and fruit stones.

Most parrots lay their eggs in the hollow of a tree, but many also nest in the cavity of a rock or wall, under the eaves of a roof, in a hole on the ground, among tufts of grass or piles of stones, in tunnels dug on a slope, or in a termite mound. The eggs, invariably white, measure between about ⅝ in (16 – 17 mm) and 2 – 2¼ in (50 – 55 mm). The minimum number is 1 – 2 and the maximum is 8 – 9. As a rule it is the female who incubates, fed at the entrance hole or in the nest by the male, but in the case of some cockatoos both sexes take turns on the eggs. In the first days of life, the chicks are fed only by the female on a cheeselike substance, rich in protein, equivalent to pigeon's milk.

As they fly, many parrots utter loud, discordant cries, repeating them in rapid succession; these calls help flocks to keep together in the course of their evening and nightly journeys. Because of their capacity for mimicry, some species, such as the gray parrot and the yellow-headed amazon (*Amazona ochrocephala*), have unhappily become the special target of dealers, and every year large numbers of adult and young birds are captured.

Gray parrot
(*Psittacus erithacus*)

Nyasa lovebird
(*Agapornis lilianae*)

Masked lovebird
(*Agapornis personata*)

AFRICA

Plum-headed parakeet
(*Psittacula cyanocephala*)

African ringed-necked parakeet
(*Psittacula krameri*)

Red-faced lovebird
(*Agapornis pullaria*)

Himalayan slaty-headed parakeet
(*Psittacula himalayana*)

Paradise parrot
(*Psephotus pulcherrimus*)

Budgerigar
(*Melopsittacus undulatus*)

Scarlet-chested parrot
(*Neophema splendida*)

Rainbow lorikeet
(*Trichoglossus haematodus moluccanus*)

Cockatiel
(*Nymphicus hollandicus*)

Kakapo
(*Strigops habroptilus*)

Ground parrot
(*Pezoporus wallicus*)

SOUTHERN ASIA

Kea
(*Nestor notabilis*)

◄| The majority of parrots are distributed through the tropical regions of the southern hemisphere, especially in South America, Australia, and New Guinea. Comparatively few species live in Africa and Madagascar, southern Asia, the Philippines, the Sunda archipelago, New Zealand, Micronesia, Melanesia, and Polynesia. The farthest point north is reached by the Himalayan slaty-headed parakeet (*Psittacula himalayana*) which, in Afghanistan, is found in the region of latitude 36° N; and in the southern hemisphere its counterpart is the austral parakeet (*Microsittace ferruginea*), which reaches the southernmost tip of Tierra del Feugo. 1) World distribution of the order Psittaciformes.

OWLS
Strigiformes

The owls or nocturnal raptors (Strigiformes) are an order of birds comprising only two families, the Tytonidae, with just over 10 species, best known of which is the barn owl, and the Strigidae, with more than 120 species, further divided into two subfamilies, Buboninae and Striginae.

Owls have large, relatively immobile eyes situated at the front of the head and encircled by large concave zones known as facial disks. All this gives them a most distinctive appearance. The feathers that grow inside the disks are soft, with few barbs and lacking barbules, while those on the edges, forming a kind of border, are small, stiff and slightly curved. In the center of the face there are two areas shaped like a half-moon, usually white, which touch each other to form the inner margin of the eyes. The beak is strongly curved, quite large and fairly broad at the base. The head of an owl, as a rule, is large and rounded, and in certain species adorned with special feathers which form hornlike tufts, that have a mimetic function. The claws are always powerful in proportion to the size of the species. The fourth toe is opposable both to the rear toe and the front ones.

Broadly speaking, an owl's plumage consists of neutral, mimetic colors, mainly gray or chestnut-brown, its uniformity broken by varied streaks and spots. Little noise is made when flying because of the very soft extensions of the barbules, which form a kind of velvety cushion for the feathers.

Sight is one of the keenest senses of nocturnal birds of prey, as is evident from the exceptionally large dimensions of their eyes; those of the tawny owl are, in fact, bigger than human eyes. Furthermore, owls' eyes are furnished with a highly developed crystalline lens, a markedly convex cornea and an opaque nictitating membrane or third eyelid, a unique feature among birds. Their overall field of vision ranges virtually through 180° and a third of this is made up of binocular vision. Thus an owl is readily able to distinguish reliefs in the terrain and to estimate distances. In total or almost total darkness even these birds are unable to distinguish anything and rely wholly on their hearing to locate and

Little owl
(*Athene noctua*)

Scops owl
(*Otus scops*)

Ural owl
(*Strix uralensis*)

Short-eared owl
(*Asio flammeus*)

Tengmalm's owl
(*Aegolius funereus*)

Long-eared owl
(*Asio otus*)

Snowy owl
(*Nyctea scandiaca*)

Oriental hawk owl
(*Ninox scutulata*)

Barn owl
(*Tyto alba*)

Blakiston's fish-owl
(*Ketupa blakistoni*)

Eagle owl
(*Bubo bubo*)

catch prey. Being long-sighted, they have difficulty in seeing nearby objects, so when tearing up food they use their sense of touch, bringing into play the long whiskers growing from the base of the beak.

Owls are not exclusively nocturnal, especially in the Far North where species such as the snowy owl spend the summer in conditions of almost perpetual light. All species hunt, if they can, around dusk and dawn, in the semi-darkness. During the night they alternate active periods with intervals of song and rest; but it is generally during the day that they satisfy the latter need, retreating to remote, shady spots in order to sleep, safe from the attacks and clamor of other birds who normally display hostility toward them. Owls probably require such long periods of quiet and immobility to regulate their metabolism properly.

Food for many species consists principally of rodents, but owls hunt many other small animals including tiny mammals, birds, reptiles, amphibians, fish, insects, and various invertebrates. The largest types of prey may weigh 6 – 8 lb (3 – 4 kg) but only the eagle owl and other Strigidae or similar size can cope with victims of such dimensions. Victims are usually swallowed whole, and only when they are too big are they ripped to pieces.

Calls play an important part in the life of nocturnal birds of prey. As a rule the male emits a cry of one or more notes, repeated at regular but varying intervals. This has territorial significance and serves to entice the female, who is normally less vocal than her mate, giving out similar sounds but with different tonalities. Most of the singing occurs in the breeding season. The syrinx (vocal organ) consists only of bronchi and vibrates under the impulse of two pairs of muscles, which sometimes come into hard contact with the jaws, producing a characteristic sound.

Owls generally breed in isolated pairs and not in colonies, but they may display gregarious habits when migrating and in winter quarters. With the exception of a few species, such as the short-eared owl, they build no nest, contenting themselves in some cases with a small hollow in the ground, but generally laying their eggs and rearing their young in rock fissures, tree hollows, burrows, and nests of other animals. Many species habitually make use of buildings for these purposes.

Spectacled owl
(*Pulsatrix perspicillata*)

Pygmy owl
(*Glaucidium passerinum*)

Saw-whet owl
(*Aegolius acadicus*)

Great horned owl
(*Bubo virginianus*)

Ferruginous pygmy owl
(*Glaucidium brasilianum*)

Elf owl
(*Micrathene whitneyi*)

Barred owl
(*Strix varia*)

Hawk owl
(*Surnia ulula*)

Pell's fishing owl
(*Scotopelia peli*)

Great gray owl
(*Strix nebulosa*)

Brown wood owl
(*Strix leptogrammica*)

The Strigiformes have morphological features in common, thus differentiating them from other orders of birds. Their eyes are situated at the front of the head and are surrounded by broad concave facial disks. Some species have two hornlike ear-tufts on the head, which have a mimetic function. Because of the abundant fluffy plumage, owls typically have a stocky, rounded shape. The smallest, such as the elf owl, weigh little more than 1¾ oz (50 g), the largest such as the eagle owl, weigh around 8¾ lbs (4 kg). These nocturnal birds of prey comprise 130 different species divided into 28 genera and two families. 1) Distribution of the tawny owl (*Strix aluco*); 2) distribution of the Ural owl (*Strix uralensis*); 3) the birds belonging to the order Strigiformes are distributed in all continents, except Antarctica.

ROADRUNNER
Geococcyx californianus

Order Cuculiformes
Family Cuculidae
Size Length 23 in (58 cm)
Weight 18 oz (500 g)
Distribution Southwestern parts of North America
Habits Solitary
Nesting On bushes or cactuses
Reproductive period Spring
Incubation 18 days
Eggs 2 – 12
Chicks Inept
Sexual maturity 1 – 2 years

The roadrunner (*Geococcyx californianus*) is a well-known bird featured in many a comic strip and animated cartoon. It is medium-sized, chestnut-brown and dirty white in overall color, with a blue eye ring that is much broader at the rear. The large, powerful bill is hooked at the tip and is capable of disposing of prey such as snakes. There is a small crest on the head, the neck is moderately long and the tail as long as the rest of the body.

Speed is typical of birds that live on steppes and savannas but this is gained at the expense of flight capacity. The roadrunner, although a very fast runner, is an extremely awkward flier, and in any event the small wings only carry it short distances. It scampers nimbly over rocky and sandy terrain, accomplishing leaps of up to 10 ft (3 m). Maximum running speed is about 15 mph (24 kmh) but as a rule the average rate is 10 mph (15 – 6 kmh).

The roadrunner eats grasshoppers, snails, birds, mice, lizards, and snakes, including venomous species such as young rattlesnakes. It also has a habit of heaping up snail shells, and this activity often signals its presence.

The species is found in southern California, Texas, and central Mexico. It nests on cactuses, trees, and tall bushes to a height of up to about 17 ft (1 to 5 m); the female lays 2 – 12 dirty white eggs at intervals of alternate days.

Incubation, unusually, begins soon after the first egg is laid, and it is possible to find eggs and chicks together in the same nest. Incubation lasts 18 days and the babies, although helpless at birth, are able to walk about on the ground and perch on bushes at the age of 7 – 8 days.

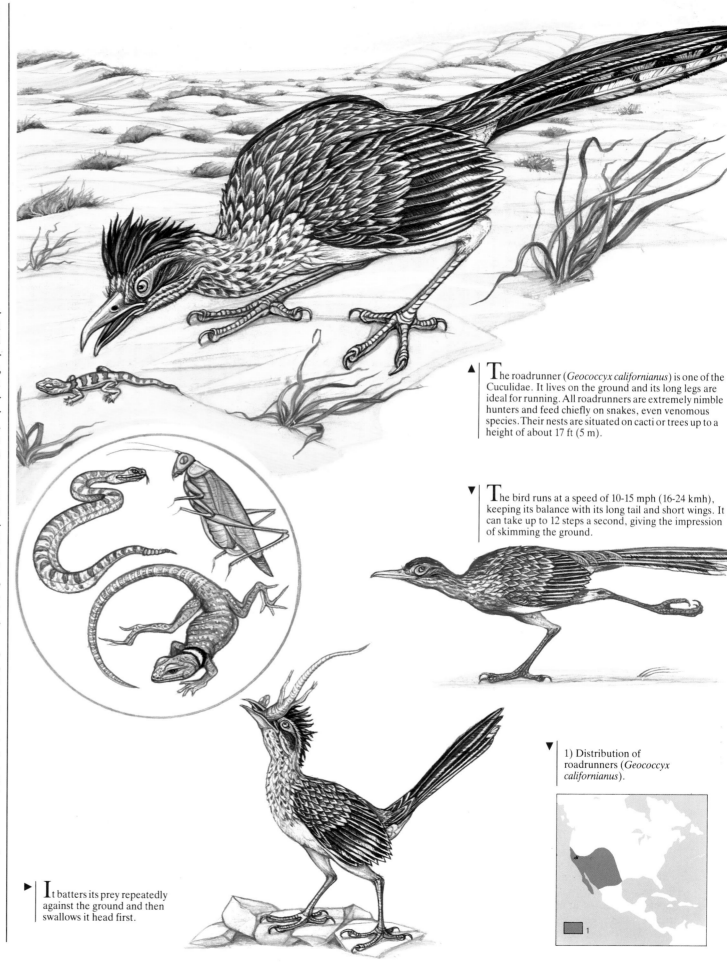

▲ The roadrunner (*Geococcyx californianus*) is one of the Cuculidae. It lives on the ground and its long legs are ideal for running. All roadrunners are extremely nimble hunters and feed chiefly on snakes, even venomous species. Their nests are situated on cacti or trees up to a height of about 17 ft (5 m).

▼ The bird runs at a speed of 10-15 mph (16-24 kmh), keeping its balance with its long tail and short wings. It can take up to 12 steps a second, giving the impression of skimming the ground.

▼ 1) Distribution of roadrunners (*Geococcyx californianus*).

▶ It batters its prey repeatedly against the ground and then swallows it head first.

SWIFT

Apus apus

Order Apodiformes
Family Apodidae
Size Length 6 – 7 in (16 – 18 cm)
Distribution Old World; absent from polar regions and South Africa
Habits Markedly gregarious
Nesting In colonies on high rocks and buildings
Eggs 2 (rarely 3)
Chicks Nidicolous

The swift has a streamlined body with long, slender wings and a relatively short, forked tail. The mouth when open, is squarish in shape, with a very wide gap; the bill is rather short and strongly hooked. When the bird is perched, the wings, much longer than the tail, cross each other above the upper tail.

The swift's habitats are extremely varied; they are found equally commonly in cities, up in the mountains and along the seashore. Food consists of a vast range of insects, from flies and gnats to small butterflies.

The swift is one of the most perfectly formed of all flying birds. Its normal speed through the air is 38 – 56 mph (60 – 90 kmh) and at times it reaches up to 125 mph (200 kmh). Swifts, in fact, spend roughly half of their life in the air, accomplishing most basic activities, hunting insects, courting and mating, on the wing.

The material for building a nest (feathers, bits of straw, hair) is likewise snatched up on the wing; and even when drinking, swifts merely skim the water surface and make off. The only occasion when the birds remain perched for any length of time is at night and when incubating.

These birds, perfectly streamlined for catching insects in midair, possess a variety of special structures which enable them to fly very fast, for long periods and with the sudden changes of direction that are vital for capturing any insects trying to escape pursuit. The mouth, so extraordinarily large, is held wide open during flight and can thus easily trap the tiniest insects.

The swift is a migratory bird, settling only temporarily in regions where insects are present at certain seasons, as in continental Europe.

▲ Swifts normally fly at about 35-55 mph (60-90 kmh) but can for short distances reach a speed of over 125 mph (200 kmh). The varied flight pattern alternates periods of flapping with glides and wheeling movements. Thanks to certain structural adaptions which they have in common, swifts and hummingbirds are unsurpassed in performing complex aerial maneuvers.

▼ Insects are caught in the air as the bird flies with mouth agape.

▲ The swift is one of the most specialized hunters of flying insects, and because it destroys a large number of harmful insects it is protected in many lands. The small creatures on which it feeds, such as flies and butterflies, make up the so-called aerial plankton.

HUMMINGBIRDS
Trochiliformes

The family Trochilidae, comprising the hummingbirds, contains not only the smallest living bird but also the smallest warm-blooded animal, namely the bee hummingbird (*Calypte helenae*), scarcely 2 in (5 cm) long, half of this length being made up of tail and bill. At the opposite extreme is the giant hummingbird (*Patagonia gigas*), as big as a starling and weighing about ¾ oz (20 g), roughly ten times heavier than the bee hummingbird.

With 315 – 320 species, the family Trochilidae is the second largest bird family in the New World. The majority of these species are concentrated in a narrow equatorial belt, extending no more than 10° in breadth. Some hummingbirds live exclusively in the lower stratum of the primary forest, others in the upper stratum. There are those adapted to arid regions, where the vegetation consists principally of flowering cactus, and those that regularly visit parks and plantations.

Many hummingbirds set off on true migrations: the rufous hummingbird (*Selasphorus rufus*) has its breeding grounds in Alaska and flies south to winter in southern Mexico, a journey of almost 2,000 miles (3,000 km), a tremendous distance for a bird that weighs a mere 3 – 4 g.

When hummingbirds hover motionless, the wings move forward and backward as well as up and down, and the tips trace a flat, horizontal figure-of-eight pattern. The wing movements are so rapid that in the smaller species they are almost invisible and certainly cannot be followed by the human eye. Frequencies have been registered, according to species, of between 8 and 80 beats per second, increasing to 200 at moments of particular excitement. The smaller the species, the greater the frequency of wing beats. The speed of a hummingbird's flight does not normally exceed 30 mph (50 кmh), but under certain stimuli, as when courting or defending territory, some species, although only for brief instants, reach 60 mph (100 кmh).

Apart from their tiny dimensions and flight capacities, hummingbirds are notable for their vivid, shining colors. The beak, whether black, reddish or yellowish, is always slender and delicate, but size and curvature vary

Ruby-throated hummingbird
(*Archilochus colubris*)

The future of the hummingbirds looks somewhat gloomy. Most of them live in tropical forests which are fast disappearing, and this directly threatens the survival of many species. Yet they have an advantage over many birds from the same regions. Because of their natural lack of fear, their comparative intelligence, and their ability to adapt, various species have been able to make the most of parks and gardens in and around the villages and towns that are gradually springing up in place of the primary forests.

enormously. Thus the tiny beak of the purple-backed thornbill (*Ramphomicron microrhynchum*) is not more than a centimeter in length, while that of the sword-billed hummingbird (*Ensifera ensifera*) is almost 4 in (10 cm), virtually the same length as body and tail combined.

Hummingbirds manage to conserve energy, in some measure, by falling into a miniature state of lethargy in the course of the night. Like other birds, but in contrast to mammals, their body temperature varies, depending on whether they are at rest or fully active, from 102° to 108°F (39° to 42°C). During this phase of torpor this may drop to almost the same level as the outside temperature, but never down to freezing point, with heart-rate falling to around 40 per minute from the normally active 500 – 1,300 per minute.

Lethargy occurs when the nocturnal temperature drops by at least 10°F (5 – 6°C) below the norm, but it also depends upon the reserves of subcutaneous fat, state of health, and other psychological factors.

Males of some species sing all day long, with brief intervals for feeding, while others sing mainly in the morning or evening. Most hummingbirds merely produce a few sharp, shrill notes, tirelessly repeated, but the males of the little hermit (*Phaethornis longuemareus*), the wedge-tailed saberwing (*Campylopterus curvipennis*) and the wine-throated hummingbird (*Atthis ellioti*) all have a decidely varied and harmonious song.

In temperate latitudes most courtship displays occur in spring and summer, but in tropical zones the breeding season tends to be more irregular, linked as it is to the flowering periods of the various plants on which the different species feed.

The female usually builds a nest on her own, and will generally lay only two white eggs, noticeably elongated in form.

The bill of the newly hatched chick is very short. To feed it the mother buries her own beak in the bottom of the baby's throat and regurgitates nectar and small half-digested insects.

Hummingbirds often have two consecutive broods, sometimes making use of the old nest, sometimes building a new one above the other or some distance from it.

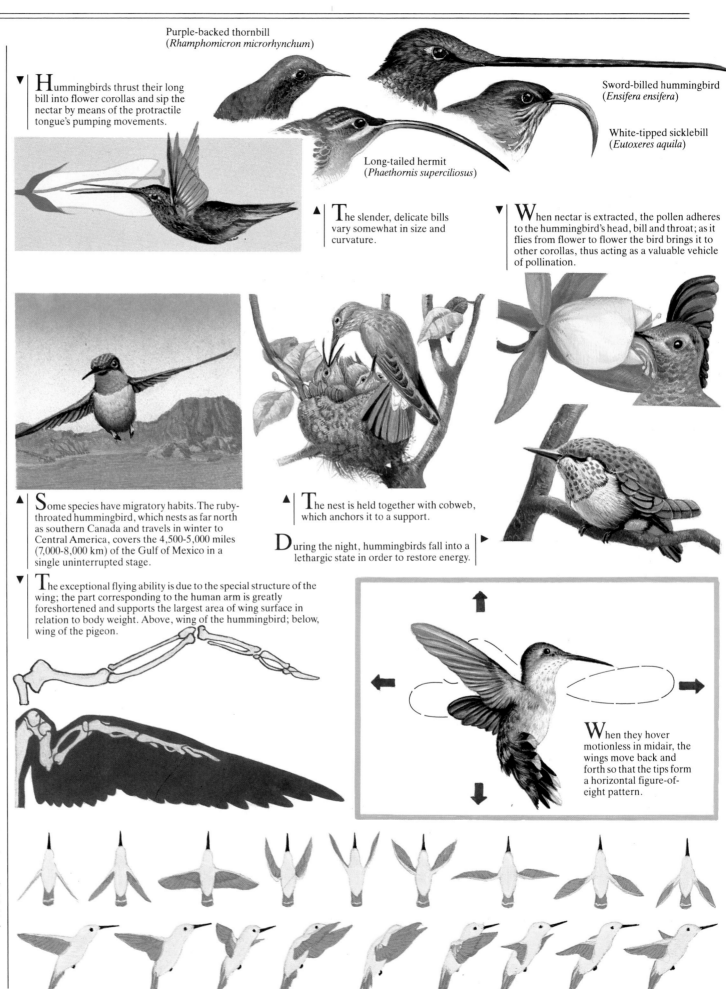

Purple-backed thornbill
(*Rhamphomicron microrhynchum*)

Sword-billed hummingbird
(*Ensifera ensifera*)

Long-tailed hermit
(*Phaethornis superciliosus*)

White-tipped sicklebill
(*Eutoxeres aquila*)

▼ Hummingbirds thrust their long bill into flower corollas and sip the nectar by means of the protractile tongue's pumping movements.

▲ The slender, delicate bills vary somewhat in size and curvature.

▼ When nectar is extracted, the pollen adheres to the hummingbird's head, bill and throat; as it flies from flower to flower the bird brings it to other corollas, thus acting as a valuable vehicle of pollination.

▲ Some species have migratory habits. The ruby-throated hummingbird, which nests as far north as southern Canada and travels in winter to Central America, covers the 4,500-5,000 miles (7,000-8,000 km) of the Gulf of Mexico in a single uninterrupted stage.

▲ The nest is held together with cobweb, which anchors it to a support.

During the night, hummingbirds fall into a lethargic state in order to restore energy. ▶

▼ The exceptional flying ability is due to the special structure of the wing; the part corresponding to the human arm is greatly foreshortened and supports the largest area of wing surface in relation to body weight. Above, wing of the hummingbird; below, wing of the pigeon.

When they hover motionless in midair, the wings move back and forth so that the tips form a horizontal figure-of-eight pattern.

QUETZAL

Pharomachrus mocino

Family Trogonidae
Size Total length of male 40 – 47 in (100 – 120 cm), tail up to 41½ in (105 cm); female 16 in (40 cm)
Weight 5½ – 6¼ oz (160 – 180 g)
Reproductive season April – August
Incubation period 17 – 18 days
Eggs 2, sky-blue
Sexual maturity Probably at 3 years old
Maximum age 22 years

The quetzal has conspicuous plumage, glossy green above, and red below. The upper tail coverts in the male are lengthened, forming plumes of up to 3 ft (1 m) long.

The quetzal is found only from Mexico to Panama. It lives in the dark mountain forests up to an altitude of 10,000 ft (3,000 m) but comes down to 3,500 ft (1,000 m) in the rainy season.

Adult quetzals feed mainly on fruit, which they pluck in flight. They require large amounts of food, consuming on average 3¾ oz (105 g) per day, or more than half their own body weight. They swallow whole fruits as large as cherries, and fruit 1¾ in (4.5 cm) long has been found in a quetzal's crop. The young birds are fed chiefly on insects during their first few days, and later supplement their fruit diet with small vertebrates such as frogs and lizards, as well as snails. Other members of the family live mainly off butterflies and their larvae.

Outside the breeding season, quetzals frequently live in small groups. Only older males are seen alone in winter. They mostly stay in the treetops of tropical forests, 160 ft (50 m) or more above the ground, and in spite of their conspicuous plumage, they are hard to see, especially as they often sit quietly on a branch for long periods. Occasionally they betray their presence by their call, which is most frequently heard during the breeding season.

The male quetzal has an impressive mating flight. It soars above the jungle treetops and flies in circles, uttering a call of several notes. The birds then make their breeding holes, which resemble those of woodpeckers, high up in the soft wood of rotten tree trunks. Males and females share the incubation of the eggs, and bring up the young birds together.

The very beautiful iridescent green feathers of the quetzal were used by Pre-Colombian civilizations of Central America to adorn the head-dresses of kings and chieftains. After the European invasion of the continent, intensive hunting decimated the species so that nowadays the bird is very rare, an additional reason being deforestation which has destroyed much of its traditional habitat.

It feeds principally on large amounts of fruit, daily equivalent to about half its body weight. The bird also eats small vertebrates and snails. Some species of the family mainly consume butterflies and their larvae.

It scoops out a nest in the soft wood of rotting treetrunks, high above the ground. Both male and female (shown here) share incubation and rear the chicks together.

The Trogonidae live in the primary forests of Central and South America, Africa and southern Asia. 1) The quetzal (*Pharomachrus mocinno*) lives only in America, in a zone that includes southern Mexico and Panama.

BAR-BREASTED MOUSEBIRD

Colius striatus

Family Coliidae
Size Full length 9¾ – 14¼ in (25 – 36 cm); tail 6¼ – 9¾ in (16 – 25 cm)
Weight 1½ – 2½ oz (42 – 71 g)
Reproductive season During a large part of the year
Incubation period 10½ – 14 days
Eggs 1 – 6 eggs, usually 2 – 3
Sexual maturity 6 – 10 months
Maximum age 11 years

The mousebirds owe their name to their unremarkable gray-brown plumage, which looks like fur underneath, and their long tails, giving them the look of mice. They have strong feet with very mobile toes, and their strong claws are very well adapted to climbing trees.

The bar-breasted mousebird is found in Africa south of the Sahara from Nigeria to the Sudan and from Ethiopia down East Africa and southern Africa to the Cape. It is found on the edges of forests, in forest galleries beside the rivers, and in the savanna, but not in dense tropical jungles of the Congo basin or in dry and treeless zones.

Mousebirds are overwhelmingly vegetarian, and live off fruit, young shoots, leaves, and flowers. They are social birds, and live in family groups and larger parties outside the mating season. They prefer to sit in the branches of leafy trees and bushes, which they are well adapted to climbing. They shoot like tiny arrows from one bush to another, but never fly far at a time. They come only rarely to the ground, to take a dustbath or eat some earth.

The male has no song, but flies and hops back and forth like a tiny ball of feathers, until the female is ready to mate. They build open, bowl-shaped nests in the trees and bushes of small twigs and roots, lined with kapok and green leaves. The 2 – 4 white eggs are incubated by both sexes from the moment the first egg has been laid, so that the young chicks hatch one after another. The chicks are blind at first, and nearly naked, but their first quills grow and their eyes open after only a few days.

Blue-naped mousebird
(*Colius macrourus*)

Red-faced mousebird
(*Colius indicus*)

▲ The birds derive their name from the gray-brown color of their plumage. Mainly vegetarian, they feed on fruit, leaves, and flowers in large quantities, often raiding orchards. Now and then they also catch insects.

▼ They live in Africa south of the Sahara to Cape Province, but are not found in the dense jungles of the Congo basin or in arid treeless zones.
1) Distribution of order Coliiformes.

◄ During the night they roost on branches, tail perpendicular to the ground, clustering close to each other.

RHINOCEROS HORNBILL

Buceros rhinoceros

Family Bucerotidae
Size Full length 48 in (120 cm)
Weight Male 5½ – 6½ lb (2.5 – 3 kg);
female 4½ – 5 lb (2 – 2.3 kg)
Reproductive Season January – April
Incubation period 30 – 40 days
Eggs 1 – 2 white eggs, exceptionally 3
Maximum age 33 years

The plumage of the rhinoceros hornbill is almost entirely black, only its tail being white with a black band. It has an enormous yellow beak tinged with red on the base, with a prominent casque, which reaches the tip of the beak in some subspecies. As with all the hornbills, with the exception of the helmeted hornbill (*Rhinoplax vigil*), which has a solid casque, the casque is hollow so that the beak is relatively light in spite of its size. Hornbills also have extremely aerated bones in their extremities, so that they are lighter than their size would suggest. The plumage of both sexes of the rhinoceros hornbill is alike, but the female is a little smaller. The iris of the eye is also red in the male, and white in the female. Other species of the hornbill family are distinguished by differentiation of the plumage between the sexes, and in the coloring of the bald patches around the eyes and throat.

The hornbills are found in Africa, southern Asia and across the neighboring archipelagos as far as New Guinea. However, the rhinoceros hornbill is found only from the Malacca peninsula across Sumatra and Borneo as far as West Java. It inhabits the great primeval forests, but does not live higher than 4,000 ft (1,200 m) up its native mountains. Forest clearance is threatening the species since they require undisturbed woodlands with large trees in which to find the holes they will nest in, in order to survive. Only the smaller species of the family, such as the tokos, inhabit the African savannas and similar habitats in India. Other representatives of the hornbills live in tropical forests on the slopes of the African volcanoes up to a height of more than 6,500 ft (2,000 m) above sea-level.

Hornbills live in pairs, or in small

Rhinoceros hornbill
(*Buceros rhinoceros*)

◀ The most spectacular feature of the rhinoceros hornbill is the enormous beak, surmounted by an equally remarkable casque. The latter is a horny sheath supported inside by spongy bone, so that in spite of appearances it is fairly lightweight. The presence of a casque distinguishes hornbills from toucans, whose bills are otherwise slightly similar.

▼ Most of the hornbill's food consists of fruit but sometimes it also eats animal prey.

Toucan

Rhinoceros hornbill

parties outside the breeding season. They prefer to sit in treetops 150 – 200 ft (50 – 60 m) above the ground. They require a large amount of food, and so seek out the fruit-bearing trees over a large surrounding area, often flying in from all directions. Their wings are rounded, making their flight difficult, and unusually noisy for a bird. Many species call continuously while they are in the air. The rhinoceros hornbill has a resonant call like a goose which the two partners of a pair emit alternately while they are in the air, and this is one of the most characteristic bird calls of the Borneo forest. The pairs stay very close together throughout the year, and the females are often fed by their mates even outside the breeding season.

Hornbills have very remarkable breeding behavior. All species breed in holes in trees, but the special feature of the rhinoceros hornbill's behavior is that it fills up the entrance of the hole with droppings and bits of food until only a narrow slit remains. The female remains in the hole throughout the incubation period and even after her young are hatched, and is fed during the whole of this period by the male. When the young hatch, the male must provide food for them as well. The rhinoceros hornbill needs a large hole to nest in, and these can measure up to 20 in (55 cm) long, 15 in (40 cm) wide, and 50 in (120 cm) deep.

Generally, 2 eggs are laid. These are incubated for more than a month, and the young need another 2½ – 3 months before they can leave the nest. The female leaves the hole somewhat earlier however, after molting her wing and tail feathers. If anything should happen to the male during this period, then both the female and her young will die. It has been observed, however, that other unmated males will then start to tend the birds in the nesting-hole. After the female has left the hole, the young close up the entrance again to the size of a narrow slit. They continue to be fed by their parents for a long time after leaving the nest, and remain in the family group until the next breeding season. They can be distinguished for a long time by their smaller casques. Those species which inhabit the tropical forests and can find sufficient food throughout the year breed more or less all year round. A single breeding-hole may be used for several broods, or else used by different pairs in alternation.

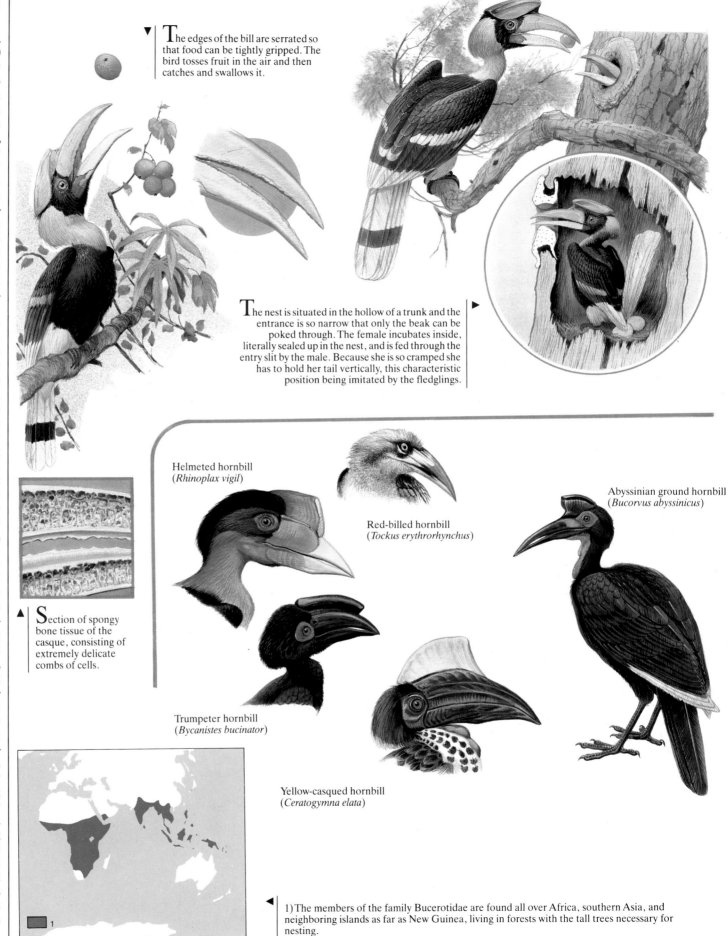

▼ The edges of the bill are serrated so that food can be tightly gripped. The bird tosses fruit in the air and then catches and swallows it.

The nest is situated in the hollow of a trunk and the entrance is so narrow that only the beak can be poked through. The female incubates inside, literally sealed up in the nest, and is fed through the entry slit by the male. Because she is so cramped she has to hold her tail vertically, this characteristic position being imitated by the fledglings. ▶

▲ Section of spongy bone tissue of the casque, consisting of extremely delicate combs of cells.

Helmeted hornbill (*Rhinoplax vigil*)

Red-billed hornbill (*Tockus erythrorhynchus*)

Abyssinian ground hornbill (*Bucorvus abyssinicus*)

Trumpeter hornbill (*Bycanistes bucinator*)

Yellow-casqued hornbill (*Ceratogymna elata*)

◀ 1) The members of the family Bucerotidae are found all over Africa, southern Asia, and neighboring islands as far as New Guinea, living in forests with the tall trees necessary for nesting.

WOODPECKERS

Piciformes

There are some 210 species of woodpeckers, the most agile of the tree-climbing birds. In the first and most important group there are, ecologically, three types, namely the tree woodpeckers, easily the most numerous and highly specialized (as, for example, the great spotted woodpecker and the three-toed woodpecker), who spend virtually their whole life on the trunks and branches of trees; then come the ground woodpeckers (such as the green woodpecker), finding most of their food on the ground, and finally the large woodpeckers that occupy an intermediate position (such as the black woodpecker). Size varies from 3¼ in (8 cm) for the tiniest piculets to 22 in (56 cm) in the case of the imperial woodpecker from Mexico.

The woodpeckers inhabit every continent except Antarctica; nor are they found in the Arctic, on the island of Madagascar, in Australia, New Guinea, New Zealand, and throughout Oceania. The eastern limit of their distribution is to the east of Celebes and Alor, these being the last islands where the family is present. In the northern hemisphere woodpeckers range to the northernmost limits of the coniferous forests (the taiga); and in the southern hemisphere they extend to the forests of southern beech (*Nothofagus*) in Patagonia. The majority of species live in Southeast Asia and tropical America.

The coloration of woodpeckers' plumage ranges from black, mingled in varying measure with white and red, to green and to chestnut with red or yellow patches. Males and females often differ by virtue of the presence or absence of small colored marks, usually on the head. Various anatomical modifications provide evidence of the birds' climbing capacities, and other physical changes have come about because all woodpeckers, apart from the wrynecks, nest in cavities which they drill themselves in hard or rotting wood. Among such features are a strengthening of the neck muscles; the presence of special mechanisms designed to deaden the repercussions caused by the hammering of the bill against wood, so as to avoid possible damage to the brain; a

Male great spotted woodpecker (*Dendrocopos major*), recognizable by the red patch on the nape, here shown feeding one of his babies. The young remain in the nest for 20-23 days. Below, some of the insects eaten by the great spotted woodpecker: beetles, ants, and their larvae.

lengthening of the projections of the hyoid bone supporting the tongue, so that it can be fully extended from the beak to capture prey; and a modification of the structure of the tail feathers, so that the tail can be used as a prop whenever they interrupt their climbing activity.

Woodpeckers are closely associated with environments such as woods and forests. A few take up residence in parks, gardens, thickets, copses, and orchards in open country.

Feeding basically on insects, which they are able to find all year round because they capture them beneath the bark and in the wood, the woodpeckers of cold and temperate zones apparently have no need to migrate. An exception is the wryneck (*Jynx torquilla*) which winters in Africa south of the Sahara. Although most woodpeckers are insectivores, many species also feed generously on seeds or fruit.

The majority of woodpeckers nest in holes which, with a few exceptions, they make with their beaks in wood.

Tropical woodpeckers most often lay 2 or 3 eggs while those from temperate regions lay 4 to 10. Incubation normally lasts from 12 to 16 days. This is the shared responsibility of male and female, who change places regularly, but among European species it has been observed that it is always the male who sits on the eggs first during the night. When the eggs hatch the chicks are naked and pinkish. The fledglings, according to species, take 3 or 4 weeks to grow.

Almost all woodpeckers are solitary by habit and, except in the breeding season, males and females live separately. During the breeding season the woodpeckers defend their territory. Even though boundaries are not clearly defined, others of the same species are strictly forbidden to venture too near a stranger's nest. Woodpeckers announce their presence and communicate with one another by giving out sharp call notes and also by tapping their bill repeatedly and very rapidly against the dead wood of a tree, producing a drumming sound which can be heard for quite a distance.

▲ The great spotted woodpecker can extend its tongue several inches beyond the tip of the beak in order to capture insect larvae concealed in the wood.

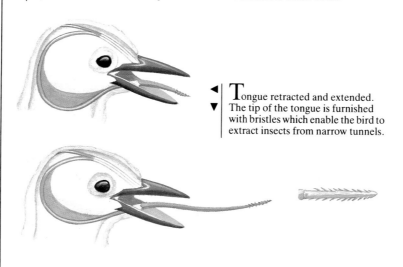

◀ Tongue retracted and extended. The tip of the tongue is furnished with bristles which enable the bird to extract insects from narrow tunnels.

▲ Pair of great spotted woodpeckers (male on left, female on right) exchanging places to incubate the eggs.

▼ Some North American woodpeckers. The acorn woodpecker is noted for its habit of stocking acorns in single cavities along the treetrunk.

◀ Great spotted woodpeckers keep their nest very clean; after each feed, the adult waits for the chick to produce its droppings (wrapped in a kind of capsule) and then carries them away.

Acorn woodpecker
(*Melanerpes formicivorus*)

Yellow-bellied sapsucker
(*Sphyrapicus varius*)

Common flicker
(*Colaptes auratus*)

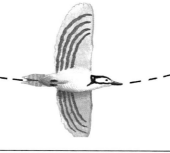

F light trajectory of a woodpecker. Because the bird beats its wings intermittently, this tends to be undulating.

BOWERBIRDS
Ptilonorhynchidae

The size of the bowerbirds varies from that of a thrush to that of a rook, namely from about 7 to 12 in (18 to 30 cm). Males are, as a rule, brightly colored and ornamented in various ways. Among certain species the plumage takes on the most astonishing changes of tone depending on the angle of light incidence. Only rarely do the sexes look alike, the females being much more modest and subdued in color.

The bowerbirds are forest dwellers who spend the greater part of their time in the foliage, except when they come down to the ground to display. Although they eat fruit they may also consume insects and snails. The nest is a cup-shaped affair of roughly interlaced branches, situated up in a tree. The 1 – 3 eggs are white, with typical hieroglyphic markings. So far as is known, only the female incubates and rears the brood.

The bowerbirds are known only from New Guinea and Australia and have derived their vernacular name from the males' extraordinary habit of building special display grounds, known as bowers, avenues, and maypoles, designed simply to attract females for the complex phases of courtship ceremonies. Genuine bowers and avenues are constructed only by some species; they are always situated at ground level and often surrounded by exhibition arenas, and they have no connection with the nest which, as mentioned, is invariably placed in a tree. Some species assemble brightly colored objects inside their bower. The species of the genera *Ptilonorhynchus*, *Chlamydera* and *Sericulus* perform the almost incredible feat of "painting" the walls of their bower with the colored juices of certain berries, mingled with bits of charcoal and pulped grass held together with saliva, using as a tool a wad of leaves or bark.

The basic structure of a bower is a central post with a circular roof descending toward the base. Avenues have a basal platform, walls and an arch or roof of interlaced twigs and branches. Bowers, avenues and their immediate surroundings may be decorated at various points with fruit, flowers, beetles, and other colored objects.

Having completed his avenue, the male bowerbird assembles his collection of colored objects, even using artificial items such as matchboxes and pieces of glass. Everything is chosen with the greatest care. The satin bowerbird has a special fondness for blue articles.

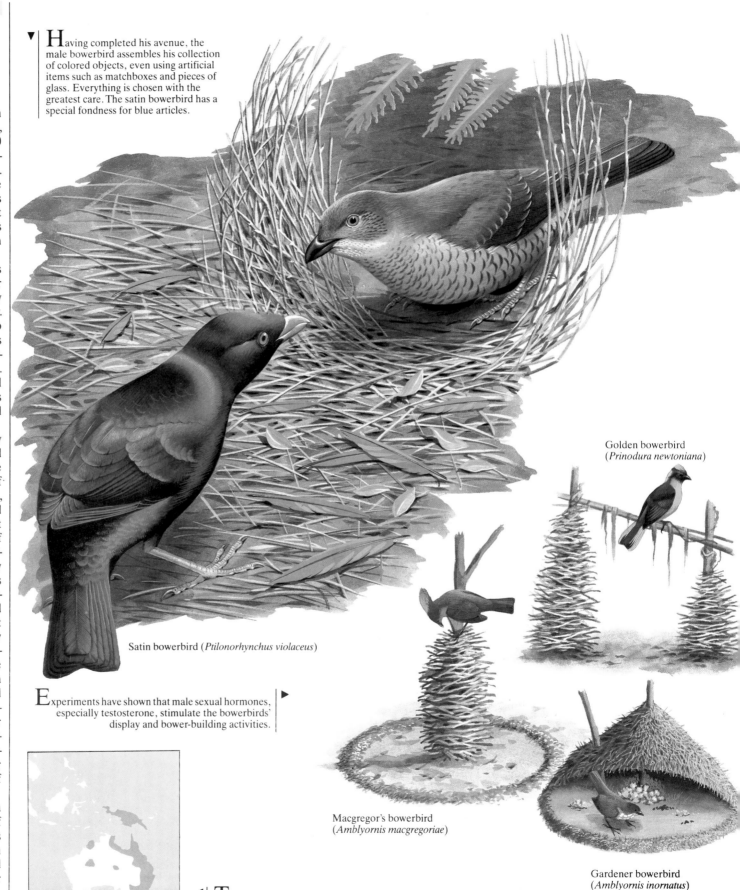

Golden bowerbird (*Prinodura newtoniana*)

Satin bowerbird (*Ptilonorhynchus violaceus*)

Experiments have shown that male sexual hormones, especially testosterone, stimulate the bowerbirds' display and bower-building activities.

Macgregor's bowerbird (*Amblyornis macgregoriae*)

Gardener bowerbird (*Amblyornis inornatus*)

The bowerbirds spend most of their time in the heart of the forest, feeding mainly on fruit. They appear to be related both to the crows and the birds of paradise, and they live only in Australia and New Guinea. 1) Distribution of family Ptilonorhynchidae.

BIRDS OF PARADISE

Paradisaeidae

The birds of paradise constituting the family Paradisaeidae are universally famous for the colorful, decorative splendor of their plumage and for their extraordinary private or collective ceremonial displays. It is not so well known, however, that these astonishing birds are very closely related to the Corvidae, which are notable, for the most part, for their lack of color. New Guinea and the adjacent islands form the evolutionary center of the Paradisaeidae, a few species of which are found in the northernmost parts of Australia and the Moluccas.

All species of birds of paradise are tree dwellers, inhabiting the most inaccessible mountain zones, often at very high altitudes. Food consists of insects, small vertebrates, and other animals, and some species also consume fruit. As a rule the birds are not gregarious by habit, being observed in small groups only where food is very plentiful or, in some cases, on display grounds. Certain species have black plumage, without special ornamentation save the metallic reflections of the feathers and the odd caruncle or wattle, the males differing hardly at all from the females. At the other extreme are species in which the females have fairly drab plumage while the males are either black with an adornment of strangely formed feathers or brightly colored in a blend of beautiful hues, further embellished by a variety of curious ornamental features.

The form of breed-behavior depends on the type and extent of sexual dimorphism. Species in which there is little or no distinction between sexes form monogamous pairs. But among species where sexual dimorphism is very marked, there is no pair formation. The males assemble in groups of varying numbers or exhibit themselves individually on display grounds. Some birds of paradise prepare an arena on the forest floor, clearing it of all large objects in order to perform their private displays. Others go through the ritual on a branch high above the ground; and the males of some species come together to perform collective dances.

For a long time Europeans believed birds of paradise to be divine because they were thought to lack legs and thus to have come from heaven. Actually they have very sturdy legs, but the skins which were dispatched to Europe had the limbs removed so as to avoid damaging the flimsy feathers.

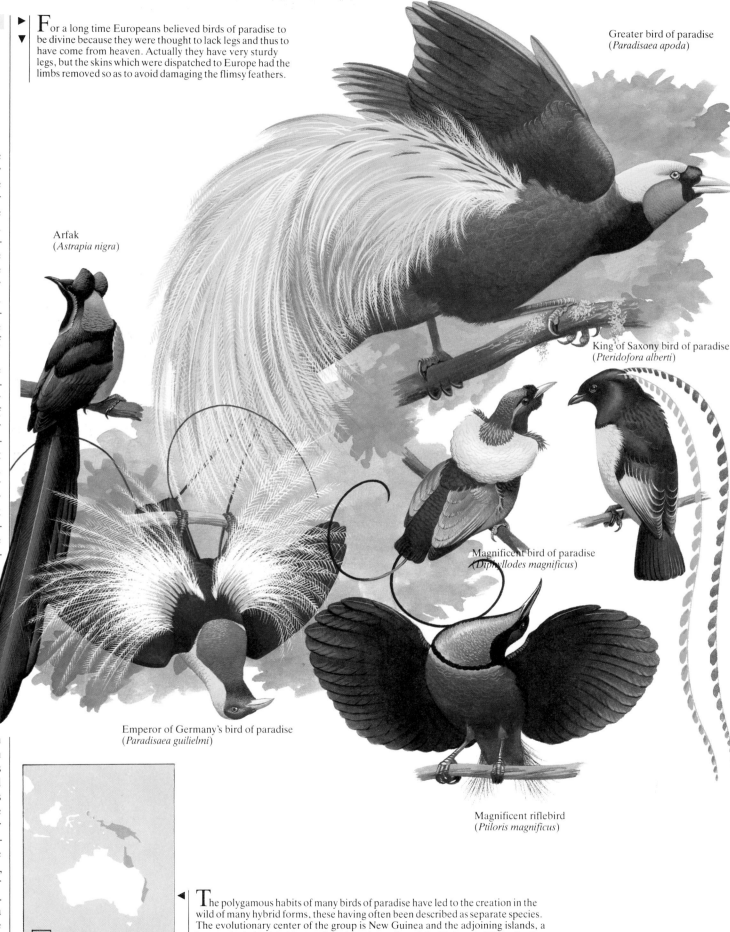

Greater bird of paradise
(*Paradisaea apoda*)

Arfak
(*Astrapia nigra*)

King of Saxony bird of paradise
(*Pteridofora alberti*)

Magnificent bird of paradise
(*Diphyllodes magnificus*)

Emperor of Germany's bird of paradise
(*Paradisaea guilielmi*)

Magnificent riflebird
(*Ptiloris magnificus*)

The polygamous habits of many birds of paradise have led to the creation in the wild of many hybrid forms, these having often been described as separate species. The evolutionary center of the group is New Guinea and the adjoining islands, a few species being inhabitants of northern Australia and the Moluccas. 1) Distribution of the family Paradisaeidae.

DUCKBILLED PLATYPUS

Ornithorhynchus anatinus

Order Monotremata
Family Ornithorhynchidae
Size Length, head to rump, 24 in (60 cm), tail 6 in (15 cm), height 6 in (15 cm). Male considerably bigger than female
Weight Up to 4½lb (2 kg)
Reproductive period July to October
Size of egg Length 0.6 – 0.7 in (16 – 18 mm), width 0.55 in (14 – 15 cm)
Number of young 1 – 3, most commonly 2
Sexual maturity 2½ years
Maximum age 17 years, in captivity

The duckbilled platypus is a very strange-looking animal. Its stout body is covered in thick fur, with long bristles and a soft undercoat. The back, flanks, legs, and tail are dark or very dark brown, while the belly is a yellowish-brown or light gray. The most remarkable feature is the broad, flat beak, which looks at first like a duck's bill. Adult platypuses have no proper teeth, but when the young animals are developing they can be shown to have 12 teeth in the upper mandible and 22 in the lower mandible. Fine lateral channels can be seen at the edges of the lower mandible which the animal uses to strain the food it has taken from the water without having to open its bill. Platypuses have cheek-pouches at the side of the mouth in which they store their prey.

The legs are very short. The feet have five toes, with powerful claws. There are webs stretched between the toes. On the inner side of the two hindleg ankles are hollow, horny spurs, which in the males are connected with a poisonous gland in the thigh. Female platypuses have mammary glands, but they have no nipples, only two glandular areas.

Platypuses are quite common in the brooks, rivers, and lakes of Tasmania and eastern Australia.

The female lays 1 – 3 eggs, which have strong shells like parchment. After an incubation of 10 – 12 days, the young hatch; they are about 1 in (2.5 cm) long, and are suckled by the mother for 4 months.

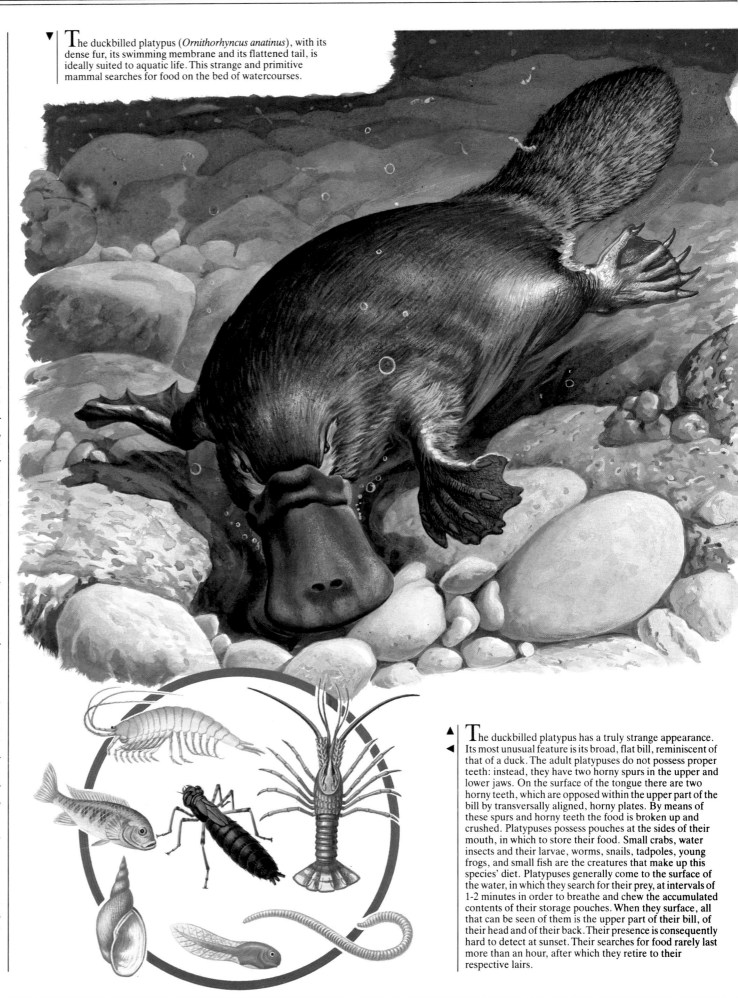

The duckbilled platypus (*Ornithorhyncus anatinus*), with its dense fur, its swimming membrane and its flattened tail, is ideally suited to aquatic life. This strange and primitive mammal searches for food on the bed of watercourses.

The duckbilled platypus has a truly strange appearance. Its most unusual feature is its broad, flat bill, reminiscent of that of a duck. The adult platypuses do not possess proper teeth: instead, they have two horny spurs in the upper and lower jaws. On the surface of the tongue there are two horny teeth, which are opposed within the upper part of the bill by transversally aligned, horny plates. By means of these spurs and horny teeth the food is broken up and crushed. Platypuses possess pouches at the sides of their mouth, in which to store their food. Small crabs, water insects and their larvae, worms, snails, tadpoles, young frogs, and small fish are the creatures that make up this species' diet. Platypuses generally come to the surface of the water, in which they search for their prey, at intervals of 1-2 minutes in order to breathe and chew the accumulated contents of their storage pouches. When they surface, all that can be seen of them is the upper part of their bill, of their head and of their back. Their presence is consequently hard to detect at sunset. Their searches for food rarely last more than an hour, after which they retire to their respective lairs.

MARSUPIALS

Infraclass Metatheria

The marsupials (Marsupialia), make up a sub class of mammals (Mammalia). They include an extraordinary variety of creatures. There are marsupials that hop and marsupials that go on all fours, marsupials that climb, burrow, glide or swim. They include carnivores, herbivores, and omnivores. Many species have no pouch, but are still recognized as genuine marsupials on account of other characteristics. The smallest species are some 1¾ in (4.5 cm) long and weigh barely ¼ oz (5 g), the biggest are as tall and as heavy as an adult man. Most of them have a thick, woolly coat. The tail is generally long; in some possums and phalangers it is prehensile. Others use the tail as an aid to balancing. The characteristic feature of female marsupials is the marsupian or incubating pouch, containing nipples, in which the minute newborn babies are suckled by the mother and accommodated until they are able to fend for themselves. While many species have a well-developed pouch, some have no more than a fold of skin, and in others even that is missing. The dentition reflects the animals' feeding habits, and the number and arrangement of the teeth differ widely. Marsupials often have elongated hindlegs.

After a gestation period of from eight to 42 days, according to the species, up to 25 young are born. They are hardly developed, and only ¼ – 1¼ in (0.5 – 3 cm) long. These little creatures have to find their way to their mother's nipples without help. To that end they are equipped with a very fine sense of smell and strong forelegs with sharp claws. As soon as one of these little animals reaches a nipple, it seizes it firmly in its mouth.

Marsupials have moved into every environment except the sea. There are now marsupials living in America from the south of Canada down to Patagonia and, in Australasia, in the Australian continent, Tasmania, New Guinea, Celebes, Halmahara, the Bismarck Archipelago, and the Solomon Islands.

The present-day marsupials comprise nine families and 237 species.

Woolly opossum
(*Caluromys lanatus*)

Large spotted-tailed native cat
(*Dasyurus maculatus*)

Tasmanian wolf
(*Thylacinus cynocephalus*)

Crested-tailed marsupial mouse
(*Dasyuroides byrnei*)

Narrow-footed marsupial mouse
(*Sminthopsis crassicaudata*)

Thick-tailed dormouse possum
(*Ceraertus nanus*)

Tasmanian devil
(*Sarcophilus harrisi*)

Marsupial anteater
(*Myrmecobius fasciatus*)

Marsupial mole
(*Notoryctes typhlops*)

Common wombat
(*Vombatus ursinus*)

Pig-footed bandicoot
(*Chaeropus ecaudatus*)

Spotted cuscus
(*Phalanger maculatus*)

Koala
(*Phascolarctos cinereus*)

Honey glider
(*Petaurus breviceps*)

Striped phalanger
(*Dactylopsila trivirgata*)

NORTHERN OPOSSUM

Didelphis marsupialis

Order Didelphida
Family Didelphidae
Size Length from head to rump, 13 – 20 in (32 – 50 cm), tail 10 – 21 in (25 – 53 cm)
Weight Up to 12 lb (5.5 kg)
Dentition $\frac{5.1.3.4}{4.1.3.4}$ = 50
Reproductive period Twice a year
Gestation 12 – 13 days
Time in pouch 10 weeks
Number of young 8 – 25
Sexual maturity 6 – 8 months
Maximum age 8 years

The true opossum is an animal about the size of a well grown cat, with a head more like that of a rat. Opossums have pointed snouts and big round ears, almost hairless and so thin as to be almost transparent. They fold them flat when they sleep. Coarse bristles partly cover the thick, soft fur of the belly. They differ considerably in length and thickness, giving a shaggy and unkempt look. The fur is pale gray to gray-black. As in most of the opossums, the long tail is prehensile. It is dark in color but yellowish-white at the tip. Opossums have a well-developed pouch, opening forward. Each of the hands and feet has five toes. There are no claws on the thumbs and big toes, which can be opposed to the other fingers and toes. With their four "prehensile" hands and a prehensile tail, they are outstanding climbers. The ears are considerably more sensitive than those of humans and can hear sounds in the ultrasonic range. The opossum relies mostly on its hearing when hunting.

Opossums live in plains and mountains, steppes, tropical rainforest, and even city parks. They can live just as well on the ground as in the trees. The northern opossum (*Didelphis marsupialis*) inhabits almost the whole of America from the Great Lakes in southern Canada across North and Central America as far as Uruguay and Paraguay in the south. In South America their habitat to a great extent overlaps that of the southern opossum (*Didelphis paraguayensis*).

Opossums are mostly solitary animals. A group will nearly always consist

Northern opossum
(*Didelphis marsupialis*)

▲ The opossum is the best known and most widely distributed of the American marsupials. It is for this reason that the name "opossum" is generally given to all members of the family *Didelphidae*. Characteristic features of these animals are the pointed snout and the rounded ears, which are translucent and almost completely hairless. Opossums have a well-developed pouch with an anterior opening. Their feet have five digits, and the big toe is clawless and opposable. Being thus equipped with four prehensile "hands," as well as a prehensile tail, they are excellent climbers.

▶ Opossums feed on mice, birds, eggs, reptiles, frogs, insects and their larvae, and various types of fruit. Their range of diet is very varied, as is also their range of habitat. They are omnivorous, but they meet most of their dietary requirements with animal foodstuffs. They often search for food scraps near human habitations. Whereas they spend the daytime sleeping in secure hiding places, during the night and evenings they emerge to search for food.

of a mother and her young. They sleep by day in some safe hiding-place, going out in the evening and at night to look for food. The opossums' diet is as varied as their habitat. They are omnivorous. While they feed chiefly on animal food, they also often consume considerable amounts of vegetable food. Those that live near human habitations often look for scraps in the dustbins.

Twice a year, after a gestation of 12–12 days, females give birth to 8–18, sometimes as many as 25, young, which weigh only 0.15 g at birth and are only ¼ in (7.5 mm) long. These tiny, hardly developed creatures have to find their way unaided along the 3 in (8 cm) passage that leads from the genital aperture to the protecting pouch. But there are only 13 nipples there, so only the strongest and swiftest survive; the weaker go under. They leave their mother's pouch for the first time at the age of about 10 weeks. At 3–4 months they are independent of their mother, but still get her to carry them on her back and run to her in case of danger. They are already sexually mature at 6–8 months and can make their own contribution to the preservation of the species.

The opossums are a very big family. Originally they lived only in the New World. Most species occur only in Central and South America. The murine opossums (genus *Marmosa*) are found from central Mexico to northern Patagonia. They are sometimes called dwarf opossum; but the largest species may be as big as a rat. The animals are arboreal, very skillful climbers, but are also found in the Argentinian pampas and in mountains to a height of 12,000 ft (3,700 m). They have prehensile tails sometimes twice as long as their bodies. Most species have dark borders round their eyes. They mostly live on insects and fruit.

Four-eyed opossum (*Metachirops opossum*) range from central Mexico to southeastern Brazil and northern Argentina. They may be as much as 14 in (35 cm) long. These nocturnal animals are excellent climbers but can also move very swiftly on the ground and in water. They are omnivorous.

The water opossum or yapok (*Chironectes minimus*) occurs from southwest Mexico to southern Brazil and northern Argentina. It always lives near water, digging burrows for itself in sloping banks. The hindfeet have elongated toes and are webbed.

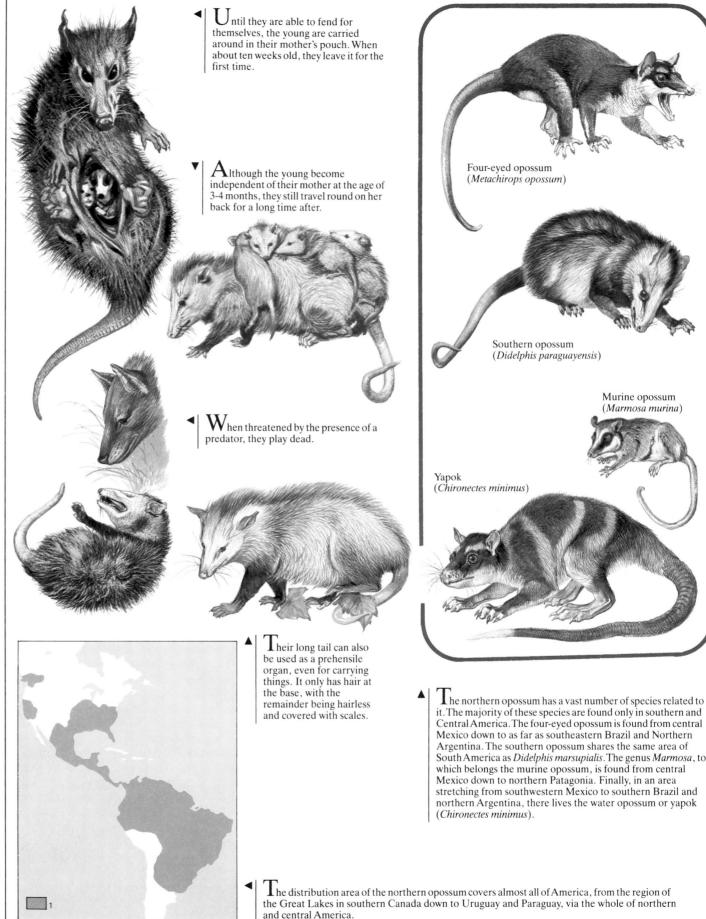

Until they are able to fend for themselves, the young are carried around in their mother's pouch. When about ten weeks old, they leave it for the first time.

Although the young become independent of their mother at the age of 3-4 months, they still travel round on her back for a long time after.

When threatened by the presence of a predator, they play dead.

Their long tail can also be used as a prehensile organ, even for carrying things. It only has hair at the base, with the remainder being hairless and covered with scales.

Four-eyed opossum (*Metachirops opossum*)

Southern opossum (*Didelphis paraguayensis*)

Murine opossum (*Marmosa murina*)

Yapok (*Chironectes minimus*)

The northern opossum has a vast number of species related to it. The majority of these species are found only in southern and Central America. The four-eyed opossum is found from central Mexico down to as far as southeastern Brazil and Northern Argentina. The southern opossum shares the same area of South America as *Didelphis marsupialis*. The genus *Marmosa*, to which belongs the murine opossum, is found from central Mexico down to northern Patagonia. Finally, in an area stretching from southwestern Mexico to southern Brazil and northern Argentina, there lives the water opossum or yapok (*Chironectes minimus*).

The distribution area of the northern opossum covers almost all of America, from the region of the Great Lakes in southern Canada down to Uruguay and Paraguay, via the whole of northern and central America.

RED KANGAROO

Macropus rufus

Order Phalangeria
Family Macropodidae
Size 32 – 64 in (80 – 160 cm)
Weight 60 – 155 lb (27 – 70 kg)
Dentition $\dfrac{3.0.2.4}{1.0.2.4} = 32$
Reproductive period All the year round
Gestation 33 days
Number of young 1
Time in pouch 190 days
Sexual maturity At about 28 months
Maximum age 16 years

Red kangaroos, 32 – 64 in (80 – 160 cm) from head to rump, are the biggest marsupials still living. Standing upright they may reach a height of more than 6½ ft (2 m) at the shoulder. Females are generally from a third to a quarter smaller than males. The tail, up to 44 in (110 cm) long, is very muscular. The forelegs are astonishingly small, yet surprisingly strong. Contrasting with them are the exceedingly powerful, elongated hindlegs, on which the animal bounds along when moving quickly.

Red kangaroos which are strictly vegetarian, live and feed on the wide plains of the Australian grasslands where the annual rainfall is more than 15 in (380 mm). These areas lie inland and include semidesert, prairies, and parklands. The settlers increased the range of the red kangaroo's distribution when they cleared woods and burned bushes.

When the living conditions are good, kangaroos can often be seen in very large flocks. If they are startled it becomes clear that these actually consist of a number of smaller groups that have congregated because of the favorable environment. The big flock immediately breaks up into smaller compact groups, known as "mobs." These most commonly comprise 2 – 4 animals. Comprehensive investigations have shown that they are probably family groups, since they nearly always consist of one male and one or more females, with their young. But solitary animals do also sometimes attach themselves to the groups without causing any disruption.

Red kangaroos are neither strictly diurnal nor nocturnal in habit. A fiery

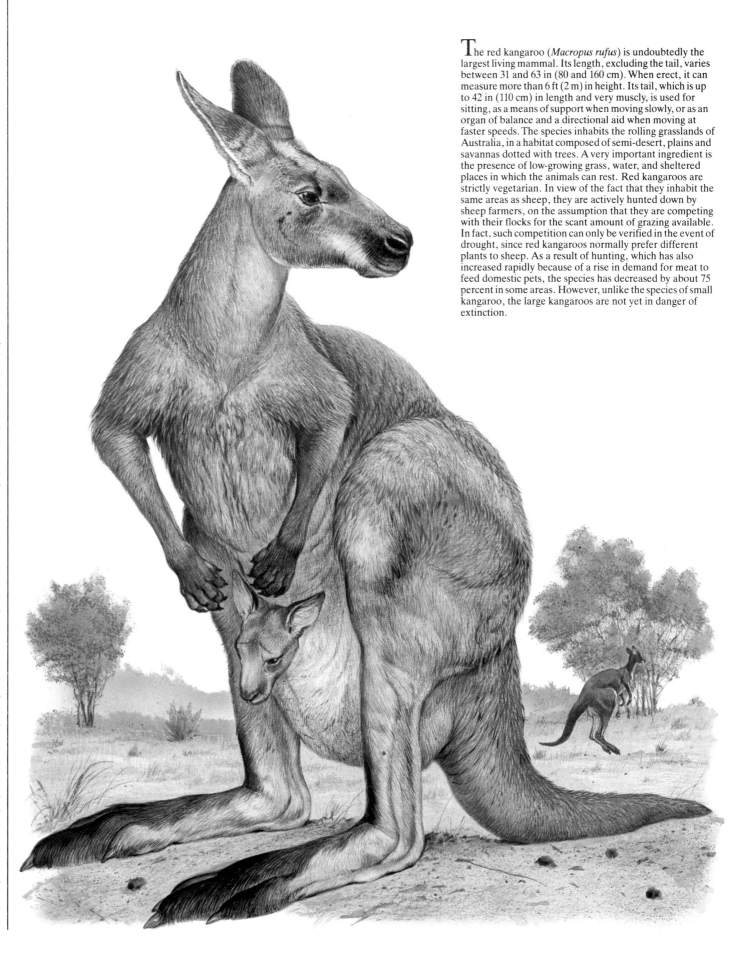

The red kangaroo (*Macropus rufus*) is undoubtedly the largest living mammal. Its length, excluding the tail, varies between 31 and 63 in (80 and 160 cm). When erect, it can measure more than 6 ft (2 m) in height. Its tail, which is up to 42 in (110 cm) in length and very muscly, is used for sitting, as a means of support when moving slowly, or as an organ of balance and a directional aid when moving at faster speeds. The species inhabits the rolling grasslands of Australia, in a habitat composed of semi-desert, plains and savannas dotted with trees. A very important ingredient is the presence of low-growing grass, water, and sheltered places in which the animals can rest. Red kangaroos are strictly vegetarian. In view of the fact that they inhabit the same areas as sheep, they are actively hunted down by sheep farmers, on the assumption that they are competing with their flocks for the scant amount of grazing available. In fact, such competition can only be verified in the event of drought, since red kangaroos normally prefer different plants to sheep. As a result of hunting, which has also increased rapidly because of a rise in demand for meat to feed domestic pets, the species has decreased by about 75 percent in some areas. However, unlike the species of small kangaroo, the large kangaroos are not yet in danger of extinction.

heat reigns all day on the prairies and semideserts of inland Australia, and naturally kangaroos stay in their shady resting places and do not go out to drink and graze until dusk, retiring again at daybreak. But in areas where the daytime temperature does not rise so high and where the animals are undisturbed, they can also be observed during the daytime. They go to rest at irregular intervals and have no definite feeding and sleeping times.

The red kangaroo's means of locomotion is very striking. When they want to move slowly they use their forelimbs and tail, but for greater speed they use their hindlegs. Moving without haste, they first lean on their forelegs and at the same time plant their powerful tail on the ground between their hindlegs, so that their body is supported at three points. They then swing their hindlegs forward and put them down beside, or slightly ahead of, the forepaws. They then lift their forelegs and straighten their body, then put down their forelegs and tail again and repeat the movements. Since the forelimbs are very much shorter than the hindlegs, this is a slow way of moving. As they go they bend their head and upper body down, so that they cannot look round them as they go. When then want to do that they stand up, leaning back on their tails. For fast movement they use their characteristic hopping gait, using only their hindlegs. Normal leaps, when they are not hurried, may measure 3 – 6 ft (1 – 2 m), but in danger red kangaroos can make enormous jumps, over 40 ft (13 m) and up to 10 ft (3 m) high. They can attain a speed of 50 mph (80 kmh).

Kangaroos generally give birth to a single offspring; twins are extremely rare. At birth the kangaroo is barely 1 in (2 cm) long and weighs less than 1 g. Through the mother's rough belly-fur the tiny creature creeps up to the pouch. When it gets there it immediately seizes a nipple in its mouth and does not let go of it until 190 days later, when it is big enough to leave the pouch.

In order to move fast, the red kangaroo hops by placing its weight exclusively on its hind legs.

Red kangaroos leave their shady shelters only at sunset, either to drink or to graze. In areas where the daytime temperature is not excessive they can also be seen during the day.

Red kangaroos can cover 42 ft (13 m) with a single jump and reach a height of 10 ft (3 m).

When fighting, kangaroos rear up in front of each other and place their weight on their hindlegs and their tail, which acts as a third leg. In trying to knock their opponent down, they kick quickly out with their hindlegs, keeping only their tail on the ground. These blows can be delivered with such force that serious injuries may result, caused partially also by their strong claws.

During birth, the female kangaroo sits on the base of her tail, thereby exposing the aperture from which her baby will arrive in such a way as to facilitate its passage into the interior of her pouch.

The red kangaroo's diet consists of grass, leaves, and tree-bark.

KOALA

Phascolarctos cinereus

Order Phalangeria
Family Phalangeridae
Size 24 – 32 in (60 – 80 cm)
Weight 35 lb (16 kg)
Dentition $\dfrac{3.1.1.4}{1.0.1.4} = 30$
Reproductive period Summer, once a year
Gestation About 1 month
Number of young 1
Time in pouch 5 – 6 months
Sexual maturity At about 3 – 4 years
Maximum age 12 years

Although the woolly fur gives the body a rather stocky appearance, the Koala is, in fact, comparatively slender. The fur is light or dark gray on top , whitish on the underside. The big round head, with its short muzzle, naked black nose-tip and big, thick, hairy ears, gives the koala an attractive appearance. The thumb and the second finger (corresponding to our index finger) can be opposed to the other three fingers, so that the hand has a very strong grip. The sharp claws also give the animals a firm grasp on smooth bark, so that they are remarkable climbers. The tail is rudimentary. There is a place above the pelvis where the fur grows particularly thick and rough, to prevent the animal from slipping when sitting on a branch. The female koala has a well-developed pouch, opening to the back and containing two nipples.

Koalas are strictly tree dwelling, seldom descending to the ground, so they are confined to areas of continuous woodland. Their range of distribution includes the eucalyptus forests from northern Queensland to southern Victoria, but they are not found on the Cape York peninsula. They spend virtually the whole of their lives in the top of eucalyptus trees. They will only come down to the ground to move from one tree to the next if it is too far for them to climb or jump. Koalas climb about the branches very well and very safely, but move extraordinarily slowly.

The name "Koala" comes from a language of the Australian aborigines, and means "it does not drink"; they get practically all the liquid they need from their food. Koalas are nocturnal; they sleep during the day, generally sitting in a forked branch, but never in hollow

The koala bear (*Phascolarctos cinereus*) is a large, climbing marsupial that lives in the woods of eastern Australia. Its thick fur gives it a squat, ungainly look. It is, however, an excellent climber, which only comes down to earth in exceptional circumstances.

1) The koala's area of distribution.

trees. They go in search of food at night. They are purely herbivorous and feed exclusively on the leaves of certain species of eucalyptus tree.

Eucalyptus leaves are very hard, and consequently indigestible. To enable them to cope with their diet, koalas have an appendix 72 – 100 in (180 – 250 cm) long, three or four times as long as the whole animal. They harbor large quantities of bacteria there, which enable them to break down their diet of leaves and convert it into a nourishing food rich in vitamins. It forms a pulpy substance, which is brought up again as nutriment and finally digested.

Koalas mark trees as their own territory by leaving their scent on them. They embrace a branch or stem with both arms and rub it with a secretion from glands in a naked spot over the breastbone. Each group's territory is thus clearly recognizable by others of the species. If possible, koalas avoid going on to the ground. These slow, clumsy-looking animals can swing from tree to tree, taking immensely long leaps. Even mothers with young on their back can jump in this way.

Koalas are peaceable animals, solitary or living in small groups. During the mating season mature males generally have a small harem, guarding and defending them jealously. After a period of gestation of some 35 days a single young is born. Apparently a female koala only gives birth every two years. The newborn koala is barely 1 in (2 cm) long and weighs 5 – 6 g. When it first becomes visible, after about 6 months, it has already grown to a length of 7½ in (18 cm). It is still another two months before it leaves the pouch, and then the mother carries it on her back. It is weaned after about a year. During the transitional period it supplements its mother's milk every 2 – 3 days with the caecotrophe, the pulp of predigested leaves, which is excreted from the anus, and so gradually gets used to a plant diet. Koalas are sexually mature at the age of 3 or 4 years.

◄ Koalas sleep seated in the forks of branches.

▲ The koala's food consists of the leaves of various types of eucalyptus.

▼ The koala's pouch opens to the rear.

▲ When the young koala has outgrown its mother's pouch it clings to her back.

▼ Koalas jump from branch to branch with surprising sure-footedness.

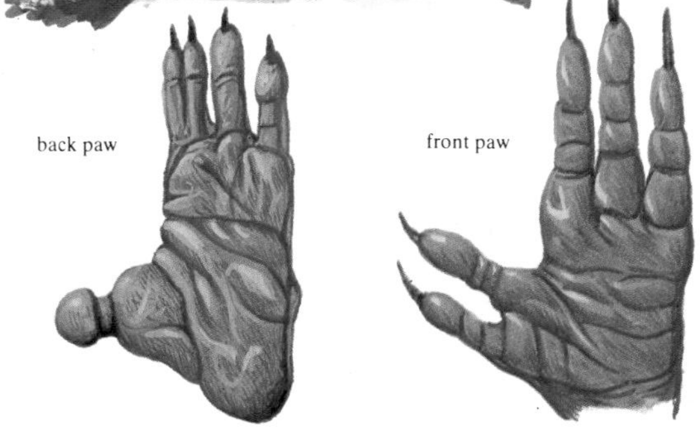

▲► The front paws have a thumb and second finger that are opposable to the other three, thereby giving the creature's powerful claws a vicelike grip. On the back paws, however, only the big toe can be spread out.

MOLES

Order Insectivora
Family Talpidae
Size Length of head and body 7 – 8½ in (18 – 25 cm), plus tail 6¾ – 8½ in (17 – 21.5 cm)
Dentition $\dfrac{3.1.4.3}{3.1.4.3} = 44$
Reproductive period Spring – summer
Gestation About 45 days
Number of young 3 – 4
Sexual maturity 6 – 12 months

The family Talpidae comprises 12 genera, with 19 species. The animals involved are typically subterrestrial: they dig tunnels and spend most of their life underground. Also included among Talpidae, however, are aquatic or semi-aquatic species, which are only occasionally subterrestrial. Generally, Talpidae have elongated, cylindrical bodies; the snout, which is overlapped by the edge of the lower lip, is sturdy, tubular, elongated and hairless. Their eyes are tiny and often covered in skin, and they possess no external ears. The paws have five digits, and in most of the genera the terminal bones of the digits have a clearly visible median groove or two lobes. The digging forms have large front paws with an additional (falciform) bone.

The subfamily Desmaninae comprises two genera, each with one species. The Russian or musk desman (*Desmana moschata*) is distributed through southeastern Europe and central-western Asia. The tail is vertically compressed, and at its base are situated odoriferous glands that give the whole animal its characteristic smell of musk. The tail is used, together with the animal's other limbs, as a means of propulsion through the water. Its coat is made up of extremely beautiful fur, whose underlayer is short, dense and very soft; its outer layer consists of longer and harder hairs. Its coloring varies from reddish-brown to gray. Desmans are aquatic animals which prefer the edges of rivers, where the current is slower. The entrance to their lairs is always underwater and deep enough down for the animal to be able to use it even in winter, when the water freezes. The lair itself is always situated above the level of the water and forms part of a system of burrows that is often shared by several animals. Their prey consists

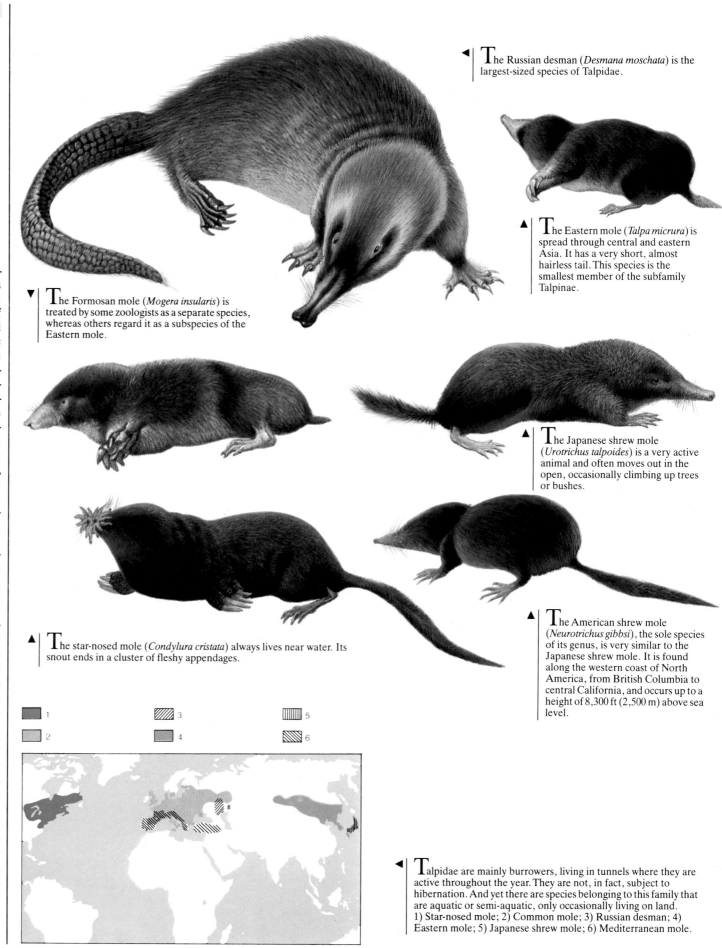

The Russian desman (*Desmana moschata*) is the largest-sized species of Talpidae.

The Eastern mole (*Talpa micrura*) is spread through central and eastern Asia. It has a very short, almost hairless tail. This species is the smallest member of the subfamily Talpinae.

The Formosan mole (*Mogera insularis*) is treated by some zoologists as a separate species, whereas others regard it as a subspecies of the Eastern mole.

The Japanese shrew mole (*Urotrichus talpoides*) is a very active animal and often moves out in the open, occasionally climbing up trees or bushes.

The American shrew mole (*Neurotrichus gibbsi*), the sole species of its genus, is very similar to the Japanese shrew mole. It is found along the western coast of North America, from British Columbia to central California, and occurs up to a height of 8,300 ft (2,500 m) above sea level.

The star-nosed mole (*Condylura cristata*) always lives near water. Its snout ends in a cluster of fleshy appendages.

1 2 3 4 5 6

Talpidae are mainly burrowers, living in tunnels where they are active throughout the year. They are not, in fact, subject to hibernation. And yet there are species belonging to this family that are aquatic or semi-aquatic, only occasionally living on land. 1) Star-nosed mole; 2) Common mole; 3) Russian desman; 4) Eastern mole; 5) Japanese shrew mole; 6) Mediterranean mole.

of leeches, worms, earthworms, crustaceans, insects, fish eggs, amphibia, tadpoles, and fish. Often, however, they eat vegetable matter. The gestation period lasts some 45 days, after which 3 – 4 young are produced, blind, toothless and almost completely hairless. These are suckled for roughly 30 days. The musk Desman occurs sporadically in an area along the basins of the Volga, the Don, the central Urals, and the upper Dnieper.

Members of the subfamily Talpinae include the common European mole (*Talpa europaea*). The related Eastern mole (*Talpa micrura*) is slightly smaller; it is found in Sikkim and India and as far east as Mongolia, Manchuria, Korea, Japan, and Taiwan.

The subfamily Scalopinae contains twelve species, none of which have an outer ear. Among them is *Urotrichus talpoides*, found throughout Japan, in forests and mountainous areas at a height of around 6,500 ft (2,000 m) above sea level. In appearance it is very like a shrew. The shrew mole (*Neurotrichus gibbsi*), is very similar and is found along the western coast of North America from British Columbia to central California, up to a height of about 8,000 ft (2,500 m).

There is only one species in the subfamily Condylurinae, the star-nosed mole (*Condylura cristata*), found in Canada and in the United States. Its area of distribution is governed by the presence of damp, muddy terrain. The length of its body is 4 – 5 in (10 – 13 cm), while its tail measures 2¼ – 3¼ in (5.6 – 8.4 cm). The adults weigh 1½ – 3 oz (40 – 85 g). Its coat is dense and tough and also fairly water-resistant, while its coloration varies from brownish-black to black. The most distinctive feature of this creature is its snout, which ends in a disk surrounded by 22 fleshy appendages (11 on each side). They all move like tentacles, particularly when the animal is searching for food. They probably contain tactile organs. Between mid-April and mid-June the female gives birth to the year's only litter, generally 2 – 7 young. Tunnels are dug out of moist ground, and some of them lead directly into water: these animals are, in fact, expert swimmers and divers, and in winter they are even able to swim under the ice. Much of their food is obtained from the bottom of ponds and streams, and this generally takes the form of earthworms, crabs, water insects, and even small fish.

◀ The Russian desman is a semi-aquatic species: it favors small and medium-sized, smooth-flowing rivers set in forests or forested steppes.

▼ The front paws are partially palmate.

▲ The Russian desman's diet consists of crustacea, tadpoles, leeches, and earthworms, but also fish and vegetable matter.

◀ The star-nosed mole is a skillful swimmer, even underwater, with the help of all four of its paws. These resemble those of Talpinae and Scalopinae: the width of the front ones is the same as their length, and there is no interdigital membrane. The tail is compressed at the base, covered in scales, and with occasional hairs. During the winter and spring its diameter increases noticeably in both sexes, which is probably the result of an accumulation of fats that act as a reserve of energy for use during the mating season. The star-nosed mole neither hibernates nor estivates and appears to be active all round the clock. They often leave their burrows, even when there is snow, in which case they may walk along its surface or dig long tunnels underneath it.

▼ The snout ends in 22 fleshy "tentacles" that close together when the animal is eating.

▼ The diet of *Condylura cristata* includes insects, crustacea, mollusks, etc.

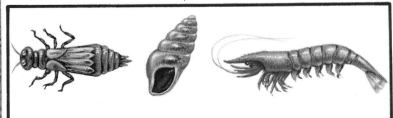

FLYING LEMUR

Genus Cynocephalus

Order Dermoptera
Family Cynocephalidae
Size Length of head and body 15 – 16½ in (38 – 42 cm), plus tail of 8¾ – 10¾ in (22 – 27 cm)
Weight 2¼ – 4 lb (1 – 1.8 kg)
Dentition $\frac{2.1.2.3}{3.1.2.3} = 34$
Reproductive period Around January
Gestation 60 days
Number of young 1, rarely 2

The order Dermoptera comprises two species of the single genus *Cynocephalus: C. volans,* found in the Philippine islands of Mindanao, Basilan, Samar, Leyte, and Bohol, and *C. variegatus,* which ranges from the island of Tenasserim and southern IndoChina to Malaysia, Sumatra, Java, Borneo, and the surrounding islands.

The principal characteristic of these animals is the way in which they are typically adapted for gliding. The skin covering their body is, in fact, much larger than the actual body itself. By extending their limbs and their tail, the flying lemurs unfold a patagium that allows them to glide once they have launched themselves into the air. The patagium is actually a single, very broad fold in the animal's coat. Despite the fact that the patagium allows for almost perfect gliding, it constitutes a great hindrance to the animal in moving its front and rear limbs while walking. .

The color of the flying lemur's coat is generally not uniform, even though the predominant shades are gray and brown. This coloring blends extremely well with the color of the branches and trunks of trees.

The front limbs are pentadactylous and the digits are long and straight, ending in rather short, curved nails. The conformation of the feet is similar to that of the front limbs. In the skull, the edges of the orbital cavity are very marked, except to the rear, where the orbital cavity remains open and communicates directly with the temporal cavity. The dentition possesses certain distinctive characteristics: it is heterodont and diphyodont, with the number and shape of the milk teeth being identical to that of the adult teeth. The substitution occurs at an

▲
▶ Dermoptera are tropical mammals capable of achieving gliding flight thanks to their body skin, which extends outward to form a patagium, or flying membrane, when the hindlimbs and tail are stretched out. Their body is of modest size – roughly 16 in (40 cm) long, plus 10 in (25 cm) of tail. Their snout is similar to that of the flying fox. They live typically in forests. However, *Cynocephalus variegatus* (illustrated above) has been seen in coconut plantations in Malaysia. Dermoptera are exclusively tree-dwelling and nocturnal. They spend the day hanging head down from branches, protected by their natural camouflage (provided by the pale, dappled markings on their body and patagium). The females give birth, after a gestation period of approximately 60 days, to a single young (rarely two), which they normally carry around with them for some time, its back legs clinging onto the fur of their underbelly and its milk teeth attached firmly onto their teats.

early age, except for the lower canine. The lower incisors are large and forward-facing; their crown, which is flattened from back to front, has the shape of a scraper and a series of vertically running, parallel grooves that make the tooth look like a comb. This configuration resembles that of lemurs' teeth.

The typical habitat of the flying lemur is made up of forests, although *Cynocephalus variegatus* has been seen in Malaysia in coconut plantations. They are totally arboreal creatures and skillful climbers, even though their movements are generally very slow. When they move along the branches of trees, the patagium is kept folded under their front limbs so as not to become entangled. On the ground, they are literally unable to move, and in these circumstances their sole preoccupation is to clamber up the first thing that they see. The animals spend their days in hollows in trees, where they hang vertically with their head at the top, gripping on with their claws. Often they assume another resting position, whereby they cling to a branch with all four limbs and with their head hanging down. Their tail appears not to be prehensile. Many of the creatures will simultaneously use the same tree as a nest.

Toward sundown they begin to come out of their refuges and start gliding into the trees where they feed. Flying lemurs appear to be creatures of habit in their movements. Their diet consists mainly of fruit, young shoots, flowers, and leaves; only vegetable matter has ever been found in the stomachs of dead individuals. After a gestation period of approximately 60 days, the female gives birth to one or rarely two young. When the mother has to move, her offspring either remains in the nest or may accompany her by attaching itself to her coat with its back legs and gripping onto her teats with its milk teeth. When faced with danger, the flying lemur emits a harsh, raucous cry.

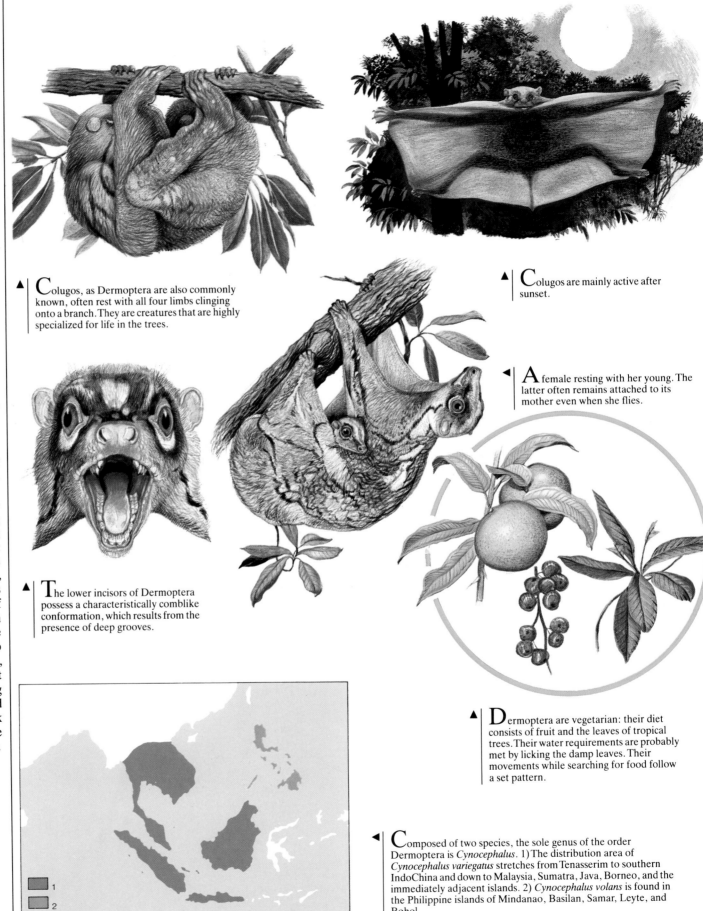

▲ Colugos, as Dermoptera are also commonly known, often rest with all four limbs clinging onto a branch. They are creatures that are highly specialized for life in the trees.

▲ Colugos are mainly active after sunset.

◄ A female resting with her young. The latter often remains attached to its mother even when she flies.

▲ The lower incisors of Dermoptera possess a characteristically comblike conformation, which results from the presence of deep grooves.

▲ Dermoptera are vegetarian: their diet consists of fruit and the leaves of tropical trees. Their water requirements are probably met by licking the damp leaves. Their movements while searching for food follow a set pattern.

◄ Composed of two species, the sole genus of the order Dermoptera is *Cynocephalus*. 1) The distribution area of *Cynocephalus variegatus* stretches from Tenasserim to southern IndoChina and down to Malaysia, Sumatra, Java, Borneo, and the immediately adjacent islands. 2) *Cynocephalus volans* is found in the Philippine islands of Mindanao, Basilan, Samar, Leyte, and Bohol.

1
2

FLYING FOXES
Suborder Megachiroptera

Flying foxes are only found in the tropics and subtropics of the Old World. Their distribution is limited by the fact that they need to find fruit all year round. To meet this need for food many species undertake seasonal migrations.

The Megachiroptera include the biggest of the bats, with a body length of 16 in (40 cm) and a wingspan of 5½ ft (1.7 m). The best known species, and one of the largest, is the Indian flying fox (*Pteropus giganteus*) with a body weight of 2¾ oz (80 g) and a wingspan of 4½ ft (1.4 m). The females are a uniform dark brown in color, the males have a light yellow mane of long, coarse hair. Like almost all flying foxes, it has no tail. The interfemoral membrane is no more than a narrow fringe. The species occurs only on the Indian subcontinent and in Sri Lanka. These bats always congregate in fairly large colonies, numbering from a few hundred to several thousand. They spend the day resting in the branches of great trees, hanging down from the branches like fruit, alternating short active periods in which the animals clean themselves with longer phases of sleep. During sleep they cling fast to a branch with one foot, the other foot being tucked into the hair of the belly. Both wings are folded round the body, so that the animal is completely enfolded up to the neck by the protecting wing membranes. Even the muzzle is pressed into the chest, and only the ears are left free. The animals remain alert even while they sleep and a vigil is kept over the surrounding country by the continually moving ears. Any unknown noise is picked up and may wake them and set them flying.

The bats wake 10 – 15 minutes after sunset and clean themselves. The animals hanging on the inner branches of the tree clamber along the branch to the outside, and 25 minutes after sunset the first of them fly off. Ten minutes later the whole colony is airborne. The animals fly round their rest tree in wide circles two or three times and then make off in little groups in different directions to their feeding grounds, often miles away. They stay in their food trees all night, then fly back to their rest trees in the early morning. Indian flying foxes live mainly on the

▲ The Indian flying fox (*Pteropus giganteus*) represents the prototype of Megachiroptera. The large eyes, the pointed ears, and the elongated snout are all reminiscent of a fox, even though the latter, of course, is in no way related to the species. In common with many Megachiroptera, *Pteropus giganteus* has no tail. The caudal flying membrane has been reduced to a narrow fringe. The female is a dark chestnut brown in color; the male has an area of long, coarse hairs around its neck, pale yellow in color, which are connected with glands containing odorous secretions. These oily secretions moisten the hairs on the neck.

► Flying foxes feed on a large number of tropical fruits, such as bananas, mangoes, guavas, and figs. They squeeze the juice from them and then spit out the tough fibers.

juice of ripe fruit. The bats fly silently into the food trees and clamber along the branches to the fruit. They pull the thin branches toward them with their thumb claws and seize the fruit with the four big, sharp canine teeth.

Although thousands of flying foxes may congregate in a single rest tree, they never hang touching one another but always stay a little distance, generally 12 – 20 in (30 – 50 cm), apart; particularly aggressive males will drive their neighbors away if they come within a few feet of them. Once they have chosen their resting place, flying foxes always return to the same place in the tree every morning. An individual's place in the tree is decided by its order of seniority; the senior flying foxes occupy the safest places at the top of the tree and on the highest branches, and weaker and younger males have to occupy the lower branches. They post sentries over the colony and if a predator or a man comes near the tree they utter loud warning cries. The order of seniority within a colony is settled by fighting, mainly between the males. Females take the rank of the males beside which they hang, and are not themselves very aggressive. The gestation period is about 5 months and the young are born between February and April, their eyes still shut; they do not open them until the third day of their life.

▲ In Megachiroptera the flying membranes stretch between the second and fifth digits, both of which are very elongated, and between the body and the outer edge of the limbs. The caudal flying membrane consists solely of a small fringe, and the tail is almost completely lacking. Unlike Microchiroptera, the flying fox's second digit also has a claw.

▲ Many species of flying fox spend the day resting in large colonies on particular trees. While sleeping, they wrap their flying membrane around their body, leaving the ears free. Even when asleep they are on their guard, and their surroundings are being constantly scanned by their ears, which move continuously. Any unknown noise is immediately picked up, thereby giving the animal the chance to wake up and fly away.

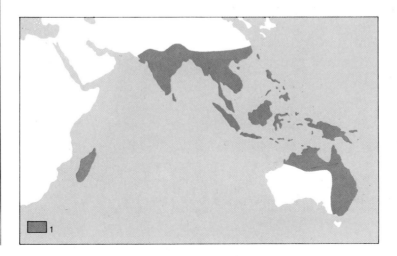

▲ Not all species of flying fox possess the vulpine head, with its pointed snout, which typifies *Pteropus* (left). In *Hypsignathus* (center), which lives in Central Africa, the male has a rectangular, hammer-shaped head with swollen lips. The large cavities in its skull act as echo-chambers for the very resonant calls that the males often emit in unison. *Nyctimene* (right) has protruding, tubular nostrils, which it can use to produce ultrasonic sounds for the purpose of echo location.

◀ 1)The distribution area of the genus *Pteropus* stretches from Madagascar to the south of the Indian subcontinent, as well as covering southern Asia and extending from eastern Australia to the islands of Fiji and Samoa. Indian flying foxes are found only in southern India and Sri Lanka. They always live in large colonies that range from several hundred to several thousand individuals. They prefer open and cultivated terrain, and are consequently not found in jungles or thickly wooded areas.

NAKED-FACED BATS

Family Vespertilionidae

The Vespertilionidae, with 38 genera and 275 species, are the biggest family of bats. They are distributed worldwide and settle in every kind of habitat from tropical rainforest to dry savannas. They are found in the whole of the temperate zones from the sea-coasts to the timber line. Characteristic of this family of bats is the sharp, smooth snout, which never has a nose-leaf. The wings of these bats are very simply constructed. The wide patagium is anchored in front to the strong upper arm, the greatly elongated forearm and the very long second to fifth fingers. The thumb is never joined to the wing membrane and carries a claw. The membrane is mostly attached to the body at the side of the rump, but in certain species it may be attached further up, at the middle of the back, giving the impression that the bat's back is naked; but in fact the back is quite normally developed, merely covered by the wing. At the back the patagium runs along the legs down to the feet. The narrow strip of skin stretching from the base of the neck along the upper arm and forearm as far as the thumb is called the propatagium, the skin between the fingers the chiropatagium, and the big wing surfaces between the side of the body and the fifth finger the plagiopatagium. There is also a membrane between the legs, the uropatagium, which may enclose the tail.

Almost all the Vespertilionidae feed on insects, generally caught on the wing. The prey is often captured with the aid of the well-developed uropatagium, which is folded forward to act as a scoop. The insect caught in this pouch is then seized with the teeth and thoroughly chewed. All these bats have needle-sharp teeth, very well adapted to breaking through the chitin of the insect's shell. Many of the Vespertilionidae also take insects, especially beetles, from the ground. One such is the North American pallid bat (*Antrozous pallidus*) which will even take scorpions and such reptiles as skinks and geckos. A remarkable specialist in its diet is the fishing bat (*Pizonyx vivesi*). It lives under stones or in empty turtle shells on the

The majority of bats of the famliy Vespertilionidae, like the species illustrated here (the common noctule bat, *Nyctalus noctula*), feed on insects that are caught in flight. Some Vespertilionidae also gather insects on the ground, particularly Coleoptera. Among the latter type is the pallid bat (*Antrozous pallidus*), found in North America. This species even succeeds in catching scorpions and small reptiles, such as skinks and geckos.

In their hunt for insects, bats sometimes catch their prey directly with their sharp teeth; often they make a sort of pouch with their uropatagium, in which the insect becomes entangled, like in a butterfly net.

Vespertilionidae will feed on all flying insects such as flies, mosquitoes, or moths. Insects living on the ground, such as Coleoptera, are caught directly there.

coasts and islands of southern California, and has long claws on its feet with which it can seize fish and crabs from the water. It is even thought that the white underside of this bat tempts fish to jump out of the water so that they are caught more easily.

The Vespertilionidae find their way almost entirely by echo-location, which accounts for the big ears found on many species. Just in front of the ear there is an earlobe, the tragus, which may be pointed or rounded; it is an important feature which helps to distinguish the different species. The eyes of the Vespertilionidae are generally quite tiny. Little research has been done on this, but it must be accepted on the evidence of the morphology that many species have only very limited, dim vision and cannot see shapes clearly. The sense of smell, however, is well developed in some species and plays a particularly important role in their social behavior.

Most of the Vespertilionidae live in caves, old buildings or hollow trees, but they can also be found under loose tree bark, and there are some that pass the day in the blossoms of tropical flowers. Many species are solitary, but most live gregariously in colonies. Mothers with young often leave the males and form separate colonies of mothers. Most commonly one or two young are born, though the American red bats of the genus *Lasiurus* produce as many as four at a birth. They are also the only bats that have four nipples; all the other Vespertilionidae have only two. The best-known genera are *Myotis*, (mouse-eared bats), *Pipistrellus* (pipistrelles), and *Plecotus* (long-eared bats).

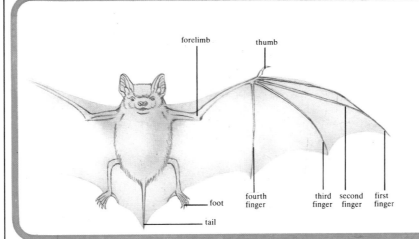

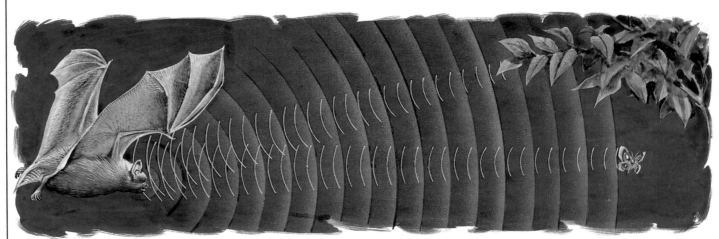

The wings of the Chiroptera are made up of a thin, elastic membrane. These patagia frame almost the whole of the animal's body. A narrow, overlapping strip runs round the front edge of the forelimb, from the neck to the thumb, which is free; most of the wing surface stretches between the very elongated fingers, the sides of the body and the hind limbs. The area between the hindlimbs is occupied by the uropatagium, which in *Vespertilionidae* also includes the long tail, right up to its tip. Before being beaten, the wings are raised well above the head and completely unfolded. A powerful downward thrust of its limbs lifts the animal up, while forward movement is controlled by the angle of the chiropatagium. While the animal is flying upwards, its fingers are folded so as to lessen wind resistance by the patagium.

▲ The most important sense in the Microchiroptera is that of hearing. Even their surroundings are identified almost exclusively by acoustic means. They emit directional signals on ultrasonic frequencies, and the returning echoes allow them to identify obstacles in their flight path, as well as insects to prey on. The theory that the echo-location system is also used during migrations should be discounted, since its range is too limited for large-scale orientation: these animals are, after all, able to return to exactly the same place after an interval of six months and a flight covering several hundreds of miles. It is thought, however, that their sense of sight plays a part in these migrations. Experiments involving bats that were taken to new locations have revealed the possibility that each individual possesses a certain "territory" around its daytime resting place, within which it can orientate itself by means of its local memory, derived from acoustically gained information. If the animal is removed from this territory, it can only regain its bearings visually and thereby try to find a point of reference for its journey back to known territory. This visual orientation seems to have allowed, in many cases, a high rate of returns, despite the bat's relatively poor sense of sight. On exactly what features the Microchiroptera base their orientation still remains a mystery. They may perhaps use salient points in the countryside or the stars, the Milky Way, or other similar points of reference.

V espertilionidae (the common noctule bat is shown above) have a pointed snout, never with any nasal appendages. Their eyes are mainly small and of limited use. Since these creatures gain their bearings mainly acoustically, their ears are often very large. In addition, these always have a tragus. ▲

◀ The majority of the Microchiroptera drink by flying low over the water and lapping the surface with their mandibles.

NINE-BANDED ARMADILLO

Dasypus novemcinctus

Order Edentata
Family Dasypodidae
Size Length of head and body 16 – 20 in (40 – 50 cm); tail 10 – 16 in (25 – 40 cm)
Weight Approximately 13 lb (6 kg)
Dentition 6 – 9 identical teeth on each side of each jaw
Reproductive period July
Gestation 4 months after the implantation of the ovum in the uterus. The implantation is delayed for a period of 3½ months
Number of young 4 (identical quadruplets)
Sexual maturity 6 months
Maximum age Not known

There are 21 species of armadillos on the American continent, ranging from the United States to Patagonia. Some species live in open country, such as savannas and pampas, while others inhabit the forests. They are exclusively ground-dwelling animals, normally living alone or in pairs, and seldom forming larger groups. They are generally nocturnal, though they sometimes come out by day.

In Spanish, the word "armadillo" is a diminutive form of the word for "armored," and refers to the protective system of bony plates, covered with horny epidermis, which protect the animal's back and sides, and form its most striking feature. The armor varies in color from brown to pink; in most species it is divided into three parts – a cephalic shield for the head, a scapular shield to protect the forepart of the body, and a pelvic shield to cover its hindquarters. These shields are separated by a number of mobile transverse bands, which do not extend across the underside of the body. They allow the various shields to articulate upon each other, and give the armadillo the freedom of movement which it requires. The number of bands varies from 3 to 30 according to the species, and their mobility is assured by the soft, flexible skin that separates them. The ventral area, where the bony plates exist only in a rudimentary form, is covered with thick and often bristly fur, the color of which varies from grayish-brown to white.

▲
► The armadillos live in a huge area which stretches from the United States to Argentina. Their bodies are protected by hard, bony scales of epidermic origin. They live on insects, small vertebrates, roots, various kinds of invertebrate, and also on carrion. The teeth are small and all of the same kind; they have no enamel and grow continually throughout the animal's life.

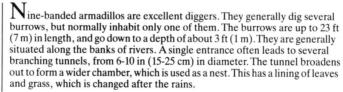

▼ Nine-banded armadillos are excellent diggers. They generally dig several burrows, but normally inhabit only one of them. The burrows are up to 23 ft (7 m) in length, and go down to a depth of about 3 ft (1 m). They are generally situated along the banks of rivers. A single entrance often leads to several branching tunnels, from 6-10 in (15-25 cm) in diameter. The tunnel broadens out to form a wider chamber, which is used as a nest. This has a lining of leaves and grass, which is changed after the rains.

The body is thickset and strong, with a robust skeleton. There are 2 – 4 vertebrae fused together in the cervical region, and 8 – 13 in the sacral region. The limbs are short, sturdy and muscular; the feet are basically five-toed, although the number of digits is often reduced. The second and third toes are dominant. They are used mainly for digging, sometimes in the search for food, and sometimes in the excavation of the burrows in which the animals live. The claws may also be used in self defense; but armadillos prefer to avoid their enemies by flight, or by rapidly digging a burrow. If they are caught in the open, some species draw up their legs inside their armor so that its edges come into contact with the ground; others roll themselves up more or less tightly. They vary greatly in size. The smallest species (*Chlamydophorus truncatus*) measures 5 in (12 cm) and weighs 3 oz (90 g), whereas the largest species reaches 40 in (1 m) in length and 110 lb (55 kg) in weight.

Armadillos are omnivorous: they live principally on insects, and also take small vertebrates such as mice, lizards, and snakes. They will eat tubers, roots, and even carrion. The nine-banded armadillo has been studied more than any other species of armadillo, partly because it destroys insects harmful to agriculture and eats poisonous snakes, and partly because its burrowing accelerates soil erosion and sometimes weakens the foundations of buildings. It is also the most numerous and the most widely distributed species, with a huge range extending from the southern United States (Oklahoma, Texas and Florida) to Argentina and Uruguay. One animal will often dig several different burrows, including a principal one in which it makes its main home. The burrow may be as much as 23 ft (7 m) in length, with a diameter of 6.8 in (15 – 20 cm). It may be situated at a depth of anything from 4 in (10 cm) to 40 in (1 m) or more below the surface of the ground. At the end of a burrow is a wider chamber containing a sort of nest lined with leaves and grass, which the armadillo renews after the rains.

Gestation lasts about 4 months and the baby armadillos are born in February or March. They are suckled for 2 weeks, and reach maturity at 6 months.

▲ The nine-banded armadillo has an excellent sense of smell, which enables it to detect the presence of insects at depths up to 8 in (20 cm) underground. It then digs them out and eats them.

▲ The nine-banded armadillo is a good swimmer. It can also cross shallow streams by running along the bottom; it has capacious bronchia and trachea, in which it can store enough air to enable it to hold its breath for 6 minutes.

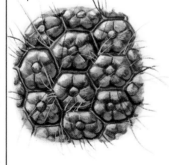

◄ The bony armor is a useful defense, but not always a sufficient one. These animals often prefer to escape danger by rapidly digging a burrow and vanishing into it.

▲ The principal enemies of the nine-banded armadillo are the jaguar, the puma, the coyote, the dog, and (more recently) the motor-car. Many of them are run over.

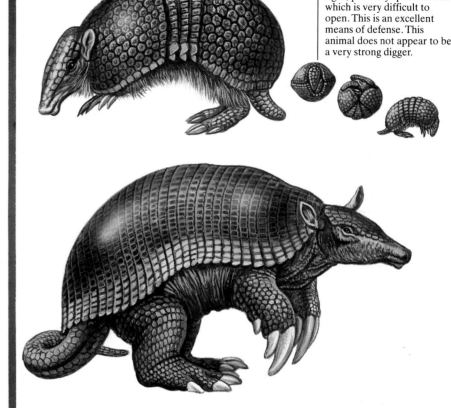

◄ The apar or three-banded bolita can roll itself up into a tight, perfectly spherical ball which is very difficult to open. This is an excellent means of defense. This animal does not appear to be a very strong digger.

▲ The giant armadillo is an excellent digger, and has huge claws on its front feet. The claw of the third digit is 8 in (20 cm) in length.

▲ The fairy armadillo is the smallest member of the family. Its armor does not extend to its flanks, which are covered by a thick, soft white fur.

◄ Geographical distribution of the armadillos. 1) The giant armadillo extends from Guyana to Argentina and Uruguay. 2) The nine-banded armadillo ranges from Oklahoma, Texas, and Florida in the United States to Argentina and Uruguay. 3) The apar or three-banded bolita lives in central and northeastern Brazil. 4) The fairy armadillo inhabits a small area of west-central Argentina.

1
2
3
4

SLOTHS

Genera Bradypus and Choloepus

Order Edentata
Family Bradypodidae
Size *Bradypus*: Length of head and body 20–24 in (50–60 cm); tail 3 in (7 cm). *Choloepus*: Total length 24–26 in (60–64 cm)
Weight *Bradypus*: 9–11 lb (4–5 kg). *Choloepus*: 20 lb (9 kg)
Dentition 5 teeth per side in upper jaw; 4 teeth per side in lower jaw. All teeth continue to grow throughout life
Reproductive period *Bradypus*: March or April *Choloepus*: Probably throughout the year
Gestation About 6 months
Number of young 1
Sexual maturity 2½ years for *Choloepus* in captivity
Maximum age Under 12 years for *Bradypus*; 23 years for *Choloepus* in captivity

Sloths are small arboreal mammals, ranging from 20–26 in (50–64 cm) in length and 9–20 lbs (4–9 kg) in weight. The thick, bristly fur varies in color from dark gray to fawn. Sloths have a short muzzle covered with short hair; the ears are small and the eyes are positioned so as to look straight ahead. There are 6–7 species of sloth grouped into 2 genera.

The three-toed sloths (*Bradypus*) called "Ai" by the natives because of the shrill, dissyllabic cry by which they keep in contact with each other have a geographical range which covers the entire area from Honduras to northern Argentina. The front legs are longer than the rear limbs, and are in fact one-third longer than the body. Whereas all other mammals have 7 cervical vertebrae, three-toed sloths have 8–10 according to the species. This allows the neck to turn through an angle of 270 degrees, and allows the animal to look straight ahead even when it is hanging under a branch.

The two-toed sloths or unau (*Choloepus*) range from Nicaragua to Bolivia and northern Brazil. They are larger than the members of the other genus. The tail of the two-toed sloth is reduced to a barely visible stump. The cervical vertebrae are 6–7 in number according to the species. The ears are larger than those of the three-toed sloth, and the hindlegs are slightly longer than the front ones.

▲
▶ Sloths spend most of their lives hanging from the branches of trees in the rainforests of Central and South America. Their fur, unlike that of other mammals, grows away from the belly and towards the back, so that rainwater can run off the animal without soaking it while it is in its usual inverted position. Another characteristic of the sloth's fur is the presence of microscopic longitudinal grooves along each hair, in which minute, unicellular green algae grow, giving the animal a general greenish hue. This makes the sloth look like a mass of leaves, and enables it to melt into the background. Sloths are completely vegetarian. The three-toed sloth lives almost exclusively on the leaves, flowers, and fruit of the Ymbahuba tree.

▶ The Ymbahuba is a tree which grows along the banks of rivers and on the edges of forests.

The sloths are exclusively arboreal animals. Three-toed sloths occupy almost exclusively the ymbahuba tree (*Cecropia lyratiloba*) while two-toed sloths will live in others as well. They find their food, copulate and bring forth their young among the branches. They seldom come down to the ground, and when they do it is always with the object of moving to a new tree. Their long limbs, though perfectly adapted for a suspended existence, are quite incapable of raising the weight of the body from the ground. They crawl clumsily along, hooking onto irregularities in the surface with their forefeet to pull themselves forward. They normally spend most of their lives hanging from the trees, hooked by their long claws onto the branches and feeding on the leaves and fruit which surround them. What strikes the observer most forcibly is the extraordinary slowness of these lazy and apathetic creatures. All their movements seem to be executed in slow motion.

Sloths are solitary animals, living in their own territories; but they maintain contact with each other by aural signals. Three-toed sloths utter shrill cries, especially during the mating season; they also snort violently when they are angry, and sometimes utter a rumbling growl. They are inoffensive when not molested. They have very slow reflexes, and poor sight and hearing – although, unlike most mammals, they do have color vision. They have a keen sense of smell. Their activity is mainly nocturnal, and they sleep about 15 hours per day, holding their limbs tightly together to avoid loss of heat. Like the other Edentata, they are imperfectly warm-blooded and their body temperature fluctuates with changes in the ambient temperature to an extent which varies with the species. Temperatures recorded vary from 97°F (36°C) to 75°F (24°C), the latter being the lowest temperature registered for a mammal.

In both genera, gestation lasts about 6 months and a single offspring is born. The mother hangs from a branch with her forelimbs while giving birth. As soon as it is born, the baby sloth attaches itself to its mother's abdomen and climbs to within reach of her two teats.

▲ A strange characteristic of the three-toed sloth is that it can turn its head through an angle of 270 degrees. This enables it to look straight ahead while hanging upside down.

▲ Sloths cannot walk on the ground, but can only drag themselves forward with their front limbs.

▲ Sloths are good swimmers and can cross a wide stream without difficulty.

◄ Sloths do not make any kind of nest. During the first months of its life, the baby sloth is carried on its mother's chest.

Two-toed sloths (1) range from Nicaragua to Bolivia and northern Brazil. Three-toed sloths (2) are found from Honduras to northern Argentina. ►

1
2

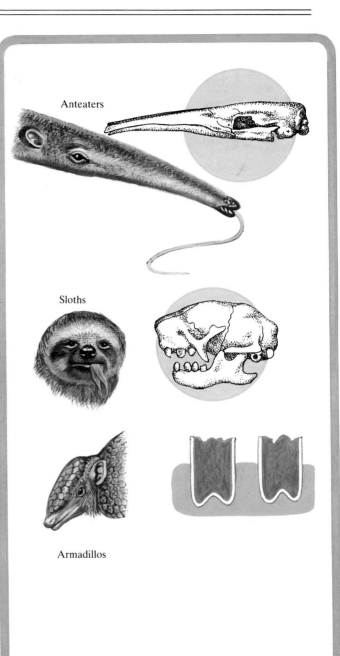

Anteaters

Sloths

Armadillos

Dentition of the Edentata
The order of Edentata includes three families – the Bradypodidae or sloths, the Dasypodidae or armadillos, the Myrmecophagidae or anteaters. Only the anteaters are completely toothless, relying on their long, sticky tongues as a specialized instrument for the capture of the ants and termites on which they live. The sloths and armadillos have teeth with no enamel, which grow continuously throughout the animal's life; they have no incisors or canines. Sloths are vegetarian, but armadillos live on insects, small vertebrates, and the leaves and stalks of plants.

GIANT ANTEATER

Myrmecophaga tridactyla

Order Edentata
Family Myrmecophagidae
Size Length of head and body 40 – 48 in (100 – 120 cm); tail 24 – 36 in (60 – 90 cm)
Weight 66 – 77 lb (30 – 35 kg)
Dentition Nil
Reproductive period Spring and fall
Gestation 6 months
Number of young 1
Sexual maturity At 2 years
Maximum age 14 years in captivity

The family Myrmecophagidae comprises three different species of anteater, one terrestrial and two arboreal, the distribution of which extends from the southern part of Mexico through central America and down to Paraguay. They live mainly in the tropical forests, but are also found in the savannas. They make their home in hollow tree trunks or in burrows excavated by other animals. They are generally solitary, but occasionally live in couples. They are completely toothless, being the only family among the Edentata which really deserve that name.

The organ with which anteaters obtain their food is the tongue, which is highly specialized and modified for extracting ants, termites and occasionally other insects. It is extremely long and thin and fully extensible. It is covered with a thick, viscous saliva to which the insects become stuck, and can be flicked in and out very rapidly – up to 160 times per minute in the case of the giant anteater. The giant anteater is up to 48 in (120 cm) in length, and measures 24 in (60 cm) at the shoulder. The forelimbs are equipped with three long claws; the claw on the third digit is particularly well developed and may measure 4 in (10 cm). The hindfeet have five smaller claws, all of the same kind. Because of the extraordinary development of the claws, anteaters walk on the thickly padded outside edge of the forefeet.

Giant anteaters are essentially ground-dwelling animals, though they can climb trees without difficulty, and are strong swimmers, capable of crossing a river of considerable size. They live in damp forests, in swampy areas

▲
◄ The giant anteater lives in the tropical forests, savannas, and swamps of Central and South America. It lives mainly on ants and termites, which it catches with its long, sticky tongue. The tongue is 40 in (1 m) in length, and can be flicked in and out at a rate of 160 times per minute. The animal detects ants' nests by its sense of smell, which is 40 times as sensitive as that of man. It tears the nests open with the powerful claws of its front feet, and thrusts its tongue inside. The total population of giant anteaters is dwindling at present, both because they are hunted by man and because of the advance of human settlements into their habitat. They are normally active by day, but tend to become nocturnal when disturbed by man.

▼ The habitat of the giant anteater.

and also in the savanna country of Central and South America, from Guatamala down to northern Argentina.

Once an anteater has discovered a termites' or ants' nest, it uses the powerful claws of its front feet to break through the hard outer wall of dried mud. It then inserts its long, thin muzzle, thrusting its tongue far into the interior. The tongue is coated with sticky saliva, which entraps the insects. Giant anteaters can eat up to 30,000 termites and ants in one day. They sometimes also eat caterpillars and other insect larvae, and worms.

The tamandua (*Tamandua tetradactyla*) is about the size of a large cat. The body is about 22 in (55 cm) in length and the tail about the same again. The eyes and the mouth are small; the muzzle is elongated but relatively short compared with that of the giant anteater. The tamandua generally has a yellowish, thick, bristly coat, with a wide black stripe round the neck and over the shoulders. The forefeet have four digits armed with claws, the third of which is particularly well developed and may be as much as 2 in (5 cm) in length. The hindfeet have five claws.

The tamandua is quite often to be found on the ground, but it is predominantly an arboreal animal. The tail – almost completely hairless and fully prehensile – is a useful extra support among the branches. Its main diet consists of ants and termites; but it will also take other kinds of insects and their larvae, sniffing them out under the bark of trees and extracting them with its powerful claws and sticky tongue. The females generally give birth to a single offspring in the spring. The tamandua lives in tropical forests and sometimes in savannas of farmland. It is common throughout a belt of land running from southern Mexico to southern Brazil and Paraguay.

The pygmy anteater (*Cyclopes didactylus*) is a tiny, graceful animal, very different from the other two species in appearance as well as size. Instead of being bristly, its coat is as soft as silk; the color is golden yellow to red-brown. The length of head and body is 6 – 8 in (15 – 20 cm), and the tail is a little longer. The weight is about 18 oz (500 g). The pygmy anteater's range extends from southern Mexico to central Brazil and Bolivia. It lives exclusively in the trees. The female gives birth to a single baby in December or January.

▲ When the giant anteater finds a nest of termites or ants, he breaks it open with the powerful claws of his front feet, and thrusts his long, sticky tongue inside.

▶ The giant anteater is not an aggressive animal, but it defends itself if attacked, inflicting deep wounds on the enemy with its sharp claws.

▲ The female gives birth to a single offspring, which she carries on her back until it is several months old.

▲ The tamandua lives mainly in the trees, and has a prehensile tail.

▲ The pygmy anteater is exclusively arboreal, and has a prehensile tail. Its fur is soft and silky.

◀ When threatened by an enemy, the animal stands up on its hindlegs, supporting itself by the tail, and defends itself with its forelimbs.

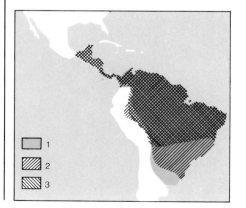

▲ Giant anteaters are excellent swimmers, capable of crossing large rivers.

◀ Distribution of the anteaters.
The giant anteater (1) ranges from Guatemala to northern Argentina. The tamandua (2) is found from the south of Mexico to Paraguay and southern Brazil. The pygmy anteater (3) lives in an area which extends from the south of Mexico to Bolivia and central Brazil.

PANGOLINS
Genus Manis

Order Pholidota
Family Manidae
Size Length of head and body from 12 in (30 cm) in the smallest species up to 32 in (80 cm) for the giant pangolin; the tail ranges from 12 in (30 cm) to 28 in (70 cm) and is generally about the same length as the body
Weight 10 – 60 lb (4.5 – 27 kg)
Dentition Nil
Number of young 1 – 3
Maximum age 2 years in captivity

Pangolins occupy the same ecological role in the Old World that armadillos and anteaters occupy in the Americas. They are found only in Asia and Africa, in the damp tropical and equatorial regions, and live more or less exclusively on ants and termites.

The outward appearance of a pangolin is rather like that of a pinecone. The animal's head, back, sides, tail, and the outer surfaces of its limbs are all covered with scales which overlap like the tiles of a roof. The muzzle is tapering and ends in a small, toothless mouth. The eyes are small, protected by thick eyelids. The earflaps are small in the Asiatic species, and non-existent in the African pangolins, which nevertheless have excellent hearing. The hind limbs are longer than the front limbs, and the feet all have five digits. The three central toes of the front feet are very long and powerful, well adapted to digging.

The African species are the white-bellied pangolin (*Manis tricuspis*), the long-tailed pangolin (*M. longicaudata or M. tetradactyla*), the giant pangolin (*M. gigantea*), and Temminck's pangolin (*M. temmincki*); and the Asiatic species are the Chinese pangolin (*M. pentadactyla*), the Indian pangolin (*M. crassicaudata*) and the Javan pangolin (*M. javanica*). They live in forests and thick bush, but are also found in savannas and open country.

Some species of pangolin live on the ground, and others in trees. They are shy animals and generally lead a solitary life, though they are sometimes found in pairs. They are nocturnal animals, except for the long-tailed pangolin, which is also active by day. Most species spend the day asleep, rolled up into a ball. The ground-dwelling species live in burrows which they dig

White-bellied pangolin
(*Manis tricuspis*)

Long-tailed pangolin
(*Manis longicaudata*)

Giant pangolin
(*Manis gigantea*)

Indian pangolin
(*Manis crassicaudata*)

There are three species of pangolin in Asia and four in Africa, living in forests and savanna regions. Some are arboreal and have a prehensile tail. Others are ground-dwelling; they are good diggers and excavate burrows to live in. Pangolins eat almost exclusively ants and termites, which they detect with the aid of their delicate sense of smell and catch with their long sticky tongue. They have no teeth with which to chew their food, but the lining of their stomach is extremely muscular and horny. The region of the pilorus is covered with minute horny projections. The stomach often contains small pebbles, which help to grind up the food. Pangolins have their body covered with horny scales.

themselves. A tunnel with a diameter of 6 – 8 in (15 – 20 cm) is excavated to a depth of 11 ft (3.5 m) ending in a large, circular chamber which may measure 6½ ft (2 m) in circumference.

Arboreal pangolins live in hollow trees. They have prehensile tails and are very good climbers. Among the branches, they move by grasping a suitable hold with both front feet and hoisting both back feet forward.

Pangolins generally move very slowly, unless they are frightened; in which case they run for a burrow or try to escape up a tree. Failing this, a pangolin will roll itself up into a ball, wrapping its tail round its body. The sharp edges of the scales, which can be moved by the animal's muscles, make this an effective means of defense, against which medium-sized predators can do little.

During the night, pangolins come out of their dens and go around looking for food. Their sense of smell is well developed, and leads them to the nests of termites or ants, which they tear open with their front feet, standing up on their hindlegs to do so, and supporting themselves with their powerful tail. The tongue, which is a very sensitive tactile organ, is then thrust into the galleries within the nest, and the insects remain attached to its sticky surface. Termites and ants are the principal food of the pangolins, which do, however, sometimes eat other insects and their larvae.

The pangolin's tongue is exceptionally interesting because it is so highly specialized in relation to its particular function. It is vermiform in shape, and its extended length may be as much as 10 in (25 cm) while the diameter is only ¼ in (0.5 cm). Pangolins are completely toothless, the insects are not chewed up before they reach the stomach, which is, however, itself an efficient masticatory organ.

Little is known about the breeding habits of the pangolin. Male and female apparently live together only in the mating season and while rearing their young; but the length of gestation is unknown. Young are born once a year. African pangolins generally have a single offspring, while the Asiatic species produce anything from one to three young.

When a pangolin is frightened, it rolls up into a tight ball, with the tail wrapped round the body. It is very difficult to unroll a pangolin in this position – especially as the scales have sharp edges.

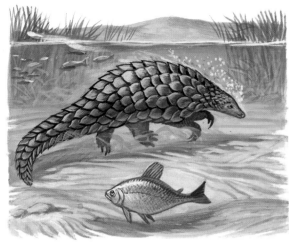

Pangolins are good swimmers.

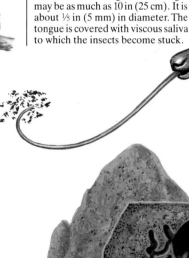

The extended length of the tongue may be as much as 10 in (25 cm). It is about ⅕ in (5 mm) in diameter. The tongue is covered with viscous saliva, to which the insects become stuck.

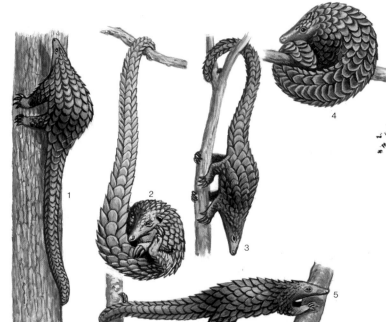

Arboreal pangolins in various positions: climbing up a tree (1); rolling up into a position of defense (2); climbing down a tree (3); resting (4); passing from one tree to another (5). The prehensile tail provides these animals with a valuable support.

Structure of a termites' nest. In the middle is the royal chamber, inhabited by the queen and her consort. The queen has an enormously enlarged abdomen, and lays hundreds of eggs every day. There are also brood cells, food stores, and other chambers, all connected by a system of tunnels.

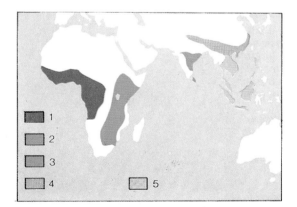

Geographical distribution of the pangolins. 1) The white-bellied pangolin, the long-tailed pangolin, and the giant pangolin live in West Africa, from Sierra Leone to Angola. 2) Temminck's pangolin lives in East Africa, in the Sudan, Kenya, Uganda, Tanzania, and southern Africa. 3) The Indian pangolin inhabits India and Sri Lanka. 4) The Chinese pangolin ranges over southern China, Sikkim, and Taiwan. 5) The Javan pangolin is found in IndoChina, Burma, Java, Sumatra, Bali, Borneo, and some other islands in the same region.

AARDVARK

Orycteropus afer

Order Tubulidentata
Family Orycteropodidae
Size Length of head and body 40 – 63
in (100 – 160 cm); tail 19 – 27 in (50 –
70 cm); height at shoulder about 24 in
(60 cm)
Weight 130 – 175 lb (60 – 80 kg),
exceptionally 220 lb (100 kg)
Gestation About 7 months
Number of young 1 – exceptionally 2
Weight at birth 4 lb (1.8 kg) – this
figure is based on a single instance

The aardvark is the only living species
representing a most unusual order of
mammals, the Tubulidentata (the
name describes the unique conformation of their teeth).

There is no other mammal with
which the aardvark could possibly be
confused. Some distant resemblances
to the pig have been detected – hence
its popular name, which means "earth-
hog." It has a long head, with a very
prominent, almost cylindrical muzzle.
The nose is mobile, and ends in a circular formation like the snout of a pig,
within which the nostrils are situated.
The aardvark can shut its nostrils at
will. The muzzle is furnished with a
large number of sensitive whiskers.
The neck is rather short and the body
extremely massive. The back is arched,
and ends in a long, powerfully muscled
tail, which may be 16 in (40 cm) in circumference at the base, and tapers
progressively down to the tip. It is not
unlike the tail of a kangaroo. The ears
are well developed, and similar in
shape to those of the ungulates; they
are 6 – 8 in (15 – 20 cm) in length and
longitudinally folded. The animal can
move them independently, and folds
them back while digging.

The limbs are of modest proportions
compared with the body. The forelimbs
are shorter than the back legs, but
extremely strong. The front feet have
four digits, the back feet five. The
claws of the front feet are exceptionally powerful, and are used for digging; the claws of the back feet are
shorter and less well developed. The
animal's highly mobile tongue is of
great biological importance. It is long
and can be fully extruded; it is slightly
flattened and constantly coated with
sticky saliva, which is produced by very
large salivary glands. The tongue is an

▲ The aardvark is a specialized insect-eater which lives mainly on termites.
◄ It is found only in Africa. It represents an archaic form of primitive
mammal, the survival of which to the present day is due to its remarkable
dietary specialization.

▼ The aardvark's habitat includes the wide grassy plains and forests of
Africa, except for some areas of dense equatorial jungle. In mountainous
country, it goes up to an altitude of about 6,600 ft (2,000 m).

▼ The aardvark's long, sticky and extensible
tongue plays an essential role in the hunt for
termites.

indispensable tool for the capture of the insects on which the aardvark lives. The teeth have a most unusual conformation. They are cylindrical in shape, and have no roots and no enamel. The dentine is arranged in parallel prisms; they grow continuously, and are covered with a sort of natural cement.

In general terms, the range of the aardvark extends over most of Africa south of the Sahara. Its distribution is largely determined by that of the termites which are its principal source of food. Savannas and grassland form the aardvark's most favored habitat; but it is also frequently found in the forests. The digging abilities of the aardvark are truly exceptional, and depend on the highly efficient musculature of the forelimbs and the special development of the claws, which perform the function of a spade and can also be used as formidable weapons of defense. The aardvark is a nocturnal animal, and normally spends the day in its burrow, which also serves it as a safe refuge at any time, and as a nest where the female can give birth and look after her young.

The aardvark's huge claws are a match even for the hard walls of a termites' nest, and tear open great breaches, measuring about 12 in (30 cm) in diameter and 16 in (40 cm) in depth. When the termites throng into the breach, the aardvark catches them by the thousands with its long, sticky tongue, which it can stick out to a distance of 12 in (30 cm), or sucks them directly into its mouth. The aardvark also takes termites, and to a lesser extent ants, on the ground outside their nests. Grubs, too, form part of its diet, especially those of the dung-beetle.

The number of young is normally one, exceptionally two. The baby aardvark is hairless at birth, and its bristly coat takes a year to develop. The first two weeks of life are spent in the burrow; then it begins to come out with its mother. At the age of 3 months it begins to eat insects, and at 6 months it digs its first burrow, next door to that of its mother, with whom it continues to circulate in search of food for a long time. Male offspring appear to leave their mother at the onset of the next breeding season, but females remain with her for a longer period. A mother is therefore sometimes seen accompanied by two offspring of different ages. The male aardvark always leads a solitary life, except in the mating season.

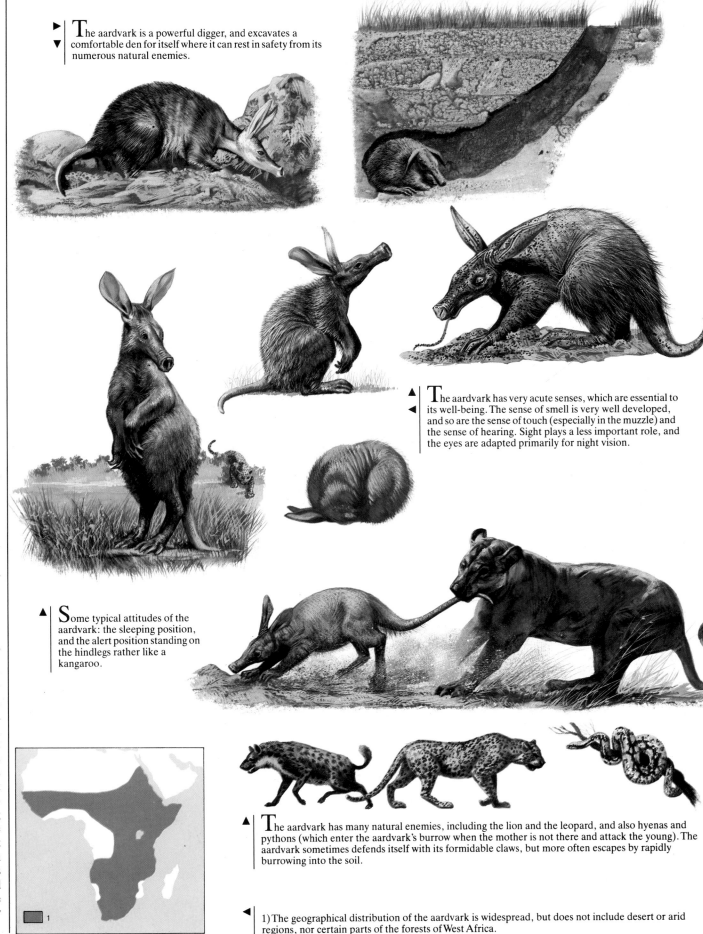

▶
▼ The aardvark is a powerful digger, and excavates a comfortable den for itself where it can rest in safety from its numerous natural enemies.

▲
◀ The aardvark has very acute senses, which are essential to its well-being. The sense of smell is very well developed, and so are the sense of touch (especially in the muzzle) and the sense of hearing. Sight plays a less important role, and the eyes are adapted primarily for night vision.

▲ Some typical attitudes of the aardvark: the sleeping position, and the alert position standing on the hindlegs rather like a kangaroo.

▲ The aardvark has many natural enemies, including the lion and the leopard, and also hyenas and pythons (which enter the aardvark's burrow when the mother is not there and attack the young). The aardvark sometimes defends itself with its formidable claws, but more often escapes by rapidly burrowing into the soil.

◀ 1) The geographical distribution of the aardvark is widespread, but does not include desert or arid regions, nor certain parts of the forests of West Africa.

CETACEANS
Order Cetacea

The cetacea make up what is perhaps the most specialized group of mammals, having broken all links with terra firma and adapted to the needs of a marine life that involves survival at extraordinary depths.

Cetaceans are the only mammals to spend their whole lives in the water; and adaptation to such an existence has brought about a series of profound transformations, which have had a striking effect on their whole morphology and skeletal anatomy. In particular, this transformation has had a substantial, although not very visible, effect on the animal's physiology, especially in relation to its respiration, blood circulation and general ability to survive extended periods of deep submersion. With the exception of a certain very small number of species that move at low speeds, such as whales, the external morphology of cetaceans reveals a perfectly hydrodynamic shape, with a fusiform body that is designed to have the least possible number of appendages, except for the fins, which are specifically developed as an aid to swimming.

In all cetaceans the mouth has a very broad opening, with a long *rima*, but without any clearly defined lips comparable to those of other mammals. They have no proper nostrils; the nasal cavities communicate with the outside by means of a vent, which is composed of two distinct orifices in Mysticeti (Balaenidae and Balaenopteridae) and of a single one in Odontoceti (all other Cetacea). This vent is situated on the top of the head, in a "periscopic" position for swimming, since it allows the most direct contact with the air with the minimum emergence of the body from the water. The eyes are small and the ears have no outer ear.

Of the quadruped terrestrial mammal, such as the far-distant ancestor of the cetaceans would have been, there remain only the front limbs, radically transformed into pectoral fins, which are almost always used solely as a directional device while swimming. The hindlimbs have disappeared, as has the pelvis, and of the latter there remain only vestigial traces, in the form of two small bones of equal size contained within the muscular mass of the abdomen.

The body of cetaceans is marvelously adapted to life in the sea, where these creatures, which originated from terrestrial forms more than 60 million years ago, have achieved colossal dimensions. The largest species is the one illustrated above, the blue whale (*Balaenoptera musculus*), which can be up to 100 ft (33 m) long.

There is relatively little fossil documentation on the ancestors of the Cetacea. Depicted here is a representative of the genus *Dorudon*, which was already fairly highly evolved and belonged to the extinct suborder Archaeoceti.

The body, more or less fusiform, decreases in diameter toward the posterior extremity, where there has developed a broad and extremely robust tailfin, which is the basic means of propulsion: it is always arranged horizontally, and not vertically, as in fish. The tail is activated by powerful motor muscles, which are inserted by means of large sinews in the posterior part of the spinal column, itself very powerful. The tailfin has no real bone structure as such, only its junction with the terminal part of the spinal column, which ends in correspondence with the interlobate sinus, in the middle of the "wings" of the fin itself. The majority of species have a well-developed dorsal fin, even though it is of modest size when compared to the overall size of the animal (especially in the case of Balaenopteridae), which is subtriangular in form. The dorsal fin is formed by a double layer of cutaneous tissue and rises up towards the center of the back, along the median line; it has no skeletal or muscular structure.

Cetaceans are nearly always large, very large or, on occasion, colossal; and the blue whale (*Balaenoptera musculus*) is, as far as we know, the largest animal ever to have existed: it can reach 100 ft (33 m) in length and more than 130 tons in weight. The minimum length is around 3 – 4 ft (1 – 1.2 m) (genus *Cephalorhynchus*), but the majority of Cetacea measure more than 6½ ft (2 m), many of them reaching 10 – 13 ft (3 – 4 m).

The skin of cetaceans is hairless and extremely smooth. The epidermis is very thin and the deep part of the derm is made up of fat or blubber, with a network of fibers enclosing enormous adipose cells. The thickness of the fat, which is always considerable, varies according to the species, the season and the part of the body; in Phocaenidae, for example, it measures roughly 1 in (2 cm); in the 85 ft (25 m) long blue whale it varies between 4½ – 5 in (11 – 13 cm), being broader in the female, while in Balaenidae it is much thicker still – maximum 20 – 28 in (50 – 70 cm).

Cetaceans have only a very few hairs in limited parts of the body, notably on the anterior part of the head in Mysticeti. None of the Cetacea have epidermal glands or nails. The animals are rarely of uniform color, being black or grayish or, in a few isolated cases, white, whereas in the vast majority of species the coloring consists of

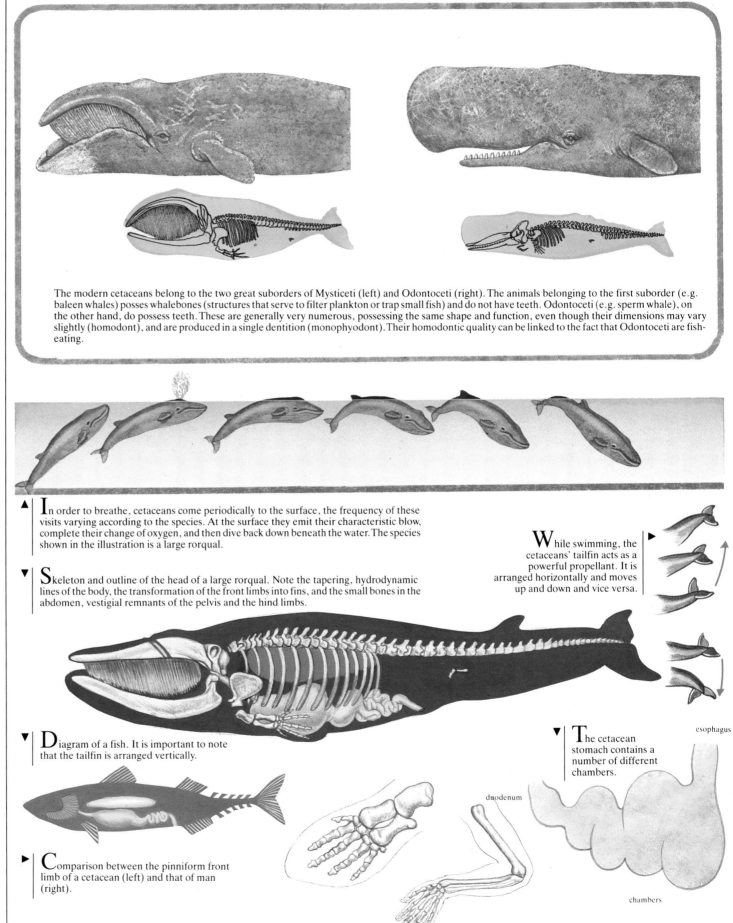

The modern cetaceans belong to the two great suborders of Mysticeti (left) and Odontoceti (right). The animals belonging to the first suborder (e.g. baleen whales) posses whalebones (structures that serve to filter plankton or trap small fish) and do not have teeth. Odontoceti (e.g. sperm whale), on the other hand, do possess teeth. These are generally very numerous, possessing the same shape and function, even though their dimensions may vary slightly (homodont), and are produced in a single dentition (monophyodont). Their homodontic quality can be linked to the fact that Odontoceti are fish-eating.

In order to breathe, cetaceans come periodically to the surface, the frequency of these visits varying according to the species. At the surface they emit their characteristic blow, complete their change of oxygen, and then dive back down beneath the water. The species shown in the illustration is a large rorqual.

Skeleton and outline of the head of a large rorqual. Note the tapering, hydrodynamic lines of the body, the transformation of the front limbs into fins, and the small bones in the abdomen, vestigial remnants of the pelvis and the hind limbs.

While swimming, the cetaceans' tailfin acts as a powerful propellant. It is arranged horizontally and moves up and down and vice versa.

Diagram of a fish. It is important to note that the tailfin is arranged vertically.

Comparison between the pinniform front limb of a cetacean (left) and that of man (right).

The cetacean stomach contains a number of different chambers.

esophagus

duodenum

chambers

257

Mammals

of mixed shades of brown and dark slate-gray with white, variously distributed: normally the upper parts of the body are darker and the lower parts either pale or white. Broken or even very striking colors are not uncommon either (as in *Orca*, for example).

Unlike terrestrial mammals, cetaceans need to be able to remain in a state of apnoea (suspended respiration), sometimes for considerable periods. Their respiratory and circulatory apparati have undergone modifications that allow for sufficient oxygenation of the various parts of the body during periods of immersion: it is particularly necessary that the supply of oxygen to the nervous system and the principal metabolic organs be maintained at a constant level. The apnoeal capacity of terrestrial mammals varies from species to species, but it is always less than in cetaceans.

There is no uniformity as to the maximum period of immersion: the common dolphin's maximum is 8 minutes, whereas that of the sperm whale is more than an hour. There are numerous factors that affect their different capabilities, but among those animals that search for their food nearest the surface, such as dolphins, there is basically no need for them to remain underwater for long periods, whereas the bottle-nosed whales and the sperm whale, which feed on cephalopod mollusks from the depths, need more time in which to dive down, hunt and then return to the surface. There are, of course, various intermediate stages within the different cetacean species, which are related to the nature of the animal's diet and the depths at which the food is obtained. However, there are also exceptions: Mysticeti, which are basically plankton-eating, stay submerged for long intervals at great depths, even though the microcrustaceans on which they feed occur only a few feet below the surface.

Macroscopic modifications to the anatomical structure also occur in the thoracic cage, which is not rigid. The hearts of marine mammals do not differ greatly from those of terrestrial mammals. In the composition of the arteries there is a great deal of elastic tissue in the walls, which may serve the purpose of alleviating internal pressure during immersion by allowing a certain degree of dilation. What is definite is that cetaceans have the capacity to achieve an impressive, peripheral

Pygmy whale
(*Caperea marginata*)

Biscayan or North Atlantic right whale
(*Eubalaena glacialis*)

Bowhead whale
(*Balaena mysticetus*)

Byrde's whale
(*Balaenoptera edeni*)

Common rorqual or fin whale
(*Balaenoptera physalus*)

California gray whale
(*Eschrichtius robustus*)

Humpback whale
(*Megaptera novaeangliae*)

Sei whale or Rudolphi's rorqual
(*Balaenoptera borealis*)

Minke whale or lesser rorqual
(*Balaenoptera acutorostrata*)

CANADIAN PORCUPINE

Erethizon dorsatum

Order Rodentia
Family Erethizontidae
Size Length from head to rump,
24 – 34 in (60 – 85 cm)
Weight 12 – 27 lb (5 – 12 kg)
Dentition $\dfrac{1.0.1.3}{1.0.1.3} = 20$

Reproductive period April to June
Gestation 7 months
Number of young Generally 1,
occasionally 2
Sexual maturity At about 15 months
Maximum age 10 years, from marked
specimens recovered in the wild

The outstanding feature of the Canadian porcupine is its spines, which make it resemble the Old World porcupines in appearance so closely. The Canadian porcupine is a stocky, compact animal. Its strong tail, used as a support in climbing, is 4 – 12 in (10 – 30 cm) long, shorter than the body. Its feet are short and strong, with powerful claws. Over 30,000 spines have been counted on a single animal; they grow only on the back, and may be up to 4 in (10 cm) long. Fine hairs grow between them, making a soft undercoat. The spines are yellowish-white at the base and brownish to black at the tip. In winter they are covered with long, dark guard hairs, so that at a distance the Canadian porcupine looks almost black until it erects its spines. The animal is found in a great part of North America, from the Pacific coast to the Atlantic, from Alaska to New Mexico. It occurs only where there are conifers growing.

Canadian porcupines are nocturnal, and feed in the trees, where they eat bark, thin twigs, leaves, and flowers. During the day, and in wet weather, it lies in a hollow tree, a cleft in the rocks, a hollow in the ground or even a roughly built nest in a tree. Mating takes place in late fall or early winter. The young are born the following summer developed to the same extent, as the young of true porcupines. Their eyes are already open and they already have spines, still soft, but hardening within half an hour.

Two related species are the coendou (*Coendou prehensilis*) and the bristly tree porcupine (*Chaetomys subspinosus*).

The Canadian porcupine (*Erethizon dorsatum*) in a typical attitude, illustrating its habit of climbing trees in search of food. It is mainly active during the night, when it gnaws bark, leaves, and soft branches.

The Canadian porcupine feeds on the leaves, buds, and the branches of sugar maple and spruce. During the summer it varies its diet to include roots, flowers, berries, and the seeds of several plants, including some aquatic plants.

Bristly tree porcupine
(*Chaetomys subspinosus*)

Prehensile-tailed coendou
(*Coendou prehensilis*)

The great horned owl (*Bubo virginianus*) is one of the most feared of the creatures that prey on the Canadian porcupine.

(1) *Chaetomys subspinosus* lives in areas of low vegetation in eastern and northern Brazil.
(2) *Coendou prehensilis* is distributed in Central America and the north of South America.
(3) *Erethizon dorsatum* lives in North America, from Alaska to New Mexico.

NORWAY LEMMING

Lemmus lemmus

Order Rodentia
Family Arvicolidae
Size Length from head to rump 5 – 6 in
(12 – 14 cm)
Weight 1 – 3 oz (30 – 90 g)
Dentition $\frac{1.0.0.3}{1.0.0.3} = 16$

Reproductive period Spring to fall, up
to 3 litters; occasionally also in winter
Gestation 16 – 21 days
Number of young 1 – 7, generally 5
Sexual maturity Females in captivity,
3 weeks at the earliest
Maximum age in wild 2 years

The lemmings have a barrel-shaped
body, short feet, ears, and tail, and
small eyes. What is unique about them
is their coloring: the top of their head
and their shoulders are black, broken
by yellow spots between the ears
which run down to the eyes to make
yellow stripes, and there are whitish
hairs inside the ears; the black goes on
to form a streak down the back. The
rest of the back is ruddy brown, the
flanks yellow to beige, while toward
the belly the coloring grows lighter to a
yellow-gray.

Norway lemmings live in the subalpine and alpine region of the Scandinavian mountains and the Kola peninsula.
They are prevalently nocturnal, even
in the northern midsummer when it
remains light all night. Even when
lemmings were put into continual
darkness in the laboratory they kept
up their night activity for two weeks.
Lemmings do not dig a very spreading
burrow, and to that extent are not typical voles. They live near the surface in
the moss and grass cover, and the galleries from the surface to their nest are
not generally more than a yard long.
The spherical nest, made in summer of
grass and lined with dry moss, is often
built under stones, tree stumps, fallen
branches, or hummocks. A short
escape tunnel with no exit runs downward from it. In winter these nests are
permanently under snow.

Lemmings are famous for the fluctu-
ation in their numbers from year to
year and the periodic migrations that
result. Like field voles, lemmings can
multiply remarkably quickly when the
conditions are favorable, and like the

▲ The Norway lemming (*Lemmus lemmus*) differs from all other species of lemming in its
bright black-and-yellow coloring. It lives in the subalpine and alpine regions of the
mountains of Scandinavia and in the Kola peninsula, but its range of distribution becomes
much wider in its migration years. Mainly nocturnal, it does not dig long underground
tunnels but lives on the ground at the level of the moss and grasses.

▶ It feeds mostly on moss and grasses, which are particularly abundant in the tundra, and
is also prepared to eat lichens.

▼ The migrations of the lemmings are always described with dramatic exaggeration. We are told that lemmings collect in groups which set off toward the
sea and there throw themselves blindly into the waves and drown, in a sort of mystic march to death. Acccurate observations have shown, in fact, that
lemmings generally move alone and at night. They follow their chosen course as closely as possible, only deviating from it if they come up against such
obstacles as rivers or lakes. When that happens, numbers of them may collect on necks of land or at points where their route becomes very narrow, and
these concentrations are very striking. It is true that, when they cannot get round the obstacle, they will not turn back from the water but try to swim
across to the opposite bank. If there are strong currents they may find it hard to maintain their direction, and the lemmings may drown, though they are
actually able to swim farther than other animals of their type, probably because their fur retains more air and so makes swimming easier. In "lemming
years" many lemmings can be found dead on the banks of lakes.

voles they reach sexual maturity quickly. The gestation period is 20–21 days and litters are of great size. Moreover, lemmings can even reproduce under the snow in winter. These factors, taken together, may explain how it is that the population can grow so quickly. About every four years the population density of the lemmings reaches a high point almost simultaneously throughout their range of distribution. Lemmings react to this situation by emigrating into areas and biotopes not previously occupied by them

The main cause for the disappearance of lemmings in areas in which they were previously particularly frequent is certainly shortage of food resulting from overgrazing. Examination of such areas after the rodents' exodus has shown that many of the plants that constitute their principal diet were completely exhausted, and even species only consumed in an emergency were becoming scarce.

The lemmings obviously have to avoid such excessive exploitation of their sources of food. Two of their characteristics help them to do this. First, lemmings are less tolerant and more aggressive toward their own kind than other rodents are. Secondly, they are more ready to move out, even into inhospitable surroundings, as the population density rises. A small-scale migration between summer and winter seems to be normal. But since all suitable habitats in the neighborhood will generally have hostile occupants, it is a long time before the migrants can find a resting place. Many of them die, others reach undefended places where there is plenty of food, settle down and live there for a long time and sometimes breed; but generally such displaced colonies die out after a time.

▲ The winter nest is made in the vegetation, just under the snow cover.

▼ Lemmings have very many enemies. Among the most dangerous of them are the skua, the snowy owl, the rough-legged buzzard, the stoat, and the Arctic fox.

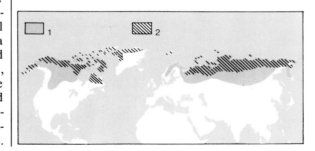

▲ The collared lemming (*Dicrostonyx torquatus*) is very much the same shape as the Norway lemming. During the summer its coat is gray-brown, notably paler on the underside of the body; in winter it turns completely white.

◄ Another peculiarity of the collared lemming occurs in the claws on the third and fourth digits of the forefeet, which in the winter grow perceptibly and divaricate, evidently as an adaptation to digging in the snow.

◄ (1) Area of distribution of the genus *Lemmus*. (2) Area of distribution of the genus *Dicrostonyx*. Both these genera, *Lemmus* and *Dicrostonyx*, contain five species. *L. lemmus*, *L. sibiricus*, and *L. amurensis* are found in Eurasia, while *L. trimucronatus* and *L. nigripes* are found in America. *D. torquatus* lives in Eurasia, while *D. groenlandicus* and *D. hudsonius* are American species.

PLAINS POCKET GOPHER

Geomys bursarius

Order Rodentia
Family Geomyidae
Size Length from head to rump 6–10 in (14–23 cm); tail 2–4½ in (5–11.5 cm)
Weight 3¾–10½ oz (125–350 g)
Dentition $\frac{1.0.1.3}{1.0.1.3} = 20$
Reproductive period In the north of its distribution range 1 litter each year, in the south 2 or more
Number of young 1–8, normally 3–5
Gestation 18–19 days
Sexual maturity At about 3 months
Maximum age Unknown

The plains pocket gopher lives in the central prairie belt of the United States, from the Great Lakes to Texas. It prefers light, brown, sandy soil or prairie soil only sparsely covered with bushes or trees. Every gopher has its own burrow, and it is only during the reproductive period (in the north, in the weeks just before the spring) that a pair can be found together in the same burrow. For the rest of the year gophers are extremely unsocial animals.

Pocket gophers are more active during the summer months than during the winter, but they do not hibernate. They can evidently maintain their strength from the food stores they gather from all around and carry in their cheek pouches. It seems that these stores may not all be eaten; decaying food has sometimes been found when burrows are dug up. Where the soil is deep enough pocket gophers burrow to a depth of 5 ft (1.5 m), and the total length of the tunnels may be over 300 ft (100 m). Their feet are narrow to allow ease of movement backward and forward. Burrows, both occupied and vacated, often provide shelter for other animals.

The young weigh about 0.06–0.1 oz (2–3 g) at birth and are fed exclusively by their mother for about ten days. They have to stay in the burrow with their mother up to the age of two months, but then they must find a territory and dig a burrow of their own, and probably also defend themselves against other young pocket gophers.

▲ It is exclusively herbivorous, feeding on roots, potato tubers, nuts, and seeds.

▲ The plains pocket gopher (*Geomys bursarius*) has a bodily structure adapted to an underground burrowing life. The body is stocky, with no recognizable neck, and the limbs are short and sturdy. Eyes and ears are strong, the pinnae very small and rounded. The two facial pouches at the sides of the muzzle are completely hairless; they are used to carry food and vegetable fibers to build the nest. The fur is fairly short and soft, and may vary in color from light yellowish-chestnut to almost black on top, with the underside rather lighter; there is no clear line of demarcation. As in nearly all the Geomyidae, the male is bigger than the female.

▲ The front paws are very muscular, with long, curved claws; these animals mainly use their forefeet for digging. Their typical rodents' teeth are strong and exposed; a membrane at the sides of the mouth enables the animal to close its mouth at the front and prevent earth from entering the oral cavity. These powerful teeth can thus be helpful for digging in the ground; but of course they are mainly used for taking food and breaking it down. The diet mostly consists of the underground parts of plants. The gopher's tail is comparatively short, sparsely haired or naked, and very sensitive; its tip contains blood vessels and nerve-ends.

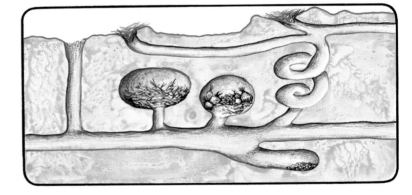

▲ The total length of the tunnels in a burrow may be well over 300 ft (100 m). Great quantities of roots, potato tubers, nuts, and seeds are found in the underground chambers.

◄ (1) The area of distribution of *Geomys bursarius*.

DESERT KANGAROO RAT

Dipodomys deserti

Order Rodentia
Family Heteromyidae
Size Length from head to rump 4–8 in (10–20 cm); tail 4–8½ in (10–21.5 cm)
Weight 1–4 oz (35–140 g)
Dentition $\dfrac{1.0.1.3}{1.0.1.3} = 20$
Reproductive period very variable
Number of young variable; in captivity 1–6, generally 2–4

The desert kangaroo rat is a small rodent, very well adapted to desert life. Its skull is as thin as paper and it has highly developed bullae. The upper part of the body varies from ocher to leather-colored, the underside and legs are pure white.

The upper incisors are flat, with a pattern of longitudinal grooves on the front surface; the lower incisors are round in section and their surface is smooth. There are five toes on the forefeet, four or five on the hindfeet, all having claws. The eyes are big, protruding and dark-colored. This species lives in parts of California, Nevada, and Arizona, and just up to the southwest corner of Utah. In Mexico the species lives in parts of California Bay, the country's furthest northeast corner, and in Sonora and parts of Chihuahua.

Kangaroo rats are strictly nocturnal, spending the hot daylight hours asleep in their burrow. They are almost entirely herbivorous, feeding on seeds, fruit, and the green parts of plants, and often use their front paws in feeding. They never drink fresh water, but obtain all the liquid they need from their food; their kidneys and even their bladder are able to extract the water from the juicy parts of the plants they eat.

They dig their burrows very flat, often in yielding soil. *Dipodomys deserti* lives only in very fine sand at least 20 in (50 cm) deep. Their tunnels often seriously undermine the ground. There is generally one nest chamber to each burrow, lined with straw, birds' feathers, and other soft materials. The storerooms are near the nest chamber and may be quite big.

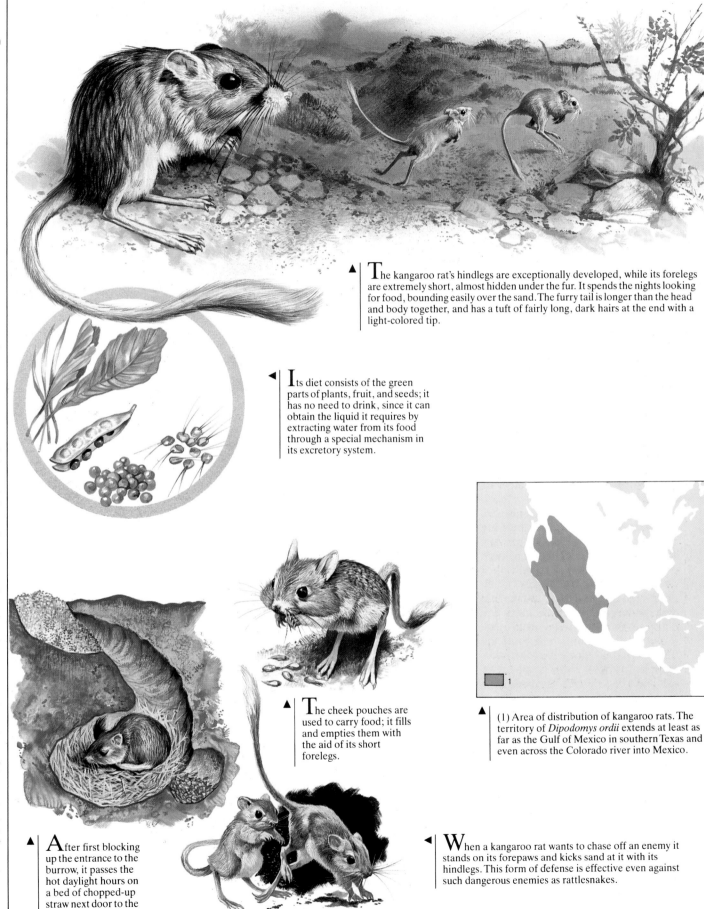

▲ The kangaroo rat's hindlegs are exceptionally developed, while its forelegs are extremely short, almost hidden under the fur. It spends the nights looking for food, bounding easily over the sand. The furry tail is longer than the head and body together, and has a tuft of fairly long, dark hairs at the end with a light-colored tip.

◀ Its diet consists of the green parts of plants, fruit, and seeds; it has no need to drink, since it can obtain the liquid it requires by extracting water from its food through a special mechanism in its excretory system.

▲ The cheek pouches are used to carry food; it fills and empties them with the aid of its short forelegs.

▲ (1) Area of distribution of kangaroo rats. The territory of *Dipodomys ordii* extends at least as far as the Gulf of Mexico in southern Texas and even across the Colorado river into Mexico.

◀ After first blocking up the entrance to the burrow, it passes the hot daylight hours on a bed of chopped-up straw next door to the food store.

◀ When a kangaroo rat wants to chase off an enemy it stands on its forepaws and kicks sand at it with its hindlegs. This form of defense is effective even against such dangerous enemies as rattlesnakes.

WHITE-CHEEKED GIANT FLYING SQUIRREL

Petaurista leucogenys

Order Rodentia
Family Sciuridae
Size Length of head and body 13 – 19 in
(34 – 48.5 cm); length of tail 11 – 15 in
(28 – 38.5 cm)
Weight 1¾ – 3¼ lb (800 – 1500 g)
Dentition $\frac{1.0.2.3}{1.0.2.3} = 22$
Reproductive period Once a year,
from February to June
Gestation Unknown
Number of young 1 – 4, usually 2
Sexual maturity Assumed to be a year
and a half
Maximum age about 14 years

The white-cheeked giant flying squirrel is much larger than ordinary squirrels, which it resembles in shape, except for its gliding membrane. This extends back from the wrist of the foreleg to the ankle of the hindleg, and is made of thin furred skin growing from each side and a long movable cartilaginous spur that extends backward from each wrist and gives it additional support. In addition, there are similar membranes developed between the wrists and the sides of the neck and between the heels and the proximal part (a quarter) of the tail. These elastic, rubber-like gliding membranes are kept to the sides when not used. The head is short and round, with large eyes. On the first short digit of the hand there is a nail, while the other digits are furnished with sharp, large claws like those of cats. The body hairs are long and soft and extremely light.

The white-cheeked giant squirrels are distributed in the Japanese main island of Honshu, also in Shikoku and Kyushu, and in western China from Kansu to Yunan. In Japan they occur in the plains or in the mountains up to 6,000 ft (1,800 m) above sea-level, inhabiting forests which consist of large, old trees.

Completely nocturnal, the white-cheeked giant flying squirrels move about at night and remain hidden in their nests during the day. When it gets dark after sunset, they come out of their nests and begin gliding. Before

Pteromys volans

Petaurista petaurista

Glaucomys volans

▲ The flying squirrels, large and small, live in the forests and can carry out flights of 100-165 ft (30-50 m) from tree to tree; there is a record of a flight of 500 ft (150 m). They stay in their nests all day and only become active at dusk. The gliding membrane is held by a cartilaginous spur stretching from wrist to ankle; it can be spread or withdrawn at will by moving the spur.

▼ Their diet is based on seeds, various kinds of nuts and acorns, bark, and moss. Sometimes they enrich this with birds' eggs.

they take off, they carefully measure the distance to the trunk of the target tree by moving their head up and down. They then leap forward by kicking hard with the hindlegs. They glide down forward, keeping the body in a horizontal position, the tail stretched backward, and the limbs extended laterally. When they near the tree marked, they bring their body into a vertical position by raising the tail and, slightly gliding upward, catch on to the tree trunk with all four feet. They rarely descend to the ground directly. Once landed, they immediately come round to the other side of the trunk to watch for enemies. Then they climb up to the treetop to glide on to the next tree.

By repeating this procedure many times, they arrive at their feeding places. The gliding distance is usually within 130 – 165 ft (40 – 50 m), sometimes extending to as far as 600 – 660 ft (180 – 200 m). Their food consists of the sprouts, leaves, and young twigs of cedars, firs, maples, and cherry trees, and of fruits such as persimmons, cherries, and raspberries, and maple seeds, acorns and chestnuts, as well as bark. They also eat beetles or young small birds.

The nest is built in a tree cavity. The entrance measures 10 – 20 cm in diameter and the nest-chamber is situated lower than the entrance, thickly matted with cedar bark, pine-needles, or sometimes dry grasses. And in an area with few large trees, twigs, barks or leaves are collected on a branch and made into a nest, which is globe-shaped from 40 to 55 cm in diameter, but a little flat vertically. In the rare case that a nest built on a branch is already sheltered from rain by other branches above, it will be dish-shaped like those of birds. Sometimes the nests are built in the attics or rafters of large buildings in temple or shrine structures, and the animal leads a solitary life there. Several nests, separated from each other by tens of meters, make up a colony in most cases. The young come out of the nest immediately after their eyes open 45 days after birth and start gliding practices on low branches.

There are many other species of flying squirrels among these the large brown giant flying squirrel (*Petaurista petaurista*), the Eurasian lesser flying squirrel (*Pteromys volans*), and the lesser American flying squirrel (*Glaucomys volans*).

A lesser flying squirrel leaps into the air, pushing off with its hindlegs and stretching its forelegs to the front as far as possible to spread the membrane. Before alighting on a tree it brings its body and tail up to the vertical position so that its legs take the shock on landing. The tail acts as a rudder during flight. When the squirrel lands on a tree it immediately moves around to the other side of the branch, head downward, to protect itself from enemies.

▲ The lesser flying squirrel gives birth to from two to five young in a litter, and they start to jump about 45 days after birth. At first they show signs of being afraid to jump into the air.

◄ J ust before it jumps into the air, it measures the distance to be covered by moving its head up and down.

◄ A young flying squirrel which has fallen to the ground during a flight is carried back to the tree by its mother, twined round her neck and held fast by her teeth.

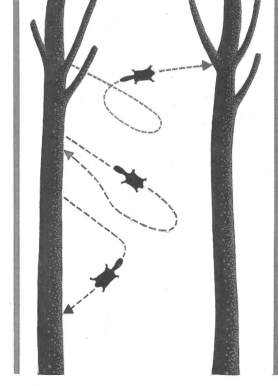

▲ The lesser flying squirrel is a virtuoso in the art of flying. From top to bottom, a spiral dive, return to the starting point after a circular flight, and return after making a right-angle turn.

◄ A rea of distribution of the flying squirrels.
(1) *Pteromys momonga*; (2) *Glaucomys volans*;
(3) *Petaurista leucogenys*; (4) other species of the genus *Petaurista*; (5) *Pteromys volans*; (6) *Glaucomys sabrinus*.

PRAIRIE DOGS

Genus Cynomys

Order Rodentia
Family Sciuridae
Size Length from head to rump 12 – 18 in (30 – 43 cm); tail about 3½ in (9 cm)
Weight 2 – 3 lb (900 – 1400 g)
Dentition $\frac{1.0.2.3}{1.0.1.3} = 22$
Reproductive period March to May
Gestation 33 – 37 days
Number of young 2 – 10
Sexual maturity At 3 years
Maximum age Unknown

All the species of Prairie dogs (*Cynomys*) are very similar. They are not really dogs, of course, but powerfully built rodents. The fur has the same coloring in all species, a yellowish beige-gray or leather-colored, with a distinct pepper-and-salt effect on the back and turning more whitish on the underside. The short tail is a little flattened, often with a suggestion of rings.

Prairie dogs once occupied vast areas in the western prairies of the central United States, from the south of the Canadian province of Saskatchewan as far south as northern Mexico. The prairies, with their almost unbroken cover of grass, are the true home of the prairie dog.

These highly social animals are diurnal, relying very much on one another and very aggressive against predators such as the American badger and snakes of all kinds. The big "towns" in which they live actually consist of family territories, each with its own feeding area. Each family territory is seized and defended by an adult, sexually mature male, and he and his "harem" of 1 – 4 females live there with their last two years' young. These family territories are called "coteries." Border disputes between coteries are always fought out or broken off by the male occupying the territory. Inside the family territory there is a strict "pecking order," which can only be readjusted by fighting. This occurs mostly in the spring; as the young – especially the males – approach sexual maturity after their third winter, they are driven from their home and have to conquer a new territory, generally on the border of a big colony.

Prairie dogs are herbivorous, feeding largely on grains. Much of the time

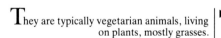

Prairie dogs (genus *Cynomys*) are stocky, thickset rodents, not of course actually related to dogs; they owe their name to a characteristic alarm call, very much like a dog's bark, that they give in case of danger. They are highly social animals, of diurnal habit, living together in big colonies which are commonly called "towns" in the vast prairies of the central United States and northern Mexico.

They are typically vegetarian animals, living on plants, mostly grasses.

When eating they adopt a characteristic attitude rather like that of the squirrels.

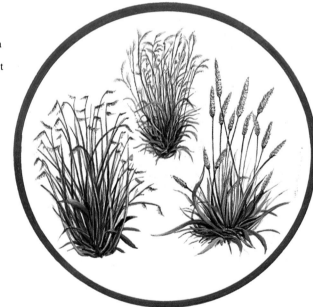

When the grass round their burrow grows too tall and dense, they cut it so that they can watch over the surrounding country and keep an eye open for potential predators.

they spend outside their burrow is devoted to gathering food. A good deal, too, is spent standing upright on watch. When an immediate danger appears, the animals instantly disappear into their burrow, or into the nearest hole. If the enemy is further away they remain sitting in the entrance or looking out of it with only the top of their head showing. All this time they give their alarm call, the call that has given them their name, like a small dog barking. Every species is said to have a range of signals. As well as the ordinary alarm call from which they get their name, they are believed to have different intonations for enemies on the ground and in the air; there is also an all-clear signal, which is used as well when they are marking out their territories. Finally there is a call for help, most commonly directed to the senior male. When seriously disturbed the whole population of a "town" disappears underground, until at last the boldest of them slowly come out to make sure the coast is clear.

There are two groups of prairie dogs. The first, rather larger and stronger, have comparatively long tails, more than a fifth of the length of the head and body, and black at the tip. There are only two species; the black-tailed prairie dog (*Cynomys ludovicianus*) and the Mexican prairie dog (*C. mexicanus*). The latter is the longer dog and can be distinguished from the common black-tailed prairie dog by its less ruddy, grayer or leather-colored fur with a high proportion of black hairs, giving the upper side a more notably grizzled look. It is found in three of the northern states of Mexico. The true black-tailed prairie dog is also a comparatively large form, but only the last third of its tail is black.

The other big group, the white-tailed prairie dogs, have rather shorter tails, less than a fifth of the length of the head and body, with a white tuft at the end and white patches on the sides, so that they also look white seen from the side. The body is usually more slender. These are not lowland species but live in higher country and in mountain valleys. The heaps of earth they make at the entrance to their burrows are untidy, not so systematically laid out as those of the black-tailed prairie dog, which are continually being reinforced and renewed. The common white-tailed prairie dog (*Cynomys leucurus*), is the biggest form in this group. The species occurs from southern Montana across central and southwest Wyoming into western Colorado and the northeast of Utah.

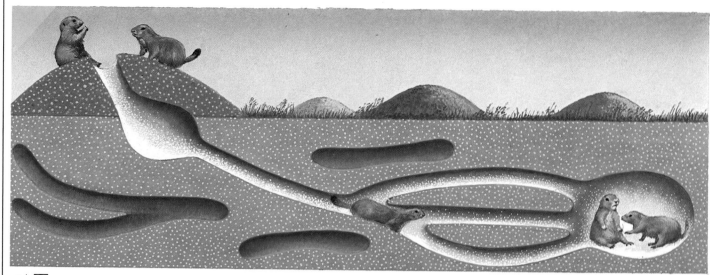

▲ The burrows are very solidly built. The tunnels, about 6 in (15 cm) wide and round in section, may go down to a depth of 10-15 ft (3-5 m) and two or three short lateral tunnels branch off, ending in closed, roundish nests. These are lined with grass, since they are always at a considerable depth in zones with a definite continental climate where there may be low temperatures. The earth dug out to make the burrow is piled up in mounds like miniature volcanic cones around the main openings of the vertical tunnels. These mounds of earth perform at least two functions; during the rains they hold up the water and prevent it from flowing into the interior, and they also act as observation posts for the animals. A few yards from the entrance there is a little platform inside the burrow used as a place to rest and as a listening post. Prairie dogs spend a lot of time improving and maintaining the exit mounds, especially when heavy rains threaten a landslide.

▲ The pictures above show some typical attitudes of prairie dogs. To assert their ownership of a particular territory, an animal stands upright on its hindfeet and utters a cry. Once the young have reached sexual maturity they are chased out by their parents and have to conquer a territory for themselves. A prairie dog stands guard at the entrance of its burrow and if danger threatens gives a kind of bark, which warns the whole colony that they should go down into the burrow. Prairie dogs are highly social animals; when two of them meet they embrace and greet each other with a sort of kiss; they often pay visits to each other.

▲ Prairie dogs are preyed on by diurnal raptors, which can easily catch them in the vast open spaces.

◄ (1) Area of distribution of *Cynomys ludovicianus* and *Cynomys gunnisoni*. The decline in the number of prairie dogs in the wide expanses of North America is mainly attributable to control measures by man. Both the farm owners, whose crops are threatened by the animals, and the cattle ranchers have for a long time systematically set out to exterminate these rodents. The range of distribution of prairie dogs, once so widespread, has been greatly reduced and some colonies are now heading for serious if not complete depopulation.

BEAVER

Castor fiber

Order Rodentia
Family Castoridae
Size Length from head to rump 32 – 40 in (80 – 100 cm)
Weight 33 – 66 lb (15 – 30 kg)
Dentition $\frac{1.0.1.3}{1.0.1.3} = 20$
Reproductive period Once a year, April to June
Gestation About 105 days
Number of young 1 – 5, average 3
Sexual maturity Usually at 3¾ years
Maximum age In wild 17 years, in captivity 35 years

The beaver is the second biggest rodent still living, next to the capybara (*Hydrochoerus hydrochaeris*). Its outward appearance bears the marks of its adaptation to life on the banks of rivers and lakes; its coat is notably soft and thick, thicker on the belly than on the back. The ears are small and the pinnae and nostrils can be closed. The hindfeet are webbed to increase the area of the feet used to drive it forward in swimming. The tail, almost naked but covered in scales, is flattened horizontally and is used as a paddle in swimming.

There are two species of beaver, the European beaver (*Castor fiber*) and the North American beaver (*Castor canadensis*). Originally the European beaver occurred all over the temperate zone of Europe, wherever there were sizeable streams, rivers, or lakes; but today only some beavers remain near the mouth of the Rhône, on the middle Elbe, in the south of Norway, in the Beresina catchment area, near Voronezh on the Don, in the northern Urals, and in Asia only on the Yenisei and Bulugun on the border between China and Mongolia.

For their habitat beavers require rivers or lakes, not too small, which do not dry up completely in summer and are not frozen to the bottom in winter. They must be at least 5 ft (1.5 m) deep, with softwood trees – willow (*Salix*), poplar (*Populus*), alder (*Alnus*), or birch (*Betula*) – on the banks, which the beavers need both as food and as building material.

Beavers move very awkwardly on land, generally walking on the whole sole of the foot. The tail swings to and fro and often trails behind along the

▲ Beaver (*Castor fiber*) felling a tree. To do this the beaver stands on its hindfeet, leans against the treetrunk with its forefeet and begins to gnaw. First it strips off the bark all round the trunk, then it attacks the wood, breaking it off in big splinters until it forms two cones balanced point to point, and cuts into the junction between these until it breaks and the tree falls.

▲ The beaver's main food consists of leaves, branches, and bark of willows, poplars, and sometimes alders. During the summer it also eats herbaceous plants – meadow sweet, reeds, waterlilies, and various kinds of thistles.

▶ The massive skull of the beaver seen from the side, showing clearly the powerful incisors, separated from the molars by the typical diastema.

ground; on soft soil it leaves a wavy track behind it. The beaver only breaks into a clumsy gallop if in danger. But when it swims it is far more skillful. It covers long stretches with only a little of its body above the surface. Since its eyes, nostrils, and auditory canals are near the top of its head, this is all it needs to find its way. When it swims it lays its forelegs and feet flat along its sides so as to obstruct its motion as little as possible. The forward thrust comes from the hindfeet; the toes are slightly spread on the backward stroke of the feet so that the webs increase their effective surface, and they work like oars. The tail serves as a steering paddle, and may be steeply angled down from the root. In case of danger the beaver slaps its tail loudly on the surface of the water as a warning signal, and then dives. It usually only stays under water for a few minutes, but dives of up to 20 minutes have been recorded.

Beavers have two characteristics that they share with no other animal; they can fell trees and bushes and they can build dams to control the current in their home waters. To fell a tree it will move round the trunk chipping out coarse splinters until the tree gives way. The direction of fall is a matter of chance. The beaver feeds on the leaves, twigs and some of the barks in summer and chops up the remainder into piles as provisions for the winter.

Beavers make two kinds of dwelling, according to the nature of the environment: burrows dug in the bank beside the water, and lodges built of branches plastered with mud, which are surrounded by water. If the water level changes frequently the tunnels may dry out, or the living chamber may be flooded. To prevent such accidents, the beaver tries to keep the water level constant by building dams. Like the lodges, they are built from logs and branches cemented with plants and mud. Beavers live as families in their burrows or lodges, each family comprising a male and female and the young of the current and of the previous year. The young normally leave the parental home at the end of the second year of life.

▲ Beavers build two kinds of dwelling, depending on their environment: simple burrows dug in banks, or structures of branches and mud with water all around them. These conical "lodges" are built of branches cemented with mud. Beavers often build dams with the same materials to keep the water-level constant. They bring in their building materials by swimming through the water.

▲ A beaver's lodge seen in section. The entrances, which open under water, lead to a roomy interior chamber carpeted with wood shavings and other plant material. This type of dwelling is generally occupied by one male and one female, with the young of the current and the past year.

▶ Diagram of a beaver's burrow dug into a bank. The entrance is always below the surface of the water. These burrows may be used for many years; the beavers maintain and repair them in the spring and fall, filling in any cracks with plants and mud. In spring this work is left to the females, but in fall the whole community takes part.

NORTHERN PIKA

Ochotona alpina

Order Lagomorpha
Family Ochotonidae
Size Head and body: 6 – 9 in (15 – 22 cm); ear: ⅝ in (1.5 – 1.8 cm)
Weight About ½ oz (10 – 13 g)
Dentition $\dfrac{2.0.3.2}{1.0.2.3} = 26$
Reproductive period From end of May to beginning of September
Gestation About 30 days
Number of young 3 – 6, usually 3 – 4 young
Sexual maturity Probably about a year
Maximum age About 3 years

Short-limbed, short-eared, tailless and small in size, the northern pikas are closer in appearance to guinea pigs than to hares or rabbits. However, they have four digits on the hindpaws, the soles being completely covered with hairs, apart from the digital pads (located under each digit); the basal parts of their round ears are cylindrical, unlike those of rodents. The hair is soft and silky and its color is conspicuously different from summer to winter. The winter coat is grayish-fuscous on the upperside of the body and yellowish-white on the underside. The summer coat is bright rufous or tawny on the upper side.

Northern pikas are widely distributed in the northeastern regions of Asia and North America. Their habitats are situated in areas with scattered large rocks, thickly covered with a growth of forbs, grasses, and alpine plants, or in rocky areas in the white fir forests.

These diurnal animals are often seen sunbathing on rocks during the day. They live in large colonies, but an individual or a pair will maintain a small territory. They inhabit subterranean nests under large rocks or in crevasses, 20 – 40 in (50 – 100 cm) below the entrance, matted with hay. There is a network of passages from each nest to the foraging ground. In winter they come and go through passages made under the snow.

In August – September they store up food for winter consumption under a large rock near their nest, bringing it by filling their mouths full. When collecting food they often climb a tall tree to gnaw off twigs. They do not hibernate, but continue their activities under the snow.

The alpine pika (*Ochotona alpina*) is a pretty little animal which first appeared about 44 million years ago and still survives. In many ways it recalls the progenitors of the lagomorphs. It lives in rock fissures in the alpine zones or in burrows dug in the ground in the steppe regions. It is mainly diurnal and forms big colonies, but each individual or pair keeps its own little territory. It can often be seen sitting on a rock enjoying the sun, with its muzzle pointed to the sky.

When frightened, it utters a cry to warn its companions of the danger. Then it disappears under the rocks.

It has a habit of cutting grass to make hay. The cut grass is made into little bundles and taken to the nest, where it is spread out to dry; when it is dry, the pika hides it under the rocks.

Area of distribution of *Ochotona alpina*. The alpine pika is widespread in northeast Asia from the Urals to the Bering Strait and in the islands of Sakhalin and Hokkaido. In North America it is found from the south of Alaska to the Yukon, from British Columbia to California, in the Rocky Mountains and as far south as New Mexico.

MOUNTAIN HARE

Lepus timidus

Order Lagomorpha
Family Leporidae
Size Length of head and tail 18 – 24 in (46 – 61 cm); tail 1½ – 2½ in (4 – 6.5 cm)
Weight 3½ – 13 lb (1.7 – 5.8 kg)
Dentition $\frac{2.0.3.3}{1.0.2.3} = 28$
Reproductive period March – April, August – September
Gestation 50 – 51 days
Number of litters per year 2
Number of young per litter 2 to 5, sometimes up to 8
Sexual maturity Between 10 and 12 months

The mountain hare, also known as the blue, alpine or varying hare is well-known for its seasonal dimorphism. In summer its thick fur is speckled brownish-gray or red-brown on the back, plain brownish on the neck and blackish on the rump. Its ears are brownish edged with black on the outside and white on the inside, with distinctive black tips. Its feet are brownish or tawny speckled with white, its tail is white on the underside and speckled brown on the upperside. The underparts of its body are white. Its winter livery is white apart from the black tips on the ears.

The area of distribution of the mountain hare includes the Alps, Ireland, Scotland, the Scandinavian peninsula, Finland, part of Poland, northern Russia, Siberia, Mongolia, and Manchuria. In North America (Greenland, Northwest Canada and Labrador) there is a similar species, the Arctic hare (*Lepus arcticus*).

The mountain hare is mainly crepuscular or nocturnal in habit, and generally a solitary animal although at times it shows gregarious behavior. It spends the day in its form usually under a bush, in a rocky crevice, between large rocks, or in some other natural cavity. In winter, it digs short runs or burrows in the snow both as a resting place and in order to find food. It is herbivorous, and in summer its diet is composed of clover, aromatic herbs, and other herbaceous plants, berries, and fungi; in the winter months it feeds on hay, roots, dry shoots, and the bark of deciduous trees.

▲▼ The alpine population of mountain hares (*Lepus timidus*) is a relic of the northern fauna that settled during the glaciations and became isolated after the last Ice Age. It is found throughout the Alps at altitudes from 4,000-12,000 ft (1,200-3,700 m). In the winter it leaves the woods and high pastures and moves down to lower forests with plentiful undergrowth. The populations which live in the northern tundra also migrate in fall, moving south to the forests and returning to the tundra in the spring. The mountain hare is dimorphic, with a white coat in winter and a speckled brownish-gray coat in summer. Its white coloration in winter is thought to be a form of camouflage as well as an adaption to harsh climatic conditions. It is a herbivorous animal, in summer feeding on herbaceous plants, berries, and fungi, and in winter eating hay, roots, and bark.

▲ Whereas the spring molt is gradual and goes through only a single stage, the winter molt goes through two stages: there is an intermediate stage when the coat is grayer in color, while beneath it is growing the white fur which very quickly replaces the gray.

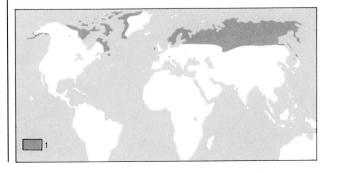

◄ 1) The different subspecies of the mountain hare are distributed in the Alps and in the northern regions of Europe and Asia. In the Arctic regions of North America and Greenland is found the Arctic hare (*Lepus arcticus*), which retains its white hair throughout the year.

DOGS

Order Carnivora
Family Canidae
Size Overall length 14 – 53 in (35 – 135 cm); length of tail 4¼ – 21 in (11 – 54 cm)
Weight 3.3 – 165 lb (1.5 – 75 kg)
Dentition $\frac{3.1.4.2}{3.1.4.3}$ = 42 (exceptionally 38 – 50)
Reproductive period Generally one a year, sometimes two
Gestation Approximately 60 days (as much as 80 in the Cape hunting dog)
Number of young 2 – 14
Sexual maturity 10 months – 3 years
Maximum age From 5 – 15

The Canidae is a relatively small and homogeneous family but it counts among its members such species as the wolf, the fox, the coyote and the domestic dog. They are specifically adapted to running and to maintaining at length a hand trot or even a gallop. The canids have elongated and semi-rigid legs which end in four well developed digits. The carnassial teeth are specially adapted for shearing but are also capable of a certain amount of grinding. As a rule there is a single litter a year, with the number of young varying from two to fourteen.

The hunting methods and patterns of social life permit three principal types of canids to be distinguished.
1) Solitary. For example, the fox, which hunts small prey, generally rodents, on its own. It is also omnivorous.
2) Solitary-social. A transitional type of canid, usually hunting and living alone but frequently associating in more or less temporary pairs.
3) Social. The wolf, the Cape hunting dog and the wild dog, for example, live in packs which may be very large and employ a method of hunting which, for the killing of large prey, relies on close cooperation.

The black-backed jackal (*Canis mesomelas*) is found in the eastern and southern parts of Africa. It is distinguished by its long, triangular ears and even more so by the black and white coat markings running along the back from the neck to the tail. The tail is reddish with a black tip.

The small-eared dog (*Atelocynus microtis*) inhabits the Amazonian forests of Brazil, Peru, Colombia,

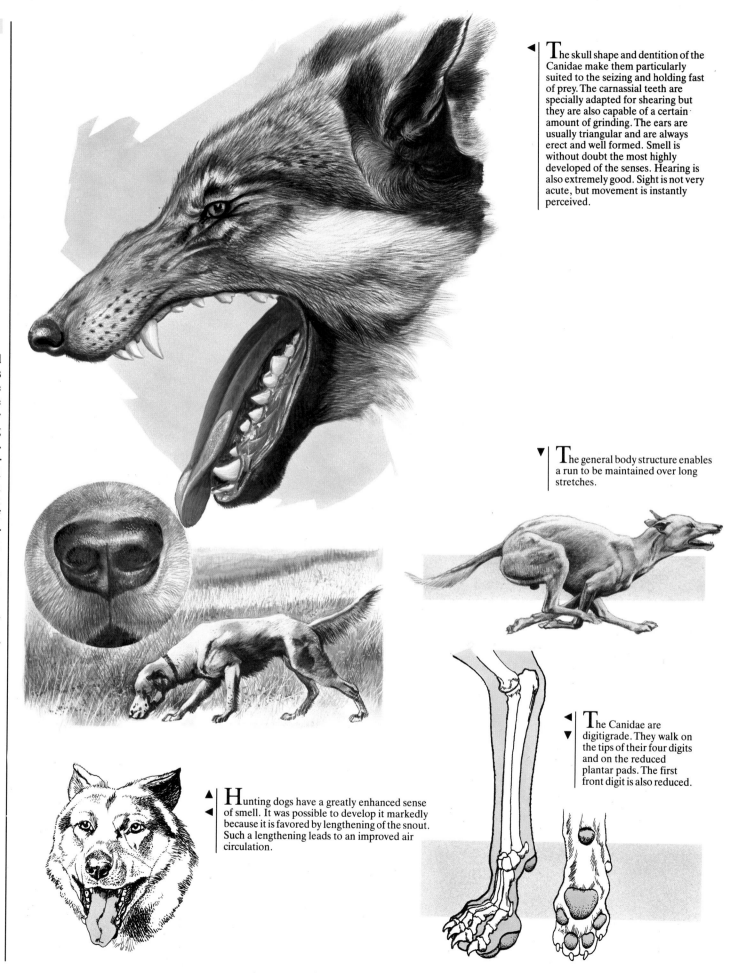

The skull shape and dentition of the Canidae make them particularly suited to the seizing and holding fast of prey. The carnassial teeth are specially adapted for shearing but they are also capable of a certain amount of grinding. The ears are usually triangular and are always erect and well formed. Smell is without doubt the most highly developed of the senses. Hearing is also extremely good. Sight is not very acute, but movement is instantly perceived.

The general body structure enables a run to be maintained over long stretches.

The Canidae are digitigrade. They walk on the tips of their four digits and on the reduced plantar pads. The first front digit is also reduced.

Hunting dogs have a greatly enhanced sense of smell. It was possible to develop it markedly because it is favored by lengthening of the snout. Such a lengthening leads to an improved air circulation.

Ecuador, and Venezuela. This canid moves through the forest with great caution, almost like a cat. It is dark in color and has short legs and a short tail which barely reaches the ground. Its ears are small and rounded and its eyes are small and slanted. Its fur is dense and harsh.

The crab-eating fox (*Cerdocyon thous*) inhabits tropical and subtropical forest from Colombia and Venezuela to Argentina. The species has been placed in a genus of its own because of the marked differences in the shape of its skull, teeth, and feet between it and the other species of South American Canidae. The crab-eating fox is omnivorous and its coat coloration is highly variable.

The maned wolf (*Chrysocyon brachyurus*) is a very slender canid with very long legs and a slight body. The head is like a fox's, the legs are dark, and the body is chestnut-yellow. Its name stems from the erectile capacity of its coat. It lives in grasslands and marshes from northeastern Brazil to northern Argentina.

The fennec (*Fennecus zerda*) is the smallest member of the family. It is pale in color, matching the sand. It looks like a small fox with large ears. It inhabits the desert and semidesert regions of North Africa and the Arabian peninsula.

The raccoon dog, or tanuki, (*Nyctereutes procyonoides*) is a small canid with very short ears, legs, and tail. The coloration of its coat resembles that of a raccoon, as indeed do many morphological and behavioral characteristics, so much so that there has been much discussion as to whether this species might not be closer to the raccoon family than the dog. Originally the raccoon dog inhabited Siberia, Japan, Manchuria, China, and northern Indochina. However, it was introduced in historical times into Russia, from where it has rapidly expanded into central and northern Europe.

The Cape hunting dog (*Lycaon pictus*) inhabits a range extending from 20°N to South Africa but is absent from the tropical jungles of West Africa and Zaire. The coloration of this large canid is extremely variable. It has large, rounded and very mobile ears, elongated paws with only four digits on both the front and rear ones, and a massive, powerful skull.

▲ | Some of the canine behavioral patterns are among the most complex in the animal world. They also have a special capacity for assimilating new information. The pack of Cape hunting dogs pictured above attacking a zebra is perfectly co-ordinated during the hunt by mechanisms which are still not fully clear.

▲ Swimming.

▲ The howl.

▲ Marking territory with urine.

▼ Play.

▼ Relationships in the hierarchy.

▲ Food preferences.

▼ Sleep.

▲ Hunting techniques.

▼ | The behavior patterns of wild dogs (some of which are illustrated on this page) can also be found in the domestic dog.

RED FOX

Vulpes vulpes

Order Carnivora
Family Canidae
Size Overall length 24 – 36 in (60 – 90 cm) height at shoulder 14 – 15½ in (35 – 40 cm)
Weight 11 – 17 lb (5 – 8 kg)
Dentition $\frac{3.1.4.2}{3.1.4.3}$ = 42
Reproductive period January to February
Gestation 53 days
Number of young 3 – 6
Sexual maturity 10 months
Maximum age 7 – 10 years; an average of 3 – 4 in the wild

The red fox has a vast range, extending through a variety of habitats and climates. In adapting itself to different situations the red fox may vary considerably in coloration and size, depending upon the habitat. In general it has a reddish back while the underparts of the body are a pale whitish-gray. The fur on the lips and on the chest is almost white or at least paler than the rest of the body. The backs of the ears and the tips of the digits are black. It has a long, thick, reddish-brown tail, the end of which is white or black.

The coloration can vary, depending upon the dryness of the habitat and the latitude, ranging from paler to more vivid shades. The fur is always rich and thick but its length is strictly dependent upon the harshness of the climate, as is the period of molt, which in warmer regions may last for many months.

The eyes of the fox are yellow and have good night vision. The pupil is vertical. All the senses are well developed, and hearing and smell are particularly so. The fox is very agile and alert. Its muscular system is very powerful in relation to the weight and structure of the animal. It enables it to leap and run with great ease and agility.

If the American red fox (*Vulpes fulva*) is regarded simply as a subspecies of *Vulpes vulpes*, then the species is found throughout almost the entire Holarctic region. In northern America it is found from the Arctic tundra to the central plains but it does not extend as far as the Mexican border. It occurs throughout Europe and is found in North Africa, Arabia, the Middle East, and the whole of Asia with

Together with the rat and man, the red fox (*Vulpes vulpes*) has been the most successful mammal on earth. Its extensive range covers a great variety of habitats and environments, some more natural than others. The secret of its success lies in its extraordinary capacity for adaptability and in its formidable mechanisms of recovery from the pressure to which it is subjected by hunters. Every attempt to exterminate the red fox is doomed to failure.

The natural diet of *Vulpes vulpes* consists of small mammals ranging from mice to hares and also birds, amphibians, and reptiles.

The pupil of the red fox is distinctive. It has a vertical opening which becomes apparent in bright light.

the exception of India, Tibet, and Indochina.

The fox has adapted to all climates and habitats with the exception of great deserts and tropical forests. It ranges from intensively cultivated lowlands to mountains (sometimes to altitudes of over 10,000–13,000 ft (3,000–4,000 m) and from marshes to tundra. It has even managed to spread into cities.

The fox breeds just once a year, the season occurring between January and March. Gestation lasts 53 days and the female gives birth to between three and six or seven young. At birth these are covered in a light, gray-brown fur. They are blind and helpless. They open their eyes at about twelve days old and a few days later their milk teeth come through. The mother suckles them for three or four weeks and then slowly begins to supplement their diet with small pieces of meat. Suckling stops completely at eight weeks of age.

The young emerge from the burrow at the age of one month, cautiously at first and then with ever increasing confidence. The adults bring them part of the kill. Initially, however, they feed them on regurgitated and already partially digested meat which is easier to absorb. Starting at the end of the second and throughout the third month, the mother also brings whole prey. The young later follow the adults in their first forays and during the hunt, but by the end of the summer they are already self-sufficient.

The behavior of the fox is highly stereotyped and repetitive, and its reputation for cunning is due to the fact that some of its behavior patterns are particularly suited to extricating it from dangerous situations. Although basically solitary, it is nevertheless a social animal.

Although a predator, the fox will eat almost anything and the range of food which it will take is among the most varied of any mammal. This abililty gives it great advantages over other predators. It is capable of hunting and killing any animal below 11 – 13 lb (5 – 6 kg) but generally it does not take wild prey larger than the size of a hare. The fox's favorite prey however, is quite definitely small mammals of the size of fieldmice or voles. It also eats insects, which, when they are most plentiful, can make up as much as 100 per cent of its diet; fruit, berries, fish, and refuse of every kind.

Arctic fox
(*Alopex lagopus*)

Swift fox
(*Vulpes velox*)

Pale sand fox
(*Vulpes pallidus*)

Fennec
(*Fennecus zerda*)

1) *Alopex lagopus*

2) *Vulpes vulpes*

3) *Vulpes macrotis*

4) *Fennecus zerda*

V arious unusual forms of *Vulpes vulpes* exist, the frequency of which varies even within a single population, thus we may distinguish the melanic fox (top), the silver fox (center), and the crossed fox (bottom). Often these are commoner in North America. They are the object of intense hunting for the fur trade. Today, however, they are bred and farmed in great numbers.

▲ T he four species of foxes: *Alopex lagopus*, which lives in polar regions; *Vulpes vulpes*, which inhabits the northern hemisphere but has no particular adaptations to warm climates; *Vulpes macrotis*, which inhabits the more southern regions of North America; *Fennecus zerda*, which inhabits the Sahara, provide an example of Allen's Law. This states that the ratio of weight to the surface area of the body increases in colder climates and that extremities of animals (tail and ears) increase in size in warmer climates because the extremities help to disperse heat. The ears of the four species conform to this rule.

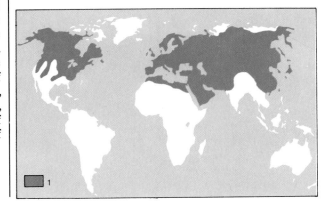

◀ T he distribution of the red fox, including the American subspecies (*Vulpes fulva*), covers virtually the entire Holarctic region. In North America it is found from the Arctic tundra to the central plains. It also inhabits Europe, North Africa, Arabia, the Middle East, and the whole of Asia apart from India, Tibet, and Indochina.

COYOTE
Canis latrans

Order Carnivora
Family Canidae
Size Overall length 39 – 48 in (100 – 120 cm); height at shoulder 18 – 21 in (45 – 53 cm)
Weight 26 – 44 lb (12 – 20 kg), sometimes as much as 66 lb (30 kg)
Dentition $\frac{3.1.4.2}{3.1.4.3}$ = 42
Reproductive period January to February
Gestation 60 – 65 days
Number of young 5 – 8

In build the coyote is generally smaller and more slender than the wolf. It has a narrower snout and its skull, legs, ears, and paws are smaller, the ears and paws being markedly so.

It has a gray-brown coat with a hint of yellow on the back, and gray underparts. The tail ends in a black tuft and the lips are very prominent, being highlighted by a distinct white surround.

There is perhaps no other species of mammal whose range extends so far from north to south. The coyote's range covers about 72° of latitude and stretches from Alaska to Guatemala. It is absent from the more eastern parts, the southeastern United States and northeastern Canada. The original habitats of this species may have been the central grasslands of North America, where there were abundant populations of wild ungulates, and the deserts of America. Today it is also found in forest, providing it is not very dense, and in the alpine environment of the northern provinces of Canada.

Female coyotes reach sexual maturity in their second year of life, at about 20 months. The mating season begins in January. The males follow the females for two or three weeks and as all the other females gradually come on heat, the males scatter to follow them. Eventually, toward the end of the mating season, each female is accompanied by just a single male. The male and female form a pair which may last for several months until the young have been raised or may endure for life.

The pair then establishes itself in its territory and within this territory it selects the old burrow of a badger, marmot, or polecat which it enlarges and adapts to its needs. Sometimes a

The coyote (*Canis latrans*) is one of the most successful members of the Canidae. Together with the red fox, it is the only species which has increased its range. The reasons for this are both biological and behavioral. The coyote has been able to profit from the changes, even the destructive ones, which man has inflicted on the environment and it has been able to adapt itself quickly to the new conditions.

The coyote's diet includes a large number of mammals, ranging from the rabbit and hare to small rodents, and from mice to prairie dogs. It also includes insects and reptiles as well as a certain amount of plant matter.

The coyote also feeds on the remains of dead animals. It is very adept at locating these because of its acute sense of smell.

completely new burrow is dug. Throughout the entire period of gestation the pair hunt and live together, although just before the birth the male will sometimes go out alone in search of food for both himself and his mate. In the week to ten days before the birth, the male and female mate several times. This behavior perhaps provides a further bond between the pair at what is a critical moment.

After a gestation period of 60 – 65 days the female gives birth to from two to twelve young. At birth the coyote cubs weigh about 7 – 9 oz (200 – 250 g); they are helpless, blind, and totally dependent upon their mother, and for about the first ten days they are fed exclusively on their mother's milk. The young are able to walk by the twentieth day and to run by the fortieth. Generally the young coyotes remain with the family until the end of October and then they gradually begin to move away until, by December, they have completely abandoned their parents. By eight or nine months of age the young coyotes are adult in size and are ready to face the lean, winter period and to withstand the dangers of their surroundings.

The fundamental unit of social organization is the family. This is built around a female which is capable of breeding. The pair bond may be permanent and it can last until one of the members of the pair is killed. The dispersal of the young during November and December makes room for the young of the succeeding generation. Not all the young, however, leave their parents and therefore a coyote family may consist of animals, generally related, of different ages. The ties which hold a family together are not, however, so strict and rigid as to prevent continual changes in the composition of the group, each individual being equally able to survive on its own.

Coyotes are not territorial in the strictest sense of the term. They do select an area in which to live and hunt but they do not defend the borders of this area against all intruders. On the other hand, they vigorously defend the burrow and the surrounding area during the breeding season. Distribution and numbers are dependent upon the quantity of food. The coyote will eat anything edible but being a carnivore it displays a distinct preference for flesh.

The coyote howls like the wolf but the sound is distinctly higher-pitched and of shorter duration. Howling serves to inform others of the individual's position and it confirms the ownership of a territory.

The cubs play at length among themselves. This activity is of fundamental importance in that it creates situations similar to those which will arise during hunting and in relations both within and between species.

The coyote can only hope to pull down and kill prey of the size of a deer if it is present in sufficient numbers. Individual coyotes are easily put to flight by these ungulates.

The young of the coyote, like those of many other mammals, treat other small animals as objects of play.

The present-day distribution of the coyote. This has extended in many regions, partly as a result of the extinction of the wolf, and it covers an area stretching from Alaska to Guatemala.

The coyote is the object of what is perhaps the most extensive campaign of population control ever mounted against a species in the wild. Every method from poison to traps has been used in the attempt to exterminate this species. While it has succeeded in certain areas, overall the campaign has been a failure.

WOLF

Canis lupus

Order Carnivora
Family Canidae
Size Overall length 51 – 63 in
(1.3 – 1.6 m); height at shoulder 24 – 36 in
(60 – 90 cm)
Weight 44 – 165 lb (20 – 75 kg)
Dentition $\frac{3.1.4.2}{3.1.4.3}$ = 42
Reproductive period From January to
May
Gestation 60 – 62 days
Number of young From 1 – 11, 5 – 6 on
average
Sexual maturity In second year
Maximum age Potentially 16 years,
10 in the wild

The wolf is the largest member of the Canidae. It is distributed almost throughout the entire northern hemisphere and its morphological characteristics vary according to the type of environment to which each population is adapted. Thus the color of the coat ranges from the pure white of the wolves living in the Arctic through various shades of gray and brown to reddish hues. Completely melanic examples are common, particularly in the populations from northwestern North America.

The wolf was at one time uniformly distributed throughout the entire northern hemisphere and it occupied a wide variety of habitats, from Arctic tundra to the deserts of the Middle East and the prairies of America to coniferous and deciduous forest. Today, as a result of the ruthless hunting to which man has subjected this species, its range has been greatly reduced.

All the wolf's senses are particularly keen but the most important is the sense of smell. Sight and hearing are, however, still highly developed. Wolves communicate with one another by means of sound. In addition to howling they will also, though more rarely, bark and yelp.

The wolf mates once a year. Mating may take place at any time from January for the more southern populations until April for populations from higher latitudes. The females are on heat for about a week and mating takes place many times during this period. In a pack where all the members are closely bound together, it is only the

The coat color of the wolf is highly variable in the various different regions and it matches the dominant colors of the environment that the individual inhabits. The measurements are also extremely variable. The largest animals live in cold climates while the smaller animals live in warmer regions. The fur is long on the neck and the tail. The tail is held hanging down parallel to the legs. The wolf's bearing is haughty and the movements of its body are restrained and well co-ordinated.

The great adaptability of the wolf is highlighted by the widely differing environments in which it is found and by the diversity of its prey: from large herbivores such as the musk ox or the elk to beavers and mice. It will also eat plant matter and refuse.

pair formed by the pack leader and his mate which mates and reproduces.

Gestation lasts 62 days. The average litter size is five to six cubs with a maximum of ten to eleven. The female gives birth in a burrow which has been dug in the ground or enlarged and adapted if, as is very often the case, it has been taken over from other animals. The birth can also take place in a lair among rocks or old, fallen tree trunks so long as the lair is both sheltered and safe. The cubs are blind and helpless at birth and they are totally dependent on their mother. They do not open their eyes until after the second week of life and begin to move, even going outside the burrow, at the end of their third week.

All the females in the pack are capable of helping the mother in watching over the growth of the cubs or of replacing her should any serious accident happen to her. In regions where the packs are continually moving around within their territories, the cubs are, from time to time, moved to new burrows in new areas where they grow and play while the pack hunts in the neighborhood. By the end of fall or the beginning of winter the cubs have already grown so much that they resemble adults and they are able to face the harsh winter climate. At this stage they also begin to follow the pack as it moves, and to learn the rudiments of hunting.

The wolf is a highly social animal which lives in packs within which there is a formidable degree of integration of individual activities and roles. The pack consists of a variable number of individuals (the average is 5 to 10, with a maximum of 25 or even 35) but in general it has a nucleus formed by a family unit. Order is maintained by a rigid hierarchy in which the males are dominant to the females and the young and the females are dominant to the young.

The wolf is a territorial animal. The territory belongs to a pack and its size ranges from ten or twenty square miles (a few tens of square kilometers) up to more than 5,000 square miles (13,000 square kilometers). The wolf will attack man only exceptionally and the few confirmed instances may well have involved rabid, atypical animals. Hence man's hatred for the wolf stems solely from competition over livestock, or possibly game.

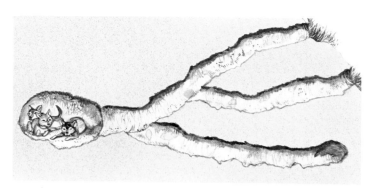

The young are born in a burrow which has been dug in the ground and which has numerous entrances. They remain in the burrow for about 15-20 days and throughout that time they are suckled by their mother. It is only after their third week that they begin to emerge and slowly learn to be independent. The mother feeds them with regurgitated food and then with small animals until they are able to catch prey for themselves.

The extremes of aggressiveness and long-suffering patience are combined in a female which has just given birth.

1) Once distributed throughout the entire northern hemisphere, the wolf has today been wiped out in almost the whole of the United States and in a large part of its European range.

The great mobility of the muscles of the snout enables the wolf to form a series of expressions which, together with the positions of the ears and the lips, enable him to signal anything from fear to aggression and submission.

BROWN BEAR

Ursus arctos

Order Carnivora
Family Ursidae
Size Length of head and body 51 – 100 in (130 – 250 cm); length of tail 2½ – 5½ in (6 – 14 cm); height at shoulder 30 – 48 in (75 – 120 cm)
Weight 130 – 880 lb (60 – 400 kg)
Dentition $\dfrac{3.1.4.2}{3.1.4.3} = 42$
N.B. 1 – 2 small premolars are often missing
Reproductive period May – July
Gestation 7 – 8 months
Number of young 1 – 3 (rarely 4)
Sexual maturity 4 – 6 years
Maximum age 25 – 30 years (up to 50 years in captivity)

The brown bear is heavily built, with a massive head and medium or small-sized ears, a stub of a tail which is practically invisible, and long, shaggy fur. The hindpaws are relatively long and resemble a human foot. They are somewhat narrower than the front paws and their claws are only half the length. The coat color of the brown bear ranges from pale golden through silver-gray, reddish-brown and chocolate brown to almost black.

At one time the brown bear was subdivided into numerous species, for example the grizzly of North America, the Kodiak or Alaskan bear, the Central Asian bear, the Himalayan bear and the European brown bear. All these forms may be crossed without any difficulty in captivity and there are also intermediate populations, so that today all the brown bears, the grizzly and the Alaskan bear are included in a single species, the brown bear (*Ursus arctos*).

Originally brown bears were found throughout Europe and the whole of Asia except for desert and steppe regions outside the tropics. The range of the brown bear in America (where it is normally known as the grizzly) was restricted to the western part of North America, stretching from Alaska in the north as far south as Mexico and east to the prairies. Over the last few centuries man has exterminated this bear from vast regions. The largest forms of the brown bear, the Kodiak or Alaskan bears, are restricted to the Pacific coast of Alaska and the northwestern coast of Canada.

The brown bears of present day show large differences between individuals and between the populations of different regions as to their size, coat color and the shape of their skull. Scientists are still not in complete agreement over the division into subspecies of the brown bear.

▲ The largest forms are the Kodiak or Alaskan bears (*Ursus arctos middendorffi*).

▲ Many grizzlies and bears from the far east of the USSR are large in size.

▲ The brown bears of western Europe (*Ursus arctos arctos*) are relatively small.

▲ During the last Ice Age, about 100,000 years ago, Europe was inhabited by the mammoth (*Mammonteus primigenius*) and the giant cave bear (*Ursus spelaeus*). These became extinct toward the end of the Ice Age. The cave bears were about a third larger than the most massive of the present-day brown bears and they were even more tied to a herbivorous diet. The cave bear did not give rise to the brown bear; instead, the two shared common ancestors.

◀ The brown bear has the most extensive range of all the species of bear and it is divided into numerous forms and subspecies.

The brown bear occupies a larger range than any other bear species. It can be found in the open forests of willow and conifer in the far north and in the broadleaved forests of temperate zones. For the most part the animal lives in forests but populations are also found in the tundra, where there are only occasional clumps of willow along the rivers or in the virtually treeless high mountain habitats of Canada, Alaska, and eastern and central Asia.

Young bears remain with their mother for at least 18 months and usually for two and a half or even three years. This long juvenile phase facilitates the formation of traditions among populations of bears. The young learn important models of reaction and habits by imitating their much more expert mothers.

Brown bears often claw and scratch with their teeth the bark of resinous trees, and then rub their neck and back over the place where the resin is welling up.

They are basically herbivorous, although they will eat animal matter if they get the chance. In early spring and summer green plants such as grasses, sedges, and shoots make up the most important part of their diet. In certain regions bears are quite happy to eat the roots of herbaceous plants. During the late summer and fall, when the bear is building up its reserves of fat for the winter, berries and nuts, such as rowan berries, bilberries, hazel nuts, beechmast, and acorns, become important. The remains of ants, wasps, and ground beetles can be found in the dung of bears between the spring and fall. Brown bears do not appear to be particularly fond of the flesh of vertebrates and they only prey on wild ungulates in certain circumstances. Several species of salmon are an important source of food for the bears living near the coast of the northern Pacific in North America and the Soviet Union.

In the late fall brown bears den up for their hibernation. Depending on the region, they may prefer to settle in a natural cavity or to dig themselves a den under the roots of a tree or among boulders. In January or February the female gives birth to her young inside the winter den.

Brown bears will sometimes fight over prey with wolves (*Canis lupus*), lynx (*Lynx* sp.), or any other predators found in their range.

The brown bear's immense strength enables it to drag the bodies even of large ungulates off into the undergrowth.

In those regions where they have never been hunted or where they have been hunted only occasionally, such as the large American national parks or wild regions remote from human habitation, brown bears show no fear of man and will even go so far as to invade campsites, having discovered that these offer the chance of finding food. In certain situations they can become dangerous because they do not take to being chased off.

285

AMERICAN BLACK BEAR

Ursus americanus

Order Carnivora
Family Ursidae
Size Length of head and body 60 – 70 in (150 – 180 cm); length of tail about 5 in (12 cm); height at shoulder 24 – 36 in (60 – 90 cm)
Weight 110 – 330 lb (50 – 150 kg); occasional specimens over 440 lb (200 kg)
Dentition $\frac{3.1.4.2}{3.1.4.3} = 42$

Reproductive period June – July
Gestation About 7 months
Number of young 2 – 3 (occasionally 1 or 4)
Sexual maturity 3½ – 5½ years
Maximum age About 30 years

The American black bear is the best known and the most widespread of the North American bears. It is of medium size and has a mainly black coat which is smooth and short haired compared to the brown bears. There are, however, also a number of well defined color variants: chocolate-brown, cinnamon and silver-gray tending to off-white.

Originally it was distributed throughout the wooded areas of North America but it has been wiped out from vast regions of the eastern, southeastern, and central United States. For a long time, however, it was not decimated to the same extent as the grizzly, and the American black bear is still found in the majority of the USA's states (about 33) as well as all the Canadian provinces and territories. It is a typical woodland animal and it prefers forests with abundant undergrowth.

The American black bear has become known to the public at large through the enormous national parks of the USA. As they are protected in these parks some bears have lost their fear of man and will even go so far as to beg for tit-bits at the roadside. Other bears congregate around rubbish tips or campsites and seize unguarded food.

The American black bear's diet is similar to the brown bear's but it is more markedly herbivorous. Depending on the season and the environment, plant matter forms between 85 and 98 per cent of its diet. During the spring (April – May) American black

The American black bear (*Ursus americanus*) is the most widespread and best known bear in North America. In the presence of grizzlies, larger members of its own species or even man it does not hesitate to take refuge in a tree.

Like the majority of bears, the American black bear is a highly adaptable omnivore. Its diet includes fruit, nuts, acorns, and sometimes small mammals or even carrion.

The American black bear has several color variants. Frequently these are found in particular parts of the bear's range.

bears feed mainly on grasses. In June they add insects to their diet, and in the fall their main sources of food are berries, beechmast, and acorns. They also readily eat mushrooms. As in other bear species, fall is a critical period as far as nutrition is concerned, in that sufficient reserves of fat must be built up for the winter. This is particularly important for those females which are going to be suckling young during the winter retreat.

American black bears are normally highly adaptable and for the month or so during the summer when the salmon swim up certain rivers in Alaska and Canada to deposit their eggs, the bears of the Pacific coastal regions gather along the rivers to fish. Occasionally they will take small domestic animals, such as sheep, goats, pigs hens, ducks, and turkeys. However, as they are attracted to carrion they are often unjustly blamed for killing animals.

Like the brown bear, the American black bear hibernates for between five and seven months each year. The preferred site for a winter den, if it is available, is a hollow in a tree; it has been calculated that compared to a cave, an optimum tree hollow enables a bear to make a saving of about 15 per cent in thermal energy. During hibernation the American black bear's body temperature falls to 12½°F (7°C) below normal and the frequency of its heartbeat falls to almost a quarter of normal. As with the brown bear, the females hibernate for longer. They retire earlier in the fall and they leave their dens later in the spring.

The American black bear's mating season is usually in June and July. The gestation period lasts about 220 days and the young are born in January or February in the mother's winter den. At birth the cubs are blind and deaf and their fur is sparse. Like brown bear cubs, they are very small, weighing only 7 – 10½ oz (200 – 300 g). However, they begin to grow rapidly on a diet composed exclusively of mother's milk. After the young have abandoned the winter den with their mother, they begin to feed on solid matter and their mother's milk becomes of less and less importance to them as a source of food. However, there have been occasional observations of the young bears continuing to suckle from time to time when they are over a year old.

In several of the North American national parks certain American black bears have lost almost all their fear of man and have started to beg for titbits from tourists at the roadside. Sometimes impatient animals try to grab the baskets of food, on other occasions individual bears may become demanding once food has run out. This can lead to serious accidents. Measures have been taken in all areas to prevent food being offered to bears and to caution tourists.

▲ Along the salmon rivers of Canada and southeastern Alaska, some American black bears, like brown bears, spend more than a month fishing.

▲ The American black bear's behavior is the result of experience. It must learn which animals are easy prey. The Canada porcupine (*Erethizon dorsatum*), for example, is an easy prey but its quills can cost an inexpert bear its life.

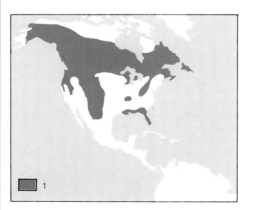

▲ American black bears hibernate in natural dens or in ones which they themselves dig. They prefer to use hollows in trees. The young are born in the winter den.

◀ 1) Present range of the American black bear.

POLAR BEAR
Ursus maritimus

Order Carnivora
Family Ursidae
Size Head and body length 48 – 60 in (120 – 150 cm); length of tail 3 – 5 in (8 – 12 cm); height at shoulder 48 – 55 in (120 – 140 cm)
Weight 330 – 1,100 lb (150 – 500 kg)
Dentition $\dfrac{3.1.4.2}{3.1.4.3} = 42$
N.B. 1 – 3 of the small premolars are often missing
Reproductive period From March to May, principally April
Gestation 7 – 8 months
Number of young 2 (more rarely 1 or 3)
Sexual maturity From 4 to 5 years
Maximum age 25 – 30 years

Although some races of the brown bear match the polar bear in size, it is, on average, the largest of the bears and therefore the largest of the Carnivora. Besides its size, its most prominent feature is the color of its coat. This ranges from yellowish to pure white. Its fur is very thick and long, and it provides an excellent protection against the cold.

The polar bear is a semi-aquatic animal and its way of life is closely tied to the sea. It is present throughout the Arctic Ocean and along the neighboring coasts, though its frequency does vary. A sighting of a mother with young has been recorded just 106 miles (170 km) away from the Pole and the species extends as far south as James Bay (the southern tip of Hudson Bay, Canada) and, occasionally, the northern coastal zone of Newfoundland. Polar bears are only found where the sea freezes during the winter. In the summer they move northward, following the limit of the drift ice, and in the winter they move southward, following the zones of open water in the fissures between the ice floes.

The polar bear has secondarily evolved back into being almost exclusively carnivorous, while its ancestors, which were similar to the brown bears, were to a large extent adapted to a diet of plant matter. Seals make up over 90 per cent of its diet.

Polar bears are strong but slow swimmers and their maximum time of submersion is about two minutes, whereas the seals, their prey, can

The polar bear (*Ursus maritimus*) is, on average, the largest of the eight species of bear. Its long thick fur provides it with excellent protection against the cold and in fact at temperatures of 50-60° F (10-15° C) the polar bear begins to feel the heat and searches for shade. It is camouflaged by the white color of its coat and this enables it to approach seals unseen.

remain underwater from 20 – 30 minutes. Therefore they cannot catch their prey while it is swimming. Instead they manage to surprise it on the ice or ambush it when it comes up to breathe at the holes in the ice. The polar bear approaches its prey with the stealth of a cat. As it closes in, it uses the cover provided by blocks of ice and then with a couple of rapid, powerful bounds it covers the last dozen yards and cuts off the seal's retreat to the water. When a polar bear attacks from the water, it swims almost totally submerged, with just its snout above water. It submerges completely for the last few yards and then leaps straight out of the sea on to the ice where the seal is sunning itself. The polar bear's favorite method, however, is to lie in wait for seals by the holes in the ice which they use for breathing.

Polar bears will even eat carrion. During the summer some also eat some plant matter. Those living along the coastline of the Arctic mainland and on the islands eat grasses, sedges, and berries, rather as brown bears do. They will also eat seaweed thrown up on the shore by the waves and have even been observed plunging into the water to gather it. They raid the nests of bird colonies, take mallard, and occasionally kill musk ox (*Ovibos moschatus*) and reindeer (*Rangifer* sp.).

Only pregnant females and sometimes those with young from the year before spend the winter in true hibernation. The males, on the other hand, are active throughout the winter and it is only during storms that they dig a temporary burrow into an ice hillock. Even then they may simply remain in one place for several days, allowing themselves to be covered by the snow. Adult polar bears are solitary and if two should chance to meet while out hunting, they will maintain a safe distance of 50 – 100 yards (meters). Fights occur only rarely.

The polar bear's mating season begins about the middle of April. The male remains in the female's company for a few days and then wanders off on his own again. It is not until October or November, when the expanses of open water begin to be covered with fresh ice, that the female heads for dry land in order to dig her winter den in a crevice in the snow. The young are born at the end of December or the beginning of January. Often there are two cubs in the litter, sometimes there is just one and exceptionally there are three.

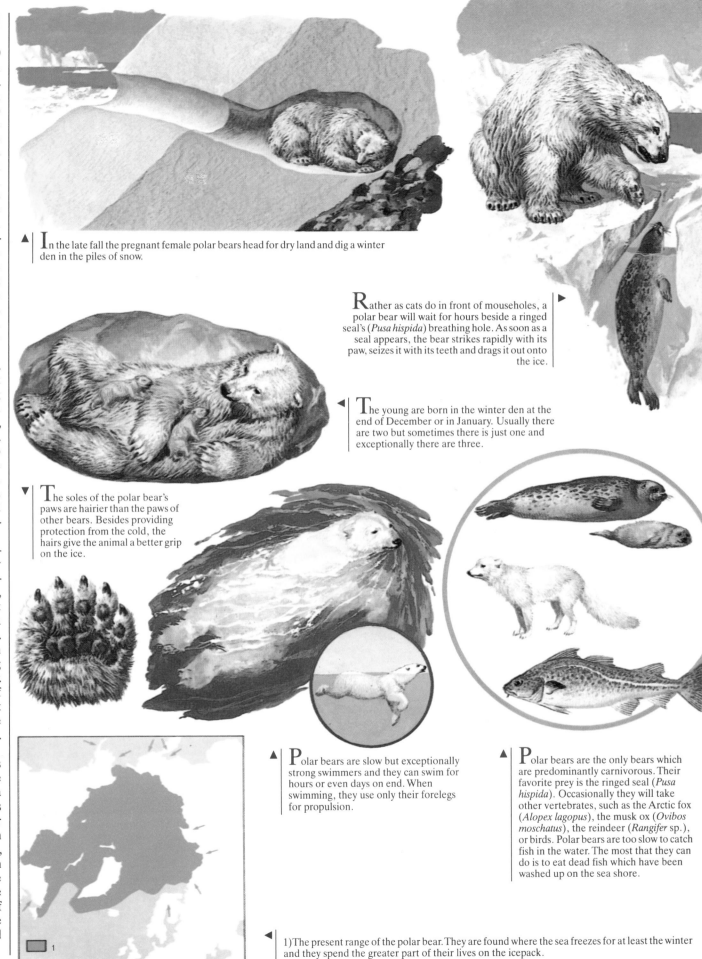

▲ In the late fall the pregnant female polar bears head for dry land and dig a winter den in the piles of snow.

▶ Rather as cats do in front of mouseholes, a polar bear will wait for hours beside a ringed seal's (*Pusa hispida*) breathing hole. As soon as a seal appears, the bear strikes rapidly with its paw, seizes it with its teeth and drags it out onto the ice.

◀ The young are born in the winter den at the end of December or in January. Usually there are two but sometimes there is just one and exceptionally there are three.

▼ The soles of the polar bear's paws are hairier than the paws of other bears. Besides providing protection from the cold, the hairs give the animal a better grip on the ice.

▲ Polar bears are slow but exceptionally strong swimmers and they can swim for hours or even days on end. When swimming, they use only their forelegs for propulsion.

▲ Polar bears are the only bears which are predominantly carnivorous. Their favorite prey is the ringed seal (*Pusa hispida*). Occasionally they will take other vertebrates, such as the Arctic fox (*Alopex lagopus*), the musk ox (*Ovibos moschatus*), the reindeer (*Rangifer* sp.), or birds. Polar bears are too slow to catch fish in the water. The most that they can do is to eat dead fish which have been washed up on the sea shore.

◀ 1) The present range of the polar bear. They are found where the sea freezes for at least the winter and they spend the greater part of their lives on the icepack.

GIANT PANDA

Ailuropoda melanoleuca

Order Carnivora
Family Ursidae
Size Length of head and body, about 60 in (150 cm); length of tail, about 6 in (15 cm); height at shoulder, about 25 in (65 cm)
Weight 154 – 265 lb (70 – 120 kg)
Dentition $\frac{3.1.4.2}{3.1.3.3.}$ = 40

N.B. The first upper premolar is often missing
Number of young 1
Maximum age 15 years in captivity

The giant panda is a medium-sized and very stout bear. It has thick fur and a striking pattern of coloration. The ears, a patch around each eye, the forelimbs and parts of the chest and back between them, and the hindlimbs are black. The head and the pelvic region are white with occasional yellowish, brownish, or reddish patches. This pattern stands out against the uniform background of a zoo cage but it blends in well with the mosaic of light and shade of its natural habitat of bamboo thickets and the leaf-covered boughs of trees. The color contrasts between the different parts of the body have a camouflaging effect by breaking up the body's shape, in much the same way as do those of the tiger (*Panthera tigris*) or the leopard (*Panthera pardus*).

The giant panda's chewing teeth (molars) are more powerful than those of any other member of the order Carnivora; an indication of the importance of plant matter in its diet. As well as its dentition, its forelimbs display adaptations to its feeding habits. A greatly enlarged sesamoid bone forms a swelling (grasping pad) opposed to the five digits, which acts as a thumb does in grasping objects.

Western science only learned of the giant panda's existence in 1869. Its discoverer, A. David, placed it among the bears. Later, certain morphological peculiarities, in particular its dentition, led most authors to regard it as the longest of the raccoons (Procyonidae). It is only very recently, with the help of modern methods, that its blood, its anatomy, and the internal structure of its teeth have been more carefully investigated. The results of all these investigations lead to the

The giant panda (*Ailuropoda melanoleuca*) is a heavily built, medium-sized bear with thick fur and a striking black and white coloration. Today it is found only in a relatively small area of southwestern China. It was discovered in 1869. The first time that one was captured alive was in the course of the first German expedition to Tibet of 1913-15. In 1937, New York Zoo became the first western zoo to obtain a living specimen of this animal. Very few giant pandas have ever been held in the West. The case of "Chi-Chi," London Zoo's female giant panda, became famous as a result of worldwide publicity concerning her refusal to mate with "An-An," Moscow Zoo's male. "Chi-Chi" later died at the considerable age of 15 without ever having given birth. However, in Peking (Beijing in Pinyin) zoo pandas have been successfully bred since 1963. A whole group of giant pandas has been bred in Peking Zoo (there were seven in 1975) and in the whole of China there were about 50 specimens in zoos. It was not by chance that the most active international animal protection organization, the World Wildlife Fund (WWF), chose the giant panda as its emblem. Quite apart from the fact that the small size of its distribution area means that its numbers are limited and that its survival is, at least potentially, threatened, it is a darling of the public: a position which it owes to its round, shortened head, which gives it an appealing resemblance to a teddy bear, its striking coloration, and its comic movements.

conclusion that the giant panda is a highly specialized bear which diverged from the main bear stock some thirteen million years ago. The similarities between its dentition and that of the Red Panda *(Ailurus fulgens)*, family Procyonidae can be explained by a process of parallel evolution due to a similar diet.

The giant panda is confined to a few mountainous areas of southwestern China. Because it is solitary and inhabits dense vegetation, it easily escapes observation by man. There are only isolated and, at times, contradictory observations on its way of life and most of these have come from hunters. The presence of giant pandas in a valley is often betrayed by their low, winding, tunnel-like paths. These paths are frequently used by other animals living in the same habitat, including Asiatic black bears *(Ursus thibetanus)* leopards *(Panthera pardus)*, takin *(Budorcas taxicolor)*, and wild pigs *(Sus* sp.). One can often come across piles of the giant panda's dung and these give an indication of its main food – the stems and young shoots of bamboo up to the thickness of a human finger. It also eats other plant matter (e.g. roots) and, when able to catch them, it is not averse to animals. In fact, the giant panda occasionally eats birds, snakes, and bamboo rats *(Rhizomys* sp.).

In captivity they have been observed marking their "territory" with urine and rubbing their anal-genital region against suitable objects. This marking is carried out by both the males and the females but more frequently by the former (in the case of a pair in captivity, the male marked the territory fourteen times more often than the female). Females have been observed to mark more frequently before and during estrus, suggesting that in the wild this behavior is connected with reproduction (identification of the sexes).

Examples in captivity have shown increased activity between ten at night and two in the morning, from which it is possible to conclude that giant pandas are mainly nocturnal. However, less rigorous observations carried out on a young pair in Paris Zoo revealed very little nocturnal activity. Up to what point giant pandas in the wild spend a period in hibernation is still the subject of discussion. It is highly likely that they reduce their activity considerably and retire into caves. On the other hand, giant panda tracks have been repeatedly seen during the winter in the snow.

▲ The giant panda is a mountain animal which prefers the ravines and valleys at altitudes of 6,500-11,500 ft (2,00-3,500 m), where a cool, humid, and misty climate prevails. The dense undergrowth of bamboo, which makes the open, subalpine conifer forests virtually impenetrable, provides it with both food and protection. Sometimes – but not frequently as happens with the Asiatic black bear – the giant panda ventures into the inhabited regions of the valleys and causes damage to the crops. The giant panda's natural enemy is the wild dog *(Cuon alpinus)* which may account for the fact that it is relatively easy to hunt the giant panda with dogs. In the presence of dogs, young pandas seek refuge by climbing trees, while larger individuals sometimes stand their ground and do not allow themselves to be pushed out of the protective tangle of plants. Giant pandas seek out the forks of large branches as resting places. Stories of pandas covering their eyes with their paws, curling up into a ball, and allowing themselves to roll down slopes when pursued, as is believed to happen in other species of bear, must be relegated to the realm of myth.

▲ About a million years ago, during the Ice Age, the giant panda was found throughout a vast area of Southeast Asia, together with the stegodon, which closely resembled the elephant, the orang-utan *(Pongo pygmaeus)*, and the tapir *(Tapirus* sp.). Today it is present in only a small sector, but this does not mean that it is a primitive form; it is, on the contrary, a highly advanced and specialized species and not a living fossil.

◀ The giant panda is mainly, though not exclusively, herbivorous. As well as bamboo shoots it eats the shoots, leaves, tubers, roots, fruits, and flowers of a whole range of other plants.

COATI

Nasua narica

Order Carnivora
Family Procyonidae
Size Length 30 – 53 in (74 – 134 cm)
Weight 6½ – 13 lb (3 – 6 kg)
Dentition $\frac{3.1.4.2}{3.1.4.2} = 40$
Reproductive period Around March
Gestation 74 days
Number of young 2 – 7
Sexual maturity Males at 2 years

The genus *Nasua* contains the following species: the whitenosed coati (*Nasua narica*), which occurs from the southwestern United States south to western Colombia and western Ecuador; the red coati (*Nasua nasua*), present in almost all the forest areas of South America; and Nelson's coati (*Nasua nelsoni*), which is found only on the island of Cozumel off the Yucatan.

All the coatis have a mobile, highly elongated nose which projects beyond the tip of the mandible almost like a trunk. The tail is long and is usually held straight, at right angles to the body. The head is elongated and the ears are short and rounded. The fur is short on the head and limbs but becomes shaggy and rough on the body. The tail fur is woolly. The coloration is highly variable, ranging from reddish to gray. A single individual will often change color considerably at the molt. The whitenosed coati has white lips and a pale band runs along the snout from the eyes. The limbs of all coatis are covered in dark fur and the paws are bare. The digits are joined together up to the last phalange and they end in long, robust claws. Depending on the species, the tail tends to have a more or less distinct pattern of rings.

The basic social unit among coatis is the mother together with her young up to two years of age. At the age of two the males leave the groups of females and disperse singly, establishing themselves in home ranges which are more or less adjacent to the home ranges of the group of females which they have left. Within the family territories of the various groups of females, there will be one area in each territory where the activity of the entire group will be concentrated.

The coatis are procyonids which are distinguished by a mobile and elongated nose. It is this feature which earned them their scientific name, *Nasua*, from the Latin *nasus*. Unlike the other members of their family, which prefer to lead a nocturnal life, the coatis are mainly active by day. They live in forest habitats and are good tree climbers. The species illustrated here is the whitenosed coati (*Nasua narica*). The inset shows the head of a red coati (*Nasua nasua*).

The coati's diet consists of reptiles, earthworms, insect larvae, other invertebrates, fruit, roots, and even rodents.

A typical posture of the coati while searching for food. Unlike the raccoons, coatis hunt for food both on the ground and in the trees. They dig into the ground with the claws on their front paws to get at insects and roots. They can also insert their long snout into holes and use it to nose out food. Rodents and lizards are dislodged by removing the material under which they are sheltering. Once dislodged, they are chased, possibly even by several coatis in a group. Occasionally they also kill birds. They have a distinctive way of killing animals which they have caught. If it is an invertebrate, they roll it with their forepaws against a hard surface (in this way, if, for example, they are dealing with an insect, they avoid being pricked or injured) and at the same time they kill it by smashing its chitinous shell. They catch vertebrates by pinning them to the ground with their forelimbs and then killing them with a bite to the head. They eat fruits in abundance; if large they strip the flesh off, using the claws of their forelegs, otherwise they are eaten whole. Coatis have even been seen catching crabs near to watercourses or preying on small agoutis. They have also been observed breaking through the shell of an egg with small bites and then licking it clean, without losing a drop.

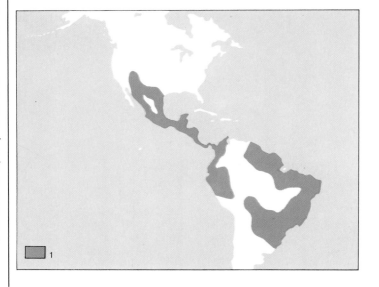

1) The distribution area of the coatis (genus *Nasua*).

KINKAJOU
Potos flavus

Order Carnivora
Family Procyonidae
Size Length 32 – 40 in (81 – 103 cm)
Dentition $\frac{3.1.3.2}{3.1.3.2} = 36$
Reproductive period Fall
Number of young 1 – 2
Sexual maturity Males at 18 months; females at 27 months
Maximum age 23 years in captivity; 19 years in the wild

The kinkajou occurs in Central and South America from Southern Mexico to the Mato Grosso. Its prehensile tail, almost as long as the rest of the body, is covered in sparse fur and round in cross section, tapering toward its tip. The limbs are short and strong. Their digits are connected together by a membrane which extends up to a third of the way along them. The claws are curved and sharp. The kinkajou is a plantigrade animal.

Breeding does not take place in any specific part of the year. At the approach of a male, a female on heat gives a distinctive cry. The female has only two nipples and after a gestation period of about 115 days she gives birth to either one or two young. These weigh about 6¾ oz (190 g) and measure about 12 in (30 cm) in length. They are covered in a very soft, silver down which is very sparse on the abdomen. The auditory passages usually open by five days while the eyes open at between 7 – 21 days. The tail becomes completely prehensile between the second and third month. The young kinkajous begin to eat solids at between 54 – 91 days. Weaning takes place at four months and by this stage the young are virtually self-sufficient.

There is almost no information available on the kinkajou's diet in the wild. Observations on animals in captivity suggest a largely insectivorous and fruit-eating diet. It does not appear to be a particularly predatory species. Its tongue can reach 5 in (12 cm) in length and is fully extendable. This enables it to remove the flesh from the fruits on which it feeds, to capture insects, either in flight or in their nests or even to extract honey from hives. It holds the food and manipulates it with its forelimbs.

The kinkajou (*Potos flavus*) is a markedly arboreal and nocturnal Procyonid. In captivity it will remain motionless throughout the day despite the noise of the public, while at night it is very active. In the wild, kinkajous occupy the same habitat by night as the *Cebus* monkey do by day. During the day they retire into a hollow in a tree or shelter in its thick foliage, covering their eyes with their forelegs. When they wake at dusk they stretch in a distinctive fashion. First they extend their arms, then they yawn and put out their tongue and, while seated, simultaneously arch their body and bring their tails round in front of their legs.

The kinkajou's diet consists of fruit, eggs, and insects.

The kinkajou has a long, extensible tongue which it uses for catching insects or extracting the flesh from fruits.

1) The kinkajou lives in the tropical forests of Central and South America.

Together with the binturong, the kinkajou is the only carnivore to have a prehensile tail. A mother may use her tail to keep her young close to her. The Procyonid moves through the trees with great ability but without ever performing what one might call acrobatics. When climbing up or down branches it always keeps its tail wrapped around the body until its feet have found a new spot to rest. It also uses its tail to help keep its balance as it roves along thin branches or lianas. It appears that fruits hanging from the branches of a tree exert a strong attraction on kinkajous. They head straight for the fruit and there will often be groups of a dozen individuals on the same plant. The individuals in such groups are all shrieking and whistling together. They grip the fruit with their forepaws and after having sniffed it they begin to eat it. Kinkajous may assume an infinite variety of positions while eating. They will even hang head downward with the fruit in their forepaws and hold on to a liana by their tail and hindlegs.

RACCOON
Procyon lotor

Order Carnivora
Family Procyonidae
Size Length 24 – 39 in (61 – 100 cm)
Dentition $\frac{3.1.4.2}{3.1.4.2} = 40$
Reproductive period January – June
Gestation 63 – 65 days
Number of young 1 – 7
Sexual maturity Male at two years, females at one

The raccoon is found from southern Canada to Central America. It has a rather stout appearance and resembles, in general form, a small bear. It has a broad head and a pointed snout; the ears are large and rounded; the limbs are rather long and are covered in short fur and the forepaws have five well separated and extremely mobile digits. This arrangement gives the raccoon a great deal of feeling in its forepaws and this is essential for a species which literally searches out crustaceans and other prey with its "hands." On the body the coat is grayish with shading that varies from yellowish to reddish chestnut, depending on the individual. The underparts are pale. The face is covered in short fur and has a distinctive dark mask which passes from one cheek to the other through the eyes. The tail is thick and has five to seven dark transverse rings on a grayish background.

Raccoons generally prefer to raise their young in hollows in trees. However, during the exploratory phase, when the young begin to emerge, there is always the chance that one will fall to the ground and be left there injured or that one will be unable to get back to the lair again. By moving to the ground, these risks are greatly reduced.

At about 60 days the young begin to eat solid foods. When the babies accompany their mother she keeps the group as close together as possible, emitting high-pitched cries at regular intervals. By about four months the young are fully weaned. During the fall the young become independent and are able to establish their own individual territories. This involves them in long journeys, often of the order of 25 miles (40 km) away from the area in which they where born. In a typical habitat in the northern

The raccoon (*Procyon lotor*) lives in wooded areas with plenty of water and its range extends from southern Canada to Central America. It does not extend above 8,200 ft (2,500 m) and it usually avoids conifer woods.

The raccoon, like the other members of the Procyonidae, has the typical forelimbs of a good tree climber. It also uses them for digging into the ground in search of worms or turning over stones and rubbish in search of insects. Typically, however, its diet consists of animals living in water. Even so, animals rarely make up 50% of the food intake of the raccoon and when they do it is only for short periods of the year. In the fall fruit forms 80% of the diet while in the winter the raccoon feeds mainly on plant matter, particularly acorns and, where possible, maize. In the spring it adds insects and amphibians, tortoise eggs, birds and rabbits. It does not appear to take carrion. Raccoons move at a trot with the head held low, the back slightly arched and the tail held downward. They are capable of reaching 15 mph (24 kmh). The raccoon has considerable economic importance both because of its highly prized pelt and because it is an animal which is hunted as game. In America raccoon hunting is an extremely popular sport. Specially bred dogs are used either to trap the raccoon up a tree or to pursue it into the water. In the water, however, the raccoon quite often manages to drown these dogs by going for their head. Its flesh is also very highly esteemed.

United States the density of raccoons can be up to eighteen individuals per square mile (seven per square kilometer).

Raccoons have an inactive phase during the winter when they retire into their lairs. They begin to become inactive when the temperature falls to around 25°F (–4°C) and in particularly harsh weather conditions they may remain in a deep sleep in their lairs for weeks on end, without taking any food. However, this is not true hibernation as there is no slowing down of their basal metabolism and their body temperature does not fall. At the slightest noise or alarm, "hibernating" raccoons are immediately able to defend themselves. Frequently several raccoons may be found together in the same lair.

In warmer weather the animals are active by night and spend the day in burrows or shelters. These may often be occupied by two individuals, presumably siblings. The abundance and distribution of these shelters seems to be determined by the distribution of the raccoon population itself. Hollows in trees are much the most popular sites but the choice does not appear to be influenced by the nearness of water or particular sources of food. The most important criterion seems to be whether or not the site is well protected. The extent of an individual's home range is highly variable and depends mainly on the degree of protection offered by the area in question and on the availability of food. So, for example, home ranges with diameters of 1 mile (1.6 km) for males and slightly less for females have been recorded, whereas in other cases home ranges of not less than 1¾ miles (3 km) in diameter have been recorded for females.

The mating season begins immediately after the end of the raccoon's winter phase. According to some zoologists, the male and the female separate after mating and the male may mate successively with two or three different females.

The specific name *lotor* (the washer) was given to the raccoon because specimens in captivity always immerse their food in water. Lyall-Watson has discovered that captive raccoons do this as a substitute for fishing. Some authors hold that this habit, which tends to recreate the conditions in the wild, also has a crucial effect on the raccoon's urge to eat.

▲ The raccoon is an extremely adaptable animal. Once used to the presence of man, it will readily move into urban areas, often causing a number of sanitary problems as well as much damage to crops.

Raccoons prefer shelters in trees. ▶

▲ Typically the raccoon does not hunt its prey but searches for it by sifting through the beds of rivers or other expanses of water.

▼ Typical postures of the raccoon. 1) When walking it holds its head down, its back slightly arched and its tail angled downward. 2) When searching for food it sieves the water with its forepaws, which are as sensitive as the hands of a human. 3) It climbs trees. 4) Before beginning to eat its prey it sniffs it. 5) The mother carries the young by seizing them by the neck. 6) It rests astride branches. 7) It suckles its young in a sitting position.

SKUNK

Mephitis mephitis

Order Carnivora
Family Mustelidae
Size Length of head and body
13 – 18 in (33 – 45 cm); length of tail 7
– 10 in (18 – 25 cm); length of hindpaw
2¾ – 3 in (8 cm)
Weight 6 – 10 lb (2.7 – 4.5 kg)
Dentition $\frac{3.1.3.1}{3.1.3.2} = 34$

Gestation 63 days
Number of young 5 or 6, up to 10
Maximum age 8 – 10 years

The skunk is of medium size for a member of the weasel family. It is elegantly shaped, with a thickset, robust body, a small, elongated head, a pointed snout, small, rounded ear pavilions, small eyes, a rather long tail and short limbs, bearing strong claws. There are highly developed anal glands whose foul-smelling secretion can be squirted an appreciable distance. The skunk can do this at will by contracting certain muscles. The body is covered in a soft, thick fur, which is very long, especially on the back and on the tail. The coat is mainly glossy black with a white pattern.

The skunk, like all the other representatives of the sub-family Mephitinae, is exclusively a New World species, being found from southern Canada to northern Mexico. It frequents prairies with varying amounts of bush, sparse scrub, forest habitats, though it avoids dense forests, cultivated land, deserts and rocky areas and both lowlands and mountains. It is not uncommon for it to come close to inhabited areas, even venturing into the outer zones of large towns. It is a gregarious animal with a very docile temperament. It is normally active by night, spending the day in one of its lairs. Using its strong claws, it will dig a fairly deep burrow in the ground but more frequently it uses the burrow of another species, such as a rabbit, fox, or badger, etc.

The skunk walks rather awkwardly, keeping its back slightly arched and its tail erect. With the onset of evening it abandons its lair and slowly wanders off in search of food, which it detects by means of its fine sense of smell. It is omnivorous and its diet varies from season to season. Among edible plant matter it shows a marked preference

▲ The skunk (*Mephitis mephitis*) is characterized by its stout, heavily built body and its long thick tail. It lives primarily in bush and grassland, extending up to the edges of villages and towns, but generally avoiding thick woods. It is nocturnal and spends the day in underground lairs.

▶ It is omnivorous and its diet consists of various plants, eggs, insects and their larvae, and small vertebrates, including rodents, which form its major food source.

for fruit. It will search for this in cultivated areas but it inflicts damage on
the crops as it is unable to climb plants
and it has to confine itself to fruit that
has fallen to the ground. It feeds on a
wide variety of vertebrate and invertebrate animals up to the size of a rabbit. It is even able to detect prey, such
as insects and their larvae, earthworms and nestfuls of mice, beneath
the ground.

The skunk displays what is known as
phaneric mimicry, in which a highly
conspicuous coat pattern and coloration is associated with the emission of
foul-smelling substances by the anal
glands as a method of defense. It is a
special adaptation against attacks by
other carnivorous animals and the
striking black and white pattern of the
coat which makes the skunk very conspicuous acts as a warning. When disturbed, the skunk goes through an
elaborate aggressive sequence, which
is intended to focus as effectively as
possible the attention of the animal
which is menacing the skunk on the latter's warning signs, before it resorts to
its defensive weapon. As a sign of
threat it turns its hindquarters towards
the aggressor and, holding its tail erect
and ruffled, drums its hind paws on the
ground. Generally this is sufficient to
make the predator back off but if it
does not, the skunk turns its head,
starts to snort, and discharges the
secretion of its anal glands.

The mating season takes place in
February and March. The young are
born in May or June in a nest which the
mother has prepared, after a gestation
period of about 63 days. The young
number five or six, although exceptionally there are as many as ten, and
they are blind and naked. They are,
however, easily recognizable as they
already bear the skin patterns which
characterize this species. They are
completely dependent on their mother
during the first stage of their life and
she looks after them and protects them
lovingly. By 20 days the young skunks
are already covered in fur and they
open their eyes before 30 days. Suckling continues for about two months
but by about 45 – 50 days, which is
before they are weaned, they are able
to walk and to leave the burrow and
follow their mother.

▲ The skunk does not allow itself to be frightened by other predators.
When confronted by them it assumes a threatening posture in which it
raises its tail and displays its hindquarters, including its highly
developed anal pouches.

▲ Position of the
skunk's anal
pouches.

▲ If this warning is not
sufficient to drive its foe
away, the skunk rises up on its
forelegs and squirts, with
great accuracy, a nauseous
liquid at the face of its
attacker over distances of up
to 10-13 ft (3-4 m).

▲ The skunk's most dangerous enemies are birds of prey and owls,
who are not in the least intimidated by the foul-smelling secretion.

▲ 1) The long-tailed skunk (*Mephitis macroura*). 2) The
spotted skunk (*Spilogale putorius*). The hog-nosed skunk
(*Conepatus leuconotus*).

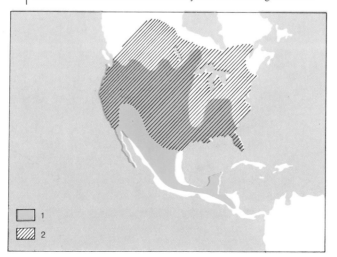

1
2

◀ The range of the skunk extends from southern Canada to northern
Mexico. (1), while the spotted skunk occurs as far south as Costa
Rica (2).

SEA OTTER

Enhydra lutris

Order Carnivora
Family Mustelidae
Size Length of head and body
47 – 54 in (120 – 150 cm); length of tail
10 – 15 in (25 – 37 cm)
Weight Males, 49 – 84 lb (22 – 38 kg);
females, 33 – 66 lb (15 – 30 kg)
Dentition $\frac{3.1.3.1}{3.1.3.2}$ = 32

Reproductive period All year round
Sexual maturity Not before three
years
Gestation 8 – 9 months
Number of young 1

The sea otter, like all the other species, is perfectly adapted in the overall build of its body to an aquatic life. It is more heavily built than other otters. Its head is broad and rounded, its neck is short and its trunk is cylindrical. The tail is short in relation to the length of its body and tends to be wedge-shaped and dorso-ventrally flattened. The coat is thick and soft and it consists of the extremely dense and soft under fur and the longer relatively stiff guard hairs. The coat has an extremely important function as the sea otter lacks the thick layer of subcutaneous fat which protects the bodies of other marine mammals from the cold of the water.

The range of the sea otter once extended along almost the whole of the coastline, together with the islands, of the northern Pacific Ocean, from the Kuril islands to Kamchatka, from the Aleutian islands to the Pribilof islands as well as others in the Bering Sea and from Alaska to southern California. It is now only found over about a fifth of its original range. Specifically, it is still present in certain areas of California, western Alaska, the Kamchatka Peninsula, and the Komandorskiye and Aleutian Islands.

The sea otter is strictly tied to a marine environment and frequents coastal waters, among the banks of floating seaweed. It is generally found in water that is between 10 – 65 ft (3 – 20m) deep but occasionally it ventures out into deep water. It carries out all its activities in the water and only comes on to dry land to give birth or when the sea is particularly rough. When it does, it always stays close to the shore, venturing only a few hundred yards (meters) inland at most. The sea otter

The sea otter (*Enhydra lutris*) is the most highly adapted of the Mustelids to an aquatic way of life, and it spends a large part of its time in the water. When the conditions of the sea permit, it will venture quite a way from the coast, but otherwise it stays close to the shore. It feeds on sea urchins, mollusks, crustaceans and fish. Occasionally it also eats seaweed.

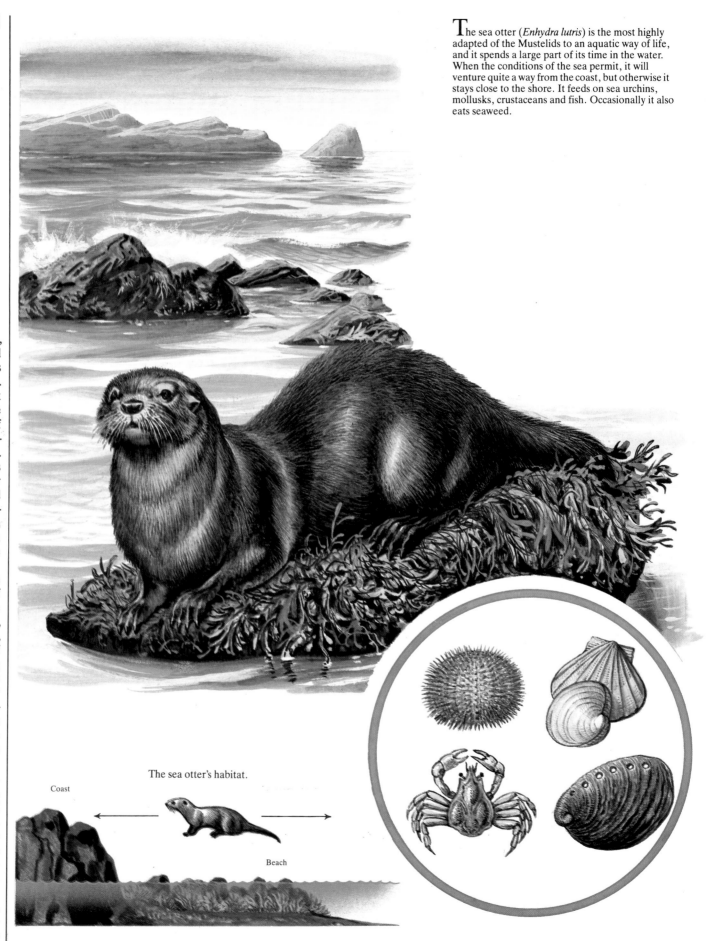

The sea otter's habitat.

Coast

Beach

is the only Fissipeda carnivore to live in the sea and it is by far the most highly adapted to an aquatic life, spending almost its entire existence in the water. It is of a lively, sociable disposition and where it has not been disturbed it shows itself to be very trusting and will even approach humans.

The sea otter has an almost exclusively carnivorous diet. It feeds off benthic marine animals which it catches on the seabed. Seaweed is eaten only accidentally. Sea urchins make up over half its food and molluscks make up almost a quarter. The remainder consists of crustaceans and fish. The stiff, tactile vibrissae on the snout and the tactile receptors on the forepaws help it to detect prey under water and so it is able to fish even in turbid waters. When searching for food it will dive as deep as 165 − 200 ft (50−60 m) at most, and it remains submerged for a few minutes. Once it has caught its prey it rises to the surface holding it closely against its chest with its forelimbs. If the dive has been particularly successful, it may surface with several animals. These are held in the folds of skin on the chest. The sea otter needs to eat a large amount of food and it is calculated that its daily intake is at least a fifth of its own weight.

The sea otter is one of the few animals capable of manipulating a tool. It uses a stone to remove shells from the rocks, wielding it like a hammer. Equally characteristic is the technique used to break gastropod shells or the calcareous plates of the dermoskeletons of sea urchins. Along with its prey, it picks up a flat stone off the bottom and carries it to the surface. It then swims on its back, positions the stone on its chest and uses it as an anvil on which to beat the shell, which it holds in its forepaws, until it breaks. Although this may appear odd, the instinctive use of a tool is not common to all sea otter populations, as this behavior has never been observed among otters of the Komandorskiye Islands. On the other hand, the sea otter does not necessarily have to use a tool to break open a sea urchin or the shell of a bivalve or gastropod, as its molar teeth have very broad crowns and are adapted to grinding. Where the shell is particularly robust and cannot be broken by any means, the otter will try, sometimes successfully, to extract the body of the mollusk and can be quite skillful at this.

▼ It swims under water with an undulating movement of the body. Every so often it assumes an almost vertical position and the forepart of its body emerges from the water.

▲ On the surface it swims on its back by making slight movements with its tail. It is in this position that it eats the animals which it has caught.

▲ During the summer it is not uncommon for it to spend the night in the water among the piles of seaweed.

▲ It rests a stone on its chest and uses it as an anvil on which to shatter the shells of its prey with its forepaws.

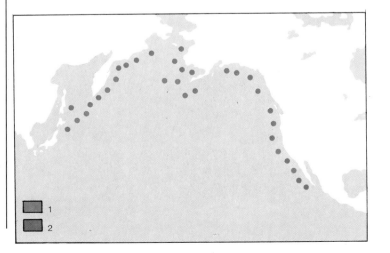

1
2

◀ It was once numerous along the coasts and islands of the North Pacific, but because of the considerable commercial value of its coat the sea otter was subjected to such intense hunting that by the beginning of this century it was believed to be extinct. Only a small number of individuals were then surviving but the protective measures which were adopted have allowed its population to increase gradually but appreciably.
1) Present range. 2) Original range.

MONGOOSES

Order Carnivora
Family Viverridae
Size Length about 13 – 43 in
(32 – 100 cm)
Weight 1½ – 7 lb (0.68 – 3.2 kg)
Dentition $\dfrac{3.1.3(4).2}{3.1.3(4).2} = 36(40)$
Reproductive period Varies, depending
upon species
Gestation From 42 days to 12 weeks
Number of young Between 1 and 6

Currently, the term mongoose is applied to about 30 species of medium-sized carnivores referred to as the civet family (Viverridae). Their distribution covers southwestern Europe, Africa and the Middle East, India, Indochina, southern China, and the Greater Sunda Islands.

The claws are non-retractile. Many mongooses use their forepaws for digging but although the claws are narrow and are progressively worn away, they always remain sharp.

The Egyptian mongoose *(Herpestes ichneumon)* occurs throughout Africa apart from the Congo region, the forests of West Africa, and the Sahara. It also occurs in Spain and Palestine. It has been introduced into Madagascar and into Italy, in the area of Circeo. It measures 43 in (110 cm) in length and it weighs 3¼ – 7 lb (1.5 – 3.2 kg). The paws are short and their soles are hairless. The coat has a woolly texture and is dark yellow except for the tip of the tail and the paws, which are black. Its diet consists of anything which it can kill: mammals up to the size of a hare, birds up to the size of a duck, snakes, lizards, insects, and worms. It also eats fruit and eggs.

Herpestes aureopunctatus occurs from northern Arabia to Afghanistan, Nepal, Assam, Burma, Malaysia, Thailand, Pakistan, India, and Hainan. Its coat has a chestnut ground color but its yellow shading gives it the appearance of having been sprinkled with gold.

The banded mongoose *(Mungos mungo)* occurs in Africa from Portuguese Guinea to Nigeria, the Sudan and Somalia, and south to the Orange River. It measures 21 – 29 in (53 – 74 cm in length.

The dwarf mongoose *(Helogale parvula)* occurs from Ethiopia and Somalia south to the Orange River.

▲
◄ The Egyptian mongoose *(Herpestes ichneumon)*. Mongooses in general search for food in groups, digging and poking about in holes, etc. and keeping in constsnt vocal contact with one other. Their diet consists mainly of insects but it also includes snakes and other reptiles and invertebrates.

▼ A typical posture of the Egyptian mongoose as it walks.

Other mongoose species.

Herpestes aureopunctatus
(Small Indian mongoose)

Banded mongoose
(Mungos mungo)

Dwarf mongoose
(Helogale parvula)

SPOTTED HYENA

Crocuta crocuta

Order Carnivora
Family Hyaenidae
Size Overall length up to 67 in (1.7 m); length of tail 13 in (33 cm); height at shoulder 36 in (90 cm)
Weight Up to 175 lb (80 kg)
Dentition $\dfrac{3.1.3.1}{3.1.3.1} = 32$
Reproductive period Once per year
Gestation 100 – 110 days
Number of young Normally 2, exceptionally 3
Sexual maturity 2 years
Maximum age Up to 40 years in captivity

The spotted hyena has a wide distribution, which includes nearly all the woodlands, savannas, and grasslands of Africa south of the Sahara.

Spotted hyenas live in packs which may number 80 – 100 individuals. The pack assembles when a prey animal is killed, and also, in the daytime, in areas selected for rest and sleep.

Spotted hyenas are predators, like the lions and hunting-dogs with which they share the African savannas, and they feed largely on prey which they have themselves killed. The animals hunted vary greatly in size, from hares to gazelles or gnus. Often hyenas do not hesitate to attack the young of the rhinoceros or lion. They may also attack a man, though they will generally run away if he puts on a bold face.

When hunting herbivorous animals of medium size, a whole group of hyenas will collaborate in the task. There is, however, no specific allocation of different roles to the various individuals. The techniques employed vary according to the species being hunted. When the prey is killed, the hyenas announce the fact by uttering a highly distinctive cry – the famous "laugh" which rings through the night to summon the other hyenas to come to the feast.

Hyenas do also eat carrion, as most Carnivora do, whenever the opportunity offers. Because of their ability to bite through and break up even the most resistant parts of a dead animal, hyenas can derive nourishment from the last remains of a kill, which may consist only if its hide or its bones.

▲ The spotted hyena is the largest member of the Hyaenidae family. Contrary to what used to be believed, it lives mainly on prey which it kills itself, and not on carrion. It hunts principally at night, though it is not so exclusively nocturnal in its habits as the other hyenas. It can often be seen moving about, if not actually hunting, by day. It is undoubtedly active at sunrise and sunset. Up to a few years ago it had never been observed and studied with proper care, because of its largely nocturnal habits. Until that time the spotted hyena was generally believed to live on carrion – an idea based on inadequate observation of the animal's behavior by day. A true picture only emerged after a painstaking survey had been carried out over a period of several years in the Serengeti plains and the Ngorongoro crater by Hans Kruuk.

◄ Animals hunted by the hyena range from small mammals to the larger antelopes.

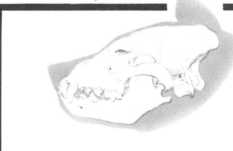

The hyena's jaws are specially adapted to produce an extraordinarily powerful bite. The huge teeth are designed for dismemberment rather than mastication. The jaws are so strong that the hyena can break the cannon-bone of a large ruminant with a single bite.

301

PUMA
Puma concolor

Order Carnivora
Family Felidae
Size Length of head and body 27 – 55 in (70 – 140 cm); length of tail 22 – 38 in (56 – 97 cm); height at shoulder 21 – 31 in (53 – 79 cm)
Weight 46 – 275 lb (21 – 125 kg)
Dentition $\dfrac{3.1.3.1}{3.1.2.1} = 30$

Reproductive period Not rigidly linked to the time of year, but more common in winter and spring
Gestation 84 – 106 days – commonly 94 days
Number of young 1 – 6 (average 3)
Sexual maturity 2 – 3 years
Maximum age 20 years

The puma is a big cat and (apart from its size) a perfect example of the basic feline type. It has spots only during the earliest part of its life.

As with many other mammals, the size of the puma varies with the climate. The smallest pumas are to be found mainly in the equatorial regions. The average size increases progressively toward both north and south, and the biggest pumas are to be found near the Straits of Magellan at the tip of South America, and in southern Canada, which is the most northerly part of the animal's range. A wide variety of coloration is to be noted. Red-brown and silver-gray specimens may be found side by side in the same region. Gray specimens are commonest in the southern parts of South America. The various shades from cinnamon to rust-red are at their brightest in the tropical regions, and take a duller form in the Andes and in the mountains of the west coast of the United States and Canada. The shorter-haired pumas of the tropical regions more often retain vestigial spots into adulthood; the long-haired pumas from the most northerly and southerly parts of the animal's range and from the mountains lose their spots completely.

Over much of its range, the main food of the puma consists of white-tailed deer and mule deer.

The tremendous strength of the puma is shown not only in its jumping ability, but also in the way it will drag heavy prey animals to a place of safety before eating them.

The puma is similar in size to the members of the panther group, but is not closely related to them. The puma is a good representative of the basic, original type of cat, without any specialized evolutionary adaptations.

The puma's wide geographical range has favored the emergence of several local races in different climatic conditions. The list of prey animals is a long one. Over most of its range, deer of medium size make the most important contribution. Larger deer, such as the wapiti and moose, play a secondary part, while other mammals of moderate size, such as hares, are also important.

LEOPARD

Panthera pardus

Order Carnivora
Family Felidae
Size Length of head and body 30 – 70 in (78 – 180 cm); length of tail 24 – 43 in (60 – 110 cm); height at shoulder 18 – 30 in (45 – 74 cm)
Weight 50 – 200 lb (23 – 90 kg)
Dentition $\frac{3.1.3.1}{3.1.2.1} = 30$
Reproductive period Not closely linked to time of year; winter or spring in northern regions
Gestation 90 – 105 days – average 96 days
Number of young 1 – 6 (average 2 – 3)
Sexual maturity 2 – 3 years
Maximum age 24 years

The leopard's markings, consisting of spots arranged in rings or rosettes, distinguish it from the other big cats.

There are races of giant leopard in Iran and West Africa and dwarf races in other areas, such as Somalia.

The leopard is very adaptable to differing habitats. This has enabled it to occupy a vast geographical territory. It is at present to be found in the whole of Africa except for the deserts in the north, in the Arabian peninsula, and in Asia Minor, spreading out through western and southern Asia to Java in the Indonesian islands, and through eastern Asia.

The leopard's preferred habitat, and presumably its original one, seems to be the forest, since the branches of a leafy tree are its favorite resting-place, and the pattern of markings on its fur provide almost perfect camouflage in broken sunlight.

The list of the leopard's prey animals is a long one, in keeping with its huge geographical range. In the savannas of East and South Africa, antelopes of various sizes make up about 85 per cent of the leopard's diet. In the diet of the leopards of the Indian jungle, the leading place is taken by the axis deer, which contributes about 60 per cent. In both Africa and Asia, monkeys also play a certain part. In India, the species most commonly eaten is the langur. Baboons are taken in Africa.

Leopard
(*Panthera pardus*)

LION

Panthera leo

Order Carnivora
Family Felidae
Size Length head to trunk 56½ – 78 in (145 – 200 cm); length of tail 26 – 39 in (67 – 102 cm); height at shoulder 28 – 43 in (73 – 112 cm)
Weight 264 – 583 lb (120 – 265 kg)
Dentition $\frac{3.1.3.1}{3.1.2.1} = 30$
Reproductive period Normally once a year but this is not determined by the seasons
Gestation About 109 days (96-119)
Number of young Between 1 and 8, on average 3
Sexual maturity In captivity around 2-3 years, in the wild about a year later
Maximum age 29 years

In other felidae, males and females are generally only differentiated by their size, but with the lion (*Panthera leo*) the mane that characterizes the male represents an evident sign of distinction between the two sexes. Many hypotheses have been put forward as to the function of the mane. The fact that it occurs in the only feline to lead a sociable existence indicates that it serves primarily as a means of social communication: the function of the mane should therefore be linked to sexual and social prowess. It is also significant that it offers protection against neck injuries that could be sustained in fights with other animals, but this is a secondary consideration.

Very young lions, as is the case with the jaguar and the leopard, the species that are most closely related to it, display a coat covered in numerous rosette-shaped spots. These are often arranged in a perpendicular fashion in relation to the longitudinal axis of the body and sometimes join together cross-wise. As the animals grow older, these tend to fade increasingly so that adult lions reveal no trace of them or at least only the merest hint.

Among all the geographical populations or subspecies, the lion of southeast and southern Asia displays the majority of the species' original characteristics, whereas the African lion to the south of the Sahara – with the exception of the Cape lions that occupy an intermediary position – appear to be those that are most evolved. The southern African lions

◀ **U**nique among all felines, the lion displays sexual dimorphism, not only as regards its body size. The male sports a mane that varies according to its geographical provenance, climatic conditions and hormonal state. The female has no mane and will at most display a few tufts of longer hair. Both males and females have long dark hairs at the tip of the tail, which form a kind of brush.

appear to be currently the largest living lions. Isolated giant examples are, however, also to be found in eastern Africa. During the Ice Age, lions of very large, almost gigantic size lived also in Europe, Siberia and in northern America, the so-called cave lions and north American lions (in the group *Panthera leo spelaea* and *Panthera leo atrox*.) At the end of the Ice Age even the southern American territory was populated by lions.

The African lion's main natural habitat nowadays is the arid landscape of the savannah. It also drifts towards semi-desert areas and thin forests. It therefore shares the same habitat as the leopard, but has a completely different ecological niche.

The leopard feeds on medium-sized game, but the lion – a more furtive hunter – attacks larger animals and will also feed on prey wrenched from other wild animals.

In order to capture large animals, the lion's success is due to the number of animals taking part in the chase. The lone hunter on average has a lower success rate than two or more individuals hunting together. Game that is heavier than the lion will generally be attacked by more than one animal. A single individual has few chances of success against, for example, a buffalo. The high degree of sociability displayed by the lion in comparison with other felines is thus an important factor in its hunting success.

This sociability, which is much greater than that of the tiger, enables groups of mothers with their young to live in groups even after sexual maturity and leads to friendly behavior between adults of both sexes. Thus packs of lions of varying size and composition are to be found, with a common link joining males who move independently of the groups made up mothers and their young. Social interaction is maintained by means of mutual smoothing of the coat, with rituals of greeting and other common actions, such as for example, roaring in unison. The rubbing of the head, one of the most fundamental behavior traits, is generally initiated by the animal who is lowest in rank in the pack. The smoothing of the coat also adheres to this. These forms of behavior are thus genreally initiated by young individuals, then by females and only rarely by adult males.

▲ The lion's sociability increases its success in hunting prey. Groups can circle and chase. The lone hunter, on the other hand, has only reduced chances of success. Ungulates, being quick to panic, are often victims. They are often hunted by groups of females, with males only taking part in an indirect way.

▲ The lion's most frequent prey are ungulates, weighing from 220 – 440 lb (100 – 200 kg), and particularly gnu and zebras. Other significant prey are large animals (440 – 1,100 lb/200 – 500 kg) such as the African buffalo and more medium-sized animals (110 – 220 lb/50 – 100 kg) such as gazelles and warthogs.

TIGER
Panthera tigris

Order Carnivora
Family Felidae
Size Length head to trunk 136 – 230 cm; length of tail 44 – 111 cm; height at shoulder 65 – 115 cm
Weight 99 – 320 kg
Dentition $\dfrac{3.1.3.1}{3.1.2.1} = 30$

Reproductive period Not determined by the seasons; in northern areas of distribution generally in winter
Gestation About 104 days (93 – 117)
Number of young Between 1 and 7, usually 3
Sexual maturity About 3 – 4 years
Maximum age 26 years

In its northern, Siberian, subspecies, the tiger (*Panthera tigris*) is the largest living feline. The lion only reached the same size in the European and northern American species, that have been extinct since the Ice Age. With a head that is small in relation to its body, the tiger substantially differs from its related species, the lion, leopard and jaguar, all of whom have rather large heads. The characteristic stripes are typical only of the tiger, among all the felines.

The tiger's coloration, which so strikes observers viewing these animals in a zoo, enables it to adapt to its habitat.

Within its territory of distribution, the tiger forms a series of clearly distinguishable geographical populations of subspecies. The existence of these, widely differing in their size, accounts for the large range of variations in the tiger's physical dimensions.

The largest are the tigers of the eastern Siberian teerritory of Amur-Ussuri and Manchuria. Among these lengths of head and trunk of up to 166 to 200 cm have been recorded, in one case of up to 290 cm. The length of the tail among these Siberian tigers ranges from 74 – 111 cm. The smallest tigers are those of Sumatra, Java and Bali. The length of the Sumatra tigers ranges from 136 to 180 cm, and the length of their tail is between 44 and 77 cm. By comparing these two extremes one may see that small Siberian females and large Sumatra males are similar in size. All the other subspecies fall within these two in terms of size. The Indian tigers are those closest to

With its Siberian population, the tiger is the largest feline alive today. Its stripes, on a rust colored background, make it impossible to confuse it with any other species. These stripes enable the tiger to conceal itself within bamboo forests and makes any habitat with yellow-brown vertical elements the perfect hiding place. Unlike the lion, which lives sociably in the open country, the tiger roams its forest environment as a solitary individual.

the Siberian species.

The distribution of the tiger spreads in a ring shape around the plateaus and desert areas of central Asia. In the dry regions of central Asia it has settled along the great rivers reaching, in the West, Turkey and the Caucasus. In southeast Asia, the Tiger may be found in Sumatra, Java and Bali. The northernmost reaches of its distribution are the eastern Siberian territory of Amur-Ussuri. Its natural habitat is a damp landscape that is rich in hiding-places such as the woods along the great Asiatic rivers, the forests and tropical parks of southern Asia and southeast Asia and the Siberian taiga. Its preferred habitat is a damp one, such as the rich vegetation of the river valleys. In the Amur-Ussuri territory, the tiger lives in a typically half-mountainous landscape in mountain regions, but rarely higher than 500 – 600 meters, always avoiding open areas and living essentially within the shelter of woods.

The tiger's sociability is scant. Generally, it leads a solitary life. Only rarely will two adult individuals join together, and if they do it is more often likely to be a male and a female. If tigers congregate in groups, it will generally be a female with young that are almost grown to adult size. A form of sociability may be witnessed when tigers join together in hunting prey, mutual intolerance being temporarily suppressed in favor of the attraction of food. This intolerance may be seen also in tigers that are in captivity. Males and females can coexist as a pair without difficulty, however, and strong links between these animals can sometimes be witnessed. When young grow up with their parents in a restricted area, such as in the captivity of a zoo, the relationship works well both with the mother and the father, until the young reach adulthood and grow to the same size. Inevitably, instances of aggression will then occur and, within the restricted space available, one individual will usually be oppressed by all the other tigers as scapegoat and will be isolated by them. There is therefore no such thing as sociability among tigers such as can be witnessed among lions.

This scarce sociability, together with a lively temperament, is a marked advantage for the tiger and its predator's life in the forests.

The tiger is a roaming hunter, which creeps forward and exploits to the full all its possibilities of concealment within the tall grass of the undergrowth. It strikes its victim by the shoulders, suddenly, with a few leaps from close range, seeking to knock it off balance by the impetus of its leap and by its weight, sinking its fangs into its scalp or throat. Its poweful canines are veritable daggers that are able to penetrate deeply and its jaw muscles are strong enough to enable the tiger to strangle even extremely large prey.

▼ Wild boar and deer, depending on the region, make up the main diet of the tiger. Its large distribution across different climatic zones, together with the differing size and strength of exemplars from different regions, mean that the animals selected as prey are wide ranging. In the eastern Siberian territory of Amur-Ussuri, tigers even attack bears.

▲ Mammals of more moderate size are also important prey.

ANTARCTIC SEALS

The true seals of the Antarctic are represented by four closely related species, all circumpolar in distribution. The most abundant and widespread antarctic phocid is the crabeater seal *(Lobodon carcinophagus)* which primarily inhabits the unconsolidated pack ice zone, but is also found on the coasts of both the north and south islands of New Zealand, on Tasmania, the southeast coast of Australia, and along the Atlantic coast of South America. The principal food of the crabeater seal is krill; the seal's cheek teeth have remarkably elaborate cusps for straining and filtering euphausiids from sea water. The body of this seal is long and slim and is covered with a pelage which changes color during the months following the molt. The crabeater is not migratory but moves with the pack ice in the winter to remain near its food source.

The Weddell seal *(Leptonychotes weddelli)* is the second most abundant Antarctic seal and inhabits the fast ice areas of the Antarctic continent although the major population components are associated with some subantarctic islands, such as the Falkland Islands and dependencies. Adult seals are dark dorsally and mottled laterally and ventrally with irregular white to gray spots. Females are larger than males. The Weddell seal is predominantly a fish-eater but is also known to feed opportunistically on benthic animals and squid. Weddell seals can dive to a maximum depth of almost 2,000 ft (600 m) and stay under for a maximum of 45 minutes.

The leopard seal *(Hydrurga leptonyx)* is dispersed over the range of the Antarctic pack ice and the coasts of Australia, New Zealand, and South America; the wider range of this species reflects its varied feeding habits including krill, fish, and penguins, and other seals. Leopard seals are not usually gregarious.

The Ross seal *(Ommatophoca rossi)* is rare in comparison to the other Antarctic species; it appears principally to inhabit the consolidated ice pack and records suggest that it is solitary.

There are three isolated breeding populations of the harp seal located in the White Sea, the east coast of

The leopard seal *(Hydrurga leptonyx)* derives its name from its spotted coat. Unlike the other pinnipeds, it has a flat head; it also differs from them in its dietary habits. It eats not only fish, but penguins and smaller seals. In the literal sense, it is the only carnivorous member of the pinnipeds.

The Weddell seal *(Leptonychotes weddelli)* lives a solitary life. Groups of this species are to be found only in the breeding season. Weddell seals are thickset in build, and live mainly on fish, although they also take squids and various animals living at great depths. They can dive to a depth of 200 ft (60 m), and can remain submerged for more than 40 minutes.

The crabeater seal *(Lobodon carcinophagus)* lives mainly on krill. Its teeth are designed not so much to crush the shells of crabs as to filter small food organisms out of the sea water.

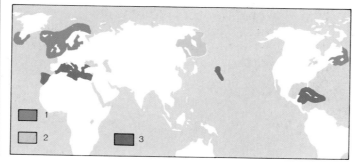

Geographical distribution of:
1) Gray seal *(Halichoerus grypus)*.
2) Ribbon seal *(Phoca fasciata)*.
3) Monk seal *(Monachus* species).

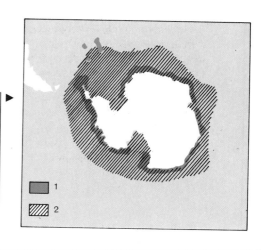

Geographical distribution of Antarctic seals:
1) Leopard seal *(Hydrurga leptonyx)*.
2) Weddell seal *(Leptonychotes weddelli)*.

Greenland, and the northern coast of Newfoundland. The species is highly migratory and seals move north in the summer to feeding grounds as the ice retreats northward. In spring and summer months juveniles feed on mysids and euphausiids while the adult diet is composed of these planktonic crustaceans as well as polar cod, capelin, herring, and squid.

The ringed seal *(Pusa hispida)* one of the smallest seals, is circumpolar in distribution and is the commonest and most widely distributed Arctic seal. A wide variety of food items (small crustaceans, as well as fishes) comprise its diet.

The bearded seal *(Erignathus barbatus)* is generally solitary and has a circumpolar distribution. It maintains a year-round association with moving sea ice in the subarctic region and is restricted to relatively shallow water. In winter, the bearded seal is found along the coast of Alaska and Siberia extending into the Arctic with the center of abundance being the ice edge of the central and southern Bering Sea.

The bearded seal is the largest of the ice-associated pinnipeds in the northern hemisphere. Males are 9 ft (2.8 m) long and weigh 900 lb (410 kg); the females are 8½ ft (2.6 m) long and weigh much less than the male.

The ribbon seal *(Phoca (Histriophoca) fasciata)* is found confined to the western half of the Bering Sea and ranges into the Okhotsk as far as Sahalin Island. It inhabits open water and ice floes but is occasionally sighted on the island and mainland shores. The species is not gregarious and usually only a few animals forming small herds are seen together.

The ribbon seal is of medium size and slender in comparison with most seals: males are 5¼ ft (1.6 m) long and weigh 210 lb (95 kg); females are 5 ft (1.5 m) long and weigh 175 lb (80 kg).

The gray seal *(Halichoerus grypus)* is a gregarious species widely distributed in temperate and subarctic waters on both sides of the North Atlantic. The species is strongly dimorphic with respect to both pelage color and size; males are much larger than females and have light spots on a darker background, while females have dark spots on a lighter background.

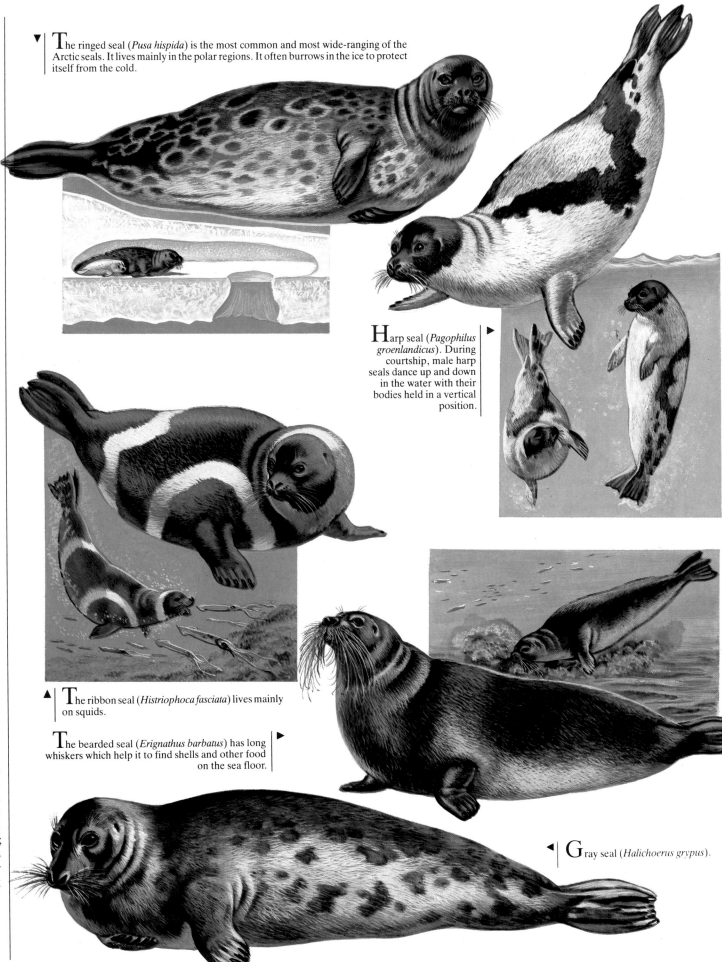

▼ The ringed seal *(Pusa hispida)* is the most common and most wide-ranging of the Arctic seals. It lives mainly in the polar regions. It often burrows in the ice to protect itself from the cold.

Harp seal *(Pagophilus groenlandicus)*. During courtship, male harp seals dance up and down in the water with their bodies held in a vertical position. ▶

▲ The ribbon seal *(Histriophoca fasciata)* lives mainly on squids.

The bearded seal *(Erignathus barbatus)* has long whiskers which help it to find shells and other food on the sea floor. ▶

◀ Gray seal *(Halichoerus grypus)*.

NORTHERN FUR SEAL/ ALASKA FUR SEAL

Callorhinus ursinus

Order Carnivora
Family Otariidae
Size Males, 8 ft (2.5 m); females, 6 ft (1.9 m)
Weight Males, 660 lb (300 kg); females 143 – 154 lb (65 – 70 kg)
Dentition $\dfrac{2.1.5-6}{2.1.5} = 34-36$
Reproductive period May – July
Gestation 10 months with 2 – 4 months delay in implantation
Number of young 1
Sexual maturity Males, 5 – 6 years; females 4 years
Maximum age 25 years

The northern fur seal, currently distributed in temperate subarctic North Pacific waters, is one of the most abundant, widely distributed and commercially important marine mammals. The main colony of northern fur seals is presently centered on St George and St Paul Islands in the Pribilof Islands and numbers approximately 1.5 million seals. Breeding colonies are also found on the Commander Islands and Robben Island in the Sea of Okhotsk, which account for approximately 200,000 – 500,000 seals. Some small groups have been recently reported on the once inhabited Kurile Islands and recolonization is believed to be underway.

The northern fur seal is a highly pelagic species and spends 300 – 330 days per year at sea. During the summer months seals congregate to pup and breed at traditional island sites. In the winter months the Pribilof population migrates south along the coasts of Canada and the United States as far south as San Diego, California. Seals from Western Pacific breeding stocks also move south in winter along the Asiatic coasts as far as Japan. During their migration, seals usually travel in small groups of up to ten animals or alone rather than in large herds.

The northern fur seal is a strongly dimorphic species; adult males generally being twice as long and weighing

The northern fur seal (*Callorhinus ursinus*) is classified among the pinnipeds and is closely related to the sea lions. Compared with the latter, however, the northern fur seal has a thicker and more luxuriant coat and a shorter and more pointed muzzle. This species exhibits pronounced sexual dimorphism. The males are darker in color than the females and are about twice as long and three to four times as heavy. The males return regularly to their island breeding-grounds between the end of May and the end of June, and fight hard among themselves to establish their individual territories, which are ready for the females when they arrive. A single male may collect a harem of 15-60 females.

Female northern fur seal.

three to four times as much as adult females. Males also differ in color and are dark black to dark brown all over except for the mane which is grayish in color. Females are slate gray above and lighter reddish gray below. The chest in both sexes bears a light patch. Seals generally darken somewhat following the annual molt. Pups are born jet black but the pelage molts to a silvery gray within a month or so of birth. The rear flippers in both sexes are greatly elongated and highly vascularized; they are waved in the air and serve to dissipate heat when the seal is under heat stress.

Most growth in females occurs during the first 4 – 5 years of life. Males begin to grow rapidly when sexual maturity is attained at 4 – 5 years of age and continue to grow until reaching sociological maturity at about 10 years; bulls generally do not achieve harem status until 10 – 12 years old. Pups leave the rookeries in September – November but migrate only relatively short distances and return to the rookeries for the following breeding season.

While at sea during the pelagic season (August – May) seals sleep during the day by floating on the surface with the rear flippers bent forward; one of the foreflippers is raised in the air and the other is extended downward, acting as a keel or centerboard. Feeding occurs at night. In the Bering Sea, capelin is important in June; gonatid squids and walleye pollack are eaten in July; gonatid squids, capelin and walleye pollack in August; and walleye pollack and gonatid squids in September. Little is known of feeding or behavior during the pelagic phase as seals are generally solitary and very widely dispersed. The only known predators of northern fur seals are sharks, killer whales, and man.

Northern fur seals have been hunted commercially since their discovery on the Pribilof Islands in 1786 by Gerassim Pribilof, a Russian fur trader and explorer. They are migratory and have been shown to exhibit strong site fidelity; in fact early sealers used this "homing" tendency to locate rookeries by following seals on their homeward migrations to summer breeding grounds.

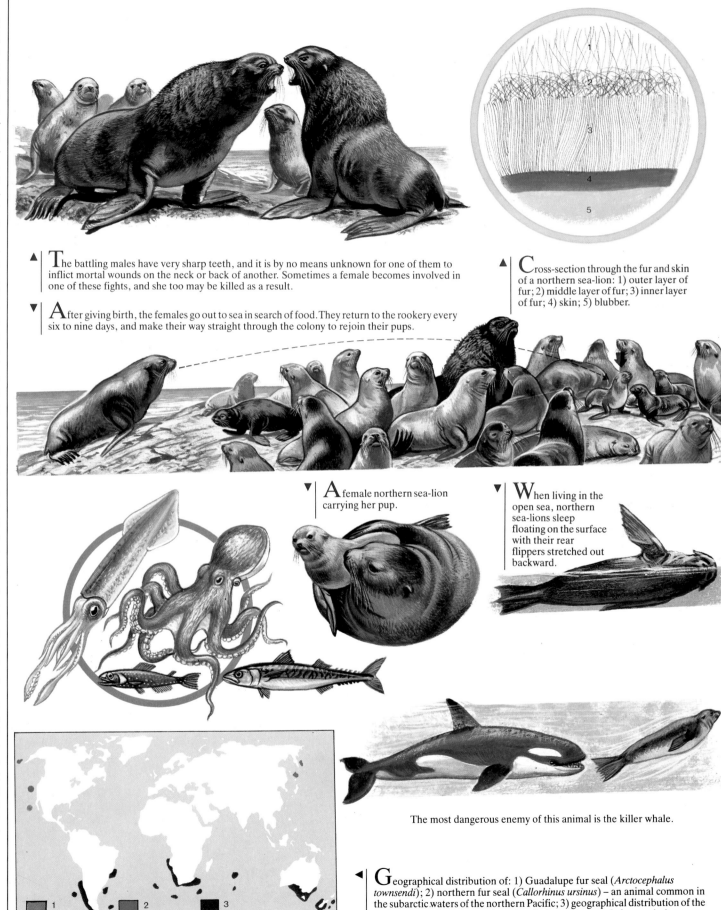

The battling males have very sharp teeth, and it is by no means unknown for one of them to inflict mortal wounds on the neck or back of another. Sometimes a female becomes involved in one of these fights, and she too may be killed as a result.

After giving birth, the females go out to sea in search of food. They return to the rookery every six to nine days, and make their way straight through the colony to rejoin their pups.

Cross-section through the fur and skin of a northern sea-lion: 1) outer layer of fur; 2) middle layer of fur; 3) inner layer of fur; 4) skin; 5) blubber.

A female northern sea-lion carrying her pup.

When living in the open sea, northern sea-lions sleep floating on the surface with their rear flippers stretched out backward.

The most dangerous enemy of this animal is the killer whale.

Geographical distribution of: 1) Guadalupe fur seal (*Arctocephalus townsendi*); 2) northern fur seal (*Callorhinus ursinus*) – an animal common in the subarctic waters of the northern Pacific; 3) geographical distribution of the various fur seals of the southern hemisphere (*Arctocephalus* species).

DUGONG
Dugong dugong

Order Sirenia
Family Dugongidae
Size Total length (8 – 13 ft (2.4 – 4 m),
more commonly 8 – 10 ft (2.4 – 3 m)
Weight 500 – 800 lb (230 – 400 kg)
Gestation Probably about 1 year
Number of young 1 – exceptionally 2
Length at birth 43 – 55 in (1.1 – 1.4 m)
Weight at birth 44 – 55 lb (20 – 25 kg)
Sexual maturity When a length of 8 ft
(2.4 m) is reached.

The dugong has a round, tapered body. The skin is smooth-looking, but has a thin covering of short hairs, 1 – 2 in (3 – 5 cm) apart. The hair on the muzzle is thicker and more bristly. The nostrils are situated well forward on top of the muzzle. Special muscles hold the nostrils shut when the animal is submerged. The forelimbs are shaped like paddles, and have no claws. The animal uses them to steer itself while swimming, to support itself while it rests, and to grasp objects to its body. When swimming rapidly, it holds them tight against its chest. The tailfin is wide, and shaped like that of the whales, with two acute-angled lobes and a strongly concave trailing edge. Adult males, and some old females, have two tusklike upper incisors, which project visibly from the mouth. Back teeth may be present to a total number of six pairs, comprising three upper and three lower molars on each side; but old specimens generally have fewer than this.

The dugong lives mainly in shallow coastal waters, only occasionally venturing a short distance upstream into the great rivers. It spends most of its time at depths of 3 – 40 ft (1 – 12 m) in the warm, often muddy, waters where it finds its food. It also makes daily journeys into deeper waters. The dugong is a sea mammal of extremely peaceable, cautious and timid character, like the manatees. When it is allowed to live in peace, it shows a tendency to a gregarious way of life. It generally swims slightly below the surface, at a speed of 6 mph (10 kmh), although it can achieve double that speed over short distances when alarmed. The length of gestation is not known exactly, but is thought to be about one year. The females give birth in shallow water.

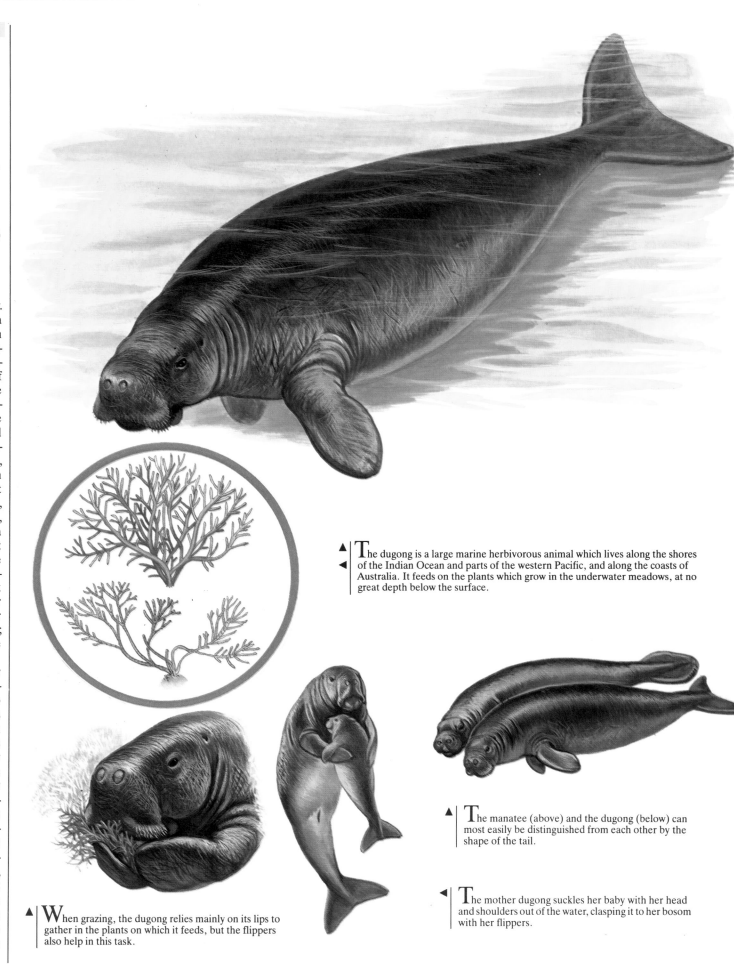

▲◀ The dugong is a large marine herbivorous animal which lives along the shores of the Indian Ocean and parts of the western Pacific, and along the coasts of Australia. It feeds on the plants which grow in the underwater meadows, at no great depth below the surface.

▲ When grazing, the dugong relies mainly on its lips to gather in the plants on which it feeds, but the flippers also help in this task.

▲ The manatee (above) and the dugong (below) can most easily be distinguished from each other by the shape of the tail.

◀ The mother dugong suckles her baby with her head and shoulders out of the water, clasping it to her bosom with her flippers.

AMERICAN MANATEE

Trichechus manatus

Order Sirenia
Family Trichechidae
Size Total length 10 – 13 ft (3.4 m)
Weight Up to 1,300 lb (600 kg)
Gestation About 13 months
Number of young 1 (exceptionally 2)
Length at birth Over 3 ft (1 m)
Weight at birth 33 – 44 lb (15 – 20 kg)
Sexual maturity 4 – 6 years, or when a length of 8½ ft (2.6 m) has been achieved

The American manatee is an aquatic mammal closely related to the dugong. The pectoral flippers are well developed, and equipped with claws. The animal lives both in coastal waters and in estuaries, canals, rivers, and similar waterways throughout the tropical and subtropical regions of the western Atlantic. It is present in Florida, the Caribbean Sea, the Gulf of Mexico, and the northern coasts of South America down to the mouth of the Amazon.

The American manatee does not seem to be particularly gregarious, although large groups are sometimes found in winter in places where the water temperature is unusually high. It normally lives in couples or small groups, the most common and stable natural association in the wild state being that of mother and young. The baby is suckled under water, and is not weaned before it reaches the age of one year, though it also begins to take solid food when only a few weeks old.

Closely related species are the Amazon manatee *(Trichechus inunguis)* and the African manatee *(Trichechus senegalensis)*. The Amazon manatee is somewhat smaller than the American manatee, with a maximum length of about 9 ft (2.8 m). Its distinctive characteristics are the absence of claws on its flippers, the smoothness of its skin, and the presence of large white patches on the underside of the body. It is a freshwater species, found only in the river basins of the Amazon and the Orinoco. The African manatee lives in the rivers and coastal waters of West Africa, from the River Senegal in the north to the River Cuanza in Angola to the south.

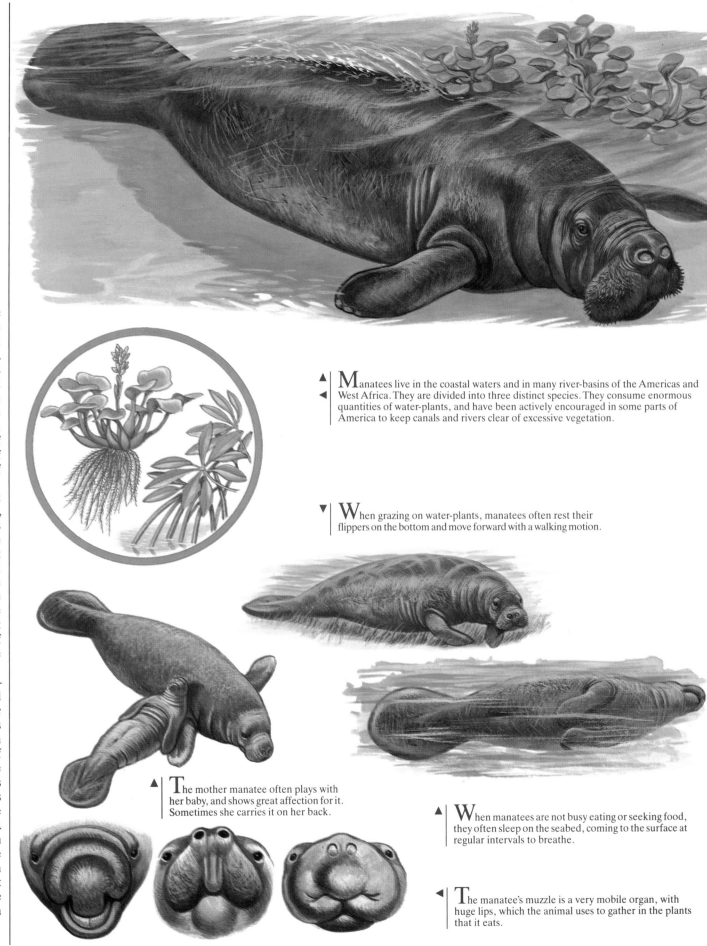

Manatees live in the coastal waters and in many river-basins of the Americas and West Africa. They are divided into three distinct species. They consume enormous quantities of water-plants, and have been actively encouraged in some parts of America to keep canals and rivers clear of excessive vegetation.

When grazing on water-plants, manatees often rest their flippers on the bottom and move forward with a walking motion.

The mother manatee often plays with her baby, and shows great affection for it. Sometimes she carries it on her back.

When manatees are not busy eating or seeking food, they often sleep on the seabed, coming to the surface at regular intervals to breathe.

The manatee's muzzle is a very mobile organ, with huge lips, which the animal uses to gather in the plants that it eats.

INDIAN ELEPHANT

Elephas maximus

Order Proboscidea
Family Elephantidae
Size Length of head and body
(including trunk) 18 – 21 ft (5.5 – 6.4
m); length of tail 4 – 5 ft (1.2 – 1.5 m);
height at shoulder 8 – 10 ft (3m)
Weight Up to 5 tons
Gestation 20 – 22 months

The geographical distribution of the Indian elephant was formerly much more extensive, reaching as far west as Arabia and as far east as China. It is now reduced to India, Burma, Thailand, the Malaysian peninsula, Sumatra, and Sri Lanka. There are also small numbers in Borneo, but these were probably introduced by man at some time in the past.

The habitat of the Indian elephant is very varied including damp tropical forests, thick jungle, open grassy plains, and dry woodlands. Water plays an important role in its life, for it drinks 15 – 20 gallons (70 – 90 liters) per day and requires substantial further supplies to keep itself cool and clean. Like the African species, it needs to refresh itself frequently by bathing, by showering itself all over with water from its trunk, or by wallowing in swamps, where the mud not only cools it down but helps it to get rid of skin parasites. It also frequently takes dust baths, picking the dust up and spraying it over the body with its trunk.

Elephants create paths through the jungle, following a perfectly rational pattern in relation to the terrain, and providing access to the animals' drinking places in the valleys and their favorite pastures higher up. These paths are wide and well marked, with great stairways going up the steep hillsides and zigzag tracks coming down them, to form a real communications network which may last for many generations. The Indian elephant, like the African species, is a good swimmer and can cross wide rivers or inlets of the sea, holding its trunk out of water to breathe.

The Indian elephant is a gregarious animal, with a social structure that resembles in some respects that of the African species. The cow elephants

▲ The trunk of the Indian elephant (left) ends in a single finger, whereas the African animal (right) has two.

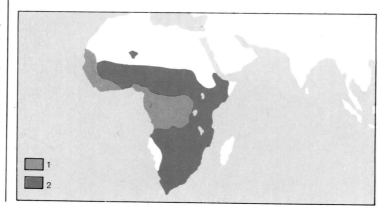

▲ Many differences of detail separate the Indian elephant (above) from the African elephant (below). The African elephant is an altogether larger animal; its forehead is fairly flat in outline, whereas the forehead of the Indian elephant has two large protuberances separated by a groove; the African species has larger ears and tusks; and the line of the back, when seen in profile, is concave for the African and convex for the Indian species.

◄ Geographical distribution of the two subspecies of African elephant: (1) *Loxodonta africana cyclotis*, the forest elephant and (2) *Loxodonta africana africana*, which is the more important subspecies, typical of the savanna country.

form small herds of their own with 8 to 20 members, led by a female and consisting of cows, half-grown young and generally, though not always, mothers with small babies. Bulls generally live alone or in small groups. When a herd is at pasture, a system of social hierarchy is observed, and the senior members are always allowed first choice of the best food. Those in the lower part of the social scale remain in the background, and approach their seniors with circumspection. A cow elephant with a baby, for example, can only be approached by a junior member if it helps to feed the baby.

The Indian elephant, like the African species, eats a very wide variety of vegetable matter from both forest and grassland, finding much of its food at ground level. Grass, roots, leaves and shoots of trees and shrubs, fruits, twigs, and bark are all taken, and various kinds of bamboo are especially appreciated. The necessity of finding, tearing down and swallowing the enormous amount of food which an elephant requires every 24 hours is the main factor in determining its daily pattern of activity. It is calculated that an adult elephant must spend 18 – 20 hours a day feeding itself.

Social and inter-individual contacts are generally maintained by means of acoustic and olfactory signals. In the forests, the members of a wild herd of elephants communicate over a distance by means of trumpeting and screams. Cow elephants call their babies to them by flapping the ears noisily against the head. Meetings between individuals are also marked by screams and gurgles of greeting; and the same sounds are used as a means of keeping in contact over a short distance by members of the same group.

Gestation lasts from 20 – 22 months, and each baby takes several years to bring up. When a cow elephant gives birth, she has the assistance of another female, or sometimes of two. An hour after birth, the baby is already able to stagger along with the herd next to his mother, who steadies him when necessary with her trunk. It is suckled for a minimum of 6 months, but generally up to an age of 2 – 3 years, although their diet is supplemented with solid food from an early stage.

The Indian elephant can be distinguished from the African by differences in the profile of the head, the profile of the back, the size of the ears, the form taken by the tip of the trunk (one-fingered in the Indian species and two-fingered in the African), and the number of toes with well-developed nails on the front and back feet.

Indian elephant

African elephant

Unlike adult animals, the newborn baby elephant has a sparse covering of hair, which disappears as it grows up.

Like the African elephant, the Indian is very fond of bathing, and of giving itself shower-baths by spraying water over its body with its trunk.

Apart from man, the tiger is the only enemy of the Indian elephant. It is a very real danger to baby elephants, but is easily put to flight by the adults.

The Indian elephant is a most valuable helper to man in many Asiatic countries, especially for heavy forestry work.

1) Geographical distribution of the Indian elephant.

AFRICAN ELEPHANT

Loxodonta africana

Order Proboscidea
Family Elephantidae
Height at shoulder Males 10 – 13½ ft (3.2 – 4 m); females 7 – 8½ ft (2.2 – 2.6 m)
Weight Males 4¾ – 6 tons; females 2 – 3¼ tons
Gestation 20 – 22 months

For the last three centuries, the range of the African elephant has included most of Africa south of the Sahara, except for the desert and semidesert regions. The disastrous effects of hunting for the ivory trade during the nineteenth and twentieth centuries and of changes in the habitat have now confined the African elephant mainly to certain isolated regions, most of which are national parks or game reserves. The elephant can adapt itself to many different environments, from semi-arid bush country to riverside tropical forest, from sea level to mountainous regions at a height of over 12,000 ft (3,600 m) or more. The most typical habitat, however, is well-wooded savanna, generally not far from water, with periodical excursions in the dry season to neighboring forest regions.

The elephant is not a selective eater, but needs a wide variety of vegetation, which it gathers at all levels – off the ground, from low shrubs, from high up in the trees, or anywhere else its versatile trunk can reach. Elephants get most of their food from ground vegetation – especially graminaceous plants – during the rains in savanna country; in the dry season they rely on the woodlands at higher altitudes. In many cases plants are eaten whole, long grass being pulled up by the animal's trunk in bundles and thrust straight into the mouth. Foliage is stripped off the high branches of trees, and the tender parts of the branch itself may also be eaten, together with fruit, bark, etc. When famine brings about a high concentration of elephants in one particular spot, the results of overgrazing may be disastrous for the vegetation. The elephants pull up shrubs by the roots, and knock down trees in order to eat their upper branches. When an elephant pulls up a shrub, he is generally careful

The African elephant is the largest living land mammal. The enormous development of the ears is to be interpreted as an adaptation the function of which is to help the animal disperse its body heat. A huge beast such as an elephant inevitably has a lower ratio of surface area to bulk than a smaller animal.

The African elephant lives in a wide variety of habitats, including river banks, grasslands, and forest. It can adapt itself to anything but excessively dry regions.

to knock the earth off the roots by beating it against his side before he eats it. An adult elephant will eat about 5 per cent of his weight and drink some 48 gallons (220 liters) per day.

Breeding takes place throughout the year, but in some regions most births take place shortly before the rains. This provides the baby elephants with favorable conditions for the first few months of life, with high humidity and rich vegetation. The young that are born in the dry season have to make long journeys with their mothers in search of water and food. Gestation lasts 21 – 22 months, and the interval between births may be from 2½ to 9 years, according to the region. The number of young is generally one. The male baby elephant weighs up to 260 lb (120 kg), and the female from 200 – 220 lb (90 – 100 kg); in both cases, the length is about 4 ft (1.2 m). The skin of the newborn baby elephant is bluish gray in color, wrinkled and hairy. About half an hour after birth, the baby elephant can get on its feet and accompany its mother back to the herd. When about to give birth, the mother leaves the herd and goes off on her own, often accompanied by a female "helper." The baby stays with its mother for a long time, and is suckled for a period of 2 – 3 years.

The social organization of the elephant is of the matriarchial type. The unit on which it is based is the family group of 3 – 5 members, comprising one female and her offspring. The herd consists of a number of family groups, generally led by sisters or daughters of an old cow elephant who is head of the entire herd. This may have anything from 6 to about 70 members. Solitary bulls are also to be found; they are generally old animals, and are sometimes accompanied by a younger male with whom they have a friendly relationship. Old bulls tend to be relegated to an existence on the margin of the social structure, one reason being that their worn-down teeth limit them to a diet of tender vegetation, which can only be found near watercourses. Old females, on the other hand, remain in the herd after they have given up their role as leaders, but generally go into a rapid physical decline.

▲ Elephants love water, and are good swimmers. Access to water is absolutely essential for the elephant, which often gives itself copious shower-baths with its trunk, to cool itself down.

▲ In addition to showering itself with water, the elephant often sprays large quantities of earth or dust over its skin with its trunk, in order to free itself from parasites.

▲ When the elephant wants to rest, it sometimes lies down on its side. It may also go to sleep standing up, often leaning against a tree.

▲ Elephants often indulge in ritual combat, but sometimes also fight seriously. Young males wrestle with interlocked trunks as a form of play.

▲ Cow elephants take great care of their babies, and guide them when the herd is on the move. Sometimes they hold their babies by the tail with their trunk.

▼ In their daily travels, elephants adopt a marching order based on precedence, led by an old female. Baby elephants always stay with their mothers.

▼ Thanks to its great height and long trunk, the elephant can eat the leaves of quite tall trees. The balanced variety of vegetable products consumed by the elephants alleviates its impact on the environment.

◄ In times of drought, the elephant will dig holes in the ground with its powerful tusks in search of water.

▼ Because of their size, African elephants have virtually no natural enemies. Various predators (including the lion) may form designs against baby elephants; and it then falls to the mother to drive them off.

WARTHOG

Phacochoerus aethiopicus

Order Artiodactyla
Family Suidae
Size Length 56 – 76 in (140 – 190 cm);
height to shoulder 26 – 34 in (65 – 85 cm)
Weight 110 – 330 lb (50 – 150 kg)
Dentition $\frac{3.1.4.3}{3.1.4.3}$ = 44
N.B. It only has 32 at maturity
Reproductive period Almost all year
round
Gestation 170 days
Number of young 2 – 7, normally 3
Sexual maturity At 1 year
Maximum age 15 – 18 years

This member of the hog family has a very distinctive appearance. It is a slender animal with fairly long legs, a well-proportioned body and a very long tail terminating in a tuft. What gives it an almost prehistoric look is the head, which is long, broad, and heavy. The eyes are positioned very high, and below them are two huge, symmetrical warty growths, those of the male being particularly big. Further down, almost at the angles of the mouth, are two more, smaller warts. The canines of the lower jaw are quite long but those of the upper jaw are far longer, arching upward, inward and back, so as to form a semicircle. A fair-sized mane covers the neck and shoulders.

The warthog is widely distributed in Africa south of the Sahara to the southernmost parts of the continent, with the exception of South Africa proper. Its habitat is steppe and savanna, open regions where the highly placed eyes on the top of the head are certainly of great selective advantage, enabling the animal to avert danger more easily. Food consists almost entirely of grass.

The warthog is essentially a sedentary animal which seldom strays far from its home. Because it lives in surroundings where predatory attacks are common, it deliberately turns tail and seeks refuge in underground burrows, preferably those already excavated by an aardvark. Its only possible defense is to confront an aggressor face to face by interlocking tusks and relying on its own superior strength.

▲
◄ The warthog (*Phacochoerus aethiopicus*), unlike other Suidae, lives in the wide open spaces. It has fairly long legs and its eyes are situated high on the head, an adaptation for guarding against predators on the savannas. The tusks are quite long and the facial warts are prominent. It is active, too, during the day and feeds on vegetation. One unique feature of warthogs is their manner of fighting among themselves. Their weapons (namely the tusks) are among the most fearsome anywhere in the world of mammals; and their skin is not thick, but rather soft, not nearly so strong or bristly as that of wild boars. It is mainly for this reason that combats have a ritualized quality and are always conducted face to face. The only possible defense is to lock tusks with the adversary. After fighting in this position for a while, the weaker animal gives ground, lowering its head or kneeling, looking for a safer foothold, giving out brief grunts and aiming to keep the head down. When the dominant animal breaks off the struggle, the loser turns and flees at top speed. The winner may follow for a short distance but without any particular offensive intentions.

▼| **H**abitats of the warthog.

swamps   open plains   bush   forest

OTHER SUIDAE

Babirusa

The babirusa (*Babyrousa babyrussa*) is one of the strangest mammals. The body, unlike that of other Suidae, is most highly developed towards the rear, the back being arched and the legs long and thin. The grayish hairs that cover the body are so sparse that the animal looks completely hairless. The tail lacks a characteristic terminal tuft. The distinctive feature of the species is the extreme length of the canine teeth. While those of the lower jaw are directed straight up and may curve backward, those of the upper jaw perforate the bones of the skull and thus, after growing up to about a foot in length (in older males) they turn backward and downward so as to form a semicircle.

The babirusa's range is restricted to the island of Celebes and a few other neighboring islets, the faunas of which, not merely for this reason, may be regarded as quite unusual. The preferred habitat consists of wet, swampy zones made up of woods, reed-covered river banks, and similar areas. The babirusa is, of all pigs, the one most at home in water: it swims freely and does not have any hesitation in crossing rivers and even arms of the ocean.

Food generally consists of plant substances such as leaves, grass, fruit and shoots, but also insects and invertebrates. It communicates in much the same way as others of the family, with grunts and squeaks and, when irritated, gnashing of teeth and tusks. Social organization is determined by the birthrate, actually the lowest in the family. Mating occurs in September; and as a rule, 1 – 2 babies are born after 5 months' gestation. Sexual maturity, at least among females, is reached at around one year.

Fights among members of the species are clearly influenced by the peculiarities of physical structure. The powerful tusks, in fact, are used for defensive rather than offensive ends, being turned backward and thus only dangerous in the case of cuts and blows to the softer parts of the body. Because the babirusa does not possess epidermic plates, defensive swellings, or a mane for deadening blows, confrontations are necessarily face onward.

▲ **M**ale babirusas (*Babyrousa babyrussa*) have incredibly long tusks. They are rather primitive Suidae, with long legs and a body with very little hair. The outward appearance of the animal is somewhat different from the norm, and the natives call it the "pig-deer." It stands about 26-32 in (65-80 cm) tall, the length of the head and body is around 36-44 in (90-110 cm) and the weight ranges from 130 to 220 lbs (60-100 kg).

◀ **T**he babirusa's food is less varied than that of other members of the family, being made up of vegetation, leaves, grass, fruit, and shoots.

▲ **B**abirusas swim very well and have a liking for wet places.

▲ **T**he over-developed tusks, measuring 12 in (30 cm) certainly have an importance other than that of merely digging in the soil.

▲ **T**he female possesses only one pair of teats, and the babies have no stripes.

◀ 1) The babirusa's range is restricted to the island of Celebes. It prefers a wet, swampy environment, made up of woods, riverside reeds and similar habitats. Unlike most Suidae, the babirusa is an endangered species, both by reason of drastic changes to its surroundings, by certain features typical of the animal itself, and, also, of course, by the direct influence of other, human, activities. The animal is not difficult to rear in captivity, but there are few specimens in zoos.

1

COLLARED PECCARY

Tayassu tajacu
Dycotiles tajacu

Order Artiodactyla
Family Tayassuidae
Size Length 30 – 40 in (75 – 100 cm);
height to shoulder 16 – 20 in (40 – 50 cm)
Weight 40 – 55 lb (18 – 25 kg)
Dentition $\frac{2.1.3.3}{3.1.3.3} = 38$
Reproductive period Throughout year
Gestation 140 – 150 days
Number of young Normally 2 (1 – 4)
Sexual maturity Females at 33 – 34 weeks, males at 46 – 47 weeks
Maximum age About 15 years, perhaps up to 20 years in wild

The peccaries are fairly similar, in outward appearance, to the true hogs. Like them, the body is sturdy, the legs are of average size and the neck is short. The muzzle is elongated, terminating in a snout, like that of the wild boar. The short coat consists mainly of bristles which are longest on the top of the head, the neck, and the back. The tail, however, is very short. The peccaries have a dorsal scent gland, the secretion of which is situated in a glandular pouch covered with fairly long hairs.

The collared peccary (*Tayassu tajacu*) is a small hog with a dark, brownish-black coat and a very conspicuous, contrasting white collar. The species is widely distributed in the more southerly parts of the United States down to Argentina, comprising about seven subspecies. Its ecological requirements are very varied: it inhabits forests but also arid scrubland, and may range quite high into the mountains.

Food is in the main herbaceous or based on plant substances. But the peccary also feeds on fruit, roots, insects, and other small animals, and even snakes.

The commonest and most important social unit is the herd. Although numbers may range from 2 to 50, most herds contain about 5 – 15 individuals. Naturally the total varies considerably according to zone and season. Rain and snow exert a strong influence on these groups, in some measure determining the birthrate and, in

The collared peccary (*Tayassu tajacu*) is an inhabitant of North and South America. Although it much resembles Suidae, it has many affinities, too, with tylopods and ruminants.

The peccary's diet consists mainly of grassland vegetation, but also fruit, roots, insects, and small animals, even snakes. It is virtually omnivorous, in fact, rather like Old World Suidae.

The tusks of wild boars grow upward, while the upper canines of peccaries grow downward. Another difference is the regression of the fifth toe, almost invisible.

tusks

hind foot

Wild boar

Peccary

Wild boar

Peccary

winter, the mortality rate as well. The herd, therefore, apart from fluctuations caused by climatic and seasonal conditions, tends to remain fairly stable over a period. Occasionally single animals wander off to join another herd, but such instances are rare.

Movements of the herd depend almost wholly on food supply and external disturbance factors. If food is easily obtainable and abundant, the herd will be compact, but in the dry season rather more scattered, with animals concentrated in particular spots, around certain edible plants. As a rule peccaries are active all day long, most often at dawn or dusk and also at night, especially during the summer. They are very sensitive to atmospheric conditions and regulate their movements accordingly.

The breeding period is not limited to any fixed season. Births generally occur during the summer rainy season, so that mating should take place in late winter. Reproduction in no way affects the composition of the herd. There are no harems or pair formations. Nor do the males engage in combat for females on heat more fiercely than at any other time of year. The mother will sometimes defend her litter quite fiercely but as a rule danger is averted either by flight or collective attack.

Although they are sociable, peccaries do not observe any type of fixed hierarchy. Leadership of the herd is not assumed by any particular animal, and members of the group follow or imitate virtually any adult individual who takes a decision. The close links uniting all members of the herd, typically expressed by mutual recognition of the clan scent, have had a significant effect on social behavior. Peccaries are territorial, inasmuch as the zone belonging to a clan will be defended against outsiders and is demarcated in certain ways. The dorsal gland plays a very important role in social relationships and in the determination of territory. The glandular region is nuzzled by both partners and two peccaries will often rub their chin on the other's back. It is very likely that, in addition to impregnating each other with scent, this action helps to stimulate the production of the secretion: such activities reinforce the group odor.

▼ Peccaries have a very keen sense of smell and can detect bulbs at depths of up to about 10 ft (3 m).

White-lipped peccary (*Tajassu albirostris*)

The white-lipped peccary is larger than the collared peccary and more aggressive. It is an omnivore which often feeds on flesh.

▲ The white-lipped peccary forms herds of 100-150 individuals. Apart from climatic and seasonal fluctuations, the herd remains fairly stable over a period. This is a relatively rare phenomenon for artiodactyls.

◄ Babies lack the stripes of wild boars and are soon active.

▲ The glandular region is liberally nuzzled by the partner and two peccaries often rub their chin on the other's back. Stimulation of the dorsal gland helps to strengthen the herd odor.

Peccaries roll in sand or dust rather than in mudbaths. ►

◄ 1) The collared peccary, with seven subspecies, has a vast range extending from the southernmost parts of the United States to Argentina. 2) The white-lipped peccary, with five subspecies, is distributed from central United States to Argentina.

325

HIPPOPOTAMUS

Hippopotamus amphibius

Order Artiodactyla
Family Hippopotamidae
Size Length over 13 ft (4 m); height up to 68 in (170 cm)
Weight 3 tons and more
Dentition $\frac{2.1.4.3}{2.1.4.3} = 40$
Reproductive period Until end of dry season
Gestation 240 days
Number of young 1
Sexual maturity Females at 9 years, males at 8 years
Maximum age 40 – 45 years and more

The hippopotamus is an extremely heavy, stocky mammal. The head is strong and weighty, with a huge mouth. The ears are small, and the nostrils and eyes are positioned high on the head. When the animal is under water the nostrils are capable of being sealed. The body is long and fat, with a prominent belly. The legs are short and heavy, with four well-developed toes, joined at the base by a membrane, clearly designed for swimming. The tail is short, rolled up and flattened at the tip. The body is practically devoid of hair, although there are a few bristles on the lips and at the tip of the tail. The general color of the adults is deep reddish-brown, the upper parts being darker; but the young tend to be less brown and more pinkish.

In theory the hippo is distributed all over Africa south of the Sahara and in the Nile basin south of Khartoum. It is absent from almost the entire southern part of the continent and from the western equatorial forests. In practice, however, the range of the species is limited to rivers, swampy zones, and lakes. Although this mammal certainly spends most of its time in wet areas, it does not confine itself to water, and much of its activity takes place on dry land. Much of the hippo's food consists of land plants and vegetation; in some places, for example, although this is not a general rule, virtually all its food is found on land. The daily quantity of food consumed is about 65 – 90 lb (30 – 40 kg) for an adult individual.

Even though the hippopotamus is an aquatic animal, its body is in no sense hydrodynamic, and although the animal can swim and dive very well, it prefers shallow water where it can

The hippopotamus (*Hippopotamus amphibius*) is an African artiodactyl partly related to the Suiformes. It spends most of its time in the water and ventures onto dry land toward evening to feed on grass. The species lives in very large herds of males, females, and young, the males remaining on the outside. Courting and mating take place in the water, and it is here, too, that the single baby is born.

Hippos, both of the pygmy and common species, are derived from common ancestors (*Anthracotheridae*) who lived in the Oligocene and Miocene eras.

Pygmy hippopotamus

Anthracotheridae

Hippopotamus

easily wade on the bottom. For this reason it lives quite happily in places where the water is not more than 3 ft (1 m) or so in depth, quiet backwaters of rivers, creeks where the water is calm or stagnant, and even ponds and mudholes. Water, nevertheless, has decisively influenced the animal's shape and physiology. The position of the nostrils, eyes, and ears is a fundamental adaptation. A hippopotamus can, without emerging or scarcely appearing above the surface of the water, so that it can hardly be seen, perform all its vital functions, such as breathing, seeing, and hearing. On dry land the hippo is an impressive sight and not lacking in agility. Lions have been known to attack, but almost always unsuccessfully if the intended prey is a healthy adult.

The hippo is obviously a fairly sociable creature, living in groups of at least 10 individuals. The females and their babies keep together on the inside of the herd. Babies will stay close to their own mothers or in groups with others of a similar age. The males wander around the edge of the herd with youngsters grouped together and adults preferring to be secluded.

The breeding period coincides with the rainy season. The baby is born in the water and very quickly comes to the surface for its first gulps of air, after which it begins to suckle.

The hippo's closest relative is the pygmy hippopotamus (*Choeropsis liberiensis*). This species is much smaller than its relative and about one-tenth its weight: it measures 28 – 34 in (70 – 85 cm) in height and 60 in (150 cm) in length, weighing 400 – 660 lb (180 – 300 kg). Its body is less bulky, the head is smaller and the tail longer, with terminal hairs. The structure of the head shows that the animal is less adapted to aquatic life. The animal ranges from Liberia to the Ivory Coast, but this is not a continuous distribution and the species is actually in danger of extinction. It lives in the equatorial rain forests near rivers, lakes, and swamps. Food consists in the main of various vegetables, soft shoots, roots, grass, and fallen fruits.

▲ The hippo's hide must be kept constantly moist. The movement of the animal in the water enables it to keep its body clean, which would otherwise be impossible.

▼ Hippos are excellent swimmers and divers, capable of staying underwater for 4-5 minutes.

▲ Although they are herbivores, hippos have strong canine teeth, up to 2 in (5 cm) long. Opening the mouth wide to reveal jaws is not a yawn but a sign of intimidation.

Hippopotamus

Frog

Crocodile

The hippo, the frog, and the crocodile have similar adaptations (eyes and nostrils) for underwater life.

▶ Combats are very violent and almost always take place in the water.

▲ The female takes good care of her baby and does not allow it to wander too far away.

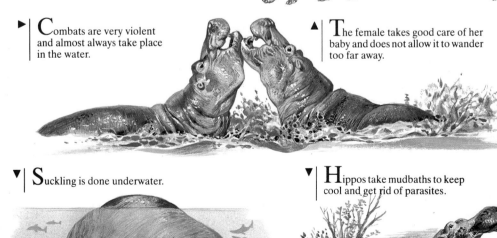

▼ Suckling is done underwater.

▼ Hippos take mudbaths to keep cool and get rid of parasites.

CAMELS

Genus *Camelus*

Order Artiodactyla
Suborder Tylopoda
Family Camelidae
Size Length of head and body 7½ – 11¼ ft (2.25 – 3.45 m); length of tail 22 – 30 in (55 – 75 cm); height (including hump) 6¼ – 7½ ft (1.9 – 2.3 m)
Weight 1,000 – 1,430 lb (450 – 650 kg)
Dentition $\frac{1.1.3.3}{3.1.2.3} = 34$

N.B. There are sometimes 2 or 4 upper premolars and 3 lower premolars
Reproductive period January – March
Gestation About 13 months
Number of young 1

Camels are the largest of the artiodactyls. The legs are long (longer in dromedaries than camels), with broad soles. There are two teats on the mammary glands. The typical gait is the amble, whereby the front and hind legs on the same side move simultaneously, touching the ground alternately on either side. When they increase speed, there are moments when all four legs actually leave the ground at the same time.

Unlike other artiodactyls, which walk on the tip of their last phalanx, protected by a hoof, the camels rest their weight wholly on the last and last but one phalanx of the third and fourth toes, the first, second and fifth toes having disappeared. These phalanges are protected at the front by a rudimentary hoof, similar to a nail, while the hind parts of the feet have developed two thick, fleshy pads.

Camels digest by ruminating, but they have developed this capacity quite independently of the true ruminants, like cows and antelopes. This type of digestion is useful in that it allows animals to swallow large quantities of food in a short period of time, not having to grind it up with the teeth, and thus to be less vulnerable to predatory attack.

Camels have to face extremely difficult living conditions in the desert. For this reason they have developed a series of adaptations, to cope with their environment. To avoid sand penetrating, they have small, hairy ears, nostrils that can be completely sealed, and eyes protected by long lashes. When drinking, the camel is able to saturate all its tissues with

Camels (genus *Camelus* survive today almost exclusively in their domesticated form. There are two distinct species, the one-humped dromedary and the two-humped Bactrian camel, both remarkably well adapted to the dry, inhospitable desert climate. The animals have for centuries helped desert populations (especially Tuaregs and Bedouins) to survive. They were used for riding and transporting merchandise for long distances, and they provided milk, meat, and wool. They still perform such functions today but are not nearly so indispensable.

water and not store it in the stomach, as is still commonly believed. Water retention is mainly achieved by a special system of body temperature control. The body temperature goes down during the night to 93°F (34°C), while by day it gradually rises to 104°F (40°C); and only at that point does the animal begin to sweat heavily. So water loss through sweating is reduced to a minimum. Moreover, camels, if forced to fast and go without water for any length of time, can use the fats contained in the hump to produce this "water." The hump, which is the camel's most conspicuous feature, is formed of adipose, fibrous tissue, constituting the reserve of fat utilized in case of need, and helping to insulate the body against excessive solar radiation.

The gestation period of a camel is about 13 months, and slightly less, about 12 months, for the dromedary. After a birth lasting several hours, the single baby is unsteady on its legs but able to move around, and as time passes it becomes increasingly secure.

There are two species of camels, the Bactrian camel (*Camelus bactrianus*) and the dromedary (*C. dromedarius*), with one and two humps, respectively.

Wild camels were once widely distributed in the arid zones of central Asia, but today, much reduced in numbers, their range comprises certain parts of the Gobi Desert in Mongolia and the region lying between this zone and China. Despite enjoying a fair measure of protection, the wild camel seems doomed to rapid extinction. It inhabits arid regions of steppe or semidesert, up to an altitude of 6,000 – 6,600 ft (1,800 – 2,000 m). In summer they live in the valleys where they can find grass, shrubs, and bushes in plenty, while in winter they move away to oases. The animals can withstand extreme fluctuations of climate, both seasonal and nyctemeral (contrasts of night and day).

The dromedary lives in the dry and desert regions of North Africa and the Middle East, from Afghanistan to the Caucasus. In Anatolia and the Caucasus its range overlaps that of the camel; and in these regions there may be mating between the two species, producing many hybrids. The dromedary exists only in the domesticated state, and in its wild form it may perhaps have inhabited the northern belt of the Sahara and Arabia.

Bactrian camel
(*Camelus bactrianus*)

▼ Two-humped camels live in desert regions of Mongolia, Central Asia, and Anatolia. They have tremendous stamina, and are capable of carrying weights of 530 lbs (250 kg) for whole days on end.. The coat is of variable color and shaggy; the hair, short in summer, lengthens in winter, with the longest fringes on the lower neck, the humps and the knees. The humps are large and sometimes droop to one side. There are callosities on the knees, as in dromedaries.

Alpaca
(*Lama guanacoë pacos*)

Vicuña
(*Lama vicugna*)

Llama
(*Lama guanacoë glama*)

▲ In the arid steppe and semidesert regions of the Gobi Desert, there are still a few dozen individuals who are believed to be genuinely wild (*Camelus bactrianus ferus*). They have smaller legs and humps than the domesticated form of Bactrian camel (*C.b. bactrianus*) and lack callosities on the knees. In summer they inhabit the valleys where they can find grass, bushes, and shrubs; and in winter they move off toward oases.

◀ In addition to *Camelus bactrianus* and *C. dromedarius*, there are two other species of the Camelidae family: the guanaco and the vicuña. The former may have been the ancestor of two domesticated breeds, the llama and the alpaca.

GUANACO AND VICUÑA

Lama guanacoë
Lama vicugna

The guanaco (*Lama guanacoë*) is the largest living South American mammal. The body, measuring 6 – 7½ ft (180 – 220 cm) in length, is stocky, the legs long and slender. The tail is 6 – 10 in (15 – 25 cm) long, rounded and hairless on the lower side. The animal's height to the shoulder is 28 – 52 in (90 130 cm) and it weighs 132 – 165 lb (60 – 75 kg). It is probably the ancestor of two domestic breeds, the llama and the alpaca.

The guanaco, like the vicuña, has an enormous geographical range. Normally the animal frequents arid terrain, especially in regions near the equator, south to the Gran Chaco lowlands. Formerly the savannas and semidesert zones of Patagonia and Tierra del Fuego were also inhabited by the animal, but today it has almost completely vanished from these regions and has a local distribution high up in the Andes, from southern Peru to Tierra del Fuego.

The guanaco lives in small herds containing, at most, 20 – 30 individuals. One male fulfils the role of guide and protector of such groups. After an 11-month gestation period, the female gives birth to one baby which she suckles for 4 months.

Of the two domesticated subspecies, the llama is mainly used as an indispensible beast of burden, being capable of carrying loads of around 110 lb (50 kg) and traveling more than 15 miles (25 km) a day over mountain tracks. The alpaca, on the other hand, has for centuries been selectively bred only for its wool.

Closely related to the guanaco is an elegant, slim animal, the vicuña (*Lama vicugna*). It is 50 – 76 in (125 – 190 cm) in length, plus a 6 – 10 in (15 – 25 cm) tail. It stands 28 – 44 in (70 – 110 cm) at the shoulder, and it weighs about 110 lb (50 kg). Until a short time ago, the vicuña inhabited the plateaux and higher ranges of the Andes, up to an altitude of 14,000 ft (4,300 m), from southern Ecuador to northwest Argentina, but nowadays the animal has completely disappeared from many regions because of unrestricted hunting.

Llama
(*Lama guanacoë glama*)

Alpaca
(*Lama guanacoë pacos*)

Guanaco
(*Lama guanacoë*)

The guanaco's habitat, as well as that of its two subspecies, is made up of localized arid and semidesert zones both in the lowlands and up in the mountains. The two domesticated varieties bred from the guanaco are the alpaca, bred for its fine wool, and the llama, used as a beast of burden, and capable, in fact, of carrying some 110 lbs (50 kg) of baggage, covering over 15 miles (25 km) daily over mountain tracks.

Llamas differ from camels by virtue of their lesser size and absence of humps; the head is small, the eyes are large, the ears pointed and the lips much more prominent.

OKAPI

Okapia johnstoni

Order Artiodactyla
Family Giraffidae
Size Length about 80 in (200 cm);
height 60 – 68 in (150 – 170 cm)
Weight 550 lb (250 kg)
Dentition $\frac{0.0.3.3}{3.1.3.3}$ = 32
Gestation 14½ – 15 months
Number of young 1

The okapi is a fairly large artiodactyl with long legs and long neck, standing higher at the shoulder than the rump. The coat is uniformly dark (brown-black) but the hind and forelegs are white with horizontal black stripes. The okapi only inhabits the rainforest in a restricted region of Zaire with an area of about 15,000 sq. miles (40,000 km^2) bounded by the Ituri, Uele, and Congo rivers. It feeds mainly on foliage, including the leaves of trees normally shunned by other animals, such as euphorbias.

Like virtually all forest animals, the okapi is solitary or lives in pairs (male and female in the breeding period, mother and baby at other times). It would appear that after mating the adults separate and continue living on their own or with the babies. The long gestation lasts more than a year, but there is no saying what advantage this may bring. A newborn okapi weighs 44 lb (20 kg) and stands 32 in (80 cm) at the shoulder. Apparently the mother initially keeps at a distance from her offspring; suckling, for example, is prolonged, and it is almost 2 months before the baby begins to feed on vegetation. Weaning starts at the age of about 9 months.

Okapis fight with one another by pushing with their shoulders or shoving neck to neck, and their skin is thicker at those points where bodies come into contact. They threaten with head lowered and neck outstretched and bowed, the exact opposite of the dominance posture. The okapi does not strike the adversary directly with its head but tries to make contact, for example, by positioning the head under the other's neck and then jerking violently upward.

The okapi (*Okapia johnstoni*) is similar to its primitive ancestor *Palaeotragus*, and in this sense is virtually a living fossil. It was only discovered at the end of the 19th century and details of its life are still little known. The white stripes on the body provide excellent camouflage as rays of sunlight filter through the foliage of the forest. The okapi feeds mainly on leaves and plants normally disdained by other animals, such as euphorbians. The first notification of its existence came from the English explorer Henry Stanley, writing of his travels. He stated that, according to local lore, animals resembling horses were living in the impenetrable Congo jungles. In 1899, under the auspices of the British governor of Uganda, an expedition was sent out to ascertain whether this was true. The first attempt at classification, based on a skin fragment, mistakenly placed the okapi among the Equidae, but this initial error was remedied after the arrival in Europe, in 1901, of a hide and two skulls. The species, in fact, bore a strong resemblance to ancient extinct giraffes, and was therefore given a separate subfamily. This discovery, one of the last in the world of mammals, aroused enormous curiosity and the species was in danger of becoming extinct, because of the demand by collectors and zoos, before really being known. Fortunately, although quite rare, the fact that the okapi lives in virtually inaccessible surroundings is a reasonable guarantee of its survival.

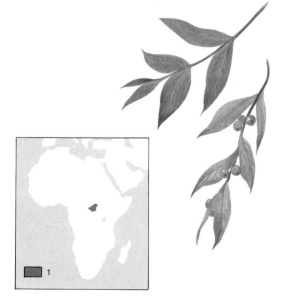

1) The okapi lives only in a restricted area of Zaire. Its habitat is the equatorial forest. It is estimated that the okapi population, occupying an area of some 15,000 sq. miles (40,000 km^2), numbers around 10,000 animals.

GIRAFFE

Giraffa camelopardalis

Order Artiodactyla
Family Giraffidae
Size Height to shoulder about 10 ft (3 m); height to top of head 15 – 19 ft (4.5 – 5.8 m)
Weight 1,100 – 1,650 lb (500 – 750 kg)
Dentition $\frac{0.0.3.3}{3.1.3.3}$ = 32
Reproductive period Throughout year
Gestation 14 – 15½ months (about 450 days)
Number of young 1 – 2
Sexual maturity 3 (5) years
Maximum age 20 – 30 years

The giraffe is an extremely strange-looking animal. The shoulder is much higher than the rump, and the small head is situated at about double the shoulder height. The eyes are large and expressive, but the ears are small, short, and pointed. There are 2 – 5 small horns, a few inches long, on the head, the number varying with sub-species. These are rounded, slightly thicker at the tip and covered with skin. The tongue is very long, measuring about 16 in (40 cm).

At one time the giraffe roamed almost all suitable zones of Africa with the exception of the most arid regions (central Sahara), the wettest areas (equatorial forests), and the mountains. Nowadays the animal's distribution is more restricted, discontinuous in the west and only continuous in the central-eastern part of the continent.

The giraffe is an animal of the tree-covered steppes, and the size and consistency of a herd depends on whether tree growth is abundant or sparse. It is the only animal, apart from the elephant, which can feed on the highest leaves of a tree, normally between 5½ – 20 ft (2 – 6 m) above the ground. With its long, prehensile tongue and large upper lip it can break off leaves and twigs and transfer them to the mouth. Its preference is for leguminous species, particularly the acacia, and it has no problems with the thorns.

Giraffes are gregarious animals and their forms of association are modeled on those of other plain-dwelling artiodactyls. Females and young form separate herds numbering a few dozen and sometimes up to 40 (or exceptionally 70) individuals. Adult males remain on their own, occasionally in

Reticulated giraffe
(*Giraffa camelopardalis reticulata*)

company with younger males; but the latter tend more readily to form all-male groups.

In these herds there is a form of hierarchy, dominance being asserted by stretching the head high and raising the chin. When rivals clash, they first threaten with lowered head, then take up positions side by side, swaying their necks and eventually striking each other, often quite violently, with head, neck, or shoulder. The small, rounded horns are not very dangerous and combats are never too bloody, but it may happen that one giraffe, sustaining injury to the blood vessels of the neck, will lose consciousness. After the clash, the loser, recognizing his inferiority, will wander off and not be pursued.

As a rule, the giraffe walks slowly, but to speed up it breaks into a trot, moving both legs on each side simultaneously. When galloping, however, the animal looks ungainly because the neck swings like a pendulum, since it has to balance the forward thrust of the legs. The giraffe looks as if it is running in slow motion, yet because of its enormous stride it can reach a speed of 30 mph (50 kmh) over short distances.

Being so large and so wary, the giraffe is less troubled than other species by the attentions of predators. Now and then a leopard will attack a giraffe, but such an incident is likely to be unplanned; and apart from assaults on sick or very young animals, the only carnivore with any real prospect of success against a healthy, adult giraffe is the lion. The surest defense for the giraffe is to run away, but in extreme situations and against less dangerous enemies, kicks are most effective.

The breeding period does not occur at any determined season and varies from place to place. Giraffes do not form harems and their system of courtship appears to be based on hierarchic links among the males which are reinforced during the phases preceding copulation. Gestation lasts a long time, more than a year. This fact, coupled with successions of births virtually once every two years, ensures that the giraffe population is normally well balanced.

The giraffe's tongue is more than 16 in (40 cm) long and very useful for feeding on leaves.

Giraffes amble, moving both legs on one side simultaneously.

Giraffe resting.

The giraffe eats mimosa and acacia leaves, including thorns.

Deep sleep lasts only a few minutes, the head being supported by hindlegs.

To establish rank, giraffes push with their necks.

A giraffe drinking.

The giraffe runs awkwardly but can reach a speed of 30 mph (50 kmh).

Giraffes, zebras, and antelopes graze together and can thus detect predators more easily.

RED DEER
Cervus elaphus

Order Artiodactyla
Family Cervidae
Size Height 40 – 52 in (100 – 130 cm), females slightly smaller
Weight 330 – 660 lb (150 – 300 kg); in some subspecies under 220 lb (100 kg)
Dentition $\frac{0.1.3.3}{3.1.3.3} = 34$
Reproductive period Mid September to mid October
Gestation About 8 months
Number of young 1
Sexual maturity 2 (3) years for females, 5 (at least) for males
Maximum age 15 – 20 years

The red deer is a well-proportioned animal with long legs and a sturdy body. The young are spotted at birth and only after a few months does this pattern fade into the uniform reddish-brown of the adults. The males (stags) vary somewhat from the females (hinds) and not only in color. Antlers apart, their general appearance is heavier and, when mature, almost bull-like. The neck is thick and sturdy, with a mane of long hairs which is conspicious during the mating season and in winter. Some parts of the body, such as the legs and belly, turn darker in color during the estral phases, and at this period males freely plunge themselves into mud.

The principal charateristic of deer is the pair of antlers, which are basically bony formations, growing rapidly (and seasonally), becoming solid and then being shed. The knobs or bosses that later develop into spikes or tines sprout from the frontal bone of the males when they are quite young, and at 14 – 17 months the initial growth is complete, soon to become solidified. The shedding of the antlers usually occurs in spring. The first antler is generally formed of a simple spike or tine. Year after year the antlers become steadily stronger and longer, with an increasing number of tines: at the age of 2 years there are 4 – 6 in all, at 3 years there are 8, and at the age of 4 years the stag may have attained its normal full growth of 12 tines.

Deer are widely distributed over Europe, Asia, and Northern America: the New World form is known as the wapiti. Deer are fairly eclectic ungulates, living in large forests, both

The family Cervidae, which of course includes the deer, is represented by more than 50 species from Eurasia and America. They are herbivorous ungulates who vary in size from that of a dog to that of a horse; and the stags bear antlers that are shed annually. The red deer (*Cervus elaphus*), shown here, has a powerful build. The rough coat is reddish brown in summer, dark-gray in winter (when it is also thicker). The fawns have a white-spotted coat. the large, imposing antlers are cylindrical in form. The red deer is an inhabitant of deciduous and mixed woodlands, preferring zones that are near water. The animal is mainly active at dawn and dusk. During the day, particularly in summer, it usually rests among the trees. In the rutting season stags fight one another for possession of the hinds who gather in harems of varying size, depending on the conditions of the environment and numbers in the herd. The stags are polygamous.

The red deer feeds on all types of vegetation, fruit, acorns, shoots, and grasses.

lowland and montane, and in more open areas, including partly swampy zones. Although not specifically adapted to life in the mountains, in summer they venture well beyond the treeline and can withstand snow quite well. Typically herbivorous, deer feed on anything that grows in woods and meadows, including grasses, fruits, foliage, shoots, twigs, and even bark.

Deer are social animals, spending their life in herds that are variously structured. There are three principal types – male herds, family herds, and mixed herds. The first of these is made up exclusively of males of varying ages but usually barring animals that are too young and thus still remain with a family herd, or older individuals who lead an isolated life. Family herds contain separate family groups, constituting a mother with a baby of that year and a daughter of the previous year. Mixed herds, however, are less stable in structure, for they are almost wholly associated with the mating season or the period immediately afterwards.

In late spring gravid females leave the herd. The birth takes place in a secluded and well-protected spot, and the female tolerates no other deer in the vicinity. After a few days, when the fawn is more confident of its own powers, mothers tend to approach one another and eventually form a herd. This usually happens in late summer.

Deer are not difficult to rear and can also be domesticated quite easily, even though, notwithstanding some positive experiments, they would seem to have no real practical value as beasts of burden. Stags are liable to be dangerous in the mating season: otherwise deer are very tolerant of human presence and live quite contentedly in public parks, in close contact with visitors. In Siberia some races have been bred in collective farms, mainly because of their antlers in velvet, and there have been breeding experiments in the Soviet Union and Scotland for the purpose of meat production.

The deer family is widely distributed in the Old World, especially in Asia and in the New World. A well known Asian species is the Axis (*Axis axis*) widespread in India and in Bangladesh. Very characteristic is its coat, sprinkled with white dots, even in the adult.

*S*ome representatives of the family Cervidae.

Muntjac
(*Muntiacus muntjak*)

Sika
(*Cervus nippon*)

Sambar
(*Cervus unicolor*)

Chinese water deer
(*Hydropotes inermis*)

Musk deer
(*Moschus moschiferus*)

Axis
or Indian spotted deer
(*Axis axis*)

Mule deer
(*Odocoileus hemionus*)

Pampas deer
(*Ozotoceros bezoarticus*)

Virginian deer
(*Odocoileus virginianus*)

▼1) Sika; 2) Sambar; 3) Red deer.

▼ 1) Mule deer; 2) Virginian deer; 3) Muntjac; 4) Pampas deer; 5) Musk deer; 6) Chinese water deer; 7) Axis deer.

1
2   3

1
2   4   6
3   5   7

REINDEER
Rangifer tarandus

Order Artiodactyla
Family Cervidae
Size Height 40 – 52 in (100 – 130 cm)
Weight Very variable, because there are also domesticated races. Generally from 200 – 600 lb (90 – 270 kg) for males, rarely more. The Eurasian subspecies are smaller
Dentition $\frac{0.0.3.3}{3.1.3.3} = 32$
Reproductive period From mid September to mid October; Eurasian subspecies to end-September
Gestation About 7½ – 8 months
Number of young 1, occasionally 2
Sexual maturity Females at 2 years, males later
Maximum age 15 – 20 years

The reindeer has an elongated body with well-developed legs. The coat is thick but not woolly, and there is a pronounced mane on the neck; the appearance of the coat differs markedly according to season. Muzzle and nostrils are covered with hair, this being an adaptation making it possible for the reindeer to hunt for food even under snow.

The reindeer's hoofs are unusually broad and widespread, making it easier for the animal to walk over muddy or snowy terrain. As the reindeer moves, the action of the sinews produces a characteristic sound.

Antlers are present in both sexes, the basal rose being somewhat flattened, and the long beams furnished with many branches. In North America the reindeer is commonly known as the caribou. The barren ground caribou, inhabiting the open spaces, has long, slender antlers with rounded branches and fairly short tines; the antlers of the woodland caribou are thicker and shorter, with flattened branches and a broader span. The maximum length is 5 ft (1.5 m) in the North American subspecies, but nearer 4 ft (1.2 m) in the Eurasian races.

Eurasian reindeer inhabit the northern countries of the Old World from Scandinavia to Siberia, whereas their American relatives, the caribous, live in Greenland, Canada and Alaska. They were once widely distributed in many parts of the United States but today there are only a few individuals

The reindeer (*Rangifer tarandus*), known in North America as the caribou, is a typical Arctic ungulate. A feature of the animal is the antler formation. Antlers are, in fact, present in both sexes, the base being somewhat flattened and the beams rather long and with many branches. The reindeer appeared during the Pleistocene, at the time of the last Ice Age, and it was then that the species had its widest distribution.

Food consists not only of grass, leaves, and fungi but also mosses and, especially, lichens.

Reindeer hoofs, here shown alongside those of the fallow deer, are highly adaptable, functioning like miniature rafts on muddy or snow-covered ground. The animal is a good swimmer.

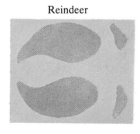

Reindeer

Fallow deer

left in northern Idaho, Nevada, and Washington.

The typical habitat of the reindeer is the tundra, but it also roams the woodlands to the south of this belt, and these, according to subspecies, generally constitute its winter quarters. The reindeer's chances of survival in the bitterest Arctic winters depend on its ability to find food, even beneath the snow. The animal kicks the snow cover away with its hoofs and then digs deeper with the forefeet to lay bare the underlying plant growth. One of its main food sources is the lichen *Cladonia rangiferina*, but many other types of vegetation are also consumed.

Harsh climatic conditions compel reindeer to undertake migrations of thousands of miles. The distances covered vary, in fact, according to the environment; thus the reindeer of Terra Nova Island, in Newfoundland, move from higher to lower ground but obviously within fixed geographical limits.

The longest journeys are those of the tundra caribou, making three migrations every year. The spring migration occurs in April-May. At the end of July the species returns from its summer quarters, and by the end of August it has again reached the southernmost bounds of the tundra. Then follows a last brief journey, interrupted by the breeding season: when this comes to an end, in late October or November, the migration is speedily resumed and the species arrives back at its winter quarters in December or January. The more southerly subspecies, which inhabit the forests, move around much less; and in some, winter and summer quarters almost overlap.

As a rule, reindeer herds are quite open in structure, so that any individuals can join or leave it without any particular consequences, except, of course, in the mating season. But there is a fairly complex hierarchy within the herd, whereby the adult males dominate other juvenile and too-elderly males and, the females. Strength of antlers is an important decider of rank among the males, as it is among the females, and the latter, in fact, will even get the better of juvenile males up to the age of two years. Dominance within the herd or class may have special relevance at particular times, as, for example, when competition for food is intense, during especially hard winters.

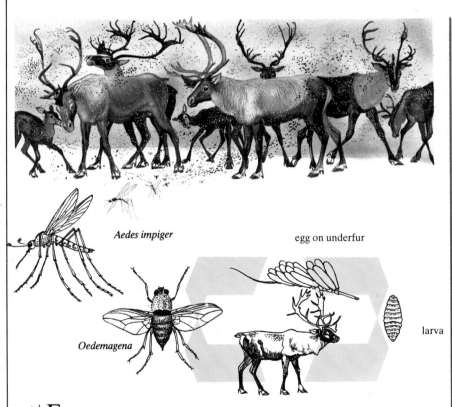

Aedes impiger

egg on underfur

Oedemagena

larva

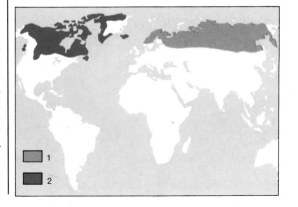

▲ Flies and mosquitos (*Aedes impiger*) are terrible scourges for reindeer and may force them to travel long distances. A species of fly called *Oedemagena* also lays its eggs at the base of the hairs, its larvae penetrating the skin and causing much pain.

▲ In their mass springtime migrations, female and young reindeer are followed by the males. Distances covered vary with the surroundings: those from Terra Nova in Newfoundland shift from higher to lower ground but obviously within geographic bounds. The more southerly races, from the forests, move about very little. Thus in the case of some subspecies (*R.t. granti*) winter and summer quarters almost overlap.

▼ Summer (1) and winter (2) quarters of the caribou (*R.t. groenlandicus*). In the hardest winters the animals winter even farther south (3).

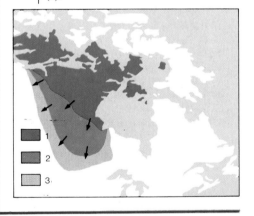

◀ 1) In Europe and Asia there are three subspecies of reindeer (*R.t. tarandus, R.t. fennicus and R.t. platyrhynchus*), inhabiting Norway, Sweden, northern Finland, the Soviet Union, Siberia, and Spitzbergen. 2) The North American caribou, with four subspecies (*R.t. groenlandicus, R.t. pearyi, R.t. granti and R.t. caribou*) live in southwestern and northwestern. Greenland (and adjacent islands), Alaska, and Canada. *R.t. caribou*, which once ranged widely over the United States, is now represented by only a few individuals in northern Idaho, Nevada, and Washington. The reindeer's characteristic habitat is the tundra. Its chances of surviving the most rigid Arctic winters depend on its finding food, even below the snow. The latter is removed with kicks and then the forelegs are inserted to uncover the plant layer underneath.

PRONGHORN ANTELOPE

Antilocapra americana

Order Artiodactyla
Family Antilocapridae
Size Height to shoulder 36 – 42 in (90 – 105 cm)
Weight About 110 lb (50 kg): female is smaller than male
Dentition $\frac{0.0.3.3}{3.1.3.3}$ = 32
Reproductive period October
Gestation 7½ months
Number of young 2 (1 – 3)
Sexual maturity Females 2 – 3 years, males later

Outwardly the pronghorn looks like many African antelopes (gazelles) but its hair is rough, the neck quite long and the head also fairly elongated. In general structure and physique, this is evidently a ruminant splendidly adapted for running, with broad chest, strong heart, and powerful muscles. The horn is unique. Like all true horns, it is made up of epidermal tissue, with many hairs cemented together with the protein keratin; in effect, therefore, it consists of a bony core enclosed in a horny sheath. Normally such horns are permanent, but the pronghorn sheds them annually and grows new ones. Actually it sheds only the outer sheath, which is not hard and compact, but covered with hairy tissue, giving it the consistency of a soft, rubbery membrane.

The pronghorn antelope is an animal of the New World, and specifically North America. Its former range extended from Canada to Mexico and California, from the Rocky Mountains to just west of the Mississippi-Missouri, but indiscriminate killing plus the opening up of the broad prairies for agriculture and livestock raising, brought the species to the brink of extinction within about a century.

The pronghorn's habitat was, above all, the open prairie and the neighboring arid zones; but the animal also roamed fairly high mountain areas and rocky ground, though necessarily open and without tree cover. As a result of this, its diet consists in the main of grasses of all kinds, including, for lack of anything better, the toughest and almost thorny species to be found in semidesert regions.

Pronghorn antelope
(*Antilocapra americana*)

▲
▶ The pronghorn is a distinctive ungulate, belonging to a family which was fairly widespread in ancient times, but nowadays represented by this species alone. Its distribution is confined to the North American continent, specifically the great plains and prairies. Its diet is made up to a large extent of various types of grass, including those that are tough or thorny. This makes life easier in steppe or semidesert regions. Social organization of the species is, in many respects, complex. At first glance the animal has the general appearance of other ungulates living in open spaces; but territory plays an important part in the pronghorn's group life. Adult males are territorial only from late March to October, the latter date coinciding with the end of the breeding season. The zone defended by such a male is very large but contains broad tracts of terrain which do not belong to any individual animal and are therefore "free"; these communal zones separate the various occcupied areas. Territory is marked with secretions from scent glands, but the mere presence of the male is also to be regarded as a visual sign of ownership.

▶ Vision is the best-developed sense. The pronghorn's eye is as big as that of a horse. The shape of the head, however thanks also to the horns, has many affinities with that of the chamois. The ears are long and pointed, with the tips slightly turned inward. The muzzle is rather slender.

The social organization of the pronghorn is fairly complex, being, in broad outline, much like that of other ungulates of the open spaces. In spring the animals live in scattered groups which become fewer in number as the time comes nearer for births. The adult males live apart in individually demarcated territories which are, of course, defended. Territory is a very important aspect of the pronghorn antelope's social life. Adult males are not territorial throughout the year, for this would make winter grouping impossible, but only from late March to October, up to the time of reproduction. The defended zone is quite large, ranging from 60 to 400 acres. Territories do not border on one another but are separated by broad tracts of ground which belong to no individual male and are therefore "free."

Territories are marked by scent from glandular secretions, or visually, in the sense that the presence of the male is itself a signal. If territory is invaded, owners will show their displeasure with puffs and snorts, punctuated by pauses for breath. If the intruder is an adult male and does not immediately withdraw, various behavior patterns may ensue. The occupier will approach, stand in his rival's way and execute a sucession of rhythmic movements which are rather like the steps of a courtship parade. The head is turned slightly toward the intruder and held down, although always above the horizontal, ears pricked back. Thus, by rotating the head a little, the pronghorn exposes the white patches on neck and cheeks as signals of intimidation.

Direct confrontations, with use of horns, are rare. In nineteen out of twenty encounters the above-mentioned rituals resolve matters, the intruder beating a retreat and, if he happens to be young, taking to his heels. Naturally, territory is at a premium during the breeding season, for it is almost exclusively the territorial males who succeed in copulating. When a female enters male territory, she is approached by the occupant who swings his head from side to side and gives out sounds of varying loudness (rumbles, gurgles, and intakes of breath), opening and half-closing the mouth and flicking the tongue to and fro. As his excitement mounts, he also emits strongly smelling gusts of breath and literally erects the sacral gland so that it visibly protrudes above the rump.

The horn of the pronghorn antelope, although consisting of genuine horny material, is shed and renewed every year.

Pronghorns are excellent runners and can keep up an average of 30 mph (50 kmh).

The white rump patch is an excellent signal, displayed when the animal is tense.

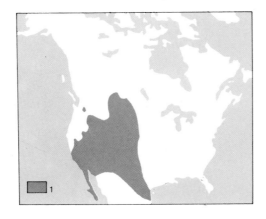

The baby is well camouflaged and only follows the mother around after a certain lapse of time.

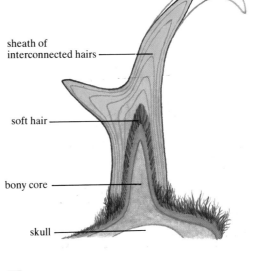

potential growth limit of horn

sheath of interconnected hairs

soft hair

bony core

skull

The animal's horns are embedded in a permanent bony core. They are about 10 in (25 cm) long, with few branches, terminating in one small, forward-turned tip and another, bigger point growing upward. Each horn is made up of an inner, permanent bony core and a sheath of epidermic tissue, full of hairs, held together by the protein keratin. The sheath is shed and renewed annually in much the same manner as a deer's entire antler.

Among extinct members of the family Antilocapridae are *Osbornoceros osborni* (above) and *Ilingoceros alexandrae* (below).

The pronghorn is an extremely inquistive animal.

1) There are five recognized subspecies of *Antilocapra americana*: *A.a. peninsularis*, *A.a. americana* (the one with the biggest range), *A.a. sonoriensis*, *A.a. aregona*, and *A.a. mexicana*. They have a discontinuous distribution across parts of North America. Nowadays the total number of pronghorns is under half a million, rather low considering that in former times, when it ranged from Canada to Mexico and California, continuously, there were approximately 40 million of them. Indiscriminate hunting brought the species to the verge of extinction, and it was only due to the strenuous action of certain naturalists that the pronghorn was restored to its present numbers.

INDIAN BUFFALO

Bubalus arnee

Order Artiodactyla
Family Bovidae
Size Height at shoulder 5 – 6 ft (150 – 180 cm)
Weight Average 1,600 – 1,900 lb (720 – 850 kg), up to a ton
Dentition $\dfrac{0.0.3.3}{3.1.3.3} = 32$
Reproductive period Varies according to area
Gestation 300 – 340 days
Number of young 1
Maximum age About 25 years

The Indian buffalo is a powerfully built animal, high at the shoulders and with a slightly hollow back, more apparent in the domestic breeds. It has a short neck with folds of skin at the front but no dewlap. Its head is large and roundish, its legs are large and relatively long, and it has a fairly long tail. Its hooves are very wide and strong, giving it a good grip on soft muddy ground.

Its coat is dark gray, iron-gray or black, in some subspecies also brown. The hair is thin and bristly, leaving the skin almost naked on some parts of the body. Domestic breeds may also be pale-colored and flecked, but these are less common. The horns are very large and sickle-shaped, with a triangular section at the base. They lie almost flat, with only the tips curving upward, and are about 4 ft (120 cm) long.

Indian buffaloes were originally widely distributed from India to Indochina, including several islands in the same region. In the past, buffaloes were present in Mesopotamia, North Africa and Egypt, and even in Europe. In these areas the wild breeds became extinct and only domestic breeds remained or were imported. Today the buffalo in the wild state is found only in protected areas, in parks or reserves. They favor a wet environment where they spend most of their day. They live mainly near rivers, in marshes, swampy lowlands and humid jungle country, and even near coastal saltwater lagoons. Buffaloes feed mainly on grasses and aquatic plants, and any marsh vegetation.

The social organization is based on

The Indian buffalo (*Bubalus arnee*) is little known in the wild, where it lives in marshy areas with plenty of reeds and thickets. Of all the bovids it is the one which most likes to live in water. It is a rather docile animal (and has therefore been widely domesticated), but if irritated it can be dangerous.

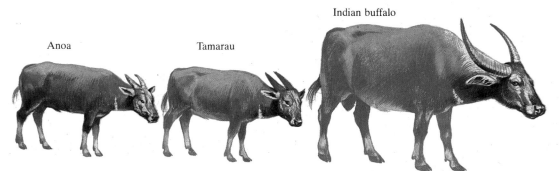

Anoa · Tamarau · Indian buffalo

Very close to the buffalo on the ladder of evolution are the anoa (*Bubalus depressicornis*) and the tamaran (*Bubalus arnee mindorensis*). All three species have a whitish half-collar.

herds of 10 – 20 individuals or more, composed mainly of young animals of both sexes, calves and cows. A few adult bulls may also live in these groups, but generally, and especially when they are older, they prefer to live separately.

The mating period does not occur at a fixed season, except for those populations that inhabit the most northerly extremes of their area distribution. For them, mating takes place toward fall and the young are born at the beginning of summer, after a gestation period of about 10 months. The cow gives birth close to the herd, and within a short time the calf can keep up with its mother.

Indian buffaloes spend most of the day in water or mud. When danger threatens, the buffaloes do not take refuge in the water but make a wide circuit through the wet grass and then stop to check on the cause of the disturbance. It is almost invariably caused by a tiger or, even more likely, by man. The tiger is certainly able to attack and overpower young animals that have become separated from the herd, but it can by no means compete with a whole herd. It also appears that the buffaloes are greatly angered by the scent of the tiger, and so are able to track it in their turn.

Related to the buffalo is the anoa, (*Bubalus depressicornis*) considered the most primitive of the bovines. In appearance it is more like an odd kind of antelope than a true bovine. It is of dwarf stature compared with buffaloes: 23 – 35 in (60 – 90 cm) at the shoulders, with a weight of 330 – 660 lb (150 – 300 kg). Its coat is brownish-gray with faint white stripes, and one clearly visible white stripe on the lower part of the neck. There are 2 – 3 known subspecies. *B.d. fergusoni* inhabits the hilly areas of Celebes, while *B.d. depressicornis* inhabits the lowland. The anoa lives in marshy or humid woodland and areas of dense undergrowth, but its natural habitat is being destroyed by land reclamation, so it is threatened by environmental changes as well as by poachers. The anoa is not a gregarious animal, living at most in pairs, so much so that if bred in captivity care must be taken to separate the bulls from the other animals. Like all *Bubalus* species, it is very aggressive and does not hesitate to attack when wounded, otherwise it is calm and slow in its movements, typically bovine.

▲ Tigers or leopards can successfully attack only very young or sick animals.

▼ Baths and mudbaths are a useful means of ridding themselves of parasites.

▼ Buffaloes have been domesticated for over 5,000 years. The horns of the domestic breeds are shorter and flatter. There are many varieties distinguishable by their coat.

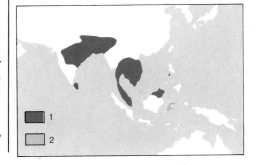

▲
▼ The anoa (*Bubalus depressicornis*) is one of the most primitive bovines, morphologically somewhere between the bovines and the antelopes. It is a solitary animal, found in the island of Celebes. The tamarau, a similar species, is classified by different authors either as a subspecies of the anoa or as a race of the Indian buffalo.

Antelopes

Anoa

Indian buffalo

Eotragus

◄ Geographical distribution of : 1) Indian buffalo (*Bubalus arnee*); 2) Anoa (*Bubalus depressicornis*). The former is found in India and southeast Asia; it populates the humid jungles and fertile valleys, especially near rivers and marshes, more rarely forests with dense undergrowth. According to some authors, Indian buffaloes are the ancestors of various domestic breeds imported also into Europe. The anoa, on the other hand, lives only in the island of Celebes and, being the smallest and most primitive of all existing species of bovids, is also known as the pygmy buffalo.

AFRICAN BUFFALO

Syncerus caffer

Order Artiodactyla
Family Bovidae
Size Height varies according to subpecies: from 3½ – 4½ ft (1.1 – 1.4 m) (*Syncerus caffer nanus*) to 5¾ ft (1.8 m) (*Syncerus caffer caffer*)
Weight 770 lb (350 kg) (*nanus*) to 2,000 lb (900 kg) (*caffer*)
Dentition $\dfrac{0.0.3.3}{3.1.3.3} = 32$
Reproductive period In relation to the rainy season
Gestation 10 – 11 months
Number of young 1
Sexual maturity Females at 2 – 3 years; males later
Maximum age About 20 years

The African buffalo (*Syncerus caffer*), is an extremely strong, heavy animal with muscular legs, a short neck and a broad, powerful head. Its horns are very thick and heavy at the base, curving upward and outward after an initial, fairly pronounced downward curve. They are over 3 ft (1 m) long, and have an even wider span. Its tail is quite long, reaching down to its hocks. The cows are smaller and their horns are not so large.

The subspecies *caffer* is dark brown to black in color, while the younger individuals are lighter, brownish red or brown. The subspecies *nanus* is smaller and differs mainly in the shape of its horns and head. Its horns are distinctly separate at the base, and smaller, 29 in (75 cm). They never curve downward, but rather outward, backward, and upward. Its ears are therefore never partially concealed by its horns, and they also appear larger because of their conspicuous fringe of hair. Its coat is mainly reddish in color, slightly darker on the shoulder.

The African buffalo is distributed throughout Africa south of the Sahara, except for the Cape region. It feeds mainly on various kinds of grasses, graminaceous plants, and tubers. It does not normally eat foliage and branches, except in real forest areas where it also feeds on buds, shoots, and leaves. In general it shows remarkable adaptability and can live in different environments. Water is always of great importance, especially during

The African buffalo (*Syncerus caffer*) is considered one of the most dangerous animals existing in Africa. However, it is aggressive only when seriously disturbed or wounded; in such cases a fatal outcome is not uncommon. There are two main types of African buffalo: the plains and the forest buffalo. The former is the larger animal, dark blackish-brown in color.

the dry season: the African buffalo must drink every day, so this is a limiting factor. Buffaloes are mainly nocturnal animals, except in areas where they are not disturbed. Broadly speaking, they remain in thick vegetation during the hottest hours, preferably near water. When dusk falls they emerge to feed, grazing for most of the night.

Their social organization is closely linked to environmental conditions. The black African buffaloes form very large herds, always numbering more than 50 head. The largest herds are composed of cows and young animals up to two years of age. The adult bulls also live mainly (80 per cent) in the herds of cows and only rarely form small separate groups of 3 to 20 individuals. Only after the age of 10 years do the males nearly always leave the herd to return to it only occasionally.

The courtship season varies according to locality. At such times the older bulls return to the herd and try to reestablish their rank, which is not always easily or peacefully accomplished. After some ceremonial threatening behavior, there are also violent clashes, when the adversaries furiously butt each other, although without causing serious injury. Gestation lasts about 300 – 330 (even 345) days, and a single calf is born, generally shortly before the rainy season, which basically determines the annual cycle.

Given their great size and courage, buffaloes have few dangerous enemies. Their principal foe is the lion. However, lions do not prey mainly on the calves and immature buffaloes, but on the older, adult solitary males, in a ratio disproportionate to the percentage of such individuals in the population. This shows that the herd is a highly effective defense against predators. Occasionally buffaloes may also fall prey to crocodiles, when they are swimming across rivers, and – even more rarely – to leopards. However, buffaloes have been observed to defend themselves very well against attacks by lions; in bloody encounters that may well result in the predator's death. A wounded buffalo will fight to the death and is a highly dangerous animal, as many African hunters have found. Left to themselves, buffaloes are not excessively aggressive, but given their size and the speed at which they can move over short distances, they are very dangerous when irritated or disturbed at close quarters.

▲ Although they are not as fond of water as the Indian buffalo, these animals often spend their time in water and take mudbaths. These activities not only serve to rid them of parasites, but also help them to keep cool: the dried mud gives effective protection against the heat.

▼ An African buffalo can even kill a lion.

▲ The dwarf forest buffalo (*Syncerus caffer nanus*), also called the red buffalo because of the color of its coat, is smaller than the plains buffalo and has shorter horns. In the past it was not considered to be a subspecies of *Syncerus caffer*, but a separate species.

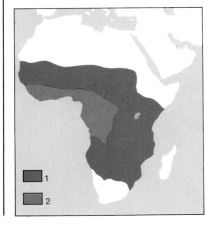

◄ Geographical distribution of: 1) the true African buffalo (*Syncerus caffer caffer*); 2) Dwarf forest buffalo (*Syncerus caffer nanus*). African buffaloes are found throughout almost all of Africa south of the Sahara. They frequent grasslands and dry plains up to swampy river mouths. They also live in the tropical and equatorial forests and in mountainous areas up to altitudes of around 10,000 ft (3,000 m). The true African buffalo is a typical ungulate of the grassy plains and inhabits East Africa, Namibia, and Angola; *Syncerus caffer nanus* is found in the forests of central and West Africa; lastly, *Syncerus caffer brachyceros*, considered by many to be an intermediate form, is the subspecies found in the most northerly areas of distribution, which is roughly from the Sudan to Senegal.

GAUR
Bos gaurus

Order Artiodactyla
Family Bovidae
Size Height at shoulder 5¼ – 6¾ ft (1.65 – 2.1 m)
Weight 1,500 – 2,200 lb (700 – 1,000 kg)
Dentition $\frac{0.0.3.3}{3.1.3.3} = 32$
Reproductive period According to the rainy season; generally from November to March (India)
Gestation 9 months
Number of young 1
Sexual maturity Males at 5 years; females at about 3 years
Maximum age 20 years

The gaur is a heavy bovine, characterized, like all members of the subgenus *Bibos* (banteng, gayal, and kouprey), by the huge development of the apophyses of the third to eleventh thoracic vertebrae. These support a great muscle mass which also adds to the distinctive hump on the back of this animal. The horns are directed upward and inward at the tips, after initially dipping down and then out into a fairly wide curve. In adult animals the horns are a dull olive color: they are often blunted at the tips and quite ridged.

The environment frequented by the gaur is forest land with plenty of plants such as bamboo, shrubs, and small trees, interspersed with large clearings. They also frequent the open lowlands not far from forest. Gaurs also inhabit hill country up to altitudes of 6,500 – 10,000 ft (2,000 – 3,000 m), but the presence of water is essential to them. In the past the gaur was widely distributed throughout India and Indochina. Today, due to various factors, its area is considerably limited, with a large number of gaps. In the Indian region the species is present in three areas: southwest India, the central upland plains, and the slopes of the Himalayas up to Assam, along the Bramaputra basin. Farther east its survival is ensured only in the few parks and nature reserves. The gaur feeds on grasses and bamboo shoots, shrubs, and undergrowth. Unlike other wild bovines, it does not damage plantations. Gaurs live in relatively large herds.

The gayal (*Bos gaurus frontalis*) is a more stocky and compact animal than the gaur, representing a domesticated

Gayal

Kouprey

Banteng

▲ The gaur (*Bos gaurus*) is a bovine of larger dimensions than domestic cattle. Through being so widely hunted, especially in the past, and because of diseases caught from its domestic relations, it is threatened with extinction.

◄ Together with the gaur, the banteng (*Bos javanicus*), the gayal (*Bos gaurus frontalis*), and the kouprey (*Bos sauveli*) also belong to the subgenus *Bibos*, one of the three genera into which the true bovines are subdivided. They are all very powerful ungulates which can be overpowered by large carnivores such as the tiger, or occasionally the leopard, only in particular circumstances.

form of the latter animal, with shorter legs and a less pronounced dorsal hump. It is smaller, too, its height at the shoulder not exceeding 5¼ ft (1.6 m).

The banteng (*Bos javanicus*) is another wild bovine from the Indochina region. It is smaller than the gaur, and more elegant in build and coloring. Its height at the shoulder is up to 5½ ft (1.7 m), and its maximum weight is 2,000 lb (900 kg). The dorsal hump is less pronounced, and the dewlap is also less prominent. Its coat is often paler, especially in some local forms, and it has a vivid whitish patch in the anal area.

The banteng's ecological requirements are similar to those of the gaur: like the latter, *Bos javanicus* lives in forest land with wide clearings, and is found up to altitudes of 6,500 ft (2,000 m).

The kouprey (*Bos sauveli*) is among the most recently described mammals, its discovery dating back only to 1935. Its origins are still uncertain and it is thought to be a bovine that returned to the wild, given the existence of a domesticated animal of this type during the period of Khmer domination. The kouprey is between the gaur and the banteng in size, and is similar in coloring. Its distinguishing feature is the shape of its horns, which curve very like a yak's. The pronounced inward hook of the tips apparently prevents the shedding of the juvenile horn sheaths, as occurs in other bovines. Unfortunately, the kouprey, too, is a species in danger of extinction. Its area of distribution is northeast Cambodia on the borders of Laos and Vietnam.

The yak (*Bos mutus*) looks very different from all the other bovines, but this is due to the unusual length of its hair. Its tail is long and its limbs well developed, its hooves broad and wide-splaying. The coat, particularly long in the area of the shoulders and the flanks and relatively short elsewhere, is dark or black in color. The tail ends in a large tuft. Its height is over 6½ ft (2 m) at the shoulder, and it weighs about 2,200 lb (1,000 kg).

The yak grazes on pasture grass, and if necessary will also eat marsh grasses, lichens, or even tubers. It can survive under the bleakest conditions. It has been domesticated since earliest times and is an irreplaceable help to the inhabitants of Nepal, Tibet, Bhutan, and the Mongolian interior.

▲ If a tiger attempts to attack gaur or gayal calves, they present a united front and force the tiger to flee.

▼ Geographical distribution of: 1) Gaur; 2) Kouprey; 3) Banteng. The gaur is a typical huge bovine of the Indian jungle, found in the forests of India, Burma, and Indochina as far as the Malay peninsula. The kouprey is limited to an area of northeast Cambodia on the borders of Laos and Vietnam, and is in danger of extinction. The banteng is found in Burma, Java, and Borneo, and is also in danger of extinction. There are three known subspecies of banteng: the banteng of Java (*Bos javanicus javanicus*), which survives only in Java in a few protected areas (Udjon Kulon and Baluran); the banteng of Borneo (*Bos javanicus lowi*), also on the verge of extinction, and protected only in the National Park of Kinabalu; and the banteng of Burma (*Bos javanicus birmanicus*), which is scattered over more or less the same protected areas where the gaur lives, in Burma and Thailand. Scholars finally distinguish the banteng of Bali, a domestic race which by now survives only in the domesticated form.

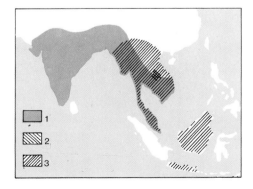

▲ The yak (*Bos mutus*) can live up to an altitude of 20,000 ft (6,000 m), and is the only pack-animal that can work at those heights. It has been domesticated for centuries, to such an extent that the wild forms are disappearing. It is an extremely economical ungulate, with a very thick and highly prized coat that has often made it the victim of hunters. Its horns are very developed, up to 3 ft (90 cm) long, and with almost the same span.

▼ The yak is a bovine that has been domesticated since very ancient times. Today it is still an irreplaceable help to peoples of Nepal, Tibet, Bhutan, and the Mongolian interior. It probably once roved throughout the upland plains of Tibet, but its present area of distribution (1) is very limited, being confined almost certainly to northen Tibet (Altyn Tag and Cuen-lun), where only a few thousand survive in the wild state.

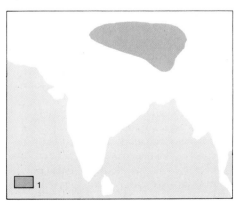

AMERICAN BISON
Bison bison

Order Artiodactyla
Family Bovidae
Size Height at shoulder up to 6¼ ft (1.9 m)
Weight About 1 ton
Dentition $\frac{0.0.3.3}{3.1.3.3} = 32$
Reproductive period July – August
Gestation 9 months
Number of young 1
Sexual maturity Females at 2 years; males much later
Maximum age 20 – 25 years

The bison is certainly the most striking-looking of the bovines. Its forequarters are much larger and more powerful than its hindquarters. The legs are of medium length and fairly strong. The head seems small in contrast, and the horns are rather small, smaller than in all other bovines. Its coat is thick and shaggy, up to 20 in (50 cm) long over the area comprising the head and forelimbs. There is a kind of tuft of hair on the head which almost covers the eyes, while a beard and mane cover the chin and dewlap. The forelimbs are covered with hair that looks like a pair of trousers. The tail ends in a tuft and is not as long as in other species, not reaching the hocks.

In the past, at the time of the European colonization, the bison inhabited almost the entire continent of North America from the Rocky Mountains to the eastern coast, and from the Great Slave Lake (in the North) to Mexico. Today, after being almost exterminated and then slowly re-established, they are still to be found in many parks in Canada and the USA.

The plains bison feed mainly on grass and similar plants; wood bison, on the other hand, feed on leaves, buds, shoots, small branches, and bark, and in cases of necessity also on mosses and lichen. Water is always necessary to bison, although in winter they can manage with snow.

The social organization of bison has much in common with that of other bovines or ungulates that inhabit open spaces. The males are often solitary or else live in small herds of males only, not far from the female herd; the females live in large herds, together

▲ The European bison and the American bison (illustrated) are the only wild bovines that exist today on the two continents. Both came close to extinction through man's activities, especially hunting, but fortunately today they are protected species.
The American bison lives in forest areas and prairies, while the European subspecies is essentially a forest-dwelling animal.

◄ During the conquest of the West, bison hunting (even by train) was fecklessly successful. It was connected with the determination to deprive the Indians of their means of survival.

with their young and the immature males. The size of the herd varies according to area: where there is a large population, an average herd is composed of more than 100 individuals. It does not seem that the herds are closed units or at all events bound together in some way, as is the case, for example, with the African buffalo. The only ties that can be assumed to exist are those of the family groups. Individual relationships among bison are also of the hierarchical kind. In general, adult males rank above all other individuals, but there is also a hierarchy among females, often linked to the presence of a calf. In this case the relationships change as the calf grows older and becomes more independent.

The largest herds form during the mating season. The bulls then become highly aggressive and fierce fights break out, with the bulls charging and wounding each other. Several bulls may fight each other several times within the space of a few dozen minutes. They charge each other head on, but their massive forehead and thick skull covered with shaggy hair afford good protection against injury. The horns are of much less importance.

The European bison (*Bison bonasus*) has had an even more dramatic history than its American counterpart. Compared with the American bison, it is slightly higher at the shoulder, 6½ ft (about 2 m), but has about the same weight of about a ton (the bulls); it is more graceful, less shaggy, has longer horns, and in short is more like a typical bovine than *Bison bison*.

The European bison, or wisent, was already very rare at the beginning of the nineteenth century, when the few surviving individuals, perhaps 300 – 500, were living in the forest of Bialowieska (Poland), whereas in ancient times they were found in almost all the forests of Europe. Today the herds of European bison must add up to a thousand individuals. Their environment is certainly a forest one, either conifer or mixed forest with large clearings, on plains or low hilly areas.

In many ways the European bison is similar to the American species. Its social organization is more or less the same as that of the American wood bison, but the herds are smaller. Gestation lasts about nine months and, as with the American species, only a single calf is born.

▲ | Bison are extremely curious and even the birth of a calf is a strong attraction.

▲ | During winter they have to dig under the snow to find food.

▲ | During the mating season the bulls fight fiercely.

The European bison (*Bison bonasus*) is slighty taller than the American species and relatively graceful in shape. It became extinct in the wild state, but was fortunately preserved through the individuals living in zoos. The present populations all stem from these. They feed mainly on poplar and ash leaves.

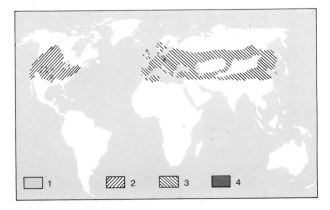

◄ | Present distribution (1) of the American bison (*Bison bison*) and original distribution (2).
Original area (3) of the European bison (*Bison bonasus*) and its present distribution (4).
The opening of the trans-American railroad (1865) played a definitive role in the fate of the bison. In 1901 the "Friends of the Bison" society was formed and, through campaigning by ardent naturalists, public opinion supported the battle for the conservation of the bison. By 1907 a reserve (Wichita) had already been created where a herd of bison could breed. Protection measures increased until, between 1915 and 1920, the parallel initiatives of the governments of the United States and Canada resulted in various parks and reserves.
The European bison has also come close to extinction this century, especially in the wake of war. Today about a thousand individuals survive in the forest of Bialowieska in Poland.

1   2   3   4

GAZELLES

Gazelles and antelopes are bovines comprising many species which are mostly notable for their agility and which carry long, slender horns. The majority come from Africa, but certain species are inhabitants of Asia. The true gazelles (genus *Gazella*), of which there are 12 species, are divided into three groups. In the great gazelles or mirror gazelles, the white patch on the rump surrounds the root of the tail like a "mirror," contrasting sharply with the darker colors of the haunches. Both males and females have horns. In the male Grant's gazelle (*Gazella granti*) the horns are 20 – 30 in (50 – 80 cm) long, lyrate, with the points generally curving forward. The female's horns are similar but not so long, 12 – 17 in (30 – 43 cm), and thinner. The upper parts of the body are yellowish-gray or rufous, the underside white.

Sömmering's gazelle (*Gazella soemmeringi*) is a little smaller. Both sexes have lyrate horns, wide apart and slightly inclined to the rear, with the points generally hooking inward. The female's horns are thinner and shorter than those of the males.

In the dama gazelle (*G. dama*) both sexes have horns, lyrate, slightly inclined backward and 6 – 16 in (16 – 41 cm) long. The color of the body varies widely from one region to another.

In the Edmi gazelle (*Gazella gazella*) the bucks have slightly S-shaped horns 8 – 14 in (20 – 35 cm) long, flat, oval in cross-section, curved backward and upward. The female's horns are the same shape but the cross-section at the base is round; they are shorter, 6 – 8 in (15 – 20 cm) and thinner, are more parallel and not so deeply ringed.

The dorcas gazelle (*G. dorcas*) is light brown or reddish brown on the upper parts of the body, and there is a brown or sepia stripe between the bottom edge of the lighter flanks and the white underside. The buck's horns are 10 – 15 in (26 – 38 cm) long and lyrate, curved in an S-shape, with the ends hooking inward. The female's horns are thinner and shorter, 6 – 10 in (16 – 25 cm), and more nearly parallel.

The forehead and top of the nose of the red-fronted gazelle, (*G. rufifrons*), are rufous or brown. The length of the horns in the males reaches 8½ – 14 in (22 – 35 cm), in the females 6 – 8 in (15 – 20 cm).

Some of the best known antelopes

Springbok
(*Antidorcas marsupialis*)

Thomson's gazelle
(*Gazella thomsoni*)

Klipspringer
(*Oreotragus oreotragus*)

Gerenuk
(*Litocranius walleri*)

Kirk's dik-dik
(*Rhyncotragus kirki*)

Zebra duiker
(*Cephalophus zebra*)

Oribi
(*Ourebia ourebi*)

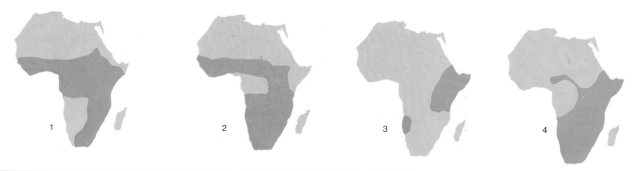

The habitat of the majority of gazelles is to be found in open grassy or bushy plains and in desert and semidesert, both in the lowlands and on mountain slopes up to 6,500 ft (2,000 m). The maps below show the range of distribution of some antelopes: (1) Klipspringer (*Oreotragus oreotragus*); (2) Oribi (*Ourebia ourebi*); (3) Dik-dik (genus *Rhyncotragus*); (4) Duikers (genus *Cephalophus*).

1

2

3

4

In Thomson's gazelle (*G. thomsoni*) there is a distinct difference between the horns of the male and female animals. While the male's horns, 10 – 17 in (25 – 43 cm) long, are lyrate and slightly S-shaped backward and upward, with 15 – 18 rings on the lower three-quarters, those of the female, 3 – 6 in (7 – 15 cm) long and often no thicker than a pencil, are nearly all smooth and almost parallel; sometimes they are absent altogether, are unequal in size or twisted, or cross over each other. The upper parts of the body are light brown, with dark brown stripes on the thighs and a dark lateral stripe on the body; the tail also has black tuft hairs.

Speke's gazelle (*G. spekei*) is a little smaller, and has 3 – 5 transverse, inflatable skin flaps on top of the nose above the muzzle. When giving its alarm call, both males and females blow up this front part of the nose to give greater resonance, and the sound goes off like a pistol shot. The S-shaped horns, sharply inclined backward with the points hooking upward, diverge from each other slightly; on bucks they are 10 – 12 in (25 – 30 cm) long with 15 – 20 rings, on females only 6 – 8 in (15 – 20 cm) long with 10 – 12 rings.

In the goitered gazelle species (*G. subgutturosa*), the bucks have a swelling under the throat that suggests a goiter; it is particulary evident during the mating period. The females usually have no horns. The buck's horns are 10 – 17 in (25 – 43 cm) long, lyrate, S-shaped toward the back and curved upward.

These gazelle species occur over the whole of North Africa as far south as 10°S in the west and 5°S in the east, in Arabia, Asia from Transcaucasia south to Central India, and eastward from Syria and Palestine across Iran, Afghanistan, Turkestan, and northern Tibet as far as northern China and eastern Mongolia.

In temperate subtropical latitudes the mating period generally comes in late fall and winter; in the tropics it varies from region to region. Many species of gazelle give birth twice a year. Gestation periods are between 5 months (Thomson's gazelle) and 7 months (Sömmering's gazelle).

The impala (*Aepyceros melampus*) is almost the size of a red deer, but slimmer and more elegant, with a long, narrow head, straight back and the crupper a little higher than the withers. The overall length is around 62 – 88 in (155 – 220 cm). Only the bucks have horns;

Eland
(*Taurotragus oryx*)

Nilghau
(*Boselaphus tragocamelus*)

Bongo
(*Taurotragus euryceros*)

Bushbuck
(*Tragelaphus scriptus*)

Brindled gnu
(*Connochaetes taurinus*)

Beisa
(*Oryx gazella beisa*)

Sable antelope
(*Hippotragus niger*)

Hartebeest
(*Alcephalus buselaphus*)

The antelopes, like the zebras and giraffes, are an essential element in African wildlife. Often apparently similar to other ungulates, they nevertheless belong to the numerous family Bovidae. The ancient antelopes were extremely adaptable animals and adjusted to life in many different environments through a great number of specializations. As a result there are now many forms, sometimes very different. They mostly live gregariously, in couples or in small family groups of one male and a number of females with their young. It is generally in the dry season that these smaller groups join together to form big herds, which then, as in the case of Grant's gazelle, may number several hundred head. In the rainy season these concentrations break up; some of the older males then become territorial and collect "harems" of 5-12 females.

they are dark brown and lyrate, 20–36 in (50 – 92 cm), with the top quarter smooth and the rest deeply ringed. The coat is short and smooth, yellowish on the upper parts and whitish below. A narrow dark brown stripe runs from the middle of the back to the tip of the bushy tail. A narrow dark brown or black stripe runs vertically up the back of the haunches, and the pads of hair round the side-toes and on the carpal joint and metatarsus are blackish brown.

The impala lives in the bush country and parklands of East and South Africa. It avoids open grasslands with no bushes or trees and places where there is no water. With its diet of leaves, buds, fresh shoots, grasses, and herbs, it needs water every day. They live gregariously either in small herds of 6 – 24 or bigger herds of 30 – 50 head. The smaller groups usually consist of a number of females with their young and one strong buck. Impalas in flight can make amazing leaps, up to 33 ft (10 m) long and 10 ft (3 m) high.

In southwestern and southern Africa the mating period is mainly from February to March, in East Africa from October to November. The mothers leave the herd to give birth after a gestation period of 6½ months (195 days). Usually they produce only one baby. The mothers of very young animals generally form maternal groups just after the birth, only joining up later with the larger groups together with their young.

Impalas are often seen in company with elephants and Grant's gazelles, but there is no genuine association. In southern Africa larger herds, up to 200 head, are found in winter, but in East Africa such congregations are only found in the dry season.

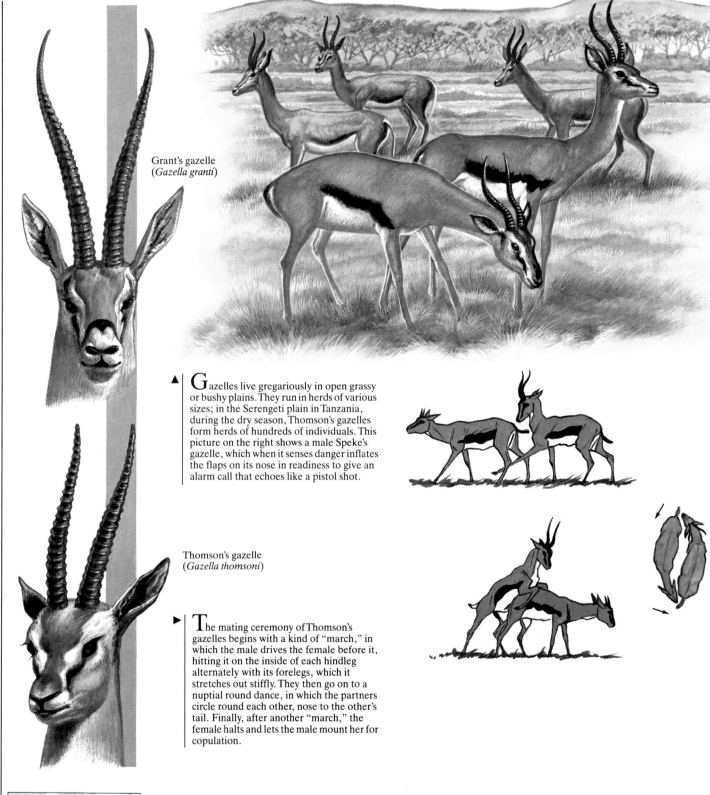

Grant's gazelle
(*Gazella granti*)

Thomson's gazelle
(*Gazella thomsoni*)

▲ Gazelles live gregariously in open grassy or bushy plains. They run in herds of various sizes; in the Serengeti plain in Tanzania, during the dry season, Thomson's gazelles form herds of hundreds of individuals. This picture on the right shows a male Speke's gazelle, which when it senses danger inflates the flaps on its nose in readiness to give an alarm call that echoes like a pistol shot.

▶ The mating ceremony of Thomson's gazelles begins with a kind of "march," in which the male drives the female before it, hitting it on the inside of each hindleg alternately with its forelegs, which it stretches out stiffly. They then go on to a nuptial round dance, in which the partners circle round each other, nose to the other's tail. Finally, after another "march," the female halts and lets the male mount her for copulation.

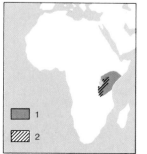

1
2

◀ (1) The range of distribution of Grant's gazelle (*Gazella granti*) extends northward from Tanzania to southern Ethiopia and Somalia, northwest to Lake Victoria and north to Lake Rudolf and eastward to the coast. (2) Thomson's gazelles (*Gazella thomsoni*) live from the southern Sudan (7°N) and Kenya, in the area of Lake Rudolf, as far as northern Tanzania (5°S). The eastern limit of the range is around 38°E.

GERENUK OR WALLER'S GAZELLE

Litocranius walleri

Order Artiodactyla
Family Bovidae
Size Total length 65 – 77 in (165 – 195 cm); length of head and trunk, male 61 – 63 in (155 – 160 cm), female 55 – 61 in (140 – 155 cm); height at shoulder, male 37 – 41 in (95 – 105 cm), female 35 – 39 in (90 – 100 cm); length of tail 10 – 14 in (25 – 35 cm)
Weight Male 88 – 115 lb (40 – 52 kg); female 77 – 100 lb (35 – 45 kg)
Dentition $\frac{0.0.2(3).3}{3.1.2.\quad 3} = 28 - 30$
Reproductive period Once a year, more rarely twice
Number of young 1
Sexual maturity between 12 and 18 months
Maximum age Probably 8 – 10 years

The gerenuk is a graceful giraffe antelope with a remarkably long neck and long legs. The head is small and narrow, elongated and flat. Only the bucks have horns, which are 10 – 17 in (25 – 43.5 cm) long. It lives in the semidesert and arid plains of northeast and eastern Africa. It avoids mountains and hill forest, preferring sandy and stony terrain with scattered trees and bushes or areas of long, dry grass on plains and rolling country up to 6,000 ft (1,800 m). Their food supply from trees and bushes appears to cover all their water needs as they have never been seen to drink.

Gerenuks live socially in small groups of varying size. Generally there are a few females with their young, led by a single buck. Now and again these little groups join together to form small herds of 25 – 30 head. Gerenuks are generally active in the morning and evening; during the midday heat they stand motionless in the shade of the trees.

The female apparently gives birth standing, generally producing a single offspring weighing about 6½ lb (3 kg), which can stand, run, and suckle after three hours. The period in which births take place varies in different regions – in October and November in Somalia, April to May in Harar.

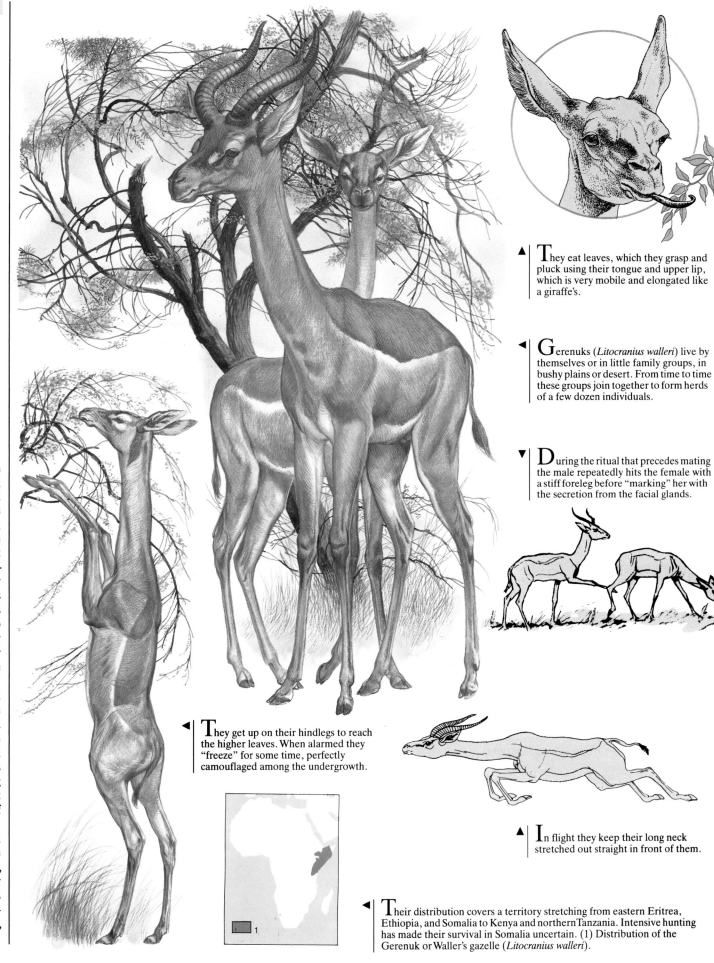

They eat leaves, which they grasp and pluck using their tongue and upper lip, which is very mobile and elongated like a giraffe's.

Gerenuks (*Litocranius walleri*) live by themselves or in little family groups, in bushy plains or desert. From time to time these groups join together to form herds of a few dozen individuals.

During the ritual that precedes mating the male repeatedly hits the female with a stiff foreleg before "marking" her with the secretion from the facial glands.

They get up on their hindlegs to reach the higher leaves. When alarmed they "freeze" for some time, perfectly camouflaged among the undergrowth.

In flight they keep their long neck stretched out straight in front of them.

Their distribution covers a territory stretching from eastern Eritrea, Ethiopia, and Somalia to Kenya and northern Tanzania. Intensive hunting has made their survival in Somalia uncertain. (1) Distribution of the Gerenuk or Waller's gazelle (*Litocranius walleri*).

TAKIN

Budorcas taxicolor

Order Artiodactyla
Family Bovidae
Size Height at shoulder 3¼ – 4¼ ft
(1 – 1.3 m)
Weight 500 – 700 lb (230 – 350 kg)
Dentition $\frac{0.0.3.3}{3.1.3.3}$ = 32
Reproductive period July – August
Gestation 8 months
Number of young 1
Sexual maturity Females at 2 years;
males probably at 4 – 5 years
Maximum age Perhaps 15 – 20 years

The takin is a ruminant, heavily built, with a thickset, clumsy appearance, the forelimbs being longer than the hindlimbs. The horns are stout, especially at the base, and somewhat resemble those of the buffalo. Horns are carried by both sexes, and are directed outward, without any noticeable curve. The average length of the horns is about 24 in (60 cm).

There are three known subspecies of takin. The Assam takin has a coat of particularly striking color. It inhabits Assam, Nepal, and Bhutan at altitudes between 8,200 and 13,000 ft (2,500 and 4,000 m), living in woodland or areas where there are dense thickets. The Szechwan takin lives in the area of the same name, in dense thickets of rhododendron and bamboo which it is able to penetrate because of its heavy build and thick coat. The Shansi takin inhabits the corresponding mountainous region in China.

Takins live in large herds of several dozen individuals. Their diet consists of plants of various kinds, graminaceous plants and grasses in summer, or else leaves, buds, and herbaceous plants. In winter they feed mainly on bamboo leaves. When it snows heavily or during particularly harsh winters, they descend to grassy valleys where climatic conditions are more favorable, down to altitudes of 6,500 ft (2,000 m). They frequent the dense vegetation creating their own paths through the thicket. They only feed in the cooler parts of the day.

The mating season begins in July, when the adult males approach the herd of females and young animals. Gestation lasts about 8 months and the young are born in March-April.

▼ Takins, gorals and serows live at different altitudes in the Himalayas.

▲ Takins (*Budorcas taxicolor*) are stoutly built animals with large strong feet. They live on steep mountain slopes at altitudes between about 6,500 and 10,000 ft (2000 and 3000 m) but during the summer they may even move up to over 13,000 ft (4000 m). Their bulk does not impede their movement in areas of dense thickets and shrubbery; they are in fact extremely agile animals.

▲ Takins are particularly fond of saline deposits.

◄ Their hooves are large, strong and wide and the spurs are also highly developed.

◄ Area of distribution of the takin (*Budorcas taxicolor*).

CHAMOIS

Rupicapra rupicapra

Order Artiodactyla
Family Bovidae
Size Height at shoulder about 36 in (90 cm)
Weight 66 – 110 lb (30 – 50 kg) according to subspecies
Dentition $\dfrac{0.0.3.3}{3.1.3.3} = 32$
Reproductive period November
Gestation 6 months
Number of young 1
Sexual maturity Female at 3 years; males at 5 years
Maximum age 20 years

The chamois is a robust and well-proportioned ungulate. The trunk is stout and muscular; the neck is of average length, the head triangular with fairly large eyes and narrow, rather small ears. The limbs are well-proportioned; the hooves are widely divaricate and of the consistency of hard rubber. The coat undergoes a seasonal molt; in summer it is short and rough, brownish-red or light-red; in winter it becomes longer and thicker, and brown-black or grayish-black. The muzzle, however, is always pale, whitish-yellow with a characteristic black mask. Horns are carried by both sexes. The overall length of the horns does not usually exceed 12 – 31 in (30 – 32 cm).

The chamois originated in Europe and in Asia Minor. It has been introduced into New Zealand. Its habitat is high mountains beyond the treeline, especially the great Alpine meadows and rocky areas. However, it frequently descends to much lower altitudes, and also spends much of its time in woodland.

The diet of the chamois consists largely of graminaceous plants and whatever grazing the high mountain pastures will yield. During winter, and also in summer for those animals that live in woodland, they feed also on the leaves and shoots provided by the undergrowth. Chamois are gregarious animals with a high degree of sociability. According to situation, the herds may be very large, numbering several dozen individuals. Generally, however, they are much smaller (10 – 20 head). After a short gestation, females give birth to a single offspring, which is able to follow the mother within a few hours of birth.

▲ There are nine (or according to some, ten) known subspecies of the chamois, which inhabit the high mountains of Europe and Asia Minor. The main species, *Rupicapra rupicapra rupicapra*, lives in the Alps, from France to northern Yugoslavia. The subspecies *balcanica* lives in southern Yugoslavia, Greece, and Albania. In the Carpathians (Transylvania, Rumania) and the Caucasus are found the subspecies *carpatica* and *caucasica*, while the *cartusiana* lives in the Chartreuse massif (France). The Spanish subspecies *pyrenaica* (Pyrenees) and *cantabrica* (Cantabrica Cordillera) have various features in common (including the enlarged throat marking, like a pale bib ringed with a vertical black edge) with the subspecies *ornata* of the central Apennines in Italy. The sole Asiatic subspecies, *asiatica*, survives in Asia Minor.

▲ Chamois are perfectly adapted to life in high mountains, thanks to their widely splayed and flexible hooves and muscular almost double jointed limbs. They are able to run very swiftly on the sheerest rock faces and within a few minutes can climb over 3,300 ft (1000 m). Their agility is proverbial, and they can even keep their footing on rocks no larger than the palm of a hand.

◄ 1) Area of distribution of the chamois.

ROCKY MOUNTAIN GOAT

Oreamnos americanus

Order Artiodactyla
Family Bovidae
Size Height at shoulder 36 – 40 in (90 – 105 cm)
Weight 132 – 280 lb (60 – 130 kg); the females are markedly smaller than the males
Dentition $\dfrac{0.0.3.3}{0.1.3.3} = 32$
Reproductive period November – early January
Gestation 147 – 178 days
Number of young 1, sometimes 2
Sexual maturity Female at 2 years, males later
Maximum age 14 – 18 years

The Rocky Mountain goat is a stocky, muscular animal which looks larger than it is because of the length of its hair. Its back is higher at the withers than the croup, and has a thick mane. Its neck is fairly long, as is its muzzle. The ears are narrow and of average length. The eyes are placed rather high, close to the base of the horns, which emphasizes the length of the nasal bones. The tail is rather short, measuring little more than 4 in (10 cm). The hoof is highly unusual, being so widely divaricate that the two parts diverge at right angles. The soles are not hard and rigid but rubbery for deftness. The spurs are well developed and further add to its surefootedness. The coat is white, rather long and woolly, and shows no seasonal dimorphism. It is particularly thick around the neck and shoulders, as well as on the joints of the legs. There is a medium-sized beard, about 5 in (13 cm) long, beneath the chin.

The Rocky Mountain goat's original area of distribution stretched from western Montana, from southern Idaho and the Columbia River in Washington as far as Alaska. However, the species has been introduced into other parts of the United States and Canada. The environment these animals frequent is high mountains, generally above the treeline. They feed on grasses and herbaceous plants and also, in summer, on willows. Their enemies are the puma, lynx, black and grizzly bears, even the coyote and golden eagle.

▲ The Rocky Mountain goat resembles, in external appearance, a woolly goat, but it is in fact closely related to the chamois. Horns are consequently carried by both males and females. They are exceptionally good climbers, able to take advantage of every foothold. They feed on grasses, mosses, and lichens that grow among the rocks or on mountain plateaux.

BARBARY SHEEP

Ammotragus lervia

Order Artiodactyla
Family Bovidae
Size Height at shoulder, males 35 – 40 in (90 – 105 cm); females 27 – 36 in (70 – 90 cm)
Weight Males, 220 – 300 lb (100 – 140 kg); females 88 – 100 lb (40 – 45 kg)
Dentition $\frac{0.0.3.3}{3.1.3.3} = 32$
Reproductive period November
Gestation 150 – 165 days
Number of young 1 – 2 (rarely 3)
Sexual maturity Females at 2 years; males later
Maximum age About 15 years

The barbary sheep is a very sturdy ungulate. The horns are triangular in section, rather heavy, thick at the base, with an average length of 25 in (65 cm), up to a maximum of 31 in (80 cm). The horns of the females are about 15 in (40 cm). There is a small short mane on the upper part of the neck and the withers. On the front of the neck there is very long thick hair that continues down the breast to the knee joint, covering and almost concealing the front legs.

The barbary sheep, also called the arni or the aoudad, inhabits the northern areas of Africa, more precisely north of the Niger as far as the Sudan and the Red Sea. Its usual habitat is rocky desert country. It feeds on plants of various kinds, shrubs and tubers. Although it inhabits areas where water is always scarce, it willingly drinks when water is available.

Barbary sheep are not very gregarious ungulates, and usually live in groups of 3 – 6 individuals, occasionally as many as 20 at the end of the dry season. As is customary among nearly all ungulates, the older males are solitary except during the mating season.

The animals are excellent leapers and climbers. During the day they stay in the shade, and emerge to feed only in the cooler hours of the day or at night. The scarcity of food in their environment means that they have to look for it in every nook and cranny.

The mating season mainly falls in November. Gestation takes about 5½ months, and the female gives birth to one or two, sometimes even three young.

Barbary sheep live in the desert areas of Africa and show features that belong both to goats and sheep. They survive on very poor grazing, and so are not difficult to raise in captivity. The color of their coat is so similar to that of the rocks on which they live that, when danger threatens, they simply remain motionless, trusting to their camouflage for protection.

◄ Barbary sheep have a characteristic mode of fighting with locked horns.

◄ During sandstorms they can use the long hair on their neck and chest as an efficient protective filter.

◄ The area of distribution of the Barbary sheep is rather fragmented and covers a strip running across the north of the continent of Africa.

◄ They also use their horns to groom themselves.

ALPINE IBEX

Capra ibex ibex

Order Artiodactyla
Family Bovidae
Size Height at shoulder, males 33 – 37 in (85 – 95 cm); females 27 – 31 in (70 – 80 cm)
Dentition $\dfrac{0.0.3.3}{3.1.3.3} = 32$
Reproductive period December – January
Number of young 1
Sexual maturity Females at 4 years; males at 7 – 8 years
Maximum age About 20 years

The Alpine ibex is a sturdy, heavily built animal with a powerful head, particularly the brow region. The limbs are muscular and the tail is short. The hair is very short, never very thick. The males have a "beard," a tuft of hair about 1½ – 2½ in (4 – 7 cm) long beneath the chin. In the males the color of the coat is gray in summer, with brown, black, reddish, beige, and cream tints. The winter coat is a much darker brown-black. The females are generally less dark in color. The young may be beige or reddish but are most often offwhite. The long horns curve backward in a scimitar shape, and are triangular in section. The length of the horns in the male averages between 30 – 36 in (75 – 90 cm) but may be more than 40 in (100 cm), while the horns of the female rarely exceed 10 – 12 in (25 – 30 cm) in length.

It is known that the Alpine ibex long ago inhabited the entire Alpine chain, above the treeline, as far as Yugoslavia. By the end of the nineteenth century the ibex was present only in the Gran Paradiso massif, in Italy. At the present moment there are many colonies of ibex apart from the Gran Paradiso. The majority are probably in Switzerland, but there are many others in France, Italy, Austria, Germany, and Yugoslavia.

During the summer ibex live very high up, well beyond the treeline. In winter they prefer steep, rocky places with a southerly exposure, which get the most sunshine and where the snow cannot settle. Only in spring may the ibex move down in search of new grass, although they may also be seen on the lower slopes in winter if there is exceptionally heavy snowfall. Glaciers and deep valleys seem to constitute

► The environment of the Alpine ibex is, generally speaking, high mountain above the treeline. However, this animal is closely tied to a rocky environment, needing steep rock walls, crags, peaks, cavities, and caves. Such features are to be found not only in high mountains, but the Alpine ibex cannot withstand the heat of summer, so the ideal climate for this species is at high altitudes. In prehistoric times it certainly lived at much lower altitudes, for example in the Italian Apennines, but the climate then was very different and much harsher.

▼ On smooth or almost level surfaces, only the soles of the hooves are placed on the ground (right); on sloping surfaces, however, the spurs are also placed on the ground (left).

impassable geographical limits for the ibex in its area of distribution.

The ibex feeds mainly on meadow plants and grasses. Sometimes, especially in winter, it will eat roots which it digs up with its hooves. Its tastes are fairly eclectic and, like all members of the genus *Capra*, it will even eat tough and spiny plants. The social organization of the ibex is based mainly on a very clear distinction between sexes. The males live in all-male herds, especially after the age of four years. Ibex of 12 – 15 years of age, on the other hand, are nearly always solitary. The females form their own herd, which includes pregnant females, females with kid, and even females too young to have given birth.

The courtship season occurs in late fall or even winter. Birth occurs about 6 months later, usually during the first half of June. A single kid is born, weighing 4 – 7 lb (2 – 3.5 kg). Within a very short time it is able to follow its mother, never leaving her side. The females give birth in particularly inaccessible places and for some time the mothers remain apart with their kids. Only towards the end of June or in July do they re-form the female herd.

The Nubian ibex (*Capra ibex nubiana*) is smaller than the Alpine ibex and has more slender but very long horns. It lives in Israel, in the rocky areas of Sinai, at about 9,000 ft (2,800 m), in Judaea, in the Negev desert, as well as in isolated areas in Egypt and the Sudan.

The Abyssinian ibex (*Capra ibex walie*) is a larger and heavier animal, with shorter but heavier horns. Of all species, this one is in great danger of extinction. It is confined to a small area of the Semien mountains (Ethiopia) at altitudes of about 9,800 – 14,700 ft (3,000 – 4,500 m).

The Siberian ibex (*Capra ibex sibirica*) is a large animal with extremely long horns. This ibex lives in the mountains of central Asia, between 1,650 and 16,500 ft (500 and 5,000 m).

The Spanish ibex, more commonly called the Pyrenean ibex, is distinguished by its horns which have a triangular section and are twisted inward. The coloring of its coat is more contrasting and the males have a very noticeable beard. They live at an altitude of 3,300 – 6,500 ft (1,000 – 2,000 m).

▼ Ibexes enjoy curling up on a rocky outcrop and basking in the sun.

▲ They can leap over distances of several meters from one precipice to another.

▼ Ibexes use their horns to keep themselves clean.

▲ When fighting they lock their horns and shove against each other: however, they rarely inflict serious injury.

▲ The different shape of the horns shows how the various subspecies have diversified.
1) *Capra ibex sibirica*; 2) *Capra caucasica*; 3) *Capra sibirica sakeen*

◄ Distribution of ibexes:
1) Pyrenean ibex (*Capra pyrenaica*);
2) Alpine ibex (*Capra ibex ibex*);
3) Nubian ibex (*Capra ibex nubiana*);
4) East Caucasian ibex (*Capra ibex cylindricornis*);
5) Himalayan ibex (*Capra sibirica sakeen*);
6) Siberian ibex (*Capra ibex sibirica*);
7) Abyssinian ibex (*Capra ibex walie*);
8) West Caucasian ibex (*Capra ibex severtzovi*).

▲ They can climb up the most inaccessible rock faces in search of a bit of grass or saline deposits.

MARKHOR
Capra falconeri

Order Artiodactyla
Family Bovidae
Size Height at shoulder, males 33 – 40 in (85 – 100 cm); females considerably smaller
Weight Males 175 – 220 lb (80 – 100 kg); females 66 – 100 lb (40 – 45 kg)
Dentition $\frac{0.0.3.3}{3.1.3.3} = 32$
Reproductive period December
Gestation 6 months
Number of young 2
Sexual maturity Females at 2 years; males at 4 – 5 years
Maximum age About 15 – 20 years

The markhor is a sturdy species of goat, notable for the splendid coat of the males. In winter this is long and thick on the back, the lower part of the flanks, the chest, and the neck. The beard is also very long. The horns are remarkably long and may measure as much as 5 ft (1.6 m); they are twisted along their axis into a number of spirals that varies according to subspecies. They are usually divergent, forming a V or U shape.

Markhors live in the mountains of central Asia in Turkestan (USSR) in Pakistan and India, as well as Afghanistan. The environment frequented by markhors is fairly varied, and may be above or below the treeline. The areas they inhabit are very rugged, with deep gorges, rock walls, and precipices.

Markhors feed on various types of plants, grasses, graminaceous plants, leaves, leaf tips, and buds. In some areas (Kashmir) their winter diet consists largely of ilex leaves which they can reach even at considerable heights. Markhors are, in fact, excellent climbers and can reach branches even 22 – 26 ft (7 – 8 m) above the ground by climbing the trunks.

Their social organization is similar to that of other goats. The herds are smaller, however, at the most numbering about 20 individuals. During the courtship period the males join the female herds and form a certain hierarchy within them. A rutting male remains close to a female in estrus, standing beside her and adopting certain stances particular to courtship behaviour.

▶ The markhor (*Capra falconeri*) is the largest of the wild goats. Its horns are twisted along their axis, in some species so much so that they look like a corkscrew. Like many other Caprinae, markhors are also a species to be considered in danger of extinction, partly because their distribution is rather fragmented and separated.

▼ The markhor's area of distribution includes the mountainous regions of Turkestan, Afghanistan, Pakistan, and northern India.

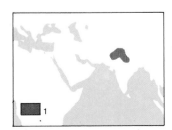

1

BIGHORN

Ovis canadensis

Order Artiodactyla
Family Bovidae
Size Length of head and body 3¼ – 3¾ ft (100 – 110 cm); height at shoulder 2¾ – 4 ft (80 – 120 cm)
Weight 330 – 440 lb (150 – 200 kg)
Dentition $\frac{0.0.3.3}{3.1.3.3} = 32$
Reproductive period June – July
Gestation 6 months
Number of young 1 – 2

The bighorn is a solid, thickset wild sheep. The head is heavy and the profile straight. Males bear a large pair of symmetrical, spiral-shaped horns some 28 – 32 in (70 – 80 cm) long, and 12 – 14 in (30 – 35 cm) in circumference at the base. Females carry horns which are considerably smaller, measure some 8 in (20 cm) in length, are slenderer, and form a single curve.

This species of wild sheep was originally found from northeastern Siberia to the mountainous strip of North America stretching from Alaska as far south as Mexico. Its present distribution in the American continent has been considerably reduced as a result of human activities and of competition with other ungulates, and today it is restricted to British Columbia and Saskatchewan in Canada, and to the states of North Dakota, Nebraska, Colorado, and New Mexico in the United States. The habitat favored by *Ovis canadensis* varies from the cold regions of Siberia and the Rocky Mountains to the hot deserts of New Mexico.

The social behavior of the bighorn has been well studied. In general the populations consist of two flocks, one of males and the other of females. Young lambs of both sexes live with the females, young males remaining there until they are 3 years old, when they join the adult males. Each flock consists of some 25 – 30 individuals. The bighorn does not roam freely, but has a precisely delimited territory which varies according to the season. The territory of the males is separate from that of the females.

Gestation takes about 6 months. The young are born in the first months of summer, the females retiring into solitude and giving birth to a single lamb.

The bighorn has a grayish-brown coat some 2 in (5 cm) long, which is darker on the back. In winter the whole coat darkens, with the exception of the stomach, the inside of the legs, the rump, chin, and the inside of the ears.

The length of the horns is a measure of status in the male hierarchy. Only individuals with horns of equal length will fight; they strike their heads together with a great noise.

The powerful horns of the male bighorn can reach 3 ft (90 cm) in length. The manner of growth is illustrated above, in individuals of (from the left) two, six, and twelve years of age.

1) Geographical distribution of the bighorn.

WILD SHEEP
Ovis ammon

Order Artiodactyla
Family Bovidae
Size Total length 4 – 7 ft (1.2 – 2.1 m); length of head and trunk 3¾ – 6¾ ft (1.1 – 2 m); height at shoulder 25 – 50 in (65 – 125 cm); length of tail 1½ – 5 in (3.5 – 13 cm)
Weight 44 – 500 lb (20 – 230 kg)
Dentition $\frac{0.0.3.3}{3.1.3.3}$ = 32

Reproductive period Once a year
Number of young 1 or 2; only 1 in primiparous ewes
Sexual maturity 18 or 30 months; in the males of larger races, not before 3½ years
Maximum age 12 – 18 years

Female wild sheep are as a rule one-quarter to one-third smaller than males. The forehead is vaulted, the head sometimes short, sometimes quite long. The ears are short and pointed, with a tuft of hair at the tip. The neck is short and strong, the trunk thickset, with a straight ridge line sloping down at the back. The narrow hooves on the slender or sturdy legs have a pearshaped outline, with the small side-toes lying flat. Both sexes have horns. The horns of the ewe, in contrast to those of the ram, are between 4 – 12 in (10 – 30 cm) long, curving backward in the shape of a saber. There are annular ribs on the surface of the horns; the annual growth marks are not very distinct. The horns of different types of rams may be from 12 in (50 cm) to 75 in (190 cm) long. The most impressive horns among Old World sheep are found on the subspecies of the Pamirs and the neighboring Central Asian mountains.

The distribution of Eurasian wild sheep extends from the Mediterranean across western and central Asia and thence northward across Transcaucasia and Kazakhstan to southern Siberia; in the south wild sheep are found in the Himalayas and thence eastward to Shensi and the Great Khingan. In Europe the true distribution is limited to Sardinia and Corsica, but the wild sheep is almost extinct there, surviving only in small numbers in reserves. The mouflon (*Ovis ammon musimon*) has been reintroduced in many parts of Europe – in the Crimea, in Poland, Hungary and Czechoslovakia, in

Argali
(*Ovis ammon ammon*)

▲ The argali, or Altai wild sheep (*Ovis ammon ammon*) is the biggest subspecies of wild sheep and lives in the mountainous regions of central Asia. The males of this species may be 50 in (125 cm) tall at the withers.

Armenian wild sheep

Punjab sheep or urial

Argali

▶ Difference in size of some wild sheep.

Yugoslavia, Italy, Switzerland, Germany, Luxembourg, and Holland. Small groups of mouflon have also been able to survive in Cyprus.

Besides the mouflon, this group comprises the following subspecies: the Elbrus wild sheep (*O.a. orientalis*) in Asia Minor; the urial or Punjab sheep (*O.a. vignei*) from the Elbrus mountains to eastern Iran, Turkestan, Afghanistan, Pakistan, and Kashmir; the Jabaira wild sheep (*O.a. kozlovi*) in the Jabarai mountains and inner Mongolia; the Himalayan wild sheep (*O.a. hodgsoni*) in the Himalayas, Tibet, Sinkiang, and Manchuria; the Pamirs wild sheep, named *O.a.polii* after the Venetian explorer of the Orient, Marco Polo, found in the Pamirs, the Karatau, Tien Shen, and northward from the Alatau to the Tarbatagai mountains; and the biggest form, in which rams may be as tall as 50 in (125 cm) at the shoulder, the Argali or Altai wild sheep (*O.a. ammon*), which lives in the Altai and the Sayan mountains.

While the European mouflon and Cyprus mouflon live in lightly wooded areas with plenty of undergrowth on the middle slopes of the mountains, the other wild sheep subspecies are predominantly found in open rough terrain at medium or high altitudes, up to 20,000 ft (6,000 m). They live on steppes, semidesert, stony crags, and the slopes and pasture near the mountain tops. In the summer these forms retreat to the highest levels beneath the snowline, and only come down to the valleys in winter.

Wild sheep live socially in small or medium-large flocks. In the summer rams are also found solitary, or in small groups apart from the ewes. For most of the year wild sheep are more or less sedentary, traveling no further than is necessary to find grazing in their immediate surroundings. In most of their distribution, grasses and a variety of plants form the main part of the diet; at extreme altitudes, as in the Pamirs, they also eat sedge, and in the semidesert salt-bearing herbs.

The period of gestation lasts about 5 months, generally from mid March to mid June; before lambing, gravid ewes leave the herd and look for a safe and sheltered place. A single lamb is generally born, though twins are not uncommon. Sexual maturity is reached by ewes at 18 months by rams at 30 months, and by rams of bigger species at 3½ years.

Mouflon
(*Ovis ammon musimon*)

Bighorn
(*Ovis canadensis*)

▲ During a mating season the males fight, first confronting each other standing up on their hindlegs, then butting each other. Their horns clash violently together, but without causing serious wounds, brain disturbance or fracture of the skull.

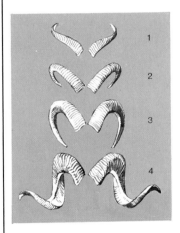

▲ When in danger, wild sheep give a hissing warning sound; this alarm call is often accompanied by loud pawing with the forefeet.

▲ Different shapes of horns: (1) Armenian wild sheep; (2) Elbrus wild sheep; (3) Urial; (4) Pamirs wild sheep.

◄ Four Asian subspecies of wild sheep are included in the "*canadensis* group", which also includes all the races in the New World. The Asian snow sheep and the American bighorns are closely related. (1) Present distribution of *Ovis canadensis*: (2) range of distribution of *Ovis canadensis dalli*; distribution of *Ovis canadensis nivicola*.

MUSK OX

Ovibos moschatus

Order Artiodactyla
Family Bovidae
Size Height at shoulder 50 – 58 in (130 – 150 cm)
Weight 700 – 900 lb (320 – 410 kg)
Dentition $\frac{0.0.3.3}{3.1.3.3} = 32$
Reproductive period August
Gestation About 8 months
Number of young 1
Sexual maturity Females at 2 years; males later
Maximum age About 20 years

The musk ox is a thickset, sturdy animal with an elongated trunk. The limbs are short and muscular; the hooves are broad and short, as also are the spurs. The general proportions of the body are difficult to distinguish because it is covered with long thick hair. The neck is of medium length and the withers are markedly higher than the croup. The head is large, with a straight profile; the muzzle is quite broad. The ears are small and pointed, the eyes are also small and placed close to the base of the horns. The tail is no longer than 4 in (10 cm). The entire body of the musk ox is covered by a thick coarse coat which even hangs down and half conceals the legs, and long hair hangs from the chin to the neck. The basic coloring is dark brown, tending to black in winter but lighter in spring. The brow is darker, but the feet are paler, offwhite or brownish-yellow. It is a very compact animal with powerful shoulders. Horns are also carried by the females.

The musk ox was first discovered in 1869, at the time of the Polar expeditions. In ancient times, during the Ice Age, it was distributed throughout most of Europe, Siberia, and the United States. Subsequently, after the last glaciation, its area shrank increasingly, until it became confined to northern Canada, including a few offshore islands, a small part of Alaska, and part of Greenland. The total number of musk ox is estimated to be over 13,000 head. The environment this animal frequents is tundra, covered with snow for most of the year but not normally to prohibitive depths.

There are three known subspecies. The Alaskan musk ox (*Ovibos moschatus*

▼ The physical build, the broad hooves and above all the thick and extraordinarily long coat of the musk ox represent a clear adaptive response to the environment in which this animal lives; the tundra of Greenland and northern Canada.

▼ The musk ox feeds on the few Arctic plants and grasses, lichens, and mosses.

lichens

Arctic plants

mosses

hoofprint

moschatus) was once on the verge of extinction but today it seems that this subspecies survives in sufficient numbers. The subspecies *O.m. niphoecus* lives in Canada and has become very rare. The Greenland musk ox (*O.m.wardi*) is the most widespread of the three: it has also been introduced into several other areas.

The musk ox is an animal adapted to the severe Arctic climate. Its food consists of the few Arctic grasses and plants, lichens, and mosses. Musk oxen live in mixed groups of males, females, and young: however, there are also herds composed solely of immature males, formed when the oldest male drives them out of the mixed herd. This occurs at the approach of the mating season and when the young males have reached a certain maturity. These herds are fairly small, not usually exceeding 10 in number.

The mixed herds are a little larger, with an average of 10 – 12 individuals, including very few calves (10 – 20 per cent). However musk oxen do sometimes form much larger herds of about 60 head. The herds are very compact units and have developed a very effective strategy to defend themselves from predators. When the latter approach, the musk oxen try to reach slightly higher ground and then – whether or not higher ground is available – close ranks in a circle, facing outward. The calves and yearlings, however, are inside the circle, and so protected from the wolf or bear that would prey on them. This form of defense, which is a characteristic of the species, is not effective against a human enemy. Musk oxen, however, fight so fiercely that they are sometimes mortally wounded, a rare occurrence in the animal world.

The mating season falls in August. During this period the bull fiercely defends his harem against other males. The fighting is particularly fierce, the two rivals first facing each other, seeking to impress and bellowing loudly. Gestation lasts about 8 months and births consequently occur in April, when the nights are still longer than the days. However the growth rate of the wild populations is very low, the more so as musk oxen in the wild apparently only give birth every two years.

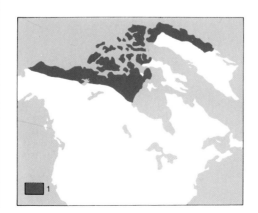

▲ These animals belong to almost the same ecological system in which the now extinct mammoth and hairy rhinoceros used to live.

▲ When they are attacked by wolves, they close together in a circle with the young protected in the middle. This defense is totally effective, whereas if an individual is caught alone, it is almost invariably killed.

▲
► The long hair provides effective protection against the cold and snow and enables the musk ox to rest even on icy ground and keep its young warm. The diagram shows the proportions of different layers which provide these animals with protection against the harsh climatic conditions in which they live: 1) layer of fat; 2) skin; 3) thick underfur; 4) long outer hair.

◄ 1) Area of distribution of the musk ox (*Ovibos moschatus*).

BLACK RHINOCEROS

Diceros bicornis

Order Perissodactyla
Family Rhinocerotidae
Size Length of head and trunk 9¾ – 12¼ ft (3 – 3.75 m); length of tail 28 in (70 cm); height at shoulder 4½ – 5¼ ft (1.4 – 1.6 m)
Weight 1 – 1.8 tons
Dentition $\frac{0.0.3(4).3}{0.0.3(4).3} = 24 - 28$
Gestation 16 months
Number of young 1 (every 3 – 4 years approx)
Sexual maturity 5 – 6 years
Maximum age About 50 years

The black rhinoceros is the most common species of rhinoceros in Africa. It is slightly smaller than the white rhino, but like it has two horns. The head is small in relation to the size of the body, shorter than that of the white rhinoceros, and generally held rather higher. The lips are not square but pointed, ending in a prehensile digitiform appendage. The nostrils are narrow and rounded, the eyes small, and the ears short with wide apertures.

The skin is hairless and covered on the flanks with a great number of tiny folds resembling wrinkles. The skin color varies through brownish shades of slaty gray or yellowish-gray. The black rhinoceros is frequently covered with mud in which it rolls and bathes, and which dries on its skin. The two horns are of different length, the front horn being longer and curved inward, normally some 20 in (50 cm) long, sometimes shorter, the maximum recorded length being about 50 in (130 cm). The rear horn is much shorter and rises vertically upward. There are very few cases of rhinoceroses with three horns, the third usually being rudimentary, but in exceptional cases it may be slightly developed.

In earlier times the black rhinoceros was extremely widespread throughout Africa, with the exception of the great tropical rainforests. Both their numbers and the areas they inhabit have been tremendously reduced by appallingly destructive hunting for sport and financial gain. Like all large animals whose existence is threatened by the insensate behavior of mankind, the black rhinoceros is now more or

▲ The black rhinoceros (*Diceros bicornis*) is slightly smaller and less impressive than the white rhinoceros, but, similarly, it has two horns and lives in Africa. The head is shorter in the black rhinoceros, the lips are pointed, and it carries its head high.

▼ The black rhinoceros inhabits forest with open clearings, the edges of woods, and thick scrub. It cannot venture far from water.

▶ Black rhinoceroses have a very varied diet, even feeding off thorny shrubs. Unlike the white rhinoceros, they rarely lower their head.

less restricted in its distribution to the game reserves and national parks, particularly south of Zambesi, where it is only to be found in protected areas. The species is more numerous in East Africa, notably in the famous national parks there.

The black rhinoceros inhabits thick scrub, wooded savanna, thorny thickets, and thickly vegetated forest clearings. It is also occasionally found in more arid areas, but it is never far from watercourses, waterholes, or muddy hollows. The presence of water is essential. The black rhinoceros is also found in mountain forests, where it climbs the slopes with great agility, despite its size; in Kenya it is found up to 9,000 ft (2,700 m). The only areas which it does not inhabit are the great tropical rainforests and shrubless grassy plains, the latter because of its dietary requirements. In the dry season its territory may extend up to 15 miles (25 km) from water, but in the rains, when water is freely available, it may roam more widely.

The black rhinoceros is a browser, the shape of its lips, and especially the prehensile digitiform appendage on its upper lip enabling it to feed off twigs, leaves, and shoots. Even in the grassy plains it seeks out small bushes, and its usual food consists of the branches of thorny shrubs. During the hottest part of the day, the rhinoceros retreats into thick vegetation or lies in the sun. Feeding is mostly done in the morning and evening. The black rhino is quite active and swift, and can reach speeds of up to 30 mph (45 kmh) at full charge; it is also surprisingly agile for so large an animal, and capable of turning abruptly as it runs. The sense of smell is very acute, and plays an important part in social life, being used, for example, for mutual recognition between mother and young, or for members of a particular home-range to keep in contact. Signals connected with smell therefore play a fundamental role. Rhinoceroses mark bushes, tufts of grass, and treetrunks with their urine.

The black rhinoceros is not very sociable and rather aggressive. The males are solitary, except under certain abnormal circumstances. The females, in contrast, live with their young, even when the latter are quite large. Mating can take place during any month. The period of gestation is 15 – 16 months, after which a single calf is born.

▼ They bathe frequently in swamps in order to cool themselves and gain relief from their parasites, covering themselves with mud, which forms a dry crust over their body.

▲ During the hottest part of the day they lie down on one side or stretch themselves out.

◄ Their paths lead through the dense and thorny undergrowth, in which they move with ease.

▼ They are very curious, and sniff out anything unfamiliar. Turtles sometimes climb over them while they are bathing to eat the parasites on their skin.

▲ Black rhinoceroses can move rapidly, and quite often charge in anger or curiosity. They are unpredictable animals, but do not usually cause damage in areas where they are not disturbed.

The young of the black rhinoceros always stays close to its mother, remaining close to her hindquarters. ►

▲
► The horn of the rhinoceros has an unusual structure, being formed of an agglutinated mass of horny fibers.

TAPIRS
Tapiridae

The tapirs are related to rhinoceroses and horses, but in outward appearance they most closely resemble a hippopotamus or a pig. Their bodies are fairly thickset and short, and seen from the side they look somewhat compressed. The upper part of the profile of the head is curved. The head is small, and the muzzle is prominent, ending in a short, conical, and extremely mobile proboscis formed by the elongated nose and upper lip. At the end of this are the nostrils, which consist of two characteristic lateral slits. The eyes are small and well protected, the ears are short and rounded, erect, and not particularly mobile. The coat of the young is covered with broken whitish-yellow stripes, and spots on a dark background, a coloring with obvious mimetic value in the undergrowth. The tapir have 42 – 44 teeth.

The neck is very muscular, and of average development; the body is sturdy and higher at the croup than at the withers, so that the spine is slightly hollow. The legs are relatively short and not very thick, with four toes on the forefeet, the first being absent and the fifth very short, so that it touches only very soft ground, and three on the hindfeet, the first and fifth being absent. The average dimensions of the four species are as follows: length of head and body (excluding tail) 6 – 8 ft (1.8 – 2.5 m); tail 2 – 4 in (5 – 10 cm); height at shoulder 2½ – 4 ft (75 – 120 cm); weight 500 – 650 lb (225 – 300 kg) and over. The females are generally larger than the males.

Tapirs inhabit wet tropical forests and jungles. They prefer habitats near watercourses, but thick vegetation is essential to them, and there they retreat during the middle of the day.

Tapirs usually live alone or in pairs, and can move without difficulty through dense undergrowth and in the open. They are excellent swimmers and can cross large rivers with ease. They love water, and the Malay tapir is particularly fond of standing immersed in water, eating aquatic plants, and will walk submerged along the bottom for quite long periods.

Tapirs have very acute senses of smell and hearing, and their proboscis is an extremely efficient tool for exploring the immediately surrounding world,

▲ The tapirs are archaic perisodactyls which have survived in the tropical forests. Illustrated above is the Malay tapir (*Tapirus indicus*) with its unmistakable white saddle on back and rump. Food consists mainly of leaves, shoots, and forest fruits.

▼ The tapir's habitat is dense tropical forest near water, along the banks of rivers.

◄ The tapir grasps shoots in its mouth, using its short and extremely mobile proboscis.

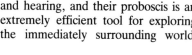

notably the plants which form their diet. They eat leaves, young branches, buds, fruits, and water-plants. It also has developed a sense of touch, since it has vibrissae which extend right to the tip, and is used for making contact with other members of the species.

All four living species belong to the single genus *Tapirus*. One species is Asiatic and the other three Central and South American. The Malay tapir (*Tapirus indicus*) is larger than the others, reaching a length of 8 ft (2.5 m). It has an unmistakable coat, which is ebony-black with a wide, dirty-white saddle of an almost silvery hue on the croup and belly. The young have a brown coat with white spots and stripes on the upper parts and flanks until at least 5 months old. The species was once very widespread in the wet forests and swampy jungle tracts of Burma, Thailand, Indochina, the Malay peninsula, and Sumatra.

The three American species of tapir are slightly smaller and slimmer, with narrower legs. The adult coat is a uniform yellowish-brown and chestnut. The proboscis is a little longer, while the young have similar striped and spotted coats. The commonest and most widespread species is *Tapirus terrestris*, the common South American tapir. It is not very large, and reaches 6 ft (2 m) in length and 3 ft (1 m) in height. It is found from Colombia and Venezuela as far as the Grah Chaco of Paraguay and the state of Rio Grande del Sul in Brazil. It chiefly inhabits the dense equatorial forests.

The remaining two American species are rarer and more restricted in their distribution. The more interesting is the mountain tapir (*Tapirus pinchaque* or *T. roulini*) which is smaller and more graceful. It is 7 ft (1.8 m) long, 30 – 34 in (75 – 80 cm) high at the shoulder. It lives at altitudes of 6,500 – 13,000 ft (2,000 – 4,000 m) in the Andes of Colombia and Ecuador, and perhaps also in parts of northern Peru and western Venezuela. The other species, Baird's tapir (*Tapirus bairdi*), is also very rare and threatened with extinction. It is found from southern Mexico as far south as Colombia and Ecuador west of the Andes. It is the largest of the American species, standing 4 ft (1.2 m) at the shoulder, and weighing over 650 lb (300 kg). It has a short mane on the neck.

▶ Tapirs frequently rest sitting on their hindquarters.

◀ They often paw the ground.

▲ They take dust and mudbaths and scratch themselves to rid themselves of parasites. Another strange habit is the way they scratch their chests and forelimbs with their hindfeet.

American tapir (*Tapirus terrestris*)

◀ The Malay tapir likes to stand submerged in rivers and swamps, where it feeds off aquatic plants and moves along the bottom; it can go for long stretches completely under water.

▲ Young tapirs: The striped coat is typical of young tapirs; it is lost after a few months. Left, a young American tapir (*Tapirus terrestris*), right (1,2,3), successive stages in the Malay tapir, showing the gradual appearance of the white saddle.

◀ 1) Distribution of the American tapir (*Tapirus terrestris*).
2) Distribution of the Malay tapir (*Tapirus indicus*).

1
2

PRZEWALSKI HORSE

Equus ferus przewalskii

Order Perissodactyla
Family Equidae
Size Height at shoulder 51 – 56 in (130 – 142 cm)
Weight 55 – 660 lb (250 – 300 kg)
Dentition $\dfrac{3.1.3(4).3}{3.1.3.\quad 3} = 40 - 42$
Reproductive period In the spring
Gestation 11 months
Number of young 1
Sexual maturity 3 years
Maximum age 34 years

The body of the Przewalski horse is, typically, a color that may vary from yellow to light red-brown, generally darker at the neck and head. The muzzle area is white, or at least light (the so-called "floury muzzle"). The mane, tail, and feet are dark brown or black. Faint transverse stripes sometimes appear above the hocks and behind the knees of the forelegs. A dark dorsal stripe always runs from the mane to the root of the tail, and there is generally also a dark stripe or patch across the shoulders. A relevant difference between the wild forms and the domestic horse lies in the way the long hairs grow; all wild forms have a short mane standing stiff and a tail with short hairs at the root or on the whole of the upper part (as in the zebra and the African and Asian wild asses), while the domestic horse characteristically has a long, flowing mane and a tail with hairs up to the root.

In the Przewalski horse the distinctive growth of the long hairs is not so extreme; the mane, though still stiff, often falls to one side, especially just before the molt. It has no forelock such as we see on domestic horses; the forehead is always bare, as in the zebras and the African and Asian wild asses. The hairs on the tail are not as short as in other wild species; whereas there are no long hairs up to the root as in the domestic horse, the hairs show a distinct tendency to form a sort of "bell" shape from the root to a third of the way down, making a short-haired tail such as is sometimes found in the primitive races of domestic horse like the fjord pony and Iceland pony.

The overall appearance of the Przewalski horse, and its skeleton,

Some members of the family Equidae

Przewalski horse
(*Equus ferus przewalskii*)

Grant's zebra
(*Equus quagga boehmi*)

Arab saddle horse
(*Equus caballus*)

Domestic donkey
(*Equus asinus asinus*)

Shetland pony
(*Equus caballus*)

All living species of the family Equidae – horses, asses, and zebras – have been placed together in the single genus *Equus* in view of the great homogeneity in their appearance and their physical conformation. Elegant and agile, graceful and tall, they are all single-toed, each leg ending in a hoof which is nothing more than the highly developed nail of the foot's single digit. The coat is smooth, with growths of longer hair forming bushy tails and manes that are upright in the wild forms but long and flowing in the domestic horse. All the Equidae are herbivorous; the wild forms live on the grassy steppes and plains of the Old World, while man has taken the many varieties of domestic horse and ass with him all over the world.

differ in many respects from those of a small horse of one of the domestic races of about the same size. One notices at once the rather clumsy look given by the strong neck and thick, heavy head. The very powerful bones of the lower jaw give the head a particularly square look. Then there is the beard, the hair that grows strongly, especially in winter, on the underside of the head as far as the throat, emphasizing the "box" shape of the skull.

Przewalski horses bred in captivity for 20 generations, being descended from only a few (8 – 10) animals, also exhibit other features of domestication, including small white stars on the forehead, and gray or roan coloring, which have occasionally appeared in some herds. However, it is impossible to say for certain whether or not some of these changes may be partly due to imported animals (from Askania Nova in southern Russia) which have been crossed with domestic horses.

The withers are not very prominent, the croup is round with the tail deeply set, the legs comparatively short, slender, and not very powerful – all features of the outward appearance of the original wild horse. In captivity and in enclosures where the ground is soft, the hooves can very quickly grow so deformed that the animals have difficulty in trotting and galloping. Old accounts say that the wild horse of Poland, the forest tarpan, was even liable to develop a handicap when its hooves grew too long.

The Przewalski horse is most probably completely extinct in the wild. According to reports by Russian scientists, the numbers of Mongolian wild horses in the border area between Mongolia and China between 1942 and 1945 had still not fallen to a disastrous level. In the area between 89° and 94°E and 44° 30′ and 45° 30′ N, i.e. between the Batyak-Bogdo and the Takhin-Shara-nuru mountains, a few herds could still be seen, and a few foals were actually caught there and taken to Ulan Bator. Only one more stallion was seen in 1955 on the Takhin-Shara-nuru, and according to accounts by shepherds only about 15 horses were still in the Ulan Shilin-choolai valley in 1964. As their habitat continues to shrink, especially as they are driven from their waterholes, the fate of these last free Przewalski horses seems to be sealed.

▲ When troubled by skin parasites, they rub the parts of the body that are hardest to reach on account of the long mane and tail hairs against the trunks of trees.

▲ Przewalski horses, or Mongolian wild horses, are the only wild horses still living. Characteristic are their yellow coloring, stiff black mane, pure black tail and feet, thick head with no forelock and the patch of white round the mouth. They live in the bushy steppes of central Asia.

▲ This Persian ivory statuette, which came from excavations at Susa in Iran and dates from about 5,000 years ago, represents a Przewalski horse in the act of yawning.

◄ The surviving wild populations are already reduced to such small numbers as to be on the verge of extinction. The last Przewalski horses may still be living in a small area of central Asia along the frontier between Mongolia and China, on two slopes of the Altai mountains, but reports are doubtful and contradictory. (1) Probable present distribution of the Przewalski horse (*Equus ferus przewalskii*).

ZEBRAS

Genus Equus
Subgenera Hippotigris
and Dolichohippus

Order Perissodactyla
Family Equidae
Size Height at shoulder 42 – 61 in
(106 – 155 cm)
Weight 265 – 950 lb (120 – 430 kg)
Dentition $\dfrac{3.1.3(4).3}{3.1.3.\quad 3} = 40 - 42$
Gestation about 1 year
Number of young 1
Sexual maturity At 2 – 4 years
Maximum age 20 – 25 years in
captivity; the steppe zebra has been
known to live for 40 years

Zebras are typical African equids and
all of the three known species have the
unmistakable black-and-white striped
coat.

Grevy's zebra (*Equus grevyi*) is the
biggest living zebra, with a long, narrow head and remarkably big, wide,
rounded ears, black at the edges and
white at the tip, with thick white hairs
inside. The head has very narrow black
stripes on a white ground, with a black
muzzle. There is a brown patch, and a
white patch above it, at the edge of the
striped area just above the nostrils.
The stripes on the neck are considerably wider, those on the body narrower
again, and often branching. There are
no stripes on the belly. Most striking of
all is the pattern of stripes on the
croup, which, unlike those of all other
zebras, do not run parallel to one
another down from the median line
but follow a different direction on the
hind part of the croup, like a series of
concentric circles drawn in chalk
round the base of the tail.

Grevy's zebra occurs from northern
Kenya and southern Somalia northward to southern Sudan, but is now
almost extinct in Somalia. Its territorial behavior is very much like that of
the wild ass. An adult male commands
a territory that may be as big as 4 sq.
miles (10 km²), although there will be
other males living there as well as
mares and foals. The stallion marks the
boundaries by loud braying and conspicuous behavior, also by piles of
droppings, sometimes of immense
size, though these do not, in fact, keep
other stallions out. The females are
prevented as far as possible from leaving the territory, because coupling

Grant's zebra (*Equus quagga boehmi*)

▲ A herd of zebra in the African savanna. The coat of these animals has a conspicuous striped pattern, which one might expect would make them very easy to see on the open plains; but in fact this is a remarkable example of cryptic coloring and makes the outlines of the animal's body completely disappear when seen from a distance.

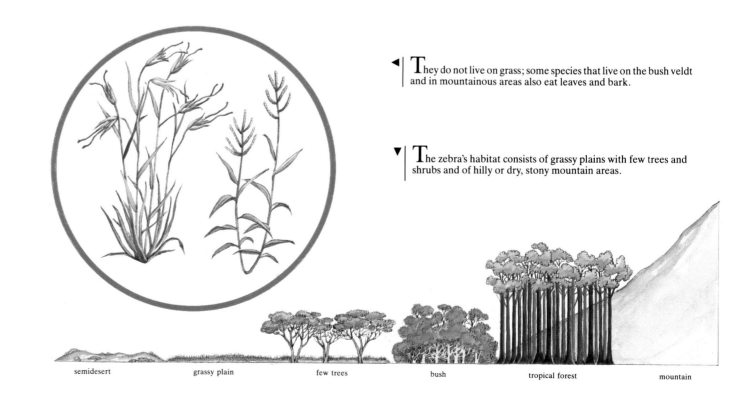

◄ They do not live on grass; some species that live on the bush veldt and in mountainous areas also eat leaves and bark.

▼ The zebra's habitat consists of grassy plains with few trees and shrubs and of hilly or dry, stony mountain areas.

semidesert   grassy plain   few trees   bush   tropical forest   mountain undisturbed by other males can only take place within it. A male may keep his territory for years, and even in severe drought will always be the last to leave it.

Zebras graze at two main times in the day, in the morning and in late evening. They rest at midday, in the shade if possible, standing in a close group. Like all the Equidae, they sleep standing; only very young foals lie down. They eat nothing but grass. Normally they will try to drink every day; they cannot go more than three days without water. The gestation period is generally said to be 390 days, but in fact it may be assumed that it lasts about a year, as with other equids.

The very rare mountain zebra (*Equus zebra*) differs from the generally similar steppe zebra in the pattern of the stripes; the moderately broad black stripes that run down the sides from the back remain more or less parallel as far back as the flanks, and only begin to change direction with the much broader stripes that run obliquely forward over the croup and hindquarters. On the steppe zebra these oblique stripes start much further forward, so that the animal looks quite different seen from the side. The stripes on the mountain zebra's legs go down as far as the fetlocks, there are no stripes on the belly and the stripes on the face, the top of the croup and the tail are narrower. There are two known subspecies, one of which, extremely rare, lives in South Africa, the other from Angola to southwest Africa. These zebras feed mainly on grass but will eat leaves and bark if necessary. They normally live in small herds of 2 – 5 adult mares with their foals, and a single stallion as their leader. The period of gestation is apparently 362 – 365 days, with the main foaling period in the rainy season, between November and April.

The steppe zebra (*Equus quagga*) is the most numerous and most widely distributed of the zebras, occurring throughout East Africa. Its main distinctive feature is the gradual fading out of the stripes on the legs and hindquarters. The further north the zebras live, the more distinct are the markings on these parts of the body.

There are four subspecies of steppe zebra: Selous's zebra, Chapman's zebra, Purchell's zebra, and the now extinct quagga.

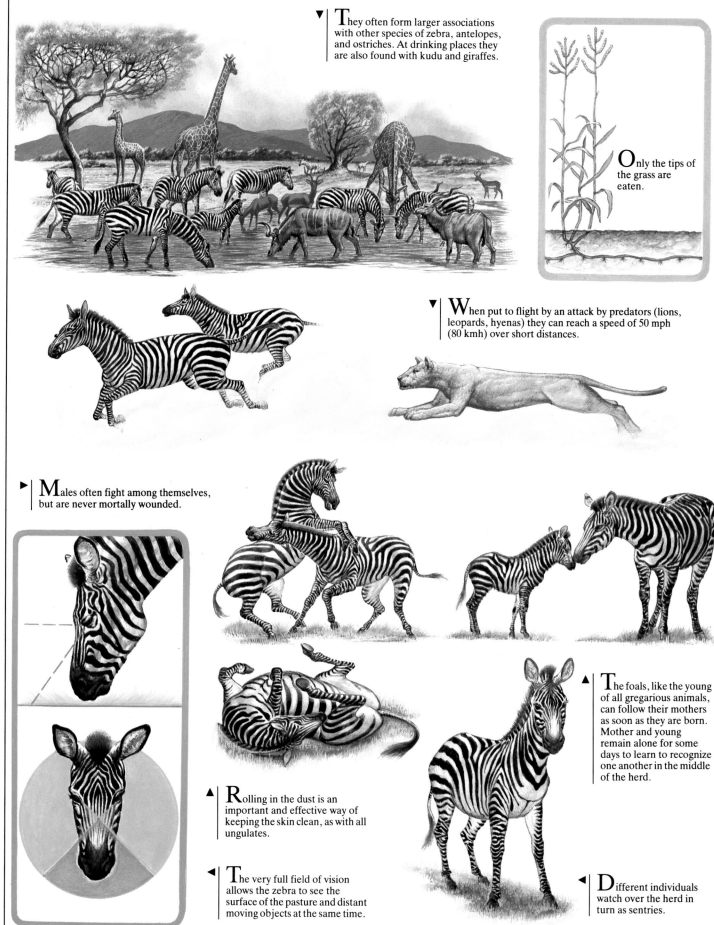

They often form larger associations with other species of zebra, antelopes, and ostriches. At drinking places they are also found with kudu and giraffes.

Only the tips of the grass are eaten.

When put to flight by an attack by predators (lions, leopards, hyenas) they can reach a speed of 50 mph (80 kmh) over short distances.

Males often fight among themselves, but are never mortally wounded.

The foals, like the young of all gregarious animals, can follow their mothers as soon as they are born. Mother and young remain alone for some days to learn to recognize one another in the middle of the herd.

Rolling in the dust is an important and effective way of keeping the skin clean, as with all ungulates.

The very full field of vision allows the zebra to see the surface of the pasture and distant moving objects at the same time.

Different individuals watch over the herd in turn as sentries.

TREE-SHREWS
Genus Tupaia

Order Primates
Family Tupaiidae
Size Length of head and body 4 – 8 in (10 – 20 cm); length of tail 4 – 10 in (10 – 25 cm)
Weight about 4¼ – 6½ oz (120 – 180 g), with variations according to species
Dentition $\frac{2.1.3.3}{3.1.3.3} = 38$
Reproductive period Throughout year
Gestation 45 – 50 days
Number of young 1 – 4 (generally 2)
Sexual maturity 4 months
Maximum age Over 2 years in captivity

The tree-shrews are small animals, similar to ordinary shrews or to small squirrels. The body is fairly slim and the pentadactylous limbs are of equal length and quite short. All the toes are furnished with thin, sharp nails, molded into claws, extremely useful for climbing up and down branches. The tail is more or less the same length as the body, thick and bushy in most members of the subfamily Tupaiinae. The dense, soft fur varies slightly in color according to species: it is generally ocher or reddish-brown above (with shades of gray, chestnut, green or black) and lighter (white or fawn) below.

Found exclusively in Asia, the tree-shrews live mainly in the tropical forests of the southeast, from India to southern China, the whole Indochinese peninsula, the Malaysian archipelago, and the Philippines. Despite their vernacular name, tree-shrews do not live exclusively in trees, and some species prefer life on the ground and in the bush. Higher up, tree-shrews may be encountered at altitudes of as much as 10,000 ft (3,000 m) in Nepal.

With the exception of the pen-tailed tree-shrew (*Ptilocercus lowii*), all the tree-shrews have diurnal habits. The animals are quite agile, showing much skill in running and jumping, and performing leaps of over 3 ft (1 m). As a rule they live alone or in pairs, being highly intolerant of other individuals of the same species. Their diet is mainly insectivorous but they also eat worms and other small animals as well as eggs, nestlings, and vegetable substances.

The best known member of the family Tupaiidae is certainly the common tree-shrew (*Tupaia glis*), about 6-8 in (15-20 cm) long, with a tail of the same length, and much studied in captivity. The outward appearance does not immediately suggest a link with the prosimians. Indeed, after their discovery they were immediately classified in the order Insectivora, mainly because of their long, pointed snout and their diet, consisting chiefly of insects and other invertebrates. Later, thanks to accurate studies of their internal structure and their physiology, affinities with the primates became clear, and the tree-shrews were classified either as prosimians or, at least, as intermediate forms between insectivores and primates.

These animals live on their own or in pairs. They are extremely intolerant of other individuals of the same species; consequently they mark out private territory and defend it fiercely against intruders. Inside this territory some species build a circular nest, fashioned mainly of moss.

AYE-AYE
Daubentonia madagascariensis

Order Primates
Family Daubentoniidae
Size Length from head to rump 14 – 17 in (36 – 44 cm); tail 20 – 24 in (50 – 60 cm)
Weight 3½ – 6 lb (1.6 – 2.8 kg)
Dentition $\frac{1.0.1.3}{1.0.0.3} = 18$
Reproductive period unknown
Gestation unknown
Number of young 1
Sexual maturity Probably in the 3rd year
Maximum age 23 years

The aye-aye must surely be the oddest and most aberrant species of all the lemurs – indeed of all the primates. When it was first discovered it was actually regarded as a rodent, largely on account of its front teeth, which are very much like a rodent's teeth. There are only two incisors in the lower jaw, and two in the upper, chisel-shaped and, especially in the lower jaw, highly developed. Canines are completely absent. But most remarkable of all is the structure of the hands and feet, which are thin and clawed, except for the big toes, which have flat nails. The second to fifth digits on hands and feet are long and thin. The third and fourth fingers on the hands are nearly twice as long as the others, and the third is particularly thin, giving the impression of a skeleton finger only covered in skin.

The two main components of the diet of the strictly nocturnal aye-aye are fruit and the larvae of insects taken out of the bark of trees. First it bites or gnaws through the rind of a fruit with its incisors, then as soon as it has made a hole in it the long middle finger comes into play, reaching into the fruit and scooping out the soft flesh. The aye-aye in search of insect larvae taps on bark or rotting wood with its middle finger, then sometimes tries to trace their movement by listening. The sense of smell also plays a part here. Once the prey is located, the bark or wood over it is gnawed away with the incisors, and the skeleton finger gets to work again, reaching into tunnels made by the larvae while feeding, and scooping the larvae out rather in the form of a pulp, which is quickly licked off the finger each time it is withdrawn.

The aye-aye (*Daubentonia madagascariensis*) lives in the rain forests of the eastern coastal zones of Madagascar; the animal feeds on insects extracted from bark and soft wood.

Although all the fingers of the hand are long and thin, the middle finger looks positively skeletal. With this particularly long, slender tool, the aye-aye extracts pulpy insect larvae from the tunnels they have dug in wood and also pierces the rind of fruit to get at the edible contents.

The two principal items of the aye-aye's diet are fruit and larvae of insects living concealed under tree bark. Thus the animal's feeding habits are quite different from those of other lemurs.

The front teeth of the aye-aye have the same function as the skeletal middle finger, being reduced to two canines in the upper jaw, matched by the same arrangement in the lower jaw; these are shaped like scalpels, like the continuously growing teeth of a rodent. Because of the very small snout and broad skull, the head appears rounded.

The aye-aye is the strangest looking of all primates and appears to have few features in common with prosimians.

1) The aye-aye was once well distributed in the east and in a small northwestern zone of Madagascar, but is nowadays seriously threatened with extinction. Its habitat is in danger of vanishing as woods continue to be destroyed. At the same time it is persecuted by local people who regard it as the harbinger of bad luck.

LEMURS

Order Primates
Families Cheirogaleidae, Lepilemuridae, Lemuridae, Indriidae, and Daubentoniidae
Size Length from head to rump, from a minimum of 4 – 6 in (10 – 15 cm), plus 5 – 7 in (12 – 17 cm) for the tail, in *Microcebus murinus*, to a maximum 24 – 28 in (61 – 71 cm) plus 1¼ – 2½ in (3 – 6 cm) for the tail, in *Indri indri*
Weight From 1¼ – 3½ oz (40 – 100 g) for *Microcebus murinus*, to 11 – 14 lb (5 – 6.3 kg) for *Indri indri*
Dentition $\frac{2.1.3.3}{2.1.3.3}$ = 36 in *Microcebus murinus*. The lower canine and one upper and one lower premolar are absent in *Indri indri*
Reproductive period August to March for *Microcebus murinus* (in captivity in the northern hemisphere, March – July, often 2 litters a year); January to March for *Indri indri*
Gestation Average of 63 days for *Microcebus murinus*; probably 120 – 155 days for *Indri indri*
Number of young 1 – 3 for *Microcebus murinus*; 1 for *Indri indri*
Weight at birth 0.08 – 0.15 oz (2.7 – 5 g) for *Microcebus murinus*; unknown for *Indri indri*
Sexual maturity At 7 – 10 weeks for *Microcebus murinus*; unknown, possibly in the third year, for *Indri indri*
Maximum age 6 years for *Microcebus murinus*; unknown for *Indri indri*

The general term "lemurs" is used here for the Prosimii living in Madagascar. The only members of this very primitive suborder of the primates found outside this big island off the southeastern coast of Africa today are the bushbabies of Africa and the lorises and related species in Africa and South and Southeast Asia. The lemurs of Madagascar used commonly to be classified in three families, the true lemurs (Lemuridae), the indris and related species (Indriidae) and the aye-ayes (Daubentoniidae).

Lemurs embody a stage in the evolution of apes and provide an excellent source of information on the social and environmental development of man's earliest ancestors.

The lemurs inhabit the forests, nowadays increasingly diminished in area, of Madagascar. They are descended from a group of prosimians which lived at the beginning of the Tertiary both in Europe and North America. They managed to retain their primitive multiplicity of forms thanks to the separation and isolation of their territorial range from the African continent – an event which occurred gradually during the Tertiary and which prevented the rivalry of other, more highly evolved monkeys. In particular, the smaller and less evolved species, such as the lesser mouse lemur (*Microcebus murinus*), shown center left, lead a nocturnal life either singly or in small groups. More evolved species, with larger dimensions, are diurnal, and belong to the genus *Lemur*, such as the ring-tailed lemur (*Lemur catta*), lower left, and the mongoose lemur (*L. mongoz*), upper left. The Indriidae, including the largest living lemur, the indri (*Indri indri*), upper right, live in small communities, or, in the case of the sociable Verreaux's sifaka (*Propithecus verreauxi*), in rather more numerous groups.

The ring-tailed lemur feeds mainly on various types of fruit (about 70 per cent of its diet), leaves (about 25 per cent), and flowers.

RING-TAILED LEMUR

Lemur catta

Order Primates
Family Lemuridae
Size Length from head to rump about 18 in (45 cm), tail about 22 in (55 cm)
Weight 3½ – 8 lb (1.7 – 3.7 kg)
Dentition $\frac{2.1.3.3}{2.1.3.3} = 36$

Reproductive period April to June; in captivity in the northern hemisphere more widely spread, from August to January
Gestation 132 – 138 days
Number of young generally 1, about 15% twins, rarely triplets
Weight at birth 1½ – 2½ oz (50 – 85 g)
Sexual maturity At about 1½ to 2 years
Maximum age 20 years

One of the best known lemurs is the ring-tailed lemur, rather strange-looking, mainly because of its black and white ringed tail. Its face, too, looks like a black and white mask, with its black nose, black-tipped muzzle and black rings round the eyes. The fur on the body is gray to reddish-gray, with the underside whitish. This distinctive coloration might be expected to make the ring-tailed lemur easy to pick out from a distance in the wild. But the opposite is true. Under the brilliant sun of southern Madagascar, the leaves and twigs of the light dry forest draw an intricate pattern of lines and dots of bright light and deep shadow on the ground, in which the ring-tailed lemur's black and white mask and tail camouflage it completely.

The ring-tailed lemur lives in south-western Madagascar, in dry wooded country and the trees lining the rivers, where the annual rainfall does not exceed 40 in (1,000 mm) and the dry season lasts as much as 8 months. During the day it strays now and again out of the light woodland into nearby open ground, rocky or sandy. The ring-tailed lemur most sociable of all living lemur species, forming groups 13 to 17 strong comprising several adult males and females and their young. The species forming the next largest troops, of 9 – 10 individuals, are the brown lemur (*Lemur fulvus*) and black lemur (*L. macaco*).

The ring-tailed lemur frequents the ground more often than other lemurs. A sociable species, it is immediately recognizable by its ringed black-and-white tail, which is held in a raised position.

The tail is moistened with the secretion of glands situated in the inner arm, and used for scent-marking individual territory.

The foot of lemurs, like that of larger monkeys, has an opposable big toe, which enables the animal to grip. Whereas all the other toes have flat nails, the second is clawed.

After dawn the ring-tailed lemur can often be seen seated in an upright position, arms extended, basking in the sun.

Lesser mouse lemur
(*Microcebus murinus*)

Indri
(*Indri indri*)

hand

foot

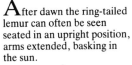

The ring-tailed lemur frequently shows its state of excitement by marking branches and leafy boughs with the glandular secretions of its genital organs. This activity, more pronounced than among other lemur species, is in keeping with the highly socialized behavior of the animal.

The smallest of the lemurs is the lesser mouse lemur, assumed to be modeled on primitive ancestrial forms. The indri, for its part, is the biggest living prosimian. Its thumb and big toe are much enlarged so as to take a firm grip when climbing.

MARMOSETS AND TAMARINS

Genera Callithrix, Cebuella, Saguinus, Leontideus

Order Primates
Family Callithricidae
Size Length of head and body 6¼ – 12¼ in (16 – 31 cm); tail 7 – 16½ in (18 – 42 cm)
Weight 3 – 20 oz (85 – 560 g)
Dentition $\frac{2.1.3.2}{2.1.3.2}$ = 32
Reproductive period Potentially all year round; appears to be more restricted in wild, depending on environmental factors
Gestation 130 – 160 days, according to species
Number of young Generally 2; more rarely 1 or 3
Sexual maturity 12 – 15 months
Maximum age 16 years or more in captivity

By reason of their outward appearance, marmosets and tamarins might seem to a layman to be more akin to squirrels than to monkeys. Their size is fairly small (somewhere between that of a rat and a squirrel), and they are, with the exception of a few prosimians, the smallest of all primates. The pygmy marmoset (*Cebuella pygmaea*), about 6 in (15 cm) long, with a tail 7 – 8 in (18 – 20 cm) in additional length, and weighing about 2¾ oz (70 – 80 g), is the smallest and lightest of them all. The head is rounded, the large eyes are placed frontally and the nostrils typically open sideways. The ears are quite big but almost always concealed by hair. The limbs are slender, those of the tamarins being comparatively longer, and well suited for jumping, especially in the case of the pinché marmoset (*Saguinus oedipus*).

Hands and feet are furnished with five digits, particularly long among the lion-headed or golden marmosets of the genus *Leontideus*; fingers and toes are equipped with thin, curved nails shaped like claws, except for the big toe, in which the nail is flat; this big toe is totally opposable, whereas the thumb is only partially so. On the other hand, by reason of their small dimensions (and thus the modest size of the hands and feet), these animals can only take a grip on the thinnest

▲ The precise classification of the marmosets and tamarins is still partly controversial, mainly in respect of the exact number of species and subspecies. Because the Callithricidae are so extremely varied, authors have tended to coin a large number of specific and even generic names, most of them probably unjustified. The trend nowadays is to limit these groups as much as possible, reducing many forms (especially those hailing from different regions) to the rank of mere subspecies.
1) Pygmy marmoset (*Cebuella pygmaea*); 2) Common marmoset (*Callithrix jacchus*); 3) Pinché marmoset (*Saguinus oedipus*); 4) Golden marmoset (*Leontideus rosalia*); 5) Emperor tamarin (*Saguinus imperator*).

▶ The varied diet of marmosets and tamarins comprises plant food and, to an even greater extent, animal food. In this context it is interesting to note that some species, such as the pinché marmoset and the silvery marmoset, are skillful hunters of small creatures (birds, mice, etc).

branches; both marmosets and tamarins usually climb trunks like squirrels, using their claws. The tail is long, quite bushy but never prehensile.

Marmosets and tamarins inhabit Panama and large parts of tropical South America. The pinché marmosets have the most northerly distribution, living in eastern Panama and neighboring zones of Colombia up to the Rio Magdalena; they are also the only species found west of the Andes, in Colombia and, partially, in Ecuador. The other species live mainly in the huge Amazon basin, from the Atlantic shores to the eastern slopes of the Andes.

All the Callithricidae are typical inhabitants of tropical rainforests, with their luxuriant tangles of epiphytic plants, both in well-drained terrain and in regularly flooded areas. They are at home in the secondary forests and in the marginal zones of thick undergrowth where there are plenty of thin treetrunks and branches, and they often adapt, too, to regions that man has partly degraded and modified. In the vertical sense, these animals cover a broad belt from 10 ft (3 m) to 65 ft (20 m) above ground level, only seldom descending to the forest floor.

The marmosets and tamarins live, for the most part, in groups of average number, socially somewhere between the small family group and the large tribe of more gregarious species. It is really a large, extended family, formed of parents and young of various ages, or perhaps also the descendants of all intermediate pairs.

The little Callithricidae are unaggressive animals, even though there is a form of hierarchy and a territorial tendency within the group. They are active throughout the day, with a possible rest period in the hottest midday hours; at night they sleep in groups inside tree cavities, waking up quite late and immediately setting off to look for food. They move about in different ways, depending on the species. Most of them climb like squirrels, helping themselves along with their claws and pursuing a spiral course up and down the trunks. The tamarins have longer limbs and are good jumpers.

The diet of these animals is quite varied, including vegetable matter but consisting mainly of animal food, such as insects, spiders and other, small arthropods, snails, worms, small lizards, birds' eggs and, occasionally, small birds and mammals.

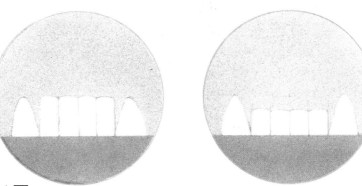

▲ The lower canines of marmosets (left) are not larger (or only slightly) than the incisors, whereas those of tamarins (right) are noticeably longer.

▼ The Callithricidae have claws on all their digits, except for the big toe with its flat nail.

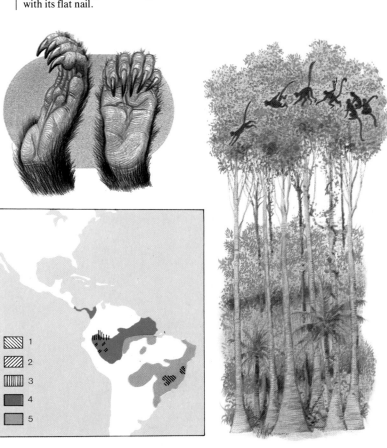

▲ Although they prefer the treetops, marmosets and tamarins often come down lower to shrub level but rarely right down to the ground. Rivers, grassy and arid zones generally constitute impassable barriers for these small animals, and the natural geographical isolation which the various populations have long experienced explains the large number of species and subspecies found in the immense Amazon basin. The map shows the distribution of the various present-day genera. 1) *Leontideus*; 2) *Callimico*; 3) *Cebuella*; 4) *Saguinus*; 5) *Callithrix*.

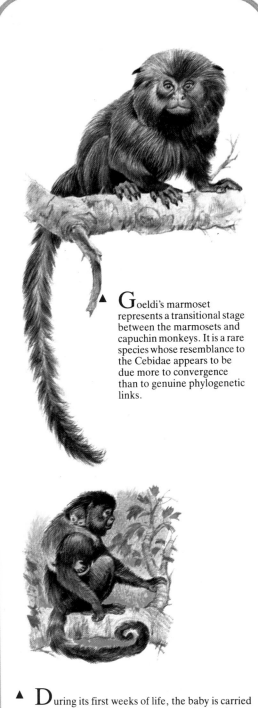

▲ G oeldi's marmoset represents a transitional stage between the marmosets and capuchin monkeys. It is a rare species whose resemblance to the Cebidae appears to be due more to convergence than to genuine phylogenetic links.

▲ D uring its first weeks of life, the baby is carried about on its mother's back; it grasps her back putting its arms around her neck, clinging tightly with its hindlegs and tail. At the age of about one year it is fully grown and within six months more is sexually mature. The thumb of this species is short but opposable, and all digits (as in other marmosets) have long, thin claws, except for the flat-nailed big toe.

SPIDER MONKEYS AND HOWLER MONKEYS

Genera Ateles and Alouatta

Order Primates
Family Cebidae
Size Head and body 14 – 24 in (35 – 60 cm); tail 20 – 36 in (50 – 90 cm)
Weight Up to 13½ lb (6 kg)
Dentition $\frac{2.1.3.3}{2.1.3.3}$ = 36
Reproductive period Potentially throughout year
Gestation About 140 days
Number of young 1
Sexual maturity 2 – 3 years
Maximum age 20 years or more in captivity

The spider monkeys owe their name to the unusual structure of their limbs, which are long and supple, and to their extraordinary agility up in the trees, comparable only to that of the gibbons from Southeast Asia. They are obviously suited for life in trees. The body is typically slender and the limbs are relatively long compared with the body, the hindlegs being longer than the arms. The hands are strikingly modified, the thumb being reduced or wholly absent, and the other fingers long and almost always curving so as to get a firm grasp of branches. The long tail is prehensile, the lower tip having a bare surface and so a tactile function; it can truly be said to serve as a fifth limb. The length of head and body is 14 – 24 in (35 – 60 cm), plus the tail which measures 20 – 36 in (50 – 90 cm). The weight is up to 13½ lb (6 kg).

Spider monkeys inhabit southern Mexico, Central America, and a large part of the tropical belt of South America (excluding southeastern Brazil) from the plains to the high mountains (Andes and mountains in Central America and Mexico).

The breeding period is not confined to any fixed time of year and may occur at any season; nevertheless, most babies appear to be born in fall. Just prior to giving birth, the female leaves the group, only returning 2 – 4 months later with her baby. The young spider monkey becomes independent after around 10 months.

Black spider monkey (*Ateles paniscus*)

The agility of the spider monkeys up in the trees is quite astonishing, comparable only to that of the Old World gibbons. The earliest travelers to Panama, seeing these creatures, described the way they formed "living chains," gripping one another's tails to swing across wide spaces from tree to tree or to ford a river. Even though such tales may be exaggerated and fanciful, they give a good idea of how the first observers of these strange monkeys reacted to their acrobatic feats.

Food consists almost wholly of fresh fruit, as well as other vegetation such as leaves, shoots, and flowers. Protein is, to a lesser degree, included in the diet, in the form of insects, eggs, and nestlings.

Forming a separate subfamily, the howler monkeys display similar behavior to the spider monkeys, although they differ somewhat in physical appearance. Far from being slender in build, they are rather tubby, heavier than almost all other New World monkeys, weighing 15½ – 20 lb (7 – 9 kg), and also among the biggest, averaging 24 in (60 cm) in length, with a tail of about 24 – 28 in (60 – 70 cm). The limbs are long but sturdy, with well-developed thumbs and big toes. The first two fingers of the hands are well separated from the other three and opposable to them. The tail is prehensile, with a tactile tip. The muzzle is prominent, with a bulging forehead; and the dilated hyoid bone and thyroid cartilage together form a kind of soundbox which enables these monkeys, uniquely, to give out cries of very high intensity and power, which can be heard in the forest for more than a mile, and twice that distance in open regions. This remarkable vocal apparatus is best developed among adult males who use their powerful voices to mark out territory.

Groups, in which females predominate, vary in number from 8 – 10 to up to 20, and a maximum of 40, individuals. The monkeys roam their territory slowly and cautiously, for there is plenty of food to be had. Howler monkeys, in fact, are the only platyrrhines to eat large quantities of leaves. They also consume fruits, shoots, and flowers, ripping them directly from the trees, as well as small quantities of insects and other arthropods. Strict tree-dwellers, they do not move as rapidly as spider monkeys, proceeding comparatively slowly and warily, usually walking along large branches on all fours, and using the tail to help them swing from one branch to another. Breeding does not appear to be confined to any particular part of the year; one baby is born after a gestation period of about 140 days, is carefully tended for about a year and becomes wholly independent at the age of 3 years.

The howler monkeys are divided into some six species. The Most northerly species is the mantled howler monkey (*Alouatta palliata*) of Central America, ranging into southern Mexico; the Guatemalan howler monkey (*Alouatta villosa*) is confined to a small zone in that country. The other species are widely distributed throughout almost the entire wet tropical belt of South America.

▲▶ The long prehensile tail serves virtually as a fifth hand, enabling the spider monkey to grasp branches, to move about more easily in the treetops, and also to feel objects, thanks to the sensitive bare surface along the tail's lower tip.

▲▶ The more or less complete atrophy of the thumb and the prolongation of the other fingers of the hand is a striking adaptation to life in the trees.

Red howler monkey
(*Alouatta seniculus*)

▲ The howler monkeys owe their name to their particularly loud voice, reinforced in adult males by their characteristic vocal apparatus.

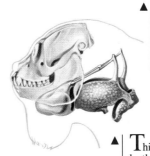

▲ This vocal mechanism is formed by the hyoid bone and the greatly enlarged thyroid cartilage of the larynx. In males, the bony vesicle formed by the hyoid bone is four to five times bigger than that of the female and functions as a sound-box; the jaw, as a result, has wider and higher side sections, giving an unmistakable shape to the skull.

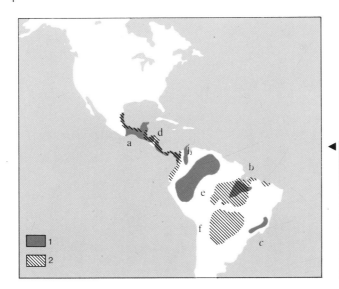

◀ The map shows the geographical ranges of some species of spider monkeys and howler monkeys. The latter, generally allotted to the separate subfamily Alouattinae, are similar to the spider monkeys but differ in certain morphological respects, being heavier and having a well-developed thumb.
1) Distribution of some spider monkeys (genus *Ateles*) and of the woolly spider monkey: a) Black-headed spider monkey (*A. geoffroyi*); b) White-bellied spider monkey (*A. belzebuth*); c) Woolly spider monkey (*Brachyteles arachnoides*).
2) Distribution of some howler monkeys (subfamily Alouattinae): d) Mantled howler monkey (*Alouatta palliata*); e) Red-handed howler monkey (*A. belzebul*); f) Black howler monkey (*A. caraya*).

BABOONS

Genus Papio

Order Primates
Family Cercopithecidae
Size Length of head and body
20 – 44 in (50 – 110 cm); tail 20 – 28 in
(50 – 70 cm)
Weight 30 – 120 lb (14 – 54 kg), average
37 lb (16.5 kg) for females, 73 lb
(33 kg) for males
Dentition $\frac{2.1.2.3}{2.1.2.3} = 32$
Reproductive period Throughout year
Gestation 6 – 7 months
Number of young 1 (rarely 2)
Sexual maturity 4 years
Maximum age 15 years and more

Baboons are animals with a stocky body, strong limbs and fairly short hands and feet. Adapting to life at ground level has caused them to adopt a quadrupedal gait, resting the soles of the feet and the palms of the hands on the ground. The overall impression is one of considerable strength, and this is reinforced by the powerful teeth, frequently bared, especially the long, pointed canines. The head is broad and the muzzle long, with voluminous cheek pouches; the eyes are small, with large, jutting brows. Males are much bigger than females and have a kind of mane or thick mantle over the shoulders. The rather coarse fur is yellowish-brown or greenish-brown, according to species, and blackish-brown in the chacma baboon (*Papio ursinus*).

Baboons nowadays live only in Africa and a few southern marginal areas of the Arabian peninsula. Inhabiting steppes and savannas, they are present almost throughout Africa south of the Sahara, with the obvious exception of the forest belt. Territory varies in extent according to the size of the troop and local availability of food; in Kenya's Amboseli Park, they occupy vast territories of 2¾ – 5¾ sq. miles (7 – 15 km²).

At night baboons gather to sleep in trees, where they feel safest; indeed, they never settle in zones where there are no trees, which provide them not only with places to rest but also shelter from the attack of a predator. In the morning they climb down from the branches and march off to look for food. The animals feed on tubers, berries, fruit, and other vegetation, as well as insects, eggs, small

Yellow baboon
(*Papio cynocephalus*)

▲
▶ Baboons have adapted to life in the wide open spaces by virtue of certain physical attributes, a strict pattern of behavior within the species and a markedly aggressive attitude; furthermore, they have tended to become omnivorous, extremely useful in a relatively poor habitat where food is not always of the highest quality. Bold and adaptable, these animals have not retreated as parts of their original environment have given way to human colonization. They are, in fact, accustomed to deriving maxium advantages from plantations and cultivated fields, such crops being regarded as easy sources of food, in this sense they often prove to be veritable pests, particularly where the leopard, their principal natural enemy, has been wiped out by man.

▼ Baboons inhabit the most varied environments. Only the mandrill and the drill live in forests (1), while the true baboons prefer wooded savannas and open plains (2). The hamadryas lives in rocky zones (3) as does the gelada who, nevertheless, can thrive in even more arid regions (4).

1   2   3   2   4

ground-nesting birds, and other vertebrates up to the size of a small gazelle. They have been seen catching hares, bringing down young Thomson's gazelles and even killing a baby vervet.

Baboons begin their social life at birth. The newborn baboons instinctively grasp their mother's breast and later transfer themselves to her back, soon learning how to stay balanced. As a rule the babies arouse the interest of the entire group and when a birth occurs, the other females, juveniles, and even adult males surround the new mother and take keen interest in her offspring; such attentions are of great importance from the social viewpoint, for after these early contacts with members of the troop they grow up to play with others of their age and with other young baboons, thus aquiring the physical and mental powers needed later when facing their hard life on the savanna.

Also belonging to the same genus as the baboons is a species adapted to even more arid environments than those of its savanna relatives, namely the hamadryas or sacred baboon (*P. hamadryas*). It, too, is a very sturdy animal, which has colonized the subdesert steppes bordering the Ethiopia plateau, as well as a few confined areas in the southwestern and southeastern tips of the Arabian peninsula. In such inhospitable surroundings, where there is little food or shelter, these animals lead a disciplined life which in some ways is even more rigidly organized than that of the true baboons. Troops are made up of 50 – 100 (or maximum 300 – 400) individuals, but within these groups there are further subdivisions into small family groups, each composed of an adult male and from 1 to 10 females with their respective young. The adult males are recognizable by the long silver-gray mane on the shoulders, which forms a kind of cloak, and by the thick hair on the sides of the head and muzzle, all giving them an impressive, commanding appearance. The pale gray females are smaller and altogether less imposing.

Hamadryas baboons spend much of the day looking for food, comprising grass, roots, seeds, and whatever else their arid habitat can offer; and sometimes they will catch small animals, especially insects. The quest for food is interrupted only for short intervals, when the animals rest and indulge in reciprocal grooming of fur.

Chacma baboon
(*Papio ursinus*)

Guinea baboon
(*Papio papio*)

Anubis baboon
(*Papio anubis*)

In addition to the common yellow baboon illustrated on the facing page, there are three other species of true baboons.

In the ordered ranks of the baboons, the females with babies travel alongside the dominant males, surrounded by other subordinate males. Potential enemies are confronted by the dominants, shoulder to shoulder with other adult males.

The long, powerful canine teeth are highly effective in defense as well as a means of intimidation during bitter disputes among members of the same species.

Partially carnivorous, baboons sometimes prey on hares, small gazelles, and even vervet monkeys.

Baboons can spend the night sitting on tree branches without feeling any soreness, thanks to the ischial callosities which virtually remove any feeling from the rump. In males theses callosities are larger and almost touch (above), whereas in females the areas are smaller and more separated (below).

The hamadryas (*Papio hamadryas*) differs from the true baboons in displaying marked sexual dimorphism, the males being much bigger and possessing a long, thick mane. It is interesting to note that among these monkeys, the submissive posture is similar, as in all baboons, to that of a female in heat, the colors and swellings of the ano-genital region being present also in the males, but without having any obvious sexual significance. Hamadryads were at one time widely found in Egypt and were worshipped by the ancient Egyptians, as is indicated by the discovery of embalmed specimens and by the numerous pictures of the animals on temples and monuments.

GIBBONS

Genera Hylobates and Symphalangus

Order Primates
Family Hylobatidae
Size Height 28 – 32 in (70– 80 cm) in upright position
Weight *Hylobates* 8¾ – 17½ lb (4 – 8 kg); *Symphalangus* 19¾ – 26½ lb (9 – 12 kg)
Dentition $\frac{2.1.2.3}{2.1.2.3} = 32$
Gestation 210 days (*Hylobates*); 235 days (*Symphalangus*)
Number of young 1
Weight at birth 14 oz (400 g)
Sexual maturity 5 – 7 years
Maximum age 30 years

Because their is no external tail and because their arms are much longer than their legs, gibbons are often included among the anthropoid apes. However, by reason of other biological and external anatomical features, this group is in some sense in between the guenons (Cercopithecidae) and the true apes (Pongidae). Some 7 species of gibbon are currently recognized.

Gibbons are distributed through parts of Southeast Asia. But whereas both genera are found in the Malaccan peninsula and on the island of Sumatra, only *Hylobates* is present in Borneo, Thailand, Laos, and Vietnam. The species belonging to the genus *Hylobates* are generally smaller than the siamangs (*Symphalangus*) and have a dense coat of fur which varies in color from black to fawn or gray. The gibbon's coat has a very important function. On winter nights, when temperatures in mountain zones fall to very low levels, thick fur is an indispensable protection against the cold.

The siamangs are larger than the species of the genus *Hylobates*; furthermore there is a membrane between the first phalanges of the third and fourth fingers, and the laryngeal sac expands in a special way, functioning as a proper soundbox, so that the voice of the animal is audible for more than a mile. The sounds emitted by the siamang are to stake out territory, to threaten possible intruders and enemies, or simply to maintain contact with members of the same family.

The habitat is basically arboreal. Gibbons live in lowland tropical forests but are also found at altitudes of up to 8,250 ft (2,500 m). As a rule

► Chart showing the typical brachiation procedure of the gibbon: the animal moves rapidly from branch to branch by swinging and alternating the positions of its long arms.

◄ Gibbons are among the smallest and most agile of all the anthropoid apes. They are highly territorial. Each pair defends its territory, which is usually quite small, with threatening howls against intruders. As a rule these cries are enough to drive the stranger off; but in some cases a bitter, bloody fight may ensue. On the occasion of each birth parents tend to enlarge their territory, so as to ensure food for all, including the new addition to the family. In fact it is normal for each couple to defend only an area that provides enough food for the sustenance of the family.

Above: detail of locomotion on a liana: the arms are held away from the body and function as points of balance. Below: gibbons can hurl themselves as much as 35 ft (12 m) from one tree to another. ►

▼ Detail (above) of the hand and foot: the thumb is small and attached low down in comparison with the other four fingers, but this helps to secure a firm grip round a branch. The gibbon can also move (below) along the thinnest branches.

hand

foot

► The gibbon feeds mainly on fruit and leaves, and also, at times, on insects and birds' eggs.

they settle around the middle or in higher parts of the trees, but when searching for food they may climb to the treetops more than 100 ft (30 m) from the ground or come right down to ground level to look for berries in the low undergrowth, and even, though more rarely, to drink. The gibbon does not usually construct a nest for the night but selects branches with dense foliage on which it will carefully settle for resting and sleeping. The diet consists in the main of fruit and leaves (90 per cent), supplemented by eggs, small birds, and insects.

Unlike many other primates, gibbons do not live in large troops, strictly organized in hierarchies, but in small groups composed of single families. The typical family is 2 – 6 in number, with one adult male, one adult female and 1 – 4 offspring. Occasionally individuals may be found living alone: these are usually old males who can no longer defend a family or young gibbons who have not yet managed to find a partner.

Gibbons are strongly territorial. Each pair will defend its own domain by shouting threats at outsiders: and such cries are generally sufficient to ward off intruders. In extreme cases, however, a real and bloody fight may take place. The territory to be defended is not very large, and each family group, in fact, will confine itself to patrolling an area which provides sufficient food for its sustenance. As confirmation of this, it has been observed that the territory defended by a family consisting only of an adult pair is smaller in area than that belonging to a couple with 2 – 3 youngsters. Indeed, whenever a baby is born, the parents will try to extend their territory to make certain there is enough food for the entire family.

The female gives birth to a single baby on average once every 2 years, after a gestation period of about 7 months. The newborn gibbon is able to take a firm grip on its mother's fur and never lets go for the first couple of months. By the eighth month it will achieve the typical brachiation.

▶ Posture adopted by the gibbon when moving over the ground.

▲ A gibbon family normally consists of father, mother, and baby. Unlike other primates, gibbons do not live in socially organized groups but in single families.

▲ Gibbons are essentially arboreal and spend the greater part of their time more than 80 ft (25 m) above the ground.

◀ Detail of saimang (*Symphalangus*) swelling its laryngeal sac to let out a cry. Such calls demarcate territory and serve to fend off potential enemies. The extremely large canine teeth are clearly visible here.

◀ Gibbons are found in parts of Southeast Asia. Both the genus *Hylobates* and the genus *Symphalangus* are present in the Malacca peninsula and on the island of Sumatra, but only the former in Thailand, Laos, and Vietnam. The geographical distribution of these animals was at one time far more extensive, as is proved by fossil finds.
Essentially tree-dwelling, gibbons live mainly on the middle and upper reaches of trees. Sometimes they come down to the ground to look for berries growing on low shrubs or to drink in pools. It is rare, however, to see a gibbon actually drinking, for as a rule the animals derive all the water they need from fruits and leaves. 1) *Symphalangus*; 2) *Hylobates*.

ORANG-UTAN

Pongo pygmaeus

Order Primates
Family Pongidae
Size Height 3¼ – 5¼ ft (1 – 1.6 m) when on all-fours
Weight Sumatra orang-utan: female 175 lb (80 kg), male 400 lb (180 kg) Borneo orang-utan: female 77 lb (35 kg), male 155 lb (70 kg)
Dentition $\frac{2.1.2.3}{2.1.2.3}$ = 32
Gestation About 250 days
Weight at birth 50 oz (1400 g)
Sexual maturity 7 – 8 years
Maximum age 30 years and more

Only one living species of orang-utan (*Pongo pygmaeus*) is known today, with two subspecies, one from northern Borneo, the other from certain parts of Sumatra. Whereas the present-day populations, although drastically reduced by reason of human intervention, are confined to these two islands of Southeast Asia, in the past there were wild populations of orang-utans throughout Indonesia, Thailand, Laos, Cambodia, Vietnam, and some parts of China.

The orang-utan, like the gibbon, is a typical tree-dwelling animal. It lives in the tree canopy at a height of 65 – 100 ft (20 – 30 m) above the ground, but may also settle on the lower branches. Occasionally it comes down to the ground, but only for short periods. At night it builds a nest at a height varying from 17 – 82 ft (5 – 25 m) ripping off branches and leaves for the purpose. The animal often covers its head and body with the same plant material so as to be completely concealed from intruders. A strange fact is that the orang-utan, even if it remains in the same area for several successive days, never makes further use of the same nest, but builds a new one every night. Sometimes a nest will be placed directly on the ground.

The orang-utan, together with the gorilla, is the largest of the anthropoid apes. Its height, when upright, is 3 – 5 ft (1 – 1.5 m) and sometimes reaches 6 ft (1.80 m). The arms are extremely long, their span often exceeding 6½ ft (2 m). Males and females differ strikingly both in size and appearance. The adult male, apart from being bigger, is distinguished from the female by virtue of the presence, on the sides of the

▲ A male adult orang-utan (*Pongo pygmaeus*). This animal, after the gorilla, is the largest living non-human primate. It is essentially arboreal. The picture shows clearly the skin pouches on either side of the face which generally develop after some ten years, the thick beard covering the chin, the short thumb and big toes separated from the other digits, the dense hair, especially on the limbs, and the flat nails on toes and fingers.

► The orang-utan's diet consists mainly of fruit, leaves, and shoots. Sometimes it also feeds on birds' eggs.

face, of two small pads of skin, either naked or covered with delicate, silky hairs, which give him a characteristic appearance.

During the season when fruit is growing, this constitutes the main food item: at other times of year the animal eats leaves, shoots, and birds' eggs.

In the typical daily round of an orang-utan, the day begins around 8.00 in the morning, when the animal, leaving the nest where it has passed the night, starts feeding on leaves and fruit. During the morning the animal generally sticks close to the nest; around midday there is an interval for building a new nest or taking a nap. In the afternoon the orang-utan may either stay in the same area or move to a neighboring zone, alternating periods of feeding with rest breaks.

The day starts drawing to an end around 6.30 pm, and then the animal settles somewhere with plenty of fruit and leaves, and after a final meal, selects the tree where it is going to spend the night and sets about preparing the nest. Nest-building is not an activity exclusive to the orang-utan, for it is common practice, too, for the gorilla and chimpanzee. Nests are also built during the daytime for the afternoon doze; but unlike those designed for sleeping in overnight, these are put together more roughly and hurriedly, as if to show that they are only temporary structures.

With respect to social organization, the orang-utan is not a gregarious animal but lives in small independent units. Such a unit may consist of one or two individuals: if the latter, it is generally a mother with her offspring. In contrast to the gibbon, the orang-utan does not form stable male and female pairs. Such pairs may form during the mating period, but the animals stay together only for a few hours, at most a day. Even when two individuals meet accidentally in the forest, they show no interest in each other and continue their separate ways.

The female orang-utan gives birth to a single baby only once every 2 – 3 years. The young ape is suckled for about 2 years. The baby spends its first year permanently attached to its mother's fur. Sexual maturity and total independence is reached at 7 – 8 years of age.

The baby is able to grasp the mother's fur almost as soon as it is born. Note how the mother wraps her feet and hands around her offspring; in fact, they are often kept in this position when not being used for gripping branches or holding food.

Variations in facial structure in the course of the animal's life: above right, newborn orang-utan; left, juvenile with beard; below, right, fully mature adult; with the characteristic skin pouches on either side.

The orang-utan builds a nest each night in trees, although cases have been observed of nests at ground level.

Orang-utan's hand and foot: note the particularly long fingers and toes, except for the thumb and big toe, which are small but opposable.

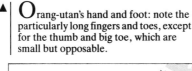

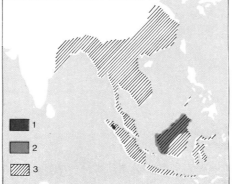

1
2
3

When moving about in a tree, the orang-utan may adopt an upright position, although it has to use its hands to maintain its balance. As a rule it grasps branches with at least three of its four limbs (no matter whether hand or foot) in order to rip off fruits and leaves.

The orang-utan, a typical tree-dwelling ape, lives in the treetops at a height of 65-100 ft (20-30 m) above ground. Nevertheless, it also settles in the lower branches, and occasionally comes right down to the ground for short periods. Progressive deforestation by man as well as hunting, have drastically reduced its numbers to a little more than a thousand or so individuals. It is believed that its current range is confined to northern Borneo and a few parts of the island of Sumatra, whereas in the past there were wild populations of orang-utans all over Indonesia, in Thailand, Laos, Cambodia, Vietnam, and some parts of China.
1) Sumatra orang-utan (*Pongo pygmaeus abelii*); 2) Borneo orang-utan (*P.p. pygmaeus*); 3) original distribution of the orang-utan.

GORILLA

Gorilla gorilla

Order Primates
Family Pongidae
Size Height 4 – 6 ft (1.2 – 1.8 m) when on all-fours
Weight Female 155 – 265 lb (70 – 120 kg); male 220 – 550 lb (100 – 250 kg)
Dentition $\frac{2.1.2.3}{2.1.2.3} = 32$
Gestation About 260 days
Number of young 1
Weight at birth 4½ lb (2 kg)
Sexual maturity Female 6 – 7 years; male 8 – 10 years
Maximum age 35 years or more

There are two subspecies of gorilla, the western gorilla (*G.g. gorilla*), living in the wet forests of the plains of Gaboon, Cameroon, and part of the Congo, and the eastern or mountain gorilla (*G.g. beringei*), from the low-land forests and in the mountains of central Africa (Congo, Uganda and the Virunga volcanos), to an altitude of 11,500 ft (3,500 m). The range of the gorilla, an animal with mainly terrest-rial habits, is limited to the forests of the plain (western subspecies) or the mountains (mountain gorilla). The females and juveniles often climb up into trees, while the males, because of their huge bulk, have tended to become ground-dwellers.

The gorilla's diet consists almost entirely of leaves, shoots, and the pith of certain plants, such as bamboo. Sometimes fruit supplements this diet.

The gorilla is the largest living monkey. When standing on all-fours, its height normally ranges from 4 – 6 ft (1.2 – 1.8 m), but it is well over 6 ft (2 m) when erect on the hindlegs. It may weigh 330 – 550 lb (150 – 250 kg), but in zoos a gorilla's weight may reach 660 lb (300 kg). The huge armspan gener-ally exceeds 6½ ft (2 m). There is a con-siderable difference between male and female: the latter is noticeably smaller and her weight does not exceed 265 lb (120 kg). The face is bare and gives an impression of massiveness because of the well-developed jaws and mandi-bles. The masticatory muscles are pow-erful and are attached to a bony (sagit-tal) crest which develops from the parietal bones of the head. The hand is very large, with a short but opposable thumb, which is used, together with the other fingers, for plucking leaves

▶ Eastern or mountain gorilla (*Gorilla gorilla beringei*); notable features are the opposable thumb and big toe, the particularly thick hair on arms and shoulders, the well-developed arches above the eyes, and the flattened nose with its broad nostrils. It is interesting to note that hair length varies according to age and altitude. The coat, in fact, tends to grow longer as years pass, and it is thicker among mountain gorillas than among gorillas living down in the plains. The hair is relatively short on the back, longer on belly and legs; but it is longest, up to 8 in (20 cm) on the arms. Males of a certain age take on a silvery color on the back, this being a sign of full maturity.

▼ 1) *Gorilla gorilla gorilla*;
2) *Gorilla gorilla beringei*.

1
2

▼ Typical habitats of the gorilla: lowland and mountain forests.

and gripping branches. The heel of the foot is of moderate development, and although the big toe is partially opposable to the others, the overall structure of the foot is better adapted for walking than for climbing. The coat color is generally black or dark gray.

The gorilla spends 80 per cent of its time on the ground. When moving, it holds the front of its body higher and supports its weight on the knuckles of its hand. On special occasions, for example when adopting a threatening attitude, it may stand upright on its legs, beating the chest with its arms. This type of posture is also adopted for short sprints, when playing and while the hands are busy collecting food. For moving about in trees, the gorilla goes on all-fours. It climbs with ease up vertical trunks, but always proceeds with careful, measured movements.

Unlike the orang-utan, who lives alone, the gorilla lives in social groups of variable size. In different areas of its distribution, groups have been observed numbering 2 – 8 animals, 10 – 20 animals or even 25 and upwards. Each group normally comprises one adult, silver-backed male, one or more subadult males, one or more adult females, and a variable number of juveniles and babies. In groups containing more than 10 – 12 individuals, there may be two adult, silver-backed males. There are always more females than males, although at time of birth the ratio appears to be even.

The gorilla's day begins around 6.00 or 7.00 in the morning, when the first rays of sun touch the nest where it has spent the night. As a rule, all members of the group keep watch on the dominant, silver-backed male, who initiates activity. They usually begin by making short journeys close to the nest, feeding on leaves and blades of grass. After this comes a period of rest which may last for little more than an hour or more than three hours. At the end of the rest period, each gorilla resumes its foraging activities in the forest, and around 5.00 or 5.30 in the afternoon starts looking for a place to build its nest and spend the night. Adult males customarily place their nest on the ground or on the lowest tree branches, while the females and young prefer to venture higher up. Once again it is the dominant male who gives the signal for this activity to commence and all the others follow his example.

▲ Family of gorillas, with a male, a female, and three babies. Unlike the orang-utan, which lives on its own, the gorilla lives in families of variable size.

▼ Gorilla on four legs: in the circle is a detail of the hand, showing how the animal supports itself on the knuckles.

▲ Example of the silver-backed adult male.

▲ Gorilla beating its chest in an aggressive posture.

▲ A gorilla running: the upright position is adopted only for brief intervals in situations such as flight or threat toward potential enemies.

▲ Gorilla resting in its nest. The animals never use the same nest for two consecutive days.

▲ Hand of a gorilla: note the very short thumb, separated from the other fingers.

◄ The gorilla feeds mainly on leaves, stems, and the pith of certain plants, such as bamboo.

▲ Female gorilla suckling her baby.

387

CHIMPANZEE
Genus Pan

Order Primates
Family Pongidae
Size Height 32 – 36 in (80 – 90 cm), on all-fours
Weight 88 – 110 lb (40 – 50 kg)
Dentition $\frac{2.1.2.3}{2.1.2.3} = 32$
Gestation About 240 days
Number of young 1
Weight at birth 3½ lb (1500 g)
Sexual maturity 7 – 8 years
Maximum age 35 years or more

In the opinion of many authors there are two distinct species, the chimpanzee (*Pan troglodytes*) and the dwarf gorilla (*P. paniscus*). The former, in its turn, comprises three subspecies. The true chimpanzee is widely distributed in Western and Central Africa, whereas *Pan paniscus* inhabits Central Africa, in the zones lying between the Zaire and Lualaba Rivers.

The chimpanzee's habitats are the tropical forests of plains and mountains up to 10,000 ft (3,000 m) and the savannas adjacent to the lowland forests. The chimpanzee can be regarded either as arboreal or terrestrial, inasmuch as some populations live mainly in trees and others predominantly at ground level. The chimpanzee is prevalently vegetarian, its principal food source (80 – 90 per cent) consisting of fruit, but it also often consumes leaves, shoots, seeds, and bark. Very occasionally it will feed on insects (ants and termites), small mammals, and fish. Of all the apes, therefore, this is the one with the most varied and least specialized diet, which most closely approximates to our own.

The chimpanzee's height ranges from 32 – 36 in (80 – 90 cm) when moving across the ground on all-fours to 60 – 68 in (150 – 170 cm) when it stands upright. Like other anthropoid apes, it has no tail. The body structure is fairly heavy, except in the case of the dwarf chimpanzee. The coat is rough, thicker on limbs and back than on the abdomen. It varies in color from brownish-black to black, although in some cases there may be reddish-brown tints. The arms are very long, though not to the extent of those of the orang-utan, terminating in a hand with long fingers. The thumb, however, is relatively short and opposable. The hindlegs are

Detail of the face of the common chimpanzee (*Pan troglodytes*) and , on right, the dwarf chimpanzee (*Pan paniscus*).

Unlike the orang-utan and the gibbon, the chimpanzee (genus *Pan*) lives in fairly large groups. The picture shows two mothers with their respective young: the latter remain with their own mother until they are 6-7 years old: but suckling lasts not more than 24 months. At lower right, a chimpanzee defends itself against a snake.

The chimpanzee has a more varied diet than any other ape. It comprises fruit, leaves, seeds, shoots, and sometimes insects (ants and termites), and meat (small mammals and birds).

shorter than the arms, but longer than the orang-utan's. The foot is long and slender, with an opposable big toe. As with the gibbon, the chimpanzee shows hardly any sexual dimorphism. The female, in fact, though smaller and lighter than the male, never differs so markedly in size as does the female gorilla and orang-utan.

On the ground the chimpanzee usually adopts a quadrupedal gait, supporting itself on the soles of its feet and bearing the weight of the front of the body on the knuckles of its hands. For short journeys or in particular circumstances, as when carrying food, the chimpanzee may adopt an upright posture and walk only on its hindlegs.

The chimpanzee is a skillful climber, and to get up to the treetops it places both legs on either side of the trunk, takes a firm grip with its long arms and moves its hands, one by one, upward. When moving along a branch, it may walk in an upright position, eventually using the hands for assistance, or will swing by the arms alone from tree to tree, like a gibbon.

Chimpanzees live in groups of variable numbers, and their social behavior is decidedly more flexible. Such groups may be formed of 40 – 50 animals (although sometimes as few as 10 or as many as 80 and perhaps more) and occupy one particular area for some length of time. Although they occupy a well-defined area, chimpanzees are not truly territorial creatures, inasmuch as when two different groups accidentally meet, there may be some signs of excitement but almost never any overt examples of hostility. There is no single dominant male in a group, but a series of "chiefs," one to each small unit within the larger group.

In the chimpanzee the gestation lasts for about 240 days, and the newborn baby weighs approximately 3¼ lb (1.5 kg). There is a close relationship between mother and baby which sometimes lasts even after it is weaned. In the first year the baby stays attached to the mother's abdomen both when feeding and moving around. It is usually suckled for more than two years but starts to feed on solid fare as early as the end of the first year. When it is three or four years old, the youngster is carried about by the mother, but in due course it becomes more independent, though sticking close to its parent.

▲ Human-like attitude of a chimpanzee: when begging a companion for a bit of food it extends its hand with the palm upward.

▲ Mother chimpanzee showing affection for her baby: body contacts are frequent, too, among adults, ranging from kisses to hand shakes designed to reassure one another.

▶ The facial muscles allow a wide range of expressions: from top to bottom, anger, joy, fear, grief.

▼ To sip water, which it collects from hollows in trunks, the chimpanzee uses a kind of sponge made by chewing leaves.

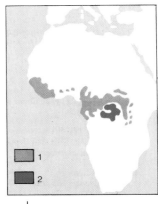

▲ A chimpanzee hunting termites: by poking a stick into the termite mound and then pulling it out, the animal can eat the insects stuck to it.

▲ Like other anthropoid apes, the chimpanzee builds a tree nest.

▲ 1) *Pan troglodytes*;
2) *Pan paniscus*.

◀ Some examples of how chimpanzees move; from top to bottom and left to right: on the ground it normally adopts the quadrupedal gait or, more rarely, the upright posture (the anatomical structure of the pelvis and the muscles does not allow the animal to maintain this position for distances of more than 220-330 yds (200-300 m), after which it has to rest its weight on the knuckles of the hand); in trees it may either adopt the erect postion, standing on a branch, or will hang by the hands from a branch overhead and swing its arms like a gibbon. The chimpanzee is a skillful climber, and can leap from tree to tree in gibbon fashion. Although less agile than the latter, it can nevertheless jump more than 20 ft (7 m). If it has to get across a ditch or a stream, it behaves much like a human, bending its legs, swinging its long arms, leaping forward and landing on the other side with its feet. In this way, from a standing start, it can jump for a distance of 6-8 ft (2-2.5 m).

PICTURE SOURCES

Walter, Aquenza, Milan: 105, 164, 165.

Oliviero Berni, Milan: 85, 93, 94, 101, 104, 162, 163, 188, 189, 199, 216, 217, 238, 239, 262, 268, 269, 270, 271, 318, 319, 320, 321, 372, 373.

Giambattista Bertelli, Brescia: 46, 60, 66.

Fausto Borrani, Brescia: 25, 116, 117, 145, 192, 193, 196, 197, 230.

Trevor Boyer / The Linden Artists Ltd., London: 170, 171, 178, 179, 180, 181, 182, 183, 184, 185, 200, 201, 222, 223, 228, 229.

Martin Camm, The Tudor Art Agency Ltd., London: 174, 175, 176, 177.

Enzo Carretti, Bagno a Ripoli (Florence): 76, 77.

Umberto Catalano, Bologna: 202, 203.

Piero Cattaneo, Bergamo: 134, 135, 136, 137, 284, 285, 286, 287, 288, 289, 290, 291, 292, 293, 294, 295, 296, 297, 368, 369, 382, 383.

Luciano Corbella, Milan: 12, 13, 14, 15, 16, 17, 20, 21, 23, 68, 69, 70, 71, 72, 73, 74, 75.

Piero Cozzaglio, Brescia: jacket, 78, 236, 237, 306, 386, 387.

François Crozat, Givors (France): 28, 29, 30, 31, 32, 33, 34, 35, 36, 37, 38, 39, 40, 41, 42, 43, 44, 45, 47, 52, 53, 54, 55, 56, 57, 58, 59, 61, 62, 63, 64, 65, 79, 156, 157.

Adriana Giangrande, Rome: 160.

Amedeo Gigli, Rome: 378, 379, 384, 385.

Ezio Giglioli, Milan: 98, 99, 100, 120, 121, 126, 127, 128, 129, 130, 131, 132, 133, 205, 206, 207, 215, 246, 247, 248, 249, 250, 251, 252, 253, 256, 257, 258, 259, 260, 261, 263, 310, 311, 312, 313, 314, 315, 316, 317.

Michel Guy, Noisy-Le-Grand (France): 95, 115, 158, 161, 204, 304, 305, 338, 339.

Francesca Jacona, Rome: 84, 214, 218, 219.

Jaromir Knotek / Art Centrum, Prague: 108, 146, 147, 152, 153.

Pavel Major / Art Centrum, Prague: 97, 154, 155, 159.

Petr Oriešek / Art Centrum, Prague: 80, 81, 103, 112, 113, 151.

Gabrielle Pozzi, Milan: 22, 48, 49, 50, 51, 67, 88, 89, 118, 119, 194, 195, 212, 213, 242, 243, 244, 245, 264, 265, 298, 299, 307, 308, 309.

John Rignall / The Linden Artists Ltd., London: 106, 107, 109, 110, 111, 166, 167, 168, 169, 172, 224, 225, 226, 227.

Aldo Ripamonti, Milan: 18, 19, 26, 27, 90, 91, 124, 125, 198, 208, 209, 210, 211, 266, 267, 274, 275, 300, 301, 322, 323, 325, 326, 327, 340, 341, 344, 345, 346, 347, 348, 349, 352, 353, 354, 355, 358, 388, 389.

Giorgio Scarato, Pressano (Verona): 114, 138, 139, 140, 141, 142, 143, 144, 254, 255, 328, 329, 330, 332, 333, 364, 365, 366, 367.

Sergio, Milan: 24, 82, 83, 86, 87, 92, 102, 122, 123, 148, 149, 150, 173, 186, 187, 190, 191, 220, 221, 231, 232, 233, 234, 235, 240, 241, 276, 277, 278, 279, 280, 281, 282, 283, 302, 303, 334, 335, 336, 337, 342, 343, 351, 356, 357, 359, 360, 361, 362, 363, 376, 377, 380, 381.

George Thompson / The Tudor Art Agency Ltd., London: 350, 370, 371.

Eva Tomkovà / Art Centrum, Prague: 96.

David Wright / The Tudor Art Agency Ltd., London: 331.

Marcello Zamarchi, Verona: 272, 273, 374, 375.